Understanding Human Behavior
and the Social Environment

Nelson-Hall Series in Social Welfare

Consulting editor: **Beulah Compton**

University of Alabama

Understanding Human Behavior and the Social Environment

Charles Zastrow
University of Wisconsin-Whitewater

Karen K. Kirst-Ashman
University of Wisconsin-Whitewater

Nelson-Hall Publishers/Chicago nh

Copy Editor: Sandi B. Schroeder
Designer: Claudia von Hendricks
Production Manager: Pamela Teisler
Cover Designer: Brand Communications Group

Sections of Chapters 2, 7, 8, 10, 12, 13 & 14 were adapted from *Introduction to Social Welfare Institutions*, 2d ed., 1982 by Charles Zastrow. Adapted by permission of the Dorsey Press, Homewood, Ill.

Sections of Chapters 2, 6, 7, 8, 10, 12, 13, 14 & 15 were adapted from *Social Problems: Issues and Solutions*, 1984 by Charles Zastrow and Lee Bowker. Adapted by permission of Nelson-Hall, Inc., Chicago.

The material on Freud in Chapter 3 and the material on parent effectiveness training in Chapter 7 were adapted from *The Practice of Social Work*, 2d ed., 1985 by Charles Zastrow. Adapted by permission of The Dorsey Press, Homewood, Ill.

Sections of the material on identity formation in Chapter 6 were adapted from "Who Am I: Quest for Identity" by Charles Zastrow. In *The Personal Problem Solver*, Charles Zastrow and Dae Chang eds., 1977, pp. 365–370. Adapted by permission of Prentice-Hall, Inc., Englewood Cliffs, N.J.

The material on the format of a Rational Self-Analysis (p. 269), the material on love relationships (p. 249); and material on the Richard Speck case (pp. 275–276) were adapted from *Talk to Yourself: Using the Power of Self-Talk*, 1979 by Charles Zastrow. Adapted by permission of Prentice-Hall, Inc., Englewood Cliffs, N.J.

LIBRARY OF CONGRESS CATALOGING-IN-PUBLICATION DATA

Zastrow, Charles.
  Understanding human behavior and the social environment.

  Bibliography: p.
  Includes indexes.
  1. Social service.   2. Behavioral assessment.
3. Life change events.   I. Kirst-Ashman, Karen Kay.
II. Title.
HV40.Z28 1987   361.3'01'9   86-23832
ISBN 0-8304-1122-4

Copyright © 1987 by Nelson-Hall Inc.

Reprinted 1987

All rights reserved. No part of this book may be reproduced in any form without permission in writing from the publisher, except by a reviewer who wishes to quote brief passages in connection with a review written for broadcast or for inclusion in a magazine or newspaper. For information address Nelson-Hall Inc., Publishers, 111 North Canal Street, Chicago, Illinois 60606.

Manufactured in the United States of America

10   9   8   7   6   5   4   3   2

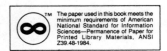

™ The paper used in this book meets the minimum requirements of American National Standard for Information Sciences—Permanence of Paper for Printed Library Materials, ANSI Z39.48-1984.

To Nick and Christopher

Preface

An 18-year-old man, who sees no reason to live anymore, threatens to kill himself. A couple suddenly separates after 23 years of marriage. A young family plagued by unemployment is evicted from their apartment and moves into a tent. A demonstration is staged because a local factory refuses to hire black workers. Why do people do what they do? The main focus of this text is on *assessment*; that is, material is presented to help readers understand the underlying reasons for why people act the way they do and to evaluate the strengths and deficits in the development of people. A wide variety of theories and research about human growth and development are presented. The theories cover both the internal and external variables that influence human behavior.

This text is especially written for use in undergraduate and graduate courses in human behavior and social environment (HBSE). As stated in the following accreditation guidelines, a curriculum requirement of the Council on Social Work Education (CSWE) is that every accredited social work program must provide content on human behavior and social environment:

> In keeping with social work's person-in-environment focus, students need knowledge of the relationships among human biological, social, psychological, and cultural systems as they affect or are affected by human behavior.
>
> The curriculum design by each program should identify a coherent approach to selecting research and theories that constitute the systems of knowledge in the social, behavioral and biological sciences to be offered to students. It should specify how this knowledge will be presented in a way that illuminates divergencies and interrelationships (Council on Social Work Education, 1984, Appendix 1, p. 7).

The person-in-environment focus is a key component of an ecological model of human behavior. For many years social work programs have struggled to develop a HBSE curriculum that covers all the extensive content desired in the Council's HBSE accreditation guideline. This text seeks to meet this guideline with the following thrusts:

- An ecological model entitled The Behavior Dynamics Assessment Model (described in Chapter 1) is used which allows the authors to present a vast array of theories and research to explain and describe human development.
- A life span approach is used which allows for a description of human growth and development from conception through later adulthood.
- For each age group, separate chapters identify biological, psychological, and sociological variables that influence development.*
- Normal developmental tasks and milestones are described for each age group.
- Theories of abnormal development are presented.
- Human diversity factors (involving racial groups, ethnic groups, gender, and sexual orientation) are described.

A final thrust of this text is to present the material in an educational and readable fashion. Numerous case examples, photographs, and line illustrations are used in presenting provocative and controversial issues about human behavior. As much as possible, jargon-free language is used so that the reader can readily grasp the theory.

■ Acknowledgments

We wish to express our heartfelt appreciation to the following people and organizations:

The illustrator, Robert Gustafson

The following who gave special permission to reproduce photographs:

Nick Ashman, Fran Buss, Kevin Drollinger, Knute Jacobson, Stirling Johnson, Marge Kaneiss, Gary Kirst, Ruth Kirst, Kristine Koch, David Runyon, Gregg Theune, United Way of America, Wisconsin State Journal

A sincere thank you to Kristine Koch, Vicki Vogel, Nick Ashman, Susan Drollinger, Kevin Drollinger, and Phil McCullough for helping to conceptualize various chapters and for assisting in a number of ways with the writing. A warm thank you to the following who were invaluable in helping us to acquire photographs: Andrea Drollinger, Kevin Drollinger, Susan Drollinger, Helen Eger, Arnold Kirst, Ella Kirst, Gary A. Kirst, Gary S. Kirst, Linda Kirst, Ruth Kirst, Christopher Koch, Kristine Koch, Jon Koch, Scott Kreider,

---

*In some cases the biological, psychological, and sociological variables overlap. For example, a midlife crisis often involves a combination of biological, psychological, and sociological variables. Therefore, the authors may, rather arbitrarily, include some material under one heading (for example, covering biological aspects) when a reader can make a strong case that it should be covered under some other heading (that is, psychological aspects or sociological aspects).

and Mabel Scholtka. Finally, we want to express our indebtedness to Ronald Warncke who encouraged us to undertake this project, and who was an invaluable consultant in helping us to write this text.

Karen K. Kirst-Ashman
Charles Zastrow

Contents

Understanding Human Behavior
and the Social Environment

Introduction:
The Behavior Dynamics
Assessment Model

A midwestern farm family goes bankrupt after federal financial support and protection is withdrawn. The family is forced to pack its belongings and move to Florida, where they can only afford to live in a tent.

A two and one-half-year-old girl has not yet begun to walk or say more than "mama" and "dada." She is an only child. Her parents become worried because she seems to be lagging behind other children her age and wonder if something is wrong.

Two teenagers, who feel they are in love, struggle with many questions: Should they "make love?" Should they use birth control? What if she should get pregnant? Should they get married?

A 75-year-old widower finds his health failing. He has trouble reading and is beginning to stumble. He has lived alone in his modest home since his wife died 12 years ago. His adult children are pressuring him to sell his house and move into a nursing home. He likes both his home and his independence. What should he do?

Each of these vignettes reflects a real-life situation. Additionally, each situation addresses different issues.

Human behavior is complicated and often confusing. The basic task of social work is to "enhance the social functioning of all age-groups" (Zastrow, 1982, p. 3). Yet, in order to enhance this functioning, one must first understand it. Only then can techniques and skills be applied to make wise decisions.

■ A Perspective

This text will explore the dynamics of human behavior and prepare a foundation of knowledge on which to build practice skills. Social workers assist people in making decisions and in solving their problems. One of the primary steps in the helping process is *assessment*. Assessment involves evaluating some human condition or situation and making decisions about what aspects of the behavior or situation need to be changed.

This chapter will

- Discuss the importance of foundation knowledge within the purpose and process of social work.

- Explain the significance of foundation knowledge for assessment.
- Describe the ecological perspective and the person-in-environment focus of social work.
- Formulate a model for viewing, assessing, and understanding human behavior.

Foundation Knowledge and the Purpose of Social Work

In order to recognize the significance of foundation knowledge, the purpose and process of social work needs to be understood. Social work may be viewed as having three major thrusts (Baer and Federico, 1978, p. 68). First, social workers can help people solve their problems and cope with their situations more effectively. Second, social workers work with public and private agencies and organizations so that people can have better access to the needed resources and services. Third, social workers can "link people with systems", so that they have access to resources and opportunities. Much of social work, then, involves social functioning. People interact with other people and other organizations, such as government and social service agencies, but also groups such as families and fellow workers. Social work targets not only how individual persons behave, but also how these other systems and people impact each other.

For example, in a family of five where both parents work at low-paying jobs in order to make a marginal living, the father works at a small, non-unionized plant and the mother as a waitress. Through no fault of his own, the father is laid off, and for a short time the family survives by collecting unemployment. However, when that runs out, they face a serious financial crisis. The father is unable to find another job, and the family applies for public assistance. But due to red tape, the payments are delayed. Meanwhile, the family is unable to pay its rent and utility bills and has to cut back drastically in its food choices. The phone is disconnected, the electricity is turned off, and the landlord threatens to evict them. Reacting to these external stresses, the parents begin to fight both verbally and physically. The children complain because they are hungry, which only intensifies the parents' sense of defeat and disillusionment. Out of frustration, the parents hit the children to keep them quiet.

This situation illustrates how people are integrally involved with other systems in their environment. A social worker reviewing this case might assess how the family and other systems in their environment have impacted each other. First, the father's life was seriously affected by his work when he was laid off. The father then sought unemployment compensation, which affected that system by dipping into its funds. When those benefits ceased, the family went to the public assistance system for help. The public assistance system, in turn, impacted the family by delaying their payments. The resulting frustration affected the entire family as the parents were unable to cope with their stress. The entire situation can be viewed as a series of dynamic interactions between people and the environments.

Foundation Knowledge and the Process of Social Work

Social work practice involves several basic steps.

1. The problem or situation should be scrutinized and understood.
2. A specific plan of action should be developed. Goals should be carefully selected and clearly specified.
3. The actual intervention occurs. This is the actual "doing" part of the process and may involve providing counseling to an individual or working with a large organization to change policies so as to better accommodate client needs.
4. The social work process calls for terminating the intervention in an organized manner (Shulman, 1981, pp. 17–28).

Accurate assessment of the person, problem, and situation is well documented as critically important in the social work process (Baer, 1979; Loewenber, 1977; Richmond, 1917). Information about the problem or situation needs to be gathered, analyzed, and interpreted.

Siporin (1975, p. 119) states that assessment is "a process and a product of understanding on which action is based." This process involves basic knowledge and assumptions about human behavior. Social workers need to have this information so that they can help clients identify and select alternatives. For example, a social worker who is trying to help a potentially suicidal adolescent needs to know why people commit suicide so that he knows what questions to ask, how to react to and treat the person, and what alternatives and supports to pursue. In working with clients of different racial and ethnic backgrounds, the worker needs to have at least general information about the clients' cultural values and potentially differential treatment they've experienced (for example, racial discrimination). Only then can the worker empathize with a particular situation and help the client identify realistic alternatives.

Bartlett (1970) calls for a common base of social work practice. This base involves common values such as the belief that each individual has the right to make his or her own decisions. This base also involves common skills. For example, social workers need skills for conducting interviews and for helping people identify and evaluate their various alternatives. Finally, a common base of knowledge is necessary. For example, social workers must have access to information for planning effective interventions, and must acquire a knowledge of human behavior before any skills can be applied.

This book focuses on how people act within the context of their environments. People are dramatically affected by the other people, groups, and organizations around them. A young child may be devastated by a sharp scolding from a parent. Which United States president is elected may affect the amount of taxes an individual is required to pay, the types of freedom a person can enjoy, and the absolute quality of life itself.

■ Child Abuse: Jimmy

The Presenting Problem

As Mrs. Green was baking Christmas cookies, she overheard Mr. Horney in the next apartment yelling at his son Jimmy. She became very disturbed. Jimmy, who was only six, was crying. She heard sharp cracks that sounded like a whip or a belt, and this wasn't the first time. However, she hated to interfere in her neighbor's business. She recalled that last summer she noticed strange-looking bruises on both Jimmy's and his four-year-old sister Sherry's arms and legs. She just couldn't stand it any more. She finally picked up the phone and reported what she knew to the public social services department. In that she was concerned that the Horneys not be told who reported the situation, she was assured that the report would remain confidential. State law protected persons who reported child abuse or neglect by ensuring their anonymity if so desired.

The Investigation

Ms. Samantha Chin, the social worker assigned to the case, visited the Horney home the same day Mrs. Green made the report. Both Mr. and Mrs. Horney were home. Ms. Chin explained to them that she was there to investigate potential child abuse.

Harry Horney was 38 years old, a tall, slightly overweight and balding man dressed in an old blue shirt and coveralls. He spoke in a gruff voice, but expressed a strong desire to cooperate. He also had a faint odor of beer on his breath.

Marion Horney was a pale, soft-spoken, thin woman of 32 years. Mrs. Horney looked directly at the worker, shook her head in a determined manner, and stated that she was eager to cooperate. However, she often deferred to Mr. Horney when spoken to or asked a question.

Ms. Chin asked to examine the children. She found slashlike bruises on their arms and legs. When Mr. Horney was asked how the children got these bruises, he replied that they had to learn discipline in order to survive in life. He just strapped them a little now and then to teach them a lesson. It's nothing different than his own father did to him when he was a boy. He also stated that his neighbors could just keep their noses out of his business and the way he wanted to raise his kids. Ms. Chin replied that the state's intent was to protect children from abuse or neglect. She continued that citizens were encouraged to make a report even if the abuse or neglect was only suspected. Ms. Chin added that the anonymity of people who made reports was protected by state law.

When asked how she felt about discipline, Mrs. Horney said she agreed with her husband regarding how he chose to punish the children. All he was doing was teaching the children a lesson or two in order to maintain control and respect.

The Children

Jimmy was an exceptionally nonresponsive child of relatively small size. When asked a question, he avoided eye contact and mumbled only one word answers. When his father asked him to leave the room, he did so immediately and quietly. His mother mentioned that he was having some reading problems in school.

Sherry, on the other hand, was extremely eager and aggressive. When asked to do something, she often initially ignored the request and refused to comply until her parent raised his or her voice. At that point she would look up and very slowly do what she was told, often requiring several proddings. At other times, Sherry would aggressively pull at her parents' clothing, trying to get their attention.

Parental History and Current Status

In order to do an accurate assessment, Ms. Chin asked them various questions about themselves, their histories, and their relationship with each other. Mr. Horney came from a family of ten. His father drank a lot and frequently used a belt in disciplining his children. He remembered being very poor and having to work most of his life. At age 16, he dropped out of high school and went to work in a steel mill.

Mrs. Horney came from a broken family where her father had left when she was three. The family had always been on welfare. She had two older brothers who often teased and tormented her; her mother was quiet and rarely stated her own opinions. Mrs. Horney had dropped out of high school to marry Mr. Horney when she was 17. At that time Mr. Horney was age 23 and had already held six different jobs in seven years.

The Horneys' marriage had not been easy and was marked by poverty, unemployment on Mr. Horney's part, and frequent moves. Mr. Horney had been laid off 19 months ago from his last assembly line job; he was very disgusted that the family had to rely on welfare. Despite his frequent job changes, he had always been able to make it on his own without getting assistance. Yet, this time he had just about given up getting another job. He didn't like to talk to his wife about his problems because it made him feel weak and incompetent. He didn't really have any "buddies." All he seemed to be doing lately was watching television, sleeping, and drinking beer.

Mrs. Horney was resigned to her fate and did pretty much what her husband told her. She had little confidence in herself and mentioned that she and her husband never really talked much.

The Horneys had lived in this apartment for six months. However, as usual, they were finding it hard to pay the rent and thought they'd have to move soon. Moving so often made it hard to get involved in any neighborhood and make friends. Mrs. Horney said she'd always been lonely.

The Assessment of Human Behavior

Factors which must be considered in the assessment of a child abuse case include physical indicators, behavioral indicators, and certain aspects of social functioning which tend to characterize abusive families. Before Ms. Chin could plan an appropriate and effective intervention, she needed to understand the dynamics of the behavior involved in this family situation.

Physical Indicators of Abuse

According to the U.S. Department of Health and Welfare (1979), physical indicators of abuse may include bruises and welts, burns, lacerations and abrasions, skeletal injuries, head injuries, and internal injuries. Often it is difficult to determine whether a child's injury is the result of abuse or a simple accident. For instance, a black eye may indeed have been caused by being hit by a baseball instead of a parent's fist. However, certain factors suggest child abuse such as an inconsistent medical history on the child's part, injuries that don't seem to coincide with the child's developmental ability (for example, an 18-month-old does not break a leg from running and falling when she is not yet old enough to walk well, let alone run), and odd patterns of injuries (for example, a series of small circular burns resulting from a burning cigarette or a series of bruises healed to various degrees).

In this case, slashlike bruises were apparent on their arms and legs. On further investigation, the worker established that they did result from disciplinary beatings by their father. Cases of discipline often involve a discretionary decision on the part of the worker. The issue concerns where parental rights to discipline leave off and abusive infringement on children's rights and well-being begins. The worker must assess the situation and determine whether abuse is involved.

Behavioral Indicators of Abuse

Not only did Ms. Chin need to know what types of physical indicators are involved in child abuse, but also the behavioral indicators of abused children. These types of behaviors differ from normal behavior. Ms. Chin needed to know the parameters of normal behavior in order to distinguish it from the abnormal behavior typically displayed by abused children.

Included in the behavioral indicators of abused children are overly compliant, passive behaviors. A child who is overly eager to obey and/or exceptionally quiet and still may only be reacting to abuse. Such children may be seeking to avoid further abuse by maintaining a low profile and avoiding notice by the abuser. Jimmy manifested some of these behaviors in that he was afraid of being disciplined and so maintained as low and innocuous a profile as possible.

Sherry, on the other hand, assumed an aggressive, attention-getting approach. She frequently refused to comply with her parents' instructions until they raised their voices and often demanded additional prodding. She also aggressively tried to get their attention by pulling at them and yelling requests at them. This approach is also typical of certain abused children. Since Sherry was not getting the attention she needed through other means, she was acting aggressively to get it, even though such behavior was inappropriate. Ms. Chin needed to be knowledgeable about the normal attention needs of a four-year-old in order to understand the dynamics of this behavior.

Abused children also lag in development. Jimmy was small for his age and was having difficulty in school. Ms. Chin needed to be aware of the normal parameters of development for a six-year-old in order to be alert to developmental lags.

Family Social Functioning

Not only must the children be assessed, but also the parents. A worker must understand the influence of both personal and environmental factors on the behavior of the parents. Only then can these factors be targeted for intervention and the abusive behaviors be changed.

Personal parental factors that are related to abuse include unfulfilled needs for nurturance and dependence, isolation, and lack of nurturing childrearing practices. Ms. Chin had discovered in her interview that both parents were isolated and alone and had no one to turn to for emotional support.

Neither parent had learned appropriate childrearing practices in their respective families. While Mr. Horney had learned to be strict and punitive, Mrs. Horney had learned compliancy and passivity.

Environmental factors are equally important in the assessment of this case. Specific factors often related to abuse include lack of support systems, marital problems, and life crises.

Neither parent had been able to develop adequate support systems. Due to frequent moves,

they had never developed relationships with their neighbors. Nor could they turn to each other for emotional support in that they had never learned how to communicate effectively with each other. Finally, they were plagued by poverty and unemployment.

Ms. Chin as the initiator of intervention needed to have substantial knowledge of normal physical and emotional development, social and emotional needs, and impacts of the surrounding physical and social environment of all family members at various life stages. Only then could she understand the dynamics of the behavior involved in the situation and plan interventions to solve the problem.

In this case, Ms. Chin considered several treatment directions. A Parents Anonymous group and various social groups were available to decrease the Horneys' social isolation. Individual and marital counseling were possible both to improve self-image and to enhance marital communication. A visiting homemaker was also a possibility. Such a person could encourage Mrs. Horney to more assertively undertake her homemaking and childrearing tasks. She could also provide personal support. Parent Effectiveness Training could be used to teach the Horneys parenting skills and alternatives to harsh discipline. Finally, Mr. Horney could be encouraged to get reinvolved in a job search. An employment specialist at the agency could help him define and pursue alternative employment possibilities.

Ms. Chin discussed these alternatives with the Horneys. Together they determined which were possible and realistic. They then prioritized which were the most critical and should be pursued first. Mr. Horney admitted that he could use some help in finding a job, which he stated was his top priority. He agreed to contact the agency job specialist to help him reinstitute his job search. Mrs. Horney liked the idea of having a visiting homemaker. She felt that not only would this help her get her work done, but it would also give her someone to talk to. Both parents agreed to attend a Parents Anonymous group on a trial basis. Both also indicated that they were not interested in pursuing marriage counseling or parent effectiveness training at this time, but would keep it in consideration for the future.

The Impinging Environment

Because the environment is so important in the analysis and understanding of human behavior, the conceptual perspective must be clearly defined. As social work has a person-in-environment focus (Council on Social Work Education, 1983), the interactions between individuals, systems, and the environment are critical. Such a conceptual perspective provides social workers with a symbolic representation of how to view the world. The ecological perspective provides a way for social workers to interpret and examine their clients' situations. A key component of such a perspective is the concept of person-in-environment. Here a person is thought of as being involved in constant interaction with various systems in the environment. These systems include the family, friends, work, social services, politics, religious, goods and services, and educational systems. The person is portrayed as being dynamically involved with each. Social work practice, then, is directed at improving the interactions between the person and the various systems. This is referred to as person-in-environment fit.

The interaction between people and their environment has tremendous impacts on human behavior. The model proposed in this text emphasizes several aspects of this interaction. The ecological perspective provides us with the basis for understanding our assessment model. Understanding the following terms and concepts is necessary for understanding the assessment approach described in this book.

Social Environment

The *social environment* involves the conditions, circumstances, and human interactions which encompass human beings. Persons are dependent on effective interactions with this environment in order to survive and thrive. The social environment includes the type of home a person lives in, the type of work that's done, the amount of money available, and the laws and social rules that must be lived by. The social environment also includes all the individuals, groups, organizations, and systems with which a person comes into contact.

Transactions

People communicate and interact with others in their environments. Each of these interactions or *transactions* are active and dynamic. That is, something is communicated or exchanged. However, they may be positive or negative. A positive transaction may be the revelation that the one you dearly love also loves you in return. A negative transaction may involve being fired from a job that you've had for 15 years.

Energy

Energy is the natural power of active involvement between people and their environments. Energy can take the form of input or output. *Input* is a form of energy coming into a person's life and adding to that life. For example, an elderly person in failing health may need substantial physical assistance and emotional support in order to continue performing necessary daily tasks. *Output*, on the other hand, is a form of energy going out of a person's life or taking something away from it. For instance, a person may volunteer time and effort to work on a political campaign.

Interface

The *interface* is the exact point where the interaction between an individual and the environment takes place. During an assessment of a person-in-situation, the interface must be clearly in focus in order to target the appropriate interactions for change. For example, a couple entering marriage counseling may first state that their problem concerns disagreements about how to raise the children. On further exploration, however, their inability to communicate their real feelings to each other is discovered. The actual problem, the inability to communicate, is the interface where one individual impacts with the other. Each person is part of the other's social environment. If the interface is inaccurately targeted, much time and energy might be wasted before getting at the real problem.

Adaptation

Adaptation refers to the capacity to adjust to surrounding environmental conditions. It implies change. A person must adapt or change to new conditions and circumstances in order to continue functioning effectively. As people are constantly exposed to changes and stressful life events, they need to be flexible and capable of adaptation. Social workers frequently help people in their process of adaptation. A person may have to adapt to a new marriage partner, a new job, or a new neighborhood. Adaptation usually requires energy in the form of effort. Social workers often help direct people's energies so that they are most productive.

Not only are people affected by their environments, but vice versa. People can and do change their environments in order to adapt successfully. For instance, a person would find it hard to survive a winter in Montana in the natural environment without people-made shelter. Therefore, those who live in Montana change and manipulate their environment by clearing land and by building heated buildings. They change their environment so they are better able to adapt to it. Therefore, adaptation often implies a two-way process involving both the individual and the environment.

Coping

Coping is a form of human adaptation and implies a struggle to overcome problems. Although adaptation may involve responses to new conditions which are either positive or negative, coping refers to the way we deal with the problems we experience in life. For example, a person might have to cope with the sudden death of a parent.

Interdependence

Interdependence refers to the mutual reliance of each person on each other person. Individuals are interdependent on or rely on other individuals and groups of individuals in the social environment. Likewise, these other individuals are interdependent on each other for input, energy, services, and consistency. People cannot exist without each other. The business executive needs the farmer to produce food and customers to purchase goods. Likewise, the farmer needs the executive for money to buy seeds, tools, and other essentials. He becomes the customer for the executive. People, especially in a highly industrialized society, are interdependent and need each other in order to survive.

■ Medical Model Versus Ecological Model of Human Behavior

Courses in social work first began to be offered at colleges and universities in the early 1900s. From the 1920s to the 1960s most social work programs used a medical model approach to human behavior. The medical model approach was developed by Sigmund Freud.

The medical model approach views clients as being "patients." The task of the provider of services is to first diagnose the causes of a patient's problems and then provide treatment. The patient's problems are viewed as being inside the patient.

In regards to emotional and behavioral problems of people, the medical model conceptualizes such problems as being "mental illnesses." People with emotional or behavioral problems are then given medical labels, such as schizophrenic, psychotic, neurotic, or insane. Adherents of the medical approach believe the disturbed person's mind is affected by some generally unknown, internal condition. That unknown, internal condition is thought to be due to a variety of possible causative factors: genetic endowment, metabolic disorders, infectious diseases, internal conflicts, unconscious uses of defense mechanisms, and traumatic early experiences that cause emotional fixations and prevent future psychological growth.

The medical model identifies two major categories of mental illness—psychosis and neurosis—and classifies a number of disorders under each of these. The medical model approach provided a more humane approach to treating people with emotional and behavioral problems. Prior to Freud, the emotionally disturbed were thought to be possessed by demons, viewed as being "mad," blamed for their disturbances, and often treated by being beaten or locked up. The medical model approach emphasized intrapsychic processes and focused on enabling patients to adapt and adjust to their social situations.

In the 1960s social work began questioning the usefulness of the medical model. Environmental factors were shown to be at least as important in causing a client's problems as internal factors. Research also was demonstrating that psychoanalysis was probably ineffective in treating clients' problems (Stuart, 1970).

In the 1960s social work shifted at least some of its emphasis to a reform approach. A reform approach seeks to change systems to benefit clients. The antipoverty programs, such as Headstart and the Job Corps, are examples of efforts to change systems to benefit clients.

In the past several years social work has increasingly focused on using an ecological approach. This ecological approach integrates both treatment and reform by conceptualizing and emphasizing the dysfunctional transactions between people and their physical and social environments. Human beings are viewed as developing and adapting through transactions with all elements of their environments. An ecological model gives attention to both internal and external factors.

It tries to improve the coping patterns of people and their environments so that a better match can be attained between an individual's needs and the characteristics of his/her environment. One of the emphases of an ecological model is on the person-in-environment. The person-in-environment conceptualization is depicted in the following diagram.

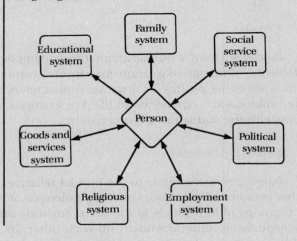

This diagram suggests that people interact with many systems. With this conceptualization, social work can focus on three separate areas. First, it can focus on the person and seek to develop his problem-solving, coping, and developmental capacities. Second, it can focus on the relationship between a person and the systems he or she interacts with and link the person with needed resources, services, and opportunities. Third, it can focus on the systems and seek to reform them to more effectively meet the needs of the individual.

The ecological model views individuals, families, and small groups as having transitional problems and needs as they move from one life stage to another. Individuals face many transitional changes as they grow older. Examples of some of the transitions are learning to walk, entering first grade, adjusting to puberty, graduating from school, finding a job, getting married, having children, having children leaving home, and retiring.

Families also have a life cycle. The following are only a few of the events that require adjustment: engagement, marriage, birth of children, parenting, children going to school, children leaving home, and loss of a parent (perhaps through death or divorce).

Small groups also have transitional phases of development. Members of small groups spend time getting acquainted, gradually learn to trust each other, begin to self-disclose more, learn to work together on tasks, develop approaches to handle interpersonal conflict, and face adjustments to the group eventually terminating or some members leaving.

A central concern of an ecological model is to articulate the transitional problems and needs of individuals, families, and small groups. Once these problems and needs are identified, intervention approaches are then selected and applied to help individuals, families, and small groups resolve the transitional problems and meet their needs.

An ecological model can also focus on the maladaptive interpersonal problems and needs in families and groups. It can seek to articulate the maladaptive communication processes and dysfunctional relationship patterns of families and small groups. These difficulties cover an array of areas, including interpersonal conflicts, power struggles, double binds, distortions in communicating, scapegoating, and discrimination. The consequences of such difficulties are usually maladaptive for some members. An ecological model seeks to identify such interpersonal obstacles and then apply appropriate intervention strategies. For example, parents may set the price for honesty too high for their children. In such families children gradually learn to hide certain behaviors and thoughts, and even learn to lie. If the parents discover such dishonesty, an uproar usually occurs. An appropriate intervention in such a family is to open up communication patterns and help the parents to understand that if they really want honesty from their children, they need to learn to be more accepting of their children's thoughts and actions.

The Behavior Dynamics Assessment Model described in this chapter incorporates all the following aspects of an ecological model: the person-in-environment conceptualization; individuals, families, and small groups having transitional problems and needs as they move from one life stage to another; and identification of the maladaptive communication processes and dysfunctional relationship patterns of families and small groups.

The Behavior Dynamics Assessment Model

People are constantly and dynamically involved in social transactions. There is constant activity, communication, and change. Social work assessment seeks to answer the question, "What is it in any particular situation that causes a problem to continue despite the client's expressed wish to change it?" An ecological approach provides a perspective for social workers to assess many aspects of a situation. The Behavior Dynamics Assessment Model targets three major aspects of the transactions between people and environment. These three aspects are intended to provide a base of dynamic understanding for assessment purposes. The first aspect of the model considers normal developmental milestones. The second emphasizes common life events which tend to occur at certain times of life. Finally, the third aspect deals with human diversity and its effects on human behavior.

For a coherent approach to the life span, a chronological perspective is taken. Starting with conception and ending with old age and death, human behavior will be examined within the framework of the different phases or age periods in a person's life. These periods range from conception through infancy, childhood, adolescence, youth, and adulthood, to old age and death.

The Behavior Dynamics Assessment Model takes the three orientations and relates this information to the individual's resulting behaviors. Behavior is then examined with a problem-solving focus. As a result of conditions which include the normal phase of development, various life events, and the additional effects of human diversity, each person exhibits various adaptive behaviors.

The model then applies all of this information to social work practice. Assessment involves analyzing situations in terms of transactions between people and their social environments. In practice, social workers help initiate effective change where problems are identified. One aspect of the intervention process involves helping people define the various behavioral alternatives available to them within the context of their social environments. The probable consequence of each alternative needs to be determined and evaluated. Finally, the most viable alternative behavior needs to be chosen.

The Behavior Dynamics Assessment Model is depicted in Figure 1.1. The following paragraphs describe each element in more detail.

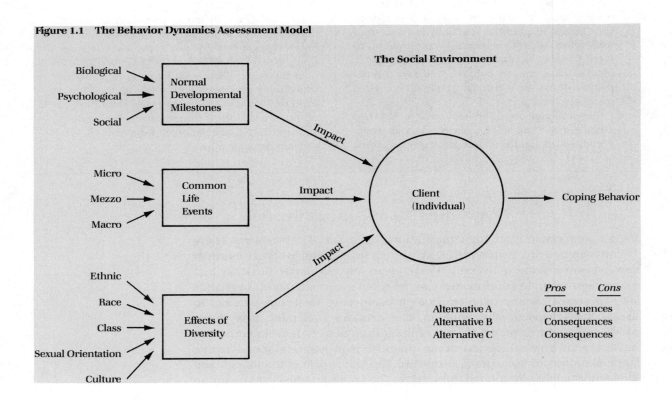

Figure 1.1   The Behavior Dynamics Assessment Model

Normal Developmental Milestones

Normal developmental milestones include those significant biological, psychological, emotional, and intellectual points of development that normally occur in a person's lifespan. This category focuses on the individual as a distinct entity. It provides a perspective on what can be considered normal. Topics include motor development, personality development, motivation, and learning.

For example, take a baby's normal motor development. The average baby can walk like an adult by age 18 months (Kaluger and Kaluger, 1979, p. 116). Or, consider the normal developmental occurrences for the elderly. Older persons tend to have important changes in their sleeping patterns, such as lighter sleep and more frequent awakenings (Kimmel, 1974, p. 371).

In order to distinguish between what is pathological and what is normal, normal developmental milestones must be recognized. The term *normal* is used here to refer to levels of functioning which are considered appropriate for a particular age level. Social work of necessity is frequently problem oriented. Practitioners must be able to distinguish between situations which merit intervention and those which do not. Much time and effort can be wasted on trying to solve problems when they are really not problems at all.

For instance, worrying about a baby who is not walking at the age of 12 months is needless. However, if that same baby is still not walking at the age of 24 months, it may merit investigation.

Likewise, take the elderly person with sleeping problems. At age 80, it may be senseless to worry about the tendency to sleep lightly. Social workers may help people adjust expectations so that these expectations are more reasonable. On the other hand, sleeping problems at the age of 50 may merit further concern in that they may be caused by stress or some abnormal physiological problem.

Normal developmental milestones provide a baseline for assessing human behavior. The extent of the problem or the abnormality can only be assessed to the extent that it deviates from what is normal.

Life Events

Each stage of life is marked by certain life events. For example, adolescence is a time for establishing an identity. Life is marked by a striving for independence and a search for a place to fit into social peer groups. Sometimes adolescence is even more stressful and may be marked by running away from home or delinquency.

Marriage and having children are characteristic of early and middle adulthood. Sometimes people face unplanned pregnancy and single parenthood during this time of life. Other people must face and deal with divorce.

Life events in later life include retirement and readjustments to married life when the children leave home. Although many elderly people remain deeply involved in family and community life, disengagement theory predicts that many others become increasingly isolated and detached from the bustling remainder of society (Cumming and Henry, 1961). Many elderly must also cope with serious health problems and illnesses.

These experiences or life events—identity crises, marriage and children, retirement and detachment—all tend to happen during certain periods of life. Each of these common events will be addressed within the context of the time of life when it typically occurs.

Throughout the life span, this book will talk about life events in three basic categories. First there are micro-events. These are experiences which involve primarily the behavior of the individual person as a distinct entity. Behavior always occurs within the context of the social environment. However, some experiences are personal. There is no immediate transaction with other people. The individual is alone and is acting on his own. The experience is mainly a private experience. Examples of micro-events might include chemical dependency, suicide attempts, or depression. The primary focus is on the behavior of the individual.

The second basic category of life events will focus on the individual's transactions with other individuals and small groups within the social environment. These will be termed mezzo-events. "Mezzo" means medium or moderate. Frequently these experiences will target intimate interpersonal relationships. This is the interface where the individual and those most immediate and important to him/her meet. These events will involve families, peer groups, and immediate work groups.

The third category of life events will include macro-events. Here people's transactions with large organizations and systems are targeted. An individual's place within the total scheme of things is analyzed. This type of life event includes poverty, discrimination, social pressures, and the effects of social policies.

Figure 1.2 depicts the ecological approach. An individual client, within the context of the surrounding social environment, copes with micro-events. The individual also copes with mezzo- and macro-events. Wherever an interface exists between the individual and other systems, the individual must adapt to or cope with these experiences.

This book will examine micro-, mezzo-, and macro-events typical of each phase of life. The variety of experiences which may be considered typical is probably infinite. However, there are some life events which social workers are frequently called on to help people cope with.

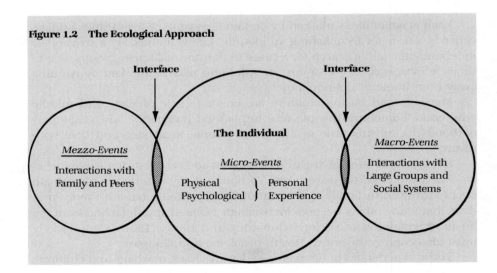

Figure 1.2   The Ecological Approach

The Effects of Human Diversity

"Diversity in ethnic background, race, class, sexual orientation, and culture in a pluralistic society" has serious effects on human behavior (Council on Social Work Education, 1983, p. 10). Any time a person can be identified as belonging to a group that differs in some respect from the majority of others in society, that person is subject to the effects of diversity. This includes being a woman in an all-male business establishment. It includes being a 62-year-old person applying for a sales job in a department store where everyone else is under 40. It also includes being a black person applying for membership in an all white country club.

Membership in any diverse group provides a different set of environmental circumstances. A Chicano adolescent from an inner city neighborhood has a different social environment than an upper middle-class adolescent of Jewish descent living in the well-to-do suburbs of the same city.

This orientation of sensitivity to group differences is critical in understanding any individual's behavior. This is important from two perspectives. First, the values or orientation of a particular diverse group will affect how an individual chooses or is pressured to behave. For instance, a single individual with a sexual preference for the same gender may very well choose to participate in social activities oriented toward others with the same preference. The individual might tend to avoid bars and nightclubs aimed primarily at helping heterosexual singles meet. Instead, this person might choose to visit nightclubs and join activities or social clubs aimed at helping people with sexual preferences for the same gender get together.

A second important perspective concerning sensitivity to group differences directs attention to how other people and groups of people in the social environment view the diverse group. Each member of the diverse group has a tendency to lose one's individual identity and assume the group identity in the eyes of others in the environment. The group characteristics become the characteristics of the individual whether the individual actually has them or not. What we're referring to here are prejudgments and stereotypes. These are not based on facts about an individual, but rather on predetermined notions about any person who happens to belong to a particular group.

Awareness of this second perspective is important for two reasons. The first is that professional values are one of the foundation blocks of social work. Devore and Schlesinger (1981) articulate basic social work values and emphasize the importance of adherence to them. These values include "the dignity of the individual, the right to self-determination, the need for an adequate standard of living, and satisfying, growth-enhancing relationships" (p. 128).

The views of those in the surrounding social environment are important for a second reason. Frequently these views, subjective opinions, and stereotypes discriminate against various diverse groups. Pressures and limitations are often placed on diverse group members. Alternatives are limited. Behavior is restricted. In the assessment of human behavior, knowing when the alternatives a person has open to him or her are limited is important.

For example, a young single black mother of three young children who is receiving public aid, applies for a service job behind the counter of a local delicatessen. The deli is run by a lower middle-class white family who hold many of the larger society's traditional values. These values include the

How important is environment to the social worker? Social work focuses on interactions between people and their environment. Environment may refer to social environment, which includes the people, groups, and organizations surrounding a client. But the social worker must also study a client's physical environment. Is there something in the client's physical setting that might be causing his or her problem? The social worker pinpoints the problem, then offers workable solutions. (Karen Kirst-Ashman)

How can the social worker help a family in times of stress? Individual family members often cope with stress in ways that are detrimental to the entire family's welfare. Enough harmful acting out of unresolved problems will cause even a solid family's foundation to crack. By assessing the family's problem, and by teaching more effective coping methods, the social worker can turn the troubled family into a functioning team. (Courtesy of United Way of America)

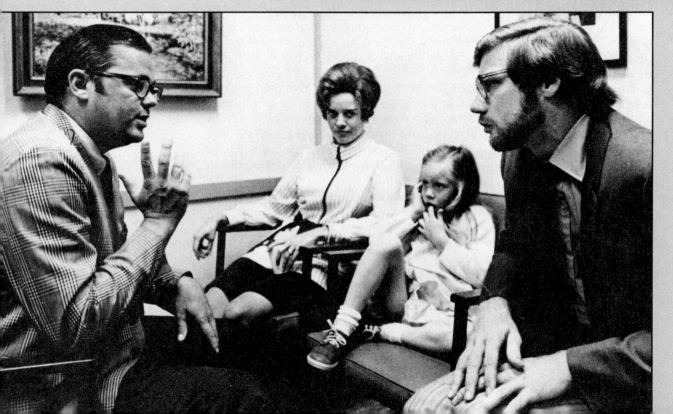

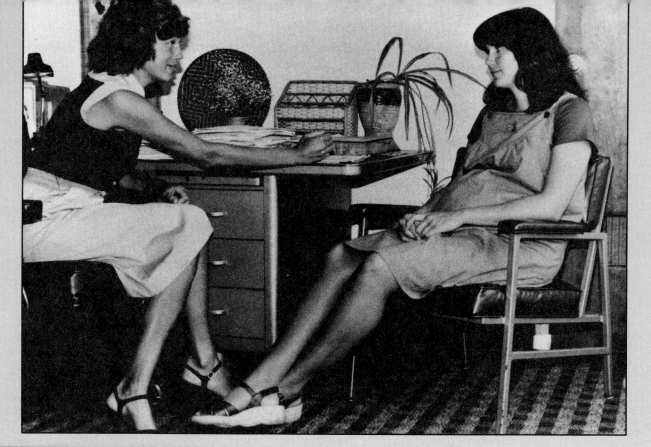

How can a social worker help this pregnant, single teenager? Early in this teenager's pregnancy, the social worker presented her with some choices to help her make the best decision for her future. She could have an abortion; keep her baby and raise it herself; keep her baby and marry the father; or give the baby up for adoption. With the social worker's help, the teenager chose independently to have the baby and give it up for adoption. (Charles Zastrow)

What type of life event is this bridal couple sharing? The couple is living out a "mezzo-event." Mezzo-events focus on an individual's transactions with other individuals or with small groups of individuals. This wedding is a mezzo-event because two individuals, the bride and groom, are experiencing an intimate, interpersonal relationship. Mezzo-events are unlike microevents, when individuals act as distinct entities, or macroevents, when they react to large systems, such as a system of social policies around them. (Knute Jacobson)

ideas that the man is the head of the household and that the woman should stay home and take care of the children. The owner of the deli and head of the family interviews the young woman and makes several immediate assumptions.

The first assumption is that the woman has no business not being married. The second is that she should be staying at home with her children. The third assumption is that the woman, because of her color, is probably lazy and undependable anyway. He uses the excuse that she has no experience in this particular job and refuses to hire her. This young woman has run up against serious difficulties in her job search. In addition, she may have problems getting adequate daycare for her young children. Taken together, all these difficulties may close to her the option of finding a job and getting off of public aid.

In assessing and understanding any person's behavior, it's critical to be aware of limitations imposed by the environment. Otherwise, impossible alternatives might be pursued. In practice, a social worker who did not understand these things might ineffectively pressure the young woman in the example to go out and get a job. Since she was already trying, failing, and becoming frustrated, this additional pressure might make her turn against the social worker and the social service system. She might just give up.

Sensitivity to human diversity is very important in social work practice. Therefore, this orientation is given a central role in the assessment of human behavior as presented here. Figure 1.3 portrays the two perspectives on human diversity.

The larger circle depicts the values and attitudes of the majority of other people in the social environment. The smaller circle which intersects and goes a bit beyond the edge of the larger circle represents the values and attitudes of some diverse group. This may be any group which is different in some way from the majority. This difference may be an ethnic diversity like being Polish. It may be a racial diversity like being native American. It may even be a diversity of sexual preference such as being gay. Diversity involves being in a group that can be distinguished from the majority in some way or another.

The diverse group circle extends beyond the larger circle of the entire social environment. This represents the separate and different values and attitudes held by the group that are not held by others in the environment.

The small central circle represents the sum total of stereotypes and prejudgments held by people in the social environment. The fact that the diverse group circle intersects the stereotype circle reflects the prejudgments held about that particular diverse group.

The diverse group circle also intersects the other general section of the social environment circle. The diverse group is still part of the total social environment. This intersection reflects the values and attitudes held in common with others in the social environment.

The two perspectives focused on here are reflected by the two shaded areas. The first is the unique perspective held by the diverse group which is different than the perspective of others in the environment. The second is where the diverse group intersects the stereotyped attitudes held in the social environment. This targets the prejudgments to which the diverse group is subjected.

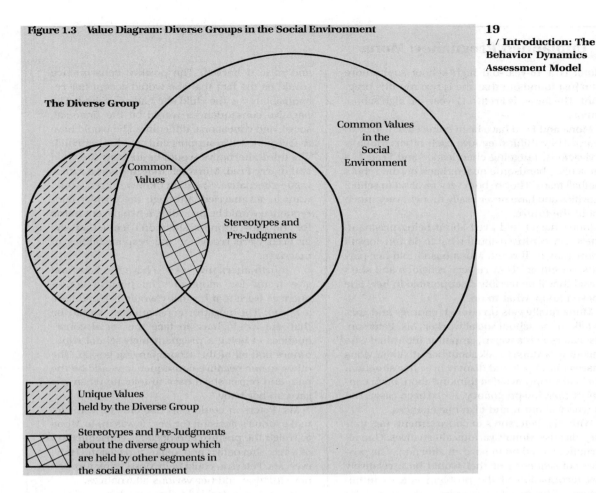

The Diverse Group

Common Values in the Social Environment

Common Values

Stereotypes and Pre-Judgments

Unique Values held by the Diverse Group

Stereotypes and Pre-Judgments about the diverse group which are held by other segments in the social environment

Coping Behaviors

As a result of a particular stage of normal development, life events, and the effects of human diversity, an individual will exhibit some type of behavior. These three orientations provide some of the ingredients for the resulting behavior. There are always reasons why people behave the way they do.

The final element in our assessment of human behavior focuses on this resulting behavior and takes it one step further. A person has reasons for behaving in certain ways. However, other alternatives are always available. A primary task of social work is to help people define the other alternatives available to them. Often people have tunnel vision. Because of stress, habit, or lack of experience, people fail to think that other alternatives exist.

Not only do other alternatives need to be defined, but they also need to be evaluated. The positive and negative consequences of each alternative need to be clearly stated and weighed.

■ Unplanned Pregnancy: Mona

Mona is a 16-year-old high school sophomore who just found out that she is two months pregnant. The father is Fred, a 17-year-old high school junior.

Mona and Fred have been going steady for two years. They think they love each other. Mona is a vivacious, outgoing cheerleader and Fred is a muscular, handsome quarterback on the school football team. They're both very involved in school activities and have never really thought very much about the future.

Mona hasn't told Fred about being pregnant. She's very confused about what to do and doesn't know how he'll react. Mona hasn't told her parents yet either. They're very religious and she's afraid they'll be terribly disappointed in her. She doesn't know what to do.

Mona finally gets up enough courage and goes to talk to the school social worker, Ms. Peterson. Ms. Peterson is a warm, empathic individual who encourages Mona to talk about her situation. Mona shares her shock and dismay over her situation. She had simply avoided thinking about birth control or possible pregnancy. It had been easier not to worry about it and take her chances.

With Ms. Peterson's encouragement, together they discuss Mona's various alternatives. One alternative would be to have an abortion. The positive consequence of that would be a relatively fast termination of the problem and its implications. The negative consequences would include the cost, any difficulty she might encounter in setting up an appointment, and any physical discomfort the procedure would cause. The most serious negative consequence for Mona was guilt in that she felt that abortions were morally wrong.

A second alternative would be to keep the baby and raise it herself. The positive consequence would be the fact that she would accept her responsibility for the child she had conceived. The negative consequences would be the financial, social, and educational difficulties she would have to face in order to support and care for her child.

A third alternative would be to keep the child and marry Fred. Mona felt that this was a rather vague alternative. She didn't know if Fred would want to get married. Although the positive consequence would be providing a two parent home for the baby, Mona really didn't feel either she or Fred were ready for the responsibilities of marriage.

A fourth alternative was to have the baby and give it up for adoption. The positive consequences were that her baby would live and have a home. The negative consequences would be that she would have to face the social consequences of being a pregnant high school sophomore and all of the accompanying gossip. The other major negative consequence would be the pain and regret she'd have to tolerate when she gave up her baby.

Ms. Peterson could not, nor did she want to, make Mona's decision for her. It was up to Mona to weigh the positive and negative consequences of each alternative and make a decision. However, Ms. Peterson could help Mona think through her situation and her various alternatives.

Mona finally decided to have the baby and give it up for adoption. After weighing each alternative within her own personal value system, she decided that this was the best route for her to take. She knew she'd have to talk to Fred first, but she felt at least she had defined her own perspective.

Text's Objectives

The intent here is not to teach practice skills. However, the goal is to provide a perspective on practice in preparation for skill acquisition. The Behavior Dynamics Assessment Model provides a systematic foundation for integrating knowledge about human behavior.

The case example of Mona's unplanned pregnancy illustrates a way of looking at human behavior. The focus is on understanding the behavior by looking at the reasons for it. The Behavior Dynamics Assessment Model does not specify how to interview or how to counsel. However, it does present a perspective on behavior and behavioral alternatives in preparation for practice.

Students who grasp the content in this text will be able to

1. Identify the normal processes of sequential physical, psychological, and socio-cultural development throughout the life span;
2. Recognize and assess the common social issues, stresses, and crises affecting normal development and maturity (e.g., emotional disturbance, delinquency, alcoholism and drug abuse, divorce, mid-life crisis, poverty) as related to social work practice;
3. Analyze the individual's functioning within various environmental systems including families, groups, and organizations;
4. Identify the environmental conditions of various diverse groups and examine the special stresses and pressures to which they are subject;
5. Apply this knowledge to social work practice.

Summary

The focus of this text is to present theories and research results which are intended to assist students in assessing human behavior and the social environment. The interaction between people and their environment has tremendous impacts on human behavior.

This chapter describes the Behavior Dynamics Assessment Model, which serves as a framework for organizing assessment content in this text. The model is based on ecological concepts, and targets three major aspects of the transactions between people and environment: normal developmental milestones, common life events which tend to occur at certain times of life, and human diversity and its effects on human behavior. Common life events include micro-, mezzo-, and macro-events. For a coherent approach to the life span, a chronological perspective is used, which ranges from conception to old age and death. In the past few decades the profession of social work has been moving from using a medical model to using an ecological approach in assessing human behavior.

Infancy and Childhood

CHILD-
HOOD

Biological Aspects of Infancy and Childhood

Juanita lovingly watched her one-year-old Enrico as he lay in his crib playing with his toes. Enrico was a first child, and his mother was very proud of him. She was bothered, however, by the fact that he could not yet sit up by himself. Living next door was a baby about Enrico's age, whose name was Teresa. Not only could she sit up by herself, but she could stand alone and was even starting to crawl. Juanita thought that it was odd that the two children could be so different and have such different personalities. That must be the reason, she thought. Enrico was just an easy going child. Perhaps he was also a bit stubborn. Juanita decided that she wouldn't worry about it. In a few weeks Enrico would probably start to sit up.

Knowledge of normal human development is critical in order to understand and monitor the progress of children as they grow. In the example Enrico was indeed showing some developmental lags which were becoming more and more striking. He was in need of an evaluation to determine his physical and psychological status so that he might receive help.

■ A Perspective

According to the Behavior Dynamics Assessment Model, the attainment of normal developmental milestones has a direct impact on the client. Biological development affects behavior as does psychological and social development. This chapter will explore some of the major aspects of infancy and childhood which are necessary both for providing information to clients and for making appropriate assessments of client behavior. This chapter will

- Describe the dynamics of human reproduction including conception, diagnosis of pregnancy, fetal and prenatal development, problem pregnancies, and the actual birth process.
- Explain normal developmental milestones as children progress through infancy and childhood.
- Examine the impacts of sensory integration on child development and describe the various types of sensory systems.

● Explore abortion and infertility, two critical decision-making situations and life events which concern the decision to have children.

The Dynamics of Human Reproduction

Chuck and Christine had mixed emotions about the pregnancy. It had been an accident. They were both in their mid-30s and already had a vivacious four-year-old daughter named Hope. Although Hope had been a joy to both of them, she had also placed serious restrictions on their personal lifestyle. They were looking forward to her beginning school. Christine had begun to work part-time and was planning on going full-time as soon as Hope turned five.

Now all that had changed. To complicate the matter, Chuck, a university professor, had just received an exciting job offer in Hong Kong—the opportunity of a lifetime. They had always dreamed of spending time overseas.

The unexpected pregnancy provided Chuck and Christine with quite a jolt. Should they terminate the pregnancy and go on with their lives in exotic Hong Kong? Should they have the baby overseas? Questions concerning foreign prenatal care, health conditions, and health facilities flooded their thoughts. Would it be safer to remain in the states as they were and turn down this golden opportunity? Christine was 35. Her reproductive clock was ticking away. Soon risk factors concerning having a healthy, normal baby would begin to skyrocket. This might be their last chance to have a second child.

Chuck and Christine did some serious soul-searching and fact searching in order to arrive at their decision.

Yes, they would have the baby. Once the decision had been made, they were filled with relief and joy. They also decided to travel to Hong Kong. They would use the knowledge they had about prenatal care, birth, and infancy to maximize the chance of having a healthy, normal baby. They concluded that this baby was a blessing which would improve, not impair, the quality of their lives.

The decision to have children is a serious one. Ideally, a couple should examine all alternatives. Children can be wonderful. Family life can involve pleasurable activities, pride, and fullness to life. On the other hand, children can cause stress. They demand attention, time, and effort and can be expensive to care for.

Information about conception, pregnancy, birth, and childrearing can only help people make better, more effective decisions.

Conception

Sperm meets egg; a child is conceived. But in actuality, it is not quite that simple. Many couples who strongly desire to have children have difficulty conceiving. Many others whose last desire is to conceive do so with ease. Some amount of chance is involved. Of women having unprotected intercourse, 25 percent conceive after one month, 63 percent after three months, and 80 percent after one year (Shane, Schiff, and Wilson, 1976). Approximately 12 percent of couples in the United States are infertile or unable to conceive (Hyde, 1982, p. 131). Regardless, knowledge of the process is critical for making clear and specific decisions.

Conception refers to the act of becoming pregnant. Sperm need to be deposited in the vagina near the time of ovulation. *Ovulation* involves the ovary's release of a mature egg into the body cavity near the end of one of the fallopian tubes. A woman is born with approximately 400,000 immature eggs, about half of which still remain alive at puberty. Usually the ovaries alternate releasing an egg on a monthly basis. Fingerlike projections called *fimbriae* at the end of the fallopian tube draw the egg into the tube by some unknown process of attraction. From there the egg is gently moved along inside the tube by tiny hairlike extensions called *cilia*. Fertilization actually occurs in the third of the fallopian tube nearest the ovary.

Conception may occur, that is, if a sperm has gotten that far. After *ejaculation*, or the discharge of semen by the penis, the sperm travels up into the uterus and through the fallopian tube to meet the egg. Sperm are equipped with a tail which can lash back and forth propelling them forward. The typical ejaculate, an amount of approximately one teaspoon full, contains about 300 million sperm. Unlike females who are born with a finite number of eggs, males continually produce new sperm. Fertilization is, therefore, quite competitive. It is also hazardous. The majority of these sperm don't get very far. Many spill out of the vagina, simply drawn by gravity. Others are killed by the acidity of the vagina. Still others swim up the wrong fallopian tube. Perhaps only as many as 200 finally reach the egg. The journey to the egg takes approximately two hours. By the time a sperm reaches the egg, it has swum a distance 3,000 times its own length (Hyde, 1982, p. 100).

Sperm can live up to three days. However, after about a day, they begin to lose their capacity to fertilize an egg (Guyton, 1981). Some reports of conception a full week after intercourse have been made, but this may have involved an inaccurate detection of ovulation (Masters and Johnson, 1985, p. 108). The egg, on the other hand, is capable of being fertilized for about 12 to 24 hours.

The actual fertilization process is thought to involve a cluster of sperm secreting an enzyme and depositing it on the egg. This enzyme apparently helps to dissolve a gelatinous layer surrounding the egg and allows for the penetration of a sperm. Recent research indicates that the egg also takes an active part in the fertilization process (Schatten and Schatten, 1983, p. 32). The egg apparently selects and embraces one specific sperm with tiny projections extended from its surface. It then expels other sperm by producing a brief electrical charge on its surface. This is followed by the production of a hard coating of protein which makes it difficult for the other sperm to penetrate.

Fertilization occurs during the exact moment when the egg and sperm combine. Eggs that are not fertilized by sperm simply disintegrate. The genetic material in the egg and sperm combine to form a single cell called a *zygote*. Eggs contain an X chromosome. Sperm may contain either an X or a Y chromosome. Eggs fertilized by a sperm with an X chromosome will result in a female; those fertilized by sperm with a Y chromosome will result in a male.

The single-celled zygote begins its cell division process approximately 36 hours after fertilization. The cell divides to form 2 cells, then 4, then 8, and so on. After 4 to 7 days, the new mass of cells, first called a *morula* and now a *blastocyst*, attaches itself to the lining of the uterus. If attachment does not occur, the newly formed blastocyst is simply expelled. From the point of attachment until 8 weeks of gestation, the *conceptus*, or product of conception, is called an *embryo*. From 8 weeks until birth, it is referred to as a *fetus*. *Gestation* refers to the time passing during a pregnancy from conception to birth.

Diagnosis of Pregnancy

Pregnancy can be diagnosed by using laboratory tests, by observing the mother's physical symptoms, or by performing a physical examination. Many women first become aware of the pregnancy when they miss a menstrual period. However, women also can miss periods as a result of stress, illness, or worry about possible pregnancy. Some pregnant women will even continue to menstruate for a month or even more. Therefore, lab tests are often needed to confirm a pregnancy. These can be done at a Planned Parenthood agency, a medical clinic, or a physician's office.

Most laboratory tests fall within two categories—immunologic or biologic. Both tests depend on the detection of *HCG* (human chorionic gonadotropin) in the mother's urine. HCG is a hormone which is secreted by the placenta.

The immunologic test is fast and accurate and is currently the most common one used. A drop of the woman's urine is mixed with specific chemicals, placed on a glass slide, and observed. HCG, if present, will prevent the substance from coagulating. This means that the pregnancy test is positive. Immunologic tests are 95 to 98 percent accurate when administered two weeks after a woman misses her menstrual period.

Newer pregnancy tests are being developed. For instance, the *beta-subunit HCG radioimmunoassay* is one which is 99 percent effective. It involves measuring the level of HCG in a blood sample. This test is sensitive enough to detect a pregnancy within eight days after conception. However, it is not yet readily available.

The biologic test also involves detection of HCG in the urine. However, here a sample of the woman's urine is injected into the bloodstream of some laboratory animal, such as a frog or rabbit. After several days the animal will ovulate if HCG was present. This ovulation indicates that the woman is pregnant.

A pelvic examination performed by a physician can also be used to diagnose pregnancy by the sixth to eighth week of gestation. Physical symptoms include a softening of the central part of the uterus just above the cervis (referred to as *Hegar's Sign*), a softening of the cervix, a bluish coloration of the cervix and vagina, and a notable increase in the size of the uterus. One problem with this type of diagnosis, however, is the tremendous variability with which women experience these symptoms. The more certain method of detection of fetal heart beat, fetal movement, or identification by using x-rays or sound cannot be done until at least the fourth month. By this time options such as abortion become more limited. Another problem is that several critical months have already passed when the fetus has been exceptionally vulnerable to substances such as drugs, alcohol, or tobacco. Without knowing it, irreversible damage may have already been done to the fetus.

Recently, the use of home pregnancy tests has become very common. These are usually referred to as *e.p.t.'s* (early pregnancy tests). These tests measure HCG levels in the urine and cost around $10. They are very convenient and can be used as early as 9 days after the menstrual period was supposed to start. The procedure involves placing three drops of urine into a plastic test tube and adding the contents of a separate vial of material. The substance is shaken for 10 seconds and placed into a test tube holder. The tube is then left alone for two hours. Pregnancy is diagnosed if a dark brown ring is visible in a mirror which is provided with the test tube holder.

However, e.p.t.'s are not always accurate. There is a 20 percent likelihood that the first test will indicate a false negative. In other words, the test indicates that the woman is not pregnant when she really is. There is also a 3 percent error rate concerning false positives. This involves an indication that the woman is pregnant when she is really not. The error rate for e.p.t.'s is relatively high when compared to the 1 percent rate for laboratory tests.

Fetal Development During Pregnancy

An average human pregnancy lasts 266 days. It is most easily conceptualized in terms of trimesters, or three periods of three months each. Each trimester is characterized by certain aspects of fetal development.

The First Trimester

The first trimester is sometimes considered the most critical. Due to the embryo's rapid differentiation and development of tissue, the embryo is exceptionally vulnerable to the mother's intake of noxious substances and to aspects of the mother's health.

By the end of the first month, a primitive heart and digestive system have developed. The basic initiation of a brain and nervous system are also apparent. Small buds which eventually become arms and legs are appearing. In general, development starts with the brain and continues down throughout the body. For example, the feet are the last to develop. In the first month, the embryo bears little resemblance to a baby, as it has just begun to differentiate into its various organs.

The embryo begins to resemble human form more closely during the second month. Internal organs become more complex. Facial features including eyes, nose, and mouth begin to become identifiable. The 2-month-old embryo is approximately one inch long and weighs about 2/3 of an ounce.

The third month involves the formation of arms, hands, legs, and feet. Fingernails, hair follicles, and eyelids develop. All the basic organs have appeared, although they are still undeveloped. By the end of the third month bones begin to replace what had been cartilage. Fetal movement is also frequently detected at this time.

During the first trimester, the mother experiences various symptoms. This is primarily due to the tremendous increase in the amount of hormones her body is producing. Symptoms frequently include tiredness, breast enlargement and tenderness, frequent urination, and food cravings. Some women experience nausea which is referred to as morning sickness.

It might be noted that these symptoms resemble those often cited by women when first taking birth control pills. This is due to the fact that the pill, by introducing hormones or artificial hormones which resemble those of pregnancy, tricks the body into thinking it is pregnant. In this way it stops the body from ovulating at all. The pill as a form of birth control will be discussed in greater detail in Chapter 5.

The Second Trimester

Fetal development continues during the second trimester. Toes and fingers separate. Skin, fingerprints, hair, and eyes develop. A fairly regular heartbeat emerges. The fetus begins to sleep and wake at regular times. Its thumb may be inserted into its mouth.

For the mother, most of the unappealing symptoms occurring during the first trimester subside. She is more likely to feel the fetus' vigorous movement. Her abdomen expands significantly. Some women suffer edema, or water retention, which results in swollen hands, face, ankles, or feet.

The Third Trimester

The third trimester involves the completed development of the fetus. Fatty tissue forms underneath the skin, thereby filling out the fetus' human form. Internal organs complete their development and become ready to function. The brain and nervous system become completely developed.

An important concept which is especially relevant during the sixth and seventh months of gestation is that of viability. This refers to the ability of the fetus to survive on its own if separated from its mother. It is generally accepted that at six months or twenty-four weeks, the fetus becomes viable. This issue becomes especially critical when referring to abortion. The question focuses on the ethics involved in aborting a fetus which, even with external medical help, would be able to survive on its own. This issue accents the importance of obtaining an abortion early in the pregnancy when that is the chosen course of action.

For the mother, the third trimester may be a time of some discomfort. The uterus becomes large, and the mother's abdomen becomes large and heavy. The additional weight frequently stresses muscles and skeleton, often resulting in backaches or muscle cramps. The large size of the uterus may exert pressure on other organs, causing discomfort. Energy levels during this time are low for most women (Leifer, 1980). Finally, a weight gain of 22 to 27 pounds is to be expected during a healthy pregnancy (Hyde, 1982, p. 112).

Prenatal Influences

Numerous factors can influence the health and development of the fetus. Among these are the mother's nutrition, drugs and medication taken during pregnancy, alcohol consumption, the mother's age, and her smoking habits.

Nutrition

A pregnant woman is indeed eating for two. Not only does the amount of food need to increase, but also the quality of food needs careful monitoring and attention. Pregnant women need approximately 300 calories a day more than normal to provide adequate nourishment (Masters and Johnson, 1985, p. 118). Additional vitamins and minerals are needed in order to provide adequate nutrition. Poor nutrition has been found to result in low birth weight and a high mortality rate (Holmes and Morrison, 1979). Labor also tends to be longer for women having poor diets (Newton, 1972).

Protein appears to be the most critical substance affecting intellectual development (McKay et al., 1978). One study showed that children born to women who suffered protein deficits during their pregnancies had average IQ scores 16 points less than their well-nourished peers (Winick, 1976).

Drugs and Medication

Since the effects of many drugs on the fetus are unclear, pregnant women are cautioned to be wary of drug use. Drugs may enter the bloodstream of the fetus after passing across the placenta. Drugs and medication should be taken only after consultation with a physician. The effects of such drugs usually depend on the amount taken and the gestation stage during which they were taken. This is especially true for the first trimester when the embryo is very vulnerable.

Teratogens are drugs which cause malformations in the fetus. Certain drugs can cause malformations of certain body parts or organs. The tragic example of the potential effects of drugs involves the so-called thalidomide babies of the early 1960s. *Thalidomide,* a type of tranquilizer, was found to produce either flipperlike appendages on newborns in place of arms or legs, or no arms or legs at all.

Long-term use of antibiotics has also been established as being harmful to the fetus (Hyde, 1982, p. 115). For example, tetracycline has been linked to stained teeth and deformed bone structures. Other antibiotics can cause deafness.

Even nonprescription, over-the-counter drugs,—aspirin, caffeine, and insulin—should be consumed with caution (Babson et al., 1980, pp. 26–27). Adequate data is as yet unavailable to determine potential harmful effects, and therefore, it is best to be cautious.

Drug addiction on the part of the mother can result in numerous problems. Such drugs may include barbituates, heroin, and amphetamines. Potential effects include low birth weight, prematurity, convulsions, and depressed breathing (Masters and Johnson, 1985, p. 114). Newborns of drug addicts tend to be addicted to the substance themselves; these infants actually suffer withdrawal symptoms during their first few days of life.

Alcohol

Alcohol has been found to have serious effects on the fetus. The condition has been termed the *fetal alcohol syndrome.* Pregnant women who are heavy drinkers can cause growth deficits, impairments of the brain and nervous system, and facial aberrations (Ouellet et al., 1977; Clarren and Smith, 1978). Mental retardation is another serious effect. It has been established that about 85 percent of children affected by fetal alcohol syndrome have IQs which are approximately 70 or below (Hyde, 1982, p. 116). This sharply contrasts with the normal IQ of 90 to 110.

Evidence substantiates that women who drink six or more drinks per day cause their unborn children to be at serious risk. Even women who drink moderately may cause some adverse effects in their babies (Abel, 1980).

Age

The pregnant mother's age may affect both the mother and the child. These effects range from difficulty in labor for the mother to impacts on the child's mental and physical ability. It appears that mothers under age 18 and over age 40 are more likely to have a retarded child than women between these ages (Kaluger and Kaluger, 1984, p. 108).

Smoking

Numerous studies associate smoking with "lower birth weights, shortened pregnancies, higher rates of spontaneous abortion, more frequent complications of pregnancy and labor, and higher rates of perinatal mortality" (Masters and Johnson, 1985, p. 120). The amount of smoking probably has varying effects. For example, infant size has been found to be associated with the number of cigarettes smoked per day; six or more cigarettes is considered very damaging (U.S. Department of Health, Education, and Welfare, 1979).

Other Factors

Other factors have been found to affect prenatal and postnatal development. For example, a woman's income and social class level tend to affect prenatal development. Lower income levels and lower socioeconomic status tend to be associated with an increased number of health risks for both the prenatal child and the mother. Birth accidents also are more likely.

Problem Pregnancies

In addition to factors which can affect virtually any pregnancy, other problems including ectopic pregnancies, toxemia, Rh incompatibility, and prematurity, can develop under certain circumstances.

Ectopic Pregnancies

When a fertilized egg implants itself and begins to develop somewhere other than in the uterus, it is called an *ectopic pregnancy* or tubal pregnancy.

This occurs approximately once in every 100 pregnancies (Franklin and Zeiderman, 1973; Rubin, 1983). In most cases, the egg becomes implanted in the fallopian tube. More rarely, the egg becomes implanted outside of the uterus somewhere in the abdomen.

Ectopic pregnancies often abort themselves, resulting in a miscarriage. However, in some cases the fetal material continues to develop, and the fetal material must be surgically removed. Otherwise, the expanding fetus can cause a serious rupture of a woman's tissues, resulting in hemorrhaging and even death. In very rare instances, an ectopic pregnancy in the abdomen, if attached to the uterus, may be carried to term. There is still a high risk of hemorrhaging. A caesarean section is necessary to remove the infant under these conditions.

Toxemia

Toxemia usually occurs late in pregnancy and is marked by high blood pressure, severe fluid retention resulting in swelling, and protein found in the urine. In its most severe form, it can cause the mother to have convulsions, coma, and even death. Approximately 6 percent of all pregnancies are characterized by this condition (Masters and Johnson, 1985, p. 137). Its cause is unknown. Toxemia is more commonly found in very young women or in women over age 35. It is also more likely to occur in women of lower socioeconomic status.

Rh Incompatibility

Rh incompatibility occurs when the mother has Rh − blood and the fetus Rh +. This can only happen when the father's blood is Rh +. Since most people have Rh + blood, the condition is fairly rare. The mother's blood forms antibodies in defense against the fetus' incompatible blood. Problems are less likely to occur in the first pregnancy than in later ones, since antibodies have not yet had the chance to form. The consequence to an affected fetus can be mental retardation, anemia, or death.

Fortunately, Rh incompatibility can be dealt with. The mother can be injected with a serum, RhoGam, which prevents the development of future Rh − sensitivity. This must be administered within 72 hours after the first child's birth, or even after a first abortion. In those cases where Rh sensitivity is already existent, the newborn infant or even the fetus within the uterus can be given a blood transfusion.

Prematurity

A baby is considered premature if born any time earlier than the 36th week of pregnancy. Sometimes, because the exact date of conception is difficult to determine, prematurity is gauged by birth weight. Prematurity and birth weight are thus often related. Usually an infant of five and one-half pounds or less is considered to have a low birth weight. Prematurity is a condition affecting approximately 7 percent of all births in the United States (Hyde, 1982, p. 131).

Premature babies, because of their lower levels of development, are much more likely to experience health problems than are full-term babies. Respiratory problems are especially common. Prematurity appears to be associated with the mother's health and nutrition, illness during pregnancy, smoking, imperfect functioning of the placenta, syphilis, and pregnancy in very young teenagers. However, in more than one-half of all premature births, no specific cause can be established (Hellman and Pritchard, 1971).

The Birth Process

Labor involves "rhythmic, regular contractions of the uterus that result in delivery of the child, the placenta, and membranes" (Masters and Johnson, 1985, p. 183). Toward the end of the pregnancy, hormonal production by the placenta decreases. *Prostaglandins* are chemical substances which appear to stimulate the uterine muscles thereby causing contractions. Additionally, *oxytocin*, a substance released by the pituitary gland late in pregnancy, apparently causes the powerful uterine contractions late in the birth process which are necessary to expel or push out the fetus.

Prior to labor, several clues appear that are especially important. First is usually a small bloody discharge of mucus. This is actually the expulsion of the plug of mucus which remained in the cervical opening throughout the pregnancy in order to prevent germs from entering the uterus. Second, the bag of water (which acts as a cushion to protect the fetus) bursts. Although this usually happens during the end of the first stage of labor, about 10 percent of women experience this warm gush of liquid usually within 24 hours of the beginning of labor (Hyde, 1982, p. 117).

The third major indication of beginning labor is the uterine contractions. These contractions have a clearly defined rhythm. Initially, they may be 10 to 20 minutes apart and last 40 to 60 seconds each. As labor progresses, these contractions increase in frequency, intensity, and duration as the body prepares to ease the fetus out during the birth process.

Sometimes women experience what is termed *false labor.* This condition also involves contractions called *Braxton-Hicks contractions.* However, unlike in true labor, they occur very irregularly and frequently far apart. Additionally, there is no hardening of the abdominal muscles in preparation for the birth. These contractions can be confusing and cause a mother a false alarm.

Stages of Labor

The birth process itself involves three stages. Initially during the first stage of labor, the cervix is dilated or opened in preparation for the baby to pass through it. Contractions begin between 10 to 20 minutes apart in the early first stage and build to 2 to 4 minutes apart. Contractions continue to build in intensity and duration, often causing substantial pain to the mother. The water bag bursts toward the end of this stage. The first stage, the longest stage of labor, averages somewhere between 12 to 15 hours for the first pregnancy and 8 hours for later babies.

The second stage of labor marks the time when the baby is actually born. This stage begins when contractions are about 2 to 3 minutes apart and last for about 60 to 70 seconds each. The cervix is completely dilated and the baby begins to move into and through the vagina. The head usually emerges first. However, depending on the baby's position, this may be some other body part. The average length of this stage is 80 minutes in first pregnancies and 30 minutes in later ones (Masters and Johnson, 1985, p. 119).

During the second stage, the mother typically feels the urge to "bear down." This pushing, if done properly, may serve to facilitate the baby's movement out of the uterus and vagina. Each contraction also helps to move the baby farther along.

Sometimes an episiotomy is performed during this stage. An *episiotomy* involves making a small incision in the skin just behind the vagina. Its purpose is to relieve pressure on the strained tissues and help to provide a larger opening through which the baby can emerge. It also tends to prevent tearing which can leave ragged edges that are difficult to heal.

The baby finally completely emerges during this second stage and frequently needs to be held by the feet with head down for a few moments in order to facilitate drainage of any mucus in the respiratory system. This, in addition to slight taps on the buttocks or feet, help to encourage the baby to breathe on its own.

Finally, the umbilical cord which still attaches the baby to its mother is clamped and severed about three inches from the baby's body. As there are no nerve endings in the cord, this does not hurt. The small section of cord remaining on the infant gradually dries up and simply falls off.

The third stage of labor involves delivery of the *afterbirth*. The placenta and other fetal material making up the afterbirth detaches itself from the uterine walls and is expelled, often with the help of a few contractions. Finally, the episiotomy, if performed, is stitched up.

Birth Positions

Approximately 95 percent of babies are born with their heads emerging first. Referred to as a *vertex presentation*, this is considered the normal birth position and most often requires no assistance with instruments. Various birth positions are illustrated in Figure 2.1.

Another 3 percent of babies are born in a *breech presentation*. Here the buttocks and feet appear first and the head last as the baby is born. This type of birth may merit more careful attention. However, usually it can be detected ahead of time and a satisfactory delivery can be made.

A *transverse presentation* occurs in about one of every 200 births. Here the baby lies crossways in the uterus. During birth a hand or arm usually emerges first in the vagina. Such positions need special attention; either the baby must be turned during labor so that a normal birth can be accomplished or a caesarean section must be performed.

A *caesarean section* or C section is a surgical procedure where the baby is removed by making an incision in the abdomen through the uterus. Caesarean sections account for about 10 percent of all births in the United States. Caesarean sections are necessary when the baby is in a difficult prenatal position, when the baby's head is too large to maneuver out of the uterus and vagina, or when the labor has been extremely long and exhausting. Today it is usually safe with only minimal risks to the mother or infant. The mother's recovery, however, will be longer in order to allow for the incisions to heal.

Natural Childbirth

In natural childbirth, the emphasis is on education for the parents, especially the mother. The intent is to maximize her understanding of the

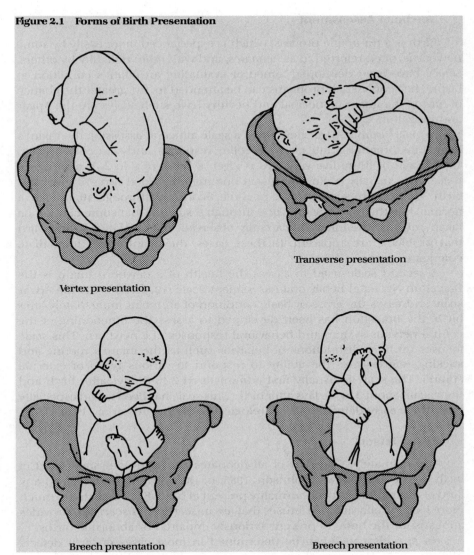

Vertex presentation

Transverse presentation

Breech presentation

Breech presentation

process and to minimize her fear of the unknown. Natural childbirth also emphasizes relaxation techniques. Mothers are encouraged to tune in to their normal body processes and learn to consciously relax when under stress. They are taught to breathe correctly and to facilitate the birth process by bearing down in an appropriate manner. The Lamaze Method is currently popular in the United States.

Many women prefer natural childbirth because it allows them to experience and enjoy the birth to the greatest extent possible. When done correctly, pain is minimized. Anesthetics are usually avoided so that maximum feeling can be attained. It also allows the mother to remain conscious throughout the birth process. Finally, episiotomies are discouraged, which prevents the mother from suffering the subsequent discomfort resulting from incisions.

Newborn Assessment

Birth is a traumatic process, which is experienced more easily by some newborns, often referred to as *neonates*, and with more difficulty by others. Scales have been developed aimed at evaluating an infant's condition at birth. The sooner such problems can be attended to, the greater the chance of having the infant be normal and healthy. Two such scales are the Apgar and Brazelton.

In 1953 Virginia Apgar developed a scale aimed at assessing the infant's heart rate, breathing, muscle tone, reflex response, and skin color (Apgar, 1958). Each of these five variables is given a score of 0 to 2. Evaluation of these signs usually occurs twice—at one minute and at five minutes after birth. A maximum score of 10 is possible. Scores of 7 through 10 indicate a normal, healthy infant. Scores of 4 through 6 suggest that some caution be taken and that the infant be carefully observed. Scores of 4 or below warn that problems are apparent. In these cases, the infant needs immediate emergency care.

A second scale used to assess the health of a newborn infant is the Brazelton Neonatal Behavioral Assessment Scale (1973). Whereas the Apgar scale addresses the gross or basic condition of an infant immediately after birth, the Brazelton has been developed to assess the functioning of the central nervous system and behavioral responses of a newborn. This scale focuses on finer distinctions of behavior such as the infant's rooting and sucking reflexes and the ability to respond to various types of external stimuli. The scale is usually first administered 2 to 3 days after birth and then again about 9 to 10 days after birth. This scale has been found especially helpful for early detection of neurological problems (Als et al., 1979).

Birth Defects

Approximately 3 percent of all neonates are born with some kind of birth defect (Masters and Johnson, 1985, p. 137). *Birth defects* refer to any kind of disfigurement or abnormality present at birth. Birth defects are much more likely to characterize fetuses that are miscarried. *Miscarriage* provides a means for the body to prevent seriously impaired or abnormal births.

No specific cause can be determined in most cases of birth defects (Wilson, 1977). However, about 20 percent can be linked to genetic factors and another 20 percent to environmental conditions such as maternal nutritional deficits, drugs, or maternal illness (Kaluger and Kaluger, 1984, p. 135). The specific types of birth defects are probably infinite, however, some tend to occur with greater frequency.

Down's Syndrome is a chromosome disorder which results in various degrees of mental retardation. Accompanying physical characteristics include slanting eyes, a broad short skull, and broad hands with short fingers. The condition is also referred to as mongolism and Trisomy 21. The probability of Down's Syndrome's occurrence is clearly related to the mother's age. It will occur in only 1 of 1,500 births for young mothers, in 1 of 300 for mothers age 35, and in 1 of 30 to 50 births for mothers age 45 (Masters and Johnson, 1985, p. 137). As these statistics indicate, after age 35 the risks of Down's Syndrome increase as the age of the mother increases.

Spina bifida is a condition in which the spinal column has not fused shut and consequently some nerves remain exposed. This birth defect occurs in approximately 1 of 500 births. Occasionally, this condition can be surgically corrected in the first months.

Rubella or German measles contracted by a pregnant woman can affect the development of the fetus. Its most serious effects on the fetus occur if contracted during the first trimester of pregnancy. These include "deafness, cataracts, heart defects, mental retardation, and retarded growth" (Masters and Johnson, 1985, p. 137). The importance of preventive vaccinations of children should be stressed. However, no pregnant woman should ever receive a vaccination.

Other Factors at Birth Affecting the Neonate

Two other conditions which have serious effects on an infant at birth are *Phenylketonuria* (PKU) and *anoxia*.

PKU refers to a genetic condition whereby an infant is unable to metabolize milk properly. It is caused by a malfunctioning of the liver so that any foods containing protein cannot be properly assimilated. Instead, substances remain and build up in the blood. These substances eventually damage the brain and result in mental retardation. Approximately 1 child in every 10,000 births is affected by this condition.

Fortunately, PKU can be detected early by a simple blood test given to the baby before leaving the hospital. On detection, a special diet can be administered which prevents the accumulation of harmful substances in the bloodstream. Mental retardation is then prevented. Eventually, some children suffering from PKU can resume a normal diet.

The other critical condition which can affect some children at birth is *anoxia*. Anoxia refers to the deprivation or absence of oxygen during birth. Oxygen deprivation can result in brain damage or even death. Anoxia can cause cerebral palsy, a condition characterized by various degrees of muscular incoordination, speech disturbances, and/or perceptual and cognitive difficulties. The Apgar rating soon after birth is helpful in identifying problems often related to anoxia.

Early Functioning of the Neonate

Most babies weigh between 5 1/2 and 9 1/2 pounds at birth. They tend to measure between 19 and 22 inches long (Specht and Craig, 1982, p. 42). Girls tend to weigh a bit less and be a bit shorter than boys. Many parents may be surprised at the sight of their newborn who does not resemble the cute, pudgy, smiling, gurgling baby typically shown in television commercials. Rather, the baby is probably tiny and wrinkled with a disproportionate body and squinting eyes. Newborns need time to adjust to the shock of being born. Meanwhile they continue to achieve various milestones in development. They gain more and more control over their muscles and are increasingly better able to think and respond.

First, newborn babies generally spend much time in sleep, although the time spent decreases as the baby grows older. Second, babies tend to respond in very generalized ways. They cannot yet make clear distinctions among various types of stimuli. Nor can they control their reactions in a very precise manner. Any type of stimulation tends to produce a generalized flurry of movement throughout the entire body.

Several reflexes which characterize newborns should be present in normal neonates. First, there is the sucking response. This obviously facilitates babies' ability to take in food. Related to this is a second basic reflex, rooting. Normal babies will automatically move their heads and begin a sucking motion with their mouths whenever touched even lightly on the lips or cheeks beside the lips. The rooting reflex refers to this automatic movement toward a stimulus.

A third important reflex is *Moro's reflex*, or startle response. Whenever infants hear a sudden loud noise, they will automatically react by extending their arms and legs, spreading their fingers, and throwing their heads back. Although the purpose of this reflex is unknown, it seems to disappear after a few months of life.

Three additional reflexes are the walking reflex, the grasping reflex, and the Babinski reflex. The walking reflex involves infants' natural tendency to lift a leg when held in an upright position with feet barely touching a surface. In a way, it resembles the beginning motions involved in walking. The grasping reflex refers to a newborn's tendency to grasp and hold objects such as sticks or fingers when placed in the palms of their hands. Finally, the Babinski reflex involves the stretching, fanning movement of the toes whenever the infant is stroked on the bottom of his or her feet.

Developmental Milestones

As children grow and develop from infants to children to adults, their growth follows certain patterns and principles. At each stage of their development, people are physically and mentally capable of performing certain types of tasks. Craig (1983, p. 10) defines development as "the changes over time in the structure, thought, or behavior of a person as a result of both biological and environmental influences." Four major principles are involved in understanding the process of human development.

Growth as a Continuous, Orderly Process

First, people progress through a continuous, orderly sequence of growth and change as they pass from one age level to another. This has various implications. For one thing, growth is continuous and progressive. People are continually changing as they get older. For another thing, the process is relatively predictable and follows a distinct order. For example, an infant must learn how to stand up before learning how to run. All people tend to follow the same order in terms of their development. For instance, all babies must learn how to formulate verbal sounds before learning how to speak in complete sentences.

Several subprinciples relate to the idea that development is an orderly process (Papalia and Olds, 1981, p. 12). One is that growth always follows a pattern from being simpler and more basic to becoming more involved and complex. Simple tasks must be mastered before more complicated ones can be undertaken.

Another subprinciple is that aspects of development progress from being more general to being more specific. Things become increasingly more specific and differentiated. For example, infants initially begin to distinguish between human faces and other objects such as balloons. This is a general developmental response. Later they begin to recognize not only the human face, but also the specific faces of their parents. Eventually, as they grow older they can recognize the faces of Uncle Horace, Mr. Schmidt who is the grocer, and their best friend Joey. Their recognition ability has progressed from being very basic to being very specific.

Two other subprinciples worthy of note involve cephalocaudal development and proximodistal development. *Cephalocaudal development* refers to development from their heads to their toes. Infants begin to learn how to use the parts of their upper body such as the head and arms before their legs. *Proximodistal development*, on the other hand, refers to the tendency to develop aspects of their body trunks first and then later master manipulation of their body extremities (e.g., first their arms and then their hands).

Specific Characteristics of Various Age Levels

A second basic developmental principle is that each age period tends to have specific characteristics (Kaluger and Kaluger, 1984, pp. 13–14). In other words, during each stage of life from infancy throughout adulthood, "normal" people are generally capable of performing certain tasks. Capabilities tend to be similar for all people within any particular age category. Developmental guidelines provide a very general means for determining whether an individual is progressing and developing normally.

Individual Differences

The third basic principle of development emphasizes the fact that people naturally have individual differences (Papalia and Olds, 1981, p. 11). Although people tend to develop certain capacities in a specified order, the ages at which particular individuals master certain skills may show a wide variation. Some people may progress through certain stages faster. Others will take more time to master the same physical and mental skills. Variation may occur in the same individual from one stage to the next. The specific developmental tasks and skills which tend to characterize each particular age level may be considered an average of what is usually accomplished during that level. Any average may reflect a wide variation. People may still be very "normal" if they fall at one or the other extremes which make up the average.

The Nature-Nurture Controversy

A fourth principle involved in understanding human development is that both heredity and the surrounding environment affect development. Individual differences, to some extent, may be influenced by environmental factors. People are endowed with some innate ability and potential. In addition, the impinging environment acts to shape, enhance, or limit that ability.

For example, take a baby who is born with the potential to grow and develop into a normal adult, both physically and intellectually. Nature provides the individual baby with some prospective potential. However, if the baby happened to be living in Ethiopia during the 1985 African famine, the environment or nature may have had drastic effects on the baby's development. Serious lack of nourishment limits the baby's eventual physical and mental potential. In severe cases, starvation results in death.

Due to the complicated composition of human beings, the exact relationship between hereditary potential and environmental effects is unclear. It is impossible to quantify how much the environment affects development compared to how much development is affected by heredity. This is often referred to as the *nature-nurture controversy.* Theorists assume stands at both extremes. Some state that nature's heredity is the most important. Others hypothesize that the environment imposes the crucial influence. From the standpoint of this book, a more intermediate approach is assumed. In other words, the Behavior Dynamics Assessment Model incorporates both hereditary and biological influences along with environmental events as impacting any individual's development and behavior.

Critical Periods

One other concept which is commonly mentioned in the developmental literature is the critical period. The critical period is "a point or stage in early development when a child is unusually receptive to influences by environmental events, objects, or persons" (Kaluger and Kaluger, 1984, p. 13). The various interpretations of how critical periods affect development all suggest that people are most susceptible to certain types of outside stimulation and influence during certain stages of life. Depending on the perspective, the particular type of development is less likely to occur or even is prevented from taking place during any other time.

The concept was initiated during psychological animal research. That is, psychological experiments focused on how animals could be imprinted with certain influences only during certain stages of development. *Imprinting* is "a kind of learning that capitalizes on an inherited tendency when the time is ripe" (Hilgard and Atkinson, 1967, p. 64). For instance, ducklings on hatching soon learn to follow their mother. This early time of life finds ducklings to be extremely susceptible to learning who their mother is. The ducklings are imprinted with this information. Subsequent experiments found that incubator-hatched ducklings could also be imprinted with inanimate objects or even people. These ducklings would follow the object or the person exactly as they would a mother duck. Once the object has been imprinted, they will only follow the object as they would their mother. After imprinting has occurred with some other object, even their mother duck would not elicit this following response (Ramsay and Hess, 1954; Hess, 1959). The learning was found to occur only during this early critical period in the ducklings' lives.

The application of the critical period concept to human development is not so clear-cut. Sometimes the term may be appropriate. For example, we have already mentioned how the human fetus is most susceptible to certain environmental conditions and their effects during the first trimester of the pregnancy (e.g. German measles). However, in general, research has not established the existence of specific critical periods during which people can best acquire specific types of information.

Relevance to Social Work

Knowledge of human development and developmental milestones can be directly applied to social work practice. Throughout the lifespan, assessment is a basic facet of intervention. In order to assess human needs and human behavior accurately, a knowledge of what is considered normal or appropriate is essential. Decisions must be made when intervention is necessary and when it is not. Comparing observed behavior with what is considered "normal" behavior provides a guideline for these decisions.

This book will address issues in human development throughout the lifespan. A basic understanding of every age level is important for generic practice. However, an understanding of the normal developmental milestones for young children is especially critical. Early assessment of potential developmental lags or problems allows for maximum alleviation or prevention of future difficulties. For example, early diagnosis of a speech problem will cue parents and teachers to provide special remedial help for a child. The child will then have a better chance to make progress and possibly even catch up with peers.

Profiles of Normal Development

The following section provides profiles of normal development for infants and young children of various ages. The intent is to provide a baseline for assessment and subsequent intervention decisions. If a child is assessed as being grossly behind in terms of achieving normal developmental milestones, then immediate intervention can be needed. If a child is assessed as being only mildly behind his or her normal developmental profile, then close observation can be appropriate. In the event that the child continues to fall further behind, help can be needed at some future time.

Gesell et al. (1940; 1946; 1956) initiated a number of studies concerning the development of children and their attainment of various developmental milestones. They studied hundreds of children to establish various indicators of normality such as when children typically can say their first word, run adeptly, or throw a ball overhand. Their findings reveal an organized sequence of behavior patterns through which children typically progress as they mature. Much of the information presented in *Developmental Milestones for Children from Age 4 Months to 11 Years* is taken from this research.

■ Developmental Milestones for Children from Age 4 Months to 11 Years

It should be emphasized that these milestones reflect only an average indication of typical accomplishments. Children need not follow this profile exactly to the letter. Normal human development provides for much individual variation. Parents do not have to be concerned if their child cannot yet stand alone at 13 months instead of the average 12 months. However, serious lags in development or those which continue to increase in severity should be attended to. This material can act as a screening guide to determine if a child might need further, more extensive evaluation.

Each age profile is divided into five assessment categories. They include motor or physical behavior, play activities, adaptive behavior which involves taking care of self, social responses, and language development. All four topics are addressed together at each developmental age level in order to reduce confusion and to provide a more complete assessment profile.

Age Four Months

Motor: Four-month-old infants typically can balance their heads at a 90 degree angle. They can also lift their heads and chests when placed on their stomachs in a prone position. They begin to discover themselves. They frequently watch their hands, keep their fingers busy, and place objects in their mouths.

Adaptive: Infants are able to recognize their bottles. The sight of a bottle often stimulates bodily activity. Sometimes teething begins this early, although the average age is closer to six or seven months.

Social: These infants are able to recognize their mothers. Other familiar faces are also recognized. They imitate smiles and often respond to familiar people by reaching, smiling, laughing, or squirming.

Language: The four-month-old will turn his/her head when a sound is heard. Verbalizations include gurgling, babbling, and cooing.

Age Eight Months

Motor: Eight-month-old babies are able to sit alone without being supported. They usually are able to assist themselves into a standing position by pulling themselves up on a chair or crib. They can reach for an object and pick it up with all their fingers and a thumb. Crawling efforts have begun. These babies can usually begin creeping on all fours, displaying greater strength in one leg than the other.

Play: At this age, the baby is capable of banging two toys together. Many can also pass an object from one hand to the other. These babies can imitate arm movements such as splashing in a tub, shaking a rattle, or crumpling paper.

Adaptive: Babies of this age can feed themselves pieces of toast or crackers. They will be able to munch instead of being limited to sucking.

Social: Babies of this age can begin imitating facial expressions and gestures. They can play "pat-a-cake," "peek-a-boo," and wave "bye-bye."

Language: Babbling becomes frequent and complex. Most babies will be able to attempt copying the verbal sounds they hear. Many can say a few words or sounds such as "mama" or "dada." However, they don't yet understand the meaning of words.

Age One Year

Motor: By age one year most babies can crawl well, which makes them highly mobile. Although they usually require support to walk, they can stand alone without holding on to anything. They

eagerly reach out into their environments and explore things. They can open drawers, undo latches, and pull on electric cords.

Play: One-year-olds like to examine toys and objects both visually and by touching them. They typically like to handle objects by feeling them, poking them, and turning them around in their hands. Objects are frequently dropped and picked up again one time after another. Babies this age like to put objects in and out of containers. Favorite toys include large balls, bottles, bright dangling toys, clothespins, and large blocks.

Adaptive: Because of their mobility, one-year-olds need careful supervision. Because of their interest in exploration, falling down stairs, sticking forks in electric sockets, and eating dead insects are constant possibilities. Parents need to scrutinize their homes and make them as safe as possible.

Babies are able to drink from a cup. They can also run their spoon across their plate and place the spoon in their mouths. They can feed themselves with their fingers. They begin to cooperate while being dressed by holding still or by extending an arm or a leg to facilitate putting the clothes on. Regularity of both bowel and bladder control begins.

Social: One-year-olds are becoming more aware of the reactions of those around them. They often vary their behavior in response to these reactions. They enjoy having an audience. For example, they will tend to repeat behaviors which are laughed at. They will also seek attention by squealing or making noises.

Language: By one year, babies begin to pay careful attention to the sounds they hear. They can understand simple commands. For instance, on request they often can hand you the appropriate toy. They begin to express choices about the type of food they will accept or about whether it is time to go to bed or not. They are imitating sounds more frequently and can meaningfully use a few other words in addition to "mama" and "dada."

Age 18 Months

Motor: By 18 months, a baby can walk. Although these children are beginning to run, their movements are still awkward and result in frequent falls. Walking up stairs can be accomplished by holding the baby's hand. These babies can often descend stairs by themselves but only by crawling down backwards or by sliding down by sitting first on one step and then another. They are also able to push large objects and pull toys.

Play: Babies of this age like to scribble with crayons and build with blocks. However, it is difficult for them to place even three or four blocks on top of each other. These children like to move toys and other objects from one place to another. Dolls or stuffed animals frequently are carried about as regular companions. These toys are also often shown affection such as hugging. By 18 months, babies begin to imitate some of the simple things that adults do such as reading a book.

Adaptive: Ability to feed themselves is much improved by age 18 months. These babies can hold their own glasses to drink from, usually using both hands. They are able to use a spoon sufficiently to feed themselves.

By 18 months, children can cooperate in dressing. They can unfasten zippers by themselves and remove their own socks or hats. Some regularity has also been established in toilet training. These babies often can indicate to their parents when they are wet and sometimes wake up at night in order to be changed.

Social: Children function at the solitary level of play. It is normal for them to be aware of other children and even enjoy having them around, however, they don't play with other children.

Language: Children's vocabularies consist of from 5 to 20 words. These words usually refer to people, objects, or activities with which they are familiar. They frequently chatter using meaningless sounds as if they were really talking like adults. They can understand language to some extent. For instance, children will often be able to respond to directives or questions such as "Give Mommy a kiss," or "Would you like a cookie?"

Age Two Years

Motor: By age two, children can walk and run quite well. They also can often master balancing briefly on one foot and throwing a ball in an overhand manner. They can use the stairs themselves by taking one step at a time and by placing both feet on each step. They are also capable of turning the pages of a book and of stringing large beads together.

Play: Two-year-olds are very interested in exploring their world. They like to play with small objects such as toy animals and can stack up to six or seven blocks. They like to play with and push large objects such as wagons and walkers.

They also enjoy exploring the texture and form of materials such as sand, water, and clay. Adults' daily activities such as cooking, carpentry, or cleaning are frequently imitated. Two-year-olds also enjoy looking at books and can name common pictures.

Adaptive: Two-year-olds begin to be capable of listening to and following directions. They can assist in dressing rather than merely cooperating. For example, they may at least try to button their clothes, although they are unlikely to be successful. They attempt washing their hands. A small glass can be held and used with one hand. They use spoons to feed themselves fairly well. Two-year-olds have usually attained daytime bowel and bladder control with only occasional accidents. Nighttime control is improving but still not complete.

Social: These children play alongside each other, but not with each other in a cooperative fashion. They are becoming more and more aware of the feelings and reactions of adults. They begin to seek adult approval for correct behavior. They also begin to show their emotions in the forms of affection, guilt, or pity. They tend to have mastered the concept of saying "No," and use it frequently. Perhaps this is the basis for the phrase, "the terrible twos."

Language: Two-year-olds can usually put two or three words together to express an idea. For instance, they might say, "Daddy gone," or "Want milk." Their vocabulary usually includes at least 25 to 50 words. Over the next few months, their acquisition of new vocabulary will be steadily increasing into the hundreds of words. They can identify common facial features such as eyes, ears, nose, etc. Simple directions and requests are usually understood. Although two-year-olds cannot yet carry on conversations with other people, they frequently talk to themselves or to their toys. It's common to hear them ask "What's this?" in their eagerness to learn the names of things. They also like to listen to simple fairy tales, especially those with which they are very familiar.

Age Three Years

Motor: At age three, children cannot only walk well, but also run at a steady gait. They can stop quickly and turn corners without falling. They can go up and down stairs using alternating feet. They can begin to ride a tricycle. Three-year-olds participate in a lot of physically active activities such as swinging, climbing, and sliding.

Play: By age three, children begin to develop their imagination. They use blocks creatively such as making them into fences or streets. They like to push toys such as trains or cars in make-believe activities. When given the opportunity and interesting toys and materials, they can initiate their own play activities. They also like to imitate the activities of others, especially those of adults. They can cut with a scissors and can make some controlled markings with crayons.

Adaptive: Three-year-olds can actively help in dressing. They can put on simple items of clothing such as pants or a sweater, although their clothes may turn out backwards or inside out. They begin to try buttoning and unbuttoning their own clothes. They eat well by using a spoon and have little spilling. They also begin to use a fork. They can get their own glass of water from a faucet and pour liquid from a small pitcher. They can wash their hands and face by themselves with minor help. By age three, children can use the toilet by themselves, although they frequently ask someone to go with them. They need only minor help with wiping. Accidents are rare, usually happening only occasionally at night.

Social: Three-year-olds tend to pay close attention to the adults around them and are eager to please. They attempt to follow directions and are responsive to approval or disapproval. They also can be reasoned with at this age. By age three, children begin to develop their capacity to relate to and communicate with others. They show an interest in the family and in family activities. Their play is still focused on the parallel level where their interest is concentrated primarily on their own activities. However, they are beginning to notice what other children are doing. Some cooperation is initiated in the form of taking turns or verbally settling arguments.

Language: Three-year-olds can use sentences which are longer and more complex. Plurals, personal pronouns such as "I," and prepositions such as "above" or "on" are used appropriately. Children are able to express their feelings and ideas fairly well. They are capable of relating a story. They listen fairly well and are very interested in longer, more complicated stories than they were at an earlier age. They also have mastered a substantial amount of information about themselves including their last name, gender, and a few rhymes.

Age Four Years

Motor: Four-year-olds tend to be very active physically. They enjoy running, skipping, jumping, and performing stunts. They are capable of racing up and down stairs. Their balance is very good, and they can carry a glass of liquid without spilling it.

Play: By age four, children have become increasingly more creative and imaginative. They like to construct things out of clay, sand, or blocks. They enjoy using costumes and other pretend materials. They can play cooperatively with other children. Simple figures can be drawn, although they are frequently inaccurate and without much detail. Four-year-olds can also cut or trace along a line fairly accurately.

Adaptive: Four-year-olds tend to be very assertive. They usually can dress themselves. They've mastered the use of buttons and zippers. They can put on and lace their own shoes, although they cannot yet tie them. They can wash their hands without supervision. By age four, children demand less attention while eating with their family. They can serve themselves food and eat by themselves using both spoon and fork. They can even assist in setting the table. Four-year-olds can use the bathroom by themselves, although they still alert adults of this and sometimes need assistance in wiping. They usually can sleep through the night without having any accidents.

Social: Four-year-olds are less docile than three-year-olds. They are less likely to conform, in addition to being less responsive to the pleasure or displeasure of adults. Four-year-olds are in the process of separating from their parents and begin to prefer the company of other children over adults. They are often social and talkative. They are very interested in the world around them and frequently ask "what," "why," and "how" questions.

Language: The aggressiveness manifested by four-year-olds also appears in their language. They frequently brag and boast about themselves. Name calling is common. Their vocabulary has experienced tremendous growth, however, there is a tendency to misuse words and they have some difficulty with proper grammar. Four-year-olds talk a lot and like to carry on long conversations with others. Their speech is usually very understandable with only a few remnants of earlier, more infantile speech remaining. Their growing imagination also affects their speech. They like to tell stories and frequently mix facts with make-believe.

Age Five Years

Motor: Five-year-olds are quieter and less active. Their activities tend to be more complicated and more directed toward achieving some goal. For example, they are more adept at climbing and at riding a tricycle. They can also use roller skates, jump rope, skip, and succeed at other such complex activities. Their ability to concentrate is also increased. The pictures they draw, although simple, are finally recognizable. Dominance of the left or right hand becomes well established.

Play: Games and play activities have become both more elaborate and competitive. Games include hide-and-seek, tag, and hopscotch. Team playing begins. Five-year-olds enjoy pretend games of a more elaborate nature. They like to build houses and forts with blocks and to participate in more dramatic play such as playing house or being a space invader. Singing songs, dancing, and playing records are usually very enjoyable.

Adaptive: Five-year-olds can dress and undress themselves quite well. Assistance is necessary only for adjusting more complicated fasteners and tying shoes. These children can feed themselves and attend to their own toilet needs. They can even visit around the neighborhood by themselves, needing help only in crossing streets.

Social: By age five, children have usually learned to cooperate with others in activities and enjoy group activities. They acknowledge the rights of others and are better able to respond to adult supervision. They have become aware of rules and are interested in comforming to them. Five-year-olds also tend to enjoy family activities such as outings and trips.

Language: Language continues to develop and become more complex. Vocabulary continues to increase. Sentence structure becomes more complicated and more accurate. Five-year-olds are very interested in what words mean. They like to look at books and have people read to them. They have begun learning how to count and can recognize colors. Attempts at drawing numbers and letters are begun, although fine motor coordination is not yet well enough developed for great accuracy.

Ages Six to Eight Years

Motor: Children ages six to eight years are physically independent. They can run, jump, and balance well. They continue to participate in a variety of activities to help refine their coordination and motor skills. They often enjoy unusual and challenging activities, such as walking on fences, which help to develop such skills.

Play: These children participate in much active play such as kickball. They like activities such as gymnastics and enjoy trying to perform physical stunts. They also begin to develop intense interest in simple games such as marbles or tiddly-winks and collecting items. Playing with dolls is at its height. Acting out dramatizations becomes very important, and these children love to pretend they are animals, horseback riders, or jet pilots.

Adaptive: Much more self-sufficient and independent, these children can dress themselves, go to bed alone, and get up by themselves during the night to go to the bathroom. They can begin to be trusted with an allowance. They are able to go to school or to friends' homes alone. In general, they become increasingly more interested in and understanding of various social situations.

Social: In view of their increasing social skills, they consider playing skills within their peer group increasingly important. They become more and more adept at social skills. Their lives begin to focus around the school and activities with friends. They are becoming more sensitive to reactions of those around them, especially those of their parents. There is some tendency to react negatively when subjected to pressure or criticism. For instance, they may sulk.

Language: The use of language continues to become more refined and sophisticated. Good pronunciation and grammar are developed according to that which they've been exposed to. They are learning how to put their feelings and thoughts into words to express themselves more clearly. They begin to understand more abstract words and forms of language. For example, they may begin to understand some puns and jokes. They also begin developing their reading, writing, and numerical skills.

Ages Nine to Eleven Years

Motor: Children continue to refine and develop their coordination and motor skills. They experience a gradual, steady gain in body measurements and proportion. Manual dexterity, posture, strength, and balance improve. This period of late childhood becomes a transitional period into the major changes experienced during adolescence.

Play: This period frequently becomes the finale of the games and play of childhood. If it has not already occurred, boys and girls separate into their respective same-gender groups.

Adaptive: Children become more and more aware of themselves and the world around them. They experience a gradual change from identifying primarily with adults to formulating their own self identity. They become more independent. This is a period of both physical and mental growth.

These children push themselves into experiencing new things and new activities. They learn to focus on detail and accomplish increasingly difficult intellectual and academic tasks.

Social: The focus of attention shifts from a family orientation to a peer orientation. They continue developing social competence. Friends become very important.

Language: A tremendous increase in vocabulary occurs. These children become adept at the use of words. They can answer questions with more depth of insight. They understand more abstract concepts and use words more precisely. They are also better able to understand and examine verbal and mathematical relationships.

Impacts of Sensory Integration on Child Development*

Jane was a 10-year-old girl who seemed constantly to be bumping into her classmates' desks. If anyone got too close to her in the lunch or recess line, she promptly proceeded to punch them. She would also frequently throw balls at others during recess. In short, she was a terror for her teacher. In desperation, her teacher finally called a parent-teacher conference which included school officials. The purpose was to suggest that Jane be placed in a special classroom for emotionally disturbed/aggressive children.

In reality, Jane was not emotionally disturbed. She was the victim of a common misconception, a misinterpretation of behavior. After more extensive testing, she was diagnosed as having disturbances in tactile and visual sensory integration—Jane was unable to perceive distances accurately and could not tolerate being touched.

Jean Ayres (1983, p. 184), a leading authority in the field, defines *sensory integration* as "the organization of sensory input for use. The 'use' may be a perception of the body or the world, or an adaptive response, or a learning process, or the development of some neural function. Through sensory integration, the many parts of the nervous system work together so that a person can interact with the environment effectively and experience appropriate satisfaction."

Sensory integration involves the ability to take in, sort out, and connect information from the world around us. Sensory integration provides children with a primary means of learning about their world. First, the senses give information about the physical conditions of our body and the environment. The subsequent sensations flow into the brain like streams flowing into a lake. Finally, the brain must organize all of these sensations if a person is to move and learn to behave normally.

The concept of sensory integration is important for social workers be-

*Many thanks are extended to Susan L. Drollinger, OTR, an occupational therapist, for her consultation and contributions to this section concerning sensory integration.

cause it helps them better understand children's behavior. Such behavioral problems as inability to follow directions accurately, inattentiveness, inability to sit still, clumsiness, bumping into people, reluctance to be touched, and aggressiveness in certain situations all may result from dysfunctions in sensory integration. When a child is said to have a sensory integrative dysfunction, there is usually no physical impairment in the sense organs or tissues themselves. Rather, it is the inability to make sense of information when it reaches the brain that is the problem.

For example, a seven-year-old boy may have 20/20 vision. However, he may find it impossible to catch a volleyball thrown to him because he is unable to integrate all of the information he's receiving from his senses. He may see the ball and wish to catch it. However, his brain may be unable to coordinate the information concerning what he sees, namely, the ball. He may not accurately perceive the size of the ball, the distance between the ball and himself, or the direction the ball is coming from. Nor may he be able to send messages from his brain to the appropriate muscles in order to catch the ball. He may not accurately determine how far apart his hands should be, in which direction they should be placed, or when he should close his hands in order to contain the ball.

The entire process of sensory integration is preprogrammed to begin at conception. Various sensory experiences or sensory inputs are necessary to activate this process. In utero, the fetus receives very special information (i.e., movement of the mother) from the uterine environment which stimulates the growth of the sensory systems. After birth, the infant is exposed to a vast variety of stimuli from contact with the family and the environment. The entire process of sensory integration takes place step by step until approximately age eight years.

In normal development, it takes place on an automatic level. In other words, children don't think about it. In this respect, development is similar to that of the respiratory or digestive systems. One breathes or digests food without overtly thinking about it. Such development simply takes place without conscious thought or control. The sensory integrative system takes in messages from the senses, sorts them out, connects them, and makes meaning out of them. This process enables us to respond appropriately and effectively to the world around us. This is a basic need in order to survive and interact comfortably with the impinging environment.

Much of the information concerning sensory integration is taken from the occupational therapy literature. *Occupational therapy* may be defined as the "art and science of directing man's response to selected activity to promote and maintain health, to prevent disability, to evaluate behavior, and to treat or train patients with physical or psychosocial dysfunction" (American Occupational Therapy Association, 1968). It involves taking both factual and theoretical scientific information and applying it to practical real-life situations and development. Therapy is designed to provide clients with appropriate experiences and activities to lessen or alleviate their dysfunctions.

Certain aspects of sensory integration are important in understanding children's behavior. These aspects include adaptive responses, infant stimulation programs, and physical aspects of the sensory integrative system. Various types of sensations are also important to understand and recognize. These involve visual sensations, auditory sensations, tactile sensations, the vestibular system, proprioceptive sensations, taste, and olfactory sensations.

Adaptive Responses

The greatest development of sensory integration occurs during an adaptive response. This involves a purposeful, goal-directed response to an environmental demand. For example, in response to the sound of a rattle, a baby may reach for and attempt to grasp it. Another example might be how a person stands in the aisle of a bus. When the bus stops, the person needs to shift her weight in order to prevent falling. An unadaptive response would be to simply fall forwards or backwards.

In an adaptive response, a challenge is mastered and something new is learned. This process helps the brain to develop and organize itself. To adults, such processes and responses may be construed simply as play. Such play might include videogames, tennis, hopscotch, or dancing. However, in reality, play consists of many adaptive responses. Play helps to make sensory integration happen. The child who learns to organize his or her play is more likely also to organize school work and develop into an organized adult.

Infant Stimulation Programs

Infant stimulation programs involve providing infants with varied experiences that are designed to stimulate their various senses. In the case of a brain-damaged child who learns more slowly than others, giving him or her as many chances as possible to practice responses is especially important. Activities involved in infant stimulation programs might include rolling, rocking, allowing the child to crawl around on surfaces of various textures, providing bright colors or a range of sounds, exposing the child to various pleasant smells, or encouraging the child to reach for objects. Infant stimulation programs are intended to encourage the infant to master situations with adaptive responses. Goals also involve supplying challenges for children and helping them deal with such challenges successfully. For example, a rattle might be held in front of an infant while encouraging the infant to reach for it and eventually placing it into his or her hand. Planning on how to obtain the rattle allows the infant to gain practical experience in both depth perception and sound orientation. The rattle also might be moved from side to side in front of the infant. The infant's head movements from side to side provide an opportunity to practice visual-motor control.

Successes in the form of healthy, normal adaptive responses are like building blocks that are necessary for more complex and mature development. Practice is necessary in order for the brain to integrate all its sensory information. The result is an adaptive response to these stimuli.

Adaptive responses by definition are both purposeful and goal directed. Some adaptive responses in adults or children may be considered inappropriate or antisocial by our general standards. For instance, a four-year-old might learn that pinching her infant sibling gains her mother's attention. However, such behavior is still goal directed and purposeful. In therapy, successes are aimed at developing healthy, normal, desired results. Therapy can be viewed as successful only if such results are achieved. Therapy is a failure if an inappropriate, deviant, or purposeless response is attained.

Physical Aspects of the Sensory Integrative System

The brain is an integrative mechanism. In other words, despite its various sources of input, it functions as one whole, interrelated system. Cognitive learning such as reading, writing, and perception takes place in the cerebral hemispheres. Such learning cannot take place without developing the brainstem. The brainstem contains the autonomic nuclei which process information from all of the other organs. It regulates the heartbeat, digestion, and breathing and is also responsible for keeping us awake or calming us down. The brainstem is the hub of the sensory integrative system.

Sensations

Sensory information is necessary for the entire sensory integration process. This information is received in the form of various types of physical sensations. Such sensations involve visual, auditory, tactile, vestibular, proprioceptive, taste, and olfactory systems.

Visual Sensations

Visual sensations involve the process of sight. The retina is sensitive to light waves. Light stimulates the retina to send visual messages to the visual processing centers located in the brainstem. These centers process the information and relate it to the other information being received. This brainstem integration forms the basis for awareness of the environment and the location of things in it.

The centers in the brainstem then send messages to other parts of the brainstem to be joined or integrated with the motor messages going to the muscles of the eyes and neck. Now the eyes and head will move as necessary to focus on the perceived object. Some visual input travels up to the cerebral cortex where the fine discrimination of visual detail occurs. Brainstem integration of the many sensations is necessary to make meaning out of what we see. For example, the pages of a book would just be perceived as small black marks if the cerebral cortex did not play its role in integrating the information.

Auditory Sensations

Auditory sensations are transmitted whenever sound waves originating from any noise stimulate the auditory receptors in the inner ear. These receptors then send messages to the brainstem auditory centers. Here auditory information is mixed in with the other sensory information being sent into the cerebral cortex.

If the auditory information did not intermingle with the other types of sensory information, we would have problems making sense out of what we hear. At each level of the brain, the message becomes clearer and more precise. The cerebral cortex refines certain sounds into meaningful syllables and words.

Tactile Sensations

Tactile sensation refers to the sense of touch. Skin contains many different kinds of receptors for distinguishing texture, heat and cold, pain, and

A fetus develops in three periods of three months each, called trimesters. During the early, embryonic stage, the fetus is exceptionally vulnerable to any noxious substances the mother ingests. It is also sensitive to food intake, drug and medication intake, and alcohol ingestion. The child in this picture is feeling her sibling's fetal movement inside their mother. What trimester (or trimesters) is the fetus in? (Charles Zastrow)

Many factors in a mother's environment can affect her fetus. If she is in a low-income bracket, she often lacks proper nourishment, bringing increased health risks to her unborn fetus. The mother in this picture gave birth to her child on a boat, while fleeing Cambodia. She was fortunate. Despite the difficult physical conditions in the birth environment, there were no complications during the mother's pregnancy, and she gave birth to this healthy child. (Fran Buss)

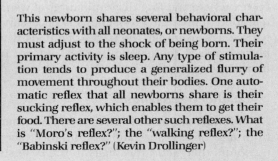

This newborn shares several behavioral characteristics with all neonates, or newborns. They must adjust to the shock of being born. Their primary activity is sleep. Any type of stimulation tends to produce a generalized flurry of movement throughout their bodies. One automatic reflex that all newborns share is their sucking reflex, which enables them to get their food. There are several other such reflexes. What is "Moro's reflex?"; the "walking reflex?"; the "Babinski reflex?" (Kevin Drollinger)

Each age period of a growing child is marked by new challenges and capabilities. The one-year-old likes to play with large balls and blocks, and can feed himself with his fingers. The five-year-old can dress and undress herself, but may need help in tying her shoes. Six-to eight-year-olds run and balance well. Most like gymnastics. What other things do six-to eight-year-olds enjoy doing? 2-I: (Karen Kirst-Ashman) 2-M: (Courtesy of United Way of America) 2-N: (Fran Buss)

the movement of the hairs on the skin. Tactile sensation plays an especially vital role in human behavior, both physical and mental. For example, having a persistent pain, regardless of how small, affects one's whole attitude.

Touch receptors below the neck send messages up the spinal cord to the brainstem. Skin receptors on the head, however, send their messages directly to the brainstem through cranial nerves. The brainstem then distributes messages throughout the brain.

Tactile sensation can be divided into two basic systems—the protective system and the discriminative system.

The Protective System. Our protective system alerts us to any potentially dangerous or harmful stimuli. It originated as a very ancient and basic survival trait in both man and animals. People must react to a dangerous situation or else be hurt. A good example of the protective system operating is how a person immediately withdraws when having touched something hot.

The Discriminative System. The primary goal of the discriminative system is to supply us with information. It responds to stimuli in the environment that give us information. This includes texture (smooth/rough, soft/hard), amount of pressure, awareness of shape and size, and weight perception. The protective system tells you immediately that something has touched the back of your head. When unexpected, the result of such a touch is often withdrawal. However, if the touch is anticipated or if the touch stimulus is maintained for some period of time, the person is then free to get further information from the discriminative system. For instance, if someone tickles your neck with a long blade of grass, the discriminative system could tell you that the grass is feathery and soft, neither hot nor cold, and that it was touching you only lightly.

Balance of the Two Systems. Both the protective and the discriminative systems are important. Two systems must work together. The protective system keeps us from harm. However, if it would be too strong, it would keep us from interacting with objects and people in the environment. The immediate reaction to any touch would be aversion and withdrawal. In the normal nervous system, protective touch is integrated early in life. It only becomes dominant when we need it in times of danger.

Tactile defensiveness can result if the two systems are not well integrated. *Tactile defensiveness* is defined as the tendency to react negatively to certain kinds of touch. For example, we might be tactilely defensive when a wasp lands on our shoulder or when someone sneaks up behind us and surprises us. People with high levels of tactile defensiveness might be overly sensitive to various types of touch that the rest of us are barely aware of.

Tactilely defensive children might be overly fidgety, hyperactive, or distractable. They might find it difficult to tolerate many of the normal tactile sensations unnoticed by the rest of us. Such children may not only react to the touch itself, but also to the fear of being touched. The fear is real; it is physically, not emotionally based. A child who is tactilely defensive may even hate to stand in line for fear that others may touch him or her. This child may crave firm pressure such as a firm pat on the back, but withdraw from any lighter touch. He or she may strike out at a person who gets too close or situate him or herself during class where others won't come anywhere near him or her. Tactile defensiveness also affects how a child plays table games, sits at the dinner table, participates in sports, and undertakes numerous other daily routine activities. Even a particular piece of clothing may make him or her irritable because of a tight sleeve or a scratchy label.

Jose, age seven, presents one example of tactile defensiveness. He typically shrinks away from other people. He hits them if they bump into him accidentally. On the other hand, he craves tactile stimulation which he can control. He is often found putting flies in his ears. He also likes to place his fingers in both nose and mouth simultaneously as he walks around attending to his daily business.

The Vestibular System

The vestibular system involves the inner ear and gives us information concerning our own movement. This inner ear includes two types of vestibular receptors which have nothing to do with hearing. One responds to the force of gravity so that people are aware of which way is up and which way is down.

The other type of vestibular receptors, called *semicircular canals*, are tiny closed tubes filled with fluid which reacts to motion. Three pairs are located in each ear. Rapid movement in any direction stimulates the receptors that lie inside the canals. Messages about this movement are then sent up the vestibular nerve to the brainstem. Messages change whenever the head changes the speed or direction of movement. These receptors are responsible for the senses of acceleration and deceleration.

The combination of the gravity receptors and the semicircular canals tells us exactly where we are in relationship to gravity. We know whether we are moving or standing still and also how fast we are moving and in what direction. Examples of how the vestibular system causes reactions include motion sickness and tolerance to spinning. A child of age eight might be able to ride the Tidal Wave roller coaster for hours on end and enjoy every minute of it. However, that same child as an adult may become nauseous on such a ride after his system has matured.

Problems in this system can have various results for either children or adults. They might have poor balance and poor protective responses. For instance, walking on a straight line may prove difficult.

People with vestibular difficulties may make clumsy and awkward movements with the large muscles operating their torso, arms, and legs. Such people may have difficulty aiming or catching a baseball.

Other people with vestibular problems might have difficulty tracking objects with their eyes or even being able to focus properly. Reading problems or trouble catching balls may result.

Some children or adults with vestibular problems may crave vestibular stimulation. Head swinging and body rocking may result. A child who zooms down the hall head first may be showing symptoms of vestibular dysfunction. Finally, gravitational insecurity may also result. This refers to "an abnormal anxiety or distress caused by inadequate modulation or inhibition of sensations that arise when the gravity receptors of the vestibular system are stimulated by head position or movement" (Ayres, 1983, p. 182).

Proprioceptive Sensation

Proprioceptive sensation concerns the sensory information caused by contraction and stretching of muscles and by bending, straightening, pulling, and compression of the joints between the bones. Proprioceptive sensation allows us to raise our hand with our eyes closed and still be able to touch our nose, even without seeing it. These sensations are especially important during movement.

Proprioceptive sensation helps us to move. Take, for example, the hands. If proprioception from your hands is insufficient, then you wouldn't know exactly where your hands were positioned in space. You would not be able to determine whether they were right in front of you or a bit toward your sides.

Children with poor integration of this proprioceptive system may show low muscle tone. This means there is less than a normal degree of vigor or tension in a muscle. They may also have difficulty with form and space perception. Likewise, they may have poor motor planning. If you don't know how you are positioned in space, you will have difficulty analyzing where other things are in relationship to you. Problems in right-left discrimination are common.

For example, you might have a girl who has difficulty catching a basketball. It's hard for her to figure out how to catch the ball because she isn't getting adequate feedback from the joints in her arms and shoulders. She must actually look at her arms and consciously think to herself: "I have to move my arms from here to here." Catching a basketball is not an automatic, almost mindless reaction for her as it is for people with normal proprioceptive sensations.

Taste and Smell

Taste and smell are the two other senses which provide information useful in sensory integration. These senses are probably well developed already at birth. For example, the sucking reflex is based on an infant's ability to taste and smell.

Smell is especially important with respect to human interaction. For example, some people are very sensitive to strong perfume and will withdraw from the person using it. Some children having an overly sensitive sense of smell will even exhibit hyperactive behavior when exposed to a strong smell.

Sensory Integration and Learning Disability

Both sensory integration and learning relate to how we take in all the various stimuli around us and respond in some adaptive behavior. Integration, or how we make sense of stimuli in our brains, enables us to learn. Learning disabilities relate to inadequate integration of various types of stimuli. A specific learning disability "implies that the youngster has a learning problem due to the dysfunction of one or more of the learning functions in one or more of the sense modalities" (McWhirter, 1977, p. 21). In other words, poor sensory integration in a specific area or specific areas results in a learning disability.

Sensory integration provides a framework by which human behavior can be analyzed. Understanding this process provides some reasons for why people behave in certain ways. Dysfunctional sensory integration in one way or another may cause an individual to have difficulties functioning in everyday life. A person may be abnormally clumsy, have difficulty reading, or abhor being touched. Sometimes these problems are physiologically, not psychologically, rooted. Many times means are available to help a person develop his or her sensory integration capacities or to compensate for some deficits in sensory integration. Therapy is often available as a means of helping an individual function more normally.

Social workers need to be aware of this alternative means of helping clients. Awareness of the types of behavioral problems exhibited by people with sensory integration problems can lead to effective referrals for appropriate testing and therapy. Many social workers will be called on to work in conjunction with occupational therapists. Understanding some of the essence and goals of this helping profession can only facilitate a good working relationship between the two.

Significant Issues and Life Events

Two significant issues will be discussed which relate to the decision of whether or not to have children. They have been selected because of the great number of people they impact and because they often pose a serious crisis for the people involved. The issues are abortion and infertility.

■ Roseanne—Single and Pregnant

Roseanne was 21-years-old and two months pregnant. She was a junior at a large midwestern state university majoring in social work. Hank, the father, was a 26-year-old divorcee she met in one of her classes. He already had a four-year-old son named Ronnie.

Roseanne was filled with ambivalent feelings. She had always pictured herself as being a mother someday. However, not now. She felt she loved Hank, but had many reservations about how he felt in return. She'd been seeing him once or twice a week for the past few months. Hank didn't really take her out much and she suspected that he was also dating other women. He had even asked her to babysit for Ronnie while he went out with someone else.

That was another thing—Ronnie. She felt Ronnie hated her. He would snarl whenever she came over and make nasty, cutting remarks. Maybe he was jealous that his father was giving Roseanne attention.

The pregnancy was an accident. She simply didn't think anything would happen. She knew better now that it was too late. Hank had never made any commitment to her. In some ways she felt he was a creep, but at least he was honest. The fact was that he just didn't love her.

The problem now was what she should do. A college education was important to her and to her parents. Money had always been a big issue. Her parents had helped her as much as they could, but they also had other children in college. Roseanne had worked odd, inconvenient hours at Arby's Roast Beef for a while. Lately she had been working as a cook several nights a week at Mickey's Diner.

What if she kept the baby? She was fairly certain Hank didn't want to marry her. Even if he did, she didn't think she'd want to be stuck with him for the rest of her life. How could she possibly manage on her own with a baby? She now shared a two-bedroom apartment with three other female students. How could she take care of a baby with no money and no place to go? She felt dropping out of school would ruin her life. The idea of "going on welfare" instead of working in welfare was terrifying.

On the other hand, the idea of an abortion scared her. She had heard so many people say that it was "murder."

Roseanne made her decision, but it certainly was not an easy one. She carefully addressed and considered the religious and moral issues involved in terminating a pregnancy. She decided that she would have to face the responsibility and the guilt. In determining that having a baby at this time would be disastrous for both herself and for a new life, she decided to have an abortion.

Fourteen years passed. Roseanne is now 35. She is no longer in social work although she had finished her degree. She does have a good job as a court reporter. She had always been interested in legal matters (reruns of the television show "Perry Mason" were still her favorite). This job suits her well.

She's been married to Tom for three years. Although they have their ups and downs, she is happy in her marriage. They love each other very much and enjoy their time together.

Roseanne thinks about her abortion every once in a while. Although she is using no method of birth control, she has not yet gotten pregnant. Possibly, she never will. Tom is 43. He had been married once before and has an adult child from that marriage. He does not feel it is a necessity for them to have children.

Roseanne is ambivalent. She is addressing the possibility of not ever having children and is looking at the consequences of that alternative. She puts it well by saying that sometimes she mourns the loss of her unborn child. Yet, in view of her present level of life's satisfaction and Tom's hesitation about having children, she feels that her life thus far has worked out for the best.

The Abortion Controversy

There are many unique sets of circumstances involved in any unplanned pregnancy. Individuals must evaluate for themselves the potential consequences of each alternative. As the Behavior Dynamics Assessment Model dictates, various life events such as an unplanned pregnancy impact individuals. At that juncture, the individual needs to define the available alternatives and assess the positive and negative consequences of each.

A basic decision involved in unplanned pregnancy is whether or not to have the baby. If the decision is made to have the baby, there is a subset of alternatives to evaluate from that point. One option is to marry the father, that is, of course, if the couple is not already married. Another alternative is for the mother to keep the baby and live as a single parent. Yet another possibility is for the father to keep the baby as a single parent. This choice, although still not very common, is becoming more legally and socially acceptable. Another alternative is to have parents (the child's grandparents) or other relatives either keep the baby or assist in its caretaking. Another option is to have the baby and place it up for adoption.

Each choice involves both positive and negative consequences. Abortion is a legal alternative in the United States. Thus, social workers may find themselves in the position of helping their clients explore abortion as one possibility open to them.

The concept of abortion inevitably elicits strong feelings and emotions in people. These feelings can be very positive or negative. People who take stands against abortion often do so on moral and ethical grounds. A common theme is that each unborn child has "the right to life." On the opposite pole are those who feel strongly in favor of abortion. They feel that women have "the right to choice" over their own bodies and their own lives.

The abortion issue provides an excellent opportunity to distinguish between personal and professional values. Each of us probably has an opinion about abortion. Some of us most likely have very strong opinions either one way or the other. The point is that in practice our personal opinions really don't matter. However, our professional approach does. As professionals it is our responsibility to help clients come to their own decisions. Our job is to assist clients in assessing their own feelings and values, in identifying available alternatives, and in evaluating as objectively as possible the consequences of each alternative.

In order to better understand abortion and its impacts, four aspects will be focused on here. First, the current legal and political situation will be described. Second, the abortion process itself and the types of abortion available will be explained. Third, some of the psychological effects of abortion will be briefly examined. Fourth, the arguments for and against abortion will be compared and assessed.

The Political Picture

The abortion controversy has now been going on for nearly two decades; but it was heightened when, in January 1973, the U.S. Supreme Court, in a 7 to 2 decision, overruled state laws that prohibited or restricted a woman's right to obtain an abortion during the first three months of pregnancy. States still have the authority to impose restrictions after the third month. States may prohibit abortions in the last ten weeks of pregnancy (a time when the fetus is probably viable, or has a good chance to live on its own) if they desire, except where the life or health of the mother is endangered.

In 1977, Congress passed, and President Carter signed into law, the so-called Hyde amendment (named for its original sponsor, Representative Henry Hyde from Illinois). This amendment bars Medicaid spending for abortions except when a woman's life would be endangered by childbirth or in cases of promptly reported rape or incest. In June 1980, this amendment was upheld on a 5 to 4 vote by the U.S. Supreme Court as constitutional. This means that the federal government and individual states do not have to pay for welfare abortions.

The Hyde amendment is significant because more than one third of the legal abortions performed in the United States between 1973 and 1977 were for women on welfare (*Wisconsin State Journal*, 1980). The passage of the Hyde amendment shows the strength of the antiabortion forces in this country. Opponents of the Hyde amendment fear that illegal "back alley" abortions may again be performed, with some women dying from medical complications.

With the election of President Reagan in 1980, there was a move toward conservatism in our society. Certain groups, such as the Catholic Church and the Moral Majority (headed by Jerry Falwell) began strongly urging that a constitutional amendment be passed to prohibit abortions, except in cases where the woman's life is endangered.

The major objection to permitting abortions is based on moral principles. The Catholic Church views abortion as one of the most important current moral issues. This church and right to life groups condemn abortions as being synonymous to murder. They assert life begins at conception and point out there is no phase during pregnancy in which there is a distinct, qualitative difference in the development of the fetus. The only time the Catholic Church views abortion as being acceptable is when it is done to save the life of the mother. The church justifies this type of abortion on the principle of "double effect," which holds that a morally evil action (an abortion) is allowable when it is the side effect of a morally good act (saving the life of the mother).

Methods of Abortion

Several different procedures are used to perform abortions. The major variable which determines whether one or the other should be used is how far the pregnancy has progressed.

Vacuum Aspiration

Vacuum aspiration, the most common method of abortion, is performed during the first trimester of pregnancy. Other terms are vacuum curettage, the suction method, and dilation and evacuation (D & E).

The procedure involves inserting an instrument into the vagina and then into the cervix. The opening of the cervix is then dilated. A plastic, tubelike instrument is inserted into the uterus. The other end of the tube is attached to an electric suction device. The interior contents of the uterus including the fetal material and placenta are suctioned out. The entire procedure takes about 10 minutes. It can be performed on an outpatient basis in a physician's office, a clinic, or a hospital.

The vacuum aspiration method is the most effective abortion method for several reasons. First of all, it is the safest for the mother. There are no additional risks posed by general anesthesia. No sutures are necessary. It is relatively fast and simple. Second, the fetal tissue is removed early in its developmental process. It is as yet nowhere near the time of viability. Third, the process is the least expensive of any of the procedures.

If this is the best type of abortion procedure, the question might be raised why it is not always used. Reasons often fall into two categories. First, the pregnant woman may not identify or acknowledge the fact that she is pregnant this early in the pregnancy. Especially if the pregnancy is un-planned and the mother is single, she may avoid thinking about the issue. She may hope that missing a menstrual period is just a fluke and that she is really not pregnant. She may also feel that by not thinking about the problem, it ceases to exist.

Some women also have difficulty deciding to have the abortion even after they realize they are pregnant. Many emotional blocks similar to those identified earlier may be operating. The decision to abort is most often a difficult one. By the time a woman verifies the fact that she's pregnant, she has only a few weeks or even days to make that decision before her preg-nancy progresses into the second trimester.

Dilation and Curettage

Another first trimester abortion technique is the dilation and curettage method, often referred to as the D & C. As with vacuum aspiration, the cervical opening is dilated or opened. An instrument made up of a sharp metal loop on the end of a long handle is inserted into the uterus. This instrument, called a curette, is used to scrape the fetal tissue and related membranes from the uterine walls.

Vacuum aspiration is considered preferable to a D & C because the latter requires hospitalization and general anesthesia. The D & C also involves greater risks than vacuum aspiration of perforation of the uterine wall, hemorrhaging, or infection.

Induced Labor

Second trimester abortions are more complicated and involve greater risks. Actual labor can be induced by injecting chemicals. One such method, the saline-induced abortion, involves inserting a fine tube through the abdomen into the amniotic sac. About seven ounces of saline (salt) solution is then injected into the sac. A second method involves prostaglandins which is a substance resembling a hormone and which acts to cause uterine contractions (Hyde, 1982, p. 164). A prostaglandin-induced abortion involves either injecting prostaglandins into the amniotic sac in a similar manner to that of a saline-induced abortion, slowly injecting it into a vein, or inserting a suppository containing prostaglandins into the vagina.

Either of these two methods results in the initiation of actual labor and the vaginal delivery of a dead fetus. Both of these methods have the disadvantages of taking hours of time, of causing the mother emotional and physical distress, of being more hazardous, and of being more expensive.

Hysterotomy

A hysterotomy is similar to a caesarean section in that the fetus is surgically removed from the abdomen. It can be done throughout the second trimester. This procedure requires general anesthesia, involves greater risks than other methods, and costs more. Another major disadvantage is that the fetus is close to attaining viability. For all of these reasons, hysterotomies are rarely performed.

Psychological Reactions to Abortion

Positive results of abortion appear to outweigh the negative psychological effects (Osofsky et al., 1971; Osofsky and Osofsky, 1972; Nadelson, 1978). Less than three of every 100,000 women who have had an abortion require serious psychiatric help (Masters and Johnson, 1985, p. 183). On the other hand, it appears that women who have requested an abortion and were denied the opportunity seem to be more likely to later suffer from a psychiatric disturbance (Forssman and Thuwe, 1966).

Despite this research, many women feel a sense of guilt, sadness, or loss, at least on a short-term basis, after having an abortion (Masters and Johnson, 1985, p. 183). This fact emphasizes the need for counseling both before and after the abortion is performed. These people need to address their feelings, deal with them, and look realistically at their own life situations.

One other frequently ignored psychological repercussion of abortion is the male's reaction to the whole process. Some evidence exists that, although men initially tend to deal with abortion in a calm, intellectual manner, after some time passes, these feelings change (Shostak et al., 1984). Perhaps a better way of putting it is that their true feelings may emerge. These men later begin to experience similar feelings to those that women initially experience, namely guilt, sadness, and even anger. The male's feelings toward abortion is an area which has traditionally been avoided. Perhaps it is one which also needs some attention.

Arguments For and Against Abortion

Numerous arguments have been advanced for permitting abortions:

- If abortions were prohibited again, women would seek illegal abortions as they did in the past. Performed in a medical clinic or hospital, an abortion is relatively safe; but performed under unsanitary conditions, perhaps by an inexperienced or unskilled abortionist, the operation is extremely dangerous and may even imperil the life of the woman.

- If abortions were again prohibited, some women would attempt to self-induce abortions. Attempts at self-induced abortions can be extremely dangerous. Women have tried such techniques as severe exercise, hot baths, pelvic and intestinal irritants, and have even attempted to lacerate the uterus with such sharp objects at hatpins, nail files, and knives.

- Recognizing abortions as being legal helps prevent the birth of unwanted babies; such babies have a higher probability of being abused or neglected.

- Permitting women to obtain an abortion allows women to have greater freedom, as they would not be forced to raise a child at a time when they had other plans and commitments.

Opponents of abortion argue that the right to life is basic and should in no way be infringed. Proponents of abortion seek to counter this view by arguing that there may be a more basic right than the right to life; that is, the preservation of the quality of life. Given the overpopulation problem and given the fact that abortion appears to be a necessary population-control technique (in some countries the number of abortions is approaching the number of live births), abortion may well be a necessary measure (although less desirable than contraceptives) to preserve the quality of life.

Regardless of one's personal view, professional social workers must be aware of arguments on both sides of the issue. Many of the points and counterpoints are presented in the accompanying discussion, *Legal Abortion: Arguments Pro and Con*.

■ Legal Abortion: Arguments Pro and Con

Antilegal Abortion	*Prolegal Abortion*
Human life begins at conception; therefore, abortion is murder. Even scientists have not reached a consensus on any other point in fetal development which can be considered the moment the fetus becomes a person. Life is a matter of fact, not religion or values.	The belief in personhood at conception is a religious belief held by the Roman Catholic Church. Most Protestant and Jewish denominations regard the fetus as a potential human being, not a full-fledged person and have position statements in support of legal abortion. When the unborn becomes a person is a matter of religion and values, not absolute fact.
We must pass a constitutional amendment to protect unborn babies from abortion. To say the law will not be followed and should not be made is like saying people still get murdered so laws against murder should be repealed.	No law has ever stopped abortion and no law ever will. The issue is not whether abortions will be done, but whether they will be done safely, by doctors, or dangerously, by back-alley butchers or by the women themselves. History has shown that antiabortion laws are uniquely unenforceable, as they do not prevent abortions.

Antilegal Abortion	Prolegal Abortion
Medicaid should not pay for abortion. It is wrong to try to eliminate poverty by killing the unborn children of the poor. Tax money should not be used for the controversial practice of aborting unwanted children. The decision not to have children should be made before getting pregnant.	The original intent of Medicaid was to equalize medical services between the rich and the poor and to help the poor become independent and self-sufficient. To make them ineligible for abortion defies justice, common sense, and rational policy. Women burdened by unwanted children cannot get job training or go to work and are trapped in the poverty/welfare cycle. Neither abortion nor childbirth should be forced on poor women.
If you believe abortion is morally wrong, you are obligated to work for the passage of a human life amendment to the Constitution.	Many people who are personally opposed to abortion, including most Roman Catholics, believe it is wrong to impose their religious or moral beliefs on others.
The right of the unborn to life supersedes any right of a woman to "control her own body."	The Supreme Court has affirmed that the constitutional right to privacy includes the right to terminate a pregnancy and that fetuses are not persons with constitutional rights.
The abortion mentality leads to infanticide, euthanasia, and killing of retarded and elderly persons.	In countries where abortion has been legal for years, there is no evidence that respect for life has diminished or that legal abortion leads to killing of any persons. Infanticide, however, is prevalent in countries where the overburdened poor cannot control their childbearing and was prevalent in Japan before abortion was legalized.
Abortion causes psychological damage to women.	The Institute of Medicine of the National Academy of Sciences has concluded that abortion is not associated with a detectable increase in the incidence of mental illness. The depression and guilt feelings reported by some women are usually mild, temporary, and outweighed by feelings of relief. Such negative feelings would be substantially lessened if antiabortion advocates were less vehement in expressing their beliefs. Women choosing abortion should be informed of the risks and benefits of the procedure and should decide for themselves what to do.
Women have abortions for their own convenience or on whim.	Right-to-life dismisses unwanted pregnancy as a mere annoyance. The urgency of women's need to end unwanted pregnancy is measured by their willingness to risk death and mutilation, to spend huge sums of money, and to endure the indignities of illegal abortion. Women only have abortions when the alternative is unendurable. Women take both abortion and motherhood very seriously.
In a society where contraceptives are so readily available, there should be no unwanted pregnancies and therefore no need for abortion.	No birth control method is perfectly reliable, and for medical reasons many women cannot, or will not, use the most effective methods. Contraceptive information and services are not available to all women, particularly teenagers, the poor, and rural women.

Antilegal Abortion	Prolegal Abortion
Abortion is not the safe and simple procedure we're told it is.	Before the 1973 Supreme Court rulings, illegal abortion was the leading cause of maternal death and mutilation. Having a legal abortion is medically less dangerous than childbirth.
Doctors make large profits from legal abortion.	Legal abortion is less costly and less profitable than illegal abortion was. Many legal abortions are done in nonprofit facilities. If it's proper to make money on childbirth, it is not wrong to earn money by performing legal abortions.
Parents have the right and responsibility to guide their children in important decisions. A law requiring parental notification of a daughter's abortion would strengthen the family unit.	Many teenagers voluntarily consult their parents, but some simply will not. Forcing the involvement of unsympathetic, authoritarian, or very moralistic parents in a teen's pregnancy (and sexuality) can damage the family unit beyond repair. Some family units are already under so much stress that knowledge of an unwed pregnancy could be disastrous.
Proabortionists are antifamily. Abortion destroys the American family.	The unwanted child of a teen-aged mother has little chance to grow up in a normal, happy American home. Instead, a new family is created: a child and her child, both destined for a life of poverty and hopelessness. Legal abortion helps women limit their families to the number of children they want and can afford and reduces the number of children born unwanted. Prochoice is definitely profamily.

Infertility

Ralph and Carol, both age 28, had been married for five years. Ralph was a drill press operator at a large bathroom fixture plant. Carol was a waitress at Chi-Chi's Mexican restaurant. They both liked their jobs well enough. They were earning an adequate enough income to purchase a small three-bedroom home and to enjoy some pleasurable amenities such as going out to dinner occasionally, taking annual camping vacations, and having cable television.

However, they felt something was wrong. Although Carol had stopped taking birth control pills over three years ago, she had still not gotten pregnant. She had read in some recent issue of *Cosmopolitan* that women over age 35 had a much greater chance of having a child with mental retardation or birth defects. Although she still had a few years, she was a little concerned. She and Ralph had always wanted to have as large a family as they could afford. This meant that they had better get going.

The couple really didn't talk much about the issue. Neither one wanted to imply that something might be wrong with the other one. The idea that one or both might be infertile was not appealing. It was almost easier to ignore the issue and hope that it would resolve itself in a pregnancy. After all, they did still have a few years.

Approximately 12 percent of all U.S. couples are infertile (Hyde, 1982, p. 131). *Infertility* may be defined as "the inability to have a baby, usually after a year or more of sexual intercourse without pregnancy" (Masters and Johnson, 1985, p. 644). Although many people assume that they will automatically be able to conceive if they don't use birth control, this is obviously not always the case.

Infertility is considered one viable explanation after a couple has been trying to conceive, by having intercourse regularly, for one year. This one-year period is frequently considered the cue for confronting the possibility of infertility. At this point, it is usually recommended that the possibility of some physical problem in one or both members of the couple be explored. Half of all fertile couples will conceive within one month of trying and 80 percent within six months (Novak et al., 1975).

Causes of Infertility

Specific causes can be identified in 85 percent of infertile couples (Masters and Johnson, 1985, p. 141). The male partner is responsible for the infertility in about 30 percent (Amelar, 1966) to 40 percent (Speroff et al., 1973) of the cases.

Female Infertility

Two major causes of infertility in women are failure to ovulate and blockage of the fallopian tubes. Many possible causes exist for not ovulating including chronic illnesses, ovarian or hormonal abnormalities, vitamin deficiency or malnutrition, and occasionally emotional stress. Whether ovulation has occurred or not can be detected by monitoring a woman's daily morning temperature. Basal body temperature charts can be used for this purpose. Immediately after ovulation, the body temperature rises and maintains this higher level for 10 to 16 days. No temperature rise at all is one indication that a woman is not ovulating. Ovulation can also be determined by examining hormonal levels or scrapings of the uteral lining.

Blockage of the fallopian tubes is another major cause of infertility. Infections such as those caused by pelvic inflammatory disease can form scar tissue which blocks the tubes. Tumors or various congenital abnormalities are other possible causes. Blockage can be detected by using x-rays after injecting a dye which outlines the internal structures. Potential blockage can also be explored by Rubin's test. Carbon dioxide is forced into the uterus through the cervix. Normal tubes will direct the gas into the abdomen, whereas blocked tubes will cause increased pressure in the uterus.

Other less common causes of female infertility include abnormally thick mucus in the cervix, sometimes referred to as "hostile mucus," which can prevent sperm from entering the uterus. Other women have an allergic response to sperm; in these cases antibodies are manufactured which destroy sperm. Structural abnormalities can also cause infertility. Finally, a woman's age may be a contributing factor. Fertility declines after age 35, with a sharper drop after age 40 (Hyde, 1982, p. 131).

Male Infertility

The most common cause of infertility in men is a low sperm count. This can be caused by numerous conditions including varicose veins in the scrotum and testes, certain infections such as the mumps when acquired in adulthood, congenital birth defects, undescended testes, and various types of drugs including alcohol, cigarettes, narcotics, and marijuana (Masters and Johnson, 1985, pp. 141–42). Even extremely tight-fitting underwear has been found to decrease sperm counts (Shane et al., 1976). One other somewhat common cause of male infertility is the decreased ability of sperm to swim.

Psychological Reactions to Infertility

Some people experience serious negative reactions to infertility. Especially for those who really desire to have children, infertility can be associated with failure. This is compounded by the fact that even the most intimate partners often don't feel comfortable talking about their sexuality, let alone the fact that something may be wrong with it. Some men associate their potency with their ability to father children. Traditionally, women have placed great importance on their roles as wife and mother. Hopefully, with the greater flexibility of women's roles today, the technological advances aimed at improving fertility, and the new options available to infertile couples, the negative psychological reactions to infertility will be minimized.

Treatment of Infertility

Various treatments are currently available for treating infertility. For treating failure to ovulate, two kinds of drugs can be used. Clomiphene is used to stimulate the pituitary which subsequently produces the hormones necessary to induce ovulation. Pregnancies result in approximately half of all women using clomiphene. Another drug called HMG (Human menopausal gonadotropins) can also be used in a series of injections to stimulate the ovaries directly. Approximately 60 to 70 percent of all women using HMG become pregnant; 20 percent of these pregnancies are multiple (Masters and Johnson, 1985, p. 145). However, a potential negative side effect is that either clomiphene or HMG can cause the ovaries to enlarge dramatically. Sometimes hospitalization becomes necessary as the ovaries may burst.

Microsurgery has been used to correct both blocked fallopian tubes and varicose veins in the scrotum and testes. Women having such surgery have a 30 to 50 percent success rate (Masters and Johnson, 1985, p. 145). The treatment of male infertility is much less advanced. The chance of correcting problems other than varicose veins with either surgery or drugs is at present much poorer.

Alternatives Available to the Infertile Couple

The first thing that needs to be done in the case of suspected infertility is to bring the matter out into the open. People need to talk about their ideas and feelings. Only then can the various alternatives be identified and a plan of action determined.

After at least one year of trying to conceive, both partners should probably pursue a medical evaluation to help determine if anything is physically wrong. The couple's sexual practices concerning pregnancy should also be discussed to make certain that they have accurate and specific information. Some suggestions are available for improving the chances of conception.

For example, a woman can monitor her temperature to help determine when she is ovulating. After doing this for several months, an ovulation pattern may be established. Sexual intercourse right around the time of ovulation may be helpful. Additionally, ejaculations should probably not occur more than once every 24 to 48 hours in order to avoid diminishing the sperm count. The best plan is probably to have intercourse every 24 to 48 hours, or about four times, during the week of ovulation (Hyde, 1982, p. 101). One other suggestion may be to have the woman assume the bottom position during intercourse, lying on her back. This helps in preventing the semen from running out of her vagina.

In those cases where treatment of infertility is impossible or unsuccessful, other alternatives, such as adoption, artificial insemination, in vitro fertilization, surrogate motherhood, and acceptance of childlessness may need to be pursued.

Adoption

Adoption is the legal, social, and psychological process which ensures a dependent child a permanent family (Friedlander, 1968). To provide a home and family to a child who has none is a viable and beneficial option. However, white infants are often in high demand and low supply. Other subalternatives within the adoption alternative include the adoption of an older homeless child or transracial adoption, the adoption of a child of another race. Foreign adoptions present yet another alternative. Each option needs to be examined.

Artificial Insemination

Artificial insemination refers to the process of "placing semen into the vagina or uterus by a means other than sexual intercourse" (Masters and Johnson, 1985, p. 146). This method can be used when the woman is fertile.

Over 20,000 babies are born annually in the United States through the process of artificial insemination (CBS Reports, 1979). Human sperm can be frozen, thawed, and used to impregnate for long periods of time. (The length of time that sperm can be frozen has not been determined; it is generally acknowledged that five years would be safe with close to 100 percent assurance.)

A sperm bank collects and maintains sperm for private citizens for a fee depending on length of time. The sperm is then usually withdrawn at some later date to impregnate (with a physician's assistance) a woman.

The sperm used in artificial insemination may be the husband's (called AIH). It is possible to pool several ejaculations from a man with a low sperm count and to inject them simultaneously into the vaginal canal of his spouse, thus vastly increasing the chance of pregnancy. AIH may also be used for family planning purposes—for example, a man might deposit his sperm in the bank, then receive a vasectomy, and then later withdraw the sperm to have children. High-risk jobs might prompt a man to make a deposit in case of untimely death or sterility.

A second type of artificial insemination, called AID, involves the donor of the sperm being someone other than the husband. AID has been used for several decades to circumvent male infertility, and also used when it is known that the husband is a carrier of a genetic disease (for example, a condition such as hemophilia). In recent years an increasing number of single women are requesting the services of a sperm bank. The usual procedure involves the woman requesting the general genetic characteristics she wants from the father, and the bank then trying to match such requests from the information known about their donors.

A third type of artificial insemination is of recent origin and has received considerable publicity. Some married couples, in which the wife is infertile, have contracted with another woman to be artificially inseminated with the husband's sperm. Under the terms of the contract this surrogate mother is paid and expected to give the infant to the married couple shortly after birth.

A number of ethical and legal questions have been raised about artificial insemination. Religious leaders object and claim that God did not mean for people to reproduce this way. In the case of AID, certain psychological stresses are placed on husbands and on marriages, as the procedure emphasizes the husband's infertility and involves having a baby that he has not fathered. On a broader dimension, artificial insemination raises such questions as: What are the purposes of marriage and of sex, and what will happen to male/female relationships if we do not even have to see each other to reproduce?

Some very unusual court cases suggest new laws will have to be written to resolve the questions that are arising. For instance, there is the case of Mr. & Mrs. John M. Prutting. He was medically determined to be sterile as a result of radiation received at work. Without her husband's knowledge, she was inseminated. After the birth of the baby, he sued her for divorce on the grounds of adultery (Rifken, 1977).

In another case a wife was inseminated with the husband's consent by a donor. They later divorced. When he requested visiting privileges, she took him to court on the grounds that he was not the father and thus had no right. In New York he won, but she moved to Oklahoma, where the decision was reversed (Rifken, 1977). And finally, there was a reported case of an engaged couple who were discovered to have had the same donor through artificial insemination, and were thus half-brother and half-sister. The marriage was called off (Rifken, 1977).

There are other possible legal implications. What happens if the sperm at a bank is not paid for? Would it become the property of the bank? Could it be auctioned off? If a woman was artificially inseminated by a donor and the child was later found to have genetic defects, could the parents bring suit against the physician, the donor, or the bank? Does the child have a right to know who his or her real father is?

Sperm banks can be used in genetic engineering movements. In the spring of 1980 it was disclosed that Robert Graham had set up an exclusive sperm bank to produce exceptionally bright children. Graham stated that at least five Nobel Prize winners had donated sperm to inseminate women. Several women have already given birth through the services of this bank (*Wisconsin State Journal*, 1980, p. 7). This approach raises questions whether reproductive technology should be used to produce superior children, and what characteristics should be defined as superior?

Surrogate Motherhood

Thousands of married couples who want children but are unable to reproduce because the wife is infertile have turned to surrogate motherhood; a surrogate gives birth to a baby conceived by artificial insemination, using the sperm of the husband. (Often the surrogate mother is paid a fee for her services.) On birth, the surrogate mother terminates her parental rights and the child is then legally adopted by the donor of the sperm and his wife.

Couples using the services of a surrogate mother are generally delighted with this medical technique and believe it to be a highly desirable solution to their personal difficulty. However, other groups assert that surrogate motherhood raises a number of moral, legal, and personal issues.

A number of theologians and religious leaders firmly believe God intended conception to occur only among married couples through sexual intercourse. These religious leaders view surrogate motherhood as ethically wrong, as the surrogate mother is not married to the donor of the sperm and because artificial insemination is viewed as "unnatural." Some religious leaders also assert that it is morally despicable for a surrogate mother to accept a fee (often from $5,000 to $10,000). They maintain procreation is a blessing from God and should not be commercialized.

Surrogate motherhood also raises complicated legal questions which have considerable social consequences. For example, surrogate mothers usually sign a nonbinding contract stipulating the mother will give up the child for adoption at birth. What if the surrogate mother changes her mind shortly before birth and decides to keep the baby? Legally, it appears she has the right to keep the baby and perhaps even sue the donor of the sperm for child support (Christopher, 1980, p. 10).

Most surrogate mothers, to date, are married and already have children. A number of issues are apt to arise. How does the husband of a surrogate mother feel about his wife being pregnant by another man's sperm? How does such a married couple explain to their children that their half-brother or half-sister will be given up for adoption to another family? How does such a married couple explain what they are doing to relatives, neighbors and the surrounding community? If the child is born with severe mental or physical handicaps, who will care for the child and pay for the expenses? Will it be the surrogate mother and her husband, the contracting adoptive couple, or society?

In 1983, a surrogate mother gave birth in Michigan to a baby who was born with microcephaly, a condition in which the head is smaller than normal and mental retardation is likely. At first neither the surrogate mother nor the contracting adoptive couple wanted to care for the child. The adoptive couple refused to pay the $10,000 fee to the surrogate mother. A legal battle ensued. Blood tests were eventually taken which indicated the probable father was not the contracting adoptive father, but the husband of the surrogate mother. Following the blood tests, the surrogate mother and her husband assumed the care of the child.

In Vitro Fertilization

The common phrase for in vitro fertilization (IVF) is test-tube babies. The process involves allowing for a sperm to fertilize an egg in a test tube. This obviously occurs in vitro or outside of the mother's body. The process was developed in order to help couples where the woman's fallopian tubes were so damaged that fertilization became impossible. After conception the fertilized egg is implanted in the woman's uterus where it continues to develop as in any other normal pregnancy.

This process is still fairly new. On July 25, 1978, the first test-tube baby was born. Louise, weighing 5 pounds, 12 ounces, was born to her parents Lesley and John Brown of Oldham, England. The world was stunned by such a feat. The physicians who developed the technique, Patrick Steptoe and Robert Edwards, had attempted the process over 30 times before, with this being the first success.

Since then, numerous IVF clinics have sprung up around the world. Forty-four have been noted in the United States alone (Masters and Johnson, 1985, p. 144). To date over 200 babies including a baby sister for Louise Brown, have been born using this technique.

However, IVF is very expensive and usually takes several attempts before being successful. Each attempt costs several thousand dollars. This financial limitation restricts this alternative only to people who can afford it.

Acceptance of Childlessness

For some infertile couples, accepting childlessness may be the most viable option. Each alternative has both positive and negative consequences which need to be evaluated. The positive aspects of childlessness need to be identified and appreciated. Increasing numbers of people are choosing to remain childless for various reasons. Not having children allows the time and energy which children would otherwise demand to be devoted to other activities and accomplishments. These include work, career, and recreational activities. A couple might also have more time to spend with and enjoy with each other, and invest in their relationship as a couple. Children are expensive. It's estimated that the cost of raising a child is over $55,000 from birth until they are age 18 (*U.S. News and World Report*, 1979). This does not include the costs of vocational school or college if the child decides to pursue these later options.

Children can provide great joy and fulfillment. On the other hand, they also can cause problems, stress, and strain. Infertile couples (and also fertile couples) may benefit from evaluating both sides of the issue. There are aspects that can be identified and appreciated when pursuing either alternative.

Summary

Human reproduction is a complex and amazing process. Prenatal influences that affect the fetus include mother's nutrition, drugs and medication, alcohol usage, age, and smoking habits. Four conditions which cause problem pregnancies are ectopic pregnancies, toxemia, Rh incompatibility, and prematurity. Stages in the birth process include initial contractions and dilation of the cervix, the actual birth, and afterbirth. Birth positions include the most common vertex position, breech presentations, and transverse presentations. Birth defects include Down's Syndrome, spina bifida, and the effects of rubella.

Reflexes of neonates include the sucking response, rooting reflex, Moro's reflex, walking reflex, grasping reflex and Babinski reflex. There are many developmental milestones as children grow older. This chapter describes "normal" motor, play, adaptive, social, and language profiles for children at various age levels. Young children are vulnerable to a variety of developmental problems, including tactile defensiveness and learning disabilities.

Significant issues related to human reproduction are abortion and infertility. Psychological reactions to abortion and the arguments for and against abortion are explored. Professional social workers have an obligation to assist pregnant clients in evaluating the various alternatives open to them so that they can make their own decisions. Twelve percent of all U.S. couples are infertile. Treatment of infertility includes drugs and microsurgery. Additional alternatives for infertility include adoption, artificial insemination, in vitro fertilization, surrogate parenthood, and acceptance of childlessness.

Psychological Aspects of Infancy and Childhood

"Hey, Barry, what did ya get on that spelling test?"

"I got an 87 percent. What did you get?"

"Aw, I only got a 79 percent. If I get a 'C' in spelling, my ma will kill me."

"Yeah, Susie got a 100 percent again. She always ruins it for the rest of us by getting straight *A*'s. I'm so sick of Ms. Butcherblock comparing us to her."

"Well, I hear Billy flunked again. He's never going to make it into fifth grade at this rate."

"Yeah, old Bill's an okay guy, but he sure isn't very smart."

"Only ten more minutes to recess. I'm gettin' out there first and get the best ball."

"Wanna bet? I'll race ya!"

Psychology is defined as the science of mind and behavior. Human psychological development involves personality, cognition, emotion, and self-concept. Each child develops into a unique entity with individual strengths and weaknesses. However, at the same time some principles and processes apply to the psychological development of all people. Likewise, virtually everyone is subject to similar psychological feelings and reactions which affect their behavior.

This example portrays two schoolboys discussing their current academic careers. Numerous psychological concepts and variables are impacting even this simple interaction. They are addressing their own and their peers' ability to learn and achieve. Learning is easier for some children and more difficult for others. Personality characteristics also come into play. Some children are more dominant and aggressive. Others are more passive. Some young people are more motivated to achieve and win. Others are less interested and enthusiastic. Finally, some children feel good about themselves and others have poor self-concepts.

■ A Perspective

The Behavior Dynamics Assessment Model proposes that many elements, including psychological variables, have important effects on individuals. They influence the potential courses of action available to a person at any

point in time. This chapter will focus on some of the psychological concepts which critically impact children as they grow up. There are four major thrusts. The first involves presenting a perspective on how personalities develop. The second concerns providing a basic understanding of how children think and learn. The third focuses on emotion, and the fourth on self-concept. This chapter will

- Summarize prominent psychological theories concerning personality development. They will include type, trait, psychodynamic, behavioral, and phenomenological theories.
- Examine major theories of cognitive development, including those of Piaget and Bruner.
- Describe the concept of emotion.
- Examine the relevance of self-concept and self-esteem especially as they affect minority children.
- Explore some life events, situations, and conditions which have serious psychological effects on children.

Theories of Personality

How many times have any of us heard someone make statements such as the following: "She has a great personality"; or "He has a personality like a wet dish rag." *Personality* refers to the complex cluster of characteristics which distinguish a person as an individual. The term may encompass a wide array of perspectives that describe people. For instance, at one extreme a person may be described as aggressive, dominant, brilliant, and outgoing. At another extreme an individual may be characterized by terms such as slow, passive, mousy, or boring.

Because personality can include such varying dimensions of personal characteristics, explaining its development can be difficult. However, a number of theorists have proposed explanations for why individual personalities develop as they do. These explanations include type theories, trait theories, psychodynamic theory, behavioral theories, and phenomenological theories.

Type Theories

Type theories include some of the earliest proposed means of categorizing or grouping different personalities. The idea here is that people can be clustered into distinct personality types. Each personality type then can be described in terms of its respective characteristics.

For example, Sheldon (1942) classifies people into three different personality types. He hypothesizes that each type is characterized by distinctive temperaments. Additionally, he contends that each personality type is manifested by people with one of three types of physique or general physical appearance. First, an *endomorph* is physically heavy set, soft, and rounded. Accompanying personality characteristics include being jovial, fun loving, social, and relaxed. Second, a *mesomorph* is a strong, muscular, athletic person. Personality characteristics include being industrious, energetic, outgoing, strong, and brave. Third, Sheldon proposes that an *ectomorph* is a fragile, tall, thin, weak person, and typically has stooped shoulders. Correspondingly, this person is typically weak willed, shy, unassertive, anxious, smart, and artistic.

Two major problems can be seen with type theories. The first is that they are overly simplistic. Considering the tremendous variety and complexity of physical types and personality configurations, classification into three basic types is overly general and probably useless. The second problem is that such a conceptualization encourages stereotypes and prejudgments on the basis of physical appearance. For example, Sheldon's type theory might assume that an overly heavy person is also a jolly person. This, in fact, may or may not be the case. As social workers it is critical to relate to people on an individualized basis. In order to maximize individual potential and choice, such stereotypes need to be avoided.

Trait Theories

Trait theories distinguish between different personalities on the basis of various personality traits. For example, an individual's personality may be described by his position or scoring on a series of trait scales (Hilgard and Atkinson, 1967, p. 470). These traits may include such characteristics as intelligence and emotional sensitivity. An individual may be scaled higher or lower on each trait dimension.

Allport (1937, 1961) postulates that each person has a series of general, relatively consistent traits that tend to characterize how that person will respond in most situations. Such personality traits exist in a hierarchy of cardinal, central, and secondary traits. Allport emphasizes individuality and the importance of any particular trait to a specific individual. A *cardinal trait* is one which is so important to the individual that it might be thought to dominate. For example, Benedict Arnold's cardinal trait might be deceitfulness, while George Washington's might be honesty.

Of more frequent occurrence, according to Allport, are *central traits.* A few major traits basically characterize any individual's personality. For instance, Aunt Mabel can be generally characterized as quiet, unselfish, sensitive, and giving.

Finally, Allport hypothesizes that people also have a series of secondary traits. These are relatively less significant traits which characterize how an individual feels in, or responds to, a particular situation. Secondary traits do not necessarily reflect a person's general personality or manner of responding. For example, Mr. Pfieffer's central personality traits might include being quiet, unassertive, and introverted. He lives alone, has few friends, and tends to avoid social and intimate situations. However, when his neighbor's home burns to the ground one night, he is the first to rush into the smoke and flames in order to save two small children. In this particular situation Mr. Pfeiffer is exceedingly courageous, although that trait is rarely displayed in other circumstances.

Like type theories, trait theories tend to be overly simplistic. A person may respond very differently depending on the situation. Human personalities are extremely complicated, perhaps too much to ever place them into neat, distinct categories.

Psychodynamic Theory

Sigmund Freud is perhaps the best known of all personality theorists. Freud's conception of the mind was two-dimensional, as is indicated in Figure 3.1. One dimension of the mind consisted of the "conscious," the "preconscious," and the "unconscious." Freud thought that the mind was composed of thoughts (ideas), feelings, instincts, drives, conflicts, and motives. Most of these elements in the mind were thought to be located in the unconscious or preconscious. Elements in the preconscious area had a fair chance to become conscious, while elements in the unconscious were unlikely to arise to a person's conscious mind. The small conscious cap at the top of this diagram indicates how Freud theorized a person was only aware of a fraction of the total thoughts, drives, conflicts, motives, and feelings in the mind.

The repressed area was a barrier under which disturbing material (primarily thoughts and feelings) had been placed by the defense mechanism of repression. Repression is a process in which unacceptable desires, memories, and thoughts are excluded from consciousness by sending the material into the unconscious under the repressed barrier. Once material has been repressed, Freud thought that material has energy and acts as an unconscious irritant, producing unwanted emotions and bizarre behavior, such as anger, nightmares, hallucinations, and enuresis.

The Id, Superego, and Ego

The second dimension of the mind was composed of the id, superego, and ego. Each of these parts is interrelated and impacts the functioning of each other.

The *id* is the primitive psychic force hidden in the unconscious. It represents the basic needs and drives on which other personality factors are built. The id involves all of the basic instincts that people need to survive. These include hunger, thirst, sex, and self-preservation. The id is governed by the pleasure principle; that is, the instincts within the id seek to be expressed regardless of the consequences. Freud believed that these basic drives or instincts involved in the id provide the main energy source for personality development. When the id is deprived of one of its needs, the resulting tension motivates a person to relieve the discomfort and satisfy the need. The id's relationship with the ego allows a person to rationally determine a means to fulfill the need.

The *ego* is the rational component of the mind. It begins to develop, through experience, shortly after birth. The ego controls a person's thinking and acts as the coordinator of personality. Operating according to the reality

Figure 3.1   Freud's Conception of the Mind

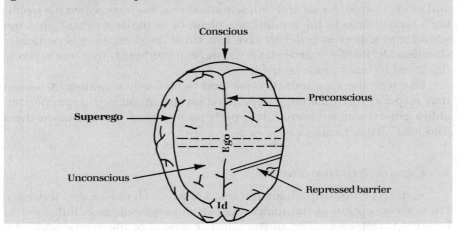

principle, the ego evaluates consequences and determines courses of action in a rational manner. The id indicates to a person what is needed or wanted. The ego then helps the person figure out how to get it.

The third component of this dimension of the mind is the *superego* or conscience. Normally developing between the ages of three to five, it consists of the traditional values and mores of society which are interpreted to a child by the parents. The superego's main function is to determine whether something is right or wrong. When an instinctual demand strives for expression which the superego disapproves of, the superego sends a signal of anxiety as a warning to the ego to prevent the expression of the instinct. The emotion of guilt is said to originate from the superego. Without the superego to provide a sense of right and wrong, a person would be completely selfish. That is, a person would use ego to rationally determine a means of getting what the id wanted, regardless of the consequences on other people.

An example of how the id, ego, and superego might function together is provided in the case of a nine-year-old girl looking at records in her favorite record store. Although the girl adores Michael Jackson, she has only 67 cents to her name. Her id, functioning by the pleasure principle, urges her to get that newly released album. Her ego reasons that she could slip the record under her jacket and race out of the store as fast as she can manage. Her ego also encourages her to look around and see if anyone, especially those "nosey" clerks, are anywhere around. She's just about to do it when her superego propels itself into action. Clearly reminding her that stealing is wrong, it raises questions such as what would her parents think about her if she were to get caught. They would be terribly disappointed. Maybe she would even be kicked out of Girl Scouts. As a result, the girl gave the album one last lingering look, sighed, and started on her way home. Her ego had already begun to work on how much lawn-mowing she would have to do to earn the money needed to purchase the album honestly.

Psychosexual Development

Freud came to realize that many people had sexual conflicts and he made sexuality a focus of his theories. The term used for the energy of the id's biological instincts was *libido*. This energy was primarily conceived as being sexual energy. Freud thought sexuality included physical love, affectionate impulses, self-love, love for parents and children, and friendship associations.

Freud further conceptualized that people in their development of personality progressed through six consecutive phases. During any one of the earlier phases, conflicts or disturbances could arise which, if not resolved, could fixate that person in some ways at that particular level of development. According to Freud, the term *fixated* meant that a person's personality development was largely, though not completely, halted at the stage that was specified. In order to develop optimal mental health, an individual would either have to resolve these crises and/or use one of several defense mechanisms. A *defense mechanism* involves any unconscious attempt to adjust to conditions that are painful. These conditions may include anxiety, frustration, or guilt. Defense mechanisms are measures through which a person preserves his self-esteem and softens the blow of failure, deprivation, or guilt. Some of these mechanisms are positive and helpful. Others only help to avoid positive resolution of conflict. Definitions of common defense mechanisms postulated by Freud are given in *Definitions of Common Defense Mechanisms Postulated by Psychoanalytic Theory*.

■ Definitions of Common Defense Mechanisms Postulated by Psychoanalytic Theory

Compensation: Making up for a real or fancied achievement or superiority. A common example is an effort to achieve success in one field after failure in another.

Repression: Mechanism through which unacceptable desires, feelings, memories, and thoughts are excluded from consciousness by being sent down deep into the unconscious.

Sublimation: Mechanism where consciously unacceptable instinctual demands are channeled into acceptable forms for gratification. For example, aggression can be converted into athletic activity.

Denial: Mechanism where a person escapes psychic pain associated with reality by unconsciously rejecting reality. For example, a mother may persistently deny that her child has died.

Identification: Mechanism through which a person takes on the attitudes, behavior, or personal attributes of another person whom he has idealized (parent, relative, or popular hero, etc.).

Reaction Formation: Development of socially acceptable behavior or attitudes which are the opposite of one's repressed unconscious impulses. Reaction formation is apparent in individuals who turn anal impulses into scrupulous cleanliness.

Regression: This mechanism involves a person falling back to an earlier phase of development in which he or she felt secure. Some adults when ill, for example, will act more childish and demanding with the unconscious goal of having others around them give them more care and attention.

Projection: Mechanism through which a person unconsciously attributes his own unacceptable ideas or impulses to another. For example, a person who has an urge to hurt others may turn it around and consciously feel that others are trying to hurt him.

Rationalization: Mechanism by which an individual, faced with frustrations or with criticism of his actions, finds justification for them by disguising from himself (as he hopes to disguise from others) his true motivations. Often this is accomplished by a series of excuses that are believed by the person. For example, a student who fails an exam may blame it on poor teaching, having long work hours, rather than consciously acknowledging the real reasons.

Freud's phases of psychosocial or personality development include the oral, anal, phallic, latency, and genital stages.

Oral Stage. This phase extends from birth to approximately 18 months. It is called oral because the primary activities of a child are centered around feeding and the organs (mouth, lips, and tongue) associated with that function. Feeding is considered to be an important area of conflict, and a child's attention is focused on receiving and taking. People fixated at this stage were thought to have the most severe personality disorders, such as schizophrenia or psychotic depression.

Anal Stage. Between the ages of one and a half and three years, a child's activities are mainly focused on giving and withholding, primarily connected with retaining and passing feces. Bowel training is an important area of conflict. People fixated at this stage have such character traits as messiness, stubbornness, rebelliousness; or they may have a reaction formation and have such opposite traits as being meticulously clean and excessively punctual.

Phallic Stage. From the third through the fifth year, the child's attention shifts to the genitals. Prominent activities are pleasurable sensations from genital stimulation, showing off one's body, and looking at the bodies of others. Also, a child's personality becomes more complex during this stage. Although self-centered, the child wants to love and be loved and seeks to be admired. Character traits which are apt to develop from fixation at this stage are pride, promiscuity, and self-hatred.

Boys and girls experience separate complexes during this stage. Boys encounter an *Oedipus complex*. This is the dilemma faced by every son at this age when he falls sexually in love with his mother. At the same time he is antagonistic toward his father, whom he views as a rival for her affections. As the intensity of both these relationships mount, the son increasingly suffers from *castration anxiety;* that is, he fears his father is going to discover his "affair" with his mother and remove his genitals. Successful resolution of the Oedipus complex occurs through defense mechanisms. A typical resolution is for the son to first repress his feelings of love for his mother and his hostile feelings toward his father. Next, the son has a reaction formation in which he stops viewing his father negatively, but now turns this around and has positive feelings toward his father. The final step is for the son to identify with his father, and thereby seek to take on the attitudes, values, and behavior patterns of his father.

Girls, on the other hand, undergo an *Electra complex* during this phallic stage. Freud believed girls fall sexually in love with their father at this age. Meanwhile, they also view their mother with antagonism. Because of these relationships, girls also suffer from castration anxiety, but the nature of this anxiety is different than for boys. Castration anxiety in a girl results from the awareness that she lacks a penis. She then concludes she was castrated in infancy and blames her mother for this. Freud went on to theorize that because girls believe they have been castrated they come to regard themselves as inferior to boys (i.e., they have penis envy). Therefore, they perceive that their role in life is to be submissive and supportive of males. Freud did not identify the precise processes for resolution of the Electra complex in girls.

Latency Stage. This stage usually begins at the time when the Oedipus/Electra complexes are resolved and ends with puberty. The sexual instinct is relatively unaroused during this stage. The child can now be socialized and becomes involved in the educational process and in learning skills.

Genital Stage. This stage, which occurs from puberty to death, involves mature sexuality. The person reaching this stage is fully able to love and to work. Again, we see Freud's emphasis on the work ethic (i.e., the idea that hard work is a very important part of life, in addition to being necessary to attaining one's life goals), which was highly valued in Freud's time. It is interesting to observe that Freud theorized that personality development was largely completed by the end of puberty with few changes hypothesized.

Psychopathological Development

Freud theorized that disturbances can arise from several sources. One source was traumatic experiences that a person's ego is not able to directly cope with and thereby strives to resolve using such defense mechanisms as repression. Breuer and Freud (1895) provide an example of a woman named Anna O. who developed a psychosomatic paralysis of her right arm. Anna O. was sitting by her father's bedside (her father was gravely ill) when she dozed off and had a nightmare that a big black snake was attacking her father. She awoke terrified and hastily repressed her thoughts and feelings about this nightmare for fear of alarming her father. During the time she was alseep, her right arm was resting over the back of a chair and became "numb." Freud theorized that the energy connected with the repressed material then took over physiological control of her arm, and a psychological paralysis resulted.

In addition to unresolved traumatic events, Freud thought that internal unconscious processes could also cause disturbances. There was a range of possible sources. An unresolved Electra or Oedipal complex could lead to a malformed superego and thus lead a person to have a variety of sexual problems—such as frigidity, promiscuity, sexual dysfunctions, excessive sexual fantasies, and nightmares with sexual content. Unresolved internal conflicts (e.g., an unconscious liking and hatred of one's parents) may be another source that causes such behavioral problems as hostile and aggressive behavior and such emotional problems as temper tantrums. Fixations at early stages of development were another source that largely prevented development at later stages and led the person to display such undesirable personality traits as messiness or stubbornness.

As indicated earlier, the main source of anxiety was thought to be sexual frustrations. Freud thought that anxiety would arise when a sexual instinct sought expression, but the ego blocked its expression. If the instinct was not then diverted through defense mechanisms, the energy connected with sexual instincts was transformed into anxiety.

Obsessions (a recurring thought such as a song repeatedly on your mind) and compulsions (such as an urge to step on every crack of a sidewalk) were thought to be mechanisms through which a person was working off energy connected with disturbing unconscious material.

Unconscious processes were thought to be the causes for all types of mental disorders. These unconscious processes were almost always connected with traumatic experiences, particularly those in childhood.

Critique of Psychodynamic Theory

Freud was virtually the first to focus on the impact of the family on human development. He was also one of the earliest, most positive proponents of good mental health. However, he was a product of the past century, and many of his ideas are subject to serious contemporary criticisms.

First, research does not support either the existence of his theoretical constructs or the effectiveness of his therapeutic method. Part of this lack may be due to the abstract nature of his concepts. It is very difficult, if not impossible, to pinpoint the location and exact nature of the superego.

The second criticism involves the lack of clarity in many of his ideas. For instance, although Freud asserts that the resolution of a boy's Oedipus complex results in the formation of the superego, he never clarifies how this occurs. The Electra complex provides another example in that the means by which girls might resolve this complex is never clearly explained.

The Electra complex leads us to a third criticism of Freud's theories. Women never really attain either an equal or a positive status within the theory. Essentially, women are left in the disadvantaged position of feeling perpetual grief at not having a penis, suffering eternal inferiority with respect to men, and being doomed to the everlasting limbo of inability to resolve their Electra complexes.

Behavioral Theories

Behavioral or learning theories differ from many other personality theories in one basic way. Instead of focusing on internal motivations, needs, and perceptions, they focus on specific observable behaviors.

Behavioral theories state that people learn or acquire their behaviors. This learning process follows certain basic principles. For example, behavior can be increased or strengthened by receiving positive reinforcement.

Behavioral theories encompass a vast array of different perspectives and applications. However, they all focus on behavior and how it is learned. More recently, greater attention has been given to the complex nature of social situations and how people react in them (Mischel, 1976, pp. 92–95). This involves people's perceptions about different situations and their ability to distinguish between one and another. More credit is given to people's ability to think, discriminate, and make choices. This perspective in behavioral theory is frequently called *social learning* or *social behavioral theory*. Behavior is seen as occurring within a social context. (Behavioral theory is described in more detail in chapter 4.)

Phenomenological Theories

Phenomenological or self-theories of personality focus on "the person's subjective, internal experiences and personal concepts" (Mischel, 1976, p. 98). A person is viewed as one who has various experiences and develops a personality as a result of these subjective experiences, instead of one who is born with a specified personality framework. It is also asserted that there are no predetermined patterns of personality development. Rather, phenomenological or self-theories recognize a wider range of options or possibilities for personality development depending on the individual's life experiences. Uniqueness of the individual personality is emphasized. Each individual will have a unique configuration of personal experiences which will result in a personality unlike any others. This is a relatively positive theoretical approach in that it focuses on growth and self-actualization.

One of the most well-known self-theorists, Carl Rogers, is the founder of client-centered (more recently termed person-centered) therapy which is based on his self-theory. One of Rogers' basic concepts in self-theory is the concept of *self*. Self is equivalent to *self-concept*. Rogers defines these terms as the "organized, consistent, conceptual gestalt composed of perceptions of the characteristics of the 'I' or 'me' and the perceptions of the relationships of the 'I' or 'me' to others and to various aspects of life, together with the values attached to these perceptions" (Rogers, 1959, p. 200). In other words, a person is the product of his own experience and how he perceives these experiences. One's self-concept is a conception of who one is (Zastrow, 1985, p. 328). Life, therefore, provides a host of opportunities to grow and thrive. Rogers maintains that there is a natural tendency toward self-actualization; that is, the tendency for every person to develop his capacities in ways which serve to maintain or enhance the person (Rogers, 1959). People are naturally motivated toward becoming fulfilled through new experiences.

Cognitive Development: Piaget

Specific theories concerning how people develop their capacities to think and understand have also been developed. Cognition involves the ability to take in information, process it, store it, and finally retrieve and use it. In other words, cognition involves the ability to learn and to think. The most noted of the cognitive theorists is probably Jean Piaget. Piaget (1952) has proposed that people go through various stages in learning how to think as they develop from infancy into adulthood. His theory, which concerns the stages through which people must progress in order to develop their cognitive or thinking ability, was derived from careful observations of his own children's growth and development.

Piaget postulates that virtually all people learn how to think in the same way. That is, as people develop they all go through various stages of how they think. In infancy and early childhood, thinking is very basic and concrete. As children grow, thinking progresses and becomes more complex and abstract. Each stage of cognitive development is characterized by certain principles or ways in which an individual thinks.

The following example does an exceptionally good job of illustrating how these changes occur. In his studies, Piaget would show children of various ages two glass containers filled with a liquid. The containers were identical in size and shape, and held an equal amount of liquid (see Figure 3.2). Children inevitably would agree that each container held the same amount of liquid. Piaget then would take the liquid from one of the containers and pour it into another taller, narrower glass container. Interestingly enough, he found that children under age six would frequently say that the taller glass held more even though the amount of liquid in each was identical. Children approximately age six or older, however, would state that despite the different shapes, both containers held the same amount of liquid. Later, it was established that the results of this experiment were the same for children of various backgrounds and nationalities.

Figure 3.2   Conservation

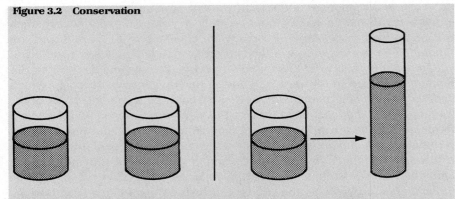

Children under age 6 would say that the taller glass holds more, even though the amount of liquid in each is identical.

This example might be explained by how children in different cognitive stages thought about or conceptualized the problem. Younger children tended to rely directly on their visual perceptions in order to make a decision about which glass held more or less liquid. Older children, however, were able to do more logical thinking about the problem. They thought about how liquid could take various forms and how the same amount could look different depending on its container. The older children illustrated a higher, more abstract or thoughtful level of cognitive development. This particular concept involving the idea that a substance can be changed in one way (e.g. shape) while remaining the same in another (e.g. quantity) is called *conservation*.

These ways of thinking about and organizing ideas and concepts depending on one's level of cognitive development are called *schema*. A person perceives the world differently and at an increasingly more abstract level during each stage. In other words, different aspects of the environment are emphasized or even noticed depending on a person's cognitive level of development. Each stage, therefore, is characterized by its own schema.

Piaget hypothesizes that all people go through the cognitive stages in the same order. The stages are continuous rather than distinct. An individual progresses through them in a continuous manner. In other words, a child does not wake up one morning and suddenly state, "Aha, I'm now in the preoperational stage of development!" Rather, children gradually progress through each stage with smooth and continual transitions from one stage to the next. Each stage acts as a foundation or prerequisite for the next stage.

Thus, organization is important in understanding Piaget's theory. People go through the various stages of cognitive development in an organized, predictable manner. Three other concepts that are also important are adaption, assimilation, and accommodation.

Adaptation refers to the capacity to adjust to surrounding environmental conditions. It involves the process of changing in order to fit in and survive in the surrounding environment. Piaget would say that adaptation is composed of the two processes, assimilation and accommodation.

Assimilation refers to the taking in of new information and the resulting integration into the schema or structure of thought. In other words, a person is exposed to a new situation, event, or piece of information. Not only is the information received and thought about at a conscious level, but it is also integrated into a way of thinking. The information is stored in a way so that it may be used later in problem-solving situations.

For example, go back to the situation where young children observe and judge the quantities of liquid in glass containers. Younger children, namely those under age six, assimilate information at a level using only their observations. Items and substances are only as they appear before their eyes. These children could not think of items as changing, as being somewhere else, or as being in a different context. They could not yet assimilate such information using higher, more logical levels of thought where some qualities of a substance could change while others remain the same. Children of age six or older can think about substances or items that are not immediately before their eyes. They can think about other different circumstances and situations.

Accommodation refers to the process by which children change their perceptions and actions in order to think using higher, more abstract levels of cognition. Children assimilate or take in new information and eventually accommodate it. That is, they build on the schema they already have and use new, more complex ways of thinking. Children aged six or older have accommodated the information about the liquid-filled glass containers. They have already assimilated information about shape, size, and quantity. Furthermore, they can think about changes in substance in a more abstract way. They can think of the liquid, not only as being held in a container of a specific shape and size, but also as it may be held in other containers of other shapes and sizes.

Piaget describes four major stages of cognitive development. These include the sensorimotor period, the preoperational thought period, the period of concrete operations, and the period of formal operations. Each stage will be described below. Major concepts characterizing the schema of each stage will be discussed.

The Sensorimotor Period

The sensorimotor period extends from birth to approximately two years of age. During this period, a child progresses from simple thoughtless reflex reactions to a basic understanding of the environment. Baldwin (1968) states that three major accomplishments are made during the sensorimotor period. First, children learn that they have various senses through which they can receive information. Additionally, they begin to understand that they can receive different kinds of sensory information about the same object in the environment.

For example, initially an infant may see and hear her parents squabbling over who will take the new Mazda RX-7 with air conditioning on a 100 degree summer day and who will take the old Dodge Dart with no air conditioning. Even though she will hear and see them squabbling, she will not be able to associate the two types of sensory information as referring to the same aspect of her environment, namely her parents. By the end of the sensorimotor period, she will understand that she can both hear and see her parents at the same time. She will perceive their interaction from both modes of sensory input.

A second major accomplishment during the sensorimotor period is the exhibition of *goal-directed behavior*. Instead of displaying simple responses on a random basis, the child will purposefully put together several behaviors in order to accomplish a simple goal. For example, a child will reach for a piece of a simple wooden puzzle in order to attempt placement into its appropriate slot. The child will plan to put the puzzle together. However, since a child's thinking during the sensorimotor period is still very concrete, the ability to plan very far ahead is extremely limited.

The third major accomplishment during the sensorimotor period is the understanding that objects are permanent. This is the idea that objects continue to exist even when they are out of sight and out of hearing range. The concept of *object permanence* is the most important schema acquired during the sensorimotor period. Initially, children immediately forget about objects as soon as they no longer can perceive them. By age two, children are generally able to think about the image of something which they can't see or hear, and solve a simple problem in relationship to that image. Children begin to use *representation*, that is, the visual imagining of an image in their minds which allows them to begin solving problems.

For example, take two-year-old Ricky who is very attached to his "blanky," an ancient, ragged, yellow blanket which he loves dearly. Ricky is in the midst of playing with his action garage toy set with his "blanky" placed snuggly next to him. Ricky's mother casually walks into the room, gently picks up the "blanky," and walks down the hallway to the bedroom. Instead of forgetting about the "blanky" as soon as it's out of sight, Ricky immediately gets up and starts actively seeking out his "blanky," calling for it relentlessly. Even though he can't presently see it and he doesn't know exactly where his mother put it, Ricky is able to think of the "blanky" and begin a quest in search of it. Furthermore, he is able to run around the house and look for it in various nooks and crannies, thinking about where it might be.

The Preoperational Thought Period

Piaget's second stage of cognitive development, the preoperational thought period, extends from approximately age two to seven. Some overlap from one stage to another should be expected. A child's thinking continues to progress to a more abstract, logical level. Although children are still tied to their physical and perceptual experiences, their ability to remember things and to solve problems continues to grow.

During the preoperational stage, children progress beyond evoking simple mental images of objects. They begin to use symbolic representations for things in their environment. Children are no longer bound to actual concrete perception. They can think in terms of symbols or mental representations of objects or circumstances.

Words provide an excellent example of symbolic representation. Children may symbolize an object or situation with words and then reflect on the object or situation later by using the words. In other words, language can be used for thought even when objects and situations are not present.

Barriers to the Development of Logical Thinking

Despite children's progress toward more abstract thinking, three major obstacles to logical thinking exist during the preoperational period. These include egocentrism, centration, and irreversibility.

Egocentrism. In *egocentrism*, a child is unable to see things from anybody else's point of view. A child is aware only of himself and needs and perspectives of others around him don't exist.

Piaget illustrated this concept by showing a child a doll in a three-dimensional scene. With the child remaining in the same position, the doll could be moved around the scene so that the child could observe it from different perspectives. The child would then be shown various pictures and asked what the scene would look like from the doll's perspective or point of view. Piaget found that the child would often choose the wrong picture. The child would continue to view the scene from his own perspective. It was difficult if not impossible for the child to imagine that the doll's perspective or point of view could be any different than the child's own.

The idea that children in this age group are so self-centered may be overly harsh. Many parents may think of the incidences where their young children appeared to show genuine empathic ability. For example, four-year-old Johnnie approaches his father after finding a robin's egg that fell from the nest. He states, "Daddy, poor birdie. She lost her baby."

Recently, some evidence has been found to show that children are not quite as egocentric as Piaget initially proclaimed (Black, 1981; Borke, 1975; Donaldson, 1979; Hobson, 1980). A child's ability to empathize with others depends somewhat on the circumstances and the issues involved. Perhaps if a child understands a situation more clearly from a personal point of view, he is better able to see another person's perspective.

Centration. *Centration* refers to a child's tendency to concentrate on only one detail of an object or situation and ignore all other aspects.

To illustrate centration, refer back to the example in which a child is asked to evaluate the amounts of liquid in two glasses. The child would observe the same amount of liquid being poured into two different shaped containers. One container was short and squat, and the other, tall and thin. When asked which container held more liquid, the child would frequently answer that the tall, thin container would. In this situation, the child was focusing on the concept of height instead of width. She was unable to focus on both height and width at the same time. Only one aspect of the situation was used to solve the problem. This is a good example of how centration inhibits more mature, logical thought.

Irreversibility. *Irreversibility* refers to a child's ability to follow and think something through in one direction without being able to imagine the relationship in reverse. For example, four-year-old Gary might be asked, "Who are your cousins?" Gary might then reply, "Sherrie, Donna, Lorrie, and Tanya." If Gary is then asked who is Sherrie's cousin, he will probably say he doesn't know. Gary is able to think through a situation in one direction, but is unable to reverse his train of thought. He knows that Sherrie is his cousin. However, he is unable to see the reverse of that relationship, namely that he is also Sherrie's cousin.

Developing Cognitive Ability

Despite barriers to the development of logical thought, several concepts illustrate ways in which children progress in their ability to think. Major changes concerning these concepts are made between the onset of the

Piaget holds that during the "sensorimotor period," which is the first stage of cognitive development, children go from having simple reflex reactions that involve no thought to obtaining a basic understanding of their environment. The sensorimotor period begins at birth and ends at about two years of age. During this period young children learn that senses bring them different kinds of information about their environment. What senses will the birthday cake stimulate for this one-year-old? (Kristine Koch)

During Piaget's second stage of cognitive development, the "preoperational thought period," children's thinking becomes more abstract and logical. This period lasts from approximately ages two to seven. Now children are increasingly able to remember things and solve problems, rather than merely evoke mental images of objects. The children can now describe these images in words. And when they do describe them, they can do so without the items being present. (Courtesy of United Way of America)

If people of one race are unfamiliar with people of another, racial prejudice can result. But familiarize children of one group with children of another, and racial prejudice disappears. Children quickly learn that just as there are all kinds of people in their own race, personalities are just as diverse in other races. By getting to know each other, the boys in this picture successfully stripped away racial barriers and became friends. (Courtesy of United Way of America)

The ability to experience emotions is an intrinsic part of a person's development. The first emotion a baby expresses is excitement. By six months, he or she experiences and can demonstrate anger or disgust. As children grow, they can express more complex emotions. The boy in this picture just caught a fish. The look on his face describes the emotion he is experiencing: happiness. (Kristine Koch)

preoperational thought period and the culmination of adult logical thinking. Children gradually improve their perceptions and grasp of these concepts.

Classification. *Classification* refers to a child's ability to sort items or stimuli into various categories according to certain characteristics. The characteristics might include shape, color, texture, or size. Children gradually develop the ability to distinguish differences between objects or stimuli and categorize them to reflect these differences.

For example, two and one-half-year-old Karen is given a bag of red, blue, and green "creepy crawlers." In this case the creepy crawlers consist of soft, plastic lizards, all of which are the same size and shape. When asked to put all the red lizards together in a heap, Karen is unable to do so. She cannot yet discriminate between the colors in order to categorize or classify the lizards according to their color. However, when Karen is given the same task at age seven, she is easily able to put the red, blue, and green lizards in their respective heaps. She has acquired the concept of classification.

Seriation. *Seriation* refers to a child's ability to arrange objects or stimuli in order according to certain characteristics. These characteristics might include size, weight, volume, or length.

For example, a child is given a number of McDonald's soda straws cut to various lengths. The child's ability to arrange such objects from shortest to longest improves as the child's cognitive ability develops (Kaluger and Kaluger, 1984, p. 242). By age four or five, a child is usually able to select both the longest and the shortest straws. However, the child still has difficulty discriminating among the middle lengths. By age five or six the child will probably be able to order the straws one by one from shortest to longest. However, this would probably be done with much concentration and some degree of difficulty. By age seven, the task of ordering the straws would probably be much easier.

The ability to apply seriation to various characteristics develops at different ages depending on the specific characteristic (Kaluger and Kaluger, 1984, p. 242). For example, children are usually unable to order a series of objects according to weight until age nine. Seriation according to volume is typically not possible until approximately age 12.

Conservation. *Conservation* refers to a child's ability to grasp the idea that while one aspect of a substance (e.g., quantity or weight) remains the same, another aspect of that same substance (e.g., shape or position) can be changed.

For example, four-year-old Hoss is given two wads of "silly putty" of exactly equal volume. One wad is then rolled into a ball and the other is patted into the shape of a pancake. When asked which wad has a greater amount of material in it, Hoss is likely to say that the pancake does. Even though Hoss initially saw that the two wads were exactly equal, he focused only on the one dimension of area. In terms of area alone, the pancake appeared to Hoss as if it had more substance. However, by the time Hoss reached age six or seven, he would probably be able to state that both wads had equal substance. He would know that matter can take different forms and still have the same amount of material.

As with seriation, children achieve the ability to understand conservation at different ages depending on the characteristic to be conserved

(Papalia and Olds, 1981, pp. 263–64). For example, whereas conservation of
substance is typically attained by age six or seven, the concept of conservation of weight is usually not achieved until age nine or ten. Conservation
of volume is usually not mastered until age eleven or twelve.

87

**3 / Psychological Aspects
of Infancy and Childhood**

The Period of Concrete Operations

The period of concrete operations extends from approximately ages
seven to eleven or twelve years. During this stage, a child develops the ability
to think logically on a concrete level. In other words, a child has mastered
the major impediments to logical thinking which were evident during earlier
stages of cognitive development.

The child now develops the capacity to see things from other people's
points of view. Understanding and empathy are substantially increased
during this period.

More complex thinking is developed. Situations and events can be viewed
and examined in terms of many variables. The child gradually becomes less
limited by centration. A child is no longer limited to solving a problem in
terms of only one variable, rather, a number of variables could be taken into
account. In the glass example, the child would begin to think in terms of
height, volume, substance, and shape all at the same time.

A child also develops his ability to conceptualize in terms of reversibility
during this period. In other words, a child can think an issue through, and
then reverse his train of thought. Relationships begin to be understood from
various perspectives. Returning to an example presented earlier, Gary would
now understand that not only was Sherrie his cousin, but that he was also
her cousin.

The concepts of classification, seriation, and conservation would also
be mastered. During the period of concrete operations a child gains much
flexibility in thinking about situations and events. Events are appraised from
many different points of view.

Additionally, children develop their use of symbols to represent events
in the real world. Their ability to understand arithmetic and to express
themselves through language greatly improves. Correspondingly, their
memories become sharper.

Despite the great gains in cognitive development made during the stage
of concrete operations, a child is still somewhat limited. Although events
are viewed from many perspectives, these perspectives are still tied to concrete issues. Children think about things they can see, hear, smell, or touch.
Their focus is on thinking about things instead of ideas. Children must enter
the final stage of cognitive development, the period of formal operations,
before they can fully develop their cognitive capability.

The Period of Formal Operations

The final stage of cognitive development is the period of formal operations. This period, beginning at approximately age 11 or 12 and extending
to approximately age 16, characterizes cognitive development during adolescence. Technically, this chapter addresses childhood and not adolescence. However, for the purposes of continuity, Piaget's fourth period of
cognitive development will be discussed here.

Abstract thought reaches its culmination during the period of formal operations. Children become capable of taking numerous variables into consideration and creatively formulating abstract hypotheses about how things work or about why things are the way they are. Instead of being limited to thought about how things are, children begin to think about how things could be. They begin to analyze why things aren't always as they should be.

For example, take Meredy, age 10, who is still limited by the more concrete type of thinking which characterizes the period of concrete operations. She is aware that a nuclear bomb was dropped on Hiroshima near the close of World War II. When asked about why this happened, she might say that the United States had to defend its own territory and this was a means of bringing the war to an end. She can conceptualize the situation and analyze it in terms of some variables. In this case the variables might include the fact that the United States was at war and had to take actions to win that war. Her ability to think through the situation might extend no further than that. When asked the same question at age 15, Meredy might have quite a different answer. She might talk about what a difficult decision such a step must have been in view of the tremendous costs in human life. She might describe the incident as one of various tactical strategies which might have been taken. She also might elaborate on the political impacts caused by the event. In other words, Meredy's ability to consider numerous variables from many perspectives would improve drastically during the period of formal operations.

Three major developments characterize adolescent thought (Gallagher, 1973). First, the adolescent is able to identify numerous variables which affect a situation. An event can be viewed from many perspectives. Second, the adolescent can analyze the effects of one variable on another i.e., hypothesize about relationships and think about changing conditions. Third, an adolescent is capable of hypothetical-deductive reasoning. In other words, an adolescent can systematically and logically evaluate many possible relationships in order to arrive at a conclusion. Various possibilities can be examined. Each possibility can be scrutinized in a conditional "if-then" fashion. For instance, the adolescent might begin thinking in terms of if certain variables exist, then certain consequences will follow.

Not all developmental theorists, however, agree with Piaget's description of cognitive development. Some research suggests that progression to the period of formal operations does not occur for all people in all instances (Keating and Clark, 1980; Super, 1980). For example, Kohlberg and Gilligan (1971) conclude that almost half of the adults in the United States don't attain this cognitive level at all. They come to this conclusion on the basis of research which evaluates the ages at which people can perform certain formal operational level tasks. One study indicates that a substantial majority of adults do not achieve this fourth cognitive level until after age 21.

Piaget (1972) has offered several possible explanations for such findings. First, an individual's social environment may influence cognitive development. Persons from deprived environments may not be offered the same types of stimulation and support necessary to achieve such high levels of cognition. Second, individual differences might have to be taken into account. Some persons might not have the necessary ability to attain the levels of thought which characterize the formal operations period. Finally, although everyone may develop a capacity for formal operational thought, this capacity may not be versatile in its application to all problems. In other words, some individuals might be unable to use formal operations with some problems or in some situations.

Effects of Diversity on Cognitive Development

Some studies indicate that some children raised in minority households do not perform as well on tests designed to measure aspects of Piaget's cognitive development. For example, in Norton's study (1969) of 109 eight-year-old children, from various socioeconomic backgrounds, she discovered a strong relationship between good language models in the home and the child's ability to overcome the cognitive barrier of irreversibility. Good language referred to language with rules conducive to the development of reversible thought. For instance, children were more likely to master reversibility in thought when they had mothers who spoke in sentences, had pastimes relating to reading, and referred to objects by using their proper names.

This was true for all subgroups except for black children from lower socioeconomic levels. These children rated poorly on reversibility despite having "good" language models in the home. On more extensive analysis it was discovered that these homes did provide effective language models. However, the models were different from those used in white homes. The tests designed to measure reversibility apparently were not effective when applied to a different type of language model.

Norton (1983) later proposes that black children from ghetto environments learn a language with a different "internal consistency" from that of standard English. She warns that such children may be penalized on entering school systems which don't acknowledge their different language model. Such children may not be considered as bright as others simply because they talk and structure their thinking somewhat differently. Finally, she suggests that schools need to sensitize themselves to such differences when helping children to learn and maximize their levels of cognitive development.

Cognitive Theory: Bruner

Jerome Bruner, another well-respected cognitive theorist, proposes an alternative theory of cognitive development. Bruner's theories are also based on the idea that cognition is developed through a series of stages. He maintains that basic information about any subject can be taught at almost any age level, if the material is presented in the appropriate manner (Bruner, 1972). Bruner, therefore, places great emphasis on the importance of education.

Bruner proposes three stages of development: the "enactive," the "iconic," and "symbolic representation" stages (Bruner et al., 1966). Each stage suggests that there is a preferred mode of learning at any particular time of life. Bruner maintains that infants learn best through physical and sensorimotor interaction with the environment. This is the enactive stage. The iconic stage follows for preschoolers and kindergarteners. This age group learns best through the use of mental pictures and imagery. Finally, children in middle school learn best through symbolic representation. This stage involves the use of language and more abstract thought in order to manipulate ideas.

Emotional Development

The concepts of *personality* and *cognition* are complicated and abstract. No one clearly specified definition is available for either. Nor is the relationship between them explicitly defined. It is not clear exactly how thinking affects personality, or how personality affects thinking. The tremendous amount of variation from one individual to another and even one individual's varying reactions from one particular situation to another makes it even more difficult to comprehend.

Emotions are also involved in a person's development. They act to complicate the profile of an individual's personality even further. For our purposes, emotion will be defined as the complex affective or feeling experience which involves subtle physiological reactions and is expressed by displaying characteristic patterns of behavior (Morris, 1979, p. 386). For example, a four-year-old boy's goldfish might be found floating belly-up one morning when the boy gets up. On hearing the unhappy news, the boy might become upset. His heart might start beating faster and his breathing might accelerate. Finally, he might run to his room and start to cry. In this case, the little boy experienced an emotion. His body responded as he became upset. Finally, the behavior of crying clearly displayed his emotional upset.

Emotional development begins in infancy at a very basic level and becomes more complex as a person matures. For example, a newborn baby displays only one emotion—excitement (Morris, 1979, pp. 400–1). The infant will react with excitement regardless of what is encountered. It may be a mother's kiss, a barking dog, or a screeching smoke alarm. All will elicit excitement.

As a baby grows older, however, emotional reactions will become more differentiated. By the age of six months, for example, anger or disgust will probably be initiated; later yet the child will experience many other emotions including affection and jealousy (Morris, 1979, p. 400). As the individual grows up and continues through life new, complex emotions will develop because of various ongoing processes and circumstances (Haith and Campos, 1977). Many emotional patterns are learned as a result of a child's experiences associated with key interpersonal relationships and life events. Emotions continue to become more complex and difficult to understand. However, Morris (1979, pp. 386–90) classifies emotional states into three basic continuums. These include approach/avoidance, intensity, and pleasant/unpleasant.

The *approach/avoidance continuum* refers to whether a person feels attracted or repelled to a person or situation. For instance, a purse snatcher may grab a woman's purse as she strolls through the local shopping center. If she feels anger, she may immediately run after the thief, screaming at him to give that purse back. Her emotions in this instance would fall toward the approach side of the continuum. If, however, she became afraid, she might flee in the opposite direction seeking a security officer. Here her emotions would fall toward the avoidance side of the continuum.

The second dimension of emotion involves *intensity*. This concerns how strongly an individual feels an emotion. For example, a young man and woman begin dating. Initially, they feel a mild attraction toward each other. This feeling is of fairly low intensity. After six months of increasing involvement, however, they may feel a strong sense of love and need for each other. The emotion here has intensified.

The third continuum of emotion is *pleasant/unpleasant*. This concerns whether the emotion being experienced is positive, enjoyable, and appealing, or negative and unpleasant. For example, two individuals might experience different emotions concerning a Sunday afternoon football game. One individual might find watching television football to be very positive. Another might feel very negative. The latter person might be bored to tears and find the experience to be exceptionally unpleasant.

Handling Emotions

Emotional aspects contribute to a person's perspective of any particular situation. As the Behavior Dynamics Assessment Model describes, psychological aspects including emotion impact an individual at any point in time. As a result of this and many other considerations, the individual will opt to behave in a certain way. Many times it is helpful for an individual to understand and be able to exert some control over his emotions. Such control may help to make more beneficial alternatives available to the individual.

Self-Concept

All individuals form impressions about who they think they are. It's almost as if each person develops a unique theory regarding who exactly she feels she is. This personal impression is referred to as the self-concept. The idea of self-concept was introduced earlier in a discussion of Carl Rogers' self-theory. A related idea is that of self-esteem. Self-esteem refers to a person's judgment of her own value. Although self-concept may include more aspects about the self than just value, many times the two terms are used interchangeably.

Self-concept is an important theme throughout mental health literature. Improving one's self-concept is often seen as a therapeutic goal for people with adjustment problems. One's self-concept is important throughout life. In order to continue working, living, striving, and positively interacting with others, one must have a positive self-concept. In other words, one must feel good enough about oneself to continue living and being productive. This is just as true for children as it is for adults.

■ The Effects of Positive and Negative Self-Concepts

Two five-year-old girls, one with a good self-concept and the other with a relatively poor self-concept illustrate the enormous effects of one's self-concept. Julie, who has a positive perception of self, is fairly confident in new situations. When she enters kindergarten, she assertively introduces herself to her peers and eagerly makes new friends. She frequently becomes a leader in their games. She often volunteers to answer her teacher's questions. Her teacher considers her happy and well adjusted.

In contrast, Mary has a relatively poor self-concept. She does not think very highly of herself or her abilities. On her first day of kindergarten, she usually stays by herself or lingers on the fringes of activities. She speaks little to others out of fear that they might criticize her. She really wants to be liked but is worried that there is nothing to like about her. Thus, it is easier for her to remain quiet and unobtrusive. For example, one day the teacher brings out pieces of colored clay for the children to play with. Being so quiet and afraid, Mary does not rush up to her teacher to get hers even though playing with clay is one of her favorite pastimes. Rather, she waits until everyone else has their clay and is returning to their seats. By the time Mary is close to the teacher, all the clay has been handed out. Instead of clay her teacher gives her a coloring book and some crayons. Mary takes them passively and begins to color a big yellow duck. All the while she is crying silently to herself. She is very disappointed that she did not get any clay. She also is hoping no one will notice that she is different from everyone else. Mary has a poor self-concept. She is afraid of others and what they might think. She does not have much self-esteem.

The self-concept is an abstract idea. It is difficult to explain exactly what it involves. However, it is still an important factor in a person's ability to function. People of virtually any age need to feel good about themselves in order to be confident and enjoy life's experiences.

Coopersmith (1967, 1968) interviewed 85 boys aged 10 to 12 and their mothers in addition to administering personality and ability tests to the boys. He concluded that self-concept is founded on four variables. The first is significance. This refers to how people feel others around them think of them and feel they are important. The second variable is competence, or their perceived ability to perform tasks which they feel are valuable. Virtue is the third variable. This involves abiding by and maintaining moral standards. The final variable is power, or the extent they feel they have power over or can influence both their own lives and the lives of others. The higher an individual scored on all of these variables, the higher was his level of self-esteem. Furthermore, it was found that a cluster of terms tended to characterize boys with low self-esteem and those with high levels of self-esteem. Children with high self-esteem might be described as successful, active, self-confident, and optimistic. Those with low self-esteem, on the other hand, might best be described by terms such as depressed, isolated, discouraged, and fearful. In other words, children with higher levels of self-esteem exhibit traits which are valued by others and, in essence, are more competent.

A few other interesting findings involved the parents of these boys (Coopersmith, 1967, 1968). Boys with higher levels of self-esteem tended to have parents who loved and accepted them, although these parents also had higher expectations concerning school work and good behavior. These parents also tended to encourage independence in terms of expressing the boys' own thoughts. The emphasis in these homes was on rewarding good behavior rather than on using excessive punishment for behavioral control. Finally, the parents themselves tended to have higher levels of self-esteem.

Gelfand (1962) hypothesized that self-esteem is based on the number of successes and failures an individual has been exposed to during past experiences. She found that such a relationship did indeed exist. The self-esteem of people experiencing success increased while the self-esteem of those exposed to failure decreased.

In summary, the evidence appears to bear out the importance of self-esteem as it relates to self-concept. Perhaps a high level of self-esteem provides a person not only with confidence, but also with emotional strength. Perhaps such strength is needed to reach out to others and gain social acceptance. Such strength might also contribute to an individual's ability to take risks, succeed, and achieve.

Self-Concepts of Minority Children

Conflicting evidence is found concerning the self-concepts of minority children, especially black children. Some studies indicate that black children tend to have poor self-concepts; others suggest that they have positive self-concepts.

Much of the evidence supporting the idea that black children have poorer self-concepts than their white counterparts originated from the mid-thirties to the early sixties (Jenkins, 1982, p. 24). One of the methods most frequently used to measure self-concept was the evaluation of a minority child's doll preference. Black children aged three to seven years typically were shown a series of pairs of dolls, one black and one white. The children were then asked various questions designed to gain insight into their racial awareness, especially as it related to their self-concepts. The children's comments and their apparent preference for the white dolls seemed to indicate that black children tended to have negative self-concepts as they related to race (Clark and Clark, 1952). Consequent studies with refined methodology appeared to draw similar conclusions (Jenkins, 1982, p. 24). Additionally, both black and white children have been found to have a preference for the color white over black (Morland, 1966; McAdoo, 1977).

Other research indicates that black children have high self-esteem (Bachman, 1970; Baughman, 1971; Taylor, 1976). Also the self-esteem of black children seems to be increasing. This research interprets children's figure drawings and indicates that black children's drawings of people are becoming much more likely to represent black as opposed to white people (Fish and Larr, 1972; McAdoo, 1977).

Several explanations can be given for this discrepancy. Methodological problems and lack of sophistication may have been involved in some of the earlier studies finding negative self-concepts. The logic used to draw conclusions in studies finding black children to have negative self-concepts may also be invalid. For example, perhaps a child's choice of a lighter color may have had nothing to do with the child's sense of self. Perhaps the preference only concerned a doll or a color. Children may have been trained to prefer lighter colors over darker through books and the media. For instance, the availability of real dolls having a darker skin color for children to play with is a relatively recent occurrence. Perhaps the children were not accustomed to seeing or playing with darker colored dolls. Finally, the complicated matter of self-concept and all that is involved might be much too complex to measure by using such simple techniques.

Two other aspects concerning minority children and self-concept merit attention. First, teachers and social workers who work with children need to be aware of their own ethnocentric perspectives when addressing the idea of self-concept. Children with other cultural backgrounds may manifest their self-confidence and self-concepts in different ways. Wise and Miller (1983, p. 350) provide a relevant illustration of an Ottawa native American girl attending an urban public school "who was referred for psychological testing and counseling because her teacher felt that she had a poor self-concept and her school work was suffering because of it." On further investigation it was determined that the teacher had made the referral because of the little girl's apparent shyness and lack of eye contact. The teacher, who had had little contact with Indian children, did not know that for many Indian subcultures, looking an adult straight in the eye for any period of time implies disrespect and is inappropriate. The little girl was only displaying the good manners and behavior which she had been taught were appropriate.

The other aspect concerning minority children and self-concept which is worthy of mention involves some suggestions for reducing racial prejudice. The idea is that if prejudice is reduced, then differences in self-concept which are based on race may no longer be an issue. After testing them on groups of second- to fifth-grade children, Katz and Zalk (1978) suggest the following four techniques to combat racial prejudice. First, positive racial contacts should be increased. In the research this was done by having both black and white children work together on teams whose task was to complete a puzzle. All of the children were then praised for their accomplishments. The intent was to reinforce and encourage both black and white children to work together. Second, vicarious racial contact should be stressed. This means that both races should be talked about within similar positive contexts. In this research, children were told a story about a black child who had many positive qualities. Here the intent was to help children think about a minority person in a positive light and yet in a way that children can understand. Third, the color black itself should be reinforced. During the study children were rewarded for choosing a picture of a black animal over a white one. Fourth, perceptual differentiation should be encouraged. In other words, children can be taught to differentiate people of the same race by looking at various personal characteristics. Here children were shown slides of a black woman whose appearance was made to vary by wearing glasses or different hairdos and by changing her facial expression. Children were encouraged to discriminate between the different slides by remembering the name respectively assigned to each.

Various positive findings were gained from this research (Katz and Zalk, 1978). Groups exposed to the techniques showed less prejudice than groups who had not been exposed. A posttest one half year later indicated that some of the gains had been maintained even over an extended period of time. One other interesting finding was that younger children were more likely to respond to the techniques and reveal less prejudice. In summary, it appears that providing some basic information about a minority group so that the unknown and strangeness is reduced can potentially have a significant effect on reducing prejudice.

Significant Issues and Life Events

Several issues and life events which can impact children have been chosen for discussion. Their selection is based on the importance of the effects they have on children and on the probability that social workers will encounter these issues in practice. The issues include intelligence testing along with its potential problems and cultural biases, mental retardation, and learning disabilities with a focus on both types and treatment.

Intelligence Testing

Intelligence may be defined as the ability to understand, to learn, and to deal with new, unknown situations. Beyond this general definition, little is known about the origins of intelligence despite many attempts to refine and clarify the definition. These attempts have ranged from primitive measurement of head size, referred to as *phrenology*, to the listing of specific mental abilities supposed to be involved in intelligence. For instance, Thurstone (1938) suggested that seven independent abilities contributed to the general level of a person's intelligence. These abilities included the ability to perceive spatial relationships, perceptual speed, memory, word fluency, reasoning, numerical ability, and verbal ability. Bouchard (1968) suggested an even more complex framework for defining intelligence. Instead of a list of mental abilities, he proposed conceptualizing intelligence in terms of how people think. This involves the systematic process aspects of thinking instead of the specific mental abilities or the contents of thinking.

Regardless, the fact is that there is no clear, specific definition of intelligence. It is at this point that it's important to distinguish between intelligence and the intelligence quotient, commonly referred to as IQ. Many might mistakenly assume that an IQ represents the absolute quantity of intelligence that a person possesses. This is not true. An IQ really stands for how well an individual might perform on a specific intelligence test in relation to how well others perform on the same test. The IQ then involves two basic facets. One is the score that a person attains on a certain type of test. The second is the person's relative standing within the peer group.

An IQ score then is apparently the best thing available to attempt measuring whatever intelligence is. Such a statement may not inspire much confidence in the value of one's IQ. However, perhaps it should elicit caution. IQ scores can be used to determine grade school placement, admission to special programs, and encouragement or lack thereof to attend college. A person who is aware of having a low IQ score may establish lower expectations. These lower expectations may act as a barrier to what actually could be achieved. She might become the victim of a self-fulfilling prophecy, i.e., what she expects is what she gets.

This could have been the case, for example, for a returning student who was the mother of three children. She was also receiving social insurance benefits because of a permanent disability. Her vocational counselor had flatly told her that her IQ was not nearly high enough to succeed in college. He suggested that she stay home and enjoy her moderate financial benefits. Although his statements discouraged her, she had the courage and stamina to enroll with a full course load at a well-respected state university. Her final grade report after her first semester indicated that she had achieved a perfect 4.0 average on a 4.0 scale. She immediately returned to her vocational counselor and requested financial assistance for a microcomputer to assist her in her coursework. He responded by mumbling in an embarrassed manner that that might be a good idea.

The Stanford-Binet IQ Test

One of the most common intelligence tests is the Stanford-Binet (Terman, 1960). First used in 1905, it has continued to be tested and refined. The value of measuring intelligence is in its usefulness in predicting success in various situations. Schools frequently use the Stanford-Binet to determine program and grade placement and potential academic success.

Perhaps one of the most beneficial uses of IQ tests is in the targeting of potential special needs for special help. For example, the following scale has been established for describing people having normal or above intellectual ability (Morris, 1979, p. 264):

IQ	Description
Above 140	Genius
120–140	Very superior
110–120	Superior
90–110	Average, normal

Morris (1979) explains that those people who score in the 90s may be able to complete eighth grade, those scoring between 100 and 109 can finish high school, and those having an IQ of 115 or above can be expected to succeed in college. People who score within any of these ranges should be able to function well in the community if there are no additional emotional or behavioral problems.

Mental Retardation

Mental retardation refers to "significantly subaverage general intellectual functioning existing concurrently with deficits in adaptive behavior and manifested during the developmental period" (Grossman, 1975, p. 11). In other words, individuals are mentally retarded to one degree or another when they are unable intellectually to grasp concepts and function as well and as quickly as their peers. Mentally retarded individuals will probably be slower at understanding ideas and concepts. They will also probably have difficulty grasping more abstract or complicated concepts. The degree of these difficulties, of course, will depend on the level of retardation.

Adaptive behavior refers to a person's ability to adapt or adjust to the social and physical environment. It involves an individual's ability to establish and maintain a good person-in-environment fit. Mentally retarded individuals are often capable of high levels of such behavior. They frequently can care for themselves physically and maintain good hygiene. Many can hold a job and support themselves to one extent or another. Mentally retarded people can often interact positively and appropriately with others. They can communicate their feelings and opinions. They can form close relationships. In summary, a person's ability to "fit in" or adapt to her surroundings is more relevant and important than absolute intellectual ability.

Nonetheless, IQ tests are used to identify the level of mental retardation. They provide one important means of determining appropriate expectations for how well a person will be able to function both academically and independently. The respective levels of expected functioning are determined by the following scores on the Stanford-Binet:

Borderline	83–68
Mild	67–52
Moderate	51–36
Severe	35–20
Profound	Less than 20

Those people scoring within the borderline range of intelligence should be capable of independent living within the community. Although they might not be able to attain high levels of academic achievement, nonetheless they should be able to live, work, have families, and function along with everyone else in their communities. With the help of special education classes, people with IQs in the 70s are able to master academic skills including reading and arithmetic to approximately a fourth- or fifth-grade level (Morris, 1979, p. 264). Frequently they are able to "blend in," that is, to present no noticeable difference between themselves and others. Labeling such people as borderline frequently is forgotten and irrelevant when these people reach adulthood.

People who are mildly mentally retarded are often able to live independently as adults except when they are under extreme stress. During those times they may have some difficulty rationally making decisions and identifying ways to cope with the stressful circumstances. People with IQs in the 60s might be expected to reach a third-grade level of academic performance, and those in the 50s, a second-grade level (Morris, 1979, p. 264). The term which has been used to describe people who are capable of learning some basic academic skills is educable.

Moderately retarded people have more difficulty understanding the world around them and mastering academic skills. These people are typically capable of learning the self-help skills necessary in physically caring for themselves. They can learn to communicate with others. Often they can develop enough skills to function in a home setting, a sheltered workshop, or even in an unskilled or semiskilled job. Supervision and guidance is usually needed when under mildly stressful conditions. People who are intellectually capable of learning to take care of many of their daily self-care activities, but are unable to master academic skills, at times have been described as trainable.

People with severe mental retardation may be able to learn some basic skills in caring for themselves. However, they will require fairly extensive supervision. Profoundly retarded people are unable to take care of themselves. They will always require almost complete supervision and attention.

The terms used to describe people are very important. In the past negative terms such as *feebleminded, moron, imbecile,* and *idiot* have been used to describe mentally retarded people. These terms emphasize what retarded people cannot do and have the flavor of name calling. The newer terms such as *borderline* or *mild* are more positive in that they focus less on the negative aspects of retardation. The more recently adapted term *developmental disability* is even less negative. This term is broader than *mental retardation* because it includes disabilities attributable to cerebral palsy, epilepsy, or other neurological conditions closely related to mental retardation or requiring treatment similar to mental retardation (Zastrow, 1982, p. 340). Placing the emphasis on the ability a person does have is much more positive than stressing retardation.

Intelligence is an important variable which impacts an individual person's behavior. In concordance with the Behavior Dynamics Assessment Model as a result of intelligence, other developmental factors, life events, and the effects of human diversity, a person has various alternatives available to him or her. A limitation on intelligence may limit some of the alternatives available to the individual. For example, a person with an IQ of 70 will probably not become a brain surgeon. However, there are still many other alternatives available to that person to construct a rich, satisfying, and fulfilling life. A basic task of the social worker might be to help that person identify his alternatives and weigh the various positive and negative consequences of each.

Potential Problems with IQ Scores

Two basic potential problems with IQ scores have already been mentioned. One is that the actual nature of intelligence is unknown. At this point in time we are talking then about a vague and subjective term. The second problem is that placing an IQ label on someone may be harmful. An individual with a low IQ may place limits on himself which may become self-fulfilling prophecies. A person labeled with a high IQ may develop an inappropriately superior attitude.

Another potential problem with IQ scores is that they do not take into account motivation or desire to work and achieve. A person with a lower IQ who works hard and is motivated to achieve may in reality attain much higher levels of achievement and success than one with a higher IQ who is not motivated to use it. Simply having the ability does not necessarily mean that it will be put to any use. Little if any information is available on the relationship between IQ and adult job performance or adult adjustment (Morris, 1979, p. 265).

IQ tests also pose a potential difficulty concerning the arbitrary manner in which people are neatly categorized purely on the basis of intelligence. Many aspects of an individual's personality, ability to interact socially, and adapt to society are not directly related to IQ. For example, can a person with a borderline IQ of 80 successfully interact with a person having a normal IQ of 100? If not, then how can a person with a normal IQ of 100 successfully interact on an equal level with a person having a superior IQ of 120? The difference for each set of individuals is 20 IQ points. Can someone with an IQ of 100 successfully interact on an equal level with a genius having a 140 IQ? What are the implications for human interaction and human rights with a 40 IQ point difference, even though both people's IQs fall at least within the normal range? How then might a person having a 60 IQ interact with one having a 100 IQ? Here is another 40 point difference.

The point is that IQ is only one facet of an individual. People have other strengths and weaknesses unrelated to IQ. Mentally retarded people are like anyone else, but with some lesser intellectual potential. All have similar feelings, joys, and needs. All have rights.

Cultural Biases and IQ Tests

Most IQ tests are culturally biased (Sinclair, 1983, p. 506). This means that white middle- and upper-class children have an unfair advantage on these tests. There are three basic types of biases (Sinclair, 1983, p. 506). First, concepts and situations might be used in the tests which are unfamiliar to minority cultures. Second, even if the minority child has heard of the word or concept, she may not understand the context in which it is used. The way the word or concept is used may not be within the realm of her experience. Third, the test may be heavily biased to emphasize measurement of vocabulary or understanding of the English language (Mercer, 1974). Children who speak either a different language or a different dialect of English will receive lower scores.

Padilla and Wyatt (1983) make the following suggestions concerning alternatives to current intelligence tests. Traditional IQ tests were developed by administering them under the same conditions to a large sample of children who are supposed to be representative of the entire population. With many of the major tests including the Stanford-Binet, minority group children were not included in the sample on which the tests were based until 1972. Therefore, an alternative to enhance the validity for such tests concerning minority group children is to include a representative number of these children in the original samples on which the test is based.

Another suggestion concerns simple translation of the test into the primary language spoken by the child. As simple as this idea seems, this has rarely been done. A similar suggestion is to adjust the way tests are worded so that children speaking different dialects of English can also understand them. Afro-American children, who are frequently more adept in Black Vernacular English (BVE), perform at a lower level on tests presented to them in standard English (Williams and Rivers, 1972). Children must be able to understand what is being asked of them in order to perform to the best of their ability on such tests.

Culture-free tests provide an additional alternative. These are tests which rely more heavily on measurement of perceptual skills than on vocabulary, language skills, and visual examples more familiar to children from some cultures than others. A related alternative idea is the culture-specific test. Such tests are purposefully designed to emphasize examples and information familiar to the minority child.

In summary, IQ tests can provide a useful means of gaining information about probable levels of a person's intellectual ability. However, extreme caution must be exercised as IQ tests do not provide information about the possible level of any individual's potential achievement.

■ The Effects of a Learning Disability

Stevie was 16. He couldn't read or add numbers. As a matter of fact, he felt he couldn't do anything right. Other people seemed to think he was dumb. He even had to go to a special school. He didn't feel dumb, though. He couldn't read, but he understood things. He could even find his way all around his hometown of Milwaukee without being able to read one street sign.

His parents and his brothers and sisters had given up on trying to help him learn to read. He knew they were tired of trying. But he never did anything right. Then they'd get mad, and he'd get mad right back. He'd go out and break some windows or shoplift. That's why he had to go to a special school. People there weren't retarded. They had what teachers and staff called behavior problems.

One time his teachers almost taught him to write his name. He must've practiced it a thousand times. After a couple of months he almost got it right. But he just forgot it again. He liked the staff at school. Sometimes they let him do jobs like washing the blackboards or taking messages to the cook. He liked having responsibility. Nobody ever trusted him with jobs at home.

Stevie didn't like to think about the future. The world looked pretty dim for someone who couldn't read or write.

Learning Disabilities

A *learning disability* is defined as an "extreme difficulty in learning, with no detectable physiological abnormality. The term is used for a wide variety of problems that may cause children to experience academic difficulty" (Craig, 1983, p. 535). Learning disabilities are not due to mental retardation. They are not caused by physical disabilities involving the senses such as vision or hearing. Nor are they caused by some type of emotional problem. Rather, learning disabilities are physiological in origin. They involve the way the brain receives, processes, and uses information.

Many times a learning disabled child is discovered when parents or teachers notice a wide discrepancy in abilities (Craig, 1983, p. 310). Perhaps the child, who appears to have a normal level of intelligence, has exceptional difficulties learning how to read. Sometimes the child will perform very well in one area but very poorly in another. Other children will display serious difficulties in their abilities to concentrate on the task at hand. A learning disability becomes a problem when it causes a child to have difficulties in school. Most learning disabled children have average or better levels of intelligence (Kaluger and Kolson, 1978). This makes the discrepancy between perceived intellectual ability and performance more obvious.

Learning disabilities range from being very mild to being very severe. Most of these children have only mild disturbances (Kaluger and Kaluger, 1984, p. 288). However, as indicated in the earlier example, some disabilities can be very severe. Frequently, learning disabled children will display unequal levels of performance. In some areas they will achieve at a normal or above normal level. In others they will show obvious deficits.

Kaluger and Kaluger (1984, p. 288) present the following facts about how learning disabilities affect school performance. First, most learning disabled children have some reading problems. Approximately 35 to 40 percent have some problems learning to write legibly. However, many of these same children are able to achieve at least average levels in math. On the other hand, another 10% do well in reading but have problems learning math.

Learning disabilities may involve language disorders, visual perceptual disorders, motor disabilities, or hyperactivity. Eaton et al. (1980) elaborate on how each of these types of learning disabilities may affect a child.

Language Disorders

Language disorders fall within three major categories. First, a child may have difficulty understanding words and meanings. This may involve not being able to grasp the individual meanings of words or how words relate to each other in terms of grammatical position.

Second, a learning disabled child with a language disorder may have auditory-processing difficulties. Some children have trouble paying attention to what is being said. The problem concerns being able to focus on the sounds most important in conveying meaning. Other children have trouble discriminating between one sound and another. For example, instead of hearing the word "bed," a child may think she heard the word "dead." The result frequently is confusion for the child and difficulty in understanding and following instructions. Still other children have trouble in recalling what has been said in the correct sequence. This also makes it difficult to follow instructions correctly if children can't understand the proper order in which they are supposed to do things. These children have special difficulties in remembering any content in a series format like months of the year.

The third type of language disorder involves children who have trouble saying what they mean or would like to say. Sometimes this involves grammatical problems. Other children may have difficulty remembering the word they want to say. Still others have trouble telling a story so that it makes sense or describing an event or situation so that the listener can understand what is meant.

Visual Perceptual Disorders

Visual perceptual disorders involve difficulties in seeing things as they really are. Some children have problems understanding spatial relationships. This might include seeing letters or words reversed. It might also involve judging distances between one item and another accurately. Other children find it difficult to complete a task that involves motor coordination. They have difficulty integrating the information they see and translating it into what they can do. They may be clumsy or inaccurate in sports activities. Their handwriting or drawing skills may be exceptionally poor. The other way in which perceptual disorders are manifested involves memory and recall. These children find it hard to remember what they have seen accurately. Misspelling is common. Forgetfulness regarding where they placed things might also result.

Motor Disabilities

Motor difficulties involve coordination of fine and/or gross motor movement. *Fine motor coordination* refers to the ability to control the more precise muscular movements. For example, activities performed by the hand such as handwriting may be affected. *Gross motor coordination*, on the other hand, involves controlling larger movements of the body such as walking or running. A child affected in this manner may be clumsy and have great difficulty performing in sports.

Hyperactivity

Hyperactivity is the fourth major type of learning disability. It may involve two main types of symptoms. One is the inability to pay attention to an ongoing activity for any reasonable amount of time. A hyperactive child may have difficulty focusing on a task. The least interruption or outside stimulation in the environment may distract him or her.

The second major type of hyperactivity involves excessive body movement. Such children are unable to keep still and are in almost constant motor movement. A hyperactive child, for example, might find it very difficult to sit at a desk for any period of time.

Dyslexia

Dyslexia refers to "a specific reading disability that causes children to perceive things differently than they really are" (Craig, 1983, p. 311). Letters and words are frequently seen in reversed or confused order. For example, the word "read" may be seen as "dear." The shapes of letters may be seen backwards such as a "d" being perceived as a "b."

Effects of Learning Disabilities on Children

Learning disabilities may psychologically affect children in several ways. Eaton et al. (1980) cite several reactions which typify responses to such disabilities. They include fear of failure, withdrawal, helplessness, and low self-esteem reactions.

Learning disabled children often become experts in failure. Through no fault of their own, they are unable to learn or do things the way other children can. Some children may fail in school or in sports so frequently that they no longer will attempt new things. They begin to assume that no matter what they do, they will just fail anyway. This fear of failure reaction often results in almost the complete avoidance of new experiences. Since the child refuses to take any new risks, potential progress is halted.

Other children take the fear of failure reaction a step further. Not only do they avoid new experiences, but they withdraw into themselves. This is called *withdrawal reaction*. People and activities seem to have caused them only failure and humiliation in the past. The safest alternative then is to withdraw into themselves. To a limited extent, this may be a healthy means of coping. However, in extreme cases children may isolate themselves and become totally preoccupied with their own thoughts.

The *helplessness reaction* is another means of responding to a learning disability. Children may use the fact that they cannot do some things in order to get out of doing other things they are capable of doing. The vague and complicated nature of learning disabilities does not help this situation. For example, a mother may ask her daughter to do her homework. The daughter responds, "Gee, Mom, I don't know how." The daughter's learning disability involves reading. Her homework is an arithmetic assignment which she has no more difficulty completing than her peers. However, because of her learning disability, the daughter is perceived as being helpless in her mother's eyes. As a result, the mother does not make the daughter do her homework.

Another possible reaction of a learning disabled child is that of low self-esteem. Learning disabled children are likely to see other children do things they cannot. Perhaps others make critical comments to them. Teachers and parents may show at least some impatience and frustration at their inability to understand or perform in the areas affected by their learning disabilities. These children are likely to internalize their failures. The result may be that they feel inferior to others, and they may develop low self-esteem.

Treatment for Learning Disabilities

In addition to observation of performance at home and in the classroom, various tests are available to help pinpoint exactly how the disability affects the child. After diagnosis, suggestions can be made for both teachers and parents to follow in order to maximize the child's progress.

A major idea is to design an individualized special education program for the child to emphasize strengths and minimize weaknesses (Papalia and Olds, 1978, p. 298). For a child with a visual perceptual disorder, emphasis might be placed on providing material that the child can hear in order to learn it. For example, instead of reading an assignment in a textbook, a tape recording of the assignment might be made available so that the child can listen to the material. On the other hand, a child with an auditory processing disorder might need extensive use of visual aids. This would allow him or her to see the material in order to learn it.

A multisensory approach can also be used (Kaluger and Kaluger, 1984, p. 289). This involves presenting material to the child using as many senses as possible. For example, a young learning disabled boy learning how to add, might be told verbally how to accomplish the task. He might also be shown on the blackboard or by using cue cards how the problem is performed. He might also be encouraged to carry out the addition task by using actual objects such as poker chips or "M & Ms." He could then manipulate the objects himself and thus use his sense of touch to enhance his learning.

A very important suggestion for treating the learning disabled child is to support and encourage development of a positive self-concept. This is important for both parents and teachers. Eaton et al. (1980, pp. 72–73) have several suggestions for enhancing self-esteem. First, the positive things that the child does should be emphasized. Problems are easy to see, but good behaviors and accomplishments often go unnoticed. Second, children should feel loved, not for their behavior, but rather for who they are. Third, confidence can be developed in children by giving them responsibility for things they are capable of accomplishing. Success at tasks helps them to develop faith in themselves. Third, comparisons to others and what they accomplish should be avoided. The learning disabled child who has probably so often failed in competition does not need to hear about how well others can do the things he can't. Rather, his own individual accomplishments should be the focus of attention. Fourth, structure in the form of clear guidelines for behavior is helpful so that the child knows what to expect. If the child knows what is acceptable and what is not, he is less likely to make mistakes. The child will also probably respond to the fact that someone cares enough to put forth the effort to provide structure.

Summary

Major theories of personality development include type, trait, psychodynamic, behavioral and phenomenological theories. Sheldon's concepts of the endomorph, mesomorph, and ectomorph personality types exemplify type theory. Allport's conception of cardinal, central, and secondary traits illustrates a trait theory. Freud's psychoanalytic theory is the predominant psychodynamic theory. Behavioral theory is one of the most useful theories of human behavior. The self theory of Carl Rogers is a phenomenological approach.

Two theories of cognitive development are Piaget's and Bruner's. The four periods characterizing Piaget's theory are sensorimotor, preoperational thought, concrete operations, and formal operations. Bruner's three stages are the enactive, the iconic, and symbolic representation.

Aspects of emotional development include approach/avoidance, intensity, and pleasant/unpleasant. High self-esteem is positively related to personality and intellectual growth. The effects of racial prejudice on the self-esteem of nonwhites are explored. Intelligence is defined, and the meaning of intelligence quotients is discussed. Various levels of mental retardation are described. Learning disabilities tend to fall into four basic categories: language disorders, visual perceptual disorders, motor disabilities, and hyperactivity. The potential reactions of children to having a learning disability include fear of failure, withdrawal, helplessness, and low self-esteem. Suggestions for treating children with learning disabilities include emphasizing strengths while minimizing weaknesses, using a multisensory approach, and enhancing self-esteem.

Social Aspects of Infancy and Childhood

"My dad could punch out your dad, I bet!" Jimmy yelled at Harry, the neighborhood bully. Harry had just bopped Jimmy in the nose. Jimmy, who was small for his age, felt hurt. So he resorted to name calling as he edged further and further away from his aggressor. Since his own house was a full two blocks away, Jimmy had to do some fast thinking about how to get there without everybody thinking he was chicken. The worst thing was that Harry was also a pretty fast runner.

To Jimmy's surprise and delight, Harry was apparently losing interest in this particular quarry. Somebody called out from the next block and was trying to interest Harry, a good fullback, in a game of football.

Scowling, Harry shouted back to Jimmy, "Oh, get out of here, you punky 'fry.' Your dad and Boy George could be sisters!" He then darted down the block and into the sunset.

That last remark was not very flattering. It referred to the famous male rock star who helped establish a name for himself by wearing women's makeup and clothing. However, Harry was running in the other direction. Any of the other guys who happened to witness this incident might just think that it was Harry who was running scared. Nonetheless, Jimmy did think it best not to reply, just in case Harry decided to change his mind.

"Whew!" thought Jimmy, "That was a close one." He was usually pretty good at staying far out of Harry's way. This meeting was purely an accident. He was on his way home from a friend's house after working on a class project. That was another story. Their project involved growing bean plants under different lighting conditions. The bean plants that were supposed to be growing good beans weren't. Jimmy secretly suspected that his partner was eating the beans.

Oh, well, Jimmy had better things to do now at any rate. He had to finish his homework. His parents had promised to buy him a new stereo boom box if he maintained at least a B$^+$ average for the whole year. Harry would probably flunk this year anyhow. He was big, but he was also pretty stupid.

Jimmy hightailed it down the street. He had visions of hearing the tones of Duran Duran, his favorite rock 'n' roll group. The horrible Harry affair was soon forgotten.

Childhood is at best a time of excitement, security, fantasy, and

fun. At its worst, it is characterized by discipline, isolation, and failure. Most children, as they grow and develop, experience a combination of these.

The Behavior Dynamics Assessment Model predicts that the attainment of primary social developmental milestones and the significant life events which tend to accompany these milestones have tremendous impacts on the developing individual and that individual's transactions with the impinging environment. Family and peer group mezzosystems are dynamically involved in children's growth, development, and behavior. Social interaction with other people in childhood provides the foundation for building an adult social personality.

■ A Perspective

The goal of this chapter is to identify and explain the major social needs, conditions, and situations affecting children and their behavior, beginning with infancy and moving to adolescence. The family environment is the fundamental setting for the learning and acquisition of interpersonal skills. The peer group and school environment also provide a training ground for social behavior.

This chapter will

- Explain the concept of socialization.
- Explore the family environment, family systems within the context of systems theory, and the family life cycle.
- Describe the basic concepts of learning theory and how such principles as positive reinforcement, punishment, and time-out can be applied to effective parenting.
- Examine some common life events which impact children including the effects of birth order and alternative family lifestyles such as single parent families, families of divorce, and families where mothers work outside of the home.
- Discuss the effects of the peer group and the school environment on children, giving special attention to the social aspects of play, freedom in the classroom, and the relationship between social class and school.

● Explore some of the ways in which society as a large social system impacts children through the provision of child welfare programs directed at helping children in need (for example, protective services, daycare, and foster family care), identify gaps in these services, and suggest new programs to fill these gaps.

Socialization

Socialization refers to "the process through which individuals learn proper ways (proper as defined by the society) of acting in a culture" (Zastrow and Bowker, 1984, p. 25). The process involves the acquisition of language, values, etiquette, rules, behaviors, and all the subtle, complex bits of information necessary to get along and thrive in a particular society.

Although socialization continues throughout life, most of it occurs in childhood. Children need to learn how to interact with other people. They need to learn which behaviors are considered acceptable and which are not. For example, children need to learn that they must abide by the directives of their parents, at least most of the time. They need to learn how to communicate to others what they need in terms of food and comfort. On the other hand, they also need to learn what behaviors are not considered appropriate. They need to learn that breaking windows with their pop guns and spitting in the eyes of other people when they don't get their way will not be tolerated.

Since children start with knowing nothing about their society, the most awesome socialization occurs during childhood. This is when the fundamental building blocks of their consequent attitudes, beliefs, and behaviors are established.

The Family Environment

Because children's lives are centered initially within their families, the family environment becomes the primary agent of socialization. The family environment "involves the circumstances and social climate conditions within families" (Kirst-Ashman, 1983). Since each family is made up of different individuals in a different setting, each family environment is unique. The environments can differ in many ways. For example, one obvious difference lies in the socioeconomic level. Some families live in luxurious 24-room estates, own a Porsche and a Mercedes in addition to the family station wagon, and can afford to have shrimp cocktail for an appetizer whenever they choose. Other families subsist in two-room shacks, struggle with time payments on their used 1977 Chevy, and have to eat macaroni made with artificial processed cheese four times a week.

However, family environments can differ in other more subtle social dimensions. Moos and Humphrey (1974) have elaborated on several of what they term "social climate dimensions." Among others, these dimensions include cohesion, conflict, and control.

Cohesion is defined as "the extent to which family members are concerned and committed to the family and the degree to which family members are helpful and supportive of each other." In families with very close relationships, children are taught that family members can turn to each other for help when they need it. Children learn that they can openly talk to their parents about their problems and comfortably ask their parents questions about things concerning them. Other families socialize their children to remain aloof from other family members and express less concern about each other's well-being. In these families, children are less able to rely on their parents for support even in times of crisis. Children must rely on themselves or on others outside of the family for support and guidance.

Another social climate dimension is that of conflict. This refers to "the extent to which the open expression of anger and aggression and generally conflictual interactions are characteristic of the family." In other words, some families see fighting almost as a way of life. Verbal and even physical aggression is seen as a primary means of relating to other people. In these families children learn that fighting, hitting, or screaming is acceptable behavior. In other families, conflict is rarely if ever found. In these families such aggression is not tolerated, and children must learn to relate to others in other ways.

A third social climate dimension is that of control. This refers to "the extent to which the family is organized in a hierarchical manner, the rigidity of family rules and procedures, and the extent to which family members order each other around." Some families adopt a strict hierarchy of control. What mother or father says is what is supposed to be done, whether the children like it or not. Other families foster a more democratic atmosphere. Children are allowed more input into their own and the family's decisions, and a greater sense of participation and freedom can be seen on the part of all family members.

Families can be compared and evaluated on many other dimensions and variables. The specific variables involved are not so important as the concept that children learn how to behave or are socialized according to the makeup of their individual family environments. The family environment is important in that children are taught what types of transactions are considered appropriate. The family environment needs to be evaluated in terms of the amount of input or energy children receive. If the level of energy and interdependence within a particular family is low, children may be deprived of the support and nurturance they need to thrive. Children may be forced to expend energy to cope with restrictive, conflictual situations. This energy may be diverted from that which is needed to grow into well-adjusted social and emotional maturity. In many of these cases, social work intervention may be warranted.

The Dynamics of Family Systems

In order to understand family functioning, it's helpful to view the family within a system's perspective. Systems theory applies to a multitude of situations, ranging from the internal mechanisms of a computer to the bureaucratic functioning of a large public welfare department to the intimate interpersonal relationships within a family. Regardless of the situation, understanding the various systems theory concepts help to understand dynamic, active, ongoing relationships among parts or among people. Systems theory helps to conceptualize or formulate a mind's eye view of how a family works.

Another important reason can be given for understanding systems theory as it relates to families. Intervention in families with problems is a major concern of social work. Family therapy is "a process through which a family as a whole is enabled to change its patterns of interaction so that all members feel less pain and become more free to develop in the directions most satisfying to them" (Zastrow, 1981, p. 379). It is based on the idea that the family is a system. In finding solutions to problems within a family, the target of intervention is the family system (Minuchin, 1974, p. 14). Whether a particular problem is initially defined as an individual member's or as the entire family's, a family therapist views this problem as one involving the entire family system. Furthermore, the entire family should be the focus of treatment (Scherz, 1970, p. 222). In order to do this, the structure of the family, that is, the specific relationships between various family members in the family system, needs to be closely observed (Perez, 1979, p. 19). *A Systems Analysis of a Family in Therapy* presents a case example illustrating this concept.

■ A Systems Analysis of a Family in Therapy

A family came in for treatment concerning a problem with 15-year-old Jimmy. Jimmy, much to his parents' dismay, had repeatedly stolen cars in the neighborhood and ran down people's mailboxes. No matter what his parents tried, nothing helped. Finally, at their wits' end, the family came in to the local family services agency for help.

The family system consisted of five members. Father was a 46-year-old businessman. Mother, age 42, was a homemaker who did not work outside the home. The children included an 18-year-old male college freshman, and a 13-year-old ninth grade daughter.

Two social work cotherapists worked at assessing this family system for several treatment sessions. No matter how they tried to find out about the other dynamics operating within the system, the family remained stubborn and was very closed. Literally and figuratively, fingers kept pointing at Jimmy as the only family problem. However, it was not logical for Jimmy to behave in this manner. He had no apparent reason to steal cars or obliterate mailboxes.

Finally, in a torrent of confessions, the family members revealed their true situations. Mother was in reality a driven alcoholic who was desperately trying to escape from her life problems. Father was a strict, closed, strong-willed individual whom other family members considered a dogmatic dictator. Emotionally, he was very lonely and felt isolated. Mother's and father's sex life had been virtually nonexistent for the past eight years. Big brother was in the process of coming out, having determined that he was really gay. Father was terrified that other upstanding members in his small town would find out and that his own reputation would be ruined. Finally, little sister was truant from school on a regular basis and as a result was in danger of flunking a grade. She was also sexually active with a variety of young delinquents, and was in almost constant fear of pregnancy.

This family system clearly illustrates how the problem was indeed owned by the entire family. This was in spite of the fact that only one member, Jimmy, had initially been identified as having a problem. In actuality, Jimmy was the healthiest individual family member. He was merely calling attention to the fact that the family had problems. Systems theory concepts help to picture conceptually and assess the interpersonal dynamics operating in families such as this one.

The Ecological Perspective versus Systems Theory

Brief comment needs to be made concerning the relationship between systems theory and the ecological perspective assumed by this book and described in Chapter 1. There is some disagreement regarding the relationship between the two perspectives, that is, to what extent the same concepts are involved. Each perspective has, at various times, been described as being a theory, model, or a theoretical underpinning. To add to the potential confusion, some of the terms, e.g., input, are very similar and have similar meanings.

However, there are two major differences. First, the ecological approach refers to living, dynamic interactions. The emphasis is on active participation. People, for example, have dynamic transactions with each other and with their environments. Systems theory, on the other hand, assumes a broader perspective. It can be used to refer to inanimate, mechanical operations such as a mechanized assembly line in a Coca-Cola bottling plant. It can also be used to describe the functioning of a human family.

The second difference between the ecological perspective and systems theory is that different terms are emphasized. For example, the ecological approach focuses on transactions between individuals and the environment at the interface or point at which the individual and environment meet. Systems theory, on the other hand, addresses boundaries of subsystems within a system, and the maintenance of homeostasis or equilibrium within a system. Some theoreticians might posit that the ecological model is an offshoot or interpretation of systems theory, as it is a bit more limited in scope and application.

Systems Theory Concepts

The following concepts are especially important as they relate to family dynamics.

Systems

A *system* is a set of elements which form an orderly, interrelated, and functional whole. Several aspects of this definition are important. The idea that a system is a "set of elements" means that a system can be composed of any type of things as long as these things have some relationship to each other. Things may be people or they may be mathematical symbols. Regardless, the set of elements must be orderly. In other words, the elements must be arranged in some order or pattern which is not simply random. The set of elements must also be interrelated. They must have some kind of mutual relationship or connection with each other. Additionally, the set of elements must be functional. Together they must be able to perform some regular task, activity, or function and fulfill some purpose. Finally, the set of elements must form a whole.

A large nation, a public social services department, and a newly married couple are all examples of systems. The most relevant example here is the family system. Any particular family is composed of a number of individuals, the elements making up the system. Each individual has a unique relationship with the other individuals in the family. Spouses normally have a special physical and emotional relationship with each other. In a family with seven children, the two oldest sisters may have a special relationship with each other that is unlike their relationship with any of the other siblings. Regardless of what the relationships are, together the family members function as a family system. These relationships, however, are not always positive and beneficial. Sometimes, a relationship is negative and even hostile. For example, a three-year-old daughter may be fiercely jealous of and resentful toward her newborn brother.

Homeostasis

Homeostasis refers to the tendency for a system to maintain a relatively stable, constant state of equilibrium or balance. A homeostatic family system functions effectively. The family system is surviving and maintaining itself and may even be thriving. However, a homeostatic family system is not necessarily a perfect family. Mother may still become terribly annoyed at father for never wanting to go out dancing. Ten-year-old Bobby may still be maintaining a D-average in English. Nonetheless, the family is able to continue its daily existence, and the family system itself is not threatened.

Homeostasis is exceptionally important in determining whether outside therapeutic intervention is necessary in a particular family situation. Absolute perfection is usually unrealistic. However, if its existence is threatened, the system may be in danger of breaking apart. In these instances, the family system no longer has homeostasis. For instance, father may abruptly lose his job. The family has just purchased a new home with high mortgage payments. If the economy is in a recession and father has difficulty acquiring a new position, the family's homeostasis is threatened. Money becomes scarce for food, clothing, and other necessities. Mother and father begin fighting with each other. Each blames the other for buying that ridiculously expensive new home to begin with. The family system itself is endangered. A new job position or some other source of financial support is necessary for the family system to regain homeostasis.

Subsystems

A *subsystem* is a secondary or subordinate system—a system within a system. The most obvious examples of this are the parental and sibling subsystems. Other more subtle subsystems may also exist depending on the boundaries established within the family system. A mother might have a daughter to whom she feels especially close. These two might form a subsystem within a family system, apart from other family members. Sometimes subsystems exist because of more negative circumstances within family systems. A subsystem might exist within a family with an alcoholic father. Here the mother and children might form a subsystem in coalition against the father.

Boundaries

A *boundary* is the separating line which encloses the elements of a system and distinguishes it from the rest of its environment. In a family system, boundaries determine who are members of that particular family system and who are not. Parents and children are within the boundaries of the family system. Close friends of the family are not.

Boundaries may also delineate subsystems within a system. For instance, boundaries separate the spouse subsystem within a family from the sibling subsystem. Each subsystem has its own specified membership. Either a family member is within the boundaries of that subsystem or he is not.

Input

Input can be defined as the energy, information, or communication flow received from other systems. Families are not isolated, self-sufficient units. Each family system is constantly interacting with its environment and with other systems. For example, one type of input into a family system is the money received for the parents' work outside of the home. Another type of input involves the communication and supportive social interaction family members receive from friends, neighbors, and relatives. Schools also provide input in the form of education for children and progress reports concerning that education.

Feedback

Feedback is a special form of input. It involves a system receiving information about the system's own performance. As a result of negative feedback, the system can choose to correct any deviations or mistakes and return to a more homeostatic state. Take, for example, a mother who works outside of the home as a computer programmer. During her job performance evaluation, her supervisor indicates that she tends to fall behind on her weekly written reports. Although she feels the reports are extraordinarily dull and tedious to complete, her supervisor's feedback gives her the information she needs to perform her job better.

A family might also receive feedback concerning its annual income tax returns. Suppose the parents failed to report some savings' interest in the hopes that no one would notice and it would save them some money. Feedback might be in the form of a terse letter informing them that they owe the Internal Revenue Service an additional amount in taxes, along with an interest penalty. This negative feedback would clearly indicate to the couple that it doesn't pay to try to cheat the government.

Not all feedback is negative. Positive feedback is also valuable. This involves a system receiving information about what it's doing right in order to maintain itself and thrive. Positive feedback can provide specific information so that members in a family system are aware of the positive aspects of their functioning. For example, the mother mentioned earlier who works as a computer programmer can receive positive feedback during the same job evaluation. Her supervisor may tell her that she has maintained the highest accuracy record in terms of her work in the entire department. This indicates to her that her conscientiousness in this respect is valued and should be continued.

Perhaps the most relevant example for social workers concerning feedback is its application in a family treatment setting. When a family comes in for help about a particular problem, feedback can raise their awareness about their own functioning. It can help them correct areas where they are making mistakes. It can also encourage them to continue positive interactions. For example, if every time a husband and wife discuss housework responsibilities, they yell at each other about what the other does not do, a social worker can give them feedback that their yelling is accomplishing nothing. Constructive suggestions might then be given about how the couple could better resolve their differences over taking out the garbage, making the breakfast orange juice, and separating the colors from the whites in the laundry.

Positive feedback might also be given. The husband and wife may not be aware that when asked a question about their feelings for each other or about how they like to raise their children, they are very supportive of each other. They immediately look to each other to check out the other's feelings. They smile at each other and encourage the other's opinions. Giving them specific positive feedback about what is occurring and describing their behaviors to them may be helpful. Such feedback may encourage them to continue these positive interactions. It may also suggest to them that they could apply similar positive means to resolving other differences.

Output

Output can be described as energy, information, or communication emitted from a system to the environment or to other systems. Work, whether it be in a job situation, a school setting, or in the home, can be considered output. Financial output is another form. This is necessary for the purchase of food, clothing, shelter, and the other necessities of life.

An important thing to consider about output is its relationship to input. If a family system's output exceeds its input, family homeostasis may be threatened. In other words, if more energy is leaving a family system than is coming in, tensions may result and functioning may be impaired. For example, in a multiproblem family troubled by poverty, illness, lack of education, isolation, loneliness, and delinquency, tremendous amounts of effort and energy may be expended simply to stay alive. At the same time, little help and support may be coming in. The result would be severely restricted family functioning and lack of homeostasis.

Entropy

Entropy is the natural tendency of a system to progress toward disorganization, depletion, and, in essence, death. The idea is that nothing lasts forever. People age and eventually die. Young families get older, and children leave to start their own families. Family systems are constantly in the process of change; conditions change.

Homeostasis itself is dynamic in that it involves constant change and adjustment. Families are never frozen in time. Family members are constantly changing and responding to new situations and challenges.

Negative Entropy

Negative entropy is the process of a system toward growth and development. In effect, it is the opposite of entropy. Goals in family treatment often involve striving to make conditions and interactions better than they were before. A relationship between quarreling spouses can improve. Physical abuse of a child can be stopped. Negative entropy must be kept in mind when helping family systems grow and develop their full potential.

Equifinality

Equifinality refers to the fact that there are many different means to the same end. It is important not to get locked into only one way of thinking, since in any particular situation, there are alternatives. Some may be better than others, but nonetheless, there are alternatives. It's easy to get trapped into an orientation of tunnel vision where no other options are apparent. Frequently, family systems need help in defining and evaluating the options available to them.

Take, for instance, the family where the father abruptly lost his job.

Instead of wallowing in remorse, other alternatives might be pursued. The family might consider relocating geographically where a similar position might be available. The mother who previously had not worked outside of the home might look into the possibility of attaining a job herself, thereby helping the family's financial situation. Moving to less expensive housing might be considered. Finally, the father might look into other types of work, at least temporarily. There are always alternatives. The important thing is to recognize them and consider them.

Differentiation

Differentiation refers to a system's tendency to move from a more simplified to a more complex existence. In other words, relationships, situations, and interactions tend to get more complex over time instead of more simplified. For example, in the life of any particular family, each day adds new experiences. New information is gathered. New options are explored. Sometimes, the basic relationships are lost in the myriad of daily details and distractions. For example, a couple might start having marital problems as their lives become more complicated. The basic fact of their affection and commitment to each other often needs to be pointed out and reinforced.

The Family Life Cycle

Before pursuing how children learn within the family system environment, one other aspect of the family needs to be examined. This book assumes a chronological framework. People functioning within their environments are not stagnant. Just as people change, so do families. Families have life cycles of their own. Each phase of family life tends to be characterized by typical life events.

Erikson (1963) identifies eight important developmental stages that individuals go through in life. Because families are made up of these individuals, the events affecting individual members also affect family systems. Erikson's stages include the following: infancy, toddler, early childhood, school age, adolescence, young adulthood, adulthood, and maturity. Each of these stages tends to be characterized by certain events. For instance, young adulthood tends to be the time when individuals enter into marriage or other intimate relationships. (Erikson's eight developmental stages are described in greater detail in Chapter 6.)

Carter and McGoldrick (1980) present a framework for conceptualizing the family life cycle. Each developmental stage is marked by emotional transitions and changes in status. The following six developmental stages are involved in the family life cycle: the unattached young adult, the newly married couple, the family with young children, the family with adolescents, the family whose children are moving on, and the family in later life.

The first phase, namely that of the unattached young adult, is marked by the separation of the young adult from the family of origin. The young adult establishes an individual identity apart from that of parents. New, intimate peer relationships are formed. The young adult also enters the world of work.

When young adults marry, they enter the second phase of the family life cycle. Adjustments need to be made concerning commitments to the new spouse. This involves realignments with extended family members and friends to accommodate the new relationship. It even involves such simple determinations as whether or not to have separate checkbooks, who makes the oatmeal in the morning, and who is responsible for taking out the garbage.

The third phase in the family life cycle involves the acquisition of young children. The couple subsystem needs to adjust to the presence and the needs of their children. They no longer are able to concentrate solely on each other. If both parents work, child care needs to be considered. Attention needs to be directed to children in the form of feeding, bathing, and playing. Babysitters need to be found in order to attend the Saturday night cocktail party at the boss's home.

As the children grow up, the family enters the fourth phase of the family life cycle, namely that of the family with adolescent children. Adolescents have needs that are very different from those of small children. A major change is the shifting of family boundaries in order to allow for the children's developing independence. A son who turns 16 may no longer want to go along on the family vacation. He may be more interested in keeping his part-time summer job so he can afford to date Laurie, a high school cheerleader.

The parents' subsystem also may need adjustment during this phase. With the children starting to separate from their nuclear family and develop their own family or lifestyle, the parents once again may focus on their own relationship. Children no longer demand the time and attention which they did when they were small. Parents may need to rediscover each other and once again establish a couple-oriented lifestyle.

Midlife career adjustment may also be necessary. Parents who have been working to establish a career may suddenly become aware that their lives have limitations. Becoming president of the corporation no longer sounds so feasible at age 45 as it may have at age 25. People must face the fact that they are mortal. If career expectations were higher than the actual career levels attained, adjustments in the level of expectations may have to be made.

In this fourth stage concern shifts toward the well-being of the parents' own mother and father. There may be important financial and health considerations on the part of aging parents and grandparents.

The fifth stage of the family life cycle is marked by the launching of children into families of their own. The changes and adjustments of the parent/couple subsystem which began in the fourth stage continue. Parents once again become a couple. Often their relationship needs renegotiation. Middle-aged parents become grandparents themselves. New relationships are developed with their children, their grandchildren, and their in-laws. Most frequently, the disability and death of their own parents must be dealt with.

Finally, the sixth stage of the family life cycle involves the family in later life. The young couple have now aged. Their own mortality becomes apparent. This is often a time for a life review. All the events that have already occurred can be reconsidered and integrated. Issues such as illness, death of a spouse, and preparation for one's own death must be dealt with. *The Family Life Cycle* summarizes the primary conditions which characterize the six phases of the family life cycle.

■ The Family Life Cycle

Phase	Primary Conditions
1	Unattached young adult
	Separation from family of origin
	Entrance into the work world
2	Marriage
	Realignments of relationships with friends and relatives
3	Acquisition and care of young children
	Adjustments to meet children's needs
4	Adolescent children
	Shifting of family boundaries as children become more independent
	Refocusing on husband/wife relationship
	Midlife career adjustments
	Concern for the well-being of their own parents who are now grandparents
5	Launching of children into their own families
	Return to the state of being a couple
	Becoming grandparents
	Dealing with disability and death of their own parents
6	Aging
	Integration of life events
	Dealing with their own disability and death

Within the context of the family system which progresses through its own life cycle, we will now turn our attention back to the social development of young children within this system. We will focus on how children become socialized into their family system and on how they learn to behave (or misbehave). Learning theory provides a relevant, conceptual base for understanding how socialization and learning occur. Thus, substantial emphasis will be placed on understanding the theoretical basis for learning theory and its applications to practical parenting.

Learning Theory

"Mom! I want a Tootsie Roll! You promised! I want one right now! Mom!" Four-year-old Huey screamed as loudly as he possibly could. He and his mother were standing in the checkout line at the local supermarket. An elderly woman was checking out in front of them. Two other women and a man were waiting in line behind them.

Huey's mother saw everybody looking at her and her young son. Huey simply would not stop screaming. She tried to "shush" him. She scolded him in as much of a whisper as she could muster. She threatened that he would never see the inside of a McDonald's again. Absolutely nothing would work. Huey just kept on screaming.

Finally, in total exasperation, his mother grabbed the nearest roll off the shelf, ripped off the wrapper, and literally stuck the thing into Huey's mouth. A peaceful silence came over the grocery store. All witnessing the event breathed a sigh of relief. Huey stood there with a happy smile on his sticky face. One might almost say he was gloating.

The family environment has already been established as a primary agent of children's socialization. It provides the critical social environment in which children learn. The next logical question to address concerns how children learn. The social and emotional development of children is frequently a focus of social work intervention. Children sometimes create behavior problems. They become difficult for parents and other supervising adults to manage. When they enter school, these management problems often continue. Teachers and administration find some children difficult to control. Frequently, as children get older, problems escalate.

Children can learn how to be affectionate, considerate, fun-loving, responsible people. But they can also learn how to be selfish, spoiled, inconsiderate hellions. This latter state is not good for parents and adults. It is certainly not good for the children themselves. Children need to cooperate with others. They need to know how to get along in social settings in order to become emotionally mature, well-adjusted adults. Social learning theory concepts are useful for recognizing why anyone, child or adult, behaves the way they do. However, the concepts are especially helpful when addressing the issue of behavior management.

In order to change behavior, it first must be understood. Learning theory provides a framework for understanding how behavior develops. Learning theory has been chosen for elaboration for several reasons. First, it emphasizes the social functioning of persons within their environments (Schwartz and Goldiamond, 1975, pp. 1–2). The total person in dynamic interaction with all aspects of the environment is the focus of attention. This is in contrast to many other theoretical approaches which focus primarily on the individual's personality or isolated history.

Second, learning theory provides "a specific conception of human behavior" (National Association of Social Workers, 1977, pp. 1309–12). It emphasizes the importance of the assessment of observable behaviors (Thomas, 1970, p. 200). It also emphasizes the use of behaviorally specific terms in defining behaviors. This helps to make any particular behavior more clearly understandable.

Finally, learning theory provides a positive approach. The underlying idea is that behaviors develop through learning them, and, therefore, can be unlearned. This allows for positive behavior changes. Instead of individuals being perceived as victims of their personal histories and personality defects, they are conceptualized as dynamic living beings capable of change.

Behavior modification is the therapeutic application of learning theory principles. Much evidence supports the effectiveness of behavioral techniques for a wide variety of human problems and learning situations (Bandura, 1969; Schutte and Hopkins, 1970; Macmillan, 1973; O'Leary and Wilson, 1975; Schwartz, 1975; Craighead et al. 1976; Fischer, 1978).

Figure 4.1   A Stimulus-Response Relationship

Lobster and German
chocolate cake   ——————————————→   Martha's salivation
(Unconditioned Stimulus)   *(Response)*

Respondent Conditioning

Respondent conditioning refers to the emission of behavior in response to a specific stimulus. It is also referred to as classical or Pavlovian conditioning. A particular stimulus elicits a particular response. The stimulus can be a word, a sight, or a sound.

For example, Martha, who has been on a strict diet for a week, stops by to visit her friend Evelyn. Evelyn is in the process of preparing a lobster dinner. She is also baking a German chocolate cake for dessert. Martha begins salivating at the thought of such appetizing food. Martha's response, salivation, occurs as a result of the stimulus, witnessing Evelyn's preparation of the wonderful, albeit fattening, food. Figure 4.1 portrays this relationship.

Much respondent behavior is unlearned. That is, a response is naturally emitted after exposure to a stimulus. This stimulus is called an unconditioned stimulus. Respondent conditioning occurs when a person learns to respond to a new stimulus which does not naturally elicit a response. This new stimulus is called a conditioned stimulus. In order to accomplish this, the new stimulus is paired with the stimulus that elicited the response naturally. The person then learns to associate the new stimulus with a particular response even though it had nothing to do with that response originally.

For example, Mr. Bartholemew, a third grade teacher, slaps students on the hand when they talk out of turn. It might be noted that he slaps them very hard on the hand. As a result of this stimulus, the slapping, students fear Mr. Bartholemew. By associating Mr. Bartholemew with getting a slap on the hand, the students eventually learned to fear Mr. Bartholemew even when he wasn't slapping them. Mr. Bartholemew himself had been paired with the hand slapping until he elicited the same response that the slapping did. Figure 4-2 helps to illustrate this relationship.

Some behavioral techniques used by social workers involve the prin-

Figure 4.2   Respondent Conditioning

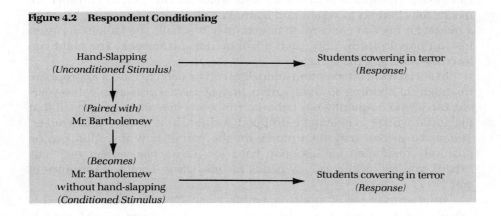

Hand-Slapping   ——————————————→   Students cowering in terror
(Unconditioned Stimulus)   *(Response)*

↓

(Paired with)
Mr. Bartholemew

↓

(Becomes)
Mr. Bartholemew
without hand-slapping   ——————————————→   Students cowering in terror
(Conditioned Stimulus)   *(Response)*

ciples of respondent conditioning. In vivo (real-life) desensitization is an example (Zastrow, 1981, pp. 225–226). This technique can be applied when a person is subject to extreme fear or anxiety over something, e.g., snakes, enclosed places, school. In vivo desensitization usually has two major thrusts. First, the client is exposed to the thing he fears very gradually. Second, while the client is being exposed to the fearful item or event, he is also taught an incompatible response. The incompatible response must be something which cannot occur at the same time as the anxiety and fear. A good example of an incompatible response is progressive relaxation.

For example, the client learns how to control his body and relax. At the same time the standard procedure is that he is exposed to the feared item or event in increasing amounts or degrees. A person who fears rats might first be shown a picture of a rat in the distance while, at the same time, using his newly acquired relaxation skills. Anxiety and fear cannot occur at the same time that the individual is in a relaxed state. They are incompatible responses.

The individual might then be shown an 8″ × 10″ photo of a rat. Once again, the individual would use relaxation techniques to prevent anxiety from occurring. The client would be exposed to rats in a more and more direct manner until the client could actually hold a rat in his hand. The client would gradually learn to use the incompatible relaxation technique to quell any anxiety that rats might once have elicited.

In addition to in vivo desensitization, other respondent conditioning techniques are sometimes used in clinical settings by social workers. However, they are not nearly as many nor are they as common as those behavioral techniques based on operant conditioning.

Modeling

The second type of learning is called *modeling*. Modeling refers to the learning of behavior by observing another individual engaging in that behavior. In order to learn from a model, an individual does not necessarily have to participate in the behavior. An individual need only to watch how a model performs the behavior in order to learn how the behavior is accomplished. For obvious reasons, modeling is also called observational behavior. A behavior can be learned simply by observing its occurrence.

Modeling is important within the context of practical parenting. Parents can model appropriate behavior for their children. This provides an effective means for children to watch and learn. For example, a father might act as a model for his son concerning how to play baseball. The father can teach his son how to throw and catch a ball by doing it himself. The child can learn by watching his father.

In social work intervention, modeling can be used to model appropriate treatment of children so that parents may observe. For example, five-year-old Larry who frequently has behavior problems may pick up a pencil that the social worker accidentally dropped and return it to the social worker. The social worker may then model for the parent how the child can be positively reinforced for his good behavior. The social worker may say, "Thank you for picking up my pencil for me, Larry. That was very nice of you."

Another example of modeling within a social work practice context is role playing. For example, a social worker might ask a parent who has trouble controlling her son to role play that son and mimic his behavior. She is instructed to act how she thinks her son would act. The social worker may then model for the parent some appropriate, effective things to say to the son when the son behaves in that way. Such modeling provides the opportunity for the parent to learn new ways of responding to her son.

Modeling can also unfortunately teach children inappropriate and ineffective behavior. For example, consider a mother who strikes other family members whenever she gets the least bit irritated with them. She is likely to act as a model for that type of behavior. Children may learn that striking others is the way to relate their anger.

Operant Conditioning

Operant conditioning is the dominant type of learning focused on in the United States (National Association of Social Workers, 1977, p. 1310). It allows for the easiest and most practical understanding of behavior. Most treatment applications are based on the principles of operant conditioning (Hosford and de Visser, 1974; Kazdin, 1975; Schwartz and Goldiamond, 1975; National Association of Social Workers, 1977).

Operant conditioning is "a type of learning in which behaviors are altered primarily by regulating the consequences which follow them" (Kazdin, 1975, p. 256). New behaviors can be shaped, weak behaviors can be strengthened, strong behaviors can be maintained, and undesirable behaviors can be weakened and eliminated. The emphasis lies on the consequences of behavior. In other words, whatever follows a particular behavior affects how frequently that behavior will occur again, as is illustrated in *Consequences and Reoccurring Behavior.*

■ Consequences and Reoccurring Behavior

The Johnsons hired their neighbor, 9-year-old Eric, to mow their lawn once a week during the summer. Eric, not being sophisticated in the ways of money management, failed to discuss how much he would be paid per hour. Eric slaved away for four hours one Saturday afternoon when he would rather have been playing baseball.

When Eric had finished, Mr. Johnson came out, complimented Eric on what a fine job he had done, and gave him $1.50 for his trouble. Unfortunately $1.50 worked out to be 37 1/2 cents per hour. Mr. Johnson thought this was more than adequate. Mr. Johnson himself had been paid only a grand total of 50 cents for doing a similar job when he was a boy. Eric, however, felt this was more than chintzy on Mr. Johnson's part. A dollar and a half would only cover three brief video games down at Video Heaven. It would not nearly begin to finance the new baseball glove he wanted.

The consequences for Eric's lawnmowing behavior were not positive. He did not receive his expected $12.00. Thus, Eric never mowed Mr. Johnson's lawn again. Instead he turned to other more generous and benevolent neighbors to upgrade his financial future. He also learned to make salary one of the first items on his business agenda. If Mr. Johnson had given him his expected rate of $3.00 an hour, Eric would have been a dependable and industrious worker throughout the summer. In other words, more favorable consequences for Eric would have encouraged his lawnmowing behavior. He would have been conditioned to mow Mr. Johnson's lawn. As it turned out, Mr. Johnson was doomed to mowing his own lawn for the remainder of the summer.

The A-B-C's of Behavior

One way of conceptualizing operant behavior is to divide it into its primary parts. These include antecedents, behaviors, and consequences (Schwartz and Goldiamond, 1975, p. 17). Another way of referring to them is the A-B-Cs of behavior.

Antecedents refer to the events occurring immediately prior to the behavior itself. These events set the stage for the behavior to occur. For instance, some individuals state that they are able to quit smoking cigarettes except when they are socializing in a bar or nightclub. The bar conditions act as a stimulus or incentive for smoking behavior, whereas other environments do not. In other words, the bar setting acts as an antecedent for smoking behavior.

The behavior refers to "any observable and measurable response or act of an individual" (Kazdin, 1975, p. 251). The important terms here are observable and measurable. There must be some way to observe the behavior in order to know when it is occurring. For example, Shirley is a six-year-old child who has been clinically diagnosed as depressed. Any thoughts she has about being depressed are not noticeable. However, she makes frequent statements about what a bad girl she is, how her parents don't like her, and what it would be like to die. These statements can be observed and noted. Such statements might be used as indicators for childhood depression.

Shirley's statements can also be measured. That is, the types of statements she makes and the frequency with which she makes them can be counted and evaluated. She might make a statement concerning what a bad girl she is 12 times per day, about how her parents dislike her 5 times per day, and about her own death 16 times per day. When her depression begins to subside, these types of verbal statements may decrease in frequency and severity. For example, Shirley may only make derogatory remarks about herself 4 times per day instead of 12. She may say her parents dislike her only once each day. Statements about death may disappear altogether.

In addition to verbal behavior, physical behavior or actions may also be observed and measured. Besides making statements which indicate she's depressed, Shirley may spend much of her time sitting in a corner, sucking her thumb, and gazing off into space. The exact amount of time she spends displaying these specific behaviors may be observed and measured. For example, Shirley initially may spend five hours each day sitting in a corner. When depression begins to wane, she may only spend one half hour in the corner.

The final component as a basis for operant conditioning involves the consequences of the behavior. A consequence may be "either something that is presented or something that is taken away or postponed" (Schwartz and Goldiamond, 1975, p. 18). In other words, something happens as a direct result of a particular behavior. Consequences are best described in terms of reinforcement and punishment.

Reinforcement

Reinforcement refers to a procedure or consequence which increases the frequency of the behavior immediately preceding it. If the behavior is already occurring at a high frequency level, then reinforcement maintains the behavior's frequency. A behavior occurs under certain antecedent conditions. If the consequences of that behavior serve to make that behavior occur more often or be maintained at its current high rate, than those consequences are considered reinforcing. Reinforcers strengthen behavior and make them more likely to occur in the future (Patterson, 1975, p. 10).

Positive Reinforcement

Reinforcement can either be positive or negative. *Positive reinforcement* refers to positive events or consequences which follow a behavior and act to strengthen that behavior. In other words, something is presented or added to a situation and encourages a particular behavior. For example, eight-year-old Herbie receives a weekly allowance of $2.00 if he straightens out his room and throws all of his dirty laundry down the clothes chute. Receiving his allowance serves to strengthen or positively reinforce Herbie's cleaning behavior.

Negative Reinforcement

Negative reinforcement refers to the removal of an event or consequence which serves to increase the frequency of a particular behavior. There are two important aspects of this definition. First, something must be removed from the situation. Second, the frequency of a particular behavior is increased. In this manner positive and negative reinforcement resemble each other. Both function as reinforcement which, by definition, serves to increase or maintain the frequency of a behavior.

A good example of negative reinforcement is a seat belt buzzer in a new car. The car door is opened and an obnoxiously loud and annoying buzzer immediately is activated. It will not stop until the driver's seat belt is fastened. The intent is to encourage people to buckle up. Conceptually, the buzzer functions as a negative reinforcer. The buzzer acts as reinforcement because it increases the frequency of buckling seat belts. The buzzer is also negative or aversive. It increases seat belt buckling behavior because people are motivated to stop it, not because they are motivated to hear it.

Another example is a snarling Doberman pinscher which inhabits a neighbor's yard. The yard, by the way, is also enclosed by a eight-foot-high, reinforced wire mesh fence which bears a sign reading, "Beware of dog." The dog serves as negative reinforcement for people entering this yard. Avoidance behavior is increased. That is, people are more likely to stay away from the yard because of their fear of being bitten.

Although at first glance this may appear obvious and simplistic, it is easy to become confused about the type of reinforcement which is occurring. In any particular situation, both positive and negative reinforcement may be taking place at the same time. Take, for instance, the example given initially to illustrate learning theory. It involved four-year-old Huey and his mother at the supermarket. Huey yelled for a Tootsie Roll. His mother finally gave in and thrust one into his mouth. His crying immediately stopped. Both positive and negative reinforcement were occurring in this example. Mother's giving Huey the Tootsie Roll served as a positive reinforcer. Huey received something positive which he valued. At the same time he learned that he could get exactly what he wanted from his mother by screaming in the supermarket. Giving him the Tootsie Roll positively reinforced his bad behavior. That type of behavior would be, therefore, more likely to occur in the future.

At the same time negative reinforcement was occurring in this situation.

Every family's environment is unique. It comprises different individuals in different settings with the social climate differing in each of those settings. While one family demonstrates a great deal of cohesion and is mutually supportive and helpful, another is in constant conflict. The conflicts lead to temperamental outbursts and ongoing arguments. In still another family where parents autocratically rule over their children, control is the operative factor. (Karen Kirst-Ashman)

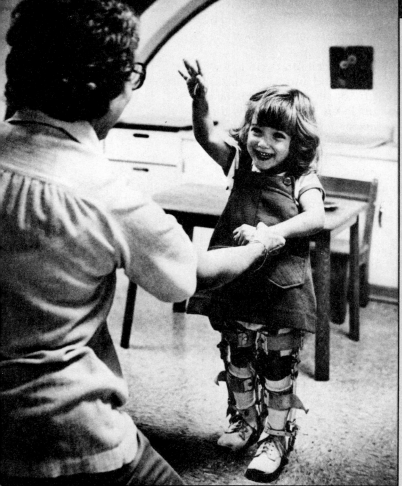

Verbal praise is positive reinforcement when directed at a specific activity or behavior. Verbal praise for a handicapped child who has taken a few steps encourages her to try walking a bit more. Another form of social reinforcement is physical praise. It can come in the form of a smile, laugh, pat, or a wink. A parent who claps when a child sings is offering physical praise. (Courtesy of United Way of America)

Different types of play characterize different age levels. At age three, children are apt to engage in parallel play. They remain near each other, but don't interact as they independently play with similar toys in a similar manner. By age five, they can share in cooperative play. They often choose to divide themselves into teams, then play together, striving for the same goal. Cooperative play enables children to see that they are part of a group. (Karen Kirst-Ashman and Charles Zastrow)

Because there is an increasing number of single-parent families, and because today's mothers are likely to work outside the home, quality day care is a modern-day essential. Even in two-parent families, a day-care situation that merely meets children's physical needs and provides custodial care is inadequate. The optimal day-care situation offers a supportive, educationally stimulating atmosphere, with each child receiving individual attention that is warm and loving. (Courtesy of United Way of America)

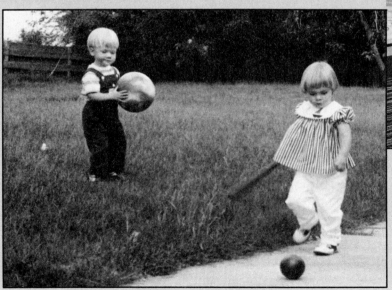

Mother's giving in behavior was encouraged or strengthened. She learned that she could stop Huey's obnoxious yelling by giving him what he wanted, namely, a Tootsie Roll. Huey's yelling therefore, acted as negative reinforcement. It increased his mother's "giving in" behavior by motivating her to stop or escape from his yelling.

Punishment

Punishment and negative reinforcement are frequently confused. Perhaps this is because they both concern something negative or aversive. However, they represent two distinctly different concepts.

Punishment is the presentation of an aversive event or the removal of a positive reinforcer which results in the decrease in frequency of a particular behavior. Two aspects of this definition are important. First, the result of punishment by definition is the decrease in frequency of a behavior. This is in direct opposition to negative reinforcement, where by definition the frequency of a behavior is increased.

Second, punishment can be administered in two different ways. One way involves presenting a negative or aversive event immediately after a behavior occurs. Negative events may include spankings, scoldings, electric shocks, additional demands on time, or embarrassing criticisms. For example, 10-year-old Susie hadn't studied for her social studies exam. Her parents had already complained about the last report card. She just hadn't given the test much thought until Ms. McGuilicutte was handing out the test papers. Susie looked over her test paper and gasped. Nothing looked even vaguely familiar. She was sitting next to Janet, whom she considered the class genius. She figured that just a few brief glances at Janet's paper wouldn't hurt anybody. However, Susie was wrong. Ms. McGuilicutte, whose vision equalled that of a hawk's, immediately noticed Susie's wandering attention. Ms. McGuilicutte swooped down on Susie and confiscated Susie's test paper. In front of the entire class Susie was told that cheating resulted not only in an F grade, but also in two weeks worth of detentions after school. Susie was mortified. She vowed to herself that she would never cheat again.

Susie received extremely aversive consequences as the result of her cheating behavior. The consequences included not only a failing test grade and two weeks of detentions, but also devastating humiliation in front of her peers. Her cheating behavior decreased in frequency to zero.

The second way in which punishment can be administered is by withdrawing a positive reinforcer. Once again, the result must be a decrease in the frequency of a particular behavior. For example, seven-year-old Robbie thought it was funny to belch at the table during dinner. Several times his parents asked him to stop belching. Each time Robbie was quiet for about a minute and then started belching again. Finally, his mother stated loudly and firmly that such belching was considered rude behavior and that as punishment, Robbie would not receive the banana split she had planned for his dessert. Robbie whined and pleaded, but his mother refused to give it to him. Robbie loved desserts, and banana splits were his favorite. Robbie never belched at the table again, at least not purposefully. Removal of the positive reinforcer, namely the banana split dessert, had served as punishment. This punishment resulted in an abrupt decrease in belching behavior. The relationships between reinforcers and punishment are summarized in *Positive Reinforcers, Negative Reinforcers, and Punishment.*

■ Positive Reinforcers, Negative Reinforcers, and Punishment

There are four basic learning principles involving positive reinforcers, negative reinforcers, and punishment:

1. If a positive reinforcer (for example, food) is presented to a person following a response, the result is positive reinforcement. With positive reinforcement the occurrence of a given behavior is strengthened or increased.
2. If a positive reinforcer is withdrawn following a person's response, the result is punishment.
3. If a negative reinforcer (for example, an electric shock) is presented to a person following a response, the result is punishment.
4. If a negative reinforcer is withdrawn following a person's response, the result is negative reinforcement. In negative reinforcement, a response (behavior) is increased through removing a negative reinforcer (for example, finishing up a homework assignment to avoid missing recess).

In sum, positive and negative reinforcement increase behavior, and punishment decreases behavior.

Extinction

Extinction involves the withdrawal of a reinforcer for a particular behavior, which results in a decrease in the frequency of that behavior. In other words, a behavior is increased or maintained by some type of reinforcement. The reinforcement is taken away. The result is a decrease in the frequency of the behavior. In this context, extinction is a form of punishment.

An example concerns the reduction of tantrum behaviors in a 21-month-old child (Williams, 1959). When put to bed, the child would scream until his parents would return to the room to comfort him. This provided positive reinforcement for the child's behavior. The parents were instructed to put the child to bed, leave the room, and ignore his screaming. The first night, the child screamed for 45 minutes. However, the next night when the parents left the room, no screaming occurred. Eventually, withdrawing the positive reinforcer of attention resulted in the total elimination of the child's tantrums. Ignoring, therefore, can be used as an effective means of extinction.

This example uses attention as a positive reinforcer. However, extinction occurs with many other reinforcers in various daily situations. For example, if putting a quarter in a coffee machine results in nothing but a gush of clear, hot water without the cup, use of that coffee machine will probably be extinguished.

One other aspect of extinction is important to note. Frequently, when reinforcement initially is stopped, a brief increase in the frequency of the behavior may occur. This is referred to as an *extinction burst* (Kazdin, 1975, p. 180). This occurs despite the eventual elimination of the behavior. For example, consider again tantrums in a small child. When the reinforcement of attention is withdrawn, the child's behavior might escalate temporarily. The intensity of the undesirable behavior can seriously strain the patience and tolerance of parents (Patterson and Crofts, 1970). One way of looking at this might be to see it from the child's perspective. If the child in the past had always received positive reinforcement through attention for his behavior, it might be very confusing suddenly to receive no attention at all for that very same behavior. The child may try exceptionally hard to get the attention to which he was accustomed. However, eventually the child will learn that the tantrums are not reinforced and are, therefore, simply not worth the effort. Thus, the tantrum behavior is extinguished.

Applications of Learning Theory to Practical Parenting

As children become socialized, they learn and assimilate various behaviors. Because learning is a complicated process, the behaviors they sometimes learn are not those that their parents would prefer. Behavior management is a major issue for many parents.

When a child behaves in a particular way, parents have various alternative ways of responding to this behavior. This conforms with the Behavior Dynamics Assessment Model. That is, at any point in time there are alternative choices concerning the plan of action an individual can take. For each alternative there are consequences. The critical task is to evaluate each alternative and select the one with the most advantageous results. Learning theory concepts provide parents with a means of understanding the alternatives open to them and of predicting the potential consequences of each alternative. It can serve to help them gain control over their children's behavior.

An example of parental alternatives in response to behavior is provided by Danny, age four. At the dinner table with his whole family present, Danny nonchalantly and without warning says an unmentionable four-letter word. Danny's parents are shocked. At this point, they can respond in several different ways. One alternative is to ignore the fact that Danny said the word. Without being given undue attention, saying the word may be extinguished. A second alternative is to tell Danny calmly that the word is not considered a very nice word. They might add that some people use it when they're angry and that other people don't really like to hear it. They might also ask him to please not use the word anymore. A third alternative is for the parents to display their horror and disbelief, scream at Danny never to say that word again, and send him up to bed without being allowed to finish his supper. When this incident actually occurred, the parents opted to respond as described in the third alternative. Poor Danny really didn't understand what the word meant. He had just heard it on the playground that afternoon. He was amazed at the response of his parents and at the attention he received. His mother reported that for the following two years, he continued to repeat that unmentionable four-letter word virtually everywhere. He said it to the dentist, to the grocer, to the police officer, and even to his grandmother. His mother reported that after a while she would've been willing to pay Danny to stop using that word, if such a strategy would have worked.

In Danny's situation, his parents' attention became a tremendously strong positive reinforcer. Perhaps if they would have stopped and thought in terms of learning theory principles, they could have gained immediate control of the situation and never thought another thing of it.

The Use of Positive Reinforcement

Positive reinforcement is based on the very fundamental idea that behavior is governed by its consequences. If the consequences of a particular alternative behavior are positive or appealing, then the individual will tend to behave that way. In other words, the frequency of that behavior will be increased.

Positive reinforcement provides a valuable means of behavioral control. It has been established as an appropriate technique for achieving positive behavioral changes in numerous situations (Kazdin, 1975, p. 105). Rose (1972, p. 87), who expresses a strong preference for positive reinforcement over the use of aversive techniques, explains that the use of positive reinforcement helps to reduce the risk that clients begin associating the negative effects of punishment, for example, with the therapist, resulting in an aversion to therapy. Positive reinforcement also provides the advantage of teaching an individual exactly how to improve his or her behavior.

Various aspects of positive reinforcement will be discussed here. First, the types of reinforcers available will be examined. The differences between positive reinforcement and the use of rewards will be explained. Finally, suggestions for maximizing the effectiveness of positive reinforcement will be presented.

Types of Positive Reinforcers

Reinforcers can be separated into two major categories, primary and secondary. Primary reinforcers are rewarding in themselves, without any association with other reinforcers (Morris, 1979, p. 152). They include objects and activities that people naturally find valuable. Food, water, candy, and sex are examples. Individuals respond positively to them naturally without having to learn their value.

Secondary reinforcers, on the other hand, have values which are learned through association with other reinforcers (Morris, 1979, p. 152). The key idea here is that they must be learned. Alone they have no intrinsic value. Money perhaps is the most easily understood example. A one thousand dollar bill in itself is nothing but a small piece of high quality paper with printed symbols on it. However, it is associated with things of value. It can be used to purchase actual items ranging from diamonds to pistacchio nuts. Money is valuable only because it is associated with other concrete primary reinforcers.

The concepts of primary and secondary reinforcers can readily be applied to treatment situations. For example, a developmentally disabled child may not initially value verbal praise. He may not yet have learned to associate verbal praise with his actual behavior. A social worker may be working with the child concerning his ability to dress himself. Initially, saying, "That's good," may mean nothing to the child. However, saying, "That's good," while at the same time giving the child a small chocolate star, may eventually give the verbal praise some meaning. The child learns to associate verbal praise with the positive value of the candy. Eventually, the praise itself becomes reinforcing to the child, even without the candy. This technique involves pairing a primary reinforcer, the chocolate star, with a secondary reinforcer, verbal praise. The secondary reinforcer becomes valuable to the child through its initial association with the candy.

Secondary Reinforcers

Five major types of reinforcers are addressed here. The first type includes food and other consumables. Food is a primary reinforcer. It has already been mentioned as a primary or unlearned form of positive reinforcement. The other four types of reinforcers are secondary or learned reinforcers. These include material, social, activity, and token reinforcers.

Material Reinforcers

Material reinforcers are specific objects or events which can be used as rewards to increase specific behaviors. Eight-year-old Herbie received an allowance for cleaning his room. Herbie's cleaning behavior was strengthened or reinforced by receiving an allowance.

Money might be considered an object or specific, tangible thing which reinforces a behavior. Other objects which might have been used as tangible reinforcers for Herbie include records, ice cream treats, and toys. Each of these items would have acquired their value through learning. Therefore, they would be considered secondary reinforcers.

Activities

Activities make up the second category of secondary reinforcers. Activities are tangible events whose value has been learned. Positively reinforcing activities for children might include watching television, playing with friends, staying up late at night, being read to, going shopping, or visiting the stock car races.

For example, 12-year-old Gina hates doing her homework at night. However, she loves going to the movies on Saturdays. Her parents positively reinforce her for doing an hour's worth of homework five nights per week by giving her money to go to the movies on Saturday. Going to the movies is an activity which serves as positive reinforcement for Gina doing her homework.

Social Reinforcers

Material and activities are not the only things that people learn to value. Various aspects of social interaction can also be considered very valuable. Social reinforcement includes words and gestures used to indicate caring and concern toward another person. This can be communicated in one of two ways, either by giving verbal or physical praise.

Verbal praise involves stating words or phrases that indicate approval or appreciation of someone's specific behavior, such as "Good job"; "You did that very well"; or "That's terrific!"

Effective verbal praise is directed at a specific behavior or activity. The person receiving the praise should be clearly aware of what the praise concerns. For instance, eight-year-old Linda did the dishes without being asked for the two days her mother was out of town attending a professional conference. Her mother, on her return home, stated, "Thank you very much for helping out and doing the dishes. I understand you did them without even being told. I really appreciate your help." Linda's mother made it very clear to Linda exactly what she did that was appreciated. When such praise acts to strengthen Linda's dish-washing behavior in the future, it is positive reinforcement. If Linda's mother instead had stated to Linda, "You're a very good girl," it may not have been clear to Linda exactly why she was good. The positive regard communicated by such a statement, of course, is valuable in itself. However, Linda may have understood her mother to mean that she was good because she didn't cry when her mother left or because she only stayed up one half hour past her bedtime. Linda may not have understood that her mother appreciated her washing dishes, and thus may never have done so without being told again.

The second type of social reinforcement is physical praise. Physical praise involves communicating appreciation or praise through physical gestures or body posture. This may simply involve a smile or a nod of the head. Hugging, clapping, or even winking can also indicate praise.

Consider, for example, how a smile might acquire significance. An infant may not initially value her mother's smile. However, the infant may soon learn to associate the smile with comfort, warmth, and food. Eventually, the smile itself becomes reinforcing. It is a secondary reinforcer. The infant learns to value it. The smile is valued not because it is of value itself, but because the infant has learned to associate it with things of value.

The effects of social reinforcement are illustrated by Beverly, age five. Beverly had acquired a role in the kindergarten play. Her part involved playing a duck whose job it was to waddle back and forth across the stage. Beverly was extremely nervous about her part, as she was an exceptionally shy child. She even had to get a new yellow dress and wear red rubbers to help characterize her role. She had been practicing her waddling for days before the play. Finally, the critical night arrived. It was almost time to initiate her waddle and dare to venture out on the stage. At the last minute, she almost backed down and started crying. However, she looked out and there were her parents in the second row, looking directly at her. They were both smiling proudly and nodding their heads. With such encouragement, she waddled across that stage like no one had ever waddled before. Her parents' obvious approval and encouragement had served to positively reinforce her acting and waddling behavior. After this experience, she became much more likely to volunteer and participate in activities which required performing before an audience.

Tokens

Tokens provide the final category of secondary reinforcers. Token reinforcers are defined as "objects that symbolize various units of value desirable to an individual that can be exchanged for something that person wants" (Fischer, 1975, p. 61). Tokens can include poker chips, slugs or artificial coins, points, checkmarks, or gold stars. In and of themselves, they mean nothing. However, they can be associated with something of value and eventually be exchanged for that item or activity.

A practical application of tokens is the use of a token economy in child management. For example, a bicycle might serve as a strong positive reinforcer for a particular child. However, it is absurd to give the child a bicycle every time the child cleans his/her room. Rather, a system can be designed where a child can earn tokens. The child can be told that if she earns a certain number of tokens, she can exchange them for a bicycle. Tokens become a secondary reinforcer. A large sum of tokens can be used to acquire a bicycle, the item of real value.

Reinforcers versus Rewards

A distinction must be made between reinforcers and rewards. A reward is not necessarily a positive reinforcer. A reward is something that is given in return for a service or a particular achievement. It may or may not increase the frequency of a particular behavior. A soldier might receive a medal of honor at the end of a war for shooting down 27 enemy planes. This is a reward. This reward does not, however, increase the frequency of this individual shooting down more planes during his civilian life.

Reinforcers, by definition, increase the frequency of a behavior. Receiving an A on an exam is a positive reinforcer for studying behavior if it serves to increase the frequency of the particular student's studying in preparation for exams. However, the student may not value the grade very much. The A may not serve to motivate him to increase or maintain studying behavior. The student becomes bored with studying and receives C and D grades on the next two exams. In this case, the grade might be considered a reward for performance on one exam. However, the grade is not a positive reinforcer because it neither maintained nor increased the frequency of his studying.

By definition, something serves as a reinforcer only if it increases behavior. A positive reinforcer needs to be valued by an individual for it to be effective. Not all items, activities, and social interactions are reinforcing to all people. For example, a roller coaster ride at Disney World may be very positively reinforcing for a third grader whose dream it is to visit Disney World. However, that same ride may not be at all reinforcing or valuable to the third grader's father who tends to become ill on roller coasters.

Suggestions for Using Positive Reinforcement

Four suggestions to enhance the use of positive reinforcement involve the quality, the immediacy, and the frequency of positive reinforcement, and the use of small steps for shaping behavior.

Quality of Positive Reinforcement

In order to be considered reinforcement, an item or event must actually increase the frequency of some behavior. It's already been established that what is reinforcing for one person may not be reinforcing for another.

A more subtle issue, however, involves the varying degrees of reinforcement value within any particular reinforcer. A particular positive reinforcer might be more reinforcing in a particular form or under certain conditions. It might be more preferable in one form than in another. For example, animals can be positively reinforced for pressing a bar by giving them food. However, they will perform with a higher frequency of bar pressing behavior if they receive foods that taste sweet than when they receive foods that are sour or neutral (Hutt, 1954). Perhaps they are not so different in this respect from human beings.

A high school senior working as a part-time janitor at a small local inner tube factory provides another example. The young man, Dave, is working to save for a downpayment on his own car. The idea of owning a car is very reinforcing to him. However, the make of the car makes a difference in terms of its value to him. Because of the tremendous costs involved in purchasing a car, Dave had decided to be satisfied with almost anything that he could reasonably afford. However, when he found a 1981 red Camaro with red flames printed on the hood for sale down the block, his working behavior sharply increased. He asked if he could double his working hours. To Dave the Camaro served as a much stronger positive reinforcer than an older, beat-up station wagon would have.

Immediacy of Positive Reinforcement

Positive reinforcement has a greater effect on behavior if it is administered immediately or shortly after the behavior occurs (Skinner, 1953). In other words, it's important that the behavior and the positive reinforcement occur very close to each other in time. Positive reinforcement loses its effect if it is delayed too long. For example, a five-year-old child brushes his teeth without being told one morning. Praising him for this behavior immediately after he's finished or even while he's brushing will have a much greater effect on whether he brushes his teeth again this way than if he's praised when he gets into bed at night. By the time bedtime arrives, he is likely to forget that he ever brushed his teeth. It becomes much more difficult for him to associate the praise with the specific teeth-brushing behavior.

Frequency of Positive Reinforcement

Positive reinforcement which is administered consistently is the most effective (Fischer and Gochros, 1975, p. 66; Patterson, 1975, pp. 36–37). In other words, the most effective way to increase a particular behavior is to reinforce it every time it occurs. This is referred to as *continuous reinforcement*. For example, Gertie, age 12, is supposed to do her math homework every night. If Gertie's teacher collects the assignments every morning and gives Gertie credit for doing them, Gertie is likely to complete her homework every night. However, if Gertie's teacher only collects the Thursday night homework, Gertie is less likely to do her homework every night.

An advantage of continuous reinforcement is that it is the most effective in establishing a particular behavior. However, a disadvantage is that if the positive reinforcement stops for some reason, the behavior is likely to extinguish rapidly. For example, Gertie's teacher collects her homework every morning for two months. Suddenly, her teacher decides that it's no longer necessary to collect the homework. As a result, there is a fairly strong likelihood that Gertie will stop doing her homework if she no longer gets credit for it.

An alternative to continuous reinforcement is *intermittent reinforcement*. This is where a behavior is not reinforced every time it is performed. Instead it is reinforced only occasionally. In the real world, continuous reinforcement is difficult to administer. It is difficult to be with a person every minute of the day in order to observe that person's behavior. Sometimes intermittent reinforcement is a viable alternative.

Intermittent reinforcement is not as powerful in initially establishing a behavior. It may take longer to establish the behavior. The behavior may not occur as regularly as it would under the conditions of continuous reinforcement. For example, Gertie might not do her homework every night because there would be a chance it wouldn't be collected the next day.

However, intermittent reinforcement is less subject to extinction. That is, suppose Gertie's teacher had only intermittently or occasionally collected her homework. Suddenly, the homework is no longer being collected. Gertie would be more likely to continue doing the homework after an intermittent schedule of reinforcement than after a continuous schedule. When she was accustomed to occasional or intermittent reinforcement, she would be more likely to continue doing her homework on the chance that it might be collected again. If homework collection stops abruptly after continuously being collected, Gertie would probably think that her teacher no longer liked to collect it. As a result, Gertie would probably stop doing her homework.

Each type of intermittent reinforcement dictates a different procedure for how frequently or in what order reinforcement should be administered. These various procedures are referred to as *schedules of reinforcement*.

Shaping Behavior

Sometimes the behavior that's supposed to be positively reinforced never occurs. It is impossible to reinforce a behavior that isn't there. Therefore, a technique called *shaping* can be used. Shaping refers to the reinforcement of successive approximations, i.e., small steps of progress, made toward the final desired behavior.

For example, seven-year-old Ralph is terrified of the water. His mother thinks that it would be valuable for him to learn to swim. However, swimming behavior cannot be reinforced because Ralph simply refuses to enter a swimming pool. In this case, shaping might be useful. Instead of attempting to positively reinforce Ralph's dogpaddle which isn't occurring, it might be useful to break down the specific behavior into smaller, more manageable pieces of behavior. For instance, swimming might be broken down into the following smaller segments of behavior: going to the beach and playing far away from the water, playing several feet away from the water, playing while sitting in one inch of water, wading, entering the water waist deep, moving arms around in the water, briefly dunking head beneath the water, and finally starting to practice beginning swimming strokes. At each step, Ralph could be positively reinforced with praise, attention, or toys for participating in that step. Eventually, his behavior could be shaped so that he would participate in behavior resembling swimming. Specific swimming techniques could then be initiated and reinforced.

The Use of Punishment

Punishment is frequently and often unwittingly chosen as the first alternative in controlling children's behavior. Often punishment is used in the name of discipline. Punishment involves either the application of an aversive consequence or the removal of a positive reinforcer. In either case the result is a decrease in the frequency of a behavior. Application of aversive events will be discussed first.

Potential Negative Consequences

Before using punishment as a means of behavioral management, it's important to consider the potential negative consequences involved. Five of them will be mentioned here. First, punishment tends to elicit a negative emotional response (Fischer and Gochros, 1975, p. 48). The child may come to dislike the learning situation. He or she may become despondent and uninterested in learning in general. For example, if a child is punished for spelling some words wrong in a composition, the child may no longer want to write at all. The child may also have a negative reaction toward the person administering the punishment.

For example, a young woman in junior high school was walking through the crowded halls from study hall to her next class. The gruff, varsity football coach grabbed her by the shoulder and shouted, "Act like a lady!" She had no idea what he was referring to. However, from that time on, she avoided both crowded hallways and that football coach whenever she could. She had developed an intense dislike for the man.

This example also illustrates the second possible negative side effect of punishment, namely avoidance of either the punishing person or the punitive situation (Kazdin, 1975, p. 161). In homes where physical punishment is used freely and regularly, children may try to stay away from the home as much as possible. Lying may provide another effective means of avoiding punitive situations. (Children sometimes learn to lie because parents set the price for honesty too high.)

The third possible negative effect of punishment is that it can teach children to be agressive (Wagonseller et al., 1977, p. 6). Another way of saying this is that a punishing agent models aggressive behavior (Kazdin, 1975, p. 161). Children can learn that the way to deal with frustration or with not getting their own way is to hit or scream. This can carry over to their interactions with peers, siblings, or adults. An example is a 16-year-old adolescent who was diagnosed as "emotionally disturbed." When he was a small child, physical punishment was used frequently and plentifully in the home. By the time he reached age 16 and grew to be 6'3" tall, a different problem became apparent in the home. The boy began to physically assault his mother whenever they had disagreements. He had learned to be aggressive.

The fourth potential problem with using punishment, specifically physical punishment, is the possibility of physically harming the child. A parent may lose control or not be aware of his or her real strength. Without initial intent, physical damage may result.

Finally, there is a fifth reason for questioning the use of punishment. Punishment teaches people what they should not do, but gives them no indication as to what they should be doing (Thorndike, 1932). Scolding a child for being impolite to her visiting Aunt Edna gives the child no indication about how she could have treated Aunt Edna more appropriately.

In summary, all five of these considerations involve losing control of the consequences of punishment. Punishment is unpredictable and, therefore, should only be used with extreme care.

Effectiveness of Punishment

Despite these considerations, there is some evidence that punishment can be effective. Punishment has been used successfully to treat specific types of problems with specific types of children. For instance, punishment using electric shock has been found to weaken the self-destructive behavior of psychotic, autistic, and developmentally disabled children (Tate and Barroff, 1966; Wolf et al., 1967; Lovaas and Simmons, 1969). When used in conjunction with reinforcement, punishment can also be used to reduce certain inappropriate behaviors in disturbed or developmentally disabled individuals (Wolpe, 1974). Punishment including reprimands and staying after school has also been used effectively in classroom programs (Hall et al., 1971). Only one day of punishment resulted in a decrease in inappropriate behavior on the part of the punished students.

Parke (1977) has concluded that superficial punishment can be an effective means of controlling behavior. However, he cautioned that punishment is a complex process with varied effects. Variables such as timing, intensity, consistency of the punishment, and the relationship between the punishing agent and the child, directly affect the results of punishment. He warns that decreasing behavior is not the only issue involved in view of the possible negative side effects.

The Nature of Punishment

Punishment has several characteristics. First, a decrease in the frequency of a behavior usually occurs immediately after the punishment is presented (Azrin and Holz, 1966; Kushner, 1968). In other words, if the behavior doesn't decrease almost immediately after the supposed punishment starts, there is a good possibility it never will. The implication is not to continue punishment if it doesn't work almost immediately.

For example, one-year-old Tyrone was crawling happily on his mother's kitchen floor when he accidentally discovered the electric socket. His mother, who was watching him out of the corner of her eye, ran over to him, slapped his hand, and raised her voice in a loud, "No!" He looked at her and returned his attention immediately to the socket. This occurred four times after which his mother slapped him even harder. He then started crying and she removed him to another room. In this incident, scolding and hitting was not effective. Tyrone's mother's attention appeared to positively reinforce Tyrone's playing with the electric socket. Scolding and hitting was not effective even after several attempts. It was not likely that it would ever work. Calmly diverting Tyrone's attention might have been a more effective approach to controlling Tyrone's behavior.

Another characteristic of punishment is that its effects, although often immediate, frequently do not last very long (Kazdin, 1975, p. 165). Relatively soon after receiving punishment, a person has the tendency to revert to the old behavior. For example, a driver may receive a speeding ticket for driving 87 m.p.h. on a 55 m.p.h. expressway. He is temporarily disgusted and takes care to drive within the speed limit. However, he soon finds it too restrictive and time consuming to drive so slowly. His speeds gradually creep up to the old levels of 85 to 90 m.p.h.

A third characteristic of punishment is that its effects are frequently limited to the conditions where the punishment occurred (Kazdin, 1975, p. 164). In other words, punishment tends to work only in the specific situation in which it occurred or only with the person who actually administered the punishment. For example, punishment which worked to suppress autistic behavior in a treatment setting was found not to work in the home (Risley, 1968). For example, Trudy, age seven, likes to spit at people as they pass by her on the sidewalk. Her mother spanks her when she sees this behavior. Therefore, Trudy never spits in front of her mother. However, when her mother is in the house or at the grocery store, or when Trudy is at the babysitter's, she continues to spit at passers-by. The babysitter tried spanking her twice, but it didn't work. Spanking functioned as punishment for Trudy, but only when her mother was present and only when her mother administered it.

Selective Use of Punishment

Perhaps the most humane and ethical perspective to assume concerning punishment is to use it sparingly and then only in certain types of severe situations. There are at least two situations when it may be appropriate.

First, it may be used to eliminate self-destructive behavior which, in itself, is dangerous to the child's well-being (Fischer and Gochros, 1975, p. 49). This might include the self-pinching or head-banging behavior of an autistic child. It might also include immediately stopping a child from ingesting a dangerous drug.

Second, punishment might be necessary where there is no other way to make a child stop a particular inappropriate behavior so that another more appropriate behavior can be reinforced (Krumboltz and Krumboltz, 1972, p. 186). For example, three-year-old Mickey's only means of relating to other children is to walk up to them and punch them. In order to reinforce more appropriate means of relating to and playing with others, Mickey's punching behavior must be eliminated or at least suppressed. Punishment might be an effective means of accomplishing this.

Suggestions for Using Punishment

When the decision is made to use punishment, Patterson (1975) makes the following four suggestions for maximizing its effectiveness. First, intervention should occur early. That is, punishment should be administered as soon as possible after the behavior that is to be punished occurs.

For example, 10-year-old Santiago had been stealing records for about six months. One sunny afternoon he decided to shoplift a record from K-Mart. Although he made it out to safety in the parking lot, his friend and colleague, Maynard, was not so lucky. A huge male clerk grabbed Maynard by the wrist as he was hoisting a record under his t-shirt. Santiago, although feeling very bad that his friend got caught, also felt very relieved that he did not.

Two weeks later Santiago's father received a phone call from the police. Apparently under duress and with the promise of a lesser punishment, Maynard had relented and given the police Santiago's name. Santiago's punishment was being grounded for the following month. Being grounded involved reporting in by 8:00 p.m. every night including weekends. Although Santiago was not particularly happy about his situation, he was unhappier about being caught than about stealing a record. He interpreted his punishment to mean, "Don't get caught." The punishment had virtually no effect on his record-stealing behavior. He continued to steal records, but did so with exceptional care. In this situation since the punishment was not administered more closely to when the stealing behavior occurred, it had little effect.

A second suggestion for using punishment is to administer the punishing consequences every time the behavior occurs. In Santiago's situation, he was punished only one time. Many other times his stealing behavior was strongly positively reinforced by getting and enjoying the records he wanted. Receiving a punishment every time a behavior occurs helps to strengthen the idea that the consequence of that particular behavior is unappealing.

The third suggestion for using punishment is to remain calm while administering it. Excessive attention directed at a particular behavior may serve as a positive reinforcer for that behavior rather than a punishment. For example, 18-month-old Petey discovered a book of matches lying on the living room coffee table. He immediately sat down and started to play with them. His mother saw him, ran over to him, and spanked him. She also took away the matches. As both of Petey's parents smoked, it was fairly likely that Petey would find more matchbooks lying around the house. As a matter of fact, he found some the next day. His mother responded in a similar manner. Petey learned that he could get a lot of attention from his mother by playing with matches. As a result, he loved to find matches and play with them. Although his mother's attention was negative, it was forceful enough to serve as positive reinforcement. Petey continued to play with matches every chance he got.

The fourth suggestion concerning the use of punishment is the most important. At the same time that punishment is used, a complimentary program should be used to reinforce other more appropriate behaviors. Punishment has been found to be most effective when an individual is being reinforced for adapting more appropriate behaviors at the same time (Azrin and Holz, 1966; Kircher et al., 1971). For example, a therapeutic goal for a profoundly retarded child was to walk instead of crawl (O'Brien et al., 1972). Punishment for crawling involved restraining him from movement for five seconds. However, this did not really serve as punishment because the child's crawling behavior didn't decrease. Nor did his walking behavior increase. Eventually, a new approach was assumed. At the same time that the child was being restrained from crawling, he was also encouraged or positively reinforced for moving his body. This included being helped to walk. As a result, his walking behavior increased and his crawling behavior decreased. In this case punishment was effective when the child was reinforced for a more appropriate behavior at the same time.

Additional Issues

In addition to the focus on positive reinforcement and punishment, three additional issues merit attention here. They concern common elements encountered in practice. The additional issues include accidental training, the use of behaviorally specific terminology, and the importance of parental attention.

Accidental Training

Thus far the discussion has emphasized planned behavioral change. The focus has been on gaining control of behavior. However, many times reinforcement and punishment affect behavior without conscious planning. Behavior can be increased or decreased without intention. When attempting to understand the dynamics of behavior, it's important to understand that accidental training does occur.

■ Accidental Training

Tommy was an only child. His parents, who were in their late 30s, had tried to have children for years without success. When Tommy came along, they were overjoyed. Both parents thought almost everything Tommy did was "simply darling." One time when Tommy was three years old, he approached some dinner guests and asked for money. He had learned that money bought ice cream, etc. Two things occurred. First, his parents thought it was just so cute so they laughed. Then they appropriately told him that asking for money was not a good thing to do. But they maintained happy, smiling faces all the while. Tommy thus received massive social reinforcement in the form of praise and attention for his begging behavior. Second, Tommy did receive fifty cents, which he later spent for choco-moca-fudge ice cream. The guests were not quite as entertained by Tommy's behavior as his parents were. However, they felt he was a cute kid and gave him money to avoid embarrassment in front of his parents.

The next time Tommy's parents had guests, Tommy did the same thing. He came out for display, said hello, and then asked them if he could have some money. He received a similar reaction. As time went on. Tommy consistently continued his begging behavior in front of guests. His parents became less entertained as the years passed. They discovered that an eight-year-old Tommy coming out and asking guests for money was no longer as cute as a three-year-old doing the same thing. However, by the time Tommy was eight, they were having a terrible time trying to decrease or extinguish his begging behavior. For an extended period of time, Tommy had accidentally been trained to beg. Such extensive accidental training had become very difficult to extinguish.

Negative attention is frequently an effective means of providing accidental training. Attention, even in the form of yelling, can function as positive reinforcement. Even though it is supposed to be negative, the social reinforcement value can be so strong that the behavior will be strengthened instead of weakened. For example, if mother yells at Freddie for picking her favorite peonies, then Freddie may learn that picking those peonies will make his mother yell. If Freddie continues to pick the peonies and his mother continues to yell at him for it, the yelling has served to reinforce his peonie-picking behavior.

Behaviorally Specific Terminology

A major advantage of conceptualizing behavior in terms of learning theory is the emphasis on specificity. A behavior must be clearly and concisely defined. This is important for three major reasons. First, a clear description of behavior allows for all involved in the behavioral management of a child to understand exactly what behavior, including problem behavior, involves.

For example, Bertha, age nine, has been described by her teachers as being too passive. It is very difficult to know what is meant by being too passive. The word "passive" is relatively abstract. The image of a passive Bertha which might be conjured up in one's mind is probably quite vague. However, if Bertha's passivism is defined in terms of her behavior, as it would be with a learning theory conceptualization, the image of Bertha becomes more distinct. Bertha's passivism might be described behaviorally in the following way:

Bertha sits quietly by herself during classes and recesses at school. She avoids social contact with peers during recess by walking to the far side of the playground away from the other children. She does not volunteer information during class. When asked a question, she typically shrugs her shoulders as if she does not know the answer. She then avoids eye contact and looks down toward the ground. She is consistently standing last in lines for lunch, for recess, or for returning to school. When other children push her out of their way, she allows herself to be pushed without comment.

Learning theory mandates clear behavioral descriptions in order to conceptualize any particular behavior. The antecedents, the behavior itself, and the consequences of the behavior must be clearly defined in order to make changes in the behavior. The behavioral description of Bertha provides a much clearer picture than merely labeling Bertha as being too passive.

Measuring Improvement

Because of the high level of specificity necessary in order to conceptualize behavior in terms of learning theory, observation of the behavior becomes much easier. Subsequently, improvements in behavior become more clearly discernable. For example, it might be difficult to establish if Bertha is becoming less passive. However, it is much easier to determine the number of times Bertha assertively raises her hand to answer a question in class.

Behavior must be observable in order to measure if it has improved. In other words, it must be very clear regarding when the behavior occurs and when it does not. In Bertha's situation, the frequency of hand-raising in class has been targeted as a behavior which involves passivism. If Bertha never raises her hand to answer a question in class, she will arbitrarily be considered passive. If she raises her hand frequently, on the other hand, she will not be considered passive.

For the sake of this illustration, hand-raising is used as a means to measure passivism. In an actual situation, Bertha's other behaviors could also be used to measure her degree of passivism. These might include behaviors such as the amount of time she spends talking to peers or the number of times she answers her teacher's questions. Her improvement might be measured by using a summation of a variety of measures.

The first step, then, is targeting a behavior to change. The next step is determining how severe the problem is in the first place. This must be known in order to tell when improvements have been made. In Bertha's case, the hand-raising must be counted and a baseline established. A baseline refers to the frequency with which a behavior occurs before a behavior modification program is started. After a baseline is established, it is easy to determine when a change in the frequency of the behavior has occurred. The change is reflected by the difference between how frequently the behavior occurred while the baseline was being established and how frequently the behavior occurs after the behavior modification program has begun.

For example, during the first month of school, Bertha raises her hand to answer a question zero times per school day. However, by the seventh month of school, she raises her hand to answer a question an average of six times per day. If one of the means of measuring passivism is considered to be the number of times Bertha assertively raises her hand in class, then Bertha can easily be described as less passive during the seventh month of school than during the first.

Clearly stated behaviors can be counted. Therefore, increases or decreases in behavior can be more clearly determined. Improvements in behavior can be established and documented. For example, in Bertha's case, each time she raised her hand above shoulder level after her teacher had asked the class a question could count as one hand-raising behavior.

The final point concerning behavioral specificity involves how the behaviors are counted in the first place. In other words, who keeps track of the frequency of the behavior and how. Behavior checklists and charts can be developed for this purpose.

A behavior checklist simply allows for a place to make note of when a behavior occurs. For example, a two dimensional chart might have each day of the week listed on the horizontal axis. Each day might be broken down into individual hours on the vertical axis on the left-hand side. The *Behavior Chart* illustrates how this might be applied to Bertha's situation.

141

4 / Social Aspects of
Infancy and Childhood

■ **Behavior Chart: Number of Times Bertha Raises Her Hand**

	Mon.	Tues.	Wed.	Thurs.	Fri.
8:00–9:00 A.M.	0	0	0	0	0
10:00–11:00 A.M.	0	0	0	0	0
11:00 A.M.–12:00 P.M.	0	0	0	0	0
12:00–1:00 P.M.	0	0	0	0	1
1:00–2:00 P.M.	0	1	1	0	1
2:00–3:00 P.M.	0	0	1	3	3

Whenever Bertha would raise her hand in class, her teacher would make a note of it on her behavior checklist. The total number of times could be counted. It could thus be clearly established if an improvement occurred.

We have not addressed the specific types of treatment that could be used in Bertha's situation to decrease her passivism. A treatment program could be established in various ways. For example, positive reinforcement could be administered whenever she raises her hand. This could be in the form of a piece of candy, verbal praise, or a token which could be applied to something she really wanted.

The Importance of Parental Attention

One of the criticisms of the application of learning theory might be that it is a rigid and somewhat cold dissection of human behavior. Warmth, caring, and human concern are not readily evident. This certainly does not have to be the case. The importance of parents communicating with their children and genuinely showing spontaneous concern for them should not be overlooked. Learning theory provides a framework for analyzing and gaining control over behavior. Other important aspects of human relationships can occur concurrently.

For example, Gordon (1975) emphasizes the importance of active listening in his suggestions for effective parenting. He describes active listening as a process where parents can become actively receptive to what a child is saying. A parent and a child often have different ways of saying things. They each have a different perspective. Active listening encourages a parent to stop for a moment and consciously examine what the child is saying. The idea is for the parent to try to look at the issue from the child's perspective. This may not be clear from the particular words the child has spoken. The parent then is urged to reflect these feelings back to the child. The end result of a parent taking the time to understand a child should be an enhancement of the warmth and caring between them.

Charlene and her mother provide an example of active listening. Charlene, age seven, comes home after school, crying. She says to her mother, "Betty invited everybody to her birthday party but me." Instead of passing it off as a simple childhood disappointment, Charlene's mother stops for a moment and thinks about what this incident might mean to Charlene. She replies to Charlene, "You really feel left out and bad about this, don't you, honey?" Charlene comes into her mother's arms and replies, "I sure do, Mom." In this instance, her mother simply reflected to Charlene her empathy and concern. As a result, Charlene felt that her mother really understood. Warmth and feeling was apparent in their relationship.

Although this interaction is not structured within learning theory terms, it certainly illustrates the basic components of warmth and empathy necessary in the parent-child relationship. Feelings and communication are ongoing, dynamic parts of that relationship. They occur simultaneously along with the ongoing management of children's behavior.

A Specific Treatment Situation: Time-out from Reinforcement

Extensive volumes have been written concerning the various aspects of learning theory and its applications. Specific concepts have already been discussed. The use of positive reinforcement and punishment have been emphasized. Two specific treatment situations have been selected to illustrate the application of these concepts by using specific techniques. They focus on concepts frequently used by social work practitioners. The treatment situation presented here involves the use of a time-out from reinforcement procedure.

The term *time-out* refers to time-out from reinforcement. In this procedure, previous reinforcement is withdrawn with the intended result being a decrease in the frequency of a particular behavior. It is a form of extinction. Instead of applying some aversive consequences such as a spanking after a behavior occurs, a child is simply removed from the reinforcing circumstances. If a child gets no attention or positive reinforcement for a behavior, that behavior will eventually diminish.

For example, four-year-old Vernite loves to play with her Tinkertoys. However, Vernite has difficulty sharing them with other children. When another child picks up one of the pieces, Vernite will typically run over to that child, pinch him, take the toy, and place it in a pile with the rest of her own Tinkertoys. As a result, other children don't like Vernite very much.

The goal here might be to decrease Vernite's selfish behavior. Selfish behavior is defined as the series of behaviors involved in pinching and taking toys away from other children. A time-out from reinforcement procedure can be used here in order to control Vernite's selfish behavior. Whenever Vernite pinches another child or takes a Tinkertoy away from that child, her mother immediately picks her up and puts her in a corner behind a screen for three minutes. At the end of that time, her mother picks Vernite up again and puts her back in the play situation. What happens is that the positively reinforcing situation filled with fun, Tinkertoys, and other children is removed. In actuality, of course, it is Vernite who is removed. Nevertheless the positively reinforcing conditions are taken away from or made unavailable to Vernite. Without receiving the reinforcement of having the toys for herself, Vernite's selfish behavior should eventually disappear. She should learn that such behavior is inappropriate, and, in effect, not worth its consequences. In other words, Vernite's selfish behavior should eventually be extinguished.

Improving Effectiveness

Several aspects of time-outs tend to improve their effectiveness. The following are suggestions for using time-outs:

1. A time-out should be applied immediately after the targeted behavior occurs in order for it to be effective.

2. Time-outs should be applied consistently. A time-out should occur as a consequence every time the targeted behavior occurs.

3. Time-outs should extend from 10 seconds to 5 minutes. Such short periods of time have been shown to be effective (Bostow and Bailey, 1969). Longer periods of time do not increase the effectiveness of the time-out (White et al., 1972). The relationship between the targeted behavior and the time-out becomes too distant. An extended time-out of an hour, for instance, may also take on some of the potential negative consequences of a more severe form of punishment such as resentment toward the person administering the time-out.

4. The time-out should take place in a very boring place (Patterson, 1975, pp. 75–76). An ideal time-out should provide absolutely no positive reinforcement. This might be a chair facing a corner or another room devoid of stimulating objects and pictures. If the time-out location is exciting or stimulating, it might serve to positively reinforce a negative target behavior rather than to extinguish it.

5. The person, frequently a parent, who is administering the time-out should be careful not to give the child positive reinforcement in the form of attention while the time-out is taking place. A parent might simply state to the child, "Time-out" (Wagonseller et al., 1977, p. 5). The child should then be removed to the time-out location with as little show of emotion as possible. No debate should take place.

6. A child should be told ahead of time exactly which behaviors will result in a time-out. The length of the time-out should also be specified (Wagonseller et al., 1977, p. 5). The intent is to help the child understand exactly what he is doing wrong and what the resulting consequences will be.

7. If the child refuses to go to the time-out location, he may have to be physically taken there. This should be done with as little show of emotion as possible. The child should be gently restrained from all activity until the time-out can begin.

8. The most important thing to remember about using the time-out procedure is that positive reinforcement should be used to reinforce more appropriate replacement behaviors at the same time. Appropriate behavior should be praised as soon as it occurs after the time-out has taken place. For example, when Vernite is returned to the play scene, she should be praised for playing with her own toys and not taking them away from other children. Her mother might simply say, "Look how well you're playing and sharing now, Vernite. Good girl."

A simple anecdote taking place in a local supermarket illustrates the ingenuity and creativity with which a time-out might be used. A mother was shopping with her two-year-old sitting in a shopping cart. Suddenly for no apparent reason the child began to scream. Much to the surprise of onlooking shoppers, the mother calmly removed her raincoat and placed it over the child's head for 20 seconds. People who are unfamiliar with the time-out technique may have thought she was trying to suffocate the child. However, she performed the procedure calmly and gently. When she removed the raincoat, there sat a peaceful and quiet child. The mother had no further problems with screaming behavior in the supermarket that day. What this mother did was to remove the child from all positive reinforcement for a brief period of time. The child learned that screaming led to no positive consequences. Thus the screaming stopped.

Related Research

When these suggestions are followed, the time-out procedure can provide an effective means of behavior change. Research has established its effectiveness in various settings. These include controlling the disruptive behavior of delinquents (Burchard and Tyler, 1965; Tyler and Brown, 1967), controlling loud classroom noise (Schmidt and Ulrich, 1969), reducing stuttering (Adams and Popelka, 1971), and curbing self-stimulating and self-destructive behaviors in developmentally disabled adults (Pendergrass, 1972).

"Grounding"

One other thing should be noted regarding the use of time-outs. Frequently, parents use grounding or sending children to their rooms to curb children's behavior. Although superficially these techniques might resemble time-outs, they don't seem to be very effective (Patterson, 1975, p. 81). Perhaps too many positive reinforcers are available in a child's room. Oftentimes this form of time-out is administered long after the actual behavior occurs. The actual time of restriction is certainly longer than the recommended time period of a maximum of five minutes.

Impacts of Common Life Events on Children

Some basic aspects of family functioning have already been examined. These included a conceptualization of family systems and an examination of learning theory applied to parenting situations. Several other social aspects of childhood merit attention. Common events or situations involving the family which frequently impact the lives of children will be discussed. These include the effects of birth order, single-parent families, families of divorce, and mothers working outside of the home. Issues concerning peers and the school will be addressed later in this chapter. Sex role identification (which is discussed in Chapter 15) is also an important aspect of socialization.

The Effects of Birth Order

Siblings compose a child's most intimate and immediate peer group. It is logical that brothers and sisters will impact the development and behavior of a child. Siblings learn how to play with each other. They act as models for each other. They also learn how to fight with each other.

An interesting body of research points to sibling order as one variable affecting children's development. Apparently, children who are first-born, middle-born, last-born, or only children tend to have certain characteristics. Other factors such as family size and sex of the siblings also have some effects.

First-Born Children

First-born children tend to be more achievement-oriented than other siblings. They are likely to speak at an early age (Koch, 1956). As preschool children, they are likely to be more creative (Lichtenwalner and Maxwell, 1969). They are also more likely to attain higher grade point averages in school in addition to being more likely to attend college (Schacter, 1963, p. 766). Finally, first-born children are more likely to achieve higher recognition in the areas of academia, science, and business (Sutton-Smith and Rosenberg, 1970).

It's interesting to note that five of the U.S. presidents frequently considered among the most notable were first-born children. They include George Washington, Thomas Jefferson, Abraham Lincoln, Franklin D. Roosevelt, and Woodrow Wilson (Schacter, 1963). Another fact is that 21 of the first 23 U.S. astronauts to venture into space were also first-borns.

Possibly this high achievement orientation is partially due to the high anxiety level and the high expectation level which might characterize new, inexperienced parents. Without having had the experience of raising children, new parents might be exceptionally anxious to see that their child is successful. The first child also is able to monopolize parental attention, at least for the first years. There are no siblings to compete with. When first-born Sherrie says the word "hippopotamus" at the age of 18 months, her parents might brim with pride. It must be obvious to the world that Sherrie is a child genius. No mention is probably made of the fact that it took many hours of careful coaching and positive reinforcement to assist Sherrie in her achievement.

The Only Child

Only children have similar characteristics as first-born children. Probably many of the same reasons apply. Only children are also able to monopolize parental attention. Parental pride and expectations tend to be focused on the only child, as they are with the first-born child. Along with first-born children, only children tend to do better in educational settings. For example, along with first-born children, only children are destined to achieve higher reading levels faster than other children (Otto, 1965).

Middle Children

Defining the characteristics of the middle child is more difficult. Middle children are not subject to the intense scrutiny and high expectations which characterize the lives of first-born children. The concept of having a child is no longer a new one for the parents. Additionally, parental attention must be divided between the first and the second child.

Middle children tend to have shorter attention spans, higher levels of distractibility, and poorer achievement levels (Cohen, 1951; Altus, 1959). These children also tend to be more extroverted. They seek the affection of others and are more pleasure oriented. Konig (1963) found middle children to be more relaxed and calm. He corroborated the fact that they have a greater tendency to be pleasure-seekers. However, despite this other-orientation, middle children tend to be perceived as less popular than children placed elsewhere in the birth order (Elkins, 1958).

In summary, it seems to be a common perception that middle children tend to hold a difficult place in the family. They are not given the attention that their older sibling receives. Yet, neither are they given the attention that a younger, even more dependent sibling demands. On the one hand, they have an older sibling to interact with and learn from. On the other hand, a middle child might be put in the hopeless situation of competing with an older and developmentally advanced first-born.

One adult middle-born child, for example, frequently tells the story of how her older sibling made her carry pails full of water to and from the sandbox to enhance their sandbox play. The first-born child was age six and the middle-born, age three. The adult middle-born reflects how she had a serious case of hepatitis at the time. Yet, the older sibling managed heartlessly to put her to work. As the middle-born adult tells the story, one could almost imagine the cruel, sharp-fanged, miniature witch of a six-year-old sister beating the middle-born with a whip in order to force her into abeyance. In reality, it was simply a matter of the older, developmentally advanced first-born using superior size and influence to manipulate the behavior of a younger sibling.

Although in middle adulthood the sisters have a very close relationship, the middle-born still dwells on the story. Perhaps this story illustrates the type of inferior situation that middle-born children frequently find themselves in. One might wonder what effects a series of this type of incident might have on a middle-born child. The fact that this particular story is so frequently repeated to the point where the older sister gets very tired of hearing it may indicate that its effects were meaningful, even if not very positive.

Last-Born Children

Parents of last-born children tend to be more relaxed in their childrearing practices and in their levels of apprehension (Sears, 1950; McArthur, 1956). In other words, parents have already gone through most of the trials, terrors, and joys inherent in raising children. They have more confidence that things will work out satisfactorily in the end.

Last-born children tend to talk at a later age, be less achievement-oriented than first-borns, and be at ease in social situations (Sears, 1950; Bossard and Boll, 1955; McArthur, 1956). They must share parental attention with other siblings. At the same time, they can learn from their siblings by watching their behavior. Perhaps this interaction teaches last-born children to be more outgoing. For example, Tomeh (1970) found that last-born girls tended to visit friends more frequently than children situated in other birth order positions.

The Effects of Family Size

Family size tends to complicate the effects of birth order. For example, children from smaller families tend to have better IQ test scores than children from larger families (Belmont and Marola, 1973; Breland, 1974; Glass et al., 1974). Perhaps this is due to the fact that parental attention can be more intensely focused when divided among fewer children. A child from a family with three children might have a better chance of her mother helping her with her geography assignment than a child from a family with nine children. Children from smaller families might receive more stimulation and individual attention than children from larger families.

Large families may dilute the specific effects of birth order. Parents may be unable to differentiate the amounts of attention given to each child when so many are present. Additionally, the fact that so many personalities are involved may complicate the picture. Relationships between specific pairs of siblings may provide special conditions. For example, in a family of 13, the oldest daughter may take special care of the youngest sibling. The result may be that this youngest sibling acquires characteristics more closely resembling those of a first-born child rather than a last-born.

Sex of Siblings

Not only does family size have an effect on the characteristics eventually acquired by children, but also the sex of siblings has an impact. The sex of the older sibling tends to influence the behavior of the younger sibling. For example, Brim (1958) found that boys who had older sisters tended to display more behaviors which might be perceived as "feminine" than did boys who had older brothers. Boys with older sisters tended to perform below their ability levels in school and to be more generally dependent and withdrawn (Koch, 1960; Hodges and Balow, 1961). Dependency and shyness or withdrawal are typically perceived as being "feminine" characteristics. (Please note that these are perceived, not necessarily actual, characteristics of females.)

On the other hand, girls with older brothers tend to show characteristics which are typically considered "masculine" (Koch, 1955). Such perceived masculine characteristics include aggressiveness, leadership ability, and self-confidence. This concurs with the idea that children learn from their older siblings. Older brothers and sisters tend to serve as models for the younger ones. Whatever types of behavior older siblings display, younger children tend to imitate.

Although birth order tends to have some effects on the characteristics manifested by children, this relationship must be viewed with caution. There is no recipe for making a particular type of personality in a child. Many variables contribute to the development of any particular personal identity. Although there seem to be some tendencies, these must be considered for what they are, that is, simply tendencies. How a child will develop cannot be predicted on the basis of birth order. At best, perhaps some guidelines for childrearing may be deduced from what we know.

For example, middle children tend to receive less attention than either first or last-borns. Parents need to realize this tendency. It might serve as a very positive influence to make special efforts to provide the middle-born child with special attention. The result might be a happier, more confident, more highly achieving adult.

Single-Parent Families

Approximately 20 percent of all children in the United States are being raised in homes with only one parent present. Several reasons account for this. They include divorce, desertion, death of a spouse, and births out of wedlock. Most of these families are headed by females. In 1979, approximately 13 percent of all white families were single-parent families headed by females (U.S. Bureau of the Census, 1980). Additionally, 43 percent of black families were female-headed, single-parent families. Another way of looking at the figures reveals that one out of every six children in the United States resides in a single-parent family (Bronfenbrenner, 1977). Regardless of the reason for the significant number of single-parent families, the fact that so many exist has become a serious issue. The traditional family configuration including two parents, frequently with the mother remaining in the home to provide child care, is becoming less and less common.

Just what effects does being raised in single-parent homes have on children? Obviously, a single parent must fulfill all of the responsibilities of running a home instead of being able to share them with a partner. A single parent must wrestle with responsibilities and tasks which are considered to make up two full-time jobs in the traditional two-parent family. The question concerning the effects on children is a difficult one to answer. Almost no research has been done on the motherless family. Many questions have been raised about the validity and reliability of the available research on fatherless families.

Some of the data has focused on psychological deficits in children produced by lack of an available father figure. When Biller (1970) reviewed the research on the effects of father absence on boys, he discovered numerous negative effects. These included poor impulse control, difficulties in achieving a strong masculine identity, and poor performance on intelligence and academic achievement tests. However, he cautioned that many of these studies failed to control for such variables as length of time a father has been unavailable, the reasons for the father's absence, or the age of the child at the time the father left.

Single-parent families headed by women are also more likely to be poor (U.S. Bureau of the Census, 1984). For example, in 1981 the mean family income for families headed by a woman was $10,078. This compared to an annual mean of $27,947 for families with a father present. This income discrepancy contributed to the fact that in 1981 over half of all U.S. children lived in families with incomes below the poverty level.

On a more positive note, research indicates that children raised in single-parent families are better adjusted than those raised in hostile, strife-ridden, intact families (Nye, 1957). Additional evidence indicates that families with a stepparent present may have more negative effects on children than families with only one parent (Bowerman and Irish, 1962). This is especially apparent with adolescent children. In other words, a stable, supportive family environment with only one parent present seems to be preferable to a family environment where a lot of fighting and strife are occurring.

Families of Divorce

Today any couple's chance of eventually getting a divorce is one out of three (U.S. Department of Commerce, 1979). Despite traditional expectations that true love and marriage will last forever, the facts do not support this idea. When such major expectations are disappointed, trauma and some struggling result. Rutter (1979), for example, found that children who came from homes broken by divorce were more likely to get into trouble than children coming from homes marked by the death of a parent. The implication is that children are affected by the emotional upheaval evident in a marriage.

Goldmeier (1980) reflects that, among other emotions, persons experiencing the divorce feel guilt and a sense of failure. Following this phase, a time of loneliness often follows. Children are bound to be affected by the strong emotions felt by the parent remaining in the home with them. The remaining parent, of course, is most frequently the mother. In nine out of ten divorces, the court still grants children's custody to the mother (Espenshade, 1979).

In effect, children of divorce have been found to suffer various negative consequences (McDermott, 1970; Sugar, 1970). Children's reactions have included depression, guilt over their perceived part in the divorce, difficulties in making friends, anger, and hostility. Physical symptoms such as insomnia, skin rashes, and loss of interest in both school and social activities have also been found.

Although the period during and immediately following the divorce is traumatic for both parents and children, the negative effects appear to lessen after two years (Hetherington et al., 1975). The worst disturbance seems to occur during the first year after the divorce. It seems that the single-parent family is able to regain its homeostasis after making adjustments to the new financial and social situation. Fathers also tend to become less and less available to their children. Perhaps children learn to accept their mother as the primary, single family leader. They have to (and do) adjust to the fact that a father is not always available.

A critical variable affecting children's adjustment to a divorce is the way the parents handle both the divorce and their children's feelings. For example, children react more negatively if the divorce proceedings are drawn out and bitter (Sugar, 1970). Children also suffer when parents use them as a buffer between each other and a means of transmitting hostility as this only fosters children's confusion and resentment. The best thing parents can do is be open with the children about the fact that the marriage has failed. Children should not be made to feel that it was their fault. Parents should clearly take responsibility for their decision to part. Finally, parents should continue to be supportive to their children and understand that the children are suffering pain and loss, too. Children need to be heard; they need to be able to express their anger, unhappiness, and shock. Only then can all family members begin to accept the new situation and start moving forward.

A social worker can be very helpful in the time following a divorce. The remaining relationships and channels of support can be strengthened and nourished. A single-parent family can be helped to define current alternatives for itself and evaluate different courses of action. A social worker can then help to emphasize a family's remaining strengths and encourage family members to maximize their level of functioning.

One other relevant aspect concerning divorce and children should be considered. Divorced women are very likely to remarry (Grady, 1980). About half of all divorced women remarry within three years. After five years, 60 to 70 percent have remarried. The implication is that frequently single parenthood is a transitional period. Family members must first adjust to the divorce and then to a new family configuration. A new parent figure and frequently new stepsiblings are involved. These new, reconstituted or blended families need to make a conscious effort to establish themselves as a new family system (Goldmeier, 1980, p. 280). The relationship between the parents becomes an important focal point (Duberman, 1975). Much of the quality of the stepsiblings' interaction will depend on the quality of the parents' marital relationship. The new parents set the stage for whether there will be strife or cooperation among all reconstituted family members.

A major break with tradition has occurred with the surge of married women entering the workforce over the past several decades. In 1948, only 11 percent of all married women with children under age six were in the labor force. In 1982, almost half of all married women with preschool children worked outside of the home (U.S. Bureau of Labor Statistics, 1982).

Many questions have been raised concerning the effects on the social and emotional development of children. The traditional view stressed the importance of a stable, supportive, caretaker being available consistently to meet the needs of children. In other words, it was important for a mother to remain in the home and coordinate the family's care and activities. However, despite attempts to prove that children of working mothers are somehow deprived, this does not seem to be the case.

Research indicates that there are few if any differences between the children of mothers who work outside of the home and those who don't (Howell, 1973; Lueck et al., 1982). No differences surface in IQ scores, school achievement levels, social relationships with peers, or amounts of independence. Perhaps it is the quality and not the quantity of a mother's attention and care that is valuable.

The Social Environment: Peers and the School

The family does not provide the only means of socialization for children. They are also exposed to other children as they play and to other adults, especially in the school setting. The transactions children have with their peers and with adults in school directly affect both the children's behavior and their social development. Children learn how to relate to others socially. They also learn what types of social behaviors others expect from them. Issues to be addressed here include the social aspects of play and the role of the school. The impact of each will be related to the social development of children.

The Social Aspects of Play with Peers

Luther, who was eight, screamed at the top of his lungs, "Red light, green light, hope to see the ghosts tonight!" He spun around and peered through the darkness. He was playing his favorite game, and he was "it." That meant that he counted to 20 and then had to find the others and tag them. The first one tagged had to be "it" the next time.

"Where were those other kids anyway?" he said silently to himself. Randy usually hides in the garbage can. He thinks that that makes him smell so unappealing that no one will look for him there. Siggy, on the other hand, likes to hide in the bushes by the drainage ditch. However, a lot of mosquitos were likely to consume anybody brave enough to venture over in that direction.

Horace was always an enigma. Luther never knew exactly where he was likely to hide. Once he had managed to squeeze into old Charlie's dog house. Charlie was a miniature mongrel.

On serious consideration of which route to take, Luther decided that the garbage can was his fastest and easiest bet. Just as Luther could've sworn that he heard Randy sneeze inside of the garbage can, he heard his mother's call. "Luther, you get in here this minute. I told you four times that you have to be home by 8:30 on week nights. Come in right now, do you hear!"

"Aw, rats," mumbled Luther. Just when he started to have some fun, he always had to quit and go home. Along came the other guys. See, he was right. Randy was in the garbage can and, sure enough, Siggy popped out from behind the bushes by the drainage ditch. As usual, he was scratching. Randy's mother was really going to give it to him when he got home. He did smell awfully bad. Horace appeared suddenly out of nowhere. He wasn't about to waste a good secret hiding place for nothing.

All four boys dragged themselves home. They walked as slowly as they could and procrastinated appropriately. Another hard summer's day of play was done, but they were already thinking about tomorrow.

Children's play serves several purposes. It encourages children to use their muscles and develop physically. It allows them to fantasize and think creatively. Finally, play enables children to learn how to relate to peers. Play can be seen as a means of socialization. Play provides a format for learning how to communicate, compete, and share. It functions as a major avenue of socialization.

Garvey (1977) defines play as activity that involves the following five qualities. First, play must be something that is done purely for enjoyment and not for a reward or because it is considered appropriate. Second, play has no purpose other than to be an end in itself. Play is done for the sake of playing only. Third, people who play choose to do it. No one can force a person to play. Fourth, play involves active participation in an activity. Either mentally or physically the individual must be involved. Pure observation does not qualify as play. Fifth, play acts to enhance socialization and creativity. Play provides a context in which to learn interaction, physical, and mental skills.

Play and Interaction

Parten (1933) observed children aged two to five during the 1920s. She examined their levels of interaction and divided play into six major levels of interaction. These included the following:

1. Unoccupied behavior. Unoccupied behavior involves little or no activity. A child might be sitting or standing quietly. Frequently, the child's attention is focused on observing something going on around him.

2. Onlooker play. A child involved in onlooker play is simply observing the playing behavior of other children. The child is mentally involved in that attention is focused on what the other children are doing. However, the child is not physically participating in the play. Onlooker play differs from solitary play in that the child's attention is definitely focused on the play of peers, instead of on simply anything that might be happening around him/her.

3. Solitary play. Solitary play involves the child playing independently. No attention is given to other children or what they might be doing.

4. Parallel play. A child involved in parallel play is still playing independently. However, the child is playing in a similar manner or with similar toys as other children in the immediate vicinity. The child is playing essentially the same way as the other children, although no interaction occurs.

5. Associative play. Here children play together in that there is some interaction. However, the interaction is not organized. For example. children may share toys or activities and talk with each other. However, their play is very individualized. Each child plays independently from the others. Attention is focused on each child's individual activities.

6. Cooperative play. Cooperative play involves organized interaction. Children play with each other in order to attain a similar goal, make something together, or dramatize a situation together. Attention is focused on the group activity. Cooperation is necessary. Children clearly feel that they are a part of the group.

Different age levels tend to be characterized by different types of play. Two-year-old children tend to play by themselves. By age three years, parallel play begins to be evident. Associative play is engaged in by more and more children as they reach the age of four years. By age five years, most children participate in cooperative play.

Parents need to be aware of the normal developmental aspects of play at different age levels. Expectations of parents and other caretakers of children need to be realistic. Children should be encouraged to play with other children in ways appropriate to their age level. Yet, children should not be pushed into activities which are beyond them. Children who are isolated in their play activities at an age when they need to be more outgoing may need encouragement in that direction. Parents and other caretakers can help children develop their play and interactional skills.

Social Class and Play

Children from different social classes seem to play differently. When Rubin et al. (1976) observed the play of preschool children, they found that children from lower socioeconomic groups tended to be characterized by parallel play. Middle-class children, on the other hand, were involved in more associative and cooperative play.

Questions may be raised about whether a socioeconomically richer environment provides greater encouragement for children to play together. An implication may be that even in their play activities, preschool children from middle-class families have a social, developmental advantage over children from lower socioeconomic classes. If such a deficit indeed exists, then it may be a future target for social work intervention.

Fantasy and "Pretend" Games

Fantasy is an important means of self-expression for young children. Saltz et al. (1977) did some interesting research on the relationship between fantasy and the development of intelligence. Economically disadvantaged preschoolers were divided into four groups. The first group of children were read fairy tales such as "The Three Little Pigs" and "The Three Billy Goats Gruff." This group was then encouraged to actually pantomime the fairy tales. The second group of preschoolers were asked to act out a series of everyday experiences such as going to the grocery store and visiting the zoo. The third group was simply read various fairy tales. Although the children discussed the stories afterward, they did not actually act out the parts. Finally, the fourth group acted as the control group. They simply participated in supervised play activities such as cutting and pasting.

The first group of children, those who actually acted out the fairy tales, had a marked improvement in intellectual functioning as measured on a variety of tests. The group that acted out everyday experiences also showed improvement, although not as great. Both the group that was read the fairy tales and the control group showed no such increases. The conclusion was that fantasy actually helps children develop their thinking ability.

An implication is that fantasy play should be encouraged in children. It is a normal part of developing their intellectual ability. Thinking things through in fantasy apparently helps them to think in real situations.

One other aspect of fantasy which frequently concerns parents is a child's imaginary friend. Between 15 and 30 percent of all children from the ages of three to ten have an imaginary playmate (Schaefer, 1969). This friend can appear as early as age two-and-one-half. Frequently the friend disappears when the child begins school (Ames and Learned, 1946). This friend usually takes the form of another child or an animal. For example, one four-year-old girl had virtually no peers to play with in her rural environment comprised mostly of farmlands. For two years, she played with "Ahkey," an imaginary friend whom she explained lived out in the forest and frequently came to play with her. Manosevitz et al. (1973) found that first-born and only children were more likely to have imaginary friends. This appears to be a normal way for a child to cope with being lonely. The friend usually disappears when other children take his/her place.

The School Environment

The school provides a major arena for socialization. Children are given information. They are taught social customs, rules, and communication skills. The family and peers help to shape a child's individual personality. The school also impacts a child's development. Schools influence children's dreams and aspirations about future careers (Walberg and Rasher, 1977). Schools help to mold the ways in which children think (Cole et al., 1971). Two specific issues related to the school environment will be discussed here. They are freedom in the classroom and the effects of social class and race.

Freedom in the Classroom

The classroom provides the major unit of structure in the school environment. One of the basic issues concerning the classroom is its atmosphere. That is, the question centers on whether an open atmosphere is more productive and beneficial for learning than a traditional closed, structured setting.

A classic study concerning leadership style in the classroom was that of Lewin et al. (1939). Ten-year-old boys participating in recreational groups were exposed to different leadership styles—authoritarian, democratic, and laissez-faire. The authoritarian leaders made all decisions and plans for the group without allowing any member input. The democratic leaders, on the other hand, structured activities so that group members had input into virtually all group decisions. Finally, the laissez-faire or permissive group leaders allowed the group complete freedom. No direction or leader involvement was apparent.

Results indicated that the boys in the democratic group were more productive, happier, and more congenial toward each other. Boys in the authoritarian groups related poorly to each other. They tended to be either passive or aggressive, and they worked poorly together. Boys in the laissez-faire groups were disorganized and bored. Disgruntlement and disputes were frequent.

Although the Lewin et al. study seemed to indicate that a democratic leadership style is the most effective, more recent evidence does not confirm this. Open classrooms which allow a lot of freedom and individual determination do not appear to enhance productivity (Featherstone, 1971). In other words, children in open classrooms don't seem to do any better academically than children in traditional classrooms. However, they do like both school and their teachers better than students in traditional classrooms. Children in open classrooms also generally are more likely to volunteer the expression of their ideas and feelings (Harvey et al., 1968). Additionally, the overall activity level is higher in open classrooms. In summary, although academic advances are not apparent, more subjective benefits seem to be derived from an open classroom atmosphere. Children appear to learn to think more independently. This may prove valuable in future decision-making situations, although this benefit would be difficult to measure.

The Effects of Social Class and Race

Children from families in lower socioeconomic levels generally do not do as well in school as middle-class children. One source estimates that lower-class children are one whole academic year behind their middle-class peers by the third grade, two years by sixth grade, and two-and-one-half years by ninth grade (Rioux, 1968, p. 92). Lower-class children are also much less likely to go to college than children raised in middle-class homes (DeLury, 1974).

Many reasons can be given for this discrepancy. First, the schools put forth and espouse middle-class values. Texts teach about middle-class parents raising middle-class children in middle-class neighborhoods. For children from other environments, the examples and reference points may be hard to comprehend. Second, the language used is middle-class language. Street terms are most frequently neither understood nor even tolerated by teachers. Street language which is the everyday tongue of many lower-class, urban youth is considered vulgar slang in the middle-class environment. How can children be expected to understand what is said if the language used is literally one that's foreign to them?

A third reason is that the school environments and level of teaching are often poorer for lower-class students. For example, Deutsch (1960) estimates that lower-class students actually receive one third less actual education time than middle-class students. He continues that this is probably due to the fact that teachers in lower-class schools spend up to 80 percent of their time either disciplining or participating in mundane activities like taking attendance.

These differences become even more severe when considering ethnic and racial minority children in schools. Minorities are disproportionately clustered in the lower class. One study showed that teacher perceptions of students were directly related to the individual teacher's race and background (Gottlieb, 1966). Black teachers were both less critical and less pessimistic about their lower-class students. It was hypothesized that perhaps teachers who were raised in similar backgrounds could better identify and empathize with the difficulties that their students faced.

How might these conditions and inequities be corrected? Not only would more financial resources benefit the poorer localities and schools, but also the targeting of teacher attitudes and skills might help. Teachers need to be made aware of other perspectives. Those teaching in lower-class schools need to understand the language of their students. They need to open their minds and be more objective. Teacher training and sensitivity sessions directed toward these ends might be one way to begin.

Child Welfare Programs

Social work addresses itself to enhancing the fit between person and environment. The social environment has tremendous impacts on children. When transactions at the interface of a child's environment are negative or destructive, the child within the family context may need help in coping. The larger social system makes up a major part of the child's environment. Laws, public policies, and government programs can either facilitate children's growth and development or seriously interfere with it. For instance, public programs aimed at redistributing wealth such as public assistance and food stamp programs can provide the extra input needed in poverty-stricken families so that the families and their children can survive. On the other hand, when such programs are cut or discontinued completely, the same families may find they lack both the financial resources and the emotional strength to provide the physically and emotionally nurturant environment their children need. This latter case is true especially when the economy is at its low ebb and employment is scarce.

Depending on the needs of the child and family, social work intervention may be warranted. Children and families may need more energy in the form of input in order to survive and thrive. Our society provides some basic types of programs aimed at enhancing the environment of children and their families. Transactions between the social system providing such services, and the children and families who receive them are often critically important to the family's and children's well-being.

Child welfare refers to one of the basic fields of social work practice. Fields of practice concern the various arenas in which social workers strive to help people achieve better conditions for living. In other words, the various fields of practice address different environmental situations where people have difficulty coping. Child welfare focuses its attention on the "well-being of children and their families" (Costin, 1979, p. 1). As a field of practice, this involves the following five aspects of practice (Maas, 1966, p. 5):

1. The children and families served.
2. The organization of agencies that serves these children and families.
3. The social policies directed toward children and their families.
4. The specific social work methods and techniques used when working with children and their families.
5. The outcomes and results of all these services.

Child welfare, in other words, involves all aspects of social workers working with children and their families. Primary child welfare goals include achieving the well-being of the child and strengthening family life (Costin, 1979, pp. 1–2). This book focuses on the functioning of persons within their environments. Since child welfare practice is aimed at improving this functioning, specifically on the behalf of children and families, child welfare programs will be discussed. Our goals here will be to define the three primary thrusts of child welfare practice, describe select critical services, and highlight major issues.

The Three Thrusts of Child Welfare

Kadushin (1980) classifies child welfare services into three major types. The first category, supportive services, involves those services directed at supporting and strengthening the family's ability to maintain children in their own homes. Examples include casework services such as counseling parents and children, protective services to address child abuse and neglect, and services to unmarried parents.

The second category of child welfare services involves supplementary services. These services are designed to supplement parents' efforts to care for their children or to compensate for the lack of parental care. These services include income supplements for families, homemaker services to help strengthen the child's home environment, and daycare services to provide child care when parents aren't available.

Substitute services make up the third category of child welfare programs. These involve services designed to substitute for parental care. They can substitute either partial or total care. These services are necessary when parents are unavailable or are unable to take adequate care of their children. Types of services include foster family care, group care, and adoption.

Current Child Welfare Programs

Specific child welfare programs fall within one of the three primary categories. These include protective services, daycare services, and foster care services.

Protective Services

Protective services provide an example of a critical type of supportive service in child welfare. The goal of protective services is to protect children from abuse and neglect. Abuse may by physical, emotional, or sexual. Neglect refers to deprivation, either of physical necessities or of emotional nurturance and support.

In practice, protective services workers first must assess the abusive or neglectful situation (Jenkins et al., 1979). They review such aspects as physical and behavioral indicators shown by the child and characteristics of the parents and family situation. Especially important is the assessment of risk to the child. A treatment plan is then established. The thrust of the plan is to enhance the goodness of fit between parents, children, and the environment. In other words, frequently an abusive or neglectful family needs greater input or energy. Their transactions with their environments most likely have been inadequate. Protective service workers would work to improve the family's transactions. Abusive and neglectful families frequently have the following needs (Jenkins et al., 1979):

- Need to develop self-esteem and self-nurturance.
- Need to overcome isolation and fear of relationships.

- Need for support systems.
- Need to deal with marital problems.
- Need for help with life crises.
- Need to learn how to care for and protect the child.
- Need to learn nurturing child-rearing practices.
- Need of the child to have adequate support and nurturing.

Protective service workers first assess the family's and individual child's needs. The next step is to provide direct service and help or to refer the family to agencies and organizations that can help it fulfill its needs. An example is presented in *Protective Services.*

■ Protective Services

Cynthia, age seven, came to school one day with odd-looking bruises on her arm. Her teacher, Mrs. Braskowicz, noticed them immediately and asked her where she got them. Cynthia, an aggressive, boisterous child who loved to get attention from her teachers, answered Mrs. Braskowicz by saying she tripped, fell down the stairs, and hit her arm on some toys at the bottom. Mrs. Braskowicz felt that this seemed a bit peculiar, but accepted Cynthia's answer and forgot the incident.

Three days later Mrs. Braskowicz again noticed some odd bruises on Cynthia's arm. She also noticed that Cynthia was having difficulty writing, as if her fingers were sprained. Again she asked Cynthia what was wrong. The child answered that it was nothing and that she probably just bumped her hand on something. This time Mrs. Braskowicz did not leave the matter at that. That same day she talked to the school social worker, who, in turn, referred the matter to a protective services worker at the local social services agency.

The protective services worker assigned the case, Mr. Bornthumper, began the case assessment almost immediately. He interviewed both Cynthia and her parents. He focused on the elements indicating that abuse was taking place and on the probable risk that Cynthia would come to further harm. He also examined the needs of the family as a whole, and of its individual members.

Mr. Bornthumper assumed as nonthreatening an approach as possible and maintained a focus on the family's and the child's welfare. He discovered that Cynthia's family had moved to the area from another state only a year before. Cynthia's mother was a shy, withdrawn person who found it difficult making new friends. She also missed her own parents and family very much. Additionally, Cynthia's baby sister, Julie, had been born only three months after the move. Julie was a very colicky baby who rarely slept more than two hours at a time and cried almost incessantly. Cynthia's father was a mop salesman who was frequently out of town. As a result, he was rarely home. When he was at home, he was either watching football and other sports on television or sleeping.

Cynthia's mother, as a result, was under severe stress. She felt lonely, isolated, and worthless. Even Julie didn't seem to love her. All the baby did was cry all of the time. Cynthia's father was hardly ever home, and when he was, he just ignored the family anyway. Cynthia's mother felt her marital relationship was deteriorating. As a result of all these stresses, the mother found herself exploding violently at Cynthia. The mother just couldn't help herself. Whenever Cynthia did the least bit wrong, the mother found herself screaming at Cynthia and often physically assaulting her.

Cynthia's family exemplified the types of needs that are common in abusive families. Loneliness, isolation, lack of emotional support, marital problems, life crises, and lack of effective parenting skills were all apparent. Mr. Bornthumper, as a protective services worker, sought to strengthen the family and enhance family members' transactions with their environment. He made various referrals of family members to the appropriate services within the community environment. He also functioned as case coordinator in order to monitor case progress.

First, he referred Cynthia's parents to a local family services agency for marital counseling. The intent was to work on improving communication within the marriage. Another issue was the lack of time the father spent at home and the lack of support he gave his wife. Among the alternatives later pursued during treatment were that he ask his employer to give him more local assignments so that his out-of-town traveling would be limited. Another alternative was that he look into getting another sales job with a different company which would not require excessive traveling.

Mr. Bornthumper also referred both parents to a parent effectiveness training group so that they might better be able to cope with and control their children's behavior. The mother was also referred to a Parents Anonymous group, a self-help group made up of abusive and neglectful parents. The thrust of the group is mutual support. Group members can also provide sugges-tions for better ways of coping with stress and children. Mr. Bornthumper also suggested that mother join a recreational group so that she could develop some friendships and have some time to herself. Mother decided to join a bowling team and to attend an aerobic dance class. Mr. Bornthumper helped her find a daycare center which would care for her children while she participated in these activities.

Finally, Mr. Bornthumper attended to Cynthia's needs. He talked with the school social worker who, in turn, helped Cynthia join a Girl Scout troop. In summary, this case illustrates how a social worker might provide supportive services to enhance an entire family's functioning within their social environment.

Daycare

As stated previously, the numbers of single-parent families are increasing. Even in two-parent families, mothers are more likely to work outside of the home. The result is a desperate need for the daytime care of children when parents aren't available. Daycare provides a good example of a supplementary service within the field of child welfare. Daycare refers to "the wide variety of arrangements which parents choose for the care of their children, of whatever age, during the day" (National Committee for the Day Care of Children, Inc., 1965, p. 2).

The best daycare situations provide much individual attention and a supportive atmosphere full of potential learning opportunities. The worst daycare situations provide no more than custodial care which serves children by providing only the bare necessities of supervision and physical care. Group daycare most frequently involves a daycare center or program which is run by a private sponsor or group. Some daycare centers are run as private businesses. Others are run by specific groups such as churches for their own parishioners or a particular industrial business primarily for its own workers.

Daycare centers are supposed to be licensed. This means that there are specific rules they are supposed to follow in order to continue operating. These rules concern many aspects of running the daycare center such as how food should be prepared, the ratio of adult supervisors to the number of children, and the amount of floor space necessary proportionately per child. These rules vary greatly from state to state, and even among communities in a particular state (Costin, 1979, p. 424). Typically, a public state licensing or regulatory agency is responsible for licensing a daycare center and for monitoring its adherence to state regulations. The intent is to ensure a satisfactory level of safety and quality for child care.

Private family daycare is another common type of daycare. This situation usually involves a mother or other family member caring for a small number of other people's children in her own home. Actually, more children are placed in private family daycare than in any other type (U.S. Department of Health, Education and Welfare, 1978, pp. II–7). It involves approximately 18 million children. A problem with this type of daycare is that very few of these settings are licensed. The potential result is a lack of quality and safety control. Another view, however, is that this type of care provides a viable, sometimes more accessible alternative to group daycare settings. Emlen (1973) concludes that private family daycare more closely resembles the quality of American family life. He reflects that the quality of such care is frequently high and that many parents prefer this to group daycare.

In actuality, most families are limited to the actual facilities or types of daycare settings available to them. Larger communities may be more likely to have group care centers available than small, rural communities. Sometimes private family daycare might be all that is available.

Regardless of the type of setting, the quality of a particular daycare setting must be evaluated. Quality varies considerably. Other factors parents must consider before selecting a daycare setting include cost and individual constraints. Such constraints might include being open only a limited number of hours, or hours which don't correspond to the family's needs. Other constraints might include placing restrictions on the age of children who are eligible for acceptance into the daycare center. For example, some daycare centers or individuals providing daycare will not accept infants because they demand excessive individual attention and care.

Foster Family Care

Foster family care is defined as "a child welfare service which provides substitute family care for a planned period for a child when his own family cannot care for him for a temporary or extended period and when adoption is neither desirable nor possible" (Child Welfare League of America, 1959, p. 5). As clearly indicated in the definition, it is a good example of a substitute service in child welfare practice. Several key terms are apparent in the definition. One of them is the fact that the care is temporary. The intent of such care is not to be permanent, but rather to provide a temporary home for a child who needs to be away from the family for any of a variety of reasons.

A second important aspect of the definition involves the reference to care being provided within a family setting. Although temporary placement for children can also be provided within institutions and group homes, our focus here is on the principle of foster family placement. The intent of such placements are to provide a family environment for a child. A family environment best provides the intimacy, support, and individual attention which children need.

A third important aspect is the idea that the placement in foster care be planned. The decision to remove a child from the original family setting should only be done for a specific and serious reason. Removing a child is a very traumatic experience for the child and for his parents.

On this note, it's logical to ask the question, "What then are the reasons for placing a child in foster care?" In fact several reasons can be stated for taking this relatively drastic step. Kadushin (1980, pp. 322–23) cites three major reasons for removing a child from the home. They include parent-related problems, child-related problems, and environmental circumstances. Seventy-five to 80 percent of children placed in foster family care are due to parent-related problems. Such problems include emotional problems, alcohol or drug abuse, child abuse or neglect, physical disabilities and basic unwillingness to care for the child. An additional 15 to 20 percent of children are placed in foster family care due to factors directly related to the children themselves. Some children are emotionally disturbed, delinquent, or participate in such aggressive behaviors that parents are unable to tolerate them. Other children are placed because of mental retardation or physical disabilities. The remaining 3 to 5 percent of children are placed because of a crisis in the family environment. These crises most frequently involve some type of serious stress such as long-term unemployment, poverty, or distressingly inadequate housing situations.

In summary, foster family care provides a means for temporarily substituting one family environment for the original. The implication is that such placement allows for a breathing space. A child can be removed temporarily from a stressful family environment. Meanwhile, the remaining family members are relieved of whatever stress the child might cause. While the child resides in a foster family placement, the family can be helped to divert its energy into more productive channels of action. Parents might need counseling or educational help. Additional financial input might also help to ease family stress and strengthen the family unit. The family might then be better able to interact in more positive ways with its environment. When the family is once again functioning satisfactorily, the child can be returned and hopefully be able to thrive.

Major Child Welfare Issues and Gaps in Service

The field of child welfare is broad. Each specific area such as family foster care or daycare has its own specific issues and gaps in service.

Costin (1979) calls for the need to emphasize child advocacy. Advocacy involves taking an active, directive role on the behalf of a client or a client group in need of help. One important aspect of child advocacy is the acknowledgement and support of the basic rights of children. The concern for children's rights can be considered on a universal level, that is, that every child should have certain specific rights such as the right to adequate food, shelter, and a home environment.

Children's rights can also be addressed concerning specific issues. For example, Goldstein et al. (1973) urge that the rights of children and their overall well-being be considered over the rights and desires of their parents concerning custody. They posit that decisions about where a child should live after a divorce or other family break-up should be based on the child's best interests, not on the parents'. Gil (1973), an advocate on the behalf of physically abused children, suggests changing the basic philosophy which supports violence as part of childrearing. He suggests establishing stronger legal sanctions against the use of physical force. He also calls for the elimination of poverty as a means of stopping child abuse, as poverty conditions seem to be related to child abuse in various ways. Wooden (1976) advocates on the behalf of incarcerated children. He calls for the abolition of jails and training schools where delinquents and status offenders are too frequently housed. Instead he calls for advocacy assuming the forms of increased monitoring of facilities which are used to house children and increased legal safeguards. Billingsley and Giovannoni (1972) point out that racial discrimination is evident in the child welfare system as it now stands. Among other things, they advocate for a system which is more sensitive to the plight of black children, for a guaranteed minimal income for every family, and for a national comprehensive program committed to child development.

In summary, children have numerous needs, many of them unmet. Two basic perspectives concerning advocacy for children can be assumed. One perspective can focus on the rights and needs of children in certain specified situations, such as those who are abused or those who are minorities. The other perspective addresses the need to advocate for the welfare of all children, regardless of their individual situations and needs. Kenniston (1977) summarizes this perspective succinctly by calling for the public support of a decent living standard for all families and for an integrated network of family services to address their needs.

Summary

Socialization refers to the process through which individuals learn proper ways of acting in a culture. Children are socialized by their families, peers, and schools. The family can be viewed as a system. A healthy family system strives to maintain homeostasis or equilibrium. Just as individuals go through developmental phases, so do families progress through life cycles.

Learning theory provides an exceptionally useful means of conceptualizing and understanding human behavior. The three basic types of learning are respondent conditioning, modeling, and operant conditioning. Learning theory concepts, such as positive reinforcement and punishment, can easily be applied to effective parenting. Although punishment is frequently used to attempt to control children's behavior, it should be used cautiously as it has several potential negative effects. Important issues in applying learning theory concepts include accidental training, the importance of behaviorally specific terminology for stating goals and measuring improvement, and the importance of parental attention. An effective behavioral technique is time-out from reinforcement.

Some life events and situations that influence the social development of children are birth order, single-parent families, divorce, working mothers, peers, and the social environment. Children raised in single-parent families tend to be better adjusted than children raised in two-parent families riddled with conflict. Children's feelings about divorce should be dealt with. Children raised in families where the mother works appear to be no worse off than children in homes where the mother does not work outside the home. The three basic types of child welfare programs are supportive, supplementary, and substitute services.

Adolescence and Young Adulthood

ADOLESCENCE
AND YOUTH

Biological Aspects of Adolescence and Young Adulthood

Roger sat in study hall gazing out of the window. He had an intense, pained expression on his face. Roger was 15 years old, and not one thing was going right for him. His arms were too long for the rest of his body. He felt like he couldn't walk from the desk to the door without tripping at least once. Homecoming was coming up soon, and his face had suddenly managed to look like a pepperoni pizza. Shirley, the light of his life, wouldn't even acknowledge his existence. To top it all off, even if he managed to get Shirley to go to homecoming with him, he'd still either have to scrounge up another older couple to drive or else have his father drive them to the dance. How humiliating. Roger continued to gaze out of the study hall window. The primary theme in his thoughts was, "Life is hard."

Change and adjustment characterize adolescence and young adulthood. Roger is not unique. Like other people his age, he is trying to cope with drastic physical changes, increasing sexual awareness, desires to fit in with the peer group, and the desperate need to establish a personal identity. As the Behavior Dynamics Assessment Model indicates, the attainment of normal developmental milestones is directly related to human behavior. Biological development and maturation affects how adolescents perceive of themselves and ultimately how they behave. Rapid and uneven physical growth may cause awkwardness. Awkwardness may result in feeling self-conscious and consequently uncomfortable in social interactions. As we will point out, for example, some psychological and behavioral differences exist between males who develop earlier and later than most others their age.

Biological development often affects the transactions between individuals and their immediate social environments. For instance, when adolescents begin to attain physical and sexual maturity, sexual relationships may begin to develop. Likewise, new and different alternatives become available to adolescents and young adults as they mature. For example, alternatives concerning sexuality may range from no sexual activity to avid and frequent sexual relations. These new alternatives merit evaluation in terms of their positive and negative consequences. Decisions need to be made about such critical issues as whether to have sexual relations or not, which if any methods of birth control to use, and whether or not to enter into marriage.

GUSTAVSON

■ A Perspective

Chapters 5, 6, and 7 will address respectively the biological, psychological, and social aspects of adolescence and young adulthood. The goal is to provide a framework for better understanding this difficult, yet exciting, time of life.

This chapter will:

- Explore some of the major physical changes that occur during adolescence and puberty.
- Describe the adolescent growth spurt, the secular trend, and both primary and secondary sex characteristics.
- Appraise some of the psychological reactions related directly to physical changes.
- Recognize the contributions of physical development, health status, and other factors to health during young adulthood.
- Explore some of the issues and life crises including sexual activity, unplanned pregnancy, teenage fatherhood, motivation for pregnancy, sex education, and methods of birth control, which tend to affect adolescents.

Adolescence

Adolescence refers to the time of life between childhood and adulthood. It's derived from the Latin verb, "adolescere," which means "to grow into maturity." It is not a very specific term. There is no precise point in time when adolescence begins or when it ends. Adolescence should be differentiated from puberty which is more specific. *Adolescence* might be considered a cultural concept which refers to a general time during life. *Puberty*, on the other hand, is a physical concept which refers to the specific time during which people mature sexually and become capable of reproduction.

Some societies have specific rites of passage or events to mark the transition from childhood into adulthood. For example, among the Mangaia of the South Pacific (Marshall, 1980), when a boy reaches the age of 12 or 13 years, he participates in a ceremony where a superincision is made on his penis. This cut is made along the entire length of the top of the penis. After the extremely painful ceremony is completed, the boy runs out into the ocean or a stream to ease the pain, and typically exclaims, "Now I am really a man."

Our society has no such distinct entry point into adulthood. Although we might breathe a sigh of relief at not having such a painful custom, we're still left with the problem of the vague transitional period we call adolescence. There are no clear-cut guidelines for how adolescents are supposed to behave. On one hand, they are children, but on the other hand, they are adults.

Some occurrences tend to contribute to becoming an adult. These include graduating from high school, getting a driver's license, graduating from college, and perhaps getting married. However, not all individuals do these things. Some young people drop out of high school, and many high school graduates don't go on to college. A substantial number of young people choose not to marry or to marry much later in life. Even people who do go through these rites do so with varying levels of maturity and ability to handle responsibility. At any rate, becoming an adult still remains a confusing concept.

Nor do the gradual, but major, physical changes help to clarify the issue. Adolescents must strive to cope with drastic changes in size and form, in addition to waves of new hormones sweeping through their bodies. Resulting emotions are often unexpected and difficult to control. Within this perspective of change and adjustment, we will look more closely at specific physical changes and at the effects of these changes on the developing personality.

Puberty

Puberty refers to the period where a person becomes physically mature and able to reproduce. It is marked by the sudden enlargement of the reproductive organs and sexual genitalia and the development of secondary sex characteristics (Tanner, 1967).

Girls begin the changes of puberty somewhere between 8 and 13 years of age. Boys generally start about two years later than girls. Girls reach their full adult height by about 17 years of age, and boys by about 21 years of age (Roche and Davila, 1970).

The two year age difference in beginning puberty causes more than its share of problems for adolescents. Girls tend to become interested in boys before boys begin noticing that girls are alive. One dating option for girls involves older men of the middle or late teens. This can serve to substantially raise parental anxiety. An option for boys is to date girls who tower over them.

There is a wide age span for both boys and girls when puberty begins. Although in general there is a two-year difference between the sexes, there are also substantial individual differences which must be taken into account. In other words, one boy may begin puberty four years earlier than another.

Acting as a catalyst for all of these changes is a marked increase in the production of hormones. Hormones are chemical substances secreted by the endocrine glands. Among other things, they stimulate growth of sexual organs and characteristics. Each hormone targets a specific area or areas and stimulates growth. For example, testosterone directly affects growth of the penis, facial skin, areas in the brain, and even cartilage in the shoulder joints (Tanner, 1971). In women the uterus and vagina respond to the female hormones of estrogen and progesterone (Garrison, 1973).

The endocrine glands which produce the hormones involved in initiating puberty form a complicated, interacting system. These hormones are either produced for the first time during puberty or are suddenly secreted in much greater amounts than before. An extensive feedback loop is created in order to both stimulate and control the growth process.

The pituitary gland, or master gland, is located directly next to a part of the brain called the hypothalamus. It is intimately connected with tiny blood vessels which carry chemical messages from the brain to the pituitary. Under the direction of the hypothalamus at the beginning of puberty, the pituitary releases hormones which have a stimulating effect on other endocrine glands in the human system. These glands then produce their own hormones which affect the growth of body parts and the hormonal production of other glands. This second set of glands in turn produce hormones which send messages back to the hypothalamus. Once again the pituitary responds to the instructions of the hypothalamus. The hormones or chemical messages sent by the pituitary to other glands in the body are monitored and regulated.

Although this is a very simplistic way of explaining the endocrine system, the basic idea is that it resembles a thermostat system. Each part of the feedback system sends information to another part of the system. The goal is to maintain a relatively stable system of hormonal production and control. A thermostat controls the temperature in, for instance, a home. The idea is to maintain a temperature that's relatively constant. When it gets too hot, the thermostat sends information to the furnace to slow down. Then when the temperature drops too low, the thermostat sends information to the furnace to speed up its heat output. In a similar fashion, the human body maintains or regulates its hormonal system. The result is an increased yet controlled production of hormones during puberty.

The Growth Spurt

The initial entrance into puberty is typically characterized by a sharp increase in height. During this spurt, boys and girls typically grow between two and five inches (Tanner, 1970). Prior to the growth spurt, boys tend to be 2 percent taller than girls. However, since girls start the spurt earlier, they tend to be taller, to weigh more, and to be stronger than boys during ages 11 to 13 years. By the time both sexes have completed the spurt, boys once again are larger than girls by about 8 percent (Papalia and Olds, 1981).

The adolescent growth spurt affects virtually the entire body including most aspects of the skeletal and muscular structure. However, boys and girls grow differently during this period. Boys' shoulders get relatively wider, and their legs and forearms relatively longer than those of girls (Tanner, 1964). Girls, on the other hand, grow wider in the pelvic area and hips. This is to enhance childbearing capability. Girls also tend to develop a layer of fat over the abdomen, hips, and buttocks during puberty. This eventually will give a young woman a more shapely, rounded physique. However, the initial chubby appearance can cause the adolescent a substantial amount of emotional stress. Crash and starvation diets can create a physical health hazard during this period.

There is the tendency toward unequal and disproportionate growth. Most adolescents have some features which look obviously uneven or disproportionate. The head, hands, and feet reach adult size and form first, followed by the legs and arms. Finally, the body's trunk reaches its full size. A typical result of this unequal growth is motor awkwardness and clumsiness. Until the growth of bones and muscles stabilizes, and the brain adjusts to an essentially new body, awkward bursts of motion and misjudgments of muscular control will result.

The Secular Trend

People now grow taller and bigger than they used to. They also reach sexual maturity and their adult height faster than in the past. This tendency toward increasing size and earlier achievement of sexual maturity is referred to as the *secular trend.* In the United States, a son is likely to be as much as an inch taller and ten pounds heavier than his father. Likewise, a daughter is likely to be one-half to one inch taller than her mother and two pounds heavier. Finally, a daughter is also likely to start menstruating ten months earlier than her mother did (Muuss, 1970).

This appears to be a worldwide trend. Muuss (1970) examined studies of children from Italy, Poland, China, New Zealand, and Japan. Increases in size and maturity were found among these various populations. Numerous causes can be given for this trend. Part of the reason might logically be due to an increase in nutrition and the general standard of living. Tanner (1968) found that during times of malnutrition and economic deprivation, this trend toward increased growth is often reversed. The lessening of disease might also contribute to the trend. One other explanation is the increase of outbreeding and the increasing evidence that genes dictating tallness are dominant over those dictating shortness (Tanner, 1978). Outbreeding involves more and more people from diverse and heterogeneous groups marrying each other instead of intermarrying people within their own extended families or smaller, isolated communities. The gene pool is increased. There might, therefore, be a greater chance for potentially dominant genes making for tallness to have a greater impact on larger populations.

This secular trend which has been going on for the past 100 years seems to have reached its peak and stopped. A 14-year-old boy of today is approximately five inches taller than a boy of the same age in 1880. However, growth has seemed to stabilize for most of the American population (Schmeck, 1976).

Primary and Secondary Sex Characteristics

As we've already indicated, a major manifestation of puberty is the development of both primary and secondary sex characteristics. Primary sex characteristics are those directly related to the sex organs and reproduction. The key is that they have a direct role in reproduction. For females these include development of the uterus, vagina, and ovaries. The uterus is an organ about the size of a fist and is shaped like an upside-down pear. It provides the environment where the fetus can develop. The vagina is the barrel-shaped organ into which a penis is inserted during intercourse and through which a baby passes when it is born. The ovaries are the major sex glands in a female which both manufacture sex hormones and produce eggs which are ready for fertilization.

For males primary sex characteristics include growth of the penis and development of the prostate gland and the testes. The penis is the male sexual organ through which urine passes out of the body as waste and through which semen passes during orgasm. The prostate gland, which is located below the bladder, is responsible for most of the ejaculate or whitish alkaline substance that makes up semen, which carries the sperm. The testes are the male sex glands which both manufacture sex hormones and produce sperm.

Secondary sex characteristics include those traits which distinguish the sexes from each other, but play no direct role in reproduction. These include menstruation, hair growth, development of breasts, voice changes, skin changes, and nocturnal emissions.

Proof of Puberty

The most notable indication that a female has achieved the climax of puberty is her first menstruation, otherwise called *menarche*. Menstruation is the monthly discharge of blood and tissue debris from the uterus when fertilization has not taken place. This initially occurs when a girl's height spurt has slowed down. The average age is 12.8 to 13.2 years. Usually, the first periods do not include ovulation, or release of a ripened egg by the ovaries. Therefore, a young girl is usually unable to conceive until 12 to 18 months after her first period (Tanner, 1978).

A wide variation in the age of occurrence for first menstruation is found from one female to another. A Peruvian girl of age five is the youngest mother ever recorded to have a healthy baby. This occurred in 1939. The baby was born by Caesarean section. At the time, physicians found that she was mature sexually, and that she apparently had begun menstruation at the age of one month. The youngest parents known are an eight-year-old mother and nine-year-old father. This Chinese couple had a son in 1910 (Hyde, 1982).

It is somewhat more difficult to establish that a boy has entered the full throes of puberty. One of the more reliable signs is the presence of live sperm in the urine. Both semen which contains sperm and urine travel through the penis via a tube called the *urethra*. Sometimes sperm remain in the urethra after ejaculating and are later transported out of the penis by urine.

Hair Growth

Hair begins to grow in the pubic area during puberty. After a period of months and sometimes years, this hair changes in texture. It becomes curlier, coarser and darker. About two years after the appearance of pubic hair, axillary hair begins to grow on the armpits. However, the growth of axillary hair varies so much from one person to another that in some people axillary hair growth appears before the appearance of pubic hair (Tanner, 1970). Facial hair also begins to grow on boys beginning on the upper lip and gradually spreading to the chin and cheeks. Chest hair appears relatively late in adolescence.

Development of Breasts

Breast development is usually one of the first signs of sexual maturity in girls. The nipples and areola, the darkened areas surrounding the nipples, enlarge. Breasts initially tend to be coneshaped and eventually assume a more rounded appearance. Breasts usually grow to their full adult size before menarche.

Some women in our culture tend to be preoccupied with breast size and feel that breasts come in one of two sizes—too large or too small. However, all breasts are functionally equipped with 15 to 20 clusters of mammary or milk-producing glands. Each gland has an individual opening to the nipple or tip of the breast into which the milk ducts open. The glands themselves are surrounded by various amounts of fatty and fibrous tissue. The nipples are also richly supplied with sensitive nerve endings which are important in erotic stimulation. There is some indication that smaller breasts are actually more erotically sensitive per square inch than larger ones (McCary, 1973).

Some adolescent boys also undergo temporary breast development. Although this may cause some anxiety concerning their masculinity, this enlargement is not abnormal. Hyde (1982) indicates this occurs in as many as 80 percent of all boys in puberty. The probable cause is small amounts of female sex hormones produced by the testes. The condition usually disappears within about a year.

Voice Changes

Boys undergo a noticeable lowering in the tone of their voices which usually occurs fairly late in puberty (Tanner, 1970). The process involves a significant enlargement of the larynx or Adam's apple and a doubling in the length of the vocal cords. Many times it takes two years or more for boys to gain control over their new voices (Garrison, 1968).

Girls also experience a slight voice change during adolescence, although it's not nearly as extreme as the change undergone in boys. Girls' voices achieve a less high-pitched, more mature tone due to a slight growth of the larynx.

Skin Changes

Adolescence brings about increased activity of the sebaceous glands which manufacture oils for the skin. Skin pores also become coarser and increase in size during adolescence. The result is frequently a rapid production of blackheads and pimples on the face and sometimes on the back, commonly referred to as acne. Unfortunately, a poor complexion is considered unappealing not only in our society, but in most cultures (Hyde, 1982). Acne adds to the stress of adolescence. It tends to make young people feel even more self-conscious about their bodies and physical appearance.

Nocturnal Emissions

Kinsey (1948) found that 83 percent of all males have nocturnal emissions at one time or another. A nocturnal emission is the ejaculation or emission of semen while a person is asleep. The highest frequency of approximately once a month tends to occur during the late teens. The number then tapers off during the twenties, and finally stops after age 30. However, occasionally a man up to age 80 will have a nocturnal emission.

Nocturnal emissions are simply a natural means of relieving sexual tension. Often, but not always, they are accompanied by sexual dreams. It's important that adolescents understand that this is a normal occurrence and that there's nothing physically or mentally wrong with them.

Some evidence indicates that females also have orgasms during sleep. However, these apparently don't occur as frequently or as early as men have nocturnal emissions. Kinsey (1953) found that 37 percent of his female sample experienced a nocturnal orgasm by the age of 45. Only 8 percent reported having orgasms during sleep more frequently than five times per year. Almost all of the women who had experienced orgasms during sleep also had experienced them knowingly while awake. In other words, it seems that females must know what an orgasm is in order to identify that it has occurred during sleep.

■ Masturbation

Masturbation refers to self-stimulation of the genitals which causes sexual arousal. Research indicates that most adolescents masturbate. Kinsey et al (1948) discovered a striking increase in the incidence of masturbation among boys aged 13 through 15 years. Twenty-one percent of all males studied had masturbated by age 12. However, this percentage drastically increased to 82 percent by 15 years of age. A substantial number of girls were also found to begin masturbating by age 15 (Kinsey, 1953). However, girls generally tended to start masturbating later than boys. A higher proportion of girls when compared to boys never masturbate at all.

More recent studies support the findings that most adolescents masturbate. Sorenson (1973) surveyed the sexual attitudes of 393 adolescents. He found that 58 percent of adolescent boys and 39 percent of adolescent girls masturbated by age 15. By age 19, virtually all boys and most girls masturbate. Boys tend to masturbate to orgasm an average of two to three times per week. Girls tend to do so approximately once a month (Hass, 1979).

One interesting difference between young men and women in the incidence of masturbation is the relationship between masturbation and sexual activity with other people. Sexually active male adolescents tend to masturbate less than those who aren't having sexual intercourse. Sexually active female adolescents, on the other hand, tend to masturbate more than their virgin counterparts (Sorenson, 1973). This may have to do with differences in sex roles and sexual expectations between males and females. It may also have to do with the fact that the sex drive of women tends to develop relatively later than men's. This sex drive continues to develop well into the adult years.

It's important to address the issue of masturbation. As we've already established, it is very common among adolescents. However, it is also looked down on. The numerous slang terms used to describe it are very uncomplimentary. These include, "beat the meat," "shoot the wad," "choke the chicken," "pound pud," and "carrot cuffing." Perhaps the negative attitude traditionally conveyed about masturbation can best be expressed by the statements of H. R. Stout in the 1885 edition of "Our Family Physician":

When the evil has been pursued for several years, there will be an irritable condition of the system; sudden flushes of heat over the face; the countenance becomes pale and clammy; the eyes have a dull, sheepish look; the hair becomes dry and split at the ends; sometimes there is pain over the region of the heart; shortness of breath; palpitation of the heart (symptoms of dyspepsia show themselves); the sleep is disturbed; there is constipation; cough; irritation of the throat; finally the whole man becomes a wreck, physically, morally, and mentally.

After such a tirade it would be a wonder if a person would dare to masturbate. This presents quite a contradiction and source of confusion for adolescents. They are actually participating in the activity of masturbation. Yet, there is some tendency for it to be considered an unappealing and even disgusting behavior. Sorenson (1973) found that many adolescents felt anxiety, defensiveness, or embarrassment over their behavior. A few felt guilty about it. Hass (1979) found that most adolescents have negative feelings about masturbation.

Adolescents need to understand that masturbation is not abnormal or harmful. In a period of their lives when they are coping with many physical changes and new life situations, they do not need to be burdened with unnecessary confusion and even guilt. Masturbation is a normal means of relieving sexual tension and other stress, allowing a means of self-discovery, developing confidence in oneself, learning to control sexual needs and impulses, and fighting isolation and loneliness (Barbach, 1980; Clifford, 1978; Sorenson, 1973). Masturbation is even a prescribed means of treatment for sexual dysfunction. Women with orgasmic dysfunctions, i.e., the inability to experience orgasms, are counseled to use masturbation (Kaplan, 1981). This provides a means for them to overcome anxiety and better understand their own sexual responses. This information can later be transferred to a partner.

Psychological Reactions to Physical Changes

One thing which marks adolescence is self-criticism. Physical imperfections are sought out, emphasized, and dwelled on. It may be a large lump on a nose. Or it may be an awesome derriere. Or it may even be a dreadful terror of braces locking unromantically during a good night kiss. Adolescents seek to conform to their peers. Any aspect that remains imperfect or too noticeable becomes the object of criticism. Perhaps it's partly because the age is filled with change and the mandatory adjustment to that change that adolescents strive to conform. Perhaps before an individual personality can develop and grow, a person needs some predictability and security.

A substantial amount of research focuses on the adolescent's perception of him/herself. Special areas of intent interest include body image, self-concept, weight level, and the condition of maturing earlier or later than what is typical.

Body Image and Self-Concept

Physical appearance is very important to an adolescent. Both males and females tend to express dissatisfaction and unhappiness about their physical attributes (Clifford, 1971). When adolescents are asked about what they like and what they dislike about themselves, physical characteristics are mentioned as dislikes more frequently than anything else (Jersild, 1952). Stoltz and Stoltz (1944) did a longitudinal study where they found that about one half of all girls and one third of all boys expressed concern about at least one of their own physical characteristics.

Perception of one's own body image and attractiveness is related to that person's level of self-esteem (Berscheid, Walster, and Bohrnstedt 1971). People who consider themselves more attractive tend to be more self-confident and satisfied with themselves. Furthermore, a person's level of physical attractiveness in adolescence seems to have some carry-over effects in adulthood. Berscheid, Walster, and Bohrnstedt (1971) did a survey of approximately 62,000 people. Although the respondents in no way could be said to represent all segments of the total population, some interesting results were obtained. People who felt they were unattractive as adolescents were the least happy group of all the people participating in the survey. On the other hand, until they reached the age of 44, people who were the most attractive adolescents made up the happiest group of people in the survey. After this age, happiness levels seemed to level out among both groups, both the more and the less beautiful.

Although both males and females feel that their physical appearance is important, there are some differences between them (Frazier and Lisonbee, 1950). For one thing, girls are more specific and detailed regarding what particular aspects they'd like to have changed. Boys, on the other hand, are more general. For example, a girl might say, "I would take away my pimples and make my complexion clear and soft," or "I'd have blue eyes and blonde hair fixed in a page-boy." Boys, on the other hand, would be more likely to say, "I'd like to be bigger and have more muscular development," or "I would change my whole physical appearance so that I would be handsome, with a good build." Some other differences also are evident. While girls are very concerned about being too fat, boys are much more worried that their upper arms or chests are too thin. Boys wonder if they're too short, and girls, that they're too tall. These differences in concerns between girls and boys are probably due to societal values as to what is a physically attractive female and what is a physically attractive male.

Weight Worries

Weight is a primary concern of adolescents, especially for females. Hendry and Gillies (1978) studied almost one thousand 15 and 16-year-old male and female adolescents. After placing them in underweight, average, or overweight categories, they compared the groups using several variables, including physical fitness, self-esteem, personality, body esteem, social class, academic attainment, extracurricular activities, and leisure companions.

Surprisingly, no major differences were found among any of the groups regarding how popular or outgoing the young people were. However, overweight adolescents were the least happy with their own bodies. They were also the least physically fit.

Teachers tended to perceive the overweight girls less positively on several dimensions. They were seen as having a less attractive appearance and as being less enthusiastic than other groups. Teachers perceived underweight males and females as being more socially nervous. Additionally, underweight girls were seen as being less competitive.

Male and female adolescents who were either overweight or underweight were less likely to be dating someone steadily than adolescents of average proportions.

Early and Late Maturation in Boys

Some adolescents mature earlier than others; others, much later. Some are lucky enough to fall within the average range of maturation. That is, these average maturers experience their physical changes at roughly the same time that many of their peers are dealing with similar changes. Tremendous importance is placed both on physical appearance and on conformity to the peer group. Average maturers are able to conform to the group, at least in this physical respect. They have others to talk to and relate to about their physical and sexual changes. Early maturers (those who mature earlier than most of their peers) have the advantages of increased physical size and athletic ability. Peers are more likely to look up to them. Adults are more likely to respond to them as if they were older. Late maturers (those who are behind most of their peer group in physical development) are not so lucky.

The timing of maturation has been found to have serious psychological effects, especially on boys. An extensive longitudinal study (Jones and Bayley, 1950; Jones, 1957) reveals some interesting differences between early and late maturing boys. The first part of the study compared two groups of boys aged 12 to 17 who were selected from the early and late extremes in maturation of their age group. They were categorized as being either early maturers or late maturers according to their skeletal age. Early maturers were found to have several advantages in that they were perceived as being more physically attractive than late maturers. They were also more likely to be treated by adults as being more mature. Finally, they were more likely to be school leaders. Differences in personality characteristics revealed them to be more relaxed, more matter-of-fact, and more able to engage in socially appropriate behavior. Early maturers look like adults at an earlier age. Therefore they are more likely to be treated like adults and in turn respond to this treatment by acting more like adults. They also tend to gain more respect from their peers. This enhances their self-confidence and their ability to interact socially.

Late maturers, on the other hand, are perceived as being less physically attractive and not as well poised. They also appear to be more tense in manner and are more likely to engage in immature, attention-getting behavior. Perhaps this behavior serves as their means of expressing themselves. Late maturers may be denied the respect and attention given more mature looking boys. Acting out behavior may provide late maturers a means of getting at least some attention and recognition, even though it may not be very positive.

A follow-up study was done using members of these groups when they were approximately 33 years of age (Jones, 1957). By adulthood most differences between the groups apparently disappeared. No differences were apparent concerning the men's adult physical size or attractiveness, marital status, number of children, socioeconomic level, or educational level.

Some differences, however, did remain between the groups despite the fact that a substantial amount of time had passed. The variations involved primarily psychological characteristics. The late maturers tended to remain less responsible, less self-controlled, and less dominating. Two personality variables showed significant differences. First, the early maturers were rated outstandingly higher in terms of making a good impression. Perhaps this follows from their apparent increased levels of self-confidence and social skills patterned in adolescence.

The second striking difference involved the increased flexibility shown by the late maturers. They appeared to be better able to tolerate situations which are less clear or out of their control. Livson and Peskin (1980) reflect on the reasons why late maturers seem to have this particular advantage. Adolescents who mature late must learn to cope early with their disadvantaged and more stressful situation. As a result, as adults they are more flexible and are better equipped with creative problem-solving skills. They paid their dues as adolescents, but reap the rewards of their experience as adults.

Other studies comparing early- and late-maturing adolescent boys show similar results. Weatherly (1964) studied groups of college students who were categorized into groups of early, average, or late maturers. These groups were compared on several measures of personality. Late-maturing boys were found to be more likely to seek attention and support from others. On the other hand, they were less likely to assume a position of leadership or dominance over other people.

Mussen and Jones (1967) administered the Thematic Apperception Test (TAT) to 33 seventeen-year-old boys. The TAT is a projective personality test where participants are shown various ink blots and asked to give impressions and tell stories about them. Their responses are then evaluated with respect to various personality traits. Of these boys, 16 were categorized as early maturers and 17 as late maturers. Some interesting differences emerged. Late-maturing boys were more likely to feel inadequate, rejected, and dominated. They also tended to be more dependent and to have poorer self-concepts. Finally, they tried harder to be socially accepted into the peer group, but were generally less successful because of their immature behavior. Early maturers, on the other hand, were generally more independent, self-confident, and acted more mature in their relationships with others.

However, this research reflects only tendencies. Much variation is found from one individual to another. Although this research can be used to give clues for better understanding human behavior, each person must be evaluated individually. It is also important to remember that these results were obtained by contrasting the two extreme groups of maturing adolescents. When either extreme is compared to the average group, these differences tend to be much less striking, and sometimes even insignificant.

Early and Late Maturation in Girls

The maturation picture for girls is more confusing and ambiguous. Differences between early- and late-maturing girls are not nearly as clear-cut and obvious as the differences between groups of boys. Faust (1960) evaluated 731 girls enrolled in the sixth through ninth grades. At each grade level girls were evaluated according to their social prestige or popularity. Early maturers were determined on the basis of early menarche. In sixth grade early maturation appeared to be a social handicap. Perhaps this was due to the confusion and disturbance that menarche is capable of causing. Girls who mature early may feel out of place compared to their peers. It may be difficult for them to communicate about their new developments with other girls who have not experienced these developments and probably don't understand them. However, as early as seventh grade the picture changed. Early maturers rapidly gained in prestige as their classmates also began to develop. These higher levels of prestige were maintained throughout the next three years.

Another study corroborated the fact that early maturing girls have an advantage. Jones and Mussen (1958) found that early maturing girls have a better total adjustment. These girls also tended to have a better self-concept and to be more secure and relaxed in their general orientation toward the world. However, two points should be noted. First, the differences were neither as clear nor as consistent as they were for boys. Second, both peer and adult observers of these girls tended to rate the late maturers as generally functioning better during the teen years.

One other study found late-maturing girls to score higher on the dimension of "manifest anxiety" (Weatherley, 1964). However, when other personality characteristics were evaluated, no differences were found. This was despite the fact that marked differences were found between early and late maturing boys.

In summary, differences between early- and late-maturing girls, when they exist at all, are not nearly as striking as the differences between early- and late-maturing boys. The reason for this difference is not clear. Perhaps boys gain their advantages due to their increased physical size which our society values in men. It could also be that there are more societal rewards for males to physically mature early than for females. There is also some indication that any advantages and disadvantages for females may vary depending on the specific time targeted during the adolescent years.

Young Adulthood

It is difficult to pinpoint the exact time of life we are referring to when we talk about young adulthood. The transition into adulthood is not a clear-cut dividing line. People become voting adults by age 18. However, in most states, they are not considered adult enough to drink alcoholic beverages until 21. A person cannot become a U.S. senator until age 30 or president until age 35. All this presents a pretty confusing picture concerning what we mean by adulthood.

Various theorists have tried to define young adulthood. Buhler (1933), for instance, clustered adolescence and young adulthood together. He felt this period included the ages from 15 to 25. During this era people focus on establishing their identities and on idealistically trying to make their dreams come true. Buhler continues that the next phase includes young and middle adulthood. This period lasts from approximately age 23 to 45 or 50. This age group focuses on attaining realistic, concrete goals and on setting up a work and family structure for life.

Levinson and his colleagues (1974), on the other hand, break up young adulthood into smaller slices. They state that in the process of developing a life structure, people go through stable periods separated by shorter transitional periods. The stage from ages 17 to 24 years is characterized by leaving the family and becoming independent. This is followed by a transitional phase from ages 22 to 28, which involves entering the adult world. The age 30 transition focuses on making a decision about how to structure the remainder of life. According to Levinson et al, a settling-down period then occurs from about ages 32 to 40.

For our purposes, we will arbitrarily consider young adulthood as including the ages from 18 to 30. This is the time following the achievement of full physical growth when people are establishing themselves in the adult world. Specific aspects of young adulthood addressed in this chapter will include physical development, health status, and the effects of lifestyle on health.

Physical Development

Young adults are in their physical prime. Maximum muscular strength is attained between the ages of 25 and 30, and generally begins a gradual decline after that (Bromley, 1975). After age 30, decreases in strength occur mostly in the leg and back muscles. Some weakening also occurs in the arm muscles.

Top performance speed in terms of how fast tasks can be accomplished is reached at about age 30 (Lehman, 1966). Young adulthood is also characterized by the highest levels of manual agility. According to Troll (1975), hand and finger dexterity decrease after the mid-thirties.

Sight, hearing, and the other senses are their keenest during young adulthood. Eyesight is the sharpest at about age 20. A decline in visual acuity isn't significant until age 40 or 45, when there is some tendency toward *presbyopia* (farsightedness). What happens is that there is a reduction in the elasticity of the lens in the eye. The result is that the lens can no longer change its curvature in order to focus on very near points of vision. When people of age 40 or more read their newspapers by holding them three feet in front of them, they are likely to be suffering from presbyopia.

Hearing is also sharpest at age 20. After this there is a gradual decline in auditory acuity, especially in sensitivity to higher tones. This deficiency is referred to as *presbycusis*. It results from a natural aging process where there is a slow degeneration and hardening of the auditory cells and nerves. Most of the other senses, namely touch, smell, and taste, tend to remain stable until approximately age 45 or 50.

Health Status

Young adulthood can be considered the healthiest time of life. Young adults are generally healthier than when they were children. Yet, they have not yet begun to suffer the illnesses and health declines which develop in middle age (Timiras, 1972). Over 90 percent of people from age 17 to 44 perceive of their health as being either good or excellent (Department of Health, Education, and Welfare, 1976). There is an increased interest on the part of many in all socioeconomic classes in health measures. For example, running and other forms of exercising, health foods, and weight control have become very popular.

Despite the fact that young adulthood is generally a healthy time of life, health differences can be seen between men and women. For example, women tend to visit physicians more than men (Howie and Drury, 1977). For those between ages 17 and 24, women made 5.6 visits to their doctors in 1977 compared to 3 visits for men. Likewise, in the group aged 25 to 44, women visited their physicians 5.8 times compared to 3.5 visits for men. However, women's more frequent visits may be attributed to health issues related to gender. These include contraception, pregnancy, or an annual pap test, instead of for more general reasons of poor health. Perhaps women are also more conscientious about preventive health care in general.

Women are more likely to be obese than are men. Obesity is dangerous to a person's health and tends to aggravate other health problems (Marieskind, 1980). Statistics taken from 1971 to 1974 indicate that for all women in the United States aged 20 to 44, 19.7 percent were obese. For men, 14.2 percent of that age group were obese (Division of Health Examination Statistics, 1971–1974). This indicates a serious health concern for both genders, although for women it is even more prevalent.

Of all the acute or temporary pressing health problems occurring during young adulthood, approximately one half are caused by respiratory problems. An additional 20 percent are due to injuries. The most frequent chronic health problems occurring in young adulthood include spinal or back difficulties, hearing problems, arthritis, and hypertension. These chronic problems occur even more frequently in families of lower socioeconomic status. People are hospitalized most frequently during young adulthood due to childbirth, accidents, digestive tract disturbances, and genital or urinary system illnesses (U.S. Department of Health, Education, and Welfare, 1979).

The death rate among young adults is not as high as among various other age groups. However, during young adulthood indications of diseases begin to appear which will plague a person later in life (Scanlon, 1979). Actual symptoms may not yet cause discomfort. Nevertheless, diseases may be gaining a foothold. Such illnesses include lung and heart problems, bone and joint difficulties, such as arthritis, kidney disease, or cirrhosis of the liver. Illnesses caused by genetic predisposition may also begin to appear during this time of life. Genetically related diseases include multiple sclerosis, rheumatoid arthritis, diabetes, and sickle-cell anemia. Even illnesses related to excessive stress such as ulcers and depression can begin to appear during early adulthood.

After the age of 30, the incidence of death rises abruptly. Fuchs (1974) compiled and discussed death rate statistics. The death rate for men is higher than for women at any age. Between the ages 15 to 24, the death rate for women is only one third that for men. The reason for this is the high rate of violent deaths for young men. Seventy-five percent of deaths for men aged 15 to 24 occur through violence such as accidents, homicide, or suicide. The difference between men and women is not nearly as great if violent deaths are excluded from the statistics.

The major cause of death at age 30 for a white male is a motor vehicle accident, many of which might be attributed to drunk driving. The next most frequent causes respectively include a heart attack, suicide, homicide and cirrhosis of the liver. Black males of that age, on the other hand, are most likely to die from a homicide. Other causes resemble those of white males. These include cirrhosis, motor vehicle accidents, heart attacks, or strokes, respectively.

Major causes of death for women provide a somewhat different profile. A 30-year-old white female is most likely to die from suicide. The causes respectively following that are breast cancer, a motor vehicle accident, a heart attack, or a stroke. A black woman of 30, on the other hand, is most likely to die from a homicide. This is the same primary cause of death for this age group as for black men. Other causes in order of their frequency of occurrence include cirrhosis, heart attacks, strokes, or breast cancer, respectively (Geller and Steele, 1977).

Lifestyle and Good Health

Good health doesn't just happen. It is related to specific practices and to a person's individual lifestyle. Several simple, basic habits have been found to prolong life (Belloc and Breslow, 1972). People who follow all of them tend to live longer than people who follow only some of them. As a matter of fact, a clear relationship seems to exist between the number of the suggested habits followed and the state of overall health.

These positive health habits include eating breakfast and other meals regularly. Snacking should be avoided. Moderate eating in order to maintain a normal, healthy weight is important. Smoking and heavy alcohol consumption are dangerous to health and should be avoided. Moderate exercise and adequate sleep are important and contribute to good health.

Different lifestyles involve different behaviors. In other words, an individual's typical way of life will involve specific types of activities. Some of these activities have been found to have direct effects on a person's health.

For instance, excessive consumption of alcohol has very negative effects on health. Alcoholics are people who have a continual and compulsive need for alcohol. Physical dependence occurs when body tissues become dependent on the continuous presence of alcohol. Approximately three quarters of all alcoholics show some impaired liver function. Cirrhosis of the liver is eventually developed by about 8 percent of all alcoholics. The chances of developing cirrhosis are about six times greater for alcoholics than for nonalcoholics (Girdano and Dusek, 1980). Cirrhosis involves gradual deterioration of the liver tissue until it no longer can adequately perform its normal functions. These functions include involvement in the process of converting food to usable energy.

Cigarette smoking is another activity that is clearly associated with health problems. Most of the deaths caused by smoking are due to heart disease. Cigarette smoke contains nicotine which acts as a stimulant. As nicotine enters the lungs, it is quickly absorbed by the small blood vessels in the lungs and immediately transported throughout the body. As a stimulant it causes both an increased heart rate and increased blood pressure. Over time the heart will be overworked and eventually be damaged (Girdano and Dusek, 1980).

Lung cancer is the second major cause of death attributed to smoking. Cigarette tars and other particles in the smoke gradually accumulate in the tubes and air sacs of the lungs. This causes a gradual change in the lung tissue's normal cells. Eventually these affected cells may reproduce new cells that are different from the original ones. The new cancerous cells begin frantic reproduction of more cancerous cells which eventually kill off and take over the normal cell tissue. The result is the growth of a malignant tumor which invades the lung and spreads to other parts of the body.

To make matters worse, it's been found that a combination of excessive alcohol consumption and tobacco usage results in an increased risk of developing cancer of the mouth, larynx, and esophagus (Winder, et al., 1976; Moore, 1971, 1965). Since approximately 90 percent of all alcoholics also smoke (Dreher and Fraser, 1968), this becomes a serious health risk.

Stress is also related to health problems. Holmes and Rahe (1976) found a strong relationship between stress and illness. The more stress a person was experiencing, the greater was the chance of becoming ill. An interesting finding was that stress was not only caused by negative occurrences such as the death of a close relative, but also by new, positive occurrences. These included outstanding personal achievements and even vacations. Apparently change in general is related to stress. Adjustment to new situations requires expending energy. This additional energy and need for adjustment is apparently related to stress regardless of whether the adjustment is related to a happy or a sad occasion.

On a more positive note, some life situations and behaviors have been found to be positively related to health. For example, marriage is apparently a healthy state. Verbrugge (1979) found that people who are married are generally healthier than people who are either separated or widowed. Married people are less likely to have long-term physical disabilities. They are also more likely to have shorter hospital stays. After those who are married, the next healthiest group are those who are single. Divorced and separated people suffer the most health problems. These latter groups are most likely to have acute illnesses, long-term disability, and long-term conditions that interfere with their social functioning.

The fact that divorced and separated people have the most health problems may be related to Holmes and Rahe's findings on stress (1976). Death of a spouse, divorce, and marital separation were respectively the causes of the highest levels of stress. Stress is a contributing cause in the development of most illnesses. Since loss of an intimate partner under any circumstances is apparently very stressful, it follows that these people would be subject to higher rates of illness.

Significant Issues and Life Events

Certain significant experiences and life events tend to characterize adolescence and young adulthood. In other words, some issues are of special concern to people in this age group. Several of these issues have been arbitrarily selected for discussion in this book. They were chosen on the basis of their relevance and impact on the physical well-being of young people. As adolescence is a period of sexual development, sexuality will be emphasized. The issues include sexual activity in adolescence, unplanned pregnancy, teenage fatherhood, motivation for pregnancy, sex education, and contraception.

Sexual Activity in Adolescence

The incidence of nonmarital sexual intercourse has dramatically increased in the past 40 years. In the 1940s, Kinsey (1948, 1953) found that about one third of all females and almost three quarters of all males in the age group under 25 reported that they had had nonmarital intercourse. Hunt (1974), on the other hand, found quite a different picture in 1972. By age 25, 97 percent or virtually all the males surveyed had had nonmarital sexual intercourse. Even more strikingly, 67 percent or approximately two thirds of the females surveyed had experienced intercourse outside of marriage. Having sexual relations outside of marriage is becoming much more common.

So far the statistics discussed have included both adolescents and young adults. In a study comparing the rates of sexual activity for adolescents in 1971 and 1976, some interesting differences emerged (Zelnik and Kantner, 1977). During this five year period, the percentage of 17-year-old women who had had intercourse at least once increased from 27 to 41 percent. Likewise, in the 15-year-old age group, the percentage of young women who experienced intercourse increased from 14 percent to 18 percent. Both of these increases support the notion that sexual activity is increasing at younger and younger ages than in the past.

Although it's very difficult to obtain accurate data about nonmarital sex for the under 15-year-old age group, it has been estimated that about one out of ten 13-year-olds have had sexual intercourse (Marieskind, 1980). One midwestern study found a substantial increase in sexual activity among 14-

year-old girls. The rate of those who had experienced intercourse rose from 10 percent in 1971 to 17 percent in 1973 (Vener and Stewart, 1974).

The increase in sexual activity among adolescents doesn't mean that they all feel positively about their sexual behavior. Some adolescents, especially girls, often feel guilty. One third of sexually active teens express at least some guilt over their behavior (Sorensen, 1973). Furstenberg (1976) found that almost half of the pregnant adolescents in his study felt that women should be virgins when they marry. This obviously points to a discrepancy between attitude, namely that of abstinence, and behavior, namely that of becoming pregnant.

The other divergence between attitude and behavior involves the importance placed on sex by adolescents. Increased sexual activity is sometimes thought to be related to increased interest in sex. But this is not the case. When asked to rank six activities according to which were most to least important in their lives, adolescent girls ranked sex last and adolescent boys, fourth (Hass, 1979). Having friendships, doing well in school, and athletics were all rated as higher priorities in terms of importance.

In summary, the frequency of sexual activity among adolescents seems to be increasing. However, it cannot be assumed that all adolescents will feel good about their sex lives. Nor can it be assumed that adolescents place sex as a high priority in their lives. This is a time of life which is full of change and adjustment. It must be especially difficult and confusing for young people to resolve the discrepancies between their attitudes toward sexuality and their actual behavior.

Unplanned Pregnancy

A staggering number of teenage pregnancies occur in the United States each year. By the age of 17, one of every ten girls gets pregnant. By the age of 19, this figure jumps up to one in every four.

Not all pregnancies are seen through to term. Approximately one third of all teen pregnancies are terminated by abortion (American Academy of Pediatrics, 1979). Miscarriages occur in approximately 100,000 (Marieskind, 1980). However, teen pregnancies still account for approximately one fifth of all the children born annually in the United States (Mothner, 1977). The actual number of babies born each year to women in their teens is over one half million.

The vast majority of these, a total of 94 percent, remain at home with their young mothers. Another 3.5 percent of the children are placed for adoption, and the other 2.5 percent, with relatives or friends (Zelnik and Kantner, 1974). This places these young women in a very different situation than that of most of their peers. Adolescence and young adulthood is the usual time of life for meeting and socializing with friends, dating, possibly selecting a mate, obtaining an education, and making a career choice. The additional responsibility of motherhood poses serious restrictions on the amount of freedom and time available to do all of these other things. Additionally, such young women are most often ill-prepared for motherhood. They are usually in the midst of establishing their own identities and learning to care for themselves.

Eighty percent of all teens who get pregnant are not married and most do not marry after becoming pregnant (Zelnik, Kim, and Kantner, 1979). Of those who do marry, the decision is often based on the fact that the young

Adolescence, the time of life between childhood and adulthood, is an exciting, but confusing time. It is a vague transitional period with neither a precise beginning nor end. In our society, there are no set guidelines for how adolescents should behave. Consequently, adolescents often alternate between acting like the children they recently were and the adults they are on their way to becoming. Levels of maturity fluctuate from one adolescent to another. (Ruth Kirst)

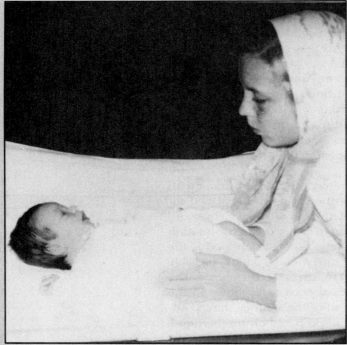

Barely out of childhood themselves, single adolescent mothers are ill-prepared for motherhood. Stress and responsibility may lead them to drop out of school or enter marriages that end in divorce. Lack of education will lessen their earning potential and finding time for social and recreational activities will be difficult. (Ruth Kirst)

Adolescents want their appearance to conform to peer standards. They are intolerant of physical imperfections that may prevent peer acceptance. Adolescent girls and boys have different physical concerns. Girls tend to be weight conscious and intent on staying thin. Boys are more concerned with body build, especially with the size of their upper arms and chests. When adolescents perceive themselves to be unattractive, they develop low levels of self-esteem and have little self-confidence. (Charles Zastrow)

Adolescent boys whose bodies mature early have several advantages over their peers. They are perceived as being attractive and viewed as leaders. Because newly increased size makes them more athletically able, they gain popularity when they do well in team sports. These early maturers are more relaxed and socially poised than their less mature peers. Adults treat them as if they were older. They, in turn, act in a more adultlike, independent fashion. (Charles Zastrow)

mother and father "have to" marry because of the pregnancy. Teen marriages have only a 50 percent chance of survival. In other words, half of them end in divorce. The chance of divorce is two to four times greater for teens who marry than for older people (Gordon, 1973).

Often the young mother will not have a spouse to help her in caring for and raising her new child. Furthermore, even if she does marry the father, it's likely that the marriage will be marred by turbulence and struggle, as the high divorce rate indicates.

Furstenberg (1976) studied the lives of 404 young mothers who had become pregnant by age 17 and compared their experiences with teens who were not pregnant. Several striking differences were discovered. Despite the fact that almost all of the young mothers expressed ambitions to complete their high school educations, approximately one half of them became high school dropouts. A five year follow-up revealed that the teen mothers had an average of two years less of school than their classmates. Teen mothers were also more likely to get married earlier. Approximately two thirds of them were married within five years of their babies' births. However, about one fifth of the marriages dissolved within a year after they had begun. A follow-up done six years after the study began revealed that three fifths of the marriages had broken up. The marriages of teen mothers were twice as likely to end in divorce as those of their peers who married without already having children.

Another variable evaluated in the study was employment status. Five years after the beginning of the study, only 48 percent of the young mothers were employed. This compared to 63 percent of their peers. The likelihood of receiving welfare or public aid was three times greater for the teen mothers than for others in their high school class. It follows logically that people with lesser education levels have lesser income potential. Poverty frequently becomes an additional burden for teenage mothers.

Thus, the added stress and responsibility of motherhood tend to impact and take a toll on teen mothers. Raising a child demands time, energy, and attention. Time taken to care for a baby must be subtracted from the time available for social, recreational, and educational activities. There are potentially serious results on the mental health and daily functioning of young mothers. This is supported by the fact that pregnant teens are more likely to attempt suicide than other girls in their age group (McKenry, Walters, and Johnson, 1979).

The consequences of teenage parenthood are emphasized here not to be cynical, but rather to provide a realistic perspective on teen pregnancy. Teenagers need to be at least intellectually aware of the impacts of motherhood. They need this information in order to make better, more realistic decisions for themselves concerning their sexual activity and their use of birth control. The other reason why it's important to focus on the consequences of teenage pregnancy concerns helping young mothers who already have their babies. Social workers need to understand the impacts of teenage parenthood. This is needed to help young mothers realistically appraise their situations, make decisions about what to do for themselves, and get involved with the supportive services they need.

Aside from the responsibilities of young motherhood, one other physical aspect of teenage pregnancy should be focused on. Such pregnancies are marked by increased physical risks, both to the child and to the mother (McKenry, Walters, and Johnson, 1979). Complications including prolonged labor, anemia, and toxemia are more likely. The babies have a much greater chance of either being premature or of having a lower than normal birth weight. The mortality rate for these babies is two to three times greater than for babies born to older mothers. Finally, these babies are significantly more likely to be developmentally disabled or to have neurological difficulties than are other babies. A related finding concerning maternal and child health is that many teenage mothers receive very little prenatal health care (National Center for Health Statistics, 1979). This fact only contributes to the health risks of the mothers and their babies.

Teenage Fathers

Unwed teenage fathers do not appear to have some deep psychological desires to father children. On measures of both personality and intellectual ability, their psychological profiles are very similar to those of other young men their age (Pauker, 1971). However, the fact remains that the unwed father is also a parent to a child. The unwed father's paternal rights and needs are now getting some attention. The male teenager's role of biological father is now being distinguished from the role of mother's potential husband.

In one survey (Robinson, 1969) of 149 unwed fathers, the men did not appear to shun responsibility. In fact, 61 percent indicated that they wanted to marry the child's mother. They indicated that these feelings went beyond pure moral obligation to do the right thing. In many of these cases, the mother decided against a marriage. The survey also found that more than 60 percent of the fathers visited the babies while they were still in the hospital. These fathers also expressed strong feelings about being the child's father.

However, relatively few unwed fathers maintain contact with the child or the child's mother after the child reaches the age of two years (Earls and Siegel, 1980). Economic and societal reasons can be given for this. When a father lives with the mother of his child, his family has less chance of receiving any income from public assistance (Stack, 1974). This would serve as an economic incentive to keep the father out of the home. Societal attitudes and pressures also may serve to discourage paternal involvement. Sawin and Parke (1976) propose that this exclusion is actually due to a prejudice against unwed teenage fathers. They hypothesize that our society has a very negative view of teenage men who have intercourse with and impregnate teenage women.

As with teenage mothers, teenage fathers also tend to do less well educationally and economically (Card and Wise, 1978). Because of the obligation to support their family, many opportunities apparently are denied them. They are more likely to leave school and have less education than others their age. They are also more likely to have lesser skilled, more poorly paying jobs than their peers. Finally, as we've already indicated, marital problems are more frequent and divorce is more likely. In other words, teenage fathers, like teenage mothers, have both more disadvantages and greater difficulties surviving than do their peers.

However, a teenage father has a role in relationship to his child. He not only has feelings concerning the birth and existence of the child, but he also has attachments and responsibilities. It is not helpful to be punitive about what he's done wrong. Rather it is important to help him express his feelings, more clearly define his role, and contribute where he can in taking over responsibilities for his child.

■ Portrait of an Unwed Father

Gary didn't know what to do. Linda just had ruined his day and probably his life. She had just told him that she was pregnant. How could this happen? What could he do?

Gary, a 17-year-old high school sophomore, had never done very well in school and had even flunked sixth grade once. Ever since then, he'd been taking "Special Ed" classes, whatever that meant, and was just barely squeaking by.

He had always considered himself a freak. He like to do a lot of drugs, that is, whenever he had the money to get them. He also liked to listen to booming punk rock and was intimately familiar with radio station WROK's top ten hits. His uniform included well-patched blue jeans, construction worker boots, and 18-inch long, healthy but somewhat scraggly, greasy hair.

Beneath this exterior, Gary was an extremely sensitive, bright person. He really cared about other people, although sometimes he had trouble showing it. This thing about Linda and a baby had really shaken him up. He really loved Linda. As a matter of fact, she was the best thing that had ever happened to him. She actually cared about him. It seemed like nobody had ever done that before. Gary really didn't have much self-confidence. The fact that Linda cared simply amazed him.

Gary lived with his mother and younger sister Shirley. Shirley was 11. He cared about her but they really didn't have much in common. There was too much of an age difference. Sometimes they stuck up for each other, though, when their mother went out with some new boyfriend and came home drunk. That happened pretty often. His mother was really something else. She was pretty nice. It seemed like she loved him, but she had always had a horrible problem accepting responsibility. A lot of times he felt like he had to take care of her, instead of vice versa. No, she wasn't one to depend on much.

Another problem was that they were dirt poor. He could never remember having a lot of things. For years he had wanted to learn how to play the guitar. He picked one up two years ago at a sleazy neighborhood auction, but it never really sounded like much. The other problem, of course, was that he felt he had absolutely no talent. He often thought the guitar looked good, though, sitting on an old peach crate in his basement room, his place of retreat.

Sometimes Gary thought about his father out in Utah. Although he only actually saw him once in the last ten years, he talked to him sometimes on the phone on holidays. His big dream was to go out and live with his dad and his dad's new family. Gary liked nature and camping. He thought that Utah would be the perfect place to go to and get away. In his more somber moments, he realized this was only a dream. His dad was pleasant enough on the phone, but he knew he really didn't care, not really. It was fun to think about sometimes, though. Sometimes when he got a better batch of drugs, he'd just sit in his room and think. He dreamed of all the wonderful things he'd do in Utah, yessirree. That's what it was though, just a dream.

Gary dreamed a lot. He didn't have much hope for the real future. He thought that was pretty hopeless. One of his teachers asked him once if he ever thought about going to college. College, hah! How could he ever afford to go to college. He couldn't even afford a K-Mart guitar. The other problem was how poorly he always did in school. He stopped studying really years ago. Now he was so far behind he knew he'd never catch up. He didn't like to think much about the future. There was no future in it.

But now Gary's problem was Linda—Linda and the baby. It's funny how he already thought of it as a baby even though it wasn't born yet. He liked the thought of having something that was really his. He liked Linda, too, and he didn't want to lose her. She was crying when she told him she was pregnant. He bet she'd like it if they lived together, or maybe even got married. Then he could move out of his mother's apartment. He could be free and on his own. He could drop out of school. School wasn't much anyhow. Maybe he could get that second shift job flinging burgers at the local hamburger shack. That wouldn't be too bad. He could see his friends there. They could have a good time.

Yeah, that's what he'd do. He'd do a good thing for once in his life. He'd marry Linda and be a father. Maybe everything would be all right then. Maybe they'd all live happily ever after.

Epilogue: Gary and Linda did get married four months later. They had a 6 pound, 8 ounce bouncing baby boy they named Billy. The problem was that things really didn't get any better. They didn't change much at all. Gary was still poor. Now, however, he was poor but with adult responsibilities. He still couldn't afford a guitar. He had to go to work at the hamburger shack every day at 5:00 p.m. just like he used to have to go to school every morning. There wasn't much money for him and Linda to have any fun with. As a matter of fact, there wasn't much money to do anything much at all. Their efficiency apartment was pretty cramped. Sometimes the baby's crying drove him almost crazy. He and Linda weren't doing too well either. When they weren't fighting, they weren't talking. Things hadn't changed much at all. He still didn't have much hope for the future.

Commentary: This case example isn't meant to portray the thoughts of a typical or representative unwed father. For example, Gary was very poor.

In reality unwed parents originate in all socioeconomic levels. However, this example is intended to illustrate the lack of experience and information adolescents often have available to them. Without information it's difficult to make insightful, well-founded decisions. A major job of a social worker is to help young people in a situation like this rationally think through the alternatives available to them. Potential services need to be talked about and plans need to be made. Young people often need both support and suggestions regarding how to proceed. They need to examine their expectations about the future and make certain that they're being realistic.

Why Do Teenagers Get Pregnant?

When adolescents are asked why they have intercourse, the most frequent answers include looking for new experiences and escaping tension (Sorenson, 1973). Other answers include using sex as a way of communicating with a partner, being more adultlike and mature, and having a way to reward or punish people close to them. An example of this latter reason would be having intercourse to reward a devoted boyfriend. Another example would be participating in sexual activity to punish parents for being too strict or too neglectful. A few adolescents state that they have sex in response to peer group expectations. In summary, adolescents give many different reasons for having sexual relations.

Becoming pregnant is not necessary. Methods of birth control are much more effective and available than ever before. The question must then be raised as to why so many adolescents get pregnant.

Part of the answer lies in the fact that 66 percent get pregnant by accident (Zelnik and Kantner, 1974). Furstenberg (1976) compared the sexual behaviors and experiences of adolescents who were mothers with those who were not mothers. He found virtually no differences in their levels of sexual activity. It appeared that some were lucky and some were not.

Young women are at their greatest risk of becoming pregnant in the very few first months after they start having sexual intercourse (Zabin, Kantner, and Zelnik, 1979). Most adolescents do not attempt to obtain and use birth control until they have been sexually active for at least a year. In fact, younger adolescent girls tend to wait even longer than their older counterparts before they think about getting some form of contraception.

Adolescent girls tend to wait until they're established in a sexual relationship before they use birth control (Settlage, 1973; Sorensen, 1973). This avoidance may be due to their unwillingness to admit to themselves that they're sexually active. Traditionally, the values of virginity in women and intercourse only within marriage were considered important. Some traces of these historic approaches may still subsist. Some young women may illogically feel that if they ignore the issue, it will cease to exist. If they don't think about their own sexual activity, then they don't have to worry about it. Other teenagers may simply want to get pregnant, even when marriage is not anticipated.

Another reason for not using contraception may be unwillingness to address the issue with their partner. Some types of birth control are more obvious than others. Other types need male assistance. A young woman may feel uncomfortable in talking to a partner about such intimate issues. Another fear may be giving her partner a wrong impression. If she appears to know a lot about contraception, she may fear her partner will think her too knowledgeable and experienced.

Adolescent females also lack adequate and accurate information on birth control. In one study, almost 1,000 sexually active adolescents were asked about what kinds of birth control they used and how they used it (Shah, Zelnik, and Kantner, 1975). A striking 80 percent admitted that they had had sexual intercourse without using any means of contraception. Almost three quarters of this 80 percent said they didn't think they could get pregnant. Their reasons ranged from thinking that they weren't old enough to conceive, to thinking they'd have to have intercourse much more often than they did to get pregnant. Some thought it was safe to have sex during some times of the month. The most frightening reason for not using contraception was a complete lack of knowledge about how reproduction occurs.

Sex Education

A heated controversy often develops over the issue of providing teens with information about sex. The fear is that giving adolescents information about sexuality will encourage them to start experimenting sexually. An underlying assumption is that adolescents won't think about sex or be interested in it unless someone around them brings up the subject.

Two fallacies can be pointed out in this approach. First, it assumes that adolescents have no access to sexual information other than that which adults around them choose to give. Hunt (1974) did an extensive study of sexual attitudes and behavior by surveying 982 males and 1,044 females. He found that 59 percent of the males and 46 percent of the females felt that they had obtained most of their sexual information from friends. An additional 20 percent of the males and 22 percent of the females gave reading material as their primary source of information. The fact that friends and reading material are the primary sources of sex information for young people has been supported by other research (Warren and St. Pierre, 1973).

Obviously, adolescents are functioning within a complex environment which exposes them to many new things and ideas. They are not locked up in a sterile cage. A tremendous emphasis is placed on sexuality and sexual behavior by the media; television, magazines, newspapers, and books are filled with sexual episodes and anecdotes. Adolescents have numerous exposures to the concept of sex.

A second fallacy is the idea that adolescents will automatically go out and try anything they hear about. If a parent tells a young person that some people are murderers, will the young person automatically go out and try murdering someone? Of course not. Although adults, especially parents, might wish they had such control over adolescents, they quite frankly do not.

Perhaps an analogy concerning sex education could be made to the situation of buying a used Chevy van. An analogous assumption would be that it would be better to have no information about how the van works prior to buying it and hope for the best. This is ludicrous. In this situation you would want as much information as possible to make the best decision about whether to buy the van or not. It would behoove you to take the van to your favorite mechanic to have it thoroughly evaluated. The point is you would both need and want information. This situation is analogous to sex education. People, including adolescents, need as much information as possible in order to make responsible decisions about their own sexual behavior and avoid ignorant mistakes. It is illogical to deprive them of information and have them act on the basis of hearsay and chance.

As stated, adolescents are exposed to the concept of sexuality and to information about sex. However, it cannot be assumed that the information they get is either accurate or specific. One study of 266 college freshmen who were enrolled in a college health course revealed some interesting findings (Warren and St. Pierre, 1973). Forty percent of the students did not understand how birth control pills prevent pregnancy, and 37 percent of the students did not understand what the word *ovulation* meant.

The primary source of information about sex is friends, and yet friends probably don't know much more about sex than they do. Information that is available is likely to be vague and inaccurate. Just because adolescents use sexual terms does not mean they are very knowledgeable about sexuality. Often these words refer to genital or sexually related body parts. Frequently these terms are vulgar and shocking. Just because teenagers use words referring to parts of the sexual anatomy does not mean that they understand how these parts function.

Another aspect of the sex education controversy is the idea that sex education should be provided by parents in the home. This is a virtuous idea. However, on closer scrutiny some problems are evident. Hass (1979, p. 166) found that approximately two thirds of both male and female adolescents felt that they were not able to talk about sexuality with their parents. Libby and Nass (1971) examined the reactions of parents to adolescent sexual activity. They discovered a tendency for parents to issue orders rather than discuss sexual issues with their children. The following statements were typical of the type of comments made by parents: "I try to keep them from knowing too much;" "I think sex education corrupts the minds of 15 or 16 year olds;" "My parents didn't tell me about it. I don't discuss it either;" "Kids know too much already (p. 230)." Needless to say, these statements reflect a negative attitude concerning talking about sex. An implication is that it's easier to avoid the whole issue. This approach interferes with open, honest communication about sex between parents and child.

One Cleveland study in the late 1970s examined the attitudes of 1400 parents toward sex education. Most parents thought it was a good idea for their children to learn about sexuality and reproduction even before they become adolescents. However, only 8 percent of the fathers studied and less than 15 percent of the mothers said that they were either comfortable enough or knowledgeable enough to sit down and talk about sexual intercourse with their children (Roberts and Holt, 1980). Even in view of these statistics, most parents are uneasy about establishing a formal sex education curriculum in the public schools.

Sex educators do not want to take the parents' place as sex educators (Dickman, 1982, p. 21). Rather, they want to ensure that children have adequate and accurate information about sex. Many times parents are uncomfortable or embarrassed talking about sex with their children. Often they feel they don't know enough of the specifics to intelligently educate a child. One student shared her eight-year-old son's reaction to her own discomfort in talking to him about sex. As she was trying to explain to him some of the basics of human reproduction, he put his hand on her arm and said, "It's okay, Mom, I get the general idea."

■ Major Methods of Contraception

Anyone who is considering becoming sexually active and who is not intentionally trying to conceive a child needs accurate and specific information about contraceptive methods. This includes adolescents. Without adequate information, responsible decisions cannot be made. Information helps to prevent people from taking unnecessary risks. We've already established the importance of sex education. Information concerning contraception is especially important. The risk of unplanned pregnancy and the resulting impact on the lives of adolescents is too critically important to ignore.

The following material describes the major methods of contraception. Their levels of effectiveness are indicated, and the advantages and disadvantages of each method are explored. No one best method of birth control exists for everybody. Each individual must select a method according to how it fits with his or her individual lifestyle. Some methods are easier to use than others. Some methods require responsible adherence to a schedule. Other methods are best suited for persons who only have occasional sexual contacts.

The Pill

Birth control pills or oral contraceptives are the most effective form of contraception other than sterilization (Masters, Johnson, and Kolodny, 1982, p. 123). They supply hormones which serve to prevent the ovaries from ovulating, or releasing a ripened egg ready for fertilization. Several brands of birth control pills are available with varying amounts and combinations of hormones. In a sense, the pill tricks the body into thinking that the person is pregnant. A pregnant woman temporarily stops ovulating in order to prevent multiple pregnancies. The pill also tends to increase the thickness of cervical mucus. This helps to stop sperm from getting through and entering the uterus.

The pill needs to be taken each day for 21 days beginning on the fifth day of the woman's menstrual period. Some pill brands include placebos or ineffective sugar pills for the remaining 7 days of the cycle. This serves to reinforce a woman's habit of taking one pill each day.

The primary advantage of the pill is that it is nearly 100 percent effective. The effectiveness rate refers to the number of women out of 100 women who will successfully contracept and not get pregnant. An effectiveness rate of 100 percent means that for every 100 women, none of them will become pregnant.

If taken regularly at approximately the same time each day, it is a very reliable means of birth control. Today's pills have relatively lower dosages of hormones than a decade ago. This is to minimize any unappealing side effects. However, the fact that they are low dosage pills make it more important that they be taken at approximately the same time each day. Otherwise there's a chance that the hormonal levels usually maintained by the pill will drop to a level which makes ovulation possible. Once ovulation occurs, pregnancy becomes possible.

The pill is relatively easy to use, in that one must be swallowed daily. Nothing needs to be inserted into the vagina. No complicated process is involved. Nothing interferes with the spontaneity of a sexual encounter. Those who are frequently sexually active are always prepared.

Disadvantages to taking the pill, include undesirable side effects, including nausea, headaches, constipation, water retention and the resulting swelling, minor increases in blood pressure, and irregular vaginal discharges. Forty percent of all women report at least one undesirable side effect (Hatcher et al., 1976). These side effects resemble those of the first trimester of pregnancy. This is because they are due to similar changes in hormonal levels. These symptoms usually disappear after two to three months, as they tend to do in pregnancy.

Another disadvantage is possible weight gain due to increased water retention. This becomes a serious concern for some women. Another undesirable effect is the increased susceptibility to vaginal infections due to changes in the vaginal mucus. Since the pill is a prescription drug, cost is somewhat prohibitive.

The most serious health risks in taking the pill are cardiovascular problems. One risk is the increased chance of blood clots in the circulatory system. The danger is that the clot can cause damage to the lungs or the brain. However, this danger must be viewed in perspective. Blood clots cause two or three annual deaths for every 100,000 women who take the pill (Rinehart and Piotrow, 1979). The death rate for pregnancy and delivery is 14 deaths per 100,000 (Hyde, 1982, p. 142). A second cardiovascular danger is the increased risk of having a heart attack. However, this is true primarily for women who smoke and for women over the age of 30 (Mann and Inman, 1975; Rosenberg et al., 1980).

Because of the associated cardiovascular problems, women over age 35 are discouraged from taking the pill. This is especially true for those who smoke (Planned Parenthood Association of Wisconsin, undated).

One important aspect to consider before using the pill as a means of contraception is a person's general approach to life. In other words, a person must be notably responsible and conscientious in order to take the pill regularly everyday. Many people, despite their good intentions, find it difficult to follow a regimented procedure. Women who are only occasionally sexually active might also find it unappealing to take the pill every day.

Although the pill is nearly 100 percent effective if used correctly, this is a misleading statement. The issue concerns the need to use the pill correctly. The actual failure rate refers to how many women actually get pregnant when using the pill. The pill's actual failure rate ranges from 4 to 10 percent. This is much different than total effectiveness. The problem lies in human error. Because of the need to take the pill religiously and because people are not perfect, mistakes occur. It is very important to consider the actual failure rate when evaluating any of the major means of birth control. How contraception works in actual practice is what is important.

Two fears about the pill have proven to be unfounded. The first unfounded fear is that the pill causes cancer (Drill, 1975; Rinehart and Piotrow, 1979). If anything, there appear to be some positive health effects from use. Newhouse et al. (1979), for instance, found that the pill may actually serve to help prevent cancer of the ovaries.

The second unfounded fear is that women who take the pill will have difficulty getting pregnant later. Although it appears that women must usually wait about three months after stopping the pill in order to get pregnant, no long-term effects in fertility have been found (Maier, 1984, p. 262).

The IUD (Intrauterine Device)

The IUD is a plastic device which is placed in a woman's uterus. IUDs are available in various shapes. They need to be inserted by a physician or trained health professional. The IUD is attached to a string which hangs out of the cervix. A woman must check this string regularly to be assured that the IUD is still in place. She can check the IUD by inserting her finger into the vagina and feel if the string is still there.

After initial insertion, a woman should check the string regularly. The IUD is most likely to be expelled during the first three months of use (Hyde, 1982, p. 144). During this time, the string should be checked prior to each sexual encounter. Women are also encouraged to use an additional form of birth control during this period to better insure protection against pregnancy. After three months, women should check the string at least once a month to ensure that the IUD is still in place.

The IUD is considered a very effective form of birth control. Its theoretical or potential rate of effectiveness is 97 to 99 percent. However, its actual effectiveness rate is 95 percent. This takes its actual or real-life failure rate into account. This is the lowest difference between theoretical and actual failure rate of any of the major methods of birth control.

Exactly how the IUD works is still a mystery. It is thought to cause an irritation in the lining of the uterus which inhibits pregnancy. The body apparently protects a potential fetus from developing in a hostile environment. Some IUDs contain hormones or elements of copper which are also believed to help inhibit pregnancy.

The major advantage of the IUD is its ease of use, and it provides continuous protection at a high level of effectiveness.

Two serious health problems when using the IUD are possible. The first is the possibility that the device will perforate or puncture the lining of the uterus. This occurs in approximately one out of every 1,000 insertions of the device (Hatcher et al., 1980). Such perforation of the uterus can cause death.

The other serious potential consequence of using the IUD is pelvic inflammatory disease (PID).

PID refers to an infection located in either the uterus or the fallopian tubes. Although PID can have many causes, the IUD appears to be one of them. Apparently, some women are more prone to acquiring PID than others. It is thought that the IUD in its role as an irritant can either aggravate minor existing infections or encourage the development of new infections in some women. The long-term danger of PID is sterility. With serious and repeated infections, scar tissue eventually builds up and blocks the fallopian tubes. This prevents sperm from meeting and fertilizing the egg. Women who are prone to pelvic inflammations are discouraged from using the IUD as a means of birth control.

Other potential side effects of the IUD include increased menstrual cramping and pain in the abdomen, increased level of menstrual flow, and irregular bleeding. Between 10 and 20 percent of women using the IUD experience at least some of these symptoms. They tend to disappear after the first couple of months, however.

Cost is another factor to consider. Although the initial cost runs somewhere from $25 to $50, the extended length of use over time makes the cost relatively reasonable.

The Diaphragm

The diaphragm is one of the barrier methods of birth control. This means that the device acts as a barrier to keep sperm from reaching and fertilizing the egg. The diaphragm is a circular thin piece of rubber stretched over a flexible ring of wire. It is shaped like a dome. A woman inserts it by squatting and pushing it with her fingers up into the vagina to cover the cervix.

Before insertion, approximately one teaspoonful of spermicidal cream or jelly should be placed at the bottom of the dome. These substances kill any sperm that manage to get around the diaphragm's barrier. The diaphragm should be left in the vagina at least six to eight hours after intercourse to make certain that all of the sperm are disposed of. An additional application of spermicide must be inserted after each act of intercourse. The diaphragm should be checked for holes before each use, which can be done by holding it up to light.

The diaphragm, when used with a spermicide, is a very effective method of birth control. Its theoretical effectiveness rating is 97 percent. However, its actual effectiveness rating is only about 83 percent. This is probably because of its inconvenience and difficulty in use. That is, it takes time to prepare for use and insert before every sexual encounter. Sometimes a woman may not have it with her when she needs it. At other times, she may not use it with a spermicide. This greatly decreases its effectiveness. Sometimes it might not be used because it would interfere with spontaneity.

A major advantage of the disphragm is its safety factor. That is, it causes virtually no health problems. No chemicals are being forced into the body. No device is inserted into delicate organs to cause irritation. The only potential difficulty suffered by only a small minority of people is an allergic reaction to a particular brand of spermicide.

Another advantage is its relatively reasonable cost. The diaphragm requires a visit to a physician. Different women need different sizes. After this initial evaluation, a diaphragm is prescribed. It can then be used over a long period of time, provided it is not damaged. In the case of a weight loss or gain of 10 pounds or more, a woman should be reexamined to make certain that her diaphragm still fits.

For individuals who are only occasionally sexually active, the diaphragm need only be used when needed. A person does not have to undergo the ongoing health risks involved in other contraceptive methods when contraception is not needed all of the time.

The major disadvantages of the diaphragm include its relatively complicated method of use and its potential interruption of spontaneity. A person must be willing to go through the correct procedure consistently for it to be an effective birth control method. As is indicated by the high failure rate, this is not always so easy.

The Cervical Cap

A relatively new form of birth control which has experienced a surge of interest in this country is the cervical cap. It resembles a small, deep diaphragm which fits snugly over the cervix and is held in place by suction. Similar to the diaphragm, it acts as a barrier to keep sperm from entering the uterus. The cap can be worn for periods of time varying from hours to weeks. Newer models are currently being tested which have a small, one-way valve in them to allow for the flow of menstrual material and cervical secretions.

Although cervical caps are relatively new in the United States, they have been fairly popular in

England and the European continent for several years. Effectiveness of the cervical cap is still being studied, although there is some evidence that it is somewhat less effective than the diaphragm (Zodhiates et al., 1981: Boehm, 1983). Initial reports have indicated several potential problems with using the cervical cap. These include the cap becoming dislodged from the cervix or causing discomfort to the male during intercourse, emitting a distasteful odor during use, and being difficult to fit for some women (Koch, 1982).

The Condom

A condom, also called a prophylactic or rubber, is a thin sheath made of latex rubber that fits over the penis. Some are also made of the thin tissue of a lamb's intestine, although these tend to be more expensive. The condom is initially rolled up into a little circular packet. This packet must be unrolled and placed on the penis. As it fits rather snugly, it acts as another of the barrier methods of birth control. After ejaculation, sperm are contained in the rubber sheath. They are never allowed to enter the vagina. Some condoms have a small bulge at the tip to allow room for semen. Otherwise some empty space must purposefully be left at the tip of the condom so that there is a place to hold the semen.

Condoms are available with a number of variations. Some are lubricated. They come with slightly different textures and in a variety of colors.

The theoretical effectiveness of a condom is 97 percent. The effectiveness level rivals that of the pill when the condom is used in conjunction with a contraceptive foam.

The actual effectiveness rate of the condom is 90 percent. Once again, this decrease in actual effectiveness can be attributed to human error. The condom must be held at the base of the penis as the penis is withdrawn from the vagina. This is to make sure that none of the semen is spilled and can enter the vagina. Condoms should not be reused.

There are many notable advantages to using the condom. First of all, it is the only nonsurgical means to giving the male some direct responsibility for contraception. Condoms are readily available at relatively low cost. They don't require a prior physical examination or a medical prescription. They are small and easy to carry along for use at any time. They cause no side effects, and serve to prevent venereal disease. One interesting advantage for some men is that the snug fit helps to maintain an erection for a longer period of time in the cases where this is desirable.

One disadvantage to using the condom is the minor intrusion of spontaneity when placing it on the penis. It is also important that it be withdrawn shortly after ejaculation to avoid spilling semen. Some young men have indicated that they hesitate to carry a condom along with them. They feel it looks to a prospective partner as if they were expecting to have intercourse. This might give a bad impression. However, the important thing is to evaluate the potential risks that are involved. The costs of an unwanted pregnancy must be weighed against risking a minor poor impression.

Spermicides

Spermicides are chemical contraceptives which function in two ways. First, the chemicals act to kill sperm. Second, the substance itself acts as a barrier which inhibits sperm from entering the uterus.

Spermicides take many different forms. They are available in creams, jellies, and foams, which are squeezed or thrust into a tube which in turn is inserted into the vagina. Spermicides are also available in tablet and suppository form which are also inserted directly into a woman's vagina.

Advantages of spermicides include their relative ease of use, their ready availability, their low cost, their use only when needed, and their lack of health risks. Unfortunately, despite these advantages, their actual effectiveness rate is only 75 percent. In other words, a woman using only a spermicide for contraception has one chance in four of getting pregnant. However, a spermicide used in conjunction with a condom is a very effective form of birth control. One notable disadvantage is that spermicides can tend to be very messy.

The Contraceptive Sponge

The contraceptive sponge is a soft, cuplike sponge device which can be inserted into the vagina and covers the cervix. Additionally, it is saturated with a spermicide to provide additional protection. Approved by the U.S. Food and Drug Association in 1983, it is the newest form of birth control to become readily available throughout the country. It is currently available without a prescription at almost any drugstore. Although in some ways it functions like a diaphragm, it does not have to be fitted by a physician. It is universally sold under the brand name, "Today."

The sponge's effectiveness is based on three principles. First it acts like a barrier to prevent sperm from entering the cervix. Second, the chemical spermicide it contains acts to kill sperm. Third, its potential for absorbing sperm is also thought to be beneficial.

The sponge is used by dampening it with a little water, squeezing it gently until the spermicidal foam appears, and inserting it into the vagina. It can be inserted up to 24 hours prior to having intercourse and should remain in place at least six hours after. Removal involves simply pulling on the attached ribbon and guiding it out of the vagina.

The sponge has an actual failure rate of approximately 15 percent, which is similar to that of the diaphragm (Masters and Johnson, 1985, p. 170). Failures may be related to problems regarding how it is used. For example, a woman may either forget or find it too inconvenient to insert prior to having sexual intercourse. Another problem may be removal of the sponge too soon after intercourse has occurred.

There are several apparent advantages of the contraceptive sponge. First, it is relatively inexpensive and easy to obtain. It is also easy to insert and use, without any messiness. Furthermore, it can be inserted a relatively long time before intercourse occurs, so that it need not interfere with spontaneity. Finally, the sponge provides protection for more than one sexual encounter without having to take any additional precautions such as adding more spermicide into the vagina.

Primary disadvantages involve the fact that there still is some 15 percent actual risk of pregnancy. This risk decreases significantly when the sponge is used concurrently with some other means of birth control such as the condom. The other potential disadvantage is a very mild irritation of the vagina or penis which occurs only in a very small percentage of users (Masters and Johnson, 1985, p. 172).

Withdrawal

Withdrawal refers to withdrawing the penis prior to ejaculating into the vagina. This is not considered a very effective means of birth control. Its actual effectiveness level ranges from 75 to 80 percent. The problem is that a few drops of semen are expelled by a pair of glands called the Cowper's glands before the full ejaculation. Both urine and semen pass through the urethra. Urine is acidic. An acidic environment is not conducive for sperm. It is thought that these few drops of liquid are discharged prior to ejaculation in order to clear the urethra of some of its acidic quality and better prepare it for sperm. However, sometimes live sperm remain in the urethra. These can be transported out through the tip of the penis by the Cowper's glands' secretion and still impregnate a woman.

The major advantage of withdrawal is that no extraneous devices or substances are needed. A major disadvantage of withdrawal is that it is not very effective. Another critical disadvantage is that a man does not always have perfect control over his ejaculation. There is the potential for him to lose control and ejaculate directly into the woman's vagina.

The Rhythm Method

The rhythm method refers to monitoring a woman's ovulation cycle and initiating sexual relations only during the safe times of her cycle. The problem is that it is very difficult to determine and accurately chart any woman's particular cycle. The theoretical failure rate is 13 percent and the actual failure rate is 21 percent. The rhythm method is considered a poor method of birth control.

There are actually three types of rhythm methods. Due to their complicated procedures, we will not address them in detail here. The calendar method is the simplest of the three. It involves counting the days of the menstrual cycle and trying to determine when ovulation occurs. The idea is to have intercourse only when it is certain that the woman is not ovulating.

The second method is the basal body temperature method. A woman's body temperature undergoes minor predictable variations depending on where she is in her ovulatory cycle. Using this method involves taking her temperature every morning as soon as she wakes up. A problem with this method is that the major temperature differential occurs only after ovulation has taken place. By this time pregnancy prevention could be too late.

The third type of rhythm method is the cervical mucus method. It necessitates that a woman examine her cervical mucus throughout her menstrual cycle. The consistency, amount, and clarity of the mucus tends to change predictably depending on where she is in her ovulatory cycle.

Many women choose to use these methods in conjunction with each other. Regardless, this can be considered a complicated, ineffective method of birth control. It is also difficult to maintain.

Contraceptive Methods of the Future

Several methods of birth control are currently undergoing research for possible use in the future. A potential method of male contraception is the development of a male birth control pill which would interfere with sperm production, maturation, or motility. Various directions for female contraception are also being explored. These include long-acting contraceptive hormones which could either be injected, implanted in small pockets under the skin, or inserted in the vagina by using plastic vaginal rings. Other experimental forms of female contraception include antipregnancy vaccines used only after conception has occurred and methods of sterilization which do not involve surgery. However, all of these methods are only in the experimental phase. Actual effectiveness and potential side effects still need careful evaluation.

Summary

Numerous physical changes mark adolescence. These include a growth spurt and the development of primary and secondary sex characteristics. Adolescents have strong psychological reactions to their physical changes. It is important for adolescents to feel they are physically attractive. Adolescents mature at different rates. Male adolescents who mature early tend to be more self-confident and are more apt to assume leadership positions among their peers. They are more apt to be perceived as physically attractive and are treated more like adults. Differences between early and late maturing females are not nearly as striking as the differences between males.

Young adulthood, arbitrarily including people from ages 18 through 30, is the time of physical prime, and the healthiest time of life. Some lifestyles contribute to good health while others have a negative effect on health.

Significant issues and life events which concern adolescents and young adults include: sexual activity in adolescence, unplanned pregnancy, teenage fatherhood, motivation for pregnancy, sex education, and methods of contraception. Of those pregnant adolescents who choose to have their babies, the vast majority keep them. There is some indication that teenage fathers are initially more psychologically involved with their offspring than they traditionally have gotten credit for. Adolescents tend not to use birth control when they first become sexually active. Sex education is very important for adolescents, as many do not have the information they need to make responsible decisions about their sexual involvement.

Psychological Aspects of Adolescence and Young Adulthood

"Teen Alcoholism Shows Dramatic Increase"

"22-Year-Old Hangs Self in Kenosha Jail"

"$200,000 Worth of Cocaine Found in College Drug Bust"

"Teen Mother Shoots Infant Daughter, Husband, and Self"

"Four Killed by Drunk Teen Driver"

These statements might all be seen in newspaper headlines. They refer to tragedies which involve adolescents and young adults. Although the media often do address sensationalistic and tragic events, the fact that such things are occurring merits our attention. What psychological variables operate to help cause such happenings?

■ A Perspective

This chapter will focus on some of the major psychological growth tasks and pitfalls confronting adolescents and young adults. As the Behavior Dynamics Assessment Model suggests, knowledge of psychological milestones normally negotiated during this period is important for the assessment of behavior and functioning. We will also discuss two categories of critical life events that affect many persons in this age group, namely suicide and substance abuse.

This chapter will

- Explore identity formation in adolescence by examining Erikson's eight stages of psychosocial development and Marcia's categories of identity.
- Explain and evaluate Kohlberg's theory of moral development, and present Gilligan's alternative model for women.
- Examine some critical issues and life events, including suicide and chemical substance abuse, which have special impacts on adolescents and young adults.

Identity Formation

Personal identities crystallize during adolescence. Through experimentation and evaluation of experience and ideas, the adolescent should establish some sense of who he or she really is. In other words, people get to know themselves during adolescence.

Erik Erikson (1950) proposed a theory of psychosocial development comprising eight stages. A key component is the development of the ego or sense of self. This theory focuses on how personalities evolve throughout life as a result of the interaction between biologically based maturation and the demands of society. The emphasis is on the role of the social environment in personality development. The eight stages are based partly on the stages proposed by Freud and partly on Erikson's studies in a wide variety of cultures. Erikson writes that the society within which one lives makes certain psychic demands at each stage of development. Erikson calls these demands crises. During each psychosocial stage, the individual must seek to adjust to the stresses and conflicts involved in these crises. The search for identity is a crisis that confronts people during adolescence.

Although Erikson's psychosocial theory addresses development throughout the life span, it is included here because of the importance of identity formation during adolescence. After the entire theory is discussed, its application to adolescence will be explored in greater depth. The stages are described in *Erikson's Eight Stages of Development*.

■ Erikson's Eight Stages of Development

Stage	Crisis	Age	Important Event
1	Basic trust versus basic mistrust	Birth to 12–18 months	Feeding

(*Continued*)			
2	Autonomy versus shame and doubt	18 months to 3 years	Toileting
3	Initiative versus guilt	3 to 6 years	Locomoting
4	Industry versus inferiority	6 to 12 years	School
5	Identity versus role confusion	Adolescence	Peer relationship
6	Intimacy versus isolation	Young adult	Love relationship
7	Generativity versus stagnation	Maturity	Parenting and creating
8	Ego integrity versus despair	Old age	Reflecting on and accepting one's life

Erikson's Psychosocial Theory

Each stage of human development presents its characteristic crises. Coping well with each crisis makes an individual better prepared to cope with the next. Although specific crises are most critical during particular stages, related issues continue to arise throughout a person's life. For example, the conflict of trust versus mistrust is especially important in infancy. Yet, children and adults continue to struggle with whether or not to trust others.

Stage 1: Basic Trust Versus Basic Mistrust

For infants up to 18 months of age, learning to trust others is the overriding crisis. To develop trust, one must understand that some people and some things can be depended on. Parents provide a major variable for such learning. For instance, infants who consistently receive warm, loving care and nourishment learn to trust that these things will be provided to them. Later in life, people may apply this concept of trust to friends, an intimate partner, or their government.

Stage 2: Autonomy Versus Shame and Doubt

The crisis of autonomy versus shame and doubt characterizes early childhood, from 18 months to three years. Children strive to accomplish things independently. They learn to feed themselves and to use the toilet. Accomplishing various tasks and activities provides children with feelings of self-worth and self-confidence. On the other hand, if children of this age are constantly downtrodden, restricted, or punished, shame and guilt will emerge instead. Self-doubt will replace the self-confidence that should have developed during this period.

Stage 3: Initiative Versus Guilt

Preschoolers aged three to six years must face the crisis of taking their own initiative. Such children are extremely active physically. The world fascinates them and beckons them to explore it. They have active imaginations and are eager to learn. Preschoolers who are encouraged to take initiative to explore and learn are likely to assimilate this concept for use later in life. They will be more likely to feel confident in initiating relationships, pursuing career objectives, and developing recreational interests. Preschoolers who are consistently restricted, punished, or treated harshly, are more likely to experience the emotion of guilt. They want to explore and experience, but they are not allowed to. Instead of learning initiative, they are likely to feel guilty about their tremendous desires to do so many things. In reaction, they may become "passive spectators" who follow the lead of others instead of initiating their own activities and ideas (Kaluger and Kaluger, 1984, p. 233).

Stage 4: Industry Versus Inferiority

School age children six to twelve years must address the crisis of industry versus inferiority. Children in this age group need to be productive and succeed in their activities. In addition to play, a major focus of their lives is school. Therefore, mastering academic skills and material is important. Those who do learn to be industrious by expending energy master activities. Comparison with peers becomes exceptionally important. Children who experience failure in school, or even in peer relations, may develop a sense of inferiority.

Stage 5: Identity Versus Role Confusion

Adolescence is a time when young people explore who they are and establish their identity. It is the transition period from childhood to adulthood when people examine the various roles they play (for example, child, sibling, student, catholic, native American, basketball star, or whatever), and integrate these roles into a perception of self, an identity. Some people are unable to integrate their many roles and have difficulty coping with conflicting roles; they are said to suffer from *role confusion*. Such persons are confused; their identity is uncertain and unclear.

Stage 6: Intimacy Versus Isolation

Young adulthood is characterized by a quest for intimacy and involves more than the establishment of a sexual relationship. Intimacy includes the ability to share with and give to another person without being afraid of sacrificing one's own identity. People who do not attain intimacy are likely to suffer isolation. These people have often been unable to resolve some of the crises of earlier psychosocial development. Various types of intimate relationships and how people experience them will be discussed in more detail in Chapter 7.

Stage 7: Generativity Versus Stagnation

Mature adulthood is characterized by the crisis of generativity versus stagnation. During this time of life, people become concerned with helping, producing for, or guiding the following generation. In a way, generativity is unselfish. It involves a genuine concern for the future beyond one's own life track. Generativity does not necessarily involve procreating one's own children. Rather, it concerns a drive to be creative and productive in a way that will aid people in the future. Adults who lack generativity become self-absorbed and inward. They tend to focus primarily on their own concerns and needs rather than on those of others. The result is stagnation, that is, a fixed, discouraging lack of progress and productivity.

Stage 8: Ego Integrity Versus Despair

The crisis of ego integrity versus despair characterizes old age. During this time of life, people tend to look back over their years and reflect on them. If they appreciate their life and are content with their accomplishments, they are said to have *ego integrity*, that is, the ultimate form of identity integration. Such people enjoy a sense of peace and accept the fact that life will soon be over. Others who have failed to cope successfully with past life crises and have many regrets experience despair.

Implications of Identity Formation in Adolescence

Achieving genital maturity and rapid body growth signals young people that they will soon be adults. They, therefore, begin to question their future roles as adults. The most important task of adolescence is to develop a sense of identity, a sense of "Who I Am." Making a career choice is an important part of this search for identity.

The primary danger of this period, according to Erikson, is identity confusion. This confusion can be expressed in a variety of ways. One way is to delay acting like a responsible adult. Another way is to commit oneself to poorly thought-out courses of action. Still another way is to regress into childishness to avoid assuming the responsibilities of adulthood. Erikson views the cliquishness of adolescence and its intolerance of differences as defenses against identity confusion. Falling in love is viewed as an attempt to define identity. Through self-disclosing intimate thoughts and feelings with another, the adolescent is articulating and seeking to better understand his/her identity. Through seeing the reactions of a loved one to one's intimate thoughts and feelings, the adolescent is testing out values and beliefs and is better able to clarify a sense of self.

Adolescents and young adults experiment with roles that represent the many possibilities for their future identity: students take certain courses to test out their future career interests. They also experiment with a variety of part-time jobs to test out occupational interests. They date and go steady to test out their relationships with the opposite sex. Dating also allows for different self-presentations with each new date. Adolescents and young adults may also experiment with drugs—alcohol, tobacco, marijuana, cocaine, and so on. Many are confused about their religious beliefs and seek in a variety of ways to develop a set of religious and moral beliefs that they can be comfortable with. They also tend to join, participate in, and then quit a variety of organizations. They experiment with a variety of interests and hobbies. As long as no laws are broken (and health is not seriously affected) in the process of experimenting, our culture gives teenagers and young adults the freedom to experiment in a variety of ways in order to develop a sense of identity.

Erikson (1959) uses the term *psychosocial moratorium* to describe a period of free experimentation before a final sense of identity is achieved. Generally, our society allows adolescents and young adults freedom from the daily expectations of role performance. Ideally, this moratorium allows young people the freedom to experiment with values, beliefs, and roles so that they can then develop a personal conception of how they can best fit into society so as to maximize their personal strengths and gain positive recognition from the community.

The crisis of identity versus role confusion is best resolved through integrating earlier identifications, present values, and future goals into a consistent self-concept. A sense of identity is achieved only after a period of questioning, reevaluation, and experimentation. Efforts to resolve questions of identity may take the young person down paths of emotional involvement, overzealous commitment, alienation, rebellion, or playful wandering.

Many adolescents are idealistic. They see the evils and negatives in our society and in the world. They cannot understand why injustice and imperfection exists. They yearn for a much better life for themselves and for others and have little understanding of the resources and hard work it takes for advancements. They often try to change the world and their efforts are genuine. If society can channel their energies constructively, their contributions can be meaningful. Unfortunately, some become disenchanted and apathetic after being continually frustrated with obstacles.

Importance of Achieving Identity

Adolescents and young adults struggle with developing a sense of who they are, what they want out of life, and what kind of people they want to be. Arriving at answers to such questions is among the most important tasks people face in life (Glasser, 1972). Without answers, a person will not be prepared to make such major decisions as which career to select; deciding whether, when, or whom to marry; deciding where to live; and deciding what to do with leisure time. Unfortunately, many people muddle through life and never arrive at well-thought-out answers to these questions. Those who do not arrive at answers are apt to be depressed, anxious, indecisive, and unfulfilled. All too often, their lives are carbon copies of Mortimer Milque's.

Mort wasn't very interested in school. He got by with Cs and Ds. He knew he wasn't as bright as others in his classes, but he was sharp enough to figure out that if he did the minimum on homework assignments, his teachers would pass him on to the next grade. He liked playing drums and was in his high school band. He hung around with students who occasionally skipped school, drank beer and smoked pot, and tried to avoid being hassled by parents and teachers.

At age 17 Mort took a job carrying out groceries in an A & P store. He used the money primarily for alcohol and drugs. After graduation he continued to live at home and worked at the A & P store. He played drums in a few rock bands, but that never paid very well as the band members neither had exceptional skills nor did they want to spend much time practicing.

Mort had begun dating at age 16. Because he was reserved and timid, the first two years he had a total of only four dates with three different girls. At age 21, he began dating Julie Mault, a fellow employee at the A & P who was recently divorced. She had an eight-month-old daughter. At age 23, Mort married Julie, partly because she had become pregnant. He and Julie soon had four people to support, as Julie gave birth to a baby girl.

They moved into an inexpensive two-bedroom apartment in a decaying area of the city near the A & P store. When bills started coming in, Mort was forced to stop going out with his buddies as he no longer could afford that. Feeling trapped and stifled, he frequently got into heated arguments with Julie—so violent at times that they occasionally slapped and shoved each other around. Mort's main entertainment gradually evolved into watching TV and drinking beer.

At age 30 he is on his way to becoming an alcoholic. Julie and he still frequently argue. He still struggles to pay the bills and tries to keep his '72 Chevelle running. Sadly, he still doesn't know what he wants out of life. He knows he really isn't happy with his present plight, but he is trapped by his lack of job skills. He is still working at A & P and has little hope of bettering himself financially. He is also ambivalent about wanting to parent the two children in his apartment. He is hopeful that when the children grow up and leave in 15 years, his life may improve. He knows that isn't much to look forward to.

The Formation of Identity

Identity development is a lifetime process. It begins during the early years and continues to change throughout one's lifetime. During the early years one's sense of identity is largely determined by the reactions of others. A long time ago, Cooley (1902) coined this labelling process as resulting in the "looking-glass self"—that is, persons develop their self-concept (who and what they are) in terms of how others relate to them. For example, if a neighborhood identifies a teenage male as being a trouble-maker or delinquent, neighbors are then apt to distrust him, accuse him of delinquent acts, and label his behavior as such. This labelling process, the youth begins to realize, also results in a type of prestige and status, at least from his peers. In the absence of objective ways to gauge whether he is in fact a delinquent, the youth will rely on the subjective evaluations of others. Thus, gradually, as the youth is identified as a delinquent he is apt to begin to perceive himself as such, and begin to enact the delinquent role.

Labels have a major impact on our lives. If a child is frequently called stupid by his/her parents, that child is apt to develop a low self-concept, anticipate failure in many areas (particularly academic) and thereby put forth little effort in school and in competitive interactions with others, and end up failing.

Since identity development is a lifetime process, positive changes are probable even for those who view themselves as failures. In identity formation, it is important to remember that what we want out of the future is more important than our past experience in determining what the future will be. The past is fixed and cannot be changed. It has brought us to where we are today. However, the present and the future can be changed. Because our past may have been painful and traumatic, it does not follow that our present and the future must be painful and traumatic. Since we are in control of our lives, we largely determine what our future will be.

A variety of approaches have been developed to help us determine who we are—transcendental meditation, biofeedback, gestalt therapy, sensitivity training, and encounter groups. (See Zastrow, 1985, for a description of these approaches.) For an approach that is particularly useful, see *How to Determine Who You Are.*

■ How to Determine Who You Are

Forming an identity essentially involves *thinking* about, and arriving at, answers to the following questions: (1) What do I want out of life? (2) What kind of person do I want to be? (3) Who am I?

The most important decisions you make in your life may well be in arriving at answers to these questions. In answering these questions, you are literally developing beliefs and attitudes about who you are and what you want out of life.

Answers to these questions are not easy to arrive at. They require considerable contemplation and trial and error. But if you are to lead a gratifying, fulfilling life, it is imperative to find answers to give direction to your life and to have a chance of living the kind of life you find meaningful. Without answers, you are apt to muddle through life by being a passive responder to situations that arise, rather than a continual achiever of your life's goals.

To determine who you are, it is very helpful to answer to the following more specific questions:

1. What do I find satisfying/meaningful/enjoyable? (Only after you identify what is meaningful and gratifying, will you be able to consciously seek involvement in activities that will make your life fulfilling, and avoid those activities that are meaningless or stifling.)

2. What is my moral code? (One possible code is to seek to fulfill your needs and to seek to do what you find enjoyable, doing so in a way that does not deprive others of the ability to fulfill their needs.)

3. What are my religious beliefs?

4. What kind of a career do I desire? (Ideally, you should seek a career in which you find the work stimulating and satisfying, that you are skilled at, and that earns you enough money to support your lifestyle.)

5. What are my sexual mores? (All of us should develop a consistent code that we are comfortable with and that helps us to meet our needs without exploiting others. There is no one right code—what works for one may not work for another, due to differences in lifestyles, life goals, and personal values.)

6. Do I desire to marry? (If yes, to what type of person and when? How consistent are your answers here with your other life goals?)

7. Do I desire to have children? (If yes, how many, when, and how consistent are your answers here with your other life goals?)

8. What area of the country/world do I desire to live in? (Variables to be considered are climate, geography, type of dwelling, rural or urban setting, closeness to relatives or friends, and characteristics of the neighborhood.)

9. What do I enjoy doing with my leisure time?

10. What kind of image do I want to project to others? (Your image will be composed of your dressing style and grooming habits, your emotions, personality, assertiveness, capacity to communicate, material possessions, moral code, physical features, and voice patterns. You need to assess your strengths and shortcomings honestly in this area, and seek to make improvements.)

11. What type of people do I enjoy being with, and why?

12. Do I desire to improve the quality of my life and that of others? (If yes, in what ways, and how do you hope to achieve these goals?)

13. What type of relationships do I desire to have with relatives, friends, neighbors, and with people I meet for the first time?

14. What are my thoughts about death and dying?

15. What do I hope to be doing 5 years from now, 10 years, 20 years?

To have a fairly well-developed sense of identity, you need to have answers to most, but not all, of these questions. Very few persons are able to arrive at rational, consistent answers to all the questions. Having answers to most of them will provide a reference for developing your views to the yet unanswered areas.

Honest, well-thought-out answers to these questions will go a long way toward defining who you are. Again, what you want out of life, along with your motivation to achieve these goals, will primarily determine your identity. The above questions are simple to state, but arriving at answers is a complicated, ongoing process. In addition, expect some changes in your life goals as time goes on. Environmental influences change (for example, changes in working conditions). Also, as personal growth occurs, changes are apt to occur in activities that you find enjoyable and also in your beliefs, attitudes, and values. Accept such changes, and if you have a fairly good idea of who you are, you will be prepared to make changes in your life goals so that you will be able to give continued direction to your life.

Your life is shaped by different events that are the results of decisions you make and decisions that are made for you. Without a sense of identity, you will not know what decisions are best for you, and your life will be unfulfilled. With a sense of identity, you will be able to direct your life toward goals you select and find personally meaningful.

Marcia's Categories of Identity

Marcia (1980) has done a substantial amount of research on the Eriksonian theory of psychosocial development. He identifies four major ways in which people cope with identity crises: (1) identity achievements, (2) foreclosure, (3) identity diffusion, and (4) moratorium. People may be classified into these categories on the basis of three primary criteria: first, whether the individual experiences a major crisis during identity development; second, whether the person expresses a commitment to some type of occupation; and, third, whether there is commitment to some set of values or beliefs.

Identity Achievement

To reach the stage of identity achievement, people undergo a period of intense decision-making. After expending much effort, they develop a personalized set of values and make their career decisions. Although there are positive and negative aspects to each identity status category, the attainment of identity achievement is usually thought of as the most beneficial.

Foreclosure

People who fall into this category are the only ones who never experience an identity crisis as such. They glide into adulthood without experiencing much turbulence or anxiety. Decisions concerning both career and values are made relatively early in life. Thus, these decisions are often based on the values and ideas of their parents rather than their own. For example, a woman might become a traditional housewife and mother, not because she makes a conscious choice, but rather because she assumes it's what she is expected to do. Likewise, a man might become a Democratic millwright in a shipbuilding factory simply because his father was also a Democratic millwright and felt that it provided a good living.

It's interesting that the term *foreclosure* is used to label this category. Foreclosure involves shutting someone out from involvement, as one would foreclose a mortgage and bar a person who mortgaged his/her property from reclaiming it. To foreclose one's identity implies shutting off various other opportunities to grow and change.

Identity Diffusion

People who experience identity diffusion suffer from a serious lack of decision and direction. Although they go through an identity crisis, they never resolve it. They are not able to make clear decisions concerning either their personal ideology or their career choice. These people tend to be characterized by low self-esteem and lack of resolution. For example, such a person might be a drifter who never stays more than a few months in any one place and defies any serious commitments.

Moratorium

The moratorium category includes people who experience intense anxiety during their identity crisis, yet have not made decisions regarding either personal values or a career choice. However, moratorium people experience a more continuous, intense struggle to resolve these issues. Instead of avoiding the decision-making issue, they address it almost constantly. They are characterized by strong, conflicting feelings about what they should believe and do. For example, a moratorium person might struggle intensively with a religious issue, such as whether or not there is a god. Moratorium people tend to have many critical, but as yet unresolved, issues.

One study of 33 college students (Orlofsky et al., 1973) supported the Eriksonian idea that there is a relationship between Stage 5 (identity versus role confusion) and Stage 6 (intimacy versus isolation). It appears that people need to confront and resolve their identity crises before they can form positive intimate relationships. Students who were found to have the best potential for developing close relationships were those falling in the identity achievement category. Shallow, stereotyped relationships tended to characterize people in both the foreclosure and identity diffusion categories. Moratorium people showed the widest variation in their ability to form relationships.

Moral Development

Adolescence is fraught with identity crises. Young adulthood is filled with avid quests for intimate relationships and other major commitments involving career and life goals. A parallel pursuit is the formulation of a personal set of moral values. Morality involves a set of principles regarding what is right and what is wrong. Many times these principles are not clearly defined in black or white, but involve various shades of grey. There is no one absolute answer. For example, is the death penalty right or wrong? Is it good or bad to have sexual intercourse before marriage?

Moral issues range from very major to minor day-to-day decisions. Although moral development can take place throughout life, it is especially critical during adolescence and young adulthood. These are the times when people gain the right to make independent decisions and choices. Often, the values developed during this stage remain operative for life.

Kohlberg's Theory of Moral Development

Lawrence Kohlberg (1963, 1968, 1969) has proposed a series of six stages through which people progress as they develop their moral framework. These six stages are clustered within three distinct levels.

■ Kohlberg's Six Stages of Moral Development

Level	Description
Level 1: Preconventional (Conventional Role Conformity)	Controls are external. Behavior is governed by receiving rewards or punishments.
Stage 1: Punishment and Obedience Orientation	Decisions concerning what is good or bad are made in order to avoid receiving punishment.
Stage 2: Naive Instrumental Hedonism	Rules are obeyed in order to receive rewards. Often favors are exchanged.
Level 2: Conventional (Role Conformity)	The opinions of others become important. Behavior is governed by conforming to social expectations.
Stage 3: "Good boy/girl morality"	Good behavior is considered to be what pleases others. There is a strong desire to please and gain the approval of others.
Stage 4: Authority-Maintaining Morality	The belief in law and order is strong. Behavior conforms to law and higher authority. Social order is important.
Level 3: Post-conventional (Self-Accepted Moral Principles)	Moral decisions are finally internally controlled. Morality involves higher level principles beyond law and even beyond self-interest.
Stage 5: Morality of Contract, of Individual Rights, and of Democratically Accepted Law	Laws are considered necessary. However, they are subject to rational thought and interpretation. Community welfare is important.
Stage 6: Morality of Individual Principles and Conscience	Behavior is based on internal ethical principles. Decisions are made according to what is right rather than what is written into law.

SOURCE: Adapted from Kohlberg (1968, 1981).

The first level, the preconventional or premoral level, is characterized by giving precedence to self-interest. People usually experience this level from ages four to ten. Moral decisions are based on external standards. Behavior is governed by whether a child will receive a reward or a punishment. The first stage in this level is based on avoiding punishment. Children do what they are told in order to avoid negative consequences. The second stage focuses on rewards instead of punishment. In other words, children do the "right" thing in order to receive a reward or compensation. Sometimes this involves an exchange of favors, a form of "I'll scratch your back if you'll scratch mine."

Level 2 of Kohlberg's theory is the conventional level, where moral thought is based on conforming to conventional roles. Frequently, this level occurs from ages 10 to 13. There is a strong desire to please others and to receive social approval. Although moral standards have begun to be internalized, they are still based on what others dictate, rather than on what is personally decided.

Within Level 2, Stage 3 focuses on gaining the approval of others. Good relationships become very important. Stage 4, "authority-maintaining morality," emphasizes the need to adhere to law. Higher authorities are generally respected. "Law and order" are considered necessary in order to maintain the social order.

Level 3, the postconventional level, concerns developing a moral conscience that goes beyond what others say. People contemplate laws and expectations and decide on their own what is right and what is wrong. They become autonomous, independent thinkers. Behavior is based on principles instead of laws. This level progresses beyond selfish concerns. The needs and well-being of others become very important in addition to one's own. At this level, true morality is achieved.

Within Level 3, Stage 5 involves adhering to socially accepted laws and principles. Law is considered good for the general public welfare. However, laws are subject to interpretation and change. Stage 6 is the ultimate attainment. During this stage, one becomes free of the thoughts and opinions expressed by others. Morality is completely internalized. Decisions are based on one's personal conscience, transcendent of meager laws and regulations. Examples of people who attain this level include Martin Luther King and Ghandhi.

Most people reach only the second level of moral functioning (Kaluger and Kaluger, 1984, p. 454). This morality is based on what others in society dictate. People respond to the pressures of the group, rather than to their own personally developed principles. Only 5 to 10 percent of all people ever reach stages 5 or 6 (Kaluger and Kaluger, 1984, p. 454).

Current Status of Kohlberg's Theory

Many questions have been raised concerning the absolute validity and general application of Kohlberg's theory (Yussen, 1977; Rubin and Trotten, 1977; Austin et al., 1977). These include potential cultural biases inherent in the categorization, limitations imposed by children's limited vocabulary and expression of their ideas, the lack of clear-cut divisions between one category and another, and the absolute order in which the levels occur.

There have been some discrepancies in findings, especially concerning the cross-cultural application of Kohlberg's theory. Kohlberg (1970) has found support for the application of his stages to the children in numerous countries including Mexico, New Zealand, Taiwan, Thailand, Kenya, and Canada. One review of the cross-cultural research supported the idea that Kohlberg's approach can apply to other countries (Edwards, 1977). This review established that people who were older in age tended to attain higher levels of moral functioning. Despite the fact that only the first four levels tended to characterize cultures that were non-Western in orientation, this still provides some support for a general application of the theory (Carroll and Rest, 1982). Questions must be raised, however, concerning the questionable application of the theory's final stage to other societies. Baumrind has criticized the theory because it does not really consider the moral development possible in other cultures. He believes that it suffers from "moral absolutism."

Another major criticism involves the idea that the distinction between moral attitudes and actual behavior is not clear (Power and Reimer, 1978). Major differences can be found between what people think is right and what they actually do. Many times the most difficult moral decisions must be made in crisis situations. If you find yourself in a burning building with a crowd of other people, how much effort will you expend to save others before yourself? What is the discrepancy between what you think is right and what you would really do in such a situation?

Kohlberg (1978) has conceded that there are valid criticisms of his theory. He has given credence to the idea that people learn and respond according to their moral context. The implication is that, depending on the specific situation and culture, morality, even true morality, may be interpreted differently. He has resolved the fact that Stage 6 may not generally be applied across all cultures, societies, and situations. Kohlberg has even dropped Stage 6 from his evaluation in view of extensive criticism, apparent cultural bias, and the infrequency with which research subjects seem to attain it even after long periods of time (Muson, 1979, p. 57).

Moral Development and Women

A major criticism of Kohlberg's theory is that virtually all of the research on which it is based used only men as subjects. As a result, women have fared poorly when measured on the traditional Kohlberg tasks, they often become fixated at Stage 3, unable to quite make the transition to Stage 4 (Papalia and Olds, 1981, p. 414–15). In other words, women tend to view morality in terms of personal situations instead of societal situations. Women often have trouble moving from a very personalized interpretation of morality to a focus on law and order. This bridge involves a generalization from the more personal aspects of what is right and wrong (how individual moral decisions affect one's own personal life) to morality within the larger, more impersonal society (how moral decisions, such as those instilled in law, affect virtually everyone). Kohlberg has been criticized because he has not taken into account the different orientation and life circumstances common to women.

Gilligan (1977) reasons that women's moral development is often based on their personal interest and commitment to the good of others close to them. Frequently, this involves giving up or sacrificing one's own well-being for others. Goodness and kindness are emphasized. Moral decisions often involve very specific personal situations. This contrasts with a common male focus on assertively making decisions and exercising moral judgments.

Gilligan targeted 29 women who were receiving pregnancy and abortion counseling. She postulated that pregnancy and birth was an area in women's lives where they could emphasize choice. Yet, it still was an intimate area to which they could relate. Gilligan interviewed the women concerning their pregnancies. She arrived at a sequence of levels which relate specifically to women. She found that women tend to view morality "in terms of selfishness and responsibility, as an obligation to exercise care and avoid hurt. People who care for each other are the most responsible, whereas those who hurt someone else are selfish and immoral. While men think more in terms of justice and fairness, women think more about specific people" (Papalia and Olds, 1981, p. 416).

Gilligan describes the following levels and transitions of moral development for women.

Level 1: Orientation to Personal Survival

This level focuses purely on the woman's self-interest. Her needs are salient. The needs and well-being of others are not really considered. At this level, a woman focuses first on personal survival. What is practical and best for her is most important.

Transition 1: Transition from Personal Selfishness to Responsibility

This first transition involves a movement in moral thought from consideration only of self to some consideration of the others involved. During this transition, a woman comes to acknowledge the fact that she is responsible not only for herself but also for others, including the unborn. In other words, she begins to acknowledge that her choice will impact others in addition to herself.

Level 2: Goodness as Self-Sacrifice

Level 2 involves putting aside one's own needs and wishes. Rather, the well-being of other people becomes important. The "good" thing to do is to sacrifice herself so that others may benefit. A woman at this level feels dependent on what other people think. Often a conflict occurs between taking responsibility for her own actions and feeling pressure from others to make her decisions.

Transition 2: From Goodness to Reality

During this transitional period, women begin to examine their situations more objectively. They draw away from their dependence on others to tell them what they should do. Instead, they begin to take into account the well-being of everyone concerned, including themselves. Some of the concern for personal survival apparent in Level 1 returns, but in a more objective manner.

Level 3: The Morality of Nonviolent Responsibility

Level 3 involves women thinking in terms of the repercussions of their decisions and actions. At this level, a woman's thinking has progressed beyond mere concern for what others will think about what she does. Rather, it involves accepting her responsibility for making her own judgments and decisions. She places herself on an equal plane with others, weighs the various consequences of her potential actions, and accepts the fact that she will be responsible for these consequences. The important principle operating here is that of minimizing hurt, both to herself and to others.

It is unlikely that this adolescent will continue wearing oversized sunglasses or even play drums forever. But it is during adolescence that teenagers experiment with roles and try to establish their own unique identity. They seek answers to such questions as "Who am I?" and "What do I want out of life?" (Gregg Theune)

All young adults examine and discover what is morally right and wrong for them. They usually extend that search further and question society's moral values, too. As they question, they reject and then selectively accept parts of their basic, learned values such as love of God and devotion to country. (Courtesy of Wisconsin State Journal)

This child sees the destructive results of her mother's alcoholism daily. Though miserably unhappy, she wants a normal family life and tries to maintain the family's status quo. She tries playing the "lost child," making herself all but disappear by being amazingly self-sufficient and requiring little attention. Acting uninvolved with her mother's problem, she never causes trouble. Children in alcoholic families frequently assume roles that will help them relieve their family's pain. (Courtesy of United Way of America)

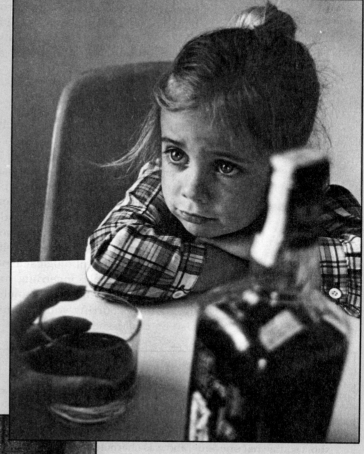

Feelings of helplessness and hopelessness, lack of a stable environment, and an overwhelming sense of internal and external pressure are some of the many causes of adolescent suicide. (Courtesy of United Way of America)

Gilligan's sequence of moral development provides a good example of how morality can be viewed from different perspectives. It is especially beneficial in emphasizing the different strengths potentially manifested by men and women. The emphasis on feelings, such as direct concern for others, is just as important as the ability to decisively make moral judgments.

Significant Issues and Life Events: Suicide and Drugs

Each phase of life tends to be characterized by issues which receive considerable attention and concern. Two command special attention as they relate to adolescence and youth. These are suicide and chemical substance use and abuse. Although these issues continue to elicit concern with respect to any age group, they have a special critical quality for those whose lives are just beginning. Young lives terminated at such an early age or thwarted by drug use represent tragic and regrettable losses of potential.

Each of these issues may be viewed either from a psychological or a social perspective. They will arbitrarily be addressed in this chapter which focuses on the psychological aspects of adolescence and young adulthood. However, material concerning some of the social aspects and implications of drug abuse will also be included (For example, the family dynamics frequently occurring within families of chemically dependent people will also be discussed).

■ Joany—A Victim of Suicide

Joany, age 15, was one of the "fries." People said that she used a lot of drugs and was wild. She did poorly in school, when she did manage to attend. Her appearance was striking. Her hair was cropped short somewhat unevenly, and was characterized by a different color of the rainbow every day, including purple, green, and hot pink. Short leather miniskirts, heavy chainlike jewelry, and dark, exaggerated makeup were also part of her style. She hung around with a group who looked and behaved much like herself. More studious, straight, upper middle-class, college-bound peers couldn't understand why she behaved that way. It was easy for them to point and snicker at her as she walked down the senior high school halls.

One day she came to school almost looking normal, noted one of her straight classmates, Karen. Karen had at times felt sorry for her in the past when people made fun of her. Today Joany was wearing an unobtrusive skirt and sweater. More noticeably, her hair was combed in an attractive manner. Today Joany finally looked like she fit in with her other classmates. Karen called out a compliment to her as she was walking down the hall, laughing with some of her other weird-looking friends. Joany turned, smiled, gave a hurried thanks, and returned to her active conversation with the others.

The next day the word spread like wildfire throughout the student population. Joany, it seemed, had hung herself in her parents' basement. The rumor was that she was terribly upset because her parents were getting a divorce. No one really knew why she had killed herself. People didn't understand the sense of hopelessness and desolation she felt. Nor did anyone know why she did not turn to friends or family or school counselors for help. There seemed to be so many unanswered questions.

All that remained of Joany several months later was an over-sized picture of her on the last page of the high school yearbook. It was labeled, "In Memoriam."

Suicide

Why do people decide to terminate their own lives? Is it because life is unbearable, painful, hopeless, or useless? Suicide can occur during almost any time of life. However, it might be considered especially critical in adolescence and youth. This is the time of life when people could enjoy being young and fresh and looking forward to life's wide variety of exciting experiences. Instead, many young people decide to take their own lives.

Incidence of Suicide

Suicide is one of the most critical health problems in the United States today. About 22,000 suicides occur every year, making suicide the ninth major cause among all deaths (Resnick, 1980). Jenson (1984, p. 12) cites the following frightening facts about suicide as it occurs within the adolescent age group alone:

- Suicide is the second leading cause of death in young people between the ages of 10 and 24. (Accidents rank first.)
- The rate of adolescent suicide began increasing in the mid-1950s and has tripled since 1960. (The rate for the rest of the population has remained constant during this same period.)
- Eighty-five percent of all adolescents think about suicide at some time. Fifty percent of these make some plan or seriously consider suicide as a means of solving their problems.

Causes of Adolescent Suicide

Freese (1979) discusses at least five variables that seem to be related to adolescent suicide.

Feelings of Helplessness and Hopelessness. As adolescents struggle to establish an identity and function independently of their parents, it's no wonder that many feel helpless. They must abide by the rules of their parents and schools. They suffer from peer pressure to conform to the norms of their age group. They are seeking acceptance by society and a place where they will fit in. At the same time, an adolescent must strive to develop a unique personality, a sense of self which is valuable for its own sake. At times such a struggle may indeed seem hopeless.

Loneliness. The feelings of isolation and loneliness also tend to characterize adolescents who attempt suicide. Kaluger and Kaluger (1984) cite one comprehensive study of adolescent suicide (Jacobs, 1971) which determined that these adolescents became increasingly detached and isolated from their relationships with others. Four variables were found to characterize the increasingly isolated lives of these young people (Kaluger and Kaluger, 1984, p. 420). One was a long duration of various problems in their lives. The second was a sharp increase before the suicide in the number of problems experienced. Third, these adolescents underwent a gradual diminishment of their ability to cope with stress which resulted in isolating themselves even more. Fourth, there seemed to be a chain reaction breakdown of one relationship after the other right before the suicide attempt.

Impulsivity. Impulsivity, or a sudden decision to act without giving much thought to the action, is yet another variable related to adolescent suicide. Confusion, isolation, and feelings of despair may contribute to an impulsive decision to end it all.

Lack of a Stable Environment. Many times, turbulence and disruption at home contribute to the profile of an adolescent suicide. Lack of a stable home environment contributes to the sense of loneliness and isolation. It also eats at the base of a person's social support. Adolescents who attempt suicide are more likely to be alienated from their parents, in addition to having experienced more problems in childhood which escalate in adolescence (Jacobs and Teicher, 1967).

Increased External and Internal Pressures. Many teenagers today express concern over the many pressures they have to bear. To some extent, these pressures might be related to current social and economic conditions. Many families are breaking up. Pressures to succeed are great. Many young people aren't even certain they will find a job when they get out of school. Peer pressures to conform and to be accepted socially are constantly operating. Suicidal adolescents may simply lose any coping powers they may have had and simply give up.

Rohn et al. (1977) studied 65 adolescents who tried to commit suicide. Subjects were selected from an inner-city suicide prevention program. Clientele were primarily black and came from backgrounds characterized by lower socioeconomic status. Three quarters of the subjects were females; one quarter were males. The youngest subject was 7, and the oldest 19; the median age was 16.

Findings revealed that these young people were troubled, isolated, and victimized by numerous pressures. About half of the subjects were labeled loners. Over half of them lived in single-parent homes. Approximately one quarter of them lived in homes without their own parents. Almost one third had at least one alcoholic parent. Additionally, school problems were common. Approximately three quarters of the subjects had academic difficulties. Over a third either did not attend school at all or were frequently truant.

■ Suicide Notes

The following are suicide notes written by people of various ages shortly before they successfully committed suicide.

Whomever—I wrote this sober, so it is what I planned, sober or drunk. I love you all and please don't feel guilty because it is what I planned drunk or sober. Life still happens whether it is today or tomorrow. But after 23 years I would think that I could have met a person that I would mean more than personal advantage. If only I meant something. People just don't seem to care. Is it that I give the impression that I don't care? I wish and want to know. I feel so unimportant to everyone. As though my presence does not mean anything to anybody. I wish so much to be something to someone. But I feel the harder I try the worse I do. Maybe I just have not run into the right person. I am still 6 feet underground. My mind just didn't want any of it obviously. Make sure _____ goes to mom. No matter what I do, in my life, I still am going to die. By someone else's hands OR MY OWN.

(Female, age 23,
of a gunshot wound).

I can't put up with this shit. I'm sorry I have to do this, but I have nothing left.

P.S. Closed casket please.
Give my guns to _____.

(Male, age 25, of a gunshot wound.)

Mom and Dad

don't feel bad—I have problems—don't feel the blame for this on you _____

(Male, age 18, of a gunshot wound.)

Please forgive me for leaving you. I love you very much, but could not cope with my health problems plus financial worries etc. Try to understand and pray for me.

I wish you all the best and that you will be able to find the happiness in life I could not.

Love and Kisses

"I can't take the abuse, the hurt, the rejection, the isolation, the loneliness. I can't deal with all of it. I can't try anymore. The tears are endless. I've fallen into a bottomless pit of despair. I know eternal pain and tears. . . ."

"No one knows I'm alive or seems to care if I die. I'm a terrible, worthless person and it would be better if I'd never been born. Tabby was my only friend in the world, and now she's dead. There's no reason for me to live anymore. . . ."

Mom and Dad, I hate you!

Love Tommy

*These notes were recorded in the manual, "A Cry for Help: Teen Suicide," prepared and presented by Tom Skinner, Edison Junior High School, Janesville, Wisconsin. Reprinted by permission of the Rock County Coroner's Office, Beloit, Wisconsin.

Suicidal Symptoms

Patterson et al. (1983) cites various risk factors that are related to a person's actual potential of carrying through with a suicide. They propose a mechanism for evaluating suicide potential which is called the "SAD PERSONS" scale (see inset). Each letter in the acronym corresponds to one of the high risk factors.

■ The SAD PERSONS Scale

S (Sex)

A (Age)

D (Depression)

P (Previous Attempt)

E (Ethanol Abuse)

R (Rational Thinking Loss)

S (Social Supports Lacking)

O (Organized Plan)

N (No Spouse)

S (Sickness)

*The SAD PERSONS scale was developed by W. M. Patterson, H. H. Dohn, J. Bird, and G. A. Patterson and is reported in the "Evaluation of Suicidal Patients: The SAD PERSONS Scale," *Psychosomatics*, April 1983, Vol. 24, No. 4, pp. 343-49. Used by permission of the Academy of Psychosomatic Medicine.

It should be emphasized that any of the many available guidelines to assess suicide potential are just that—guidelines. Any person who actually threatens to commit suicide should be believed. The very fact that they are talking about it means that they are thinking about actually doing it. This means that there is some chance that they may kill themselves. However, the following variables are useful as guidelines for determining risk, i.e., how high is the probability that they actually will attempt and succeed at suicide.

Sex

Among adolescents, females are nine times more likely to try to kill themselves than males; however, males are seven times more likely to succeed in their attempts (Jensen, 1984, p. 12). Adolescents of either gender may have serious suicide potential. However, greater danger exists if the person threatening suicide is a male. One reason for this is that males are more likely to choose a more deadly means of committing suicide.

Age

Although a person of almost any age may attempt and succeed at suicide, the risks are greater for some age groups than for others. Statistics indicate that people who are age 19 or younger, or age 45 or older are in the high-risk groups (Patterson et al., 1983).

Depression

Depression contributes to a person's potential to commit suicide. *Depression* is "a psychoneurotic or psychotic disorder marked by sadness, inactivity, difficulty in thinking and concentration, and feelings of dejection" (Webster's New Collegiate Dictionary, 1977). It doesn't involve simply feeling bad. Rather, it involves a collection of characteristics, feelings, and behaviors which tend to occur in conjunction with each other. People experiencing this collection are referred to as being depressed. These characteristics and feelings include a general feeling of being unhappy or blue, a low level of physical energy, problems in relating to and interacting with others, guilt feelings, feelings of being stressed and burdoned, and various physical problems such as sleep disturbances, headaches, and loss of appetite (Lewinsohn et al., 1978).

Previous Attempts

People who have tried to kill themselves before are more likely to succeed than people who are trying to commit suicide for the first time. One quarter to one half of all the people who succeed in killing themselves have tried before (Patel, 1974).

Ethanol Abuse

Alcoholism is related to suicide. A person who is an alcoholic is much more likely to commit suicide than one who is not (Miles, 1977).

Rational Thinking Loss

People who suffer from mental or emotional disorders, such as depression or psychosis, are more likely to kill themselves. Hallucinations, delusions, extreme confusion or anxiety all contribute to an individual's risk factor. If a person is not thinking realistically and objectively, emotions and impulsivity are more likely to take over, and a person is more likely to act in a desperate manner.

Social Supports Lacking

Loneliness and isolation have already been discussed as primary elements contributing to suicide. People who feel no one cares about them may begin to feel useless and hopeless. Suicide potential may be especially high in cases where a loved one has recently died or deserted the individual who's threatening suicide.

Organized Plan

The more specific and organized an individual's plan regarding when and how the suicide will be undertaken, the greater the risk. Additionally, the more dangerous the method, the greater the risk. A plan involving placing the loaded rifle you have hidden in the basement to your head tomorrow evening at 7:00 p.m. is more lethal than a plan of somehow getting some drugs and overdosing sometime. There are several questions which might be asked when evaluating this risk factor: How much detail is involved in the plan? Has the individual put a lot of thought into developing the specific details regarding how the suicide is to occur? Has the plan been thought over before? How dangerous is the chosen method? Is the method or weapon readily available to the individual? Has the specific time been chosen for when the suicide is to take place?

No Spouse

People who have no spouse have a greater likelihood of committing suicide than people who are married (Resnick, 1980). People who are single, divorced, widowed, or separated are included in this high-risk category. Members of this group have a greater chance of being lonely and isolated.

Sickness

Finally, people who are ill are more likely to commit suicide (Farberow and Litman, 1975). This is especially true for those who have long-term illnesses which place substantial limitations on their lives. Perhaps in some of these instances, their inability to cope with the additional stress of sickness and pain eats away at their overall coping ability; they then simply give up.

Other Symptoms

There are other characteristics which operate as warning signals for suicide. For example, drug abuse other than alcohol can affect suicide potential (Resnick, 1980).

Rapid changes in mood, behavior, or general attitude are other indicators that a person is in danger of committing suicide. A potentially suicidal person may be one who has suddenly become severely depressed and withdrawn. On the other hand, a person who has been depressed for a long period of time and suddenly becomes strikingly cheerful may also be in danger. Sometimes in the latter instance, the individual has already made up his/her mind to commit suicide. In those instances, the cheerfulness may stem from relief that the desperate decision has finally been made.

Suddenly giving away personal possessions which are especially important or meaningful is another warning signal of suicide potential. It is as if once the decision has been made to commit suicide, giving things away to selected others is a way of finalizing the decision. Perhaps it's a way of tying up loose ends, or of making certain that the final details are taken care of.

How to Use the SAD PERSONS Scale

Patterson et al (1983, p. 348) suggest a framework for using the SAD PERSONS scale when evaluating suicide potential. One point is simply assigned to each condition which applies to the suicidal person. For example, if a person was depressed, he or she would automatically receive a score of 1. Depression in addition to alcoholism would result in a score of 2, and so on. Although the SAD PERSONS scale was developed specifically to teach medical students how to evaluate suicidal potential, social workers might use it in a similar manner. The following decision-making guidelines are recommended:

Total points	Proposed clinical actions
0 to 2	Send home with follow-up
3 to 4	Close follow-up; Consider hospitalization
5 to 6	Strongly consider hospitalization, depending on confidence in the follow-up arrangement
7 to 10	Hospitalize or commit

Zero to two points might indicate a mild potential which still merits some follow-up and attention. On the other hand, a score of seven to ten indicates severe suicide potential. These cases would merit immediate attention and action. Hospitalization or commitment are among available options. Scores ranging from three to six represent a range of serious suicide potential. Although people with these scores need help and attention, the immediacy and intensity of that attention may vary. In each case, professional discretion would be involved.

Guidelines for Helping Suicidal People

Two levels of intervention are possible for dealing with a potentially suicidal person. The first involves addressing the immediate crisis. The person threatening to commit suicide needs immediate help and support literally to keep him or her alive. The second level concerns addressing the other issues which worked to escalate his or her stress. This second level of intervention might involve longer-term treatment to address other issues of longer duration which were not necessarily directly related to the suicide crisis.

For example, take a 15-year-old male who is deeply troubled over the serious problems his parents are currently experiencing in their marriage. This preoccupation, in addition to his normally shy personality, has alienated him from virtually any social contacts with his peers. The result is serious consideration regarding whether it is all worth it or not. The first priority is to prevent the suicide. However, this young man also needs to address and resolve the problems which caused the stress in the first place, namely, his parents' conflicts and his lack of friends. Longer-term counseling or treatment might be necessary.

Reactions to a Suicide Threat

You might get a phone call in the middle of the night from an old friend you haven't heard from in a while who says she cannot stand living anymore.

Or, a client might call you on late Friday afternoon and say that he is planning to shoot himself. Kiev (1980, p. 307) makes several specific suggestions for how to treat the potentially suicidal person which include the following:

Remain calm. Don't allow the emotional distress being experienced by the other person to spread and contaminate your own judgment. The individual needs help in becoming more rational and objective. The person does not need someone else who is drawn into the emotional crisis.

Be supportive. It's helpful to talk about positive qualities the person has. For example, the individual might be pleasant, unselfish, hard working, conscientious, bright, attractive, and so on. People who are feeling suicidal are most likely focusing primarily on the "bad things" they perceive about themselves and their life situations. They forget their positive characteristics. One can also focus on the positive coping skills which one has used in the past.

Focus on the problem. When working with a potential suicide the person needs help in dealing with the immediate crisis. The top priority is to prevent the suicide from occurring. A person who is overwhelmed with problems and stress may be easily sidetracked. In these instances, you can be most helpful by remaining objective and helping the person evaluate his or her situation as objectively as possible.

Identify the loss. Help the person clearly identify what is causing the excessive stress. The problem needs to be recognized before it can be examined. The individual may be viewing an event way out of perspective. For example, a 16-year-old girl was crushed after her steady boyfriend of 18 months dropped her. She felt that life was no longer worth living. In this instance, the loss of her boyfriend overshadowed all of the other things in her life—her family, her friends, her membership in the National Honor Society, and her favorite hobby of jogging. She needed help focusing on exactly what her loss had been, namely the loss of her boyfriend. To her, it felt like she had lost her whole life which was a gross distortion of reality.

Latch on to the will to live. The very fact that the suicidal person came to talk to you indicates that he or she is reaching out. Especially with adolescents, there is almost always ambivalence about wanting to die. On the one hand, they want to die; but on the other hand, they want to live. It is helpful to identify and concentrate on that part of them that clutches at life.

Don't get into a debate. Avoid arguing with the suicidal person about the philosophical values of life versus death. Don't use cliches like, "There's so much that life has to offer you," or, "Your life is just beginning." This type of approach only makes people feel like you're operating on a different wavelength, and really don't understand how they feel. People who threaten suicide have real suicidal feelings. They're not likely to be exaggerating them or making them up. What they need is objective, empathic support.

Suggest feasible options. Suicidal people may be in a rut of negative, depressing, suicidal thoughts. Talking with them about their other options may be very helpful. They may be blind to anything but their immediate crisis.

Sometimes people in this suicidal rut have hit their lowest emotional point. Their perspective is such that they feel that life has ALWAYS been as bad as this, and that it always will be as bad as this (see Figure 6.1). In reality, the old adage, "Life has its ups and downs," is true. A suicidal person

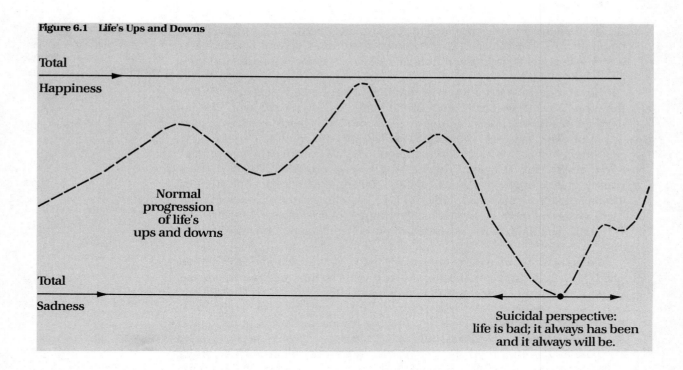

Figure 6.1   Life's Ups and Downs

Total

Happiness

Normal
progression
of life's
ups and downs

Total

Sadness

Suicidal perspective:
life is bad; it always has been
and it always will be.

has probably been "up" before and probably will be "up" again. Many times this "sense of history" can be pointed out and used beneficially.

Don't give direct advice. One of the "bottom line" dictums of social work is never, never to give advice. Each individual has the right and responsibility to make his or her own decisions. A good social worker helps clients clarify their own feelings, gain an objective perspective, and make their own decisions. The client, not you, will experience the consequences of whatever decision is made.

Referrals

One of the most useful and concrete things that can be done for suicidal people is to help them get the help they need. Because suicidal people tend to be isolated, this help often involves referring them to the various resources—both personal and professional—which are available. Personal sources of help may involve family or friends. There may be a minister or even a physician whom the individual trusts and could turn to. Referrals to police or hospital emergency rooms can be helpful when an emergency situation arises. Finally, professionals in mental health are available to provide long-term help to people in need.

Chemical Substance Use and Abuse

There was going to be a big party at Evelyn's on Saturday night. Georgia, a high school junior, couldn't wait to go. Everybody was going to be there. Evelyn said she had some great hash. Georgia didn't like to smoke all that much. However, people would think that there was something wrong with her if she didn't and that was the last thing she wanted.

Marty, age 15, liked to drink a couple of six packs on the weekend. After all, his father did, and Marty was almost an adult.

Virgil, age 18, liked to get high because then he could forget about all his problems. He wouldn't have to think about his alcoholic mother and all the problems she and his father were having. He wouldn't have to worry about all the pressures he had in school. He wouldn't even have to think about how his girlfriend recently dumped him. He just couldn't wait until the next chance he had to get high.

Drugs have become part of our daily lives. We use drugs to relax, to increase our pleasure, to feel less inhibited, to get rid of unwanted emotions, to keep awake, and to fall asleep. There are practically no Americans that do not use drugs of one kind or another. People have coffee in the morning, soda (which has caffeine) during the day, cocktails before dinner, and aspirin to relieve pain. Coleman and Cressey (1984, p. 363) summarize the extent of drug use:

> Well over 90 percent of all adults have tried alcohol, and about two thirds of the adult population are regular users. A third of all Americans regularly smoke tobacco, and about 12 percent smoke marijuana. Moreover, there has been a steady increase in drug use in the last decade. In 1972, for example, 24 percent of youths age 12 to 17 regularly used alcohol; in 1976 that figure was up to 32 percent, and by 1979 it was 37 percent. Similar increases occurred in the use of marijuana, cocaine, tranquilizers, and most other drugs, though not for tobacco or heroin.

A drug is any habit-forming substance that directly affects the brain and the nervous system; it is a chemical substance that affects moods, perceptions, bodily functions, or consciousness and that has the potential for misuse as it may be harmful to the user.

Teenage drug use has received tremendous attention in recent years. A drug may be defined as "anything that people put on their skin or swallow that can have an effect on how their mind or body works" (Finn and O'Gorman, 1981, p. 237). Drugs include alcohol, marijuana, cocaine, amphetamines, Quaaludes, PCP, tranquilizers, barbiturates, hallucinogens, narcotics, amyl nitrate, and tobacco.

Drug abuse is "the regular or excessive use of a drug when, as defined by a group, the consequences endanger relationships with other people, are detrimental to a person's health, or jeopardize society itself" (Zastrow, 1984, p. 114). All of the drugs mentioned earlier are types of chemicals. Another way of referring to drug abuse is *chemical substance abuse*. Drug or chemical substance intake becomes abusive when an individual's mind and/or body are affected in negative or harmful ways.

Chemical substance abuse is of special concern with respect to young people. Mind-altering drugs can prevent them from participating in many of the normal developmental activities which help them to mature into competent adults. For example, being high can isolate adolescents from interaction with peers and keep them floating in their own thoughts. Hangovers can interfere with the ability to think and do school work. Placing heavy emphasis on drug use can divert time and energy away from sports, recreational, academic, and social activities. Our definition identifies two key factors which determine what is considered to be drug abuse in a society—the first is the actual effects of the drug, and the second is a group's perception of the effects.

Society's perceptions of the ill effects of a drug are often inconsistent with the actual effects. In our society, moderate use of alcohol and tobacco is generally accepted; yet, moderate use can cause serious health problems. In the 1930s, our society was convinced that marijuana was a dangerous drug; it was said to cause crime, insanity, and a host of other ills. Now, available evidence suggests it may be less dangerous than alcohol (Brown, 1977).

Surprisingly, legal drugs (such as alcohol and tobacco) cause more harm in our society, than illegal drugs. Prescription drugs are also frequently abused. Among the most abused prescription drugs are sedatives, tranquilizers, painkillers, and stimulants. Americans are obsessed with taking pills. Many prescribed drugs have the potential to be psychologically and physiologically addicting. Drug companies spend millions in advertising to convince customers that they are too tense, too irritable, take too long to fall asleep, that they should lose weight, and so on. These companies then assert their medications will relieve these problems. Unfortunately, many customers accept this easy symptom-relief approach and end up dependent on pills, rather than making the necessary changes in their lives to be healthy. Such changes include exercise, stress management techniques, positive thinking, and dieting.

Prevalence of Chemical Substance Use

Alcohol is by far the most widely used chemical substance by young people. Yancy et al. (1972) surveyed over 7,000 high school students and found that 85 percent had used alcohol at one time or another. The second most popular drug was marijuana; 27 percent of those surveyed had used this drug at some time during their lives. Other drugs appear to be much less common. LSD had been used by only 8.6 percent of the sample, and heroin by less than 3 percent.

The chance of having tried alcohol and other drugs appears to increase as young people advance through the teens. This is logical, as older teens have had more time to accumulate more experiences in general. For example, one study indicates that among high school seniors, 93 percent stated that they had drunk something alcoholic in their lives (Johnston et al., 1979). Of these, 72 percent stated that they had used alcohol within the previous month. Only 7 percent stated that they drank alcohol on a daily basis. This same study found that only 1 percent of the sample used any other drugs, excluding marijuana, on a daily basis. Another recent focusing on college age students found that over two thirds of the sample had smoked marijuana (Smart and Blair, 1979).

Drug use by young people resembles the drug use patterns characterizing adults (Lennard, 1971). Alcohol usage in particular follows closely the patterns established by parents (Finn and O'Gorman, 1971, p. 34). Peer pressure appears only to be a secondary influence concerning how people drink. Periods of exceptionally heavy drinking may occur during high school, college, or military service. However, after these periods have passed, people still tend to revert to drinking practices very similar to those of their parents (Finn and O'Gorman, 1981, p. 34).

In terms of preference, beer is most popular, followed by wine, and finally by hard liquor (Rachal et al., 1975). Finn and O'Gorman (1981) cite several other trends. First, teens, on the average, are beginning to drink at a younger age. Young people may start drinking as early as age 12 or 13. Second, whereas the Northeast and the Far West used to be areas characterized by more, heavier, and earlier teen drinking, the Midwest and South are now catching up. Third, although teen drinking apparently has not increased much since its peak in 1970, the frequency of drinking to intoxication has. In other words, it appears that more adolescents are drinking heavily than a decade and a half ago. Fourth, perhaps the most striking trend in teen drinking is the increased participation by females. Unlike in the past, almost as many girls now drink as boys. However, girls still tend to drink less than boys.

Although most teenagers drink alcohol, only a very small percentage of them are alcoholics. Only about 2 percent of all teens are alcholics or alcohol abusers (Craig, 1983, p. 379). These two percent tend to have certain characteristics (Rachal et al., 1975). They are usually males who are at least age 15. Poor academic performance is common. They frequently come from homes where their parents drink. Other characteristics include association with peers who also drink, a tendency to use other drugs in addition to alcohol, a poor sense of identity, and the view that alcohol use implies maturity and adulthood (Craig, 1983, p. 379).

Finn and O'Gorman (1981) note the distinction between the use and abuse of alcohol. They indicate that experimentation is a normal part of adolescence. Seeking out new experiences helps young people learn about themselves and develop a new identity. The implication is that some experimentation with alcohol, especially in view of its generally wide social acceptance, is normal and to be expected. They stress that it is the abuse of alcohol which presents the real problem.

One other drug, tobacco, merits our attention. Significantly fewer teens are smoking cigarettes now than a decade ago. Whereas in 1972, approximately one third of all high school students smoked (Consumers Union, 1972), in 1981, the number dropped to 20.3 percent (National Institute on Drug Abuse, 1982). Additionally, those who do smoke seem to smoke less. Perhaps the downward trend in the use of this drug is related to the increased publicity about its hazards.

Specific Drugs—What They Are and Do

Knowing what a specific drug is and what it does to a person is important both in treatment and in considering its use and abuse (Zastrow and Bowker, 1984, pp. 119–34).

Alcohol

Alcohol, a depressant, is a colorless liquid that is in beer, wine, brandy, whiskey, vodka, rum, and other intoxicating beverages. The average American drinker consumes the equivalent of nearly 3 gallons of pure alcohol annually. The average drinker consumes 2.24 gallons of wine, 2.58 gallons of whiskey, and 28.08 gallons of beer each year (Keller and Gurioli, 1976, pp. 3–5). The vast majority of both teenagers and adults in our society drink.

The type of alcohol found in beverages is ethyl alcohol. (It also is called grain alcohol, as most of it is made from fermenting grain.) Many drinkers believe alcohol is a stimulant, as it relaxes tensions, lessens sexual and aggressive inhibitions, and seems to facilitate interpersonal relationships. However, it acts as a depressant to the central nervous system, as it reduces functional activity of this system. Its chemical composition and effects are very similar to ether (an anesthetic used in medicine to induce unconsciousness).

Alcohol slows down mental activity, reasoning ability, speech ability, and muscle reactions. It distorts perceptions, slurs speech, lessens coordination, and slows down memory functioning and respiration. In increasing quantities, it leads to stupor, sleep, coma, and finally death. A hangover (the aftereffects of too much alcohol) includes having a headache, thirst, muscle aches, stomach discomfort, and nausea. Alcohol can seriously affect how one drives an automobile. Behavior resulting from excessive alcohol intake can also negatively interfere in family, friend, and work relationships.

The effects of alcohol vary with the percentage of alcohol in the bloodstream as it passes through the brain. Generally, the effects are observable when the concentration of alcohol in the blood reaches one tenth of a percent. Five drinks (with each drink being 1 ounce of 86 proof alcohol, or 12 ounces of beer, or 3 ounces of wine) in two hours for a 120-pound person will result in a blood alcohol concentration of one tenth of a percent.

Alcohol also has long-term effects on a person's health. Alcoholics have a life expectancy that is 10 to 12 years less than nonalcoholics (Bliss, 1978, p. 300). There are several reasons why the life span is shorter. One is that alcohol over an extended period of time gradually destroys liver cells and replaces the cells with scar tissue. When the scar tissue is extensive, a medical condition occurs called *cirrhosis*. This is the sixth most frequent cause of death in America, numbering about 33,000 deaths per year (Metropolitan Life Insurance Company, 1977, pp. 7–11). Also, although it has no healthy food value, alcohol contains a high number of calories. As a result, heavy drinkers have a reduced appetite for nutritious food and thus frequently suffer from vitamin deficiencies and are more susceptible to infectious diseases. Heavy drinking also causes kidney problems, contributes to a variety of heart ailments, is a factor in diabetes, and also appears to contribute to cancer. In addition, heavy drinking is associated with over 10,000 suicides annually (Noble, pp. 10–12).

Interestingly, for some yet unknown reason, the life expectancy age for light-to-moderate drinkers exceeds that for nondrinkers (Noble, 1978, p. 13). Perhaps an occasional drink helps people to relax and thereby reduces the likelihood of life-threatening psychosomatic illnesses developing.

Combining alcohol with other drugs can have disastrous, and sometimes fatal, effects. Two drugs taken together may have a *synergistic interaction*—that is, they interact to produce an effect much greater than either would cause alone. For example, sedatives such as barbiturates (often found in sleeping pills) or Quaaludes taken together with alcohol can so depress the central nervous system that a coma or even death may result.

Other drugs tend to have an antagonistic response to alcohol—one drug negates the effects of the other. Many doctors now caution patients not to drink while taking certain perscribed drugs, as the alcohol will reduce, and even totally negate, the beneficial effects of these drugs.

Whether drugs will interact synergistically or antagonistically depends on a wide range of factors: the properties of the drugs, the amounts taken, the amount of sleep of the user, the kind and amount of food that has been eaten, and the user's overall health and tolerance. The interactive effects may be minimal one day and extensive the next.

When used by pregnant women, alcohol may gravely affect the unborn child by causing mental retardation, deformities, stunting of growth, and other abnormalities. This effect has been named the *fetal alcohol syndrome*.

Withdrawal from alcohol, once the body is physically addicted, may lead to the DTs (delirium tremens) and other unpleasant reactions. The DTs include rapid heartbeat, uncontrollable trembling, severe nausea, and profuse sweating.

Barbiturates

Barbiturates, another type of depressant, are derived from barbituric acid. First synthesized in the early 1900s, there are now over 2,500 different barbiturates. They are commonly used to relieve insomnia and anxiety. They are also used to treat epilepsy and high blood pressure and to relax patients before or after surgery. The purchase and use of barbiturates are illegal without a physician's prescription.

Barbiturates are used widely. Richard Blum et al. (1969, p. 242), note: "Enough barbiturates . . . are manufactured every year in the United States to provide thirty or forty doses for every man, woman, and child."

Taken in sufficient amounts, barbiturates cause effects similar to alcohol; they relax users and remove inhibitions. Typical symptoms include drowsiness and reduced coordination. Some users become hyperactive and aggressive. Prolonged high use can cause physical dependence, with withdrawal symptoms similar to those of heroin addiction. Withdrawal is accompanied by body tremors, cramps, anxiety, fever, nausea, profuse sweating, and hallucinations. Many authorities believe barbiturate addiction is more dangerous than heroin addiction, and it is considered to be more resistant to treatment than heroin addiction. Abrupt withdrawal (*cold turkey*, the sudden and complete halting of drug use) can cause fatal convulsions. One forensic pathologist noted, "Show me someone who goes cold turkey on a bad barbiturate habit, and I'll show you a corpse" (Dunning and Chang, 1977, p. 177).

Barbiturate overdose may cause convulsions, coma, poisoning, and sometimes death. Barbiturates are particularly dangerous when taken with alcohol, as alcohol acts synergistically to magnify the potency of the barbiturates. Accidental deaths due to excessive doses are frequent. Perhaps the user becomes groggy, forgets how much has been taken, and takes more until an overdose level has been reached. Barbiturates are also the number one drug used for suicide. A number of famous people have fatally overdosed on barbiturates.

Barbiturates are generally taken orally, although some users also inject them intravenously. Use of barbiturates, may also lead to traffic fatalities.

Tranquilizers

Yet another depressant is the group of drugs classified as tranquilizers. Common brand names are Equanil, Librium, Miltown, Serax, Tranxene, and Valium. Tranquilizers reduce anxiety, relax muscles, and are sedatives. Users have moderate potential of becoming physically and psychologically dependent. The drugs are usually taken orally, and the effects last four to eight hours. Side effects include slurred speech, disorientation, and behavior resembling being intoxicated. Overdoses are possible, with the effects including cold and clammy skin, shallow respiration, dilated pupils, weak and rapid pulse, coma, and possibly death. Withdrawal symptoms are similar to those from alcohol and barbiturates and include anxiety, tremors, convulsions, delirium, and possibly death. The extent of use of tranquilizers is indicated by nearly 100 million prescriptions being written each year (National Institute on Drug Abuse, 1977, p. 63).

Quaalude

Methaqualone (better known by its patent name *Quaalude*) has effects similar to barbiturates and alcohol, although it is chemically different. It has a reputation as a love drug, as users believe it makes them more eager for sex and enhances sexual pleasure. These effects are probably due to the fact that it lessens inhibitions (similar to alcohol and barbiturates). Quaaludes also reduce anxiety and give a feeling of euphoria.

Users can become both physically and psychologically dependent on Quaaludes. Overdose can result in convulsions, coma, delirium, and even death—most deaths occur when the drug is taken together with alcohol, which vastly magnifies the drug's effects. Withdrawal symptoms are severe and unpleasant. Abuse of the drug may also cause hangovers, fatigue, liver damage, and temporary paralysis of the limbs.

PCP

Phencyclindine (better known as PCP) was developed in the 1950s as an anesthetic. This medical use was soon terminated because patients displayed symptoms of severe emotional disturbance after receiving the drug. PCP is used legally today to tranquilize elephants and monkeys, as they apparently do not have the adverse side effects.

PCP is primarily used by young people who are often unaware of its hazards. It is usually smoked, often after being sprinkled on a marijuana joint. It may also be sniffed, swallowed, or injected.

PCP is a dangerous drug, in that it distorts the senses, disrupts balance, and leads to an inability to think clearly. Larger amounts of PCP may cause a person to become paranoid, lead to aggressive behavior, and may cause the user to display temporary symptoms of severe emotional disturbance. Continued use can lead to the development of a prolonged emotional disturbance. Overdose can result in coma or even death. Research has as yet not concluded whether PCP induces physical and/or psychological dependence. The drug has a potential to be used (and abused) extensively, as it is relatively easy to prepare in a home laboratory, with the ingredients and recipes being widely available.

Amphetamines

Another type of stimulant, *amphetamines*, are often called uppers because of their stimulating effect. When prescribed by a physician, they are legal. Some truck drivers have obtained prescriptions in order to stay awake and more alert while making a long haul. Dieters have received prescriptions to help them lose weight, and they often find the pills tend to give them more self-confidence and buoyance. Others who have used amphetamines to increase alertness and performance for relatively short periods of time include college students, athletes, astronauts, and executives. Additional nicknames for this drug are speed, ups, pep pills, black beauties, and bennies.

Amphetamines are synthetic drugs. They are similar to adrenalin, a hormone from the adrenal gland that stimulates the central nervous system. The better known amphetamines include dexedrine, benzedrine, and methedrine. Physical reactions to amphetamines are extensive: consumption of fat stored in body tissues is accelerated, heartbeat is increased, respiratory processes are stimulated, appetite is reduced, and insomnia is common. Users feel euphoric, stronger, and have an increased capacity to concentrate and to express themselves verbally.

Amphetamines are usually taken orally in tablet, powder, or capsule form. They can also be sniffed or injected. *Mainlining* (injecting the drug in a vein) produces the most powerful effects and can also cause the greatest harm. An overdose may cause a coma, with possible brain damage, and, in rare cases, death. Speeders may also develop hepatitis, abscesses, hallucinations, delusions, and severe emotional disturbances. Another danger is that, when sold on the street, the substance may contain impurities which are health hazards.

An amphetamine high is often followed by mental depression and fatigue. Continued amphetamine use leads to psychological dependence. It is unclear whether amphetamines are physically addictive, as the withdrawal symptoms are uncharacteristic of withdrawal from other drugs. Amphetamine withdrawal symptoms include sleep disturbances, apathy, decreased activity, and depression. Some authorities believe such withdrawal symptoms indicate that amphetamines may be physically addicting (National Clearinghouse for Drug Abuse Information, 1974, pp. 9–10).

One of the legal uses of certain amphetamines is in the treatment of *hyperactivity* in children. Hyperactivity (also called hyperkinesis) is characterized by a short attention span, extensive motor activity, restlessness, and mood shifts. Little is known about the causes of this condition. As children become older, even without treatment, the symptoms tend to disappear. Interestingly, some amphetamines (Ritalin is a popular one) have a calming and soothing effect upon hyperactive children—the exact opposite effect occurs when Ritalin is taken by adults. It should be noted that, in the past, treating uncontrollable children with amphetamines was frequently abused. Fort and Cory (1975, p. 41) note:

> Many of the children for whom Ritalin is prescribed are not really hyperactive to begin with. They are normal children who simply refuse to submit to what their teachers and parents consider orderly school and family routines. Categorizing children who are different as hyperactive often is a seductively convenient way to blame the victims for teachers' and parents' own shortcomings. Drugging these children, however, brands them as troublemakers and helps to further institutionalize drug use.

Cocaine

Cocaine is obtained from the leaves of the South American coca plant. It is rapidly replacing other illegal drugs in popularity. Although legally classified as a narcotic, it is in fact not related to the opiates from which narcotic drugs are derived. It is a powerful stimulant and antifatigue agent.

In America, it is generally taken by sniffing. It may also be injected intravenously, and South American natives chew the coca leaf. Cocaine has been used medically in the past as a local anesthetic, but other drugs have now largely replaced this use.

Cocaine constricts the blood vessels and tissues and thereby leads to increased strength and endurance. It also is thought by users to increase creative and intellectual powers. Other effects include a feeling of euphoria, excitement, restlessness, and a lessened sense of fatigue. Larger doses, or extended use, may result in hallucinations and delusions. A peculiar effect of cocaine abuse is *formication*—the illusion that ants or other bugs are crawling on or into the skin. Some abusers have such intense illusions that they literally scratch, slap, and wound themselves trying to kill these imaginary creatures.

Physical effects of cocaine include increased blood pressure and pulse rate, insomnia and loss of appetite. Heavy users may experience weight loss or malnutrition due to suppression of the appetite. Cocaine is not thought to be physically addictive. However, the drug appears to be psychologically habituating, as terminating use usually results in intense depression and despair, which drives the person back to taking the drug (Andrews and Solomon, 1975).

Serious tissue damage to the nose can occur when large quantities of cocaine are sniffed over a prolonged time period. High doses can lead to agitation, increased body temperature, and convulsions. Some people who overdose may die if their breathing and heart functions become too depressed. Little information is known about the long-term effects of cocaine.

Cocaine is known as the rich person's high, as it is extremely expensive. In 1982, it was selling for $100 a gram on the street (Paley, 1982). (A gram is equal to one-twenty-eighth of an ounce; a gram of cocaine provides between 25 and 30 average doses of the drug.)

Amyl Nitrate and Butyl Nitrate

Amyl nitrate (poppers) is prescribed for patients who risk certain forms of heart failure. It is a volatile liquid that is sold in capsules or small bottles. When the container is opened, the chemical begins to evaporate (similar to gasoline). If the vapor is sniffed, the user's blood vessels are immediately dilated and there is an increase in heart rate. These physical changes create feelings of mental excitation (head rush) and physical excitation (body rush). The drug is supposedly only sold by prescription, but (as with many other drugs) the illicit drug market has obtained access to distributing it. At the present time, the illicit sale is limited but growing in popularity with young people.

Butyl nitrate is legally available without a prescription and has an effect similar to amyl nitrate. Two of the trade names under which it is sold are Rush and Locker Room. Similar to amyl nitrate, the vapor is sniffed. It is widely available at sexual-aid stores and novelty stores.

Both these drugs have been used as stimulants while dancing and to enhance sexual excitement. The drugs have some short-term, unpleasant side effects that may include fainting, headaches, and dizziness. A few deaths have been reported due to overdoses. Both these drugs are classified as stimulants.

Narcotics

The most commonly used narcotic drugs in the United States are the opiates (such as opium, heroin, and morphine). The term *narcotic* means sleep-inducing. In actuality, drugs classified as narcotics are more accurately called analgesics, or painkillers. The principal effect produced by narcotic drugs is to create feelings of euphoria.

The opiates are all derived from the opium poppy, commonly found in Turkey, Southeast Asia, and Columbia.

The drug *opium* is the dried form of a milky substance that oozes from the seed pods after the petals fall from the purple or white flower. *Morphine* is the main active ingredient of opium. It was first identified early in the 1800s and, until rather recently, was used extensively as a painkiller. *Heroin* was first synthesized from morphine in 1874. It was once thought to be a cure for morphine addiction; but later, it was also found to be addictive. Heroin is a more potent drug than morphine.

Opium is usually smoked, although it can be taken orally. Morphine and heroin are either sniffed (snorted) or injected into a muscle or into a vein (mainlining) which maximizes the drug's effect.

Opiates affect the central nervous system and produce feelings of tranquility, drowsiness, or euphoria. Overdoses may cause convulsions, coma, and in rare cases, death by respiratory failure. All opiates are now recognized as being highly addicting.

Heroin is the most widely abused opiate. Heroin also slows the functioning of the brain. The user's appetite and sex drive tend to be dulled. After an initial feeling of euphoria, the user generally becomes lethargic and stuporous. Contrary to popular belief, most users of heroin are infrequent users and do not usually become addicted (Hunt and Zinberg, 1976)—although frequent use is highly addicting.

Opiate addiction occurs when the user takes the drug regularly for a period of time. Whether addiction will occur depends on the opiate drug taken, the strength of the dosages, the regularity of use, the characteristics of the user, and the length of time taken—sometimes as short as a few weeks. Users rapidly develop a tolerance and may eventually need a dose that is up to one hundred times stronger than a dose that would have been fatal during the initiation of the drug (Hunt and Zinberg, 1976).

The withdrawal process is very unpleasant. Symptoms include chills, cramps, sweating, nervousness, anxiety, running eyes and nose, dilated pupils, muscle aches, increased blood pressure, sometimes extreme nausea, and a fever. Most addicts are obsessed with securing a fix to avoid these severe withdrawal symptoms.

Addiction to opiates is extremely difficult to break, partly because intense craving for the drug may recur periodically for several months afterwards. Brecher et al. (1972, p. 84), note that the opiate drug:

> ... is one that most users continue to take even though they want to stop, decide to stop, try to stop, and actually succeed in stopping for days, weeks, months, or even years. It is a drug for which men and women will prostitute themselves. It is a drug to which most users return after treatment. ... It is a drug which most users continue to use despite the threat of long-term imprisonment for its use—and to which they promptly return after experiencing long-term imprisonment.

Most opiate addicts are under age 30, of low socioeconomic status, and poorly educated. A disproportionate number are black. Distribution of and addiction to narcotic drugs primarily occur in large urban centers.

When heroin was first discovered in the late 1800s, it was initially used fairly extensively as a pain killer, as a drug substitute for people addicted to morphine, and, by many, as a drug to experience euphoria. A fair number of people became addicted, and, in the early 1900s, laws were passed to prohibit its sale, possession, and distribution.

Contrary to popular belief, heroin addiction in itself has few adverse effects on the user (Brecher et al., 1972). A person who uses heroin daily (while avoiding excess doses) may continue using the drug for decades without detectable physical effects. Alcohol and tobacco unquestionably damage the human body much more than heroin. Unsanitary injections of heroin may, however, cause hepatitis and other infections. Also, the high cost of maintaining a heroin habit—often over $100 daily—may create huge financial problems.

Hallucinogens

Hallucinogens were popular as psychedelic drugs in the late 1960s. These drugs distort the user's perceptions, creating hallucinations consisting of sensory impressions of sights and sounds that do not exist. The three hallucinogens most commonly used in this country are mescaline (peyote), psilocybin, and LSD. All are taken orally—for example, in capsule form or on a sugar cube.

Peyote is derived from a cactus plant. *Mescaline* is the synthetic form of peyote. *Psilocybin* is derived from a small mushroom that grows in the southwestern part of the United States. Both peyote and psilocybin have had a long history of use by certain American Indian tribes. Members of the Native American Church, a religious organization, have won the legal right to use peyote on ceremonial occasions (Robertson, 1980, p. 450).

By far the most popular hallucinogen is *LSD* (D-lysergic acid diethylamide). LSD is a synthetic material derived from a fungus (ergot) that grows on rye and other plants. It is one of the most potent drugs known, as a single ounce will make up to 300,000 doses.

The effects of LSD vary a great deal, depending on the expectations and psychological state of the user and the context in which it is taken. A given person may experience differing reactions on different occasions. The effects that can be experienced include users having such strange sensations that they believe they are "seeing" sounds and "hearing" colors. Additional effects include colors seeming unusually bright and shifting kaleidoscopically, exaggerations of color and sound, and objects appearing to expand and contract. Bizarre hallucinations are also common. The experience may be peaceful or may result in panic. Some users have developed severe emotional disturbances that resulted in long-term hospitalization (*Chemistry and Engineering News*, 1976, pp. 44–45). Usually a trip will last 8 to 16 hours. Physical reactions include increased heart beat, goose bumps, dilated pupils, hyperactivity, tremors, and increases of sweating. Aftereffects include acute anxiety or depression. Flashbacks (returns to the hallucinatory state) sometimes occur even long after the actual drug experience. There is no data indicating whether LSD can cause either physical or psychological dependency. LSD has been used primarily as a recreational drug among the middle and upper classes. In the late 60s and early 70s, a number of college students experimented with its use.

Tobacco

The use of tobacco has now become recognized as one of the most damaging drug habits in America. Smoking can cause emphysema and lung cancer and reduces life expectancy. It significantly increases the risks of strokes and heart disease, particularly in women who use birth control pills (U.S. Department of Health, Education, and Welfare, 1979). Smoking by pregnant women sometimes leads to miscarriages, premature births, and children being born underweight. Yet, in spite of these widely publicized hazards, over one third of the adult population continues to smoke (U.S. Department of Health, Education, and Welfare, 1979).

Tobacco is highly habit forming. Nicotine, the primary drug in tobacco, has remarkable capacities, as it can act as a depressant, a stimulant, or a tranquilizer. Smokers quickly develop a tolerance for nicotine and often gradually tend to increase consumption to one or two packs or more a day. Hamilton Russell (1971, p. 9) notes:

> If we bear in mind that only 15 percent of adolescents who smoke more than one cigarette avoid becoming regular smokers and that only about 15 percent of smokers stop before the age of 60, it becomes apparent that, of those who smoke more than one cigarette during adolescence, some 70 percent continue for the next 40 years.

Special clinics and educational and therapeutic programs are available to help people quit smoking. Studies show less than 20 percent of smokers who made determined efforts to quit actually succeed (Hunt and Matarazzo, 1970). Tobacco is indeed a very habit-forming drug.

Marijuana

Marijuana (grass or pot) comes from the hemp plant, cannabis sativa. This hemp plant grows throughout the world; and its fibers are legally used to produce rope, twine, paper, and clothing.

The main use of the plant now, however, centers on its dried leaves—marijuana—and on its dried resin—hashish. Both may be taken orally but are usually smoked. Hashish is several times more potent than marijuana.

The effects of marijuana and hashish vary (as does any other drug) according to the mood and personality of the user, according to circumstances, and according to the quality of the drug. The effects are rather complicated and may induce a variety of emotions. It may induce a feeling of well-being, joyousness, hilarity, sociability, talkativeness, disconnected ideas, a feeling of floating, and laughter. It may also induce relaxation, intensify sensory stimulation, create feelings of enhanced awareness and creativity, and increase self-confidence or self-consciousness. A person may gradually experience some of these emotions, followed by others.

There is no evidence of physical addiction. If any tolerance develops, it is slight. There is considerable controversy in the literature as to whether the use of marijuana may lead to psychological dependence.

The short-term physical effects of marijuana are minor: a reddening of the eyes, dryness of the throat and the mouth, and a slight rise in heart rate. Some evidence exists that continued use by young teenagers will result in these users becoming apathetic, noncompetitive, and uninterested in school and other activities. There is also evidence that the altered thinking may continue long after the last marijuana use without the awareness of this condition by the user (up to two or three days), thus hindering educational, driving, and job performance. Users are often unaware of these effects, as many tend to associate smoking a joint with smoking a cigarette, the latter of which does not affect performance.

For years, heated debates have raged about the hazards of long-term marijuana use. Some studies claim it may cause brain damage, chromosome damage, irritation of the bronchial tract and lungs, and lower male hormone levels. These findings have not been confirmed by other studies, and the controversy rages on (Becher, 1975).

One of the most voiced fears about marijuana is that it will be a stepping stone to using other drugs. This fear appears to be groundless (U.S. Government Printing Office, 1972, p. 109). Other factors, such as peer pressure, are more crucial determinants of what mind-altering drugs people will use. The overwhelming majority of marijuana users do not progress to using other mind-altering drugs (U.S. Government Printing Office, 1972, p. 109).

In 1982, the National Academy of Sciences completed a 15-month extensive study on marijuana. The study found that a quarter of our population has tried marijuana at least once. The study found no evidence that marijuana causes permanent changes in the nervous system and concluded the drug probably does not break down human chromosomes. It also found marijuana may be useful in treating glaucoma, asthma, and certain seizure disorders and spastic conditions and in controlling severe nausea caused by cancer chemotherapy. The study warned, however, that the drug presents a variety of short-term health risks and justifies serious national concern. One of the reversible, short-term health effects is impairment of motor coordination, which adversely affects driving or machine-operating skills. The drug also impairs short-term memory, slows learning abilities, and may cause periods of confusion and anxiety. Evidence was also found that smoking marijuana may affect the lungs and respiratory system in much the same way that tobacco does and may be a factor in causing bronchitis and precancerous changes. Thus, the study found some evidence that marijuana may lead to certain adverse long-term health problems. The major recommendation was that "there be a greatly intensified and more comprehensive program of research into the effects of marijuana on the health of the American people" (National Academy of Sciences, 1982).

Dependence on Drugs

Habit-forming drugs can lead to *dependence*, which is a tendency or craving for the repeated use, or compulsive use (not necessarily abuse) of a chemical. This dependence may be physical, psychological, or both. When physical dependence occurs, the user will generally experience bodily withdrawal symptoms when drug use is discontinued. Withdrawal may take many forms and range in severity from slight tremblings to fatal convulsions.

When psychological dependence occurs, the user feels psychological discomfort if use is terminated. Dependent users also tend to believe they will use the chemical for the rest of their life, as a regular part of social/recreational activities. They also question whether the desired emotional state can be achieved without the use of the chemical, and they have a preoccupation with thinking and talking about the chemical and activities associated with using.

Users also generally develop a *tolerance* for some drugs, which means they have to take increasing amounts over time to achieve a given level of effect. Tolerance partly depends on the type of drug, as some drugs (such as aspirin) do not create tolerance.

Drug addiction is difficult to define. In a broad sense addiction refers to an intense craving for a particular substance. The problem is this definition could be applied to an intense craving for a variety of substances—pickles, ice cream, potato chips, strawberry shortcake. To avoid this problem we will define addiction as an intense craving for a drug that develops after a period of physical dependence stemming from heavy use.

Why Do People Use and Abuse Drugs?

The effects of using drugs are numerous, ranging from feeling "light headed" to death through overdosing. Drug abuse may lead to deterioration in health, relationship problems, automobile accidents, child abuse and spouse abuse, loss of job, low self-esteem, loss of social status, financial disaster, divorce, and arrests and convictions.

A distinction needs to be made between responsible drug use and drug abuse. Many drugs do have beneficial effects when used responsibly; aspirin relieves pain, alcohol helps people relax, tranquilizers reduce anxiety, antidepressant drugs reduce depression, amphetamines increase alertness, morphine is a painkiller, and marijuana is useful in treating glaucoma. Irresponsible drug use is abuse, which has already been defined.

Why do people abuse drugs? The reasons are numerous. Drug companies widely advertise the beneficial effects of their product. The media (such as television and movies) glamorize the mind-altering effects. Many popular songs highlight drinking. Taverns and cocktail lounges have become centers for socializing, and promote drinking. Through such channels, Americans have become socialized to accept drug usage as a part of daily living. Socialization patterns lead many people to use drugs, and for some the use is a stepping stone to abuse.

Attitudes toward drug use also encourage abuse. For example, some college students have a belief system that they should get blitzed or stoned after a tough exam. Ryne Duren (1979) former pitcher for the New York Yankees, raised the question: "I started becoming an alcoholic at age 4, even though I had my first drink at age 9—how can this be?" Duren went on to explain at a very young age he became socialized to believe a real man was "someone who could drink others under the table," and that the way to have fun was to get high on alcohol.

People abuse drugs for a variety of reasons. Some people build up a tolerance to a drug, and then increase the dosage to obtain a high. Physical and psychological dependence usually lead to abuse. People with intense unwanted emotions (such as intense lonliness, anxiety, feelings of inadequacy, guilt, depression, insecurity, and resentment) may turn to excessive use of drugs to relieve the intensity of their unwanted emotions. For many abusers their drug of choice becomes their best friend as they tend to personalize their drug of choice and value it more highly than they value their friends. The drug is personalized to be someone they can always count on to relieve pain or give them the kind of high they desire. Many abusers become so highly attached to their drug that they choose to continue using their drug of choice even though it leads to deterioration of health, divorce, discharges from jobs, automobile accidents, alienation from children, loss of friends, depletion of financial resources, and court appearances. Drug abusers usually feel they need their drug as a crutch to make it through the day.

Abusers develop an intimate relationship with their drug of choice. Even though this relationship is unhealthy, the drug plays a primary role in the abuser's life, dictates a certain lifestyle, fills a psychological need, and more often than not takes precedence over family, friends, and vacation. Most abusers *deny* their drug usage is creating problems for them, because they know that admitting they have a drug problem means they will have to end their relationship with their best friend, and they deeply believe they need their drug to psychologically handle their daily concerns and pressures. Drug abusers are apt to use the following defense mechanisms in order to continue using. They *rationalize* adverse consequences (such as loss of job) of drug abuse by twisting or distorting reality to explain the consequences of their behavior while under the influence. They *minimize* the adverse consequences of their drug use. They use *projection* to place the blame for their problems on others; for example, "If you had a wife like mine, you'd drink too."

There are also a variety of theories as to why people use drugs. *Biological theories* assert that physiological changes produced by the drugs eventually generate an irresistable craving for the drug. *Behavioral theories* hold that people use drugs because they find them pleasurable and continue to use them because doing so prevents withdrawal distress. *Interactionist theories* maintain drug use is learned from interaction with others in our culture; for example, people drink alcohol because drinking is widely accepted. Interactionist theories assert those who use such illegal drugs as marijuana or cocaine have contact with a drug subculture which encourages them to experiment with and to continue to use illegal drugs.

The Family Dynamics of Drug Abuse

Sharon Wegscheider (1981) maintains that chemical dependency is a family disease which involves and affects each family member. Although she focuses on the families of alcoholics, much of what she says is also frequently applied to the families of other types of chemical substance abusers.

She cites several rules which tend to characterize the families of drug abusers. First, the dependent person's alcohol use becomes "the most important thing in the family's life" (Wegscheider, 1981, p. 81). The abuser's top priority is getting enough alcohol, and the family's top priorities are the abuser, the abuser's behavior, and keeping the abuser away from alcohol. The goals of the abuser and of the rest of his or her family are at completely opposite poles.

A second rule in an alcoholic family is that alcohol is not the cause of the problem. Denial is paramount. A third family rule maintains that the dependent person is really not responsible for his or her behavior and that the alcohol causes the behavior. There is always someone or something else to blame. Another rule dictates that no one should rock the boat, no matter what. Family members strive to protect the family's status quo, even when the family is miserable. Yet other rules concern forbidding discussion of the family problem either within or outside of the family, and consistently avoiding stating one's true feelings.

Wegscheider maintains that these rules act to protect the dependent person from taking responsibility for his or her behavior, and that they actually serve to maintain the drinking problem. She goes on to identify several roles, which are typically played by family members. In addition to the chemically dependent person, there is the chief enabler, the family hero, the scapegoat, the lost child, and the mascot.

The chief enabler's main purpose is to assume the primary responsibility for family functioning. The abuser typically continues to lose control and relinquishes responsibility. The chief enabler, on the other hand, takes more and more responsibility and begins making more and more of the family's decisions. A chief enabler is often the parent or spouse of the chemically dependent person.

Conditions in families of chemically dependent people often continue to deteriorate as the dependent loses control. A positive influence is needed to offset the negative. The family hero fulfills this role. The family hero often is the perfect person who does well at everything he or she tries. The hero works very hard at making the family look like it is functioning better than it is. In this way the family hero provides the family with self-worth.

Another typical role played by someone in the chemically dependent family is the scapegoat. Although the alcohol abuse is the real problem, a family rule mandates that this fact must be denied. Therefore, the blame must be placed elsewhere. Frequently, another family member is blamed for the problem. The scapegoat often behaves in negative ways (for example, gets caught for stealing, runs away, becomes extremely withdrawn) which draws him/her much attention. The scapegoat's role is to distract attention away from the dependent person and onto something else. This role helps the family avoid addressing the problem of chemical dependency.

Often there is also a lost child in the family. This is the person who seems rather uninvolved with the rest of the family, yet never causes any trouble. The lost child's purpose is to provide relief to the family from some of the pain it's suffering. At least there then is someone in the family who neither requires much attention nor causes any stress. The lost child is simply just there.

Finally, chemically dependent families often have someone playing the role of mascot. The mascot is the person who probably has a good sense of humor and appears not to take anything seriously. Despite how the mascot might be suffering inside, he or she provides a little fun for the family.

In summary, chemical dependency is a problem affecting the entire family. Each family member is suffering from the chemical dependency, yet each assumes a role in order to maintain the family's status quo and to help the family survive. Family members are driven to maintain these roles, no matter what. The roles eventually become associated with survival.

Treatment for the Chemically Dependent Person and Family

One of the first tasks in treatment is to allow the chemically dependent person to take responsibility for his or her own behavior. The abuser must acknowledge that he or she has a problem before beginning to solve it. Several concepts involving working with the family are critical (Wegscheider, 1981). Family members must first come to realize the extent of the problem. They need to identify the chemical abuse as their major problem. Additionally, they need to learn about and evaluate their family dynamics. They need to evaluate their own behavior and break out of the roles which were maintaining the dependent person's abuse. Especially the chief enabler must stop making excuses and assuming the dependent's responsibility. If the dependent is sick from a hangover and cannot make it to school or work the next day, it must be the dependent's responsibility, not a parent's or spouse's to call in sick.

Family members eventually learn to confront the chemically dependent person and give him or her honest information about his or her behavior. For instance, they are encouraged to tell the dependent exactly how one behaved while having a blackout. If the dependent hit another family member while drunk, then this fact needs to be confronted. The confrontation should occur not in an emotional manner, but rather in a factual one.

The family also needs to learn about the progression of the disease. We've already discussed some characteristics of drug dependence. Figure 6.2 portrays the typical progression of an alcoholic's feelings and behavior. At first only occasional relief drinking occurs. Drinking becomes more constant. The dependent then begins to drink in secret and to feel guilty about drinking. Memory blackouts begin to occur and gradually increase in frequency. The dependent feels worse and worse about his or her drinking behavior, but seems to have less and less control over it. Finally, the drinking begins to seriously affect work, family, and social relationships. A job may be lost or all school classes flunked. Perhaps, family members leave or throw the dependent out. The dependent's thinking becomes more and more impaired.

Eventually, the dependent hits rock bottom. Nothing seems to be left but despair and failure, and the dependent admits complete defeat. It is at this point that the dependent person may make one of two choices. Either he or she will continue on the downward spiral to a probable death related to alcohol or may desperately struggle. Typically during this period, the dependent will make some progress only to slip back again. Vicious circles of drinking and stopping are often apparent.

Finally, the dependent may express an honest desire for help. A dependent person on the path to recovery will stop drinking. Meeting with other people who are also alcoholics or addicts is also very helpful. Support from others at this time in the process of recovery is especially critical.

Alcoholics Anonymous (AA) is a self-help organization which has provided the support, information, and guidance necessary for many dependent people to continue on in their recovery. The nationwide group is made up of other recovering alcoholics. The organization's success seems to rest on several principles. First, other people who really understand are available to give the recovering dependent person friendship and warmth. Each new member is given a sponsor who can be called for support at any time during the day or night. Whenever the dependent person feels depressed or tempted, there is always the sponsor to turn to.

Additionally, AA provides the recovering alcoholic a new social group with whom to talk and enjoy activities. Old friends with well-established drinking patterns usually become difficult to associate with. The recovering alcoholic can no longer participate in the drinking activity. Often social pressure is applied to drink again. AA provides a respite from such pressure and the opportunity to meet new people, if such an opportunity is needed.

AA also helps the recovering person to understand that alcoholism is a disease. This means that the alcoholic cannot cure himself or herself. He or she need no longer feel guilty about being an alcoholic. All that needs to be done is to stop drinking. AA also encourages self-introspection. Members are encouraged to look deeply inside themselves and face whatever they see. They are urged to acknowledge the fact that they have flaws and

Figure 6.2   Alcohol Addiction and Recovery

To be read from left to right

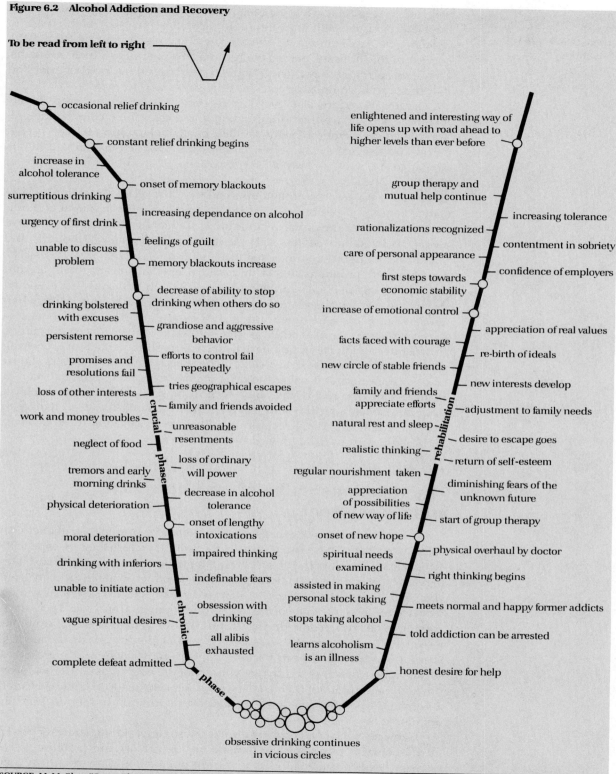

occasional relief drinking

constant relief drinking begins

increase in alcohol tolerance

surreptitious drinking

urgency of first drink

unable to discuss problem

drinking bolstered with excuses

persistent remorse

promises and resolutions fail

loss of other interests

work and money troubles

neglect of food

tremors and early morning drinks

physical deterioration

moral deterioration

drinking with inferiors

unable to initiate action

vague spiritual desires

complete defeat admitted

onset of memory blackouts

increasing dependance on alcohol

feelings of guilt

memory blackouts increase

decrease of ability to stop drinking when others do so

grandiose and aggressive behavior

efforts to control fail repeatedly

tries geographical escapes

family and friends avoided

unreasonable resentments

loss of ordinary will power

decrease in alcohol tolerance

onset of lengthy intoxications

impaired thinking

indefinable fears

obsession with drinking

all alibis exhausted

crucial phase

chronic phase

obsessive drinking continues in vicious circles

enlightened and interesting way of life opens up with road ahead to higher levels than ever before

group therapy and mutual help continue

rationalizations recognized

care of personal appearance

first steps towards economic stability

increase of emotional control

facts faced with courage

new circle of stable friends

family and friends appreciate efforts

natural rest and sleep

realistic thinking

regular nourishment taken

appreciation of possibilities of new way of life

onset of new hope

spiritual needs examined

assisted in making personal stock taking

stops taking alcohol

learns alcoholism is an illness

increasing tolerance

contentment in sobriety

confidence of employers

appreciation of real values

re-birth of ideals

new interests develop

adjustment to family needs

desire to escape goes

return of self-esteem

diminishing fears of the unknown future

start of group therapy

physical overhaul by doctor

right thinking begins

meets normal and happy former addicts

told addiction can be arrested

honest desire for help

rehabilitation

SOURCE: M. M. Glatt, "Group Therapy in Alcoholism," *The British Journal of Addiction*, 54, no. 2. Used by permission of the Society for the Study of Addiction, Edinburgh, Scotland.

will never be perfect. This perspective often helps people to stop fleeing from the pain of reality and hiding in alcohol or drugs. It helps them to redefine the expectations for themselves and to gain control. Within the context of this honesty, people often can also acknowledge their strengths. They can learn that they do have some control over their own behavior and that they can accomplish things for themselves and for others.

Organizations are also available to provide support for other family members and to give them information and suggestions. For example, Al-Anon is an organization for the families of alcoholics, and Al-Ateen is specifically for teenagers within these families. Likewise, self-help organizations similar to AA, such as Narcotics Anonymous, exist to help other types of chemical substance abusers.

Today a range of treatment approaches are available to chemical substance abusers. Types of facilities and treatment include inpatient and outpatient treatment programs at community mental health centers, chemical abuse rehabilitation centers and medical hospitals; halfway houses, and chemical treatment programs such as anabuse.

Treatment programs almost always advocate that abusers totally abstain from their drug of choice in the future, as research indicates that even one use will return the abuser to drug abuse. It should also be noted that when abusers complete a treatment program they are urged to view themselves as recovering rather than cured as they continually must work on abstaining in order to avoid the temptations of using. It is important that those receiving treatment also make lifestyle changes. The social activities of abusers almost always revolve around using the drug of choice; to successfully abstain, it is important that recovering abusers form new friendships and establish drug-free social activities and interests. Making such lifestyle changes is extremely difficult. Many recovering addicts fail in making these changes and then return to using their drug of choice.

The Relationship between Knowledge and Assessment

Considerable attention has been given to the issues of suicide and chemical substance abuse. These two issues were selected because they are especially critical and widespread. For social workers to be able to intervene and help prevent a person's suicide or help facilitate another person's recovery from chemical dependency, a base of knowledge is necessary. A social worker needs to understand some of the typical developmental and social pressures coming to bear on people during various phases of their lives. For example, it's very difficult to establish a sense of personal identity during the teenage years. It's relatively easy to become depressed, isolated, and hopeless. A social worker needs to know that young people contemplating suicide are probably serious about their threats. A worker also needs to know that such a person desperately needs social support in addition to help in logically evaluating his or her situation.

Likewise, social workers need to know some of the dynamics involved in the behavior of chemically dependent individuals and families. Social workers need to understand the concept of enabling. Only then can they assess a family accurately and know at what point intervention is needed.

With this base of knowledge, skills can be applied to help family members stop their enabling and their maintenance of false rules. Social work skills can also be used to encourage the family to realign responsibility. Other family members need to relinquish it to the chemically dependent person.

In summary, the examination of such life events and issues as we have explored here should provide social workers with a starting point on which to begin problem assessment. The intent is to provide a map or guide to begin the process of intervention.

Summary

Adolescent identity is discussed. Erikson's eight stages of psychosexual development are described. One of these stages, the crisis of identity versus. role diffusion which occurs during adolescence is discussed in some detail. Marcia's four categories of identity include identity achievement, foreclosure, identity diffusion, and moratorium. Kolberg's theory of moral development has three levels: preconventional, conventional, and post-conventional.

Two issues are discussed which are especially significant in adolescence and young adulthood—suicide and chemical use and abuse. Potential causes of suicide include feelings of helplessness, loneliness, impulsivity, lack of a stable environment, and increased external and internal pressures. Chemical substances include alcohol, barbiturates, tranquilizers, Quaaludes and PCP, amphetamines, cocaine, amyl nitrate and butyl nitrate, narcotics, hallucinogens, tobacco, and marijuana. As part of the treatment process, chemically dependent persons need to assume responsibility for their behavior.

Social Aspects of Adolescence and Young Adulthood

Laura Sardina is nineteen years old and is wondering what the future will hold for her. She still lives with her parents and has a job as a hotel maid for which she receives a minimum hourly wage. She has frequent arguments with her mother, and both of her parents have encouraged her to get a better paying job so that she can become self-supporting and move out of the house. She realizes a minimum-wage job will not enable her to live in an apartment, buy a car, buy clothes and food, and have sufficient money for entertainment.

Laura was raised in a middle-class family. Her brother is attending college to become a minister. Religion has always been an important aspect of Laura's parents' lives, but not of Laura's. She detests going to church. She would rather party. Her parents have often called her "stupid" and negatively compared her to her brother who can do no wrong. This disparagement of Laura has in many ways become a self-fulfilling prophecy. She repeated a grade in elementary school, seldom studied, and often received failing grades.

In school she saw herself as a failure and hung around with other students who viewed themselves as failures. In high school, she frequently skipped school and partied. Eight weeks before graduation, she was expelled for skipping too much school. Her parents and the school system had tried numerous times to motivate Laura to apply herself in school; she even had a number of individual sessions with three different social workers and a psychiatrist.

Laura knows her parents want her to leave home. Her parents are especially irate when she leaves home for three to four days at a time and parties in an abandoned house in the inner city of Milwaukee. She has lied to her parents about her sexual activities when the truth is she has had a variety of partners. Fortunately, she is taking birth control pills. Some of Laura's male friends are putting excessive pressure on her to prostitute herself, so that there will be more money to buy drugs and party. Laura has also had several encounters with the police, involving her friends—for shoplifting, running away from home, drinking liquor under age, kicking police officers while being arrested, and high speed auto chases after radar detected they were speeding.

Laura is asking herself a number of questions. Should she prostitute

herself? Or, should she stop associating with her friends and try to make peace with her parents by seeking a high school education and a better paying job? Whenever she has tried in the past to achieve the middle-class goals set by her parents, she always has been criticized by her parents as being a failure—she wonders what are her chances of making it this time? The one thing she has found enjoyable in life is partying with her friends, but she realizes her friends are getting her in trouble with the police. She is worried that cutting ties with her friends will result in living a life in which she will be continually rejected and put down by others. She wants a better paying job but realizes her chances are not good, especially since she hasn't completed high school. What should she do? She is deeply perplexed and confused.

■ A Perspective

This chapter will primarily focus on the social changes and social problems encountered by adolescents and young adults. (In terms of the Behavior Dynamics Assessment Model social problems and psychological problems can be viewed as subcategories of adverse life events). The social growth from puberty to roughly age 30 involves a number of passages: from being dependent on parents to becoming more independent, from adjusting to puberty to establishing a sexual identity, from beginning to date to usually marrying, from being a child with parents to perhaps parenting children, from earning money from babysitting to selecting a career and starting one's life work, from buying baseball gloves and playing ball to buying a car and traveling, from drinking Coca Cola to perhaps drinking martinis and experimenting with cocaine. The pressures and stresses of this time period have many casualties who suffer from a variety of problems. The Behavior Dynamics Assessment model enables us to examine a variety of social changes and life events encountered by adolescents and young adults. This chapter will:

• Describe the social changes that adolescents and young adults undergo.

- Describe some of the major problems encountered by this age group, including emotional and behavioral problems, births outside of marriage, crime and delinquency, and eating disorders.
- Present theoretical material on the causes of these problems and on how these problems can be treated.

Social Changes In Adolescence and Young Adulthood

During adolescence and young adulthood, people move from dependence on parents to adult independence, establish peer relationships and intimate relationships, and choose a personal lifestyle involving decisions about career, marriage, and children.

Movement from Dependence to Independence

Young people often are in a conflict between wanting to be independent of their parents and yet on another level realizing their parents are providing for many of their wants and needs: food, shelter, clothes, emotional support, spending money, and so on. Many young people see their parents as having shortcomings and conclude they know more than their parents. Yet, when their automobile breaks down and they have no idea of how to fix it, mom or dad almost always knows what to do to get it fixed.

In the pursuit of independence, adolescents often rebel against their parents' attempts to guide them and reject their views as being out of date and stupid. They sometimes do things to shock them as if to say "See, I'm my own person and I'm going to live my life my way!" Interestingly, once young people become more independent in their twenties and have to pay their own bills, they tend to have a greater appreciation of their parents' knowledge. Mark Twain noted (quoted in Papalia and Olds, 1981, p. 375) "When I was 14 my father knew nothing, but when I was 21, I was amazed at how much the old man had learned in those seven years."

Children who are raised in families where the parents have helped them in the growing-up process by providing opportunities to learn self-reliance, responsibility, and self-respect tend to make a smoother transition from dependency to adulthood interdependence. Children who are raised in families where the parents are overly permissive or where the parents take little interest in their behavior tend to have greater difficulty making the transition to adulthood as they lack structure or a system of standards and values to gauge whether their behavior is suitable and their decisions are appropriate (Scheck and El-Assal, 1973). Children who have overly protective parents also have difficulty making this transition as they usually do not learn how to assume responsibilities or make important decisions.

Some parents are wary about their children growing up. In particular, some fathers and mothers become alarmed and uncomfortable when their little girl starts dating. Many parents worry their daughter may become sexually involved and pregnant, which they believe will adversely affect her and interfere with their dreams and hopes for her having the good life. When teenagers assert their right to becoming more independent, it changes the components of the family system. Any change in the components of the system will create tension within the family. This tension is expressed by teens with such statements as "You don't understand me," "Get off my back," and "I know what I'm doing—don't treat me like a baby."

Parents may feel hurt by what they perceive as a lack of appreciation or gratitude. Common areas of conflict between parents and adolescents according to Kaluger and Kaluger (1984, p. 370) are:

Performing home chores

Use of time

Attitude toward studies

Expenditures of money

Morals and manners

Choice of friends

Clothes selection

Use of phone

Dating practices

Use of car

How should parents seek to cope with thrusts of independence from their teenagers? Kaluger and Kaluger (1984, p. 370) recommend the following:

> The most important thing for parents to keep in mind, at any time or any age of the child, is not to do or say anything that will break down or cut off the lines of communication between parent and child. All teenagers need help, even if they do not recognize this need or seem grateful for it. They must feel free to seek that help from their parents or loved ones. If teenagers cannot talk to their parents or to other acceptable adults, they have only their peers and friends to turn to. How much advice and information on serious matters can one 13-year-old or 15-year-old give to another?

Keeping the lines of communication open is admittedly easier said than done. It requires work!

■ Effective Communication between Parents and Children

Thomas Gordon (1970) in *Parent Effectiveness Training* has identified four communication techniques that are designed to improve relationships between parents and their children/youths.

Active listening. This technique is recommended for use when a youth indicates he has a problem; for example, when a 16-year-old daughter looks in a mirror and states "I'm fat and ugly—all of my friends have boyfriends, and not me." For such situations Gordon recommends that the parent use active listening. The steps involved in active listening are the receiver of a message tries to understand what the sender's message means or what the sender is feeling, and the receiver then puts this understanding into his own words and returns this understanding for the sender's verification. An active listening response to the above might be "You want very much to have a boyfriend and think the reason you don't is related to your physical appearance." An active listening response involves either *reflecting feelings* or *restating content*.

Dr. Gordon lists a number of advantages for using active listening. It facilitates problem solving by the youth, which fosters the development of responsibility. By talking a problem through, a person is more apt to identify the root of the problem and arrive at a solution than by merely thinking about a problem. When a teenager feels his parents are listening to him, a by-product is that he will be more apt to listen to the parents' point of view. In addition, the relationship between parent and youth is apt to be improved because when he feels he is being heard and understood, he is apt to feel warmth toward the parent. Finally, the approach helps a teen to explore, recognize, and express his feelings.

Dr. Gordon mentions certain parental attitudes are required to use this technique. The parent must view the youth as being a separate person with his own feelings. The parent must be able to accept the youth's feelings, whatever they may be. The parent should genuinely want to be helpful and must want to hear what he has to say. Additionally, the parent must have trust in his capacities to handle his problems and feelings.

I-Messages. Many occasions arise when a youth causes a problem for the parent: for example, a daughter may turn up the stereo so high that the music is irritating, or she may stay out after curfew hours, or she may recklessly drive an auto. Confronted with such situations many parents send either a solution message (they order, direct, command, warn, threaten, preach, moralize, or advise), or a put-down message (they blame, judge, criticize, ridicule, or name-call). Solution and put-down messages can have devastating effects on a child's self-concept and are generally counterproductive in helping a child become responsible.

Solution and put-down messages are primarily *you-messages:* "you do what I say," "don't you do that," "why don't you be good," "you're lazy," "you should know better."

Dr. Gordon advocates that parents should instead send *I-messages* for those occasions when a teenager is causing a problem for the parent. For example, take a parent who is riding in a car where the son is driving and exceeding the speed limit. Instead of the parent saying "Slow down, you idiot, do you want to get us killed," Dr. Gordon urges the parent to use an I-message: "Driving this fast really frightens me."

I-messsages, in essence, are nonblaming messages which only communicate how the sender of the message believes the receiver is adversely affecting the sender. I-messages do not provide a solution, nor are they put-down messages. It is possible to send an I-message without using the word I, as the essence of I-messages involves sending a nonblaming message of how the parent feels the child's behavior is affecting the parent.

You-messages are generally put-down messages that either convey a message to a youth that he should do something or convey to him how bad he is. In contrast, I-messages communicate to a youth much more honestly the effect of the behavior on the parent. I-messages are also more effective because they help teenagers to learn to assume responsibility for their own behavior. An I-message tells teenagers that the parent is trusting them to respect the parent's needs and that the parent is trusting them to handle the situation constructively.

You-messages frequently end up in a struggle between parent and youth, while I-messages are much less likely to produce an argument. I-messages lead to honesty and openness in a relationship, and generally foster intimacy. Teenagers, as well as adults, often do not know how their behavior affects others. I-messages produce startling results as parents frequently report that their teenagers express surprise upon learning how their parents really feel.

No-lose problem solving. In every parent-teenager relationship there are inevitable situations where the youth continues to behave in a way that interferes with the needs of the parent. Conflict is part of life and not necessarily bad. Conflict is bound to occur because people are different and have different needs and wants, which at times do not match. What is important is not how frequently conflict arises, but how the conflicts get resolved. Generally in a conflict between parent and youth, a power struggle is created.

In many families the power struggle is resolved by one of two win-lose approaches. Most parents try to resolve the conflict by having the parent winning and the youth losing. Psychologically, parents almost always are recognized as having greater authority. The outcome of the parent winning is that it creates resentment in the teenager toward his parents, leads to low motivation for him to carry out the solution, and does not provide an opportunity for him to develop self-discipline and self-responsibility. Such teenagers are likely to react by becoming either hostile, rebellious, and aggressive, or submissive, dependent, and withdrawing.

In other families, fewer in number, the win-lose conflict is resolved by the parents giving in to their teenagers out of fear of frustrating them or fear of conflict. In such families teenagers come to believe their needs are more important than anyone else's. They generally become self-centered, selfish, demanding, impulsive, and uncontrollable. They are viewed as being spoiled by others, have difficulty in interacting with peers, and also do not have respect for property or feelings of others.

Of course, few parents use either approach exclusively. Oscillating between the two approaches is common. There is evidence that both approaches lead to the development of emotional problems in children (Gordon, 1970, p. 161).

Dr. Gordon seriously questions whether power is necessary or justified in a parent-teenager relationship. For one reason, as a teenager grows older she becomes less dependent and parents gradually lose their power. Rewards and punishments that worked in younger years become less effective as the youth grows older. Teenagers resent those who have power over them, and parents frequently feel guilty after using power. Dr. Gordon believes that parents continue to use power because they have had little experience in using nonpower methods of influence.

Dr. Gordon suggests a new approach, the *no-lose approach* to solving conflicts. The approach is to have each parent and youth solve their conflicts by finding their own unique solutions acceptable to both.

The no-lose approach is simple to state—each person in the conflict treats the other with respect, neither person tries to win the conflict by the use of power, and a creative solution acceptable to both parties is sought. The two basic premises to no-lose problem solving are (a) that all people have the right to get their needs met and (b) that what is in conflict between the two parties involved is not their *needs* but their *solutions* to those needs.

Dr. Gordon (1970, p. 237) lists the six steps to the no-lose method as:

Step 1: Identifying and defining the needs of each person.

Step 2: Generating possible alternative solutions.

Step 3: Evaluating the alternative solutions.

Step 4: Deciding on the best acceptable solution.

Step 5: Working out ways of implementing the solution.

Step 6: Following up to evaluate how it worked.

This approach motivates youths to carry out the solution because they participated in the decision. It develops their thinking skills and responsibility. It requires less enforcement, eliminates the need for power, and improves relationships between parents.

Collisions of values. Collisions of values are common between parents and their children, particularly as the children become adolescents and young adults. Likely areas of conflict include values about sexual behavior, clothing, religion, choice of friends, education, plans for the future, use of drugs, hairstyles, and eating habits. In these areas emotions run strong and parents generally seek to influence their offspring to follow the values the parents hold as important. Teenagers, on the other hand, often think their parents' values are old fashioned and stupid, and declare that they want to make their own decisions about these matters.

Dr. Gordon asserts there are three constructive ways in which parents and teenagers can seek to resolve these conflicts. (For the sake of simplicity, we will use the term *mother* in describing what should be done—a father or a teenager can also use these same techniques.)

The first way a mother can influence her offspring's values is to model the values she holds as important. If she values honesty, she should be honest. If she values responsible use of drugs, she should exhibit a responsible model. If she values openness, she should be open. She needs to ask herself if she is living according to the values she professes and change either her values or her behavior, if her values and behavior are not congruent. Congruence between behavior and values is important if she wants to be an effective model.

The second way she can influence her teenagers' values is to act as a consultant to them. There are some do's and don't's of a good consultant. First of all, a good consultant finds out whether the other person would like her consultation. If the answer is "yes," she then makes sure she has all the available pertinent facts. She then shares these facts—once—so that the other person understands them. She then leaves the other person the responsibility for deciding whether to follow the advice, or not. A good consultant is neither uninformed nor a nag, otherwise she is not apt to be used as a consultant again.

The third way for a mother to reduce tensions over values issues is to modify her values. By examining the values held by her teenagers, she may realize their values have merit, and she may move toward their values or at least toward an understanding of why they hold them as values.

(It should be noted all of these techniques can be used to improve communication and relationships in practically all interactions, such as adult-adult, and counselor-client. The techniques are much broader in application than just parent-teenager.)

The task of becoming independent involves attaining emotional, social, and economic independence. Emotional independence involves progressing from emotional dependence on parents or on others, to relative independence while still being able to maintain close emotional ties; it involves moving from a parent-child relationship to an adult-adult relationship. Emotional independence involves becoming self-reliant with the knowledge that, "I am put together well enough emotionally that I can fend for myself, but I am willing to share my feelings with others and let them become part of me." Emotional independence involves receiving and sharing and being interdependent, without being emotionally dominated or overwhelmed.

Social independence involves becoming self-directed rather than other-directed. Many adolescents are other-directed as they are so strongly motivated for social acceptance that much of what the group says is what adolescents think and do. Self-directed people factor things out for themselves and make decisions based on their personal interests. Becoming socially independent does not mean becoming selfish, as socially independent people realize their best interests are served by becoming involved in political, civic, educational, religious, social, and community affairs.

Economic independence involves earning sufficient money to meet one's financial needs. Many older teenagers and young adults do not have special skills, and, therefore, obtaining good paying jobs to meet their financial needs is very difficult. Economic independence also involves learning to limit desires to ability to pay. To become economically independent it is necessary to develop at least one marketable set of skills that one can offer an employer in exchange for a job. As Prather (1970, p. 41) notes, it is important for people to realize that the more they earn, the more they will desire:

> The number of things just outside the perimeter of my financial reach remains constant no matter how much my financial condition improves. With each increase in my income a new perimeter forms and I experience the same relative sense of lack. I believe that I would be happy if only my earnings were increased by so much and I could then have or do these few things I can't quite afford, but when my income does increase I find I am still unhappy because from my new financial position I can now see a whole new set of things I don't have.

Peer Relationships

Adolescents have a strong *herd* drive and desire to be accepted by their peers. Peers are an important influence on adolescents. An extensive government study involving over 3,000 teenagers concluded that peers are more of a factor than parents in determining whether a youth will become involved in serious juvenile delinquency (Papalia and Olds, 1981, p. 376).

This study does not mean that peers are more of an influence than parents in all areas. Brittain (1963) conducted a study of teenage females which found that whether parents or peers have more influence depended on the particular situation. The respondents relied more on peers for deciding how to dress and on how to resolve school-centered dilemmas. The respondents relied more on parental opinions for deciding which job to take, on how to resolve complicated moral conflicts, and on other long-range issues.

The particular kind of peer group that an adolescent selects depends on a variety of factors: socioeconomic status (most peer groups are class bound); values derived from parents; the neighborhood that one lives in; nature of school; special talents and abilities; and the personality of the adolescent. Once an adolescent becomes a member of a peer group, the members of that subgroup influence each other in their social activities, study habits, dress, sexual behavior, use or nonuse of drugs, vocational pursuits, and hobbies.

Not all adolescents join cliques. Some prefer to be loners. Some are already pursuing what they believe will be their life goals. Some may be busy babysitting for younger children in the family. Some prefer having only one or two close friends. Some are excluded from the cliques that exist in their areas.

Adolescents tend to identify with other teenagers, rather than with adults or younger children. Sorenson (1973) suggests this identification may be due to teens believing that most other teens share their personal values and interests, while younger and older people are seen as having more divergent interests and values. Compared to people in their forties and fifties, adolescents view themselves as being less materialistic, more idealistic, healthier sexually, and better able to understand friendships and what is important in life.

Friends and peer groups help adolescents and young adults to make the transition from parental dependence to independence. Friends give each other emotional support and also serve as important points of reference for young people to compare their beliefs, values, attitudes, and abilities. In a number of cases friendships forged during adolescence endure throughout life.

Weiss and Lowenthal (1976) conducted a study on adolescent friendships and found the following five dimensions were important in selecting and maintaining friendship relationships:

1. Similarity—in values, personality, attitudes, shared activities or experiences.
2. Reciprocity—understanding, helping, accepting each other, mutual trust, and ability to share confidences.
3. Compatibility—enjoyment of being together.
4. Structure—geographic closeness, and long duration of acquaintanceship.
5. Role-modeling—respect and admiration for the friend's good qualities.

Intimacy versus Isolation

Erikson (1950) theorized that after young people develop a sense of identity, they next face the psychosocial crisis of intimacy versus isolation, which generally occurs in young adulthood (roughly during the twenties). Intimacy is the capacity to experience an open, tender, supportive relationship with another person, without fear of losing one's own identity in the process of growing close. In such a relationship the partners are able to understand, cognitively and emotionally, each other's points of view. An intimate relationship permits the sharing of personal feelings as well as the disclosure of ideas and plans that are not fully developed. There is respect for each other and mutual enrichment in the interactions. Each person perceives an enhancement of his or her well-being through the stimulating interactions with the other.

Intimacy involves being empathetic and being able to give and receive pleasure within the relationship. Although intimacy is often established within the context of a marital relationship, marriage itself does not produce intimacy. In some marriages there is considerable intimacy (including sharing and mutual respect). However, in empty-shell marriages and in marriages with considerable conflict, there is very little intimacy. There are additional contexts where intimacy is apt to develop. The work setting is one of these, where close friendships are often formulated. Close friendships are also apt to develop through membership in social and religious organizations.

Traditional socialization patterns in our society create different problems for males and females in the establishment of intimacy. Boys are taught to be restrained in expressing their feelings and personal thoughts. They are also socialized to be competitive and self-reliant. They are raised to believe that they should be sexually aggressive and seek to "go as far as possible" in order to demonstrate their virility to their male friends. Males are thus unprepared for intimate heterosexual relationships—which require that they express their feelings, be supportive rather than competitive, and have a commitment to continuing the relationship rather than piling up sexual trophies.

Traditionally, women are socialized to be better prepared for the emotional demands of intimacy. They are socialized to express their feelings and personal thoughts and to be nurturant. They may, however, enter an intimate relationship with a surplus of dependent needs; for example, by expecting their partner to be stronger or more resourceful than he is. Some women also make a more rapid commitment to a relationship than their partner does, and then they feel devastated when they discover their partner has less of a commitment. (The women's movement is fortunately changing sex role expectations and socialization practices for males and females; hopefully, the difficulties that men and women experience in forming intimate relationships will be reduced.)

The negative pole of the crisis of young adulthood is isolation. People who resist intimacy must continually erect barriers between themselves and others. Some people view intimacy as a blurring of the boundaries of their own identity and, therefore, are reluctant to become involved in intimate relationships. Some people are so busy seeking or maintaining their identity that they cannot share and express themselves in an intimate relationship.

Isolation may also result from situational factors. A young person may be so involved in studying to get into medical school that he or she may not have the time for an intimate relationship. Or, a teenage female may become pregnant, deliver and start raising the child, and then have few opportunities to become involved in a close relationship with an adult.

Isolation may also result from diverging spheres of activity and interest. Newman and Newman (1984, pp. 387–88) provide an example of how isolation may develop in a traditional marriage:

The wife stays at home most of the day, interacting with the children and the other wives in the neighborhood. The husband is away from home all day, interacting with co-workers. When the partners have leisure time, they pursue different interests. The woman likes to play cards, and the man likes to hunt. Over the years, the partners have less and less in common. Isolation is reflected in their lack of mutual understanding and their lack of support for each other's life goals or needs.

■ Romantic Love versus Rational Love

Achieving a gratifying, long-lasting love relationship is one of our paramount goals. The experience of feeling in love is exciting, adds meaning to living, and psychologically gives us a good feeling about ourselves. Unfortunately, few people are able to maintain a long-term love relationship. Instead, many people encounter problems with love relationships, including: falling in love with someone who does not love them; falling out of love with someone after an initial stage of infatuation; being highly possessive of someone they love; and having substantial conflicts with the loved one because of differing sets of expectations about the relationship. Failures in love relationships are more often the rule than the exception.

The emotion of love, in particular, is often viewed (erroneously) as being a feeling over which we have no control. A number of common expressions connote or imply that love is a feeling beyond our control, such as, "I *fell* in love," "It was love at first sight," "I just couldn't help it," and "He swept me off my feet." It is more useful to think of the emotion of love as being primarily based on our self-talk (that is, what we tell ourselves) about a person we meet.

Romantic love can be diagrammed as follows.

Event

Meeting or becoming acquainted with a person who has *some* of the overt characteristics you adore in a love.

↓

Self-talk

"This person is attractive, personable; has *all* of the qualities I admire in a lover/mate."

↓

Emotion

Intense infatuation, being romantically in love; a feeling of being in ecstasy.

Romantic love is often based on self-talk that stems from intense unsatisfied desires and frustrations, rather than on reason or rational thinking. Unsatisfied desires and frustrations include extreme sexual frustration, intense loneliness, parental and personal problems, and extensive desires for security and protection.

A primary characteristic of romantic love is to idealize the person with whom we are infatuated as being a perfect lover; that is, we notice this person has some overt characteristics we desire in a lover and then conclude that this person has all the desired characteristics.

A second characteristic is that romantic love thrives on a certain amount of distance. The more forbidden the love, the stronger it becomes. The more social mores are threatened, the stronger the feeling. (For example, couples who live together and then later marry often report living together was more exciting and romantic.) The more the effort necessary to be with each other (e.g., traveling long distances), the more intense the romance. The greater the frustration (e.g., loneliness or sexual needs), the more intense the romance.

The irony of romantic love is that, if an ongoing relationship is achieved, the romance usually withers. Through sustained contact, the person in love gradually comes to realize what the idealized loved one is really like—simply another human being with certain strengths and limitations. When this occurs, the romantic love relationship either turns into a rational love relationship, or the relationship is found to have significant conflicts and dissatisfactions and ends in a broken romance. For people with intense unmet desires, the latter occurs more frequently.

Romantic love thus tends to be of temporary duration and based on make-believe. A person experiencing romantic love never loves the real person—only an idealized imaginary person.

Rational love, in contrast, can be diagrammed in the following way.

Event

While being aware and comfortable about your own needs, goals, identity, and desires, you become well acquainted with someone who fulfills, to a fair extent, the characteristics you desire in a lover/spouse.

↓

Self-talk

"This person has many of the qualities and attributes I seek in a lover/spouse. I admire this person's strengths, and I am aware and accepting of his or her shortcomings."

↓

Emotion

Rational love.

The following are ingredients of a rational love relationship: (a) you are clear and comfortable about your desires, identity, and goals in life; (b) you know the other person well; (c) you have accurately and objectively assessed the loved one's strengths and shortcomings and are generally ac-

cepting of the shortcomings; (d) your self-talk about this person is consistent with your short- and long-term goals; (e) your self-talk is realistic and rational, so that your feelings are not based on fantasy, excessive desires, or pity; (f) you and this person are able to communicate openly and honestly, so that problems can be dealt with when they arise and so that the relationship can continue to grow and develop; (g) rational love also involves giving and receiving; it involves being kind, showing affection, knowing and doing what pleases the other person, communicating openly and warmly, and so on.

Because love is based on self-talk that causes feelings, it is we who create love. *Theoretically*, it is possible to love anyone by making changes in our self-talk. On the other hand, if we are in love with someone, we can gauge the quality of the relationship by analyzing our self-talk to determine the nature of our attraction and to determine the extent to which our self-talk is rational and in our best interests.

SOURCE: Charles Zastrow, *Talk to Yourself*. Englewood Cliffs, N.J., Prentice-Hall, Inc. 1979.

Choosing a Personal Lifestyle

Most people make decisions about how they want to live their adult years during their young adult years. (As time goes on, it is important to remember that a person has a right to make changes in the following decisions.) Decisions about lifestyles include whether to marry or stay single; whether or not to have children; what kind of career to pursue; what area of the country to live in; whether to live in an apartment, duplex or house; and so on. In choosing a lifestyle, what is actually experienced by many is not a matter of ideal choice, but rather a result of opportunities. In other words, financial resources, personal deficiencies, discrimination, etc., may greatly prevent or modify free choice. In regard to lifestyles, we will take a brief look at the following areas: marriage, cohabitation, single life, parenthood, single parenthood, childless couples, and stepparenting.

Marriage

Throughout recorded history, regardless of the simplicity or sophistication of the society, the family has been the basic biological and social unit in which most adults and children live. In addition, all past and present societies sanction the family through the institution of marriage (Glick, 1979). Clayton (1975) suggests one of the primary reasons for instituting the custom of marriage was to enable the two partners to enjoy sexuality as fully as possible with a minimum of anxieties and hazards. The natural sex drive of men and women needs to be satisfied, yet control needs to be exercised over the spread of venereal diseases. Children that result from sexual re-lationships need to be raised and cared for.

Close to 92 percent of all adults will get married in our society. Over 90 percent of all married couples will have children (Glick, 1979).

In our society people marry for a variety of reasons including desire for children, economic security, social position, love, parents' wishes, escape, pregnancy, companionship, sexual attraction, common interests, and ad-venture (Bowman, 1970). Goldin (1977) indicates other reasons for marrying include societal expectations, and the psychological needs to feel wanted more than anyone else by someone and to be of value to another person. In our impersonal and materialistic society, marriage helps meet the need to belong as it helps in providing emotional support and security, affection, love, and companionship.

■ Theories as to Why People Choose Each Other as Mates

The reasons that people choose each other as partners are complex and vary greatly. Certainly such factors as religion, age, race, ethnic group, social class, and parental pressures influence the choice of mates. In addition, many theories sug-gest additional factors. Some of these theories are summarized here. (No theory fully identifies all of the factors involved in mate selection.)

Propinquity theory asserts that nearness or being in close proximity is a major factor in mate se-lection. This theory suggests we are apt to select a mate with whom we are in close association, such as at school or at work or whom we meet through neighborhood, church, or recreational activities (Rubin, 1973).

Ideal mate theory suggests we choose a mate who has the characteristics and traits we desire in a partner. This theory is symbolized by the state-ment, "He's everything I've ever wanted."

Congruence in values theory holds that our value system consciously and unconsciously guides us in selecting a mate who has similar values (Grush and Yehl, 1979).

Homogamy theory suggests that we select a mate who has similar racial, economic, and social characteristics.

Complementary needs theory holds that we either select a partner who has the characteristics we wish we had ourselves or someone who can help us be the kind of person we want to be.

Compatibility theory asserts we select a mate with whom we can enjoy a variety of activities. This is someone who will understand us, accept us, and with whom we feel comfortable in communicat-ing because that person has similar feelings and a similar philosophy of life.

Predictors of Marital Success. A number of studies have sought to identify factors associated with marital happiness and marital unhappiness (Kirkpatrick, 1955; Campbell, 1975; Goodrich, et al., 1973; Markman, 1981; Barry, 1970; Sears, 1977; Schultz, 1980; and Snyder, 1979). Some factors are associated in a predictive manner with whether the marriage will be happy or not. Other factors are related to whether an already existing marriage is happy or not. The findings in these studies are summarized in *Predictive Factors Leading to Marital Happiness/Unhappiness.*

■ Predictive Factors Leading to Marital Happiness/Unhappiness

Marital Happiness	*Marital Unhappiness*

Premarital Factors

Parents' marriage is happy

Personal happiness in childhood

Mild but firm discipline by parents

Harmonious relationship with parents

Gets along well with the opposite sex

Acquainted more than one year before marriage

Parental approval of marriage

Similarity of age

Satisfaction with affection of partner

Love

Common interests

Optimistic outlook on life

Emotional stability

Sympathetic attitude

Similarity of cultural backgrounds

Compatible religious beliefs

Satisfying occupation and working conditions

A love relationship growing out of companionship rather than infatuation

Self-insight and self-acceptance

Awareness of the needs of one's partner

Coping ability

Interpersonal social skills

Positive self-identity

Holding common values

Factors During Marriage

Good communicative skills

Equalitarian relationship

Good relationships with in-laws

Desire for children

Similar interests

Responsible love, respect, and friendship

Sexual compatibility

Enjoying leisure-time activities together

Companionship and an affectional relationship

Capacity to receive as well as give

Premarital Factors

Parents divorced

Parents or parent deceased

Incongruity of main personality traits with partner

Acquainted less than one year before marriage

Loneliness as a major reason for marriage

Escape from one's own family as a major reason for marriage

Marriage at a young age, particularly under age 20

Predisposition to unhappiness in one or the other spouse

Intense personal problems

Factors During Marriage

Husband more dominant

Wife more dominant

Jealous of spouse

Feeling of superiority to spouse

Feeling of being more intelligent than spouse

Living with in-laws

■ Guidelines for Building and Maintaining a Happy Marriage

A successful and satisfying marriage requires ongoing work by each partner. Middlebrook (1974) provides the following guidelines—which are elaborated on here—on how to achieve and maintain a successful marriage.

1. Keep the lines of communication open. Learn to bite the bullet on minor or unimportant issues. Voice the concerns that are important to you, but in a way that does not attack, blame, or threaten the other person. Seek to use I—messages which were described in Figure 7.1

2. Seek to foster the happiness, personal growth, and well-being of your spouse as much as you seek to foster your own happiness and personal growth.

3. Seek to use the no-lose problem-solving technique to settle conflicts with partner as described in Figure 7.1, rather than the win-lose technique. Be tolerant and accepting of trivial shortcomings and annoyances in partner.

4. Do not seek to possess, stifle, or control your partner. Also, do not seek to mold your partner into a carbon copy of your opinions, values, beliefs, or of your personal likes and dislikes.

5. Be aware that everyone has up and down mood swings. When your partner is in a down cycle, seek to be considerate and understanding.

6. When arguments occur—and they will—seek to fight fair. Limit the discussion to the issue, and keep past events and personality traits out of the fight.

7. Be affectionate, share pleasant events, be a friend, and a good listener.

Benefits of Marriage. Marriage leads to the formation of a family, and the family unit has become recognized as the primary unit in which children are to be produced and raised. The marriage bond thus provides for an orderly replacement of the population. Children require care and protection until adulthood, and the family is the primary institution for the rearing of children. The family is also an important institution for socializing children into the culture; for example, in helping children to acquire a language, learn social values and mores, and learn how to dress and behave within the norms of society.

Marriage also provides an available and regulated outlet for sexual activity. Failure to regulate sexual behavior would result in clashes between individuals due to jealousy and exploitation. Unregulated sexual behavior would probably also result in the birth of many "illegitimate" (and perhaps unwanted) infants for whom no fathers could be held responsible for raising. Every society has rules that regulate sexual behavior within family units; for example, incest taboos.

A marriage is also an arrangement to meet emotional needs of the partners, such as affection, emotional support, companionship, approval, encouragement, and reinforcement for accomplishments. If people do not have such affective needs met, emotional, intellectual, physical, and social growth will be stunted. (Our high divorce rate indicates this ideal of achieving an emotionally satisfying relationship is not easily obtained).

Two alternative factors may be operating here—either a number of people do find happiness in marriage or else happy people are more apt to be married. Campbell, Converse, and Rodgers (1976) in a study of over 2,000 adults found that married people of all ages reported higher feelings of satisfaction about their lives than people who are single, divorced or widowed. The happiest of all groups were married people in their twenties with no children.

Marriage also correlates with good health. Married people live longer, particularly men (Papalia and Olds, 1981, p. 436). Widowed and divorced men have shorter life expectancies than single men, whose life expectancy is closest to the rate of married men. Fuchs (1974) suggests that widowed and divorced men may have shorter life expectancies because they lose the desire to live.

The marriage relationship encourages personal growth; it provides a setting for the partners to share their innermost thoughts.

In a marriage a lot of decisions need to be made. Should the husband and wife buy a new car or a house? Should they both pursue careers? Do they want children? How will the domestic tasks be divided? How much time will be spent with relatives? Should a vacation be taken this year; if so, where? Problems in these areas can erupt into crises that if resolved constructively can lead to personal growth. Through successful resolution, people often learn more about themselves and are better able to handle future crises. However, if the problems remain unresolved, conflict may fester with considerable discord resulting.

■ Open versus Closed Marriages

O'Neill and O'Neill (1971) in their book *Open Marriage* contrast traditional marriage with open marriage. A traditional, or closed marriage, embodies such principles as:

- Possession or ownership of spouse.
- Denial or stifling of self by putting marriage or family first.
- Playing the couples game by the expectations of doing everything together during leisure time.
- The husband being the primary decision-maker and often away from home while the wife is domestic, passive, subservient, and stays at home with the children.
- Absolute fidelity.

An open marriage, in contrast, advocates:

- Freedom to pursue individual interests.
- Flexible roles in which meeting financial responsibilities and domestic tasks are shared.
- Expansion and growth of both spouses through openness and the freedom to pursue individual goals and interests. It is expected that one person's growth will facilitate the other partner's development.
- A marriage based on open communication, trust, and respect.

A controversial element of the open marriage approach is increased freedom to have extramarital sexual relationships.

Marriage counselors are currently seeing a number of couples where serious interaction difficulties occur because one spouse wants an open marriage, while the other desires a closed marriage. The feminist movement and the changing roles of women in our society have brought into public awareness the differences between open and closed marriages. Many wives are now seeking a career, their own identity, an equalitarian relationship, and a sharing of domestic responsibilities. Meanwhile, some of their husbands with a traditional orientation still expect that a wife's place is in the home. These husbands assume their wives should be subservient, take care of the children, and do all of the domestic tasks.

Cohabitation

Cohabitation is the open living together of an unmarried couple. Most such couples live together for a relatively short time (less than two years) before they either marry or separate (Papalia and Olds, 1981, p. 443).

For some, cohabitation serves as a trial marriage. For others it offers a temporary or permanent alternative to marriage. And for many young people, it has become the modern equivalent of dating and going steady.

Interestingly, cohabitation does not appear to have much of an effect on eventual marital adjustment or marital success. Jacques and Chason (1979) found no significant differences between those who had lived with someone premaritally and those who had not.

Why then do a number of couples decide to live together without a marriage ceremony? The reasons are not fully clear. Many people want close intimate and sexual arrangements and yet are not ready for the financial and long-term commitments of a marriage. With our society being more accepting than in the past of cohabitation, some couples appear to be choosing this living arrangement. To some extent, they can have friendship, companionship, and a sexual relationship, without the long-term commitment of marriage. Living with someone helps many young adults to learn more about themselves, to better understand what is involved in an intimate relationship, and to grow as a person. Cohabitating may also help some people clarify what they want in a mate and in a marriage.

Cohabitating also has its problems, some of which are similar to those encountered by newlyweds: adjusting to an intimate relationship, working out a sexual relationship, overdependency on the partner, missing what one did when living alone, and seeing friends less. Other problems are unique to cohabitation, such as explaining the relationship to parents and relatives, discomfort about the ambiguity of the future, and a desire for a long-term commitment from their partner.

Closely related to cohabitating is a relationship in which the man and woman maintain separate addresses and domiciles, but, for several days a month, live together. This latter form is more of a trial honeymoon than a trial marriage. When people only live together for a few days a month, they are apt to seek to put their best foot forward.

In some recent instances courts have ruled that cohabitating couples who decide to dissolve their nonmarital living arrangements have certain legal obligations to one another. For example, in a much publicized case in 1979, a California court judge ruled that actor Lee Marvin must pay over $100,000 to a woman with whom he cohabitated for six years.

Single Life

Some people choose to remain single; they like being alone and prefer not being with others much of the time. Others end up being single as they do not find a partner they want to marry or because they are in relationships where their partner chooses not to marry. Historically, there was a greater expectation that people would marry than at the present time. Now, people are freer to make decisions about whether to marry and what kind of a lifestyle to seek.

Single people have fewer emotional and financial obligations. They do not need to consider how their decisions and actions will affect a spouse and children. They are freer to take economic, physical, and social risks. They can devote more time to the pursuit of their individual interests.

Adams (1971, p. 491) notes the age of 30 represents, to some extent, a turning point for the single woman who wants to marry:

> By 30 most women who are still unmarried are beginning to build up economic independence, an investment in work, and a viable value system that allows them to identify and exploit major sources of personal and social satisfaction in other areas than marriage and family. Even those whose first preference is

marriage are compelled to readjust their social sights and relationships because the number of eligible men will have thinned out and their married peers will be caught up in a web of social and domestic activities with which they cannot identify and that do not meet their needs. At this juncture the unmarried woman, if she is not to be plagued by a constant sense of dissatisfaction, must take stock of her situation and carefully evaluate both its negative features and its assets.

Stein (1976) interviewed over 60 single men and women between the ages of 22 and 62 and found the following reported advantages to being single: satisfaction in being self-sufficient, increased career opportunities, an exciting lifestyle, mobility, sexual availability, the freedom to change, opportunities to have a variety of experiences, opportunities to play a variety of roles, and opportunities to have friendships with a variety of people. The following negative aspects of being married were reported: boredom, obstacles to self-development, feeling trapped, unhappiness, having to conform to expectations, sexual frustration, poor communication, limited mobility, restriction of new experiences, and lack of friends. (It appears the respondents in this study were biased toward the single life. Different results might have been found if the researchers had interviewed single people who wanted to be married, but who as yet had not found a marriageable partner.)

Parenthood

The birth of a baby is a major life event. Caring for a baby changes lifestyles of parents and also the marriage. For some, caring for a child (who is totally dependent) is a troublesome crisis. For others, caring for a baby is viewed as a fulfillment and an enhancement of life. For many couples, parenthood has troublesome aspects, while it also enhances their lives.

What are some of the problem areas of parenthood? The birth of a baby signals to parents that they are now adults and no longer children; they now have responsibilities not only to themselves, but also in caring for someone who needs 24-hour care. A baby demands a huge amount of time and attention. If the mother is career oriented, she may resent the new demands placed on her time and energy, which now cause interruptions in her career advancement. (Even in most liberated families, the bulk of the responsibilities for caring for the children still falls on the mother.) Because wives assume the majority of the responsibilities, they tend to have more difficulties adjusting to the parental role than their husbands do (Hobbs and Cole, 1976).

Russell (1974) studied 271 middle- and working-class couples in which the children ranged in age from 6 to 56 weeks. The study found that the wives were bothered most by interrupted rest and sleep, fatigue, feeling edgy, and worry about their loss of figure and about their personal appearance. Interestingly, the more highly educated a woman was, the greater her difficulty in adjusting to parenthood. Perhaps this was due to viewing parenthood as interfering with her career goals. The wives who had the most positive reactions to the child's birth tended to be those who had easy pregnancies and deliveries, those who were in excellent health, and those who had been married a longer time.

The husbands in the Russell study tended to have different concerns than the wives, although they were also bothered by interruptions in sleep and rest. The husband's concerns included having to change lifestyle because of the baby, increased financial pressures, additional work in caring for the baby, and interference from in-laws in childrearing. Those fathers who most enjoyed the parental role were those who had prepared for parenthood by reading books and attending classes, those who had been involved in taking care of someone else's children, and those who saw being a father as being one of their most important life roles. Not surprisingly, those couples who made the most positive adjustments to parenthood were those who wanted and planned for the birth of the baby, and those who were happily married.

Why do people have children? Historically, in agricultural and preindustrial societies children were an economic asset, as their labor was important in planting and harvesting crops and in tending of domestic animals. Parents wanted large families to help out with the work. When the parents became elderly, the children tended to provide much of the care. Because children were an economic asset, values were gradually established that it was natural and desirable for married couples to want to have children. Motherhood became invested with a unique emotional aura. Some psychological theories reflected this aura by asserting that women (interestingly, not men) had a nurturing instinct that could only be fulfilled by having and caring for children. (It appears the supposed nurturing instinct was in reality a value that was learned by women through socialization practices.)

Today, children are an economic liability, rather than an economic asset. Overpopulation is increasingly being recognized as one of the world's greatest problems. In our society there is an expectation that Social Security and other government programs will primarily care for elderly parents, rather than this being a responsibility of the children. Children can have negative, as well as positive, effects on lifestyles and on marital relationships. For these, and other reasons, married couples in our society over the years have gradually decided to have fewer children; now most couples usually want zero to three children. Birth control devices now make such wishes a reality. To some extent, however, many couples still feel compelled by society to have children.

Hoffman and Manis (1979) conducted an extensive study to identify the psychological satisfactions of having children. Love of children, fun, and stimulation headed the list.

Price-Bonham and Skeen (1979) conducted a survey of 160 black and white husbands who were working full-time, were parents of at least two children, and were living with their wives. According to this study, these husbands rated the best things about being a father as having someone to love and love them, the feeling that their children made them feel respectable, and that they would have someone to care for them in old age. Discipline problems and increased responsibilities were the worst things about being a father. A number of these husbands stated that fatherhood was more demanding than they had anticipated. Many said if they had a chance to do it over again, they would not have children. They felt children made their life financially harder, interfered with their previous lifestyles, and interfered with what they had wanted to do in their lives. The study led the researchers to recommend extensive education for fatherhood in the elementary and secondary school curriculum.

Children have a pervasive influence on a marriage (Feldman, 1971). It is common for a husband and wife to have disagreements about how to raise and discipline children; such dissension is perhaps to be expected as the two partners were raised somewhat differently and, therefore, have acquired different philosophies on how to raise children. Feldman (1971) found that couples who were most likely to report an increase in marital satisfaction after the birth of the first child were those who had known each other a substantial amount of time before they were married, and those who were pursuing their individual interests in the marriage. Those who were excessively dependent on each other tended to experience a decrease in marital satisfaction following the birth of a baby.

Rollins and Galligan (1978) found that a decline in marital satisfaction after the birth of a child is more common among working-class families than among middle-class families. These researchers also suggest that children are less likely to lower marital satisfaction in families where the parents desired to have children, and where the parents have outside resources for helping to care for the children. Even when parenting has a negative influence on marital satisfaction, parenting often has a positive effect on the self-concepts of the parents and on their work roles (Feldman and Feldman, 1977). Thus, parenting appears to contribute to the personal development of an individual.

■ Parental Sex Preferences

In most countries boys are generally preferred to girls. Although it is the male's sperm that determines the sex of the child, in many developing countries and countries where the status of women is low, a woman's capacity to remain married may depend on her producing sons. In some of these countries, boys are fed better, given better medical care, and receive more schooling. The death rate for female children is significantly higher than for male children as female children are more apt to be neglected.

In this country couples who want only one child usually desire a boy. Those who want two, generally desire one of each; and those who prefer three usually want two boys and one girl. Husbands, in particular, tend to have a strong preference for a boy. The reasons a couple desires a boy or a girl vary. Those couples desiring a boy generally prefer someone to carry on the family name and bring honor to the family; those who prefer a girl want someone who is easier to raise, is lovable, is fun to dress, and is able to help with the housework (Williamson, 1978).

The Group for the Advancement of Psychiatry (1973) views parenting as a developmental process and has identified the following four stages:

1. Anticipation: This stage occurs during pregnancy and involves the expectant parents thinking about how they will raise their children, how their lives will change, and the meaning of parenthood. Some expectant parents have ambivalent feelings about what lies ahead. During this stage the expectant parents begin the process of viewing themselves as their children's parents, instead of being their parents' children.

2. Honeymoon: This stage occurs after the birth of the first child and lasts for a few months. Parents are often very happy about having and holding a baby. It is also a time of adjustment and learning, as attachments are formed between parents and child, and family members learn new roles in relation to one another.

3. Plateau: This stage occurs from infancy through the teenage years. Frequent adjustments must be made by the parents, as parents need to adapt their parenting behavior to the level of the child.

4. Disengagement: This stage occurs at the time when the child disengages; for example, when the child marries. Because the child disengages, the parents should also change their behavior and disengage from the child. Relationships change from parent-child in nature to adult-adult.

These stages illustrate the fact that children have a great effect on parents. The Group for the Advancement of Psychiatry (1973) also notes that parents often judge their parenting on how well their children turn out. When children fulfill their expectations, the parents usually pat themselves on the back for a job well done. The danger of this approach is that if the children fall short of meeting parental expectations (which sometimes are unrealistic), the parents are apt to conclude they failed. Parents need to realize the final product is not entirely under their control as children are influenced by many other factors that are external to the family.

Single Parenthood

Traditionally, marriage and parenthood have been viewed as going together. Yet, single parenthood is emerging as a prominent family form in our society. There are several ways to become a single parent: death of spouse, divorce, separation, adoption of a child by an unmarried person, and birth of a child outside of marriage.

Although an increasing number of males are becoming single parents, by far the vast majority of single parents are females. Twenty percent of children in the United States are being raised in a home with only one parent, and in 90 percent of these families that parent is the mother. (Kaluger and Kaluger, 1984, p. 508). Many reasons can be given for the female head. If a child is born outside of marriage, legal and social customs dictate that the mother rather than the father should have parental rights. In nine out of ten divorce cases, the mother is awarded custody of the children (Espenshade, 1979).

Children raised in one-parent families are more apt to develop emotional problems, to have academic difficulties, and to become involved in delinquency (Kaluger and Kaluger, 1984, p. 507). Boys raised in one-parent families headed by a female are more apt to have deficits or abnormalities in sex-role development (Biller, 1982). Many one-parent families are living in poverty, so that many of the problems manifested by the children in these families may be related to restricted opportunities and resources.

Because of low income and many financial expenses, a high percentage of female single parents are forced to apply for public assistance (generally from the Aid to Families of Dependent Children's program). However, many of these mothers have male friends and relatives who can provide adequate sex-role models. In addition, there are a variety of other programs and organizations to help single parents, such as Big Brothers, Big Sisters, and Parents Without Partners.

Schlesinger (1977) found that single parents tend to have feelings of loneliness, social isolation, and alienation. They also tend to express unhappiness about having reduced opportunities for social and sexual contact with the opposite sex. Such discontent may adversely affect the children. But home situations need to be viewed in perspective. A single parent home where there is a loving, wholesome atmosphere is probably better for a child's development than a two-parent home where there are serious con-

Children bring fun and stimulation to their parents and give their lives meaning. But parenthood is a mixed blessing, bringing troublesome aspects as well as joy and fulfillment. This new mother's lifestyle and marriage may change radically now that her child is born. Caring for her baby will take up huge amounts of time. Her baby may cause strain on her marriage as well as creating tension while she's working at her job. (Fran Buss)

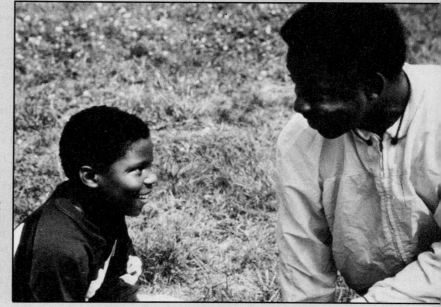

What do fathers like this one like most about parenthood? A recent survey found that, above all, both black and white fathers liked having someone to love. Being loved in return rated equally high. They felt secure in the knowledge that there was someone to care for them in their old age. What surprised them? The discipline problems and increased responsibilities of fatherhood were far greater than they had anticipated. (Courtesy of United Way of America)

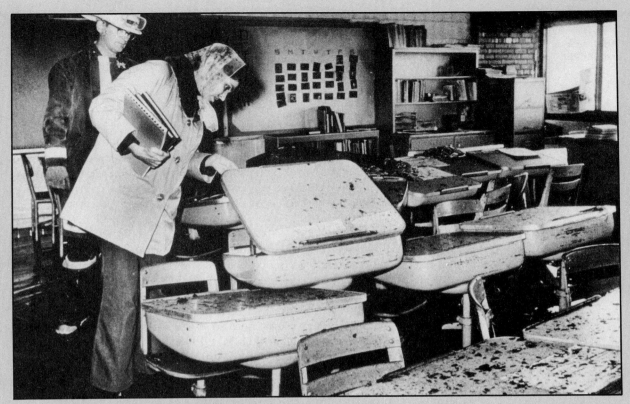

A teenage arsonist set this school building on fire. Sadly, he is not unique. He is one of many adolescents and young adults who commit the bulk of crimes in our society. Teenagers are arrested more than any other age group. When adult criminals are found guilty, they are tried and punished for their wrongdoing. Because the courts want to reorient juvenile law offenders, they advocate psychological treatment for them. (Courtesy of Wisconsin State Journal)

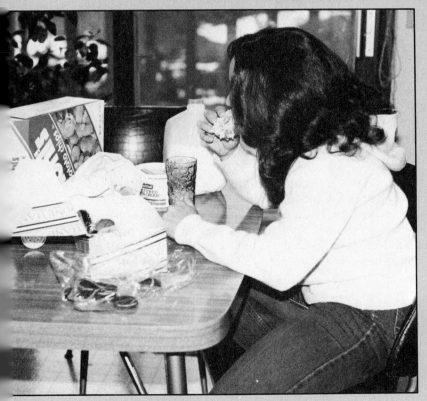

Bulemia is an eating disorder that compels the victim to go on eating binges and devour as many as forty thousand to sixty thousand calories a day. Bulemics usually eat highly caloric junk food, such as sweets and fried foods. After eating, they purge themselves of the food. Another eating disorder is anorexia nervosa. (Charles Zastrow)

flicts, tensions, strife, and unhappiness. Kaluger and Kaluger (1984, p. 508) state: "Whether the single-parent home is good or bad for the child appears to depend on the stability, the absence of strife and malcontent, and the presence of love and security that is experienced by the child."

Childless Couples

Having children is recognized legally and religiously as being one of the central components of a marriage. In our society there still continues to be a value that something is wrong with a couple if they decide not to have children; this value, however, is no longer as strongly held as it once was. Perhaps in the future this value will cease to exist due to the overpopulation problem and due to the high cost of raising children; the average cost of raising a child from birth to age 18 is estimated to be over $70,000 (*U.S. News & World Report*, 1981, p. 77).

Married couples may decide not to have children. Some feel they do not have what it takes to be good parents. Some have heavy commitments to their careers or to their hobbies and do not want to take time away from them to raise a family. Others feel that having children would be an intrusion into their marital relationship. Still others enjoy the freedom to travel, to make spur-of-the-moment plans, and do not want their lifestyle changed with having children (Papalia and Olds, 1981, p. 453).

Rollin (1970) found that marriages without children are happier. Campbell (1975) found that marriages are happiest before children are born and after the children leave home. Apparently, children place demands and strains on a marriage that can lead to some dissatisfaction.

Houseknecht (1979) compared 50 childless (by choice) wives and 50 mothers and found a very small difference in overall marital satisfaction. Childless women were slightly more satisfied. Childless couples were more likely to work together on projects, to have more frequent exchanges of stimulating ideas, to discuss things more calmly, and were more likely to engage in outside interests. The childless wives agreed more with their husbands on career decisions, leisure time activities, and division of household tasks. The childless wives also expressed a stronger desire to continue the marriage. Childless wives have also been found to be better educated, less religious, and more apt to be employed than mothers (Papalia and Olds, 1981, p. 454).

Dytrych et al. (1975) found that unwanted children are adversely affected in a variety of ways; they are more apt to be abused, have more frequent illnesses, receive poorer school grades, and have more behavior problems than children whose births are desired. Such findings suggest that if couples do not want to have children, it is probably in their best interest and that of society for them not to have children.

Stepparenting

With the high rates of divorce and remarriage in our society, an increasing number of families have children of "yours, mine, and ours." Negative stereotypes about the relationship between stepparents and stepchildren include the relationship being one of antagonism, coldness, and hostility. Images of the stepparent include his or her being abusive, competitive, and uncaring. With such stereotypes there is a danger that stepparents and stepchildren may interact according to these negative expectations.

A stepfamily differs somewhat from a natural family in that more people are involved; for example, ex-spouses, ex-in-laws, as well as an assortment of cousins, uncles, and aunts. The married couple can have both positive and negative interactions with this large supporting cast. If a prior marriage has ended bitterly, the unresolved emotions that remain (such as anger and insecurity) will affect the present relationship. Such problems may be a major reason why many of these marriages end in divorce. Einstein (1979) found that 4 out of 10 of these marriages end in divorce within the first five years of marriage.

The area of greatest stress for stepparents is that of childrearing. A stepchild, used to being raised in a somewhat different way, may balk at having to conform to a new set of rules. The stepchild may also have difficulty accepting the stepparent as someone who has the right to parent him or her. Such a difficulty is more likely to arise if the stepchild feels remorse that the missing parent is not present. If the husband and wife disagree about how to raise children, the chances of conflict are substantially increased. Stepparents and stepchildren also face the problem of adjusting to the habits and personalities of each other. Kompara (1980) recommends that stepparents should not rush into establishing a relationship with stepchildren; a gradual effort at establishing a relationship is more likely to result in a trusting and positive relationship. Kompara (1980) also notes that becoming a stepparent is usually more difficult for a woman because children tend to be emotionally closer to their biological mother and have spent more time with her than with the father.

Stinnet and Walters (1977) reviewed the research literature on stepparenthood and concluded: (1) integration tends to be easier in families that have been split by divorce than by death, perhaps because the children realize the first marriage is not working out, (2) stepparents and stepchildren come to the blended family with unrealistic expectations that love and togetherness will rapidly occur, (3) children tend to see a stepparent of the opposite sex as playing favorites with their own children, (4) most children continue to miss and admire the absent biological parent, (5) male children tend to more readily accept a stepparent, particularly if the new parent is also a male, and (6) adolescents have greater difficulty accepting a stepparent than young children or adult children.

Social Problems

In addition to going through normal phases of social development (such as developing an identity and choosing a lifestyle), there are a number of situations and life crises that tend to occur. The remainder of this chapter will focus on the following social problems: emotional and behavioral problems; crime and delinquency; births outside of marriage; and eating disorders.

Emotional and Behavioral Problems

Emotional problems (involving unwanted feelings) and behavioral problems (involving irresponsible actions) are two comprehensive labels covering an array of problems. Emotional difficulties include depression, feelings of inferiority or isolation, feeling guilty, shyness, having a low self-concept, having a phobia, and excessive anxiety. Behavioral difficulties include being sadistic or masochistic, being hyperactive, committing unusual or bizarre acts, being overly critical, being overly aggressive, abusing one's child or spouse, being compulsive, committing sexual deviations, showing violent displays of temper, attempting suicide, and being vindictive.

Everyone, at one time or another, will experience emotional and/or behavioral problems. Severe emotional or behavioral problems have been labeled as being mental illnesses by certain members of the helping professions. The two general approaches to viewing and diagnosing people who display severe emotional disturbances and abnormal behaviors are the medical model and the model which asserts mental illness is a myth.

Medical Model

This model views emotional and behavioral problems as a mental illness, comparable to a physical illness. The use of mental illness labels involves applying medical labels (that is, schizophrenia, paranoia, psychosis, neurosis, insanity) to emotional problems. Adherents of the medical approach believe the disturbed person's mind is affected by some generally unknown, internal condition. That unknown, internal condition, they assert, might be due to genetic endowment, metabolic disorders, infectious diseases, internal conflicts, unconscious use of defense mechanisms, and traumatic early experiences that cause emotional fixations and prevent future psychological growth.

The medical model identifies two major categories of mental illness: psychosis and neurosis—and classifies a number of disorders under each of these. Definitions of some of these disorders follow.

Psychosis: Fundamental mental derangement characterized by defective or lost contact with reality. Categories of psychoses include the following:

Schizophrenia: A psychotic disorder characterized by loss of contact with the environment and by disintegration of personality expressed as disorder of feeling, thought, and conduct.

Paranoia: A psychosis characterized by systematized delusions of persecution or grandeur.

Manic-depression: A psychosis characterized either by mania (i.e., mental and physical hyperactivity) or psychotic depression or by alternating mania and depression.

Neurosis: A less serious nervous disorder for which there is no known organic cause. (Some authorities consider this disorder as being a personality disturbance and not a disease.) Categories of neuroses include the following:

Anxiety reaction: Extensive anxiety that is generalized. This anxiety is displayed daily, with the patient often having no conscious awareness of the reasons for the anxiety.

Hypochondria: An erroneous belief by a person that he or she has imaginary illnesses.

Neurotic depression: Long-term depression that ranges from mild to moderate; in extreme cases the depression may lead to suicide.

Obsessive neurosis: A compulsion to think or behave in a particular way without any rational reason—for example, daily thinking about reincarnation when others around the person are conversing about something else; or daily taking 10 or more showers.

Phobia: An unreasonable fear of a specific situation or thing—for example, extreme or uncontrollable fear of water, rabbits, heights, birds, tests, authority figures, or dating.

The medical model approach arose in reaction to the historical notion that the emotionally disturbed were possessed by demons, were mad, were to be blamed for having their disturbances, and who were treated by being beaten, locked up, or killed. The medical model led to viewing the disturbed as being in need of help, stimulated research into the nature of emotional problems and promoted the development of therapeutic approaches.

Mental Illness Is a Myth Model

Critics of the medical (mental illness) approach assert such medical labels have no diagnostic or treatment value and frequently have an adverse labeling effect.

Thomas Szasz (1961a) was one of the first authorities to assert that mental illness is a myth—does not exist. Beginning with the assumption that the term *mental illness* implies a "disease of the mind," he categorizes all of the so-called mental illnesses into three types of emotional disorders and discusses the inappropriateness of calling such human difficulties mental illnesses:

1. *Personal disabilities*, such as excessive anxiety, depression, fears, and feelings of inadequacy. Szasz says such so-called mental illnesses may appropriately be considered mental (in the sense in which thinking and feeling are considered mental activities), but he asserts they are not diseases.

2. *Antisocial acts*, such as bizarre homicides and other social deviations. Homosexuality used to be in this category, but was removed from the American Psychiatric Association's list of mental illnesses in 1974. Szasz says such antisocial acts are only social deviations and he asserts they are neither mental or diseases.

3. *Deterioration of the brain with associated personality changes.* This category includes the mental illnesses in which personality changes result following brain deterioration from such causes as arteriosclerosis, chronic alcoholism, general paresis, or serious brain damage following an accident. Common symptoms are loss of memory, listlessness, apathy, and deterioration of personal grooming habits. Szasz says these disorders can appropriately be considered diseases, but are diseases of the brain (i.e., brain deterioration which specifies the nature of the problem) rather than being diseases of the mind. Szasz (1961b, p. 87) asserts the notion that people with emotional problems are mentally ill is as absurd as the belief that the emotionally disturbed are possessed by demons:

> The belief in mental illness as something other than man's trouble in getting along with his fellow man, is the proper heir to the belief in demonology and witchcraft. Mental illness exists or is "real" in exactly the same sense in which witches existed or were "real."

The point that Szasz and many other writers are striving to make is that people do have emotional problems, but they do not have a mystical, mental illness. Terms that describe behavior, they believe, are very useful; for example, depression, anxiety, an obsession, a compulsion, excessive fear, hallucinations, or feelings of being a failure. Such terms describe personal problems that people have. But the medical terms, they assert (such as schizophrenia and psychosis) are not useful because there is no distinguishing symptom which would indicate whether a person has, or does not have, the illness. In addition, Offer and Sabshin (1966) point out there is considerable variation between cultures regarding what is defined as a mental illness. The usefulness of the medical model is also questioned because psychiatrists frequently disagree on the medical diagnosis to be assigned to those who are disturbed (Koll, 1969).

In a dramatic study psychologist David Rosenhan (1973) demonstrated that professional staff in mental hospitals could not distinguish insane patients from sane patients. Rosenhan and seven normal associates went to twelve mental hospitals in five different states claiming they were hearing voices; all eight were admitted to these hospitals. After admission these pseudopatients stated they stopped hearing voices and acted normally. The hospitals were unable to distinguish their sane status from the insane status of other patients. The hospitals kept these pseudopatients hospitalized for an average of 19 days, and all were then discharged with a diagnosis of "schizophrenia in remission."

The use of medical labels, it has been asserted, has several adverse labeling effects (Scheff, 1966). The person labeled mentally ill (and frequently the therapist) believes that he or she has a disease for which unfortunately there is no known cure. The label gives the labeled person an excuse for not taking responsibility for his/her actions (for example, innocent by reason of insanity). Since there is no known cure, the disturbed frequently idle away their time waiting for someone to discover a cure, rather than assuming responsibility for their behavior, examining the reasons why there are problems, and making efforts to improve. Other undesirable consequences of being labeled mentally ill are they may lose some of their legal rights (Szasz, 1963); may be stigmatized in their social interactions as being dangerous, unpredictable, untrustworthy, or of weak character (Phillips, 1963); and may find it more difficult to secure employment or receive a promotion (Lemert, 1951).

The question of whether mental illness exists is indeed important. The assignment of mental illness labels to disturbed people has substantial implications for how the disturbed will be treated, for how others will view them, and for how they will view themselves. Cooley's "looking glass self-concept" (1902) crystalizes what is being said here. The looking glass says we develop our self-concept (our idea of who we are) in terms of how other people react to us. If someone is labeled mentally ill, other people are apt to react to him as if he were mentally ill, and that person may well define himself as being different, crazy, and begin playing that role.

Assessing and Treating Unwanted Emotions

A variety of theoretical frameworks can be used for assessing and treating emotional problems. A summary of these frameworks is in Zastrow (1985). The rational therapy approach will be described here as it is one of the more useful approaches. The primary developer of rational therapy is Albert Ellis (1962).

Many people erroneously believe that our emotions are primarily determined by our experiences (that is, by events that happen to us). On the contrary, rational therapy has demonstrated that the primary cause of all of our emotions is what we tell ourselves about events that happen to us.

All emotions occur according to the following format:

Events:

(Our experiences)

$\downarrow$

Self-talk:

(Self-talk is the set of evaluating thoughts we give ourselves about facts and events that happen to us.)

$\downarrow$

Emotions:

(May include remaining calm.)

This basic principle is not new. The stoic philosopher Epictetus wrote in *The Enchiridion* in the first century A.D.: "Men are disturbed not by things, but by the view which they take of them." (Quoted in Ellis, 1979, p. 190). An example will illustrate this process:

Event

Jane Adams studies extensively for her first human behavior exam, takes the exam, and receives a "C."

$\downarrow$

Jane's Self-Talk

"Gee, this is awful. I studied so hard for this exam, and bombed out. It sure looks like I'm going to fail this course. Human behavior is not for me. I'm simply dumber than other students. Since this is a required course in the social work major, it looks like I'll never make it as a social worker. I'm a failure. Maybe I should drop out of college right now, rather than continuing to waste my money when I'll never graduate anyway."

Jane's Emotions

Depressed, feeling of being a failure, disgusted with self.

If on the other hand, Jane tells herself the following about receiving a "C," her emotions will be very different:

Event

Jane Adams studies extensively for her first human behavior exam, takes the exam, and receives a "C."

$\downarrow$

Jane's Self-Talk

"Wow—I just got by on this exam. Nearly half the class got a "C" or lower on the exam, so it looks like I'm doing about as well as others. All I need is a grade of "C" in this course to pass the course and fulfill the requirement. I see where I made some mistakes that I shouldn't have made, so I think I will be able to do better on the next exam. I'll also talk with the instructor to get some ideas on how I can improve in this course. I feared I flunked this exam, and I wound up doing better than I expected. I'm progressing satisfactorily in the social work major, and I think I can do better."

$\downarrow$

Jane's Emotions

Mildly anxious about receiving a "C," relief that the exam was not flunked, optimistic about improving her grade on the next exam, and optimistic about passing the course.

The most important point about the above process is that our self-talk determines how we feel, and by changing our self-talk we can change any unwanted emotion. An unwanted emotion can be defined as either an emotion we want to change, or an emotion we have that others have become significantly concerned about—for example, excessive depression which has continued since a loved one died several years earlier. It is possible that an emotion which is generally viewed as being positive can be an unwanted emotion; for example, if we find we are feeling happy at a funeral, we may want to change the emotion. Also, emotions generally viewed as negative can be a wanted emotion in certain situations, for example, sadness at a funeral.

Changing Unwanted Emotions

There are only five ways to change an unwanted emotion, and only the first three of them are constructive. These three are getting involved in meaningful activity, changing the negative and irrational thinking which underlies the unwanted emotion, and changing the distressing event.

Meaningful Activity. The first constructive way is to get involved in some meaningful or enjoyable activity. When we become involved in activity that is meaningful, it provides satisfaction and structures and fills time, thereby taking our mind off a distressing event.

Practically all of us encounter day-to-day frustrations and irritations—having a class or two that are not going too well, having a job with irritations, or having a blah social life. If we go home in the evening and continue to think about and dwell on the irritations, we will develop such unwanted emotions as depression, anger, frustration, despair, or feeling of being a failure. (Which of these emotions we will have will directly depend on what we tell ourselves.)

By having an escape list of things we enjoy doing, we can nip unwanted emotions in the bud. Everyone should develop an escape list of things they enjoy doing: taking a walk, golf, going to a movie, tennis, shopping, needlework, visiting friends, and so on. By getting involved in things we enjoy, we take our mind off our day-to-day concerns and irritations. The positive emotions we will instead experience will directly stem from the things we tell ourselves about the enjoyable things we are doing.

In urging people to compile and use an escape list, the authors are not suggesting that people should avoid doing something about trying to change unpleasant events. If something can be done to change an unpleasant event, all constructive efforts should be tried. However, we often do not have control over unpleasant events and cannot change them. Although we often cannot change unpleasant events, we always have the capacity to control and change what we tell ourselves about unpleasant events. It is this latter focus that is often helpful in learning to change our unwanted emotions.

Changing Self-Talk. A second approach to changing unwanted emotions is to identify and then change the negative and irrational thinking that leads to unwanted emotions. M. Maultsby (1975) developed an approach entitled Rational Self-Analysis (RSA) that is very useful for learning to challenge and change irrational thinking. An RSA has six parts as shown in *Format for Rational Self-Analysis.*

■ Format for Rational Self-Analysis

A	D(a)
Facts and events	Camera check of A

B	D(b)
Self-talk	Rational debate of B

1. _____
2. _____
etc.

1. _____
2. _____
etc.

C	E
Emotional consequences of B	Emotional goals and behavioral goals for similar future events

---

The goal in doing an RSA is to change any unwanted emotion (anger, love, guilt, depression, hate, and so on). An RSA is done by recording the event and self-talk on paper.

Under Part A (facts and events) simply state the facts or events that occurred.

Under Part B (self-talk) write all of your thoughts about A. Number each statement in order (1, 2, 3, 4, and so on). Also write either good, bad, or neutral after each self-talk statement to show yourself how you believed each B section statement reflected on you as a person. (The RSA example which is presented in the inset "A Rational Self-Analysis of a Broken Romance" illustrates the mechanics of this, and other components, of doing an RSA).

Under Part C (emotional consequences) write simple statements describing your gut reactions/emotions stemming from your self-talk in B.

Part D(a) is to be written *only* after you have written sections A, B, and C. Part D(a) is a camera check of the A section. Reread the A section and ask yourself "If I had taken a moving picture of what I wrote was happening, would the camera verify what I have written as facts?" A moving picture would probably have recorded the facts, but not personal beliefs or opinions. Personal beliefs or opinions belong in the B section. A common example of a personal opinion mistaken as a fact is: "Marty made me look like a fool when he laughed at me while I was trying to make a serious point." Under D(a) (camera check of A) correct the opinion part of this statement by only writing the factual part: "I was attempting to make a serious point when Marty began laughing at what I was saying." Then add the personal opinion part of the statement to B (that is, "Marty made me look like a fool.").

Part D(b) is written to determine if the self-talk statements in B follow the five rational rules. Take each B statement separately. Read B-1 first and ask yourself if it is inconsistent with any of the five questions for rational thinking. It will be irrational if it does one or more of the following:

1. Does not fit the facts. For example, you tell yourself no one loves you after someone has ended a romantic relationship—and you still have several close friends and relatives who love you.

2. Hampers you in protecting your life. For example, if you decide you can drive 30 miles to some place when you are intoxicated.

3. Hampers you in achieving your short- and long-term goals. For example, you want to do well in college and you have two exams tomorrow which you haven't studied for, but instead you decide to go out and party.

4. Causes significant trouble with other people. For example, you think you have a right to challenge anyone to a fight whenever you interpret a remark as being an insult.

5. Leads you to feel emotions that you do not want to feel.

If the self-talk statement is rational, merely write "that's rational." If, on the other hand, the self-talk statement meets one or more of the guidelines for irrational thinking, then think of an alternative "self-talk" to that B statement. This new self-talk statement is of crucial importance in changing your undesirable emotion, and needs to: be rational and be a self-talk statement you are willing to accept as a new opinion for yourself. After writing down this D(b-1) self-talk in the D(b) section, then consider B-2, B-3, and so on in the same way.

Under Part E write down the new emotions you want to have in similar future A situations. In writing these new emotions that you desire, keep in mind that they will follow from your self-talk statements in your D(b) section. This section may also contain a description of certain actions you intend to take to help you achieve your emotional goals when you encounter future A's.

In order to make a rational self-analysis work, you have to put effort into challenging the negative and irrational thinking with your rational debates whenever you start thinking negatively. *With effort, you can learn to change any unwanted emotion. This capacity is one of the most important abilities you have.* (Once you gain considerable skill in writing out an RSA, you will be able to do the process in your head without having to write it out.)

This process of challenging negative and irrational thinking *will* work in changing unwanted emotions if you put the needed effort into it. Just as dieting is guaranteed to lose weight, so is this approach guaranteed to change unwanted emotions. Both, however, require an effort and commitment to use the process in order to make it work.

■ A Rational Self-Analysis of a Broken Romance

A 21-year-old male college student wrote the following rational self-analysis:

A (facts and events)	Da (camera check)
Last year I became very involved with a person named Cindy. At the beginning of our relationship	**Da.** This is all factual.

I could tell she was really more infatuated with me than I was with her. Realizing this, I sat down with her and explained that she was coming on too strong for me and that I wasn't ready for a serious relationship yet. I didn't want to hurt her. So there I was, big Joe Authority. I had been in two relationships before and dated a lot, so I knew what could happen if we got involved too quickly. But in all my relationships I had never really felt badly or pondered on them (never had my heart broken). So we went out, and I gradually started to feel more attracted toward her. We got along really well. We could talk very easily with one another, and we shared many things and experiences with each other. We had a small fight now and then, but everything seemed to be going all right. It was at this point I could have used some of my own medicine. I started to believe the things she said, like "I'll never leave you" and "I don't know what I'd ever do without you," thereby setting myself up for a big let down. Then it happened. When she came back to college after summer vacation, she said she didn't want to go steady anymore. Well, needless to say, I was pretty shocked at the suddenness of this. I asked her why, and she said it hurt her too much my being away from her (I live 50 miles away) and that she needed someone around all the time. After this, I told her how I felt and tried to change her mind. I even offered some alternatives, but it didn't work. I could not change her mind, so I left and pretended it didn't bother me, but it did.

B
(my self-talk)

B-1. That bitch! She just wants to go out with other guys. (Bad)

B-2. She's probably seeing another guy behind my back. (Bad)

B-3. This always happens to me in a relationship. (Bad)

B-4. I cannot live without her. (Bad)

B-5. I'll never find anyone like her again. (Bad)

Db
(my rational debates of B)

Db-1. She's not a bitch. A bitch is a mother dog. Cindy is someone I really love and care about. She might want to go out with other guys even though she said this wasn't the case, not to mention it would be the logical thing to do if she wasn't going out with me. I had also said the same thing, that I wanted to date others earlier in our relationship.

Db-2. I don't know this as a fact, and besides, I asked her and she said she was not.

Db-3. Yes, it usually does happen when you break up with someone. It's not bad. It's just normal.

Db-4. This is certainly not true. I lived well without her before I met her, and I can do the same in the future.

Db-5. There are over 2 million eligible women to date—surely some of those have characteristics I'll admire as much as the positives about Cindy.

B-6. She just doesn't want to put the effort into it because I live so far away. (Good)

B-7. She's just a flirt! All she wants to do is hang around in bars so she can be just like her friends. (Bad)

B-8. I'm never going to get involved with anyone again. (Bad)

B-9. I'm just going to treat girls like s— and take advantage of them. (Bad)

B-10. I'll just go out with other girls. (Good)

B-11. Maybe I'll wait and she'll call me back. (Bad)

B-12. I have never felt this bad about breaking up with someone. (Bad)

B-13. I will wait and call her in a few months from now and I can find out what the real reasons are and how she's doing. (Neutral)

B-14. I'd still like to see her, at least we could still be friends. (Good)

C
(my emotions)

Angry, jealous, confused, concerned, lonely and depressed.

Db-6. She said she needed someone around all the time and I can't be there all the time. I don't want someone who can't handle the responsibility.

Db-7. I told her from the beginning I wanted her to go out with her friends. Also, I can't really say she's a tease or a flirt. Although she did mention, commenting about a friend, how nice it must be to have guys wanting to take you out all the time. I really think she began to feel this way later on.

Db-8. Not too smart, especially if I want to get married some day. Besides, I know if I meet someone I really like I would go out with her. Besides that, I know there's a risk involved.

Db-9. This is not like me. I could never do this. Besides, it's not right to take things out on other people.

Db-10. Very good—a positive start, probably the smartest thing I've said so far. After all, there are plenty of fish in the sea.

Db-11. I don't want to do this because it will give me false hopes and lead me to feel more lousy and depressed.

Db-12. True, I have never felt this bad, but it happened. Now I know what it's like and I can learn from this experience.

Db-13. I would like to know the real reason, so if I feel like calling I will. I'm very concerned about her and know there's some very emotional things bothering her about her family life and would like to make sure that these things aren't bothering her.

Db-14. I don't want bad feelings between us, but still I shouldn't get too carried away with this, otherwise it could bring me down.

E
(my emotional and behavioral goals)

To realize that I'm not some victim of some sort of crime, and also realize that this is normal and things like this happen. I'm going to go out with other women, knowing that this is a risk I'm going to have to take.

Changing the Distressing Event. A third way to change unwanted emotions is to change the distressing event. Some distressing events can be changed by directly confronting the events and taking constructive action to change these events. For example, if we are let go from a job, we can seek another; when we find one we will feel better. Or, if we are receiving some failing grades, one way of constructively handling the situation is to meet individually with the instructors of these courses to obtain their suggestions on how to do better. If suggestions are received that appear practical and have merit, we will feel better.

Not all distressing events can be changed. For example, we may have a job that we need and be forced to interact with other employees who display behaviors we dislike. If we cannot change their behaviors, the only other constructive option is to bite the bullet and seek to adapt to the circumstances. However, when it is feasible and practical to change distressing events, we should seek to change these events; if we are successful we are apt to feel better because we will then give ourselves more positive self-talk.

Destructive Ways to Change Unwanted Emotions

There are two other ways to change unwanted emotions which, unfortunately, some people turn to. One of these ways is by seeking to temporarily relieve intense unwanted emotions through the use of alcohol and other drugs. Unfortunately, many people seek to relieve unwanted emotions through the use of such mind-altering drugs as alcohol, cocaine, tranquilizers, and so on. When the effects of the drug wear off, a person's problems and unwanted emotions still remain, and there is a danger that through repeated use a person will become dependent on the drug.

The only other way to relieve unwanted emotions is a sure-fire way— a bullet to the head (or some other form of suicide). This way is the ultimate destructive approach to changing unwanted emotions.

Assessing and Changing Deviant Behavior

Our thinking is not only the primary determinant of our emotions, but also of our actions, as depicted in the following diagram:

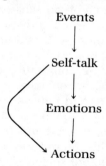

To demonstrate this principle, reflect on the last time you did something bizarre or unusual. What self-talk statements were you giving yourself (that is, what were you thinking) prior to and during the time when you did what you did? An excellent way of determining why a person did something bizarre or unusual is to determine (often through asking the person) what he was thinking prior to and during the time when he did what he did. A deduction of this principle is that in order to change unwanted behavior (such as overeating, drinking to excess, and violent displays of temper), it is necessary for the person with the problematic behavior to change his thinking patterns. These concepts are illustrated in *Our Thinking Determines Our Behavior.*

■ Our Thinking Determines Our Behavior

One of the authors was describing to a class the concept that our thinking primarily causes our emotions and our actions. A male student voluntarily self-disclosed the following:

"What you're saying makes a lot of sense. It really applies to something that happened to me. I was living with a female student who I really cared about. I thought, though, that she was going out on me. When I confronted her about it, she always said I was paranoid and denied it.

Then one night I walked into a bar in this town and I saw her in a corner in a 'clutch' position with this guy. I told myself things like 'She really is cheating on me. Both of them are playing me for a fool. That little tramp.' Such thinking led me to be angry.

I also told myself 'I'm going to set this straight. I'm going to get even with them. I'll break the bottoms off these two empty beer bottles and then jab each of them with the jagged edges.' I proceeded to knock off the bottoms on the bar, and then started walking towards them. I got to within eight feet of them and they were still arm in arm and didn't see me. I began, though, to change my thinking. I thought that if I jabbed them, the end result would be that I would get 8 to 10 years in prison, and I concluded she isn't worth that. Based on this thinking I decided to drop the beer bottles, walk out, and end my relationship with her—which is what I did."

Crime and Delinquency

A second life event or social problem frequently experienced during adolescence or young adulthood is crime or delinquency. A crime is a violation of the criminal law. Practically everyone occasionally breaks the law. For example, if a person drives a car, it is likely that person has intentionally or unintentionally broken such laws as speeding, driving the wrong way on a one-way street, or making an illegal turn. Many people have also committed such offenses as jaywalking, taking something of value from work, and perhaps some liquor violations. If a criminal is defined as someone who has violated the law, then in a broad sense all of us are criminals.

The people who tend to get arrested and spend time in jail or prison are those who generally commit more serious crimes—such as armed robbery, burglary, or rape. (At times, however, some people are arrested, convicted, and treated as a criminal for committing crimes that are no more serious than the bulk of the population commits.) On rare occasions, a person may be arrested, charged, and convicted of a crime he does not commit, with substantial adverse consequences on: his emotional well being, his trust in the justice system, his reputation, and his financial resources.

Adolescents and young adults commit the bulk of crimes, and by far are the most arrested age group in our society (Coleman and Cressey, 1984, pp. 396–438). Juveniles may be arrested for more violations than adults. Juveniles may be arrested for committing all of the same crimes as adults. However, there is an additional set of laws involving status offenses—that is, acts that are defined as illegal if committed by juveniles, but not if committed by adults. Status offenses include running away from home, being truant from school, violating curfew, having sexual relations, being ungovernable, and being beyond the control of parents.

Juveniles when arrested are generally treated differently than adults. The juvenile court tries to act in the best interests of the child, as parents should act. Juvenile courts (in conception) have a treatment orientation. In adult criminal proceedings, the focus is on charging the defendant with a specific crime, holding a public trial to determine if the defendant is guilty as charged, and if found guilty, punishing the wrongdoer via a sentence. In contrast, the focus in juvenile courts is on the current physical, emotional, psychological and educational needs of the children as opposed to punishment for their past misdeeds. Reform or treatment of the juvenile is the goal, even though the juvenile or his family may not agree that the court's decision is in the juvenile's best interest.

Of course, not all juvenile court judges live up to these principles. In practice, some juvenile judges focus more on punishing, rather than treating, juvenile offenders. Court appearances by children can have adverse labeling effects, such as youths viewing themselves as delinquent and then continuing to break the law.

Why do people violate the law? There are many theories about crime causation. For a review of these theories, see Coleman and Cressey (1984, pp. 406–12). Crime is a comprehensive label covering a wide range of offenses, such as drunkenness, possession of narcotics, rape, auto theft, arson, shoplifting, attempted suicide, purse snatching, incest, gambling, prostitution, fraud, false advertising, homicide, and kidnapping. Obviously, since the nature of these crimes varies widely, the motives or causes underlying each must vary widely.

The self-talk theory as described by Zastrow and Navarre (1979), in essence, asserts the reasons for any criminal act can be identified by discovering what the offender was thinking prior to and during the time when the crime was being committed. This theory is a derivation from rational therapy which was described earlier in this chapter. A case example of this theory is presented in *Self-Talk Explanation as to Why Richard Speck Killed Eight People*.

■ Self-Talk Explanation as to Why Richard Speck Killed Eight People

On the night of July 13, 1966, eight nurses were brutally choked and stabbed to death in the house where they lived in Chicago. Richard Speck was arrested shortly afterwards and was found guilty in a 1967 trial. The testimony of a ninth nurse who survived by hiding under a bed was crucial in convicting Speck. Speck was eventually sentenced to serve eight consecutive 50 to 150 year sentences for the eight murders.

Why did he kill these people? For nearly 12 years Speck maintained his innocence. Then, after he realized maintaining his innocence would no longer affect the length of his sentence, he admitted in March 1978, the killing of seven of these eight nurses to Robert Greene, newspaper reporter for Field Enterprises. Speck related the following events, and his thinking, which led to these murders.

It began in the afternoon of July 13, 1966, when he met another man (who later became an accomplice). The two started shooting heroin and drinking whiskey. Speck reported this was the first time he had shot heroin in his life. (The heroin and whiskey probably were a factor in reducing their inhibitions to commit crimes.) In the evening the two started thinking about getting money via burglary. Speck reports (Greene, 1978, p. 2):

The idea of making some money didn't even hit us until that night. We didn't know nothing about the neighborhood (where the women were killed, at 2319 E. 100th St.).

We didn't pick no house. We just knocked. When people answered the door, we asked for phony names and left. We were waiting for no one to answer so we could break in and burglarize it.

We knocked on the girls' door. No one answered. It wasn't planned or nothing. When we got upstairs, we seen them all in the bedrooms asleep. There were three or four bedrooms. I don't know how many.

Some girls woke up. We said, "Stickup, we want your money." I told one of them to get the money. She spit in my face and said she'd pick me out of a lineup. Ninety-nine percent of the people in this country are stool pigeons. I just blew . . . .

I can't even tell you what she looked like, to be truthful. She got stabbed in the heart.

Thus, it appears Speck and his accomplice killed these women to avoid being arrested for burglary and because one of the girls spit in his face. (Unfortunately, the reporter did not explore with Speck his further thinking about what it meant for him to be spat on.)

Speck went on to talk about the murders and what he did to his accomplice (Greene, 1978, pp. 1–2):

I stabbed them and I choked them. If that one girl wouldn't have spit in my face, they'd all be alive today . . . I killed seven of them, the other guy killed one. We left. He's frantic. He says he doesn't want any of the money at all. He's dead now . . . .

I know he's dead, because I shot him six times . . . .

He was frantic; he would have turned state's evidence on me. I was carrying a knife and a gun. We went down by the railroad tracks. He threw the money at me. He said, "Here, I don't want none of this, none of this."

I knew what he was gonna do. Turn state's. So I shot him. I shot him twice in the face. He got up. I was using a .22, a Saturday night special. I shot him four or more times in the face, and he went down.

I put him in a boxcar, and nobody ever found the body.

Thus, it appears Speck killed these people primarily because he believed such actions would cover up the burglary and the ensuing murders, and because he felt gravely offended when a nurse spit in his face. The self-talk that led Speck to do what he did was undoubtedly based on beliefs that Speck held that he would do anything (including murder) to avoid being arrested for a felony, and that "no one is going to mess with me by spitting in my face." These thinking patterns probably developed through prior experiences that Speck had. (Speck had a history of being involved in violent, criminal activity.)

Births Outside of Marriage

A third life event or social problem which frequently occurs in the lives of adolescents and young adults is the occurrence of a birth outside of marriage. Females between the ages of puberty and age 30 account for nearly all of the births outside of marriage. Unmarried teenage females are statistically most vulnerable to the problem of unplanned pregnancies. More than 1 million teenage females become pregnant each year. Most of these pregnancies are unplanned, generally unwanted, and often result from misinformation or lack of access to birth control. Roughly 60 percent of these teenagers have babies, with the remainder ending the pregnancy through an abortion or miscarriage (*Statistical Abstract of the United States: 1984*, pp. 64–72). Over half of the teenagers who carry the pregnancy to full term are still unmarried at the time of birth. Four out of five teenage marriages end in divorce; many of these marriages were preceded by a pregnancy (Furstenberg, 1976). Thus pregnant teenage females who marry are also apt in the future to become single parents. For those who are unmarried when the child is born, over 90 percent decide to keep the child, rather than to place the child for adoption (Fosburgh, 1977).

Many teenagers are not adequately informed about the reproductive process and tend not to use contraceptives. Some teenage females think if they take a birth control pill once a week, they won't become pregnant. Some believe it's safe to have sex standing up. Some are afraid birth control will harm them or their future babies. Some believe if they or their partner smoke marijuana, they are protected. Some believe if they have sex infrequently they won't become pregnant. Others believe if they do not want a baby they will not become pregnant. Some are reluctant to disturb the spontaneity of the sex act by appearing too well prepared ahead of time. Some feel it is their boyfriend's responsibility to use birth control. Some are unable to obtain access to birth control devices. Some try to pay allegiance to the sexual code of waiting until marriage to have sex. They seek to save their self-respect by considering themselves as having been so swept away by love that they could not help themselves. (In this way they maintain that unpremeditated sex is acceptable, while carefully planned sex is something only bad girls engage in.)

A few teenage women who become pregnant want to be a mother for a variety of reasons. Some get pregnant because they feel a need to love someone (a baby), or they feel a need to be loved by someone—a baby. (They are usually surprised to learn that babies usually *take* much more affection than they *give*.) Some hope to gain a husband, or to hurt their parents, or feel a need to get away from a miserable home situation, or see being pregnant as a way to gain attention/recognition/status.

Compared with their peers, teenage fathers are similar in personality and intellectual functioning (Pauker, 1971). Many teenage males automatically assume that their partner is taking precautions, since the Pill is the most common birth control method used by teenage women. Some males are afraid that if they ask a prospective partner whether she has taken birth control precautions, the potential partner will change her mind about desiring sexual intercourse (Scales, 1977). And some males do not give any thought to pregnancy being a possible consequence of unprotected intercourse.

The consequences of teenage parenthood are immense for the young mothers, their babies, and society at large. Pregnant teenagers are more prone than pregnant women in their twenties to a number of complications of pregnancy, including prolonged labor, anemia, and toxemia (McKenry et al., 1979). Teenage mothers are more likely to bear children with neurological defects; two to three times more likely to have babies who die in the first year, and twice as likely to bear premature babies and low-birth-weight babies (McKenry et al., 1979). A major reason that teenage mothers are a much higher medical risk than mothers in their twenties is a lack of early, regular, and high quality medical care (Papalia and Olds, 1981, p. 388).

A teenage woman who becomes pregnant usually is highly traumatized. Often, psychologically, she is still a child who is forced to make adult-type decisions and assume responsibilities she is ill-prepared to assume. Some of the tasks she faces are informing her parents, the father of her child, and close friends and making decisions about whether to terminate the pregnancy. The latter decision almost always involves a confrontation of some of her religious and moral beliefs. If she carries the baby to full term, she then will have to make decisions about adoption, living arrangements, and whether to seek public assistance. If she decides to raise the child she faces the tasks of learning how to physically and emotionally care for a child, how to financially support two people, how to start a career or how to continue her education while at the same time raising a child, and how to make arrangements for socializing with others.

The stigma attached to births outside of marriage has lessened, but the unwed mother and her child are still sometimes subjected to it. The unwed mother may find that some people avoid socializing with her because she has a child. Some employers may be reluctant to hire her because they fear she will not be able to come to work when her child is ill. Some males may be reluctant to form long-term relationships with her because they do not want to be involved in providing care to a baby who is not biologically their child. The stigma attached to having a child outside of marriage may create feelings of guilt and inadequacy in the mother.

A child raised by a single mother frequently has restricted opportunities. The child is substantially more apt to be raised in poverty, and thereby have reduced opportunities: to have the financial resources to eat and dress well, to obtain a good education, and to form the connections that will open up attractive career opportunities. Being raised in a home without a father may also create feelings of inferiority and shame. In some cases a teenage mother is ill prepared to raise a child; she may still psychologically be a child who is now raising a child. Being raised in such an environment increases the chances that the child's physical, emotional, intellectual, and social development may be stunted.

Most single teenage mothers are not prepared by education, experience or maturity to undertake the dual responsibility of parenthood and economic support. In many of these families society inevitably has to contribute to the support of these mothers, usually through public assistance programs, the largest of which is Aid to Families of Dependent Children.

Development and expansion of sex education programs in school systems appears to be one of the better ways to combat the high incidence of births outside marriage. Ursula Myers (1982, p. 189) recommends the components of sex education programs for teenagers should include:

1. Basic biological information about reproduction, pregnancy, birth control, venereal disease, childbirth, abortion, and the medical risks of premature pregnancy and parenthood.
2. An examination of some of the consequences of single parenthood, such as economic dependency, turmoil with parents, interruption and/or dropping out of educational programs, inadequate housing, and difficulties in meeting the role requirements of being both a mother and a teenager.
3. Information on alternatives to sexual intercourse—for example, petting.
4. Parenting skills training—that is, training on how to raise a child.
5. Family living training, role expectations of children and of husband and wife, conflict resolution, decision making, financial counseling, and dating and marriage responsibilities.

Even with over 1 million teenagers becoming pregnant each year, the question of whether to provide sex education is still a controversial issue in many school systems. Apparently many people believe sex education will lead to promiscuity and to teenage pregnancies. Advocates of sex education argue that such programs reduce the number of teenage pregnancies.

Eating Disorders

In the early 1980s Karen Carpenter died from complications resulting from anorexia nervosa. In 1984 Jane Fonda acknowledged she was bulimic for a number of years. Eating disorders have become the disease of the 1980s. Estimates are that roughly 20 percent of college females have an eating disorder (Boskind-White and White, 1983). Most of the people who have an eating disorder are female. The fourth life event or social problem addressed here which can affect adolescents and young adults is an eating disorder.

The two primary eating disorders are anorexia nervosa and bulimia. Both anorexics and bulimics have a fear of fatness, but their techniques for staying thin vary greatly.

An anorexic eats very little food. She is near starvation much of the time. Bulimics, on the other hand, binge and purge themselves. The average American's food intake is around 3,500 calories a day. Bulimics eat substantially more. They may devour as much as 40,000 to 60,000 calories a day. They typically binge on high-calorie junk foods—such as sweets and fried foods. Bulimics also want to stay thin. So they purge themselves through a variety of ways. The most common method of purging is vomiting. Vomiting may initially be induced by putting the fingers down the throat. Some bulimics rely on Q-tips, or on drinking copious amounts of fluids. Many bulimics, with practice, gain control of their esophogal muscles and are able to induce vomiting at will.

Although vomiting is the most common method used by bulimics for purging, there are other methods. These methods include laxatives, fasting, enemas, chewing food and then spitting it out, and compulsive exercise—such as swimming many laps, running many miles, and working out with barbells and weights.

The widespread incidence of bulimia has gone unrecognized until recently. Bulimia is much more common than anorexia. Bulimia has gone unrecognized for so long because binging and purging is almost always done in secret. Bulimics dread the possibility that their habit will be revealed. Very few will tell the whole story to their doctors, therapists, or family.

Anorexics and bulimics have some similarities (Boskind-White and White, 1984). Both are likely to have been brought up in middle-class, upwardly mobile families, where their mothers are overinvolved in their lives and their fathers are preoccupied with work outside the home. For the most part, bulimics and anorexics were good children eager to comply and eager to achieve in order to obtain the love and approval of others. Both tend to lack self-esteem, feel ineffective and have a distorted body image in which they view themselves as being fatter than others view them as being. Both have an obsessive concern with food.

Anorexics and bulimics are different. Anorexics are generally younger, far less socially competent, and much more isolated from and dependent on the family. The anorexic stays away from food. In contrast, bulimics, during times of stress, turn toward food. They binge and then purge. Bulimics, for the most part, are able to function in social and work contexts. Their health may be gravely affected by binging and purging, but their lives are not necessarily in imminent danger, as is often the case with anorexics. Anorexics are also *very* thin, while bulimics are not as underweight and may even be overweight.

One societal reason for the increased incidence of anorexia and bulimia may be the increasing value that our society places on being slim and trim.

Bulimics tend to have few friends. Much of their time is spent on binging and purging and keeping others from knowing about it. Bulimics are often overachievers, and in college tend to attain high academic averages.

Purging for bulimics often becomes a purification rite, as it is frequently viewed as a way to overcome self-loathing. They tend to believe they are unlovable and inadequate. Through purging, they feel completely fresh and clean again. These feelings of self-worth are only temporary. They are extremely sensitive to minor insults and frustrations, which are often used as excuses to initiate another food binge.

Why are bulimics and anorexics primarily women? Orbach (1978) makes a strong case that there are many more pressures on women to be slender and trim than on men. Our socialization practices also overemphasize the importance of women being slender.

Both anorexia and bulimia lead to serious health problems. Stating the obvious, nutritious meals are needed for good health and survival. Anorexics risk starvation, and both bulimics and anorexics risk serious health problems. Fat synthesis and accumulation are necessary for survival. Fatty acids are a major source of energy. When fat levels are depleted, the body must draw on carbohydrates (sugar). When sugar supplies dwindle, body metabolism decreases, which often leads to drowsiness, inactivity, pessimism, depression, dizziness, and fatigue.

Bulimics and anorexics are taking a number of dangerous health risks. Psychotropic drugs (such as tranquilizers and antidepressant drugs) may affect the body differently due to changes in body metabolism. Abnormalities in the electroencephalograms of people with eating disorders have been found. Chronic vomiting can lead to gum disease and innumerable cavities, due to the hydrochloric acid content of vomit. Vomiting can also lead to severe tearing and bleeding in the esophagus. Chronic vomiting may result in a potassium deficiency which then may lead to muscle fatigue, weakness, numbness, erratic heartbeat, kidney damage, and in severe instances, paralysis. Additional medical problems associated with eating disorders are described in Boskind-White and White (1983).

A variety of treatment programs are available for anorexics and bulimics. Individual and group therapy programs have been developed to change the psychological thinking patterns that initiated and are sustaining the undesirable eating patterns. For those for whom severe health problems have already developed, medical care is essential. Therapy for eating disorders includes instruction in establishing and maintaining a nutritious diet. Some elementary, secondary, and higher education school systems are now developing preventive programs which seek to inform students about the risks of eating disorders and which seek to identify and provide services for students who are beginning to develop an eating disorder.

Summary

This chapter focuses on the social changes and social problems encountered by adolescents and young adults. Young people during this time period face the social developmental tasks of moving from parental dependence to adult interdependence, establishing peer relationships, forming intimate relationships with others, and choosing a personal lifestyle. Choosing a personal lifestyle not only involves making career decisions, but also decisions about marriage, cohabitation, remaining single, having and raising children, and perhaps being a single parent or being a stepparent.

Social problems described in this chapter include emotional and behavioral problems, crime and delinquency, births outside of marriage, and eating disorders. There are a wide variety of emotional and behavioral problems. Two models of conceptualizing such problems were summarized: the medical model which views emotional and behavioral problems as being mental illnesses, and a model which holds mental illness does not exist. Adolescents and young adults commit the bulk of crimes. Juvenile courts have more of a treatment orientation than the adult criminal justice system. Unmarried teenage females are statistically most vulnerable to the problem of unplanned pregnancies. The vast majority of single teenage females who carry the pregnancy to full term decide to keep the child. Eating disorders (primarily bulimia and anorexia nervosa) have recently been recognized as a serious problem. Anorexics eat very little food, while bulimics binge and purge.

Middle Adulthood

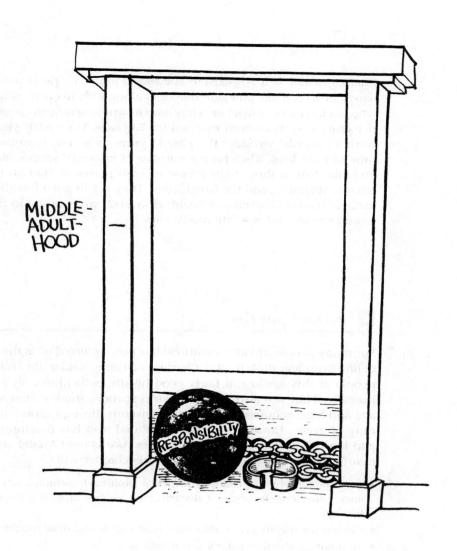

Biological Aspects of Middle Adulthood

Charles Neider is a 50-year-old successful attorney. He is married, has a daughter in college, and generally gets along with his wife, Ginny (age 47), who is a high school teacher. They have a family income in excess of $85,000 per year. They have been married for 23 years. Their early years together were a financial struggle; the past 15 years, however, have been the best time of their lives. They have a number of interests, several close friends, and take two to three trips a year to such places as Hawaii, Europe, the Orient, Acapulco, and the Greek Isles. They are in good health, stay physically fit by working out at a health club, and have a house in the suburbs, a motor boat, and two late model cars.

■ A Perspective

For many people, middle adulthood has been referred to as the prime time of life (Bromley, 1974, p. 243). Charles and Ginny Neider illustrate this. Most people at this age are in fairly good health, both physically and psychologically. They are also apt to be earning more money than at any other age and have acquired considerable wisdom through experiences in a variety of areas. However, middle adulthood also has developmental tasks and life crises. The Behavior Dynamics Assessment Model enables us to examine these tasks and life crises. This chapter will:

- Describe the physical changes in middle adulthood, including physical appearance, sense organs, physical strength and reaction time, and intellectual functioning.
- Discuss the midlife crises associated with female and male menopause.
- Summarize sexual functioning in middle age.
- Present biomedical advances that could dramatically alter our lifestyles. These advances include embryo transplants, genetic screening, cloning, and breaking the genetic code.

The Age Span of Middle Adulthood

Middle age has no distinct biological markers. The beginning of middle adulthood has been identified as ranging from 30 to 40 by different writers. The ending of this age period has been viewed as ranging from age 60 to 70. Somewhat arbitrarily, this text will view the age limits for the beginning and ending of middle adulthood to range from age 30 to age 65. This period covers a large number of years—35.

Physical Changes in Middle Age

Changes in Physical Functioning

Most middle-aged people are in good health and still have substantial energy. Small declines in physical functioning are barely perceptible. At age 48, for example, Althea Gipson, who jogs, may notice it takes her a little longer to run the course. These decreases in physical functioning may be sufficient to make people feel they are aging.

Schanche (1973) asserts the major physical change is a reduction in reserve capacity, which serves as a backup in times of stress and during a dysfunction of one of the body's systems. Schanche reports that the following changes occur:

- The heart of a 40-year-old pumps only 23 liters of blood per minute, compared to the 40 liters that it pumped at age 20.
- The gastrointestinal tract secrets fewer enzymes, which increases the chances of constipation and indigestion.
- The kidneys have a reduced capacity to concentrate waste materials.
- The diaphragm weakens, which results in an increase in the size of the chest.

In addition to gradual reductions in energy levels, middle-aged adults also have less capacity to do physical work. A longer time period is needed to recoup strength after extended and strenuous activity. Working full time at a job and socializing into the wee hours of the evening is harder. Recovering from colds and other common ailments generally takes longer. For those who begin an exercise program, it takes longer to get the body back into physical shape, and it takes longer to get the pain out of joints and muscles after extensive physical exercise. Welford (1977) notes that middle age adults are best at tasks that require endurance rather than rapid bursts of energy. These adults need to make adjustments in their physical activities to compensate for these changes in energy level.

Health Changes

In the early 40s a general slowing down in metabolism usually begins. Individuals who reach this age either begin to gain weight or have to compensate by eating less and exercising more.

Health problems are more apt to arise. Signs of diabetes may occur; and the incidence of gall stones and kidney stones increases (Lindeman, 1975). Hypertension, heart problems, and cancer also have higher rates of occurring during the middle adult years as compared to the younger years. Back problems, asthma, arthritis, and rheumatism are also more common. But because nearly all these ailments can be treated, middle age adults need to have periodic physical examinations in order to detect and treat these illnesses in their early stages of development.

Changes in Physical Appearance

Gradual changes can take place in appearance. Some people discover these changes one day by looking at themselves in a mirror and become alarmed. Gray hairs are apt to appear. The hair may thin. Wrinkles gradually appear. The skin may become dry and lose some of its elasticity. There is a redistribution of fatty tissues; males, for example, are apt to develop a "tire" around their waist, and the breasts of women may decrease in size. Minor ailments develop that cause a variety of twinges.

Some studies with interesting results have been conducted on personal appearance. Bush (1976), who showed slides of both women and men to students, found that those judged to be physically attractive were also judged to be brighter, richer, and more successful in their social and career lives.

Having a physically attractive body has become a cult in our society. Americans spend hundreds of hours and millions of dollars on grooming themselves, exercising, and dieting. The body beautiful cult leads those who judge themselves to be attractive to feel that they are superior to those they judge to be less attractive physically.

Berscheid and Walster (1975) found that women who were physically attractive during college days tended during middle adulthood to be less happy, less satisfied with their lives, and less well adjusted than women who were more ordinary looking during their college years. (Men's happiness did not appear to be related to physical attractiveness.)

Why do physically attractive women have a less satisfying life as they grow older? One explanation is that physically attractive women develop their sense of self-worth in terms of their physical features. As their physical beauty begins to fade in middle adulthood, they may feel a greater sense of loss than ordinary looking women who have developed a sense of self-worth that emphasizes other features—for example, a pleasing disposition, being friendly, being a caring and honest person, and being productive and competent. Because women are more apt to be judged on their physical features in our society than men, perhaps men are less apt in middle adulthood to be adversely affected psychologically by changes in their physical appearance. A double standard of aging is found in our society. Facial lines, gray hair, and wrinkles often are viewed as indicating distinction in men, while similar changes in women are viewed as being unattractive and no longer sexually appealing. (It is interesting to note that men tend to be more sensitive than women in a different area; men are more apt than women to feel old before their time if they have not achieved career or financial success. Apparently more pressure is placed on men in our society to have a successful career.)

Changes in Sense Organs

A gradual deterioration occurs in the sense organs during middle adulthood. Middle age adults are apt to develop problems with their vision that may force them to wear bifocals, reading glasses, or contacts. The psychological impact of being required to wear glasses may be minor or can be fairly serious if the person begins "awfulizing" about growing older.

During middle age there is also a gradual hardening and deterioration of the auditory nerve cells. The most common deterioration in middle adulthood is *presbycusis*, which is a reduction in hearing acuity for high frequency tones. Timiras and Vernadakis (1972) have found that middle-aged men generally have significantly greater losses of high frequency tones than middle-aged women. Sometimes the hearing loss is enough so that a hearing aid is needed.

Engen (1977) has found that there are generally some minor changes in taste, touch, and smell as a person grows older. Most of these changes are so gradual that a person makes adjustments without recognizing that changes are occurring.

Changes in Physical Strength and Reaction Time

Physical strength and coordination are at their maximum in the 20s, and then have slow declines in middle adulthood. Generally these declines are minor. Manual laborers and competitive athletes (boxers, football players, weightlifters, wrestlers, ice skaters) are most apt to be affected by these gradual declines. Some sports figures who have excelled in athletic contests and have been applauded and worshiped by fans may experience a traumatic identity crisis in middle adulthood when they no longer are as competitive. Their lifestyle and identity have been based on excelling with athletic skills, and now that those skills are fading they need to find new interests and another livelihood.

■ An Identity Crisis When the Applause Stops

Chuck Walters excelled in sports in grade school and high school. In high school he lettered in basketball, football, and baseball. In his senior year he was 6'1" and weighed around 220 lbs. He was a halfback on the football team and scored 10 touchdowns in eight games. He was an outfielder on the baseball team and batted .467, hitting 13 home runs. Especially good at basketball, he was quick and averaged 23.4 points a game.

He was recruited by a number of universities

for both his football and basketball skills. He chose to accept a basketball scholarship at a major midwestern university. As a bonus for accepting a scholarship, an alumnus bought him a Pontiac Firebird. He was also given a summer job by another alumnus as a construction worker, which paid well and didn't require much work. Chuck had concentrated on sports and partying in high school and college. In college he chose the easiest major (Physical Education) he could find and only occasionally went to class. By taking the minimum number of credits needed to maintain his basketball eligibility and by having a tutor, he managed to make his grades to play varsity basketball. He loved college. He had plenty of money, a new car, many dates, and was worshipped on campus as being a hero. He thought this was the way to live. In his junior year he averaged 16.7 points as a guard, and in his senior year he was an all-conference selection and averaged 22.3 points a game.

He also began experimenting with cocaine. He loved being applauded and adulated. He just knew the merry-go-round would keep whirling around.

To his surprise, he wasn't drafted by the pro's. So he went to Europe to play basketball there, hoping to excel so that some pro team would give him a try out. He played in Europe for five years and was traded several times. At age 30 he was finally cut.

This cut became a major identity crisis. He realized the applause and adulation was now coming to a screeching halt. He drank and used cocaine to excess in order to try to numb the pain of his loss. He had failed to graduate from college, having only junior standing when his scholarship eligibility ran out. He had been carried in college by his tutor, as his reading and writing skills were at the 10th grade level. He is uncertain what his career interests are—he now fears he has no saleable skills and he is worried his money may soon run out. He can no longer support his extravagant lifestyle. At the present time he is considering trying to get some fast money by smuggling cocaine into the United States. His cocaine habit is costing him $100 per day. What should he do? He doesn't know, but he's dulling the pain with cocaine.

Simple reaction time reaches its optimum at around age 25 and is then maintained until around age 60, when the reflexes gradually slow down (Woodworth and Schlosberg, 1954). As people grow older they learn more and are generally better at a number of physical tasks in middle adulthood than they were in their 20s—such tasks include driving ability, hunting, fishing, and golf. The improvement that comes from experience outweighs minor declines in physical abilities. The same is true in other areas. Persons aged 45 to 54 have been found to sort mail with the fewest mistakes (Papalia and Olds, 1981, p. 468). Skilled industrial workers are most productive in their 40s and 50s, partly because they are more careful and conscientious (Belbin, 1967). Middle-aged workers are less likely to have disabling injuries on the job—which is probably due to learning to be careful and learning to use good judgment (Hunt and Hunt, 1974).

Changes in Intellectual Functioning

Contrary to the cliche "You can't teach an old dog new tricks," mental functions are at a peak in middle age. Middle-aged adults can continue to learn new skills, new facts, and can remember those they already know well. Unfortunately, many middle age people do not fully use their intellectual capacities. Many settle in to a job and family life and are less active in using their intellectual capacities than they were in their younger years when they were attending school or when they were learning their profession or trade. Some middle-aged adults are unfortunately trapped by the erroneous belief that they can't learn anything new.

If a person is mentally active, that person will continue to learn well into later adulthood. Practically all cognitive capacities show no noticeable declines in middle adulthood. Adults who are trapped by the belief that they completed their education in their 20s are apt to show declines in their intellectual functioning in middle adulthood. There is truth in the adage "What you do not use, you will begin to lose."

In regards to specific intellectual capacities, there are variations. People in middle adulthood who use their verbal abilities regularly (either on the job or through some other mental stimulation such as reading) further develop their vocabulary and verbal abilities. There is some evidence that middle-aged adults may be slightly less adept at tests of short-term memory, but this is usually compensated by wisdom gained from a variety of past experiences (Papalia and Olds, 1981, p. 470). If middle-aged adults are mentally active, their IQ scores on tests are apt to show slight increases (Kangas and Bradway, 1971).

Creative productivity is at optimum point in middle age. In a study of scientists, scholars and artists, Dennis (1966) found the highest rate of output was generally in the 40s and that productivity remains high for many people in their 60s and 70s. Troll (1975, p. 39) suggests there are different age peaks for different types of creative production: "In general, the more unique, original and inventive the production, the more likely it is to have been created in the 20s and 30s rather than later in life. The more a creative act depends on accumulated development, however, the more likely it is to occur in the later years of life."

In the past decade an increasing proportion of middle-aged adults have been returning to college. Some want an additional degree to move up a career ladder. Some seek training that will help them to perform their present jobs better. Some are preparing to seek a new career. Some are taking courses to fill leisure time and to learn about subjects they find interesting and challenging. Some attend to expand their knowledge in special interest areas, as in photography or sculpturing. Some want to expand their interests in preparation for retirement years. Professionals in rapidly expanding fields (such as computer science, law, medicine, gerontological social work, the sciences, engineering, and teaching) need to keep up with new developments. (Social work practitioners often take workshops and continuing education courses to keep abreast of new treatment techniques, new programs, and changes in social welfare legislation.)

Stubblefield (1977, p. 351) eloquently summarizes the importance of viewing education as a lifelong process: "In our modern complex society, no one ever completes his or her education. Learning throughout the life-span is a requirement, not an option."

Life is more meaningful if one's intellectual capacities are challenged and used. College instructors are generally delighted to have returning students in their classes, as such students have a wealth of experiences to share and are highly committed to learn as much as they can. Compared to younger students, they are less apt to be majoring in partying.

When middle-aged adults return to college, it often takes a few weeks to get used to the routine of taking notes in classes, writing papers, and studying for exams. A few courses, such as mathematics and algebra, tend to be difficult, as returning students have forgotten some of the basic concepts they learned earlier. Since people at age 50 learn at nearly the same rate and in the same way as they did at age 20, most returning students do well in their courses.

Colleges are not the only places that offer adult education courses. Such courses are also provided by vocational and technical centers, businesses, labor unions, professional societies, community organizations, and government agencies. The concept of lifelong education has been a boon for many colleges and universities as the increase in returning students has generally offset the seats left empty by decreased enrollment of younger students.

There is generally only a small amount of deterioration in physical capacities, and almost no deterioration in potential for mental functioning in middle adulthood. Cognitive functioning may actually increase well into later adulthood (Kaluger and Kaluger, 1984, pp. 526–27). The sad fact is that many people fail to be sufficiently active both mentally and physically so that their actual performance, physically and mentally, falls far short of their potential performance.

Female Menopause

Menopause is the event in every woman's life when she stops menstruating and can no longer bear children. The median age when menopause occurs is 49 years, although the event may occur in some women who are as young as 36, or may not occur until a woman is in her mid 50s (Olds, 1970). The time span ranging from two to five years during which a woman's body undergoes the physiological changes that bring on menopause is called the *climacteric*. There is some evidence of a hereditary pattern for the onset of menopause, as daughters generally begin and end menopause at about the same age and in the same manner as their mothers. Menopause is caused by a decrease in the production of estrogen, which leads to a cessation of ovulation.

Menopause begins with a change in a woman's menstrual pattern: (1) periods are skipped and become irregular in their timing, (2) there is a general slowing down of flow of blood during menstruation, (3) there is an irregularity in amount of blood flow and an irregularity of timing of the periods, or (4) there is an abrupt cessation of menstruation. The usual pattern is skipped periods, with the periods occurring farther and farther apart.

During menopause there is a reduction of activity of the ovaries. This change of life affects other glands and may produce disturbing symptoms. Goodman et al. (1978) report approximately 75 percent of women undergoing menopause encounter few, if any, disturbing symptoms. Kirby (1973) notes that about 25 percent of women experience serious symptoms and need medical therapy.

During menopause a number of biological changes occur. The ovaries become smaller and no longer secrete eggs regularly. The fallopian tubes (having no more eggs to transport) become shorter and smaller. The vagina loses some of its elasticity and becomes shorter. The uterus shrinks and hardens. The urine has some changes in its hormonal content (Sherman, 1971). All of these changes are biologically related to the cessation in the functioning of the reproductive system.

A number of other internal changes also occur. The lymphatic glands and the spleen decrease in size. There are changes in the wall of the intestine which increases the chances of becoming constipated. A few women experience a lessened capacity to retain urine.

The most obvious symptoms experienced during menopause, however, are the external physical changes. These symptoms may last for a few weeks, several months, or several years.

One of the most common is hot flashes, which is also called hot flushes. During a hot flash, the body first becomes warm, perspires excessively, and then feels chilled. These hot flashes may extend over the entire body or be limited to the face and neck. Most frequently hot flashes occur during the months when periods are missed. They usually cease after the menses stop completely. Hot flashes generally last only a minute or two and can be controlled by medication.

The hair on the scalp and external genitalia may become thinner. The labia may lose their firmness. The breasts may lose some of their firmness and become smaller. There is a tendency to gain weight and the body contour may change. Some women lose weight. Itchiness, particularly after showering, may occur. Headaches may increase, and insomnia may occur. Some muscles, particularly on the upper legs and arms, may lose some of their elasticity and strength. Some masculine characteristics may appear, such as growth of hair on the upper lip and at the corners of the mouth. Many of these symptoms can be treated and minimized by the use of estrogen replacement therapy.

A variety of psychological reactions also accompany menopause, but certainly not every woman encounters psychological difficulties. If a woman is well adjusted emotionally before menopause, she is unlikely to experience psychological difficulties (Flint, 1976).

The psychological reactions that a woman has about menopause are determined by her thoughts and interpretations of this life change. If a woman sees this change as simply being one of many life changes, she is not apt to have any adverse difficulties. She may even view menopause as being a positive event in which she no longer has to bother with menstruation or worry about getting pregnant.

On the other hand, if a woman views menopause negatively, she is apt to develop such emotions as anxiety, depression, feelings of low self-worth, and lack of fulfillment. Some women believe menopause is a signal they are losing their physical attractiveness, which they further erroneously interpret as meaning an ending of their sex life. Some no longer feel needed, as their children have left the nest and they have a low paying, boring job—or no job at all. Some are widowed, separated or divorced, and regret still having to "scrimp and save to make ends meet." For many women this is a time of reexamining the past; if the past is interpreted as having been something else than what they had desired, they feel unfulfilled and cheated. Even worse, if they appraise the chances for a better life to be nil, they are apt to be depressed and have a low sense of self-worth. If they viewed their main role in life as being a mother and raising children, they now will feel a sense of rolelessness; and if their children fall far short of meeting their hopes and expectations, they are apt to view themselves as being a failure. Some women seek to relieve their problems through alcohol. Others seek out understanding lovers. Some isolate themselves, while others cry much of the time and are depressed.

There is no clear-cut way to identify the exact time when menopause ends. Most authorities agree that the climacteric can be considered as ending when there has been no menstrual period for one year. (Some women may go several months during menopause before having one of their last periods.) Physical symptoms of menopause usually end when ovulation ceases.

Some doctors urge that some type of birth control be continued for two years after the last period in order to prevent a pregnancy. "Change-of-life" babies are rare because conception, although possible, is unlikely to occur. Middle-aged pregnancies do present increased health risks. The child has a higher chance of having a birth defect. For example, the rate of Down's syndrome in the children of younger mothers is 1 in 600, while the rate for older mothers rises to 1 in every 50 births (Kaluger and Kaluger, 1984, p. 533). Spontaneous abortions are more common in women who become pregnant after the age of 40 years. In addition, older women are more apt to have a prolonged labor due to the loss of elasticity of the vagina and the cervix.

All in all, menopause does not appear to have the serious consequences for most women that are implied by old wives' tales. Neugarten et al. (1963) surveyed several hundred women and found that women who had been through it had a much more positive view than women who had not. As one woman noted, "I've been healthier and in much better spirits since the change of life. I've been relieved of a lot of aches and pains" (cited in Neugarten, 1968, p. 200).

Male Climacteric

In recent years there has been considerable discussion about male menopause. (In a technical sense the term *male menopause* is a misnomer, as menopause means the cessation of the menses. The term *male climacteric* is perhaps more accurate.) It should be noted that men who have gone through menopause still retain the potential to reproduce.

Sometime between the ages of 35 and 60 men reach an uncertain period in their lives that has been termed a *mid-life crisis*. It is a time of high risk for divorce, for extramarital affairs, for career changes, for accidents, and even for suicide attempts. All men experience it to some degree and emerge a bit changed, for better or for worse (Schanche, 1973). It is a time of questions: "Is what I'm doing with my life really satisfying and meaningful? Would I be better off if I had pursued a different vocation or career? Do I really want to be married to my wife?"

Male menopause is a time when a man reevaluates his marriage and his family life (Pierce, 1976). This period of reassessment is often characterized by nervousness, decrease in sexual activity, depression, decreased memory and concentration, decreased sexual interests, fatigue, sleep disturbances, irritability, loss of interest or self-confidence, indecisiveness, numbness and tingling, fear of impending danger, and/or excitability. Other possible symptoms are headaches, vertigo, constipation, crying, hot flashes, chilly sensations, itching, sweating, and/or cold hands and feet (Reitz, 1977).

The man going through male menopause usually encounters some event which forces him to examine who he is and what he wants out of life. During this crisis he looks back, as well as ahead, upon his successes and failures, his degree of dependency on others, the outcomes of his dreams, and his capabilities for what lies ahead. Depending on what he sees and how he deals with it, this experience can be either exhilarating or demoralizing. He sees the disparity between youth and age, between hope and reality (Schanche, 1973).

Male menopause is caused by a combination of psychological and biological factors. Biological factors will first be discussed. As a male grows older, his hair thins and begins to turn gray. He develops more wrinkles and tends to develop a tire around his waist. His physical energy gradually decreases, and he can no longer run as fast as he once did. There are changes in his heart, his prostate, his sexual capacity, his chest size, his kidneys, his hearing, and his gastrointestinal tract.

The production of testosterone gradually decreases. Testosterone is an androgen which is the most potent naturally occurring male hormone. It stimulates the activity of male secondary sex characteristics, such as hair growth and voice depth, and helps to prevent deterioration in the sex organs in later life. The male sex glands are essential for the vitality of youth. These glands are the first glands to suffer when aging occurs. Two of the more subtle changes—as compared to hair loss, wrinkles, slowing blood circulation, more sluggish digestion—are a decline in the number of sperm in an ejaculation and a reduction of testosterone present in the plasma and urine. The testes lose their earlier vigorous functioning and produce decreasing amounts of hormones (Zaludek, 1976). Older men generally take a longer time to achieve an erection. It also takes a longer time before an erection can be regained after an orgasm.

Some men do have greater hormonal fluctuations at menopause. Kimmel (1974) summarizes studies which have found evidence of monthly cycles in some men with hormonal fluctuations in a 30 day rhythm. The majority of men move into menopause gradually as far as biology is concerned. Dr. Herbert Kupperman has defined what he calls a true male climacteric. These males suffer from testicular dysfunctions, hot flashes, neurological symptoms, and psychosomatic symptoms (Reitz, 1977).

For this pure climacteric male the treatment of choice is hormone replacement therapy. Androgens which are consistently injected for four to six years can halt and actually reverse thinning of the bone that weakens the body. The treatment returns the male to potent sexual functioning and helps him to control premature ejaculation or incomplete erection. The man first undergoes a battery of laboratory and clinical tests to determine his general state of health and the depth of his hormonal needs. He is checked every four to six months. If he has a testosterone deficiency, he may need treatment for the rest of his life (Zaludek, 1976).

The biological changes (including the diminishing production of sex hormones) do play an important part in male menopause, but perhaps even more important is the problem of being middle aged in a culture that worships youth and looks down on age (Reitz, 1977). Many of the problems associated with male menopause are due to psychological factors.

There is the fear of aging, which is intensified by an awareness that his mental and physical capacities are declining, including his sexual capacities. Also involved is the fear of failure, either with his job or in his personal life. Fear of women may be a part of this. A man may think that his sexual prowess is waning, and then may fear women's greater sexual capacities. He may also have a fear of failing in his sexual activities. The man with self-doubts is especially susceptible to the fear of rejection. He is very sensitive to derogatory comments about his age, his physique, or his thinning hair. There is a fear of death as he realizes he has probably lived at least half of his life. All of these fears are apt to have an adverse impact on his emotional and sexual functioning (Zaludek, 1976).

A significant part of male menopause is due to depression, which is often brought on by the fear of aging and a recognition that his sexual

A reduction of energy accompanies middle age, manifesting itself in many ways. For example, after exercising, middle-aged women will have a harder time getting the pain out of their joints and muscles than they did when they were younger. Other middle-age slowdowns? The heart pumps less blood per minute and the kidneys have a reduced capacity to concentrate waste materials. What major physical change is thought to cause this midlife slowdown? (Gregg Theune)

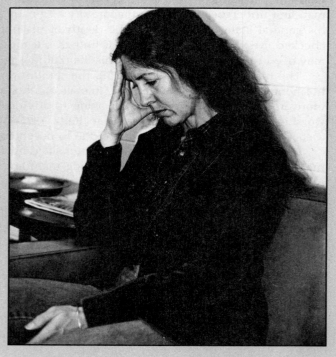

Menopause is the time in a woman's life when menstruation stops and she can no longer bear children. If a woman sees menopause as merely one of life's changes, her attitude toward it will be positive. If not, a variety of psychological reactions can accompany it. Some women feel anxious, unfulfilled, or even depressed when this life change occurs. Why does menopause cause depression in some menopausal women? (Charles Zastrow)

This mother and daughter are graduating from college at the same time. The mother represents a new breed of women who are returning to school at middle age. Some of these middle-aged women are getting the college degrees they never earned. Some are changing careers, and others are keeping up with new developments in fields they've already entered. What are some of the other reasons that prompt women to return to school in midlife?
(Gregg Theune)

Just as a satisfying marriage is likely to increase sexual pleasure in a marriage, a satisfying sexual relationship contributes to a satisfying marriage. For married couples with sexual problems, sex therapy is becoming increasingly popular. One study showed that men experience the greatest sexual satisfaction in their marriages from ages sixteen to twenty-five, while women's sexual satisfaction peaks between ages thirty-six and forty-five. What are other factors that contribute to sexual problems in marriage?
(Charles Zastrow)

powers are waning (Pierce, 1976). He also realizes that he will never achieve the successes that he envisioned for himself years earlier. His bouts with depression may be so profound that he may contemplate suicide (Zaludek, 1976). Depression during this mid-life crisis may also be triggered by: a reevaluation of childhood dreams, conflicts in need of resolution, new erotic longings and fantasies, sadness over opportunities lost, and a new questioning of values. All of this is coupled with a search for new meaning in life. He realizes half of his life may be gone, and time becomes more precious. He worries over things undone and there does not seem to be enough time for everything. He has the feeling of missing out on a big chunk of life. The man who is engaged in activities outside his daily job is a less likely candidate for depression. It is unbalanced to be so busy with getting ahead that the pleasures of life are missed (Reitz, 1977). To recapture some of his former enthusiasm and perhaps to shake some of his unsettling doubts and fears, he may drive himself to work harder, to exercise more, or to seek younger women (Zaludek, 1976).

A man at mid-life is also apt to experience a growing dissatisfaction with his job. He feels a sense of entrapment as the pressure to pay bills forces him to continue working at a job that is increasingly boring and unfulfilling. Along these lines is the fact that his personal identity is deeply entwined with his work roles. His job has provided him with an opportunity to define his self with others, to enter into a stable set of relationships with colleagues and/or clients, and to explain his place in the world. Now he questions that place. Occupational aspirations may change several times during this time period. The emphasis may shift from measuring success in terms of achievement to measuring it in terms of economic security. Also at this time, movement up the occupational ladder is largely completed. If he has not achieved his work goals by age 40 or 50, he may realize he may never achieve his goals; he may even be demoted one or two steps down the occupational ladder (Wallberg, 1978).

■ Five Stages of Adult Development Surrounding Male Menopause

Schanche (1973) describes five stages of adult male development. Stage one is Getting into the Adult World. This stage occurs in a man's early 20s. He has pretty much broken away from home by this time. He has begun to play an individual role in terms of a job, friendships, and sexual relationships. He is not yet inwardly committed to a way of life. Normally in this stage, the man acquires a mentor, usually an older man who encourages, helps, and influences him toward a truly adult commitment. The mentor provides the wise and the reassuring qualities of an older brother. The relationship is a friendship with adult equality, but the mentor also performs the fatherly tasks of teaching, caring, criticizing, and helping. This relationship normally ends when the man reaches his 30s.

Stage two occurs when the man is in his early 30s and is referred to as Settling Down. This is when he makes an adult commitment. (If the man has not made a significant start toward settling down by the age of 32, his chances of forming a reasonably satisfying life structure are diminished.) At this stage he fashions a mature life structure which includes establishing a stable home, loving and caring for a wife and children, and accepting responsibilities in the community at large.

Between the ages of 36 and 39, he reaches stage three which is Becoming One's Own Man. This is a transitional time. He becomes acutely aware of the constraints and dependencies of his life. He begins to chafe under the authority and influence that others exercise over him. He feels constrained in his marriage and his other relationships. A sense of aging and mortality become clear. He has sexual fantasies which he may act out by having affairs or he may daydream about them. He questions whether he wants the security of his marriage, or if he would rather have the freedom to pursue new relationships with other women. At this time, he rejects his mentor in order to find out where he stands on his own.

Stage four is the Mid-Life Crisis. At this time he asks himself if he has lived up to his original goals and seeks to find a way to accept the disparity between what he had hoped for and what actually happened. He also realizes there is a disparity between what he is, and what he has accom-plished. Even if nothing in his external life changes, the man does. He cannot return to or simply remain in his earlier life structure. It is inevitable that the internal changes give different meaning to his life structure.

The fifth and final stage, is Restabilization and the End of the Mid-Life Decade. This stage may involve radical changes in his lifestyle, relatively minor ones, or no apparent changes at all. Most men do remain in the same marriage, the same job, and the same lifestyle, but will begin to put more emphasis on the more fulfilling aspects of life and be reconciled to the aspects that are missing.

Midlife Crisis: True or False?

The ease or panic with which a man faces his mid-years will depend on how he has accepted his faults and his strengths throughout life. The man who has developed a strong affective bond with his family will fare better than the man who followed a more isolated and career-oriented course. To age gracefully is to realize that he has done the best he could with his life (Pierce, 1976).

Many physicians will prescribe antidepressant therapy and counseling, along with requesting the support and understanding of family and close friends (Zaludek, 1976). Men who undergo a mid-life crisis need to realize that there is still a great deal of pleasure and satisfaction to be gotten out of life. This is not the end; there are still things left for them to do.

Women go through similar psychological worries; for example, the empty nest syndrome. Recent research indicates a declining proportion of women are affected by the empty nest syndrome as more women are emphasizing careers. The behavioral changes are just more often explained away in the woman by her decreasing hormonal levels. Mid-life is a time of reassessment for both sexes as people in this age group look over their life and see where they are and how they got there. It is a time of reprioritizing one's life. With the right attitude, this time period can become a time of reappraisal, renewed commitment, and growth.

Life is full of crises and transitions: learning to walk, entering school, starting to date, marrying, becoming a parent, and being informed that someone close has died. All of these events are apt to be both a crisis and a transition to living somewhat differently. Similarly, psychologically realizing that there is slow deterioration in one's physical capacities, and realizing that there is a disparity between one's earlier dreams and present reality is apt to be a crisis for many people.

Some health evidence exists showing that midlife is a crisis for many people. Hypertension, peptic ulcers, and heart disease are most often diagnosed in middle age patients (Rosenberg and Farrell, 1976). The suicide rate for males between the ages of 40 and 60 is nearly three times as high as the rate for males in the 15 to 24 age group, and the rate of first admissions for alcoholism treatment for middle-aged individuals is higher than for younger adults (Kaluger and Kaluger, 1984, p. 539). These statistics suggest that middle adulthood can be a period of stress and turmoil.

But mid-life need not be a serious crisis. Neugarten (1970) has noted that a person who develops an inner sense of the life cycle and who is aware of expected life events is not apt to experience a mid-life crisis. Such an individual is apt to encounter a variety of normal crises and stresses, but is not apt to experience an intense identity crisis (Neugarten, 1970).

Thus, it appears that mid-life (comparable to other age periods) is a time of transition and change. For some it is a crisis, but not for others (Hutsch and Deutsch, 1981). For some women, menopause is a precipitating factor that sets off a mid-life crisis; while for other women some of the symptoms may be uncomfortable, but an identity crisis is not precipitated. For some men and women, their children leaving home precipitates an identity crisis, while other men and women delight in seeing their children grow and develop and experience a new sense of freedom in being able to travel more and in being able to pursue more vigorously special interests and hobbies. Lowenthal and Chiriboga (1972) report that most men and women look forward to the departure of the youngest child.

In an extensive study Costa and McCrae (1980) conclude that men who undergo a mid-life crisis are apt to have had adjustment problems for a long time. Kaluger and Kaluger (1984, p. 541) conclude: "Mid-life crises may be the result of unadjusted adolescents and young adults who grow up to be unadjusted middle-aged adults rather than the result of a universal crisis confined to mid-life."

Sexual Functioning in Middle Age

Sexual expression is an important part of life for practically all age groups. In this section we will focus on sexual functioning during middle adulthood: in marriage, in extramarital relationships, for those who are divorced or widowed, and for the never-married.

Sex in Marriage

A close relationship exists between overall marital satisfaction and sexual satisfaction, particularly for men (Maier, 1984, p. 325). These two factors probably influence each other. Marital satisfaction probably increases the pleasure derived from sexual intercourse; and a satisfying sexual relationship probably increases the satisfaction derived from a marriage. Women are much more likely to be orgasmic in very happy marriages than in less happy marriages (Masters, Johnson and Kolodny, 1985, p. 393).

Generally speaking, marriage partners report satisfaction with marital sex. Hunt (1974) found most spouses rated sexual intercourse with their partners to be "very pleasurable" or "mostly pleasurable." Interestingly, the ratings given by husbands were generally higher than those of the wives. For men, satisfaction was highest in the 16 to 25 age group and decreased slightly as men grew older. For women, satisfaction was highest in the 36 to 45 age group. These findings are consistent with studies which have found that a man's sex drive reaches its peak at a relatively young age, while that of a woman tends to peak in her late 30s or early 40s (Maier, 1984).

The median frequencies of marital coitus by age groups as found in the Hunt (1974) study are presented in Figure 8.1. Similar results were found in a more recent study by Trussell and Westoff (1980). The frequency of marital coitus is highest when the individuals are in their 20s (between two and four times a week), and then gradually declines to about once a week in couples over age 45. Westoff (1974) found that women who have a job because they wish to work report a higher frequency of marital intercourse than either wives without a paid job or wives who work out of economic necessity. Masters, Johnson and Kolodny (1985, pp. 393–94) note there is a strong correlation between the frequency of intercourse and satisfaction with marital sex for women. These researchers add there is a strong correlation between a wife's ability to communicate her sexual desires and feelings to her husband and the quality of marital sex.

Parents after the birth of their first child report less sexual satisfaction on the average than childless couples (Maier, 1984). The presence of children in a family generally functions as an inhibition to sexual relations (James, 1974). Contrary to popular belief, the highest frequencies of sexual intercourse occur in childless couples. Many adjustments, pressures, and problems can be associated with parenthood.

Married couples now use a greater variety of sexual techniques than couples in earlier generations. Couples now experiment with a variety of positions. The female-on-top position is increasingly being used, as it gives the female greater control over stimulation of the clitoris than the man-on-top position. Oral sex has also become more popular. Couples today also

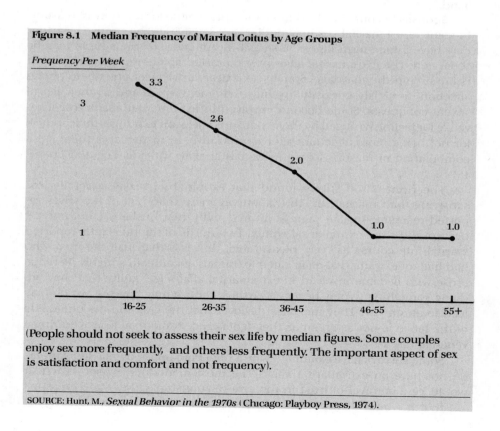

Figure 8.1   Median Frequency of Marital Coitus by Age Groups

Frequency Per Week

(People should not seek to assess their sex life by median figures. Some couples enjoy sex more frequently, and others less frequently. The important aspect of sex is satisfaction and comfort and not frequency).

SOURCE: Hunt, M., *Sexual Behavior in the 1970s* (Chicago: Playboy Press, 1974).

spend a longer time lovemaking. The amount of sex play has lengthened to an average of about 15 minutes, and the duration of actual coitus has increased from an average of two minutes in the Kinsey et al. (1948) study to about 10 minutes in the Hunt (1974) study. This change may reflect a greater awareness by married men and women at the present time that women are more likely to enjoy sex more and to be orgasmic if intercourse is unhurried.

Hunt (1974) also found that about 72 percent of young husbands masturbated, and so did 68 percent of young wives. Sex therapists generally view masturbation to be a normal and useful sexual outlet.

Extramarital Sexual Relationships

About 50 percent of husbands and approximately 40 percent of wives report having experienced extramarital coitus (Hunt, 1974; Tauris and Sadd, 1977). In spite of these fairly high rates, most Americans frown on this practice. Levitt and Klassen (1973) found that 72 percent of the people they surveyed stated extramarital sex is "always wrong," while an additional 14 percent regarded it as "almost always wrong."

For males, the frequency of extramarital coitus decreases with age, while with females there is a gradual increase up to around age 40. These sex differences may reflect differences in the peaking of the sex drive. Wives with full-time jobs are more apt to have extramarital affairs than housewives (Tauris and Sadd, 1977). Working wives have an increased opportunity to become acquainted with a variety of men who are not known by the husband.

Spouses become involved in extramarital coitus for a variety of reasons. In some cases marital sex may not be very satisfying. The spouse's partner may have a long-term illness, a sexual dysfunction, or the couple may be separated. The extramarital affair may represent an attempt to obtain what is missing in the marriage. Some seek extramarital involvements to obtain affection, to satisfy curiosity, to find excitement, or to add to their list of sexual conquests. Some become involved in extramarital affairs to get revenge for feeling wronged by their spouse. Some want to punish their spouse for not being more affectionate or appreciative. In many cases there are a combination of reasons for an extramarital affair (Greene, Lee and Lustig, 1974).

The Hunt (1974) survey found that extramarital sex is generally less satisfying than marital sex. In that survey more than half of the wives reported reaching orgasm "almost always" with their husbands, but only 39 percent did so in extramarital coitus. Two thirds of the husbands reported marital intercourse as "very pleasurable," but less than half the men who had had an extramarital affair rated extramarital coitus this highly. Perhaps those who become involved in extramarital affairs feel guilty that they are doing something wrong, or may fear their spouse may find out which may lead to an uproar. They may also discover that the grass on the other side of the fence is not as green as they fantasized. Some may fear acquiring a venereal disease.

Some surveys have examined why a high percentage of married couples do not have an extramarital affair. The most mentioned reason is that it would be a betrayal of trust in the love relationship. Other stated reasons are that it would damage the marital relationship, that it would hurt the spouse, and that the probable benefits of an affair are not worth the consequences (Hunt, 1974; Sprey, 1972).

In most cases extramarital affairs are carried out in secret. Sometimes the spouse later discovers the affair. Typical reactions to the affair are summarized by Maier (1984, p. 332) through his experiences as a marriage counselor:

> Among the most common feelings expressed by a spouse after such a discovery are anger and a sense of being deceived and betrayed. In addition, the affair is often seen as a symbolic insult to the spouse's affection and sexual adequacy. Certain subcultures consider it appropriate to seek some type of revenge or retribution.
>
> Generally speaking, isolated sexual experiences are less disturbing to spouses than prolonged extramarital affairs. Brief sexual encounters can sometimes be written off as temporary reactions to sexual frustration; however, longer affairs are seen as greater threats to the marital love relationship.

The discovery of an extramarital affair may lead to a divorce, but not always. Sometimes the discovery of an affair is a crisis that forces a couple to recognize that problems (sexual or nonsexual) exist in their marriage, and the couple then seeks to work on these to improve the marriage. Some spouses reluctantly accept and adjust to the affair without saying much. They may be financially dependent on their partner, or they may have a low sense of self-worth and have made adjustments to being emotionally abused by their spouse in the past. Others show little reaction because they realize a divorce is expensive, socially degrading, and may result in loneliness. In such marriages the relationship may become devitalized with the partners having little emotional attachment to each other.

A few spouses react to an extramarital affair by gradually entering into a consensual extramarital relationship. In such a relationship extramarital sexual relationships are permitted and even encouraged by both partners. One type of a consensual extramarital sex arrangement is *mate swapping*. In this arrangement two or more couples get together and exchange partners, either retiring to a separate place to have sexual relations or having sex in the same room with various combinations of partners.

■ The Coolidge Effect in Males Who Join Swinging Groups

Denfield and Gordon (1970) have found that some men in swinging groups report greater potency with a variety of sexual partners than with a single partner. This has been called the *Coolidge effect* because President Calvin Coolidge is said to have remarked that roosters have an unusually high potency level in the presence of many hens (Bermant and Davidson, 1974).

Some researchers on animals have reported comparable results. Maier and Maier (1970) found an average bull will copulate with a cow about ten times, resting for increasing periods of time between ejaculations and finally appearing to be exhausted. However, if additional cows are then presented to the bull, he may copulate up to 70 times in a 24-hour period. Part of the Coolidge effect may be due to novelty. Peters (1980) found that a sexually exhausted male rat again became sexually aroused when researchers provided a discolike atmosphere with intermittent musical tones and flashing lights. Interestingly, no evidence of a Coolidge effect has been found in human females or in female animals (Daly and Wilson, 1983). Also, the Coolidge effect does not appear to exist for some mammalian species (Dewsbury, 1981).

Sex Following Divorce

When matched for age, divorced men have a slightly higher frequency of coitus than married men. Divorced men also tend to have a variety of partners (Hunt, 1974). Divorced women also generally have a fairly active sex life, although the incidence of postmarital sex tends to be lower than when they were married. They also tend to have a smaller number of partners than divorced men (Hunt, 1974). Divorced women report a higher frequency of orgasm than they experienced in marital sex (Hunt, 1974). Divorced men also report sexual relationships are satisfying. These results should not be interpreted as meaning that sex following a divorce is more satisfying than marital sex. People who have a satisfying sexual relationship may be less likely to get a divorce. People who get a divorce are probably not as likely to give high ratings to their sexual relationship when they were married.

Hunt and Hunt (1977) report that divorced people are less concerned about hiding their sexual relationships from their children than were divorced people a generation ago. Divorced people apparently now have more liberal views on sexuality than was true in the past.

Sex in Widowhood

Ending a marriage by divorce can be traumatic, but ending a marriage by the death of one's spouse is usually more traumatic. In a divorce a spouse has input into the decision to part, but most widows and widowers have no input and wish their partner was still alive. They not only have to adjust to being single, but also to the death of a loved one.

Widowers are more likely than widows to establish a new sexual relationship. Around 90 percent of widowers form a new sexual relationship, while less than half of widows do (Gebhard, 1968). In middle and later adulthood there are substantially more eligible single women than single men. There is greater cultural acceptance of older men dating younger women, than vice versa. Cultural patterns also encourage widowers to establish new sexual relationships, while widows feel pressure to be sexually loyal to their deceased spouse. Widows also tend to receive more emotional support from friends and family; and therefore, may feel less need to form a new sexual relationship.

Sex among the Never-Married

Very little research has been conducted on the sexual lifestyles of never-married adults. The attitudes of singles about their status vary widely. Some plan never to marry. Some want to marry, but haven't found the right partner, or have found someone they want to marry but that person refuses to marry. Some desperately seek a partner.

The lifestyles of the never-married vary tremendously. Some contently become celibate. Others are highly involved in the singles scene—living in apartments for single people, going to singles bars, and joining singles clubs. Some singles have numerous sexual partners. Some singles, on the other hand, become involved in their careers or hobbies, and while they occasionally may date, they do not want the restrictions of a marriage. Some singles are content to date someone steadily for a few years, and when that relationship sours, they move on to another. Some occasionally cohabit with the opposite sex. Some become addicted to alcohol or to some other drug, and spend relatively little time in romantic relationships.

Celibacy

A small minority of people choose to abstain from sexual intercourse. Certain religious leaders (such as Buddhist monks and Roman Catholic nuns and priests) are required to remain celibate. In other cases, individuals choose to abstain for a variety of reasons. They may not want the entanglements of sexual relationships. They may have a low sex drive. They may enjoy other ways, such as masturbation, of expressing their sexuality. They may fear acquiring a venereal disease or have a venereal disease and do not want to risk passing on the disease to someone else. They may be in a conflictive relationship with a partner and, therefore, may not desire to become sexually intimate. They may have a partner who has a low sex drive or one who is physically incapable of intercourse.

Although some people find abstinence to be very difficult, others experience it as satisfying. Coyner (1976), a feminist, suggests that periods of celibacy may be important for self-exploration and recovery from broken romances.

Bio-Medical Advances in Human Reproduction

Changes in our lifestyles are primarily determined by technological advances (Ogburn and Nimkoff, 1955). In the past 50 years many advances have resulted in dramatic changes in our lifestyles.

Predicting what technological breakthroughs will occur in the future and how these advances will affect our lifestyles is difficult and undoubtedly filled with error. Because of the emphasis placed on research and technology in our society, future technological breakthroughs are apt to occur even more rapidly than in the past. In fact, Alvin Toffler (1970) in *Future Shock* asserts that adjusting psychologically to rapid lifestyle changes is currently a major problem and will become the most difficult adjustment people will have to make in future years.

In spite of predicted technological advances, environmentalists are predicting our civilization is in serious danger due to overpopulation, depletion of energy resources, likelihood of mass famines and starvation, and dramatic declines in the quality of life. There is also a serious danger that the technological development of nuclear weapons will result in a nuclear war which has the potential of destroying civilization as we know it.

What the future will hold is difficult to accurately predict. The worst mistake, however, is to take the "ostrich head in the sand" approach in which no effort is made to plan and control the future.

Currently a number of developments in the biomedical area have the potential of dramatically changing lifestyles, not only for middle age adults, but for all age groups. Whether these developments are desirable has not as yet been determined. Most of these advances involve developments in the area of human reproduction, and there is extensive controversy as to whether these developments will be judged to be desirable or immoral.

Embryo Transplants

A breakthrough in the human reproductive area occurred in 1984 when an egg donated by one woman was fertilized and then implanted in another woman. Australian researchers in January 1984 reported the first successful birth resulting from a procedure in which an embryo was externally conceived and then implanted in the uterus of a surrogate (*Wisconsin State Journal*, February 4, 1984, p. 2). This type of surrogate motherhood is a modern-day twist on the wet nurse of earlier times.

This type of surrogate motherhood varies from the type described in chapter 2 in which the surrogate mother contributes half of the genetic characteristics through the use of her egg. With this type of surrogate motherhood, the surrogate does not contribute her own egg (and therefore none of the genetic characteristics of the child).

Surrogate pregnancies can, on one hand, be seen as the final step in the biological liberation of women. Like men, women could sire children without the responsibility of pregnancy and childbirth.

■ Embryo Case Gains International Attention

A South American couple, Elsa and Mario Rios, amassed a fortune of several million dollars in real estate in Los Angeles. In 1981 they enrolled in a test-tube baby program at Queen Victoria Medical Center in Melbourne, Australia, after their young daughter died. Several eggs were removed from Mrs. Rios and fertilized by her husband's sperm in a laboratory container. One of the fertilized eggs was then implanted in Mrs. Rios' womb, but she had a miscarriage 10 days later. The two remaining embryos were frozen so doctors could try implantation later.

On April 2, 1983 the couple was killed in the crash of a private plane in Chile. Since doctors have successfully thawed and implanted frozen embryos (which have resulted in births) a number of social and legal questions arise. These questions include the following:

Should the embryos be implanted in the womb of a surrogate mother in the hope of developing to delivery?

Are the embryos legal heirs to the multimillion dollar estate of the Rios?

Does life legally begin at conception? If a surrogate mother carries the embryo to birth, is she legally the mother, and is she entitled to some of the inheritance?

Do embryos conceived outside the womb have rights? If so, what rights? Should these rights be the same as accorded humans?

Should experiments be conducted on fetal tissue in order to consider producing embryos for spare parts that could be used in transplants?

This case dilemma highlights how the rapid advance of in vitro fertilization has outstripped attitudes and laws.

SOURCE: "Embryo Case Opens New Debate" *Wisconsin State Journal*, June 19, 1984, pp. 1–2.

But, surrogate pregnancies promise to create a legal nightmare. Do the genetic mother and father have any binding legal rights? Can the genetic parents place reasonable restrictions on health, medical care, and diet during the pregnancy? Can the genetic parents require the surrogate mother not to smoke or drink? Can the genetic parents require the surrogate to abort? Could the surrogate abort despite the genetic parents' consent? Whose child is it—what if both the genetic mother and the surrogate mother legally want to be recognized as the mother after the child is born? Will the lower class and minorities serve as holding tanks for upper class women's children? Legal experts see far-reaching changes in family law, inheritance, and the concept of legitimacy if laboratory fertilization and child-rearing by surrogate mothers become accepted practices.

Human embryo transplants, when combined with principles of genetic selection, would also allow people who want superhuman children to select embryos in which the resultant infant would have a high probability of being free of genetic defects and allow parents to choose with a high probability the genetic characteristics they desired—such as the child's sex, color of eyes and hair, skin color, height, muscular capabilities, and IQ. A superhuman embryo would be formed from combining the sperm and egg of a male and female who are thought to have the desired genetic characteristics. This breakthrough will raise a number of personal and ethical questions. Couples desiring children may face the decision of having a child through natural conception or selecting in advance superhuman genetic characteristics through embryo transplants.

Another question that will arise is whether our society will attempt to use this new technology to control human evolutionary development. If the answer is affirmative, decisions will need to be made about which genetic characteristics should be considered as being desirable, and questions will arise about who should have the authority to make such decisions. Although our country may not desire to control human evolutionary development in this manner, will we not feel a necessity to do so if a rival nation begins a massive evolutionary program? In addition, will parents have the same, or somewhat different, feelings toward children who are the result of embryo transplants as compared to children who result from natural conception?

Genetic Screening

Almost all states now require mandatory genetic screening programs for various disorders. About 2,000 human disorders are caused by defective genes, and it is estimated that each of us carries two or three of them (Reilly, 1977). Mass genetic screening could eliminate some of these disorders. One screening approach that is increasingly being used with pregnant women is amniocentesis, which is used to determine chromosomal abnormality. *Amniocentesis* is the surgical insertion of a hollow needle through the abdominal wall and uterus of a pregnant female to obtain amniotic fluid for the determination of chromosomal abnormality.

A new test called *chorionic villi sampling* (CVS) has recently been developed to determine if fetuses are normal. The test, which can be performed right in a physician's office as early as the fifth week of gestation, is painless and relatively simple. It provides a viable alternative to amniocentesis, which cannot be performed until the sixteenth or seventeenth week of pregnancy, relatively far into the second trimester of pregnancy.

CVS involves inserting a long suction tube through the vagina into the uterus. A sampling of the embryonic tissue which will later develop into the placenta is then taken. The tissue sample is composed of long, fingerlike projections called chorionic villi. They serve as a passageway for nutrients, oxygen, and waste to pass between mother and embryo. Since the tissue is made up with the same cells as the fetus, consequent laboratory analysis should detect genetic abnormalities.

CVS, however, is not yet readily available. Another potentially prohibitive factor is that costs run from $550 to $800 or more (which is about the same as that of amniocentesis). More and more pregnant women are being pressured to terminate the pregnancy of a high-risk or proven genetically inferior fetus. Also, some genetic disorders can be corrected if caught in time.

Several years ago *Fortune* magazine carried an article with the heading "How to Save $100 Billion" which urged genetic screening be used much more extensively to reduce the incidence of persons with genetic diseases. Bylinsky (1974, p. 152) notes "if we allow our genetic problems to get out of hand by not acting promptly . . . we can run the risk of overcommitting ourselves to the care and maintenance of a large population of mentally deficient patients at the expense of other urgent social problems."

Genetic screening programs raise serious issues regarding questions such as: Who shall live? Who shall be allowed to have children? Who shall make such decisions? Is this a direction which our country ought to take?

The eugenics movement was proposed late in the 19th century and embraced by many scientists and government officials. Similar to today, eugenics was designed to improve humanity or individual races by encouraging procreation by those deemed most desirable and discouraging those judged as deficient from having children. The movement fell into disfavor for a while when Adolf Hitler used it to justify the Holocaust, which exterminated millions of Jews, gypsies, mentally retarded people, and others. Are we headed in a similar direction again?

Cloning

Cloning refers to the process whereby a new organism is reproduced from the nucleus of single cell. The resultant new organism has the same genetic characteristics as the organism contributing the nucleus; that is, it probably will be possible to make biological carbon copies of humans from a single cell. Biologically, each cell is a blueprint containing all the genetic code information for the design of the organism. Cloning has already been used to reproduce cows, frogs, and mice.

One type of cloning amounts to a nuclear transplant. The nucleus of an unfertilized egg is destroyed and removed. The egg is then injected with the nucleus of a body cell by one means or another. It should then begin to take orders from the new master, begin to reproduce cells, and eventually manufacture a baby with the same genetic features as the donor. The embryo would need a place to develop into a baby—either an artificial womb or a woman willing to supply her own. The technology for a complete artificial womb has not as yet been developed. The resultant clone would start life with a genetic endowment identical to that of the donor, although learning experiences may alter the physical development or personality. The possibilities are as fantastic as they are repulsive. For example, imagine a basketball team of two Kareem Abdul-Jabbars and three Magic Johnsons, or a baseball team with nine Dave Winfields in the batting order and ten Steve Carletons on the pitching staff. With a quarter-inch piece of skin, one could produce 1,000 genetic copies of any noted scientist, or of anyone else!

Cloning could, among other things, be used to resolve the ancient controversy of heredity versus environment. On the other hand, there are grave dangers and undreamed-of complications. What is to prevent the Adolf Hitlers from making copies of themselves? Will cloning fuel the population explosion? What legal rights will clones be accorded (inheritance for example)? Will religions recognize clones as having a "soul"? Who will decide who will be able to have clones made of themselves? Couples may face the choice of having children naturally or raising children who are copies of themselves.

Breaking the Genetic Code

Genes are the chemical blueprints of all living things. Genes determine whether an organism will grow into a plant, an animal, or a human being. They also determine our sex, color of our eyes and hair, and in part, how intelligent we are.

These genes are located inside the cell nucleus. Scientists now know there are about 100,000 genes inside each human cell and have now isolated over 20,000 of these genes and identified the specific jobs they do in the body (Ubell, 1985).

Genes are largely composed of long spiraling double strands of atoms. These strands are DNA (deoxyribonucleic acid), which is the master chemical of genes. The sequence or layout of these atoms contains all the instructions the cell needs to function.

Genes control the chemistry of every cell. When a gene is malformed, missing, or out of place, the chemical activity of the cell is affected. In humans, such genetic defects can lead to diseases, or to such problems as cancer, Down's syndrome, cystic fibrosis, diabetes, anemia, atherosclerosis, Tay-Sachs disease, and many other diseases.

For example, it has been discovered that each of us probably carries one or more cancer-causing genes, called *oncogenes* (*onkos* is Greek for "mass" as in the massing of malignant cells in a tumor). Undisturbed, oncogenes are harmless. However, if something comes along that triggers the oncogenes, they make a chemical that causes cells to divide and multiply uncontrollably, forming millions of additional cells that invade and choke our organs. Ubell (1985, p. 12) notes: "Researchers have yet to unravel exactly what turns on an oncogene, how to prevent it from turning cancerous or, once it has turned cancerous, how to turn it off. Once they do, they can cure and prevent cancer."

It appears that scientists are on their way with genetic engineering to unbelievable breakthroughs. Ubell (1985, p. 11) summarizes some of these:

> Imagine a new world, a world in which disease no longer kills or maims. Cancer is cured—even prevented before it invades and destroys body tissue. All bodily infections, from malaria to viral pneumonia, are eliminated or effectively treated. And every inherited disease, from Down's syndrome . . . to diabetes, is cured in the womb so that the individual is born healthy.
>
> Imagine in that same world of the future that there is ample food to feed all people because crops also resist disease, grow under bad weather and soil conditions and provide more nourishment than any of today's fruits, vegetables, and grains. And that hardier, disease-resistant cows, chickens, and other livestock turn feed into milk or meat more effectively.

One approach that may be used to alter the genetic makeup of an organism is gene splicing. An illustration is provided in *Super Livestock: A Likely Breakthrough in Food Production*. One way to affect all genes in an organism is to splice the desired gene into the genes of a virus. Since a virus infects all the body cells, it would transfer the desired gene to all genes in the body.

■ Super Livestock: A Likely Breakthrough in Food Production

Using genetic-engineering techniques, scientists have successfully transferred human growth hormone genes into fertilized mice eggs. As a result they have produced super mice that have grown more than twice as large as their litter mates without the genes. Within the next few years, scientists are predicting this same technique will produce super livestock. The hope is a breakthrough that will allow farmers to produce livestock that grow faster and bigger and that more efficiently convert feed into meat.

Kim McDonald speculates on the possibilities:

- Giant sheep, cattle, and poultry that eat normal amounts of feed but grow faster and put less fat and more protein on their bodies than do ordinary livestock.
- Pigs that produce mammoth porkchops at no extra charge to the farmer.
- Dairy cows that can, at the farmer's command, increase their milk production 30 percent over normal amounts with the simple addition of a harmless chemical to their feed.

SOURCE: Kim McDonald, "Rapid-Growth Genes Could Yield 'Super Livestock' ", *Chronicle of Higher Education*, February 8, 1984, p. 1.

When genes are more fully understood, it may be possible sometime in the future to keep people alive, young, and healthy almost indefinitely (Rorvik, 1969). Aging can be controlled, and medical conditions (such as allergies, cancer, and arthritis) can be relatively easily treated and eradicated. Such possibilities stagger the imagination. Many legal and ethical questions will arise; perhaps two of the more crucial will be who shall live and who shall die, and who shall be permitted to have children. Such a fountain of youth may occur within some of our lifetimes.

These biomedical advances have the potential of dramatically altering the values and lifestyles of not only middle-aged adults, but all age groups. In terms of the Behavior Dynamics Assessment Model, the future advances in biomedical technology can be viewed as future life events that will impact on all individuals in the world. The technology will provide people with a wide range of new decisions; for example, whether to make clones of themselves, whether to terminate a pregnancy if the embryo is found to have chromosomal abnormalities, and whether to have superhuman children.

Summary

For many people, middle adulthood is the prime time—most middle-aged adults are in good health (both physically and psychologically) and tend to earn more money than at any other age. Middle adulthood covers a range of years; somewhat arbitrarily, the authors consider middle adulthood to range from age 30 to age 65. Some decline in physical capacities occurs in middle adulthood. There is also a higher incidence of health problems than in younger years. Cognitive functioning may actually increase during middle adulthood. The sad fact is that many people fail to be sufficiently active both mentally and physically so that their actual performance *mentally* falls far short of their potential performance.

Female menopause is the event in every woman's life when she stops menstruating and can no longer bear children. For a few women menopause is a serious crisis, but for many it is just another of life's developmental changes. It appears that many males reach an uncertain period in their lives which is referred to as a mid-life crisis. The ease or panic with which a man faces his mid-years will depend on how he has accepted his weaknesses and strengths throughout life.

A man's sex drive reaches it peak in the early twenties, while that of a woman tends to peak in her late thirties or early forties. There appears to be a close relationship between overall marital satisfaction and sexual satisfaction. Extramarital sex is usually reported as being less satisfying than marital sex. There are some dramatic technological advances occurring in biology and medicine which include embryo transplants, genetic screening, cloning, and breaking the genetic code.

Psychological Aspects of Middle Adulthood

It is Saturday night on Michigan Avenue in Chicago and Doug and Shirley Peepers are engaged in a favorite activity on a warm summer evening: strolling down this Gold Coast street and watching the thousands of other people who are also strolling and people watching. Americans have a fascination with people watching. While strolling, Doug and Shirley enjoy gossiping about what makes people tick; that is, discussing why people do what they do. For example, they look at the elderly bag lady dressed in a moth-eaten red plaid overcoat, knee-high nylon hose, and ancient, shaggy blue sneakers. They wonder how she got to be this way. Is she the victim of some tragic story? Where is her family, or doesn't she have any? Likewise, Doug and Shirley look at the sleek, jet-set millionaire pulling up to the curb in his Maserati Biturbo so that a fastidiously neat, uniformed doorman can help him out of the car. The millionaire is striking with his fashionable haircut, glowing gold jewelry, and Gucci clothes. Doug and Shirley wonder if he is a self-made computer magnate displaced from Silicon Valley, or if he's the by-product of generations of wealth.

■ A Perspective

Figuring out the underlying reasons that cause others' actions often has substantial payoffs. If a salesperson knows what motivates people to buy a certain product, he or she can then structure the sales pitch around this focus. If a counselor knows why a father is abusing his child, the counselor then knows what has to be changed to stop the abuse. If a mother knows what discipline techniques will be effective with her children, she is then better prepared to curb unwanted behavior in her children.

The primary focus of this human behavior and social environment text is to provide theoretical frameworks that will help the reader to observe and assess human behavior. The Behavior Dynamics Assessment Model described in Chapter 1 provides a model for identifying a multitude of variables that influence human behavior.

Shirley Peepers is a computer programmer, and her husband Doug is a mechanical engineer. Although they have had little formal training in assessing human behavior, playing amateur psychologist is one of their favorite leisure time activities. As with anything else, assessments of human

behavior are apt to be more accurate when one has greater knowledge and awareness of the significant cues to attend to. Professional social workers who will be planning interventions with people and organizations have a special need to develop their assessment skills. Middle adulthood provides as critical a stage as earlier developmental periods to examine some of the psychological dynamics of human behavior. Consistent with this focus, this chapter will:

- Describe Erikson's (1963) and Peck's (1955) theories of psychological development during middle adulthood. Because there is a paucity of psychological theories specifically directed at middle adulthood, the primary focus will be on describing contemporary theories and models for assessing human behavior throughout the life span.
- Summarize Maslow's theory on hierarchy of needs.
- Discuss human behavior in terms of game analysis and script analysis.
- Describe nonverbal communication cues.
- Summarize Glasser's control theory explanation of human behavior.
- Summarize the neuro-linguistic programming approach to assessing communication.

Generativity versus Stagnation

Erikson's (1963) seventh life stage developmental crisis is generativity versus stagnation. Generativity involves a concern and interest in establishing and guiding the next generation. The crisis of generativity versus stagnation is perceived by a middle-aged adult to involve a commitment to improve the life conditions of future generations. The achievement of generativity involves a willingness to care about the people and the things that one has produced. It also involves a commitment towards protecting and enhancing the conditions of one's society.

The achievement of generativity is important for the survival and development of any society. It involves having the adult members committing themselves to contributing their skills, resources, and creativity to improve the quality of life for the young.

The contributions may be monumental, as were Martin Luther King, Jr.'s and Gandhi's, to equality and human rights. For most people, however, the contributions are less well known, as, for example, the work done by volunteers for human service organizations. Adults serve on school boards, are active members of parent-teacher associations, serve on local government boards, are active in church activities, and so on. In each of these roles, adults have opportunities to positively influence the quality of life for others. To some extent it is a reciprocity situation—when these adults were younger they were recipients of such services from other adults; now they are providers of such services. In this regard, Newman and Newman (1984, p. 445) note:

> Adults serve as advisers, government leaders, religious leaders, and educators. In each of these roles, individuals have opportunities to extend the impact of their values and goals to others. Through their loving response to their children, through the care they take to perform their work at a high standard of excellence, and through their expressed respect for the diverse people they encounter, adults model a capacity for generativity that promotes optimism and perseverance among younger generations.

The opposite of generativity is stagnation. Stagnation indicates a lack of psychological movement or growth. Some adults are self-centered and seek to maximize their pleasures at the expense of others; such people are stagnated as they have difficulty in looking beyond their own needs or experiencing satisfaction in taking care of others. Having children does not necessarily guarantee generativity, as adults who are unable to cope with raising children or with maintaining a household are likely to feel a sense of stagnation. Burnout has been identified as being one of the signs of stagnation (Pines and Aronson, 1981).

The experience of stagnation appears to be somewhat different in the narcissistic adult and the depressed adult. The narcissistic individual is egocentric, and generally relates to others in terms of how others can serve him. Such an individual may be fairly happy until the physical and psychological consequences of aging begin to occur. Such individuals often then experience an identity crisis when they realize their beautiful bodies and other physical attributes are waning. Many of these individuals experience a conversion to finding other meanings in living than a totally self-involved lifestyle. For example, they may become a coach for a little-league softball team or become active in church activities.

On the other hand, a depressed person is likely to perceive himself as having insufficient resources to make any contribution to society. Such a person is apt to have low self-esteem, to be pessimistic about opportunities for improvement in the future and, therefore, to be unwilling to invest effort into improving himself or in seeking to help others.

Peck's Theories of Psychological Development

Peck (1955) expanded Erikson's concepts by suggesting that there are four psychological advances critical to successful adjustment in middle adulthood:

1. Socializing versus sexualizing in human relationships.   Peck suggests it is psychologically healthy for middle age adults to redefine the men and women in their lives so that they value them as individuals, friends, and companions, rather than primarily as sex objects. (The women's movement and other groups have been advocating that all age groups should view people as being individuals worthy of respect, rather than as being sex objects.)

2. Valuing wisdom versus valuing physical powers. Peck views wisdom as the capacity to make wise choices in life. He suggests well-adjusted middle-aged adults are aware that the wisdom they now have more than compensates for decreases in stamina, physical strength, and youthful attractiveness.

3. Cathectic flexibility versus cathectic impoverishment. Cathectic flexibility is the capacity to shift emotional investments from one activity to another, and from one person to another. Middle-aged adults are apt to experience breaking of relationships due to the deaths of friends, parents, and other relatives and the growing independence of children and their moving out of the home. Physical limitations may also necessitate a change in activities.

4. Mental flexibility versus mental rigidity. By middle age, most people have completed their formal years of education and have been sufficiently trained for their jobs or careers. They have also arrived at a set of beliefs about an afterlife, religion, politics, desirable forms of entertainment, and so on. Some middle-aged adults stop seeking new information and ideas and become set in their ways and closed to new ideas. Such people are apt to be stymied in their intellectual growth and are apt to view life as mundane, unfulfilling, and unrewarding. Others are apt to continue to seek new experiences and be challenged by additional learning opportunities. They use their prior experiences and answers they've already arrived at as provisional guides to the solution of new issues. Such people are likely to view life as being meaningful, rewarding, and challenging.

Maslow's Hierarchy of Needs

Abraham Maslow (1954, 1968, 1971) viewed humans as having tremendous potential for personal development. He believed it was human nature for people to seek to know more about themselves and to strive to develop their capacities to the fullest. He viewed human nature as being basically good and saw the striving for *self-actualization* as a positive process as it leads people to identify their abilities, to strive to develop them, to feel good as they become themselves, and as being beneficial to society.

Maslow saw most people as being in a constant state of striving. Very few people fully attain a state of self-actualization. The vast majority of people are in a state of disequilibrium and are striving to satisfy their needs.

Maslow identified a hierarchy of needs which motivate human behavior. When people fulfill the most elemental needs, they strive to meet those on the next level, and so forth, until the highest order of needs is reached. In ascending order, these needs are:

1. Physiological: food, water, oxygen, rest and so on.
2. Safety: security; stability; and freedom from fear, anxiety, threats and chaos. A social structure of laws and limits assists in meeting these needs.
3. Belongingness and love: intimacy and affection provided by friends, family, and lover.
4. Self-esteem: self-respect, respect of others, achievement, attention, and appreciation.
5. Self-actualization: the sense that one is fulfilling one's potential and is doing what one is individually suited for and capable of. This need results in efforts to create and to learn. A fully developed, self-actualized person displays high levels of all of the following characteristics: acceptance of self, of others, and of nature; seeks justice, truth, order, unity, and beauty; has problem-solving abilities; is self-

directed; has freshness of appreciation; has a richness of emotional responses; has satisfying and changing relationships with other people; is creative, and has a high sense of moral values.

Maslow's hierarchy of needs is illustrated in Figure 9.1. The needs at each level must be fairly well satisfied before the needs at the next level become important. Thus, physiological needs must be fairly well satisfied before safety needs become important, and so on.

Maslow did not offer an age-stage approach to development. Striving for self-actualization is seen as a universal process that can be observed at nearly all ages. However, it is likely that there is some progression among age groups. Infants probably have a strong emphasis on physiological needs. As a person gradually grows older, safety needs are emphasized, and then belongingness and love needs, and so on. Since middle-aged adults have had a variety of learning experiences and tend to be at the peak of their earning potential, they tend to have a greater opportunity to focus on meeting self-actualization needs. However, such crises as unemployment, prolonged illness, and broken relationships can switch the emphasis to a lower area of need.

Game Analysis and Script Analysis

Analyzing human behavior in terms of games and scripts provides another useful theoretical framework for understanding and changing human behavior. Both game analysis and script analysis were developed by Eric Berne, who is recognized as being the founder of Transactional Analysis (TA), which is a psychotherapy approach. (See Dusay and Dusay, 1984, for a summary of TA.)

Game Analysis

A game (Berne, 1964) can be defined as a set of transactions with a gimmick (that is, a hidden scheme for attaining an end). In a game one or more participants are consciously or unconsciously striving to achieve an

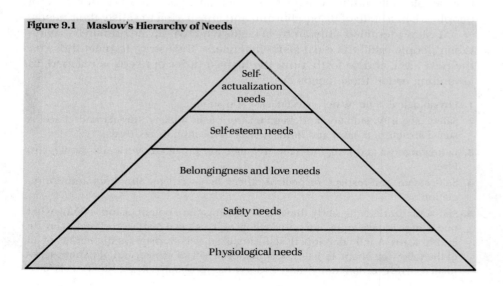

Figure 9.1   Maslow's Hierarchy of Needs

Self-actualization needs

Self-esteem needs

Belongingness and love needs

Safety needs

Physiological needs

ulterior outcome by using a hidden scheme. For example, in the following exchange a salesperson uses a gimmick to sell the product:

Salesperson: "This one is better, but you can't afford it."
Male Customer: "That's the one I'll take."

The salesperson arouses the customer's pride by telling him that he is unable to afford the better, but more expensive item. Psychologically, the customer says to himself, "I'll buy the expensive item just to show that arrogant so-and-so that I'm as good as anyone."

People who are attempting to achieve a hidden outcome may or may not be aware of their intentions—or aware of the gimmick they are using. For instance, a husband who has a vague fear his wife may desert him may not be aware he is playing a game when he says to her, "Honey, why don't you quit work and stay home to take care of the house? I can earn enough to support both of us." He may not be aware with this communication that he wants his wife to stay home so that she becomes financially dependent on him, and so that she has less opportunity to meet other men.

Although some games may lead to substantial financial loss or mental anguish for some participants, not all games are necessarily undesirable. For instance, an individual having a strong need for social approval may perform many altruistic and charitable deeds.

A game may also be repeated over and over. A few people, for instance, continually play "one-up." For some, playing a certain game may become so much a part of their personality that it can aptly be called their style of life. A male alcoholic who denies that he has a drinking problem is an example of this. (The alcoholic's payoffs for denying his drinking problem are the rewards he receives from drinking—such as feeling high and as a way to temporarily escape facing his problems.)

The alcoholic game also illustrates another aspect of games—several people may be involved. In the traditional alcoholic game described by Berne (1964), there may be a nagging, masochistic wife who literally drives her husband to drink so he will abuse her when inebriated. This wife receives two sets of payoffs. The abuse received is a form of recognition or attention.[1] The second reward the wife receives is that the day after the drunken episode the wife has ammunition to belittle and berate her husband, and to get him to do things for her to atone for his behavior. The alcoholic is also apt to have companions who frequently say: "Let's go have a drink—a drink will be good for you." Their payoff is the fun and partying they have. Then there may also be a sympathetic listener to the alcoholic—perhaps a bartender who listens in order to get the alcoholic to spend his money.

Some people are involved in playing games that have destructive outcomes for themselves and for others. Often, people are unaware that a destructive game is being played. For example, family members of an alcoholic may make elaborate efforts to keep the drinking problem hidden from others, without realizing they are continuing to make it possible for the alcoholic to drink.

---

[1]Transactional analysis makes an important psychological point by asserting that in the absence of receiving positive strokes, a person will seek negative strokes. Strokes are forms of human recognition. Positive strokes include greetings, smiles, approval, cheers, and applause. Negative strokes include cold looks, disapproval, criticism, and frowns.

Two levels of communication—social and psychological—are involved in games. The social level is the overt or manifest, and the psychological level is the covert or latent. Prochaska (1979, pp. 237–38) gives the following example of these two levels of communication in a game:

> For example, if a woman asks a man, "Why don't you come by my place to see my collection of sculpture?" and the man responds, "I'd love to. I'm really interested in art," they may be . . . communicating a message at a different level, such as . . . "Boy, I'd really like to get you alone in my apartment" and "I'd sure love to look at your curves."

For a game to progress at least one of the participants has to pull a switch, as further described in this example by Prochaska (1979, p. 238):

> For the payoff to occur, one of the players has to pull a switch. In this case, after fixing drinks and sitting close on the couch examining a reproduction of Rodin's The Kiss, the woman still seems to be sending a seductive communication. The man's vanity convinces him to proceed, and he puts his hand on her leg, only to be rebuffed by a slap on the face and an irate "What kind of woman do you think I am?"
>
> The couple has just completed a heavy hand of RAPO.[2] Besides gaining mutual recognition, excitement, and some structured time together, there is also a strong emotional payoff for each. The woman is able to proudly affirm her position in life that she is OK, while feeling angry toward men for not being OK, just as her mother always said. The payoff for the man is to feel depressed and thereby reaffirm his conviction that he is not OK.

Eric Berne (1964) lists a large number of psychological games in *Games People Play*. People tend to have a repertoire of favorite games they play; many people base their social relationships on finding suitable partners to play the corresponding opposite roles. The following are common games played by people.

In the game "Why don't you? Yes but . . .," a person consistently asks for suggestions or advice, and then consistently rejects any that is offered. The other participants in this game assume the principal player is attempting to solve a real problem in a concrete manner, so they offer suggestions. The principal player in this game is able to get at least two payoffs—one is attention from other people, and the other is a payoff that comes from being able to put others down by implying "That's really a dumb suggestion." The other participants may get a payoff through telling themselves "I must be a warm, caring person as this person respects and trusts me enough to share this problem with me."

In the "one-up" game, one person seeks to top whatever someone else says. If the conversation is about big fish, the one-upper always has a story about how he caught this mammoth fish. If the topic is about bad grades received, the one-upper seeks to amaze everyone with how bad his or her grades are. If jokes are being told, the one-upper begins by saying "I've got one that'll top that. Have you heard about . . ."

"Wooden leg" is a game in which people attempt to manipulate others to not expect too much from them because of such wooden legs as having a physical handicap, being raised in a ghetto, having had a tragic romance, having emotional problems such as being depressed, and so on. Closely

---

[2]Eric Berne defines RAPO in its milder forms as "Kiss Off" or "indignation."

related, "If it weren't for ..." is a cop-out game in which players seek to rationalize not succeeding at a variety of tasks and goals.

A person who plays "poor me" is seeking sympathy and may at times try to get others to do things for him or her. Closely related is someone who plays "ain't it awful" by taking a negative view of events. Such a person is usually seeking attention and sympathy. In the game "there I go again," the player seeks to excuse away his or her ineffective behavior without taking responsibility.

Some clients enjoy playing "confession" where they seek to tell all their personal and interpersonal troubles in the hope of receiving recognition and help from others. Some unhappily married men get together and enjoy discussing "wives are a pain" as a way of ventilating their unhappiness. Some unhappily married wives enjoy discussing "men aren't worth it" as a way of ventilating their frustrations. Parents enjoy discussing "look how hard I've tried" when a home situation is particularly uproarious and hostile as a way to relieve their frustrations that the goals for their family have not been achieved. Many people seek to avoid assuming responsibility for their failures and shortcomings by placing the blame on others and playing "it's all them."

Some individuals who have received few positive strokes end up seeking a lot of negative strokes, which to them is better than receiving no strokes. One game that is played to receive negative strokes is "kick me" in which the player seeks to do things which will elicit negative reactions from others.

People who enjoy creating trouble for others are apt to play "let's you and him/her fight," with the payoff being the spectator pleasure they receive in watching others tangle.

People who receive psychological rewards in analyzing others and in giving advice often play "psychiatry." A person who seeks to see how many different sexual relationships he or she can have often seeks to play "love em and leave em." Traditionally, men in our society have been socialized to play "Mr. Macho" and women "Miss America."

"Monday morning quarterbacks" seek to make themselves feel important by telling you what you should have done differently after things have not turned out well for you.

The number of different games that can be played is best described as infinite. Only a few of the more typical ones have been summarized here.

Game analysis can be defined as a treatment technique in which a counselor enables clients to gain insight into some of their interactions through the use of game concepts. The kinds of games which are the main focus of game analysis are those which lead to undesirable outcomes for clients.

The social worker's role in analyzing games is to teach clients the terminology of game analysis. This perhaps can best be accomplished at the first occasion in which a worker helps a client to gain insight into a game. The social worker needs to point out to the clients that playing games is not necessarily undesirable. This may be therapeutically valuable as some clients may feel it is wrong to play games because games have an exploitative connotation. Such a feeling may cause resistances to examining games. These resistances may be reduced by informing clients that everyone plays games, with some games having beneficial outcomes, while others have undesirable outcomes. Social workers must help clients recognize those games which are destructive for them or for other players and also enable them to gain insight into how these games are being played. Clients must be encouraged to explore new ways of responding after they are aware of how their role in a game leads to undesirable consequences. Clients need help in assigning specific names to those undesirable games they are playing. Using colloquial names for games is often acceptable and advantageous as they may be more precise and have more meaning for clients. Social workers can teach people the kind of games they need to play in order to achieve their goals. Some people have goals considered beneficial for themselves and society, but do not know what they have to do to achieve these goals. Often such people can be instructed in ways to use game concepts. For example, a person seeking a job may need to learn to play "how to get an interview," and "how to sell yourself in an interview." Or, a couple who is frequently feuding may need to learn "how to fight fairly" and "how to give in a relationship to get what you want."

There are three reasons why game analysis appears to be a useful therapeutic approach: (1) One of the important functional values of naming something (in this case a certain kind of game) is that it increases clients' capacities to identify when similar transactions are occurring in the future. Once clients recognize and have insight into a game which is causing them difficulty, they are in a better position to cease their destructive behavior and to explore alternative modes of behavior. (2) Analyzing behavior in terms of games is apt to be intriguing to clients and, therefore, may lead to greater personal involvement in therapy and increase their motivation to resolve their difficulties. (3) Game analysis provides clients with a method of analyzing certain problematic interactions. After learning how to analyze such interactions, clients should be better able to analyze other problematic games beyond those specifically discussed in counseling.

Life Scripts

Every person has life scripts (plans) which are formed during childhood and are based on early beliefs about oneself and others. These plans are developed from early interactions with parents and others and are largely determined by the pattern of strokes that are received.

Many details of a life script are supplied by parental opinions, suggestions and encouragements: Examples include "She's such a cute girl, everyone loves her," "He's stupid and will never amount to much," "He'll be famous some day," "He's sure nutty," "All the girls will want to date him." Fairy tales, myths, TV shows, early life experiences, and children's stories are also important sources of life scripts. While parental influences and fairy tales are important contributing factors, the life script is still the creation of a young child. One's life script may be either winning or losing, being a success or a failure, exciting or dull. Each script also includes specific roles, such as heroes and heroines, villains and victims, etc.

Harris (1969) has identified four general life scripts that a person chooses to view him or herself in comparison with others. These four positions are (1) I'm OK—You're OK; (2) I'm OK—You're not OK; (3) I'm not OK—You're OK; and (4) I'm not OK—You're not OK.

People who decide "I'm OK—You're OK" tend to be productive, law-abiding people who are successful and who have positive, meaningful relationships with others.

People who decide "I'm OK—You're not OK" predispose themselves to exploit others, cheat others, rob others, or succeed at the expense of others. This type of person may be a criminal, a ruthless business executive, or a destructive lover who loves them and leaves them.

People who decide "I'm not OK—You're OK" feel inferior in the presence of those they judge as superior. Such a life script frequently leads to withdrawal from others as a way to avoid being reminded of not being OK. Withdrawal is not the only alternative. The person can write a counterscript based on lines borrowed from early authority figures: "You can be OK if . . . ." The person is then driven to achieve the "if" contingencies. Examples of such contingencies include: making huge sums of money, being submissive, being entertaining through making others laugh, etc. Such a person then strives to meet these contingencies in order to receive strokes and approval from others.

People who decide "I'm not OK—You're not OK" tend to be the most unhappy and disturbed. Prochaska (1979, p. 241) states:

> The extreme withdrawal of schizophrenia or psychotic depression is their most common fate. They may regress to an infantile state in the primitive hope that they may once again receive the strokes of being held and fed. Without intervention from caring others, these individuals will live out a self-destructive life of institutionalization, irreversible alcoholism, senseless homicide, or suicide.

Decisions about life scripts are generally made early in childhood. James and Jongeward (1971, pp. 84–85) provide an incident in the life of a client, now 43, that led her to conclude "I'm not OK and men are not OK either."

> My father was a brutal alcoholic. When he was drunk he would hit me and scream at me. I would try to hide. One day when he came home, the door flew open and he was drunker than usual. He picked up a butcher knife and started running through the house. I hid in a coat closet. I was almost four years old. I was so scared in the closet. It was dark and spooky, and things kept hitting me in the face. That day I decided who men were—beasts, who would only try to hurt me. I was a large child and I remember thinking, "If I were smaller, he'd love me" or "If I were prettier, he'd love me." I always thought I wasn't worth anything.

Based on this script, she married an alcoholic at age 23 and for the next 20 years had been living her life drama of feeling worthless and living with a "beast."

Scripts (as in a play in a theatre) are plans which we learn and then carry around in our heads. These scripts enable us to conceptualize where we are in our activities, and are plans for directing what we need to do to complete our activities and to accomplish our goals. Scripts are also devices for helping us to remember what we have done in the past.

One of the areas where our behavior is largely guided by scripts is sexual behavior. Sexual scripts result from elaborate prior learning in which we acquire an etiquette of sexual behavior. Scripts tell us who are appropriate sexual partners, what sexual activity is expected, where and when the sexual activity should occur, and what should be the sequence of the different sexual behaviors.

Scripts vary greatly from one culture to another. Powdermaker (1933, pp. 276–77) provides the following description of a script about female masturbation which is generally held by the Lesu of the South Pacific:

> A woman will masturbate if she is sexually excited and there is no man to satisfy her. A couple may be having intercourse in the same house, or near enough for her to see them, and she may thus become aroused. She then sits down and bends her right leg so that her heel presses against her genitalia. Even young girls of about six years may do this quite casually as they sit on the ground. The women and men talk about it freely, and there is no shame attached to it. It is a customary position for women to take, and they learn it in childhood. They never use their hands for manipulation.

A life script and a theatrical script have many similarities. Each has a cast of characters, dialogue, themes and plots, acts and scenes, and generally both move towards a climax. Often, however, a person is unaware or only vaguely aware of the life scripts he or she is acting out. Public stages on which people act out their scripts include home, social gatherings, church, school, office, and factory. As Shakespeare wrote, "All the world's a stage."

Most life scripts are learned at an early age. As children grow they learn to play roles—villains, law enforcers, heroes, heroines, victims, and rescuers—and seek others to play complementary roles. Through playing roles, children integrate new themes and parts into their roles and gradually develop their life scripts. The particular scripts that are developed are substantially influenced by the reactions they receive from significant people in their lives.

Individuals follow scripts and so do families and cultures. Cultural scripts are expected patterns of behavior within a society. In our culture, for example, only men are expected to fight in military conflict, while in Israel both sexes are expected to fight wars. In regards to cultural scripts, James and Jongeward (1971, p. 70) note:

> Script themes differ from one culture to another. The script can contain themes of suffering, persecution, and hardship (historically the Jews); it can contain themes of building empires and making conquests (as the Romans once did). Throughout history some nations have acted from a "top-dog" position of the conqueror; some from an "underdog" position of the conquered. In early America, where people came to escape oppression, to exploit the situation, and to explore the unknown, a basic theme was "struggling for survival." In many cases this struggle was acted out by pioneering and settling.

Historically, women are socialized in our society to have different life scripts than men. American women traditionally are expected to be affectionate, passive, conforming, sensitive, intuitive, dependent, and "sugar and spice and everything nice." They are supposed to be primarily concerned with domestic life, to be nurturing, to instinctively love to care for babies and young children, to be deeply concerned about their personal appearance, and to be self-sacrificing for their family. They should not appear to be ambitious, aggressive, competitive or more intelligent than men. They are expected to be ignorant of and uninterested in sports, economics or politics. In relationships with men they should not initiate forming the relationships. Additionally, women are expected to be tender, feminine, emotional and appreciative.

Males also have a number of traditional sex role expectations in our society. A male is expected to be tough, fearless, logical, self-reliant, independent, and aggressive. He should have definite opinions on the major issues of the day and is expected to make authoritative decisions at work and at home. He is expected to be strong, to never be depressed, vulnerable, or anxious. He is not supposed to be sissy, or feminine. He is expected not to cry or openly display emotions. He is expected to be the provider and to be competent in all situations. He is supposed to be physically strong, self-reliant, athletic, to have a manly air of confidence and toughness, to be daring and aggressive, to be brave and forceful, to always be in a position to dominate any situation, to be a Clint Eastwood. He is supposed to initiate relationships with women and is expected to be dominate in relationships with them. (The women's movement is now initiating changes in these sex role scripts. The ultimate result would be to take pressure off both men and women to conform to rigid sex role stereotypes. Each individual, either male or female, would then be free to develop the personality characteristics and strengths naturally fitting that person. Sex role stereotypes will be discussed further in Chapter 15.)

In our society (as well as in other large and complex societies) there are a number of subcultures, and each subculture has its own scripts. Street gangs, Chicanos, Jews, dentists, and college students each have their own subcultural scripts. For example, common aspects of scripts for college students include cramming at the last moment for exams, procrastination, partying, idealism, shortage of money, and expectation of success, happiness, and money following graduation.

Families also have scripts. These scripts provide a set of directions for family members. Examples include:

We Winships have always been pillars of the community.
We Navarres have always been rowdy.
We Hubbards have always been in trouble with the police.
We Schomakers have always been gamblers.
We Hepps have never had to ask for a handout from anyone.
We Rices have always been Democrats.

If a family member does not live up to the script expectation, he or she is often viewed as a deviant. The importance of scripts in determining human behavior is emphasized by Berne (1966, p. 310):

> Nearly all human activity is programmed by an ongoing script dating from early childhood, so that the feeling of autonomy is nearly always an illusion—an illusion which is the greatest affliction of the human race because it makes awareness, honesty, creativity, and intimacy possible for only a few fortunate individuals. For the rest of humanity, other people are seen mainly as objects to be manipulated. They must be invited, persuaded, seduced, bribed or forced into playing the proper roles to reinforce the protagonist's position and fulfill his script.

There are an infinite number of script themes. A few of the more common themes are the following:

I must be loved by everyone.
I've got to be perfect.
My purpose in life is to save sinners.
People will only love me if I make them laugh.
My life will always be one big party.

I'm cut out to be a leader.

I'll never get anywhere.

I will never let anyone get the best of me.

I'm headed for fame and fortune.

James and Jongeward (1971, pp. 84–85) provide the following example of how a life script is played:

> . . . a woman, who had taken the position "Men are bums," marries a sequence of bums. Part of her script is based on "Men are not OK." She fulfills her own prophecy by nagging, pushing, complaining, and generally making life miserable for her husband (who has his part to play). Eventually, she manipulates him into leaving. Then she can say, "See, I told you. Men are bums who leave you when the going gets rough."

Often people play games as part of their life scripts. A person who has a script of being a Casanova plays the game "love em and leave em." A person who has a script of "I won't leave anyone get the best of me" is apt to play "one up." A person who has a script of "I'll always find a way to seduce people into helping me" is apt to play "poor me."

Script analysis can be defined as a treatment technique in which a counselor enables clients to gain insight into the scripts they are acting out through the use of script concepts. The types of scripts which are the primary focus of script analysis are those which lead to undesirable outcomes for clients or for others.

The counselor's role in analyzing scripts is to: (1) Teach clients the terminology of script analysis. (2) Point out to clients that everyone is playing a variety of scripts, and that scripts largely determine human behavior. (They need to indicate that some scripts have beneficial outcomes, while others have undesirable outcomes.) (3) Help clients to recognize those scripts which have undesirable outcomes. (4) Help clients to assign names to the scripts they are playing so that they can be more readily identified when they are being acted out in the future. (5) Help clients to develop new, desirable scripts to act out and to encourage and teach clients more effective ways of responding in the future.

Nonverbal Communication

In seeking to assess human behavior, it is important to attend to nonverbal communication. Sigmund Freud (1981, p. 253) noted, "He that has eyes to see and ears to hear may convince himself that no mortal can keep a secret. If his lips are silent, he chatters with his finger tips; betrayal oozes out of him at every pore."

It is impossible not to communicate. No matter what we do, we transmit information about ourselves. Even an expressionless face communicates messages. As you are reading this, stop for a minute and analyze what nonverbal messages you would be sending if someone were observing you. Are your eyes wide open or half closed? Is your posture relaxed or tense? What are your facial expressions communicating? Are you occasionally gesturing? Do you occasionally roll your eyes? What would an observer deduce you are now feeling from these nonverbal cues?

At times nonverbal cues (such as sweating, stammering, blushing and frowning) convey information about feelings that we desire to hide. Through developing our skills in reading nonverbal communication, we will be more aware of what others are feeling and be better able to interact effectively. Since feelings stem from thoughts, nonverbal cues such as blushing also transmit information about what people are thinking.

In literature, perhaps the greatest reader of nonverbal cues was Sherlock Holmes. In the following exchange Holmes (Doyle, 1974) makes certain deductions about his friend and colleague Watson:

> "How do I know that you have been getting yourself very wet lately, and that you have a most clumsy and careless servant girl?" . . . "It is simplicity itself," said he; "my eyes tell me that on the inside of your left shoe, just where the firelight strikes it, the leather is scored by six almost parallel cuts. Obviously they have been caused by someone who has very carelessly scraped round the edges of the sole in order to remove crusted mud from it. Hence, you see, my double deduction that you had been out in vile weather, and that you had a particularly malignant boot-slitting specimen of the London slavery."

The Functions of Nonverbal Communication

Nonverbal communication interacts with verbal communication. Nonverbal communication has the following functions in relation to verbal communication:

1. Nonverbal messages may *repeat* what is said verbally. A husband may say he is really looking forward to becoming a father and repeat this happy anticipation with glowing facial expressions.

2. Nonverbal messages may *substitute* for verbal ones. If a close friend has just failed an important exam, you can get a fairly good idea what he or she is thinking and feeling by looking at the facial expressions.

3. Nonverbal messages may *accent* verbal messages. If someone you are dating says he or she is angry and upset with something you did, the depth of these feelings may be emphasized by pounding a fist and pointing an accusing finger.

4. Nonverbal messages may serve to *regulate* verbal behavior. Looking away from someone who is talking to you is a way of sending a message that you are not interested in talking.

5. Nonverbal messages may *contradict* verbal messages. An example of such a double message is someone with a red face, bulging veins, and a frown on the face, yelling, "Angry! Hell no, what makes you think I'm upset?" When nonverbal messages contradict verbal messages, the nonverbal messages are often more accurate. When receivers perceive a contradiction between nonverbal and verbal messages, they usually believe the nonverbal (Adler and Towne, 1981, p. 257).

While nonverbal messages can be very revealing, they can also be unintentionally misleading. Think of the times when people have misinterpreted your nonverbal messages. Perhaps you tend to say little when you first wake up, and others have interpreted this as meaning that you are troubled. Perhaps you have been quiet on a date because you are tired or because you're thinking about something that has recently happened. Has your date at times misinterpreted such quietness to mean you are bored or unhappy with the relationship? While thinking deeply on a subject, have you had an expression on your face that others have interpreted as being a frown? The point is that nonverbal behavior is often ambiguous in the messages that can be interpreted as being sent. A frown on the face, for

The members of this therapy group are concentrating on each other's nonverbal communication. Whether we speak or remain silent, our nonverbal communication interacts with and intensifies our verbal messages, repeating and accenting them. Such nonverbal cues as blushing or stammering are comments on our feelings. Even an expressionless face transmits feelings. If someone were to watch you reading this book right now, what nonverbal communication would he or she observe? (Charles Zastrow)

In the picture shown, two long-time friends are creatively comparing their life transitions to the changes in the mulch pile before them. They don't miss the physical stamina and youthful appearance they had when younger. As mature, middle-aged adults, they're more appreciative of the wisdom they've gained as they've aged. As they continue to seek new life experiences and find new learning opportunities, they view life as meaningful and rewarding. (Knute Jacobsen)

This volunteer, working in a nursing home, demonstrates "generativity," Erikson's seventh life stage developmental crisis. Generativity means raising the next generation to be caring individuals by acting as a role model for them. Thus, adults who involve themselves in selfless causes generate offspring who emulate them. The flip side of Erikson's generativity is "stagnation," a lack of psychological movement or growth. Stagnated adults are self-centered and unable to look beyond their own needs. (Courtesy of Untied Way of America)

From infancy to old age, human beings need physical contact. Holding hands, pats on the back, and hugs and kisses are physical demonstrations of warmth and caring. Direct physical contact is so vital to infants that without it their emotional, intellectual, and physical development can be severely stunted. Rene Spitz discovered that children raised in institutional settings in the nineteenth century who were cared for properly nevertheless died. The reason? Lack of adult physical contact. (Karen Kirst-Ashman)

example, may represent a variety of feelings: being tired, angry, feeling rejected, confused, unhappy, irritated, disgusted, bored, or simply lost in thought. *Nonverbal messages should not be interpreted as facts, but as clues that need to be checked out verbally to determine what the sender is thinking and feeling.*

The remainder of this section will examine some examples of how we communicate nonverbally through posture, body orientation, gestures, touching, clothes, personal space, territoriality, facial expressions, eye movements, voice, physical appearance, and the environment.

Many of these examples are taken from white middle-class American nonverbal communication. Nonverbal communication is strongly culture based. In other words, the identical nonverbal behavior may be interpreted differently depending on the cultural/ethnic/racial background of the observer. For example, a comfortable interpersonal distance may be six inches in some cultures and six feet in others. Awareness of these differences is especially critical when communicating with clients of different cultural/ethnic/racial backgrounds. Such awareness is the only thing that makes accurate understanding possible. To illustrate, direct eye contact by a worker is usually considered desirable by white clients, but is usually considered rude and intimidating by many Native Americans. Kissing between adult males is usually interpreted as indicating a homosexual relationship in our culture, but such kissing is a greeting custom in some European cultures. Adult males who wear skirts in our culture are viewed as weird, but kilts (knee-length pleated skirts) are commonly worn by men in Scotland and by Scottish regiments in the British armies.

Posture

In picking up nonverbal cues from posture, one needs to note the overall posture of a person and the changes in posture. We tend to take relaxed postures in nonthreatening situations and to tighten up when under stress. Some people never relax, and their rigid posture shows it.

Watching the degree of tenseness has been found to be a way of detecting status differences. In interactions between a higher status person and a lower status person, the higher status person is usually more relaxed, while the lower-status person is usually more rigid and tense (Mehrabian, 1981). For example, note the positions that are usually assumed when a faculty member and a student are conversing in the faculty member's office.

Teachers and public speakers often watch the posture of listeners to gauge how the presentation is going. If members in the audience are leaning forward in their chairs, it is a sign the presentation is going over well. If the audience is slumping in their chairs, it is a cue the presentation is beginning to bomb.

An indication of how posture communicates is the large number of verbal phrases which use posture as a metaphor:

"He is able to stand on his own two feet."
"I've got a heavy burden to carry."
"She won't take that lying down."
"She's got a lot of backbone."

Body Orientation

Body orientation is the extent to which we face toward or away from someone with our head, body, and feet. Facing directly towards someone signals an interest in starting or continuing a conversation, while facing away signals a desire to end or avoid conversation. The phrase "turning your back" on someone concisely summarizes the message that is sent when you turn away from someone. Can you remember the last time someone signaled they wanted to end a conversation with you by turning away from you?

Gestures

Most of us are aware that our facial expressions convey our feelings. When we want to hide our true feelings, we concentrate on controlling our facial expressions. We are less aware that our gestures also reveal our feelings, and, therefore, we put less effort into controlling our gestures when we want to cover up our feelings. As a result, our gestures are sometimes better indicators of how we really feel.

People who are nervous tend to fidget. They may bite their fingernails, tap their fingers, rub their eyes or other parts of their body, bend paperclips, or tap a pencil. They may cross and uncross their legs. They may rhythmically swing a leg back and forth while crossed or may rhythmically move a foot back and forth.

Many gestures provide cues to a person's thoughts and feelings. Clenched fists, whitened knuckles, and pointing fingers signal anger. When people want to express friendship or attraction to us they tend to move closer to us. Hugs can represent a variety of feelings: physical attraction, good to see you, best wishes in the future, and friendship. Shaking hands is a signal of friendship and a way of saying "Hello" or "Goodbye."

Albert Scheflen (1974) notes that a person's sexual feelings can be signaled through gestures. He describes preening behavior which is designed to send a message that the sender is attracted to the receiver. Preening behavior includes rearranging one's clothing, combing or stroking one's hair, and glancing in a mirror. Scheflin cites a number of invitational preening gestures that are specific to women: Exposing or stroking a thigh, protruding the breast, placing a hand on the hip, and exhibiting a wrist or palm. Naturally these gestures do not always suggest sexual interest, as they may occur for a variety of other reasons. (It is interesting to note that comparable research has not been conducted on males. Conducting this research only on women may indicate a sexist bias.)

Gestures are also used in relation to verbal messages for a variety of purposes: repeating, substituting, accenting, contradicting, and regulating. Some people literally speak with their hands, arms, and head movements. Many people are unaware of the number of gestures they use, and then (if videotaped) are surprised to view the extent to which they communicate with gestures.

■ Nonverbal Behavior among Poker Players

Oswald Jacoby has noted poker players use non-verbal messages extensively. He has divided poker players into three classes: (1) ingenuous players, (2) tricky players, and (3) unreadable players.

Ingenuous players. These players are usually beginning players who possess few skills. When they look worried, they probably are. When they have a mediocre hand, they take a long time to bet. When they like their hand, they bet quickly. When they dislike their hand, they frown and scowl and look like bad luck has bit them. When they bluff, they look a little guilty. When they have a really good hand they immediately seek to raise the bet. This ingenuousness is seldom found in veteran players. Ingenuous players reveal their hands by their body language. Players of this type usually quit poker at an early stage because of their bad luck.

Tricky players. Most poker players fall into this category. Tricky players act opposite of the way they really feel. When they have a poor hand they exude confidence, and when they have a good hand they tremble a little and look nervous as they bet. Sometimes they do a triple cross by acting the way they feel their hand is.

Unreadable players. Unreadable players have no consistency. They will randomly exude confidence or look nervous, and such nonverbal messages will give no clue to the nature of their hand. Unreadable players are excellent players.

SOURCE: Oswald Jacoby, *Oswald Jacoby on Poker* (New York: Doubleday & Company, 1974)

Touching

Rene Spitz (1945) has demonstrated that young children need direct physical contact, such as being cuddled, held, and soothed. Without such direct physical contact, the emotional, social, intellectual and physical development of children will be severely stunted. Spitz observed that in the 19th century high proportions of children died in some orphanages and other child care institutions. The deaths were not found to be due to poor nutrition or inadequate medical care, but instead to lack of physical contact with parents or nurses. From this research came the practice of nurturing children in institutions—picking the baby up, holding it close, playing with it, and carrying it around several times a day. With this practice, the infant mortality rate dropped sharply in institutions.

Ashley Montagu (1971) describes findings which suggest that eczema, allergies, and certain other medical problems are in part caused by a person's lack of physical contact with a parent during infancy. Physical stimulation of children will facilitate their intellectual, social, emotional, and physical development.

Adults also need physical contact. People need to know that they are loved, recognized, and appreciated. Touching (through holding hands, hugging, pats on the back) are ways of communicating warmth and caring. Unfortunately, we have been socialized to refrain from touching, except in sexual contacts.

Our language is a mirror of our culture. Common phrases suggest that more importance is placed on the senses of sight and hearing than on touch:

"Seeing is believing."

"It's good to see you again."

"It's really good to hear from you."

"I've got my eye on you."

We have coined few phrases that include words for touch. For example, when leaving someone we say "See you again soon" rather than "Touch you again soon." If we should say the latter, it would be apt to be interpreted as having sexual connotations.

Touching someone is in fact an excellent way of conveying a variety of messages, depending on the context. A hug at a funeral will connote sympathy, while a hug when meeting someone connotes "It's good to see you." A hug between parent and child conveys "I love you," while a hug on a date may have sexual meanings. A number of therapists have noted *communication and human relationships would be vastly improved if people reached out and touched others more—with hugs, squeezes of the hand, kisses, and pats on the back.* Touch is crucial for the survival and development of children, and touch is just as crucial for adults to assure them that they are worthwhile and loved.

Clothing

Clothes keep us warm, protect us from catching colds and other illnesses, and cover certain areas of our body so we are not arrested for indecency. But clothes have many other functions. Certain uniforms tell us what a person does and who we can receive services from: for example, uniforms of police officers, fire fighters, nurses, physicians, and waiters. The way we dress sends signals about sexuality. People intentionally and unintentionally send messages about themselves by what they wear. Clothes give messages about our occupations, personality, interests, groups we identify with, social philosophies, religious beliefs, status, values, mood, age, nationality, and personal attitudes. For example, the way an instructor dresses sends messages to the class as to the kind of atmosphere he or she is seeking to create.

There are numerous "wardrobe engineers" (tailors, manufacturers, and sellers of clothes) who assert we can better obtain what we want by improving our selection of clothes. There is truth to the phrase "Clothes make a person."

The importance of clothes in determining judgments that people make about strangers was demonstrated in a study by Hoult (1954, pp. 324–28). Hoult began by having 254 students rate the photos of male strangers on such things as "best-looking," "most likely to succeed," "most intelligent," "most like to date or double date with," and "best personality." For these photos, Hoult obtained independent ratings of clothes and the models' heads. Hoult then placed high-ranked outfits on models with low-ranked heads. Lower-ranked clothing was placed on models with higher-ranked heads. He found through a reranking that higher-ranked clothing was associated with an increase in rank, while lower-ranked clothing was associated with loss of rank.

Any given item of clothing can convey several different meanings. For example, the tie a man selects to wear may reflect sophistication or nonconformity. In addition, the way the tie is worn (loosened, tightly knotted, thrown over one's shoulder, soiled and wrinkled) may provide additional information about the wearer.

A problem often encountered by women is that they lack a socially dictated business uniform. Men wear ties and three piece suits in bland, dark colors. Women interested in developing professional and business careers are still seeking clothing which will convey the best impression. Often they must choose between masculine-looking, unattractive, bland clothing and clothing which is more colorful and aesthetically attractive.

Clothes also affect our self-image. If we feel we are well dressed in a situation, we are apt to be more self-confident, assertive, and outgoing. If we feel we are ill dressed in a situation, we are apt to feel more reserved, less confident, and be less assertive. When we're feeling at a low tide, dressing up will make us feel better about ourselves and raise our spirits.

There is a real danger of misreading nonverbal messages. We often stereotype others on skimpy information, and frequently our interpretations are in error. Sometimes we get burned by our interpretations. One of the authors remembers a client he interviewed in a correctional facility who for the previous four years had lived in an elegant fashion, traveled all over Europe and North America, and stayed in the finest hotels. He financed this lifestyle by writing bad checks. He stated that whenever he needed money, he would carefully dress in an expensive suit and would have no trouble cashing his checks.

Personal Space

We dislike uncomfortable crowding and other perceived invasions of our personal space. We can sometimes tell how people are feeling toward each other by noting the distance between them. Each of us carries around a kind of invisible bubble of personal space wherever we go. The area inside this bubble is perceived as our private territory. The only people we are comfortable in allowing to enter our private territory are those who we are emotionally close to. We feel we are being invaded when strangers and people we are not emotionally close to enter our private territory.

Edward Hall (1969) has identified four distances or boundaries that we set in our daily interactions. We use these distances to guide us in setting the type of interactions we want to have with others. The particular boundary we choose depends on the context of the conversation, how we feel toward the other person, and what our interpersonal goals are. These include the intimate zone, the personal zone, the social zone, and the public zone.

Intimate Zone

This zone begins with skin contact and goes out about eighteen inches. We generally only let people we are emotionally very close to enter this boundary, and then mostly in private situations—comforting, conveying caring, making love, and showing love and affection. When we voluntarily let and want someone to enter this distance, it is a sign of trust. We lower our defenses. Think back to dates you have had. If the person moves within this zone and sits tight against you, it is a signal he or she is comfortable with the relationship and may want it to progress further. On the other hand, if the person seeks to maintain a safe distance of two or more feet, it is a cue that the person is still sorting out the relationship, or is wanting a more distant relationship.

When someone moves into this intimate zone without our wanting them to, we feel invaded and threatened. Our posture becomes more upright, and our muscles tense. We may move back, and avoid eye contact, as a way of signaling we want a more distant relationship. When we are forced to get close to strangers (on crowded buses and elevators), we generally avoid eye contact and try not to rub against others, probably as a way of saying "I'm sorry I'm forced to invade your territory. I'll try not to bother you."

Personal Zone

This zone ranges from about eighteen inches to approximately four feet. This zone is the distance at which couples stand in public. Interestingly, if someone of the opposite sex at a party stands this close to someone we are dating or are married to, we tend to contemplate whether this person is seeking to move in. Also, if we see our spouse or date move close to someone of the opposite sex at a party, we also may become suspicious and sometimes jealous.

The far range of the personal zone (from about two and a half to four feet) is the distance in which we convey we are seeking to keep the other at arm's length. It is the distance just beyond the other person's reach. Interactions at this distance may still be reasonably close, but they are much less personal than the ones that occur at a closer distance. Sometimes the communication at an arm's length distance represents a testing out by people regarding whether they want the relationship to become emotionally closer.

Social Zone

This zone ranges from about four feet to about twelve feet. Business communications are frequently in this zone. The closer part of this zone (from four to about seven feet) is the distance at which people who work together usually converse, and it is the distance at which salespeople and customers usually interact.

Hall (1969) indicates the seven to twelve foot range is the distance for more impersonal and formal situations. For example, this is the distance that our boss talks to us from behind his or her desk. If we were to pull our chair around to the boss's side of the desk in order to sit closer, a very different kind of relationship would be signaled. (The way furniture is arranged, and the kind of plants and wall hangings that people have in their office convey signals about their values and interests, and the type of relationship they want to convey. For example, an office in which the office-holder has a desk between the customer/client/student suggests a formal and impersonal interaction is being sought. An office in which a desk is not used as a barrier and one which has plants suggests a warmer, less formal interaction is being sought.)

Public Zone

This zone runs outward from twelve feet. Teachers and public speakers generally use a closer range of public distance. In the farther distances of public space (beyond twenty-five feet) two-way communication is very difficult. Any speaker who voluntarily chooses to have considerable distance from the audience is not interested in having a dialog.

Territoriality

Territoriality is behavior characterized by identification with an area in such a way as to indicate ownership and defense of this territory against those who may invade it (Knapp, 1978, p. 115). Many birds and animals will strike back against much larger organisms if they feel their territory is being invaded.

Territoriality also exists in humans. Traditionally, dad has his chair, mom has her kitchen, and each child has his or her own bedroom.

There are things which we feel we own which we really do not own. Students tend in each class to select a certain seat to sit in. If someone else should happen to sit in your chosen seat, do you not feel your ownership rights are being violated, and that you are being invaded? Clearly, the college/ university owns the chairs, and not us.

What we acquire to be our property are strong indicators of our interests and values. The things we acquire are often topics of conversation—our cars, our homes, our leisure-time equipment, our plants, our clothes.

The material things we acquire also communicate messages about our status. Wealthy people acquire more property. Interestingly, we generally grant more personal space and greater privacy to people of higher status. For example, we will knock at the boss's office and wait for an invitation to walk in before entering. With people of a similar status to us or of a lower status, we frequently walk right in.

Facial Expressions

Most people select the face and eyes to be the primary source to receive nonverbal communication. Facial expressions often are mirrors which reflect our thoughts and feelings. Yet, facial expressions are a complex source of information for several reasons. First, facial expressions can change rapidly. Slow motion films have found that a fleeting expression can come and go in as short a time as a fifth of a second (Adler and Towne, 1981, p. 266). In addition, researchers have found that there are at least eight distinguishable positions of the eyes and lids, at least eight positions for the eyebrows and forehead, and at least ten for the lower face (Adler and Towne, 1981, p. 266). Multiplying these different combinations together leads to several hundred different possible combinations. Therefore, compiling a directory of facial expressions and their corresponding emotions is almost impossible.

Ekman and Friesen (1975) have identified six basic emotions that facial expressions reflect—fear, surprise, anger, happiness, disgust, and sadness. These expressions appear to be recognizable in all cultures. People seeing photos of these expressions are quite accurate in identifying these emotions. Therefore, although facial expressions are complex, these six emotions can fairly accurately be identified.

A word of caution should be noted about reading facial expressions. Because people are generally aware that their facial expressions reflect what they are feeling and thinking, they may seek to mask their facial expressions for a variety of reasons. For example, a person who is angry and doesn't want others to see the anger, may seek to hide this feeling by smiling. Therefore, in reading facial expressions we should be aware the sender may be seeking to conceal his or her real thoughts and feelings.

The eyes are also great communicators. When we want to end a conversation, or avoid a conversation, we look away from the other person's eyes. When we want to start a conversation we often seek out the other's eyes. We may wait until the receiver looks at us, as a signal to begin.

The eyes also communicate dominance and submission. When a high status person and a low status person are looking at each other, the low status person tends to look away first. Downcast eyes signal submission or giving in. (Downcast eyes may also signal sadness, boredom, or tiredness.)

Good salespeople are aware that eyes are a sign of involvement. They seek to catch our eye. When they know they have caught our eye, they begin their pitch and seek to maintain eye contact. They know there are social norms in our society such as the courtesy of hearing what a person has to say once we allow the person to begin speaking. These social norms trap us into hearing the sales pitch once eye contact has been made. Good salespeople watch eyes in a store in another way. They observe what items we are most looking at, and then seek to emphasize these items in their sales pitch.

The importance of eyes in communicating are reflected in common phrases:

"He could look right through you."
"He's got shifty eyes."
"Did you see the gleam in her eye."
"His eyes shot daggers across the room."

Eye expressions suggest a wide range of human expressions. Wide open eyes suggest wonder, terror, frankness, or naiveté. Raised upper eyelids may mean displeasure. A constant stare connotes coldness. Eyes rolled upward suggest another's behavior is unusual or weird.

When we become emotionally aroused or interested in something, the pupils of our eyes dilate. Some counselors are sufficiently skilled in reading pupil dilation they can tell when they touch on a subject that a client is sensitive about.

E. H. Hess and J. M. Polt (1960, pp. 349–50) measured the amount of pupil dilation while showing men and women various kinds of pictures. The greater the subject's interest in the picture, the larger the eyes dilated. Women's eyes dilated an average of 20 percent when looking at pictures of nude men. Men's eyes dilated an average of 18 percent when looking at pictures of nude women. Surprisingly, the greatest increase in pupil size occurred when women looked at a picture of an infant and a mother.

Voice

The same word or phrase may have many meanings. Therefore, the way we say the word is the meaning we give to the word. For example, Knapp (1978, p. 323) shows how the meaning of the following sentence is changed by the word which is emphasized.

He's giving this money to Herbie. (HE is the one giving the money; nobody else.)
He's *giving* this money to Herbie. (He is GIVING, not lending, the money.)
He's giving *this* money to Herbie. (The money being exchanged is not from another fund or source; it is THIS money.)

He's giving this *money* to Herbie. (MONEY is the unit of exchange, not a check or wampum.)

He's giving this money to *Herbie*. (The recipient is HERBIE, not Eric or Bill or Rod.)

When we ask a question, we usually raise our voice at the end of the sentence. When we make a declarative statement, we usually lower our voice at the end of the sentence. Sometimes we intentionally manipulate our voice to contradict the verbal message.

In addition to which words are emphasized in a sentence, our voice can communicate in many other ways. These ways include length of pauses, tone, pitch, speed, volume, and disfluencies (such as stammering or saying "uh," "um," and "er"). All of these factors together have been called *paralanguage.* Paralanguage deals with how something is said and not with what is said (Trager, 1958).

Using paralanguage we can communicate the exact opposite of what the verbal message is. You might practice through changing your voice how you would seek to convey literally, and then sarcastically, messages such as:

"I really like you."
"I'm having a perfectly wonderful time."
"You're really terrific."

Albert Mehrabian (1981) has found that when the paralanguage and the verbal message are contradictory, that the former will carry more meaning. When there is a contradiction between words and the way something is said, subjects usually interpret the message in terms of the way it was said.

An excellent way to learn more about the way you are using paralanguage is to videotape one of your conversations or speeches, and then watch the replay. Such a process will also give you valuable feedback about your other forms of nonverbal communication.

Physical Appearance

While it is common to hear people say that it is only inner beauty that really counts, research shows that outer beauty (physical attractiveness) plays an influential role in determining responses for a broad range of interpersonal interactions. Singer (1964) found that college professors tended to give higher grades to females who were physically attractive than to those who were less attractive. Mills and Aronson (1965) found attractive females could modify attitudes of male students more than less attractive females could.

Widgery and Webster (1969) have found that attractive persons, regardless of sex, will be rated high on credibility. If attractive people are rated high initially on credibility, it greatly increases their ultimate persuasiveness in a variety of areas—sales, public speaking, changing attitudes, being recognized as a credible counselor, and so on.

Unattractive defendants are more likely to be judged guilty in courtrooms and more likely to receive longer sentences (Solender and Solender, 1976). The evidence is clear that *initially* we respond much more favorably to those perceived as physically attractive than those seen as less attractive. Attractiveness serves to open doors and create greater opportunities.

Physically attractive people have been found to outstrip less attractive people on a wide range of socially desirable evaluations, including personality, popularity, success, sociability, persuasiveness, sexuality, and often happiness (Knapp, 1978, p. 156). For example, attractive women are more apt to be helped and less likely to be the objects of aggressive acts (Berscheid and Walster, 1974). Less attractive people are at a disadvantage from early childhood on. Teachers, for example, interact less (and less positively) with unattractive children (Algozzine, 1976). Physical attractiveness is also a crucial factor in determining who we decide to date and who we decide to marry. In many situations practically everyone prefers the most attractive date regardless of her or his own attractiveness and regardless of being rejected by the most attractive date (Knapp, 1978, p. 159).

Interestingly, unattractive men who are seen with attractive women are judged higher in a number of areas than are attractive men who are seen with attractive partners (Bar-Tal and Saxe, 1976). They are judged as making more money, as being more successful in their occupation, and as being more intelligent. Apparently, the evaluators reasoned that unattractive males must have to offset this imbalance by succeeding in other areas to be able to obtain dates with attractive women.

Being physically attractive does *not* mean that a person will be more intelligent, more successful, better adjusted, and happier than less attractive people. Attractiveness *initially* opens more opportunities to be successful, but after a door is opened, it is performance that determines outcome.

The shape of our body suggests certain stereotypes. (These stereotypes may or may not be accurate). People who are overweight are judged to be older, more old-fashioned, less strong physically, more talkative, less good-looking, more agreeable and good natured, more sympathetic, more trusting of others, more dependent on others, and more warm-hearted and sympathetic. People who are muscular are rated as being stronger, better-looking, younger, more adventurous, more self-reliant, more mature in behavior, and more masculine. People with a thin physique are rated as younger, more suspicious of others, more tense and nervous, less masculine, more pessimistic, quieter, more stubborn, and more inclined to be difficult (Parnell, 1958). Overweight people and very thin people have been found to be discriminated against when seeking to obtain jobs, obtain life insurance, adopt children, and receive entrance into college (Knapp, 1978, p. 166).

Being tall is a strong advantage in the business world for men, but not for women. Shorter men are shortchanged on salaries and job opportunities (Knapp, 1978, p. 167).

Everyone has considerable capacity to improve their physical appearance. Dieting, exercising, learning to manage stress, learning to be assertive, getting adequate sleep, improving our grooming habits, and improving our choice of clothes will substantially improve our physical appearance. Practically all of us have the opportunity to improve our physical appearance, which will open more doors and create more opportunities.

The Environment

Perhaps all of us have been in immaculate homes that have "unliving rooms" with furniture coverings, plastic lamp coverings, and spotless ashtrays which send nonverbal messages of: do not get me dirty, do not touch, do not put your feet up, and stay alert to avoid a mistake. In such homes we are not able to relax. Owners of such homes wonder why guests cannot relax and have a good time. They are unaware that the environment is communicating messages which lead guests to feel uncomfortable.

A study by Maslow and Mintz (1956) found the attractiveness of a room shapes the kind of communication that takes place and also influences the happiness and energy of people working in it. The researchers used an unattractive room which looked like a janitor's closet and a beautiful room which was furnished with curtains, carpeting, and comfortable furniture. Subjects were required to rate a series of pictures in order to gauge their energy level and feelings of well-being. When subjects were in the ugly room, they became tired and bored sooner and took longer to complete their task. They described the room as producing fatigue headaches, monotony, and irritability. When the subjects moved to the beautiful room, they displayed a greater desire to work, they rated the faces they were judging higher, and they communicated many more feelings of comfort, importance, and enjoyment. This experiment provides evidence supporting the common sense notion that workers do a better job and generally feel better when they are in an attractive environment.

The color of rooms apparently affects mood and productivity. Mehrabian found that children who were tested on an I.Q. test scored about 12 points higher in rooms they described as being beautiful in contrast to rooms they described as having ugly colors (Mehrabian, 1976). Blue, orange, yellow, and yellow-green were considered beautiful colors; black, brown and white were considered ugly. The beautiful rooms appeared to stimulate alertness and creativity. Friendly words and smiles increased in the beautiful rooms, while irritability and hostility decreased. Mehrabian says the most pleasant colors are, in order, blue, green, purple, red and yellow. The most arousing colors are, in order, red, orange, yellow, violet, blue, and green. The pastel colors of pink, baby blue, and peach are thought to have a calming effect. Some prisons and jails are now painting cells in pastel colors, hoping that it will calm and relax inmates.

Businesses have found they can control the rate of customer turnover by environmental design. Dim lighting, comfortable seats, and subdued noise levels will encourage customers to talk more and spend more time in a bar or restaurant (Sommer, 1969). If the goal is to run a high-volume business (as in a fast food place) businesses can encourage customer turnover by bright lights, uncomfortable seats, and high noise levels (for example, by having poor soundproofing). Chairs can be constructed to be comfortable, or to be uncomfortable by putting pressure on the sitter's back. Airports seek to get travelers into the restaurants and bars where they will spend money by having comfortable chairs, tables where people can converse, and dim lighting. They discourage travelers from sitting in waiting areas by bright lighting, and by having uncomfortable chairs bolted shoulder to shoulder in rows facing outward which make conversation and relaxation next to impossible.

Casino owners in Las Vegas have built their facilities without windows or clocks so that customers will be less aware how long they have been gambling. The aim is to keep people gambling as long as possible. Without windows, some customers are unaware they are gambling into the next day.

The shape and design of buildings affect interaction patterns in many ways. In apartment buildings people who live near stairways and mailboxes have more contact with neighbors than those who live in less heavily traveled parts of the building. Access to neighbors increases communication. Fences, rows of trees, and long driveways increase privacy.

Wall decorations, types of furniture, and placement of furniture in offices convey messages as to whether the officeholder wants informal, relaxed communications, or wants formal, to-the-point communications. A round table, for example, suggests the officeholder is seeking to have the communication be seen as equalitarian, while a rectangular table suggests the communication should recognize status and power differentials. With a rectangular table, the high-status people generally sit at one end of the table. If the meeting is between sides of equal strength, one side tends to sit at one end, and the other at the other end, rather than intermingling the members. A classroom in which the chairs are in a circle suggests the instructor wants to create an informal, discussion atmosphere. A classroom with the chairs in rows suggests the instructor wants to create a formal, lecture-type atmosphere.

Control Theory

William Glasser (1984) has developed a control theory explanation of human behavior. A major thrust of the theory is that we have pictures in our heads of what reality is like, and pictures of how we would like the world to be. Glasser (1984, p. 32) asserts ". . . all our behavior is our constant attempt to reduce the difference between what we want (the pictures in our heads) and what we have (the way we see situations in the world)."

An example may illustrate the process. Keith Fitzpatrick (age 37) has been dating Sonja Noddelson (age 38) off and on for three and one-half months. Keith was divorced 19 months ago; Sonja has never been married. Gradually Keith discovers he is becoming more and more attached to Sonja. He develops a picture of them making a commitment to each other and perhaps getting married in a year or two. This picture motivates him one night when they are having dinner to inform her that he increasingly feels attracted to her, and asks how she views their relationship. Sonja indicates she enjoys being with him, but also wants her independence. She adds she occasionally is dating others. Keith's reaction to the last statement is to feel crushed, as he realizes there is a wide discrepancy between the way he wants their relationship to be, and what Sonja wants out of the relationship. After several moments of small talk, Keith gradually regains his composure. He concludes that he will try a variety of strategies to entice Sonja into making a commitment to him.

In the next few weeks he seeks to wine and dine her. He also unobtrusively observes what she likes and dislikes. He tries to present himself in the way that he thinks she likes. For example, she mentions she detests men who drink and smoke to excess. So he cuts down on his drinking when he is with her, and also announces to her that he has given up smoking. He discovers she likes theatrical plays, so (even though he dislikes such plays) he buys tickets and takes her to some plays, and then tells her that he really loves going to them.

When Sonja mentions she has had a date with someone else, he feels hurt and jealous. In an attempt to also make her feel jealous, he then asks someone else on a date. Afterwards, he informs Sonja that the date really went well (even though it didn't).

He also shows his interest in her by sending her cards and flowers. Three weeks later, when he asks her to go with him to Thanksgiving dinner at his parent's house, she indicates she thinks that will give the wrong impression as she does not at this time want to make a commitment to anyone. At this point Keith feels he has put a lot into this relationship and realizes that she is remaining rather uninvolved. To attempt to force her to make more of a commitment to him, he displays by his verbal and nonverbal communication that he is angry, and that he thinks she has an obligation to go with him. He adds that his folks will be really disappointed if she fails to attend.

Unfortunately for Keith, Sonja has learned in the past that it is a mistake to be controlled in relationships by guilt trips and obligations. She tactfully and politely informs Keith that she not only will not go with him to the Thanksgiving dinner, but that she has decided that their present noncommittal dating relationship is not working, and, therefore, she no longer will date him. Keith immediately gives up the tactics of angering and making her feel obligated to go. Instead, he pleads with her to continue dating him. However, Sonja adheres to her decision. When Keith realizes this latest strategy is not going to work, he feels he has to regain some of his honor in this lost cause. He proceeds to resort to name-calling, four letter words, and pointing out her faults as he perceives them. At this point, their relationship ends in an uproar. In this example, all of Keith's efforts to achieve the picture of an ongoing relationship with Sonja fail. After the uproar, he chooses to start dating others, hoping to find someone to replace the picture in his head of being with Sonja.

How do we develop the pictures in our heads that we believe will satisfy our needs? Glasser asserts that we begin to create our picture albums at an early age (perhaps even before birth), and that we spend our whole lives enlarging these albums. Essentially what happens is that whenever what we do gets us something that satisfies a need, we store the picture of what satisfied us in our personal picture albums. Glasser (1984, p. 19) gives the following example of this process by describing how a hungry child added chocolate-chip cookies to his picture album:

> Suppose you had a grandson and your daughter left you in charge while he was taking a nap. She said she would be right back, because he would be ravenous when he awoke and she knew you had no idea what to feed an eleven-month-old child. She was right. As soon as she left, he awoke screaming his head off, obviously starved. You tried a bottle, but he rejected it—he had something more substantial in mind. But what? Being unused to a howling baby, and desperate, you tried a chocolate-chip cookie and it worked wonders. At first, he did not seem to know what it was, but he was a quick learner. He quickly polished off three cookies. She returned and almost polished you off for being so stupid as to give a baby chocolate. "Now," she said, "he will be yelling all day for those cookies." She was right. If he is like most of us, he will probably have chocolate on his mind for the rest of his life.

When this child learned how satisfying chocolate chip cookies are, he placed the picture of these cookies in his personal picture album.

Glasser notes by the term *pictures*, he means *perceptions* from the five senses of sight, hearing, touch, smell, and taste. When we get hungry, or thirsty, or have some other needs or wants, we select one or more pictures from our albums and then seek to obtain what that picture represents. For example, if we are really hungry we may select a picture of a prime rib dinner (or lobster, or two hamburgers) from our album and then seek to obtain what our picture represents.

The pictures in our albums do not have to be rational. Anorexics have a picture that they are too fat and starve themselves to come closer to their irrational picture of unhealthy thinness. Alcoholics have a picture of themselves satisfying many of their needs through alcohol. Child molesters have pictures of satisfying their sexual needs through sexual activities with young children. Rapists have pictures of satisfying their power and perhaps sexual needs through sexual assault. To change a picture, we have to replace it with another that will at least reasonably satisfy the need in question. People who are unable to replace a picture may endure a lifetime of misery. Some battered women, for example, will endure brutal beatings and humiliations in marriage because they do not believe they can replace their husbands in their albums.

Glasser notes that whenever there is a difference between the picture we now see and the picture we want, a *signal* is generated by this difference which starts us behaving in a way to obtain the picture we want. In order to obtain what we want, we examine our behavioral systems and select from these behaviors one or more that we judge as being the best available behaviors to reduce this difference. These behaviors not only include straightforward problem-solving efforts, but also such manipulative strategies as becoming angry, pouting, and trying to make others feel guilty. People who are acting irresponsibly or ineffectually have either failed to select responsible behaviors that they have in their behavioral repertoires or as yet have not learned responsible courses of action for the particular situation they are facing.

Glasser believes humans are driven by five basic, innate needs. As soon as one need is satisfied, another need (or perhaps more than one acting together) pushes for satisfaction. The first basic need is *to survive and reproduce*. Included in this need are such vital functions as breathing, digesting food, sweating, regulating blood pressure, and meeting the demands of hunger, thirst, and sex.

A second need is *to belong—to love, share, and cooperate*. This need is generally met through family, friends, pets, plants, and material possessions such as a beloved car or boat.

A third need is *power*. Glasser says this need involves getting others to obey us and to then receive the esteem and recognition that accompanies power. The drive for power is sometimes in conflict with the need to belong. For example, two people in a relationship may struggle to take control of the relationship, rather than seeking an equalitarian relationship.

A fourth need is *freedom*. People want the freedom to choose how they live their lives, to express themselves, to read and write what they choose, to associate with whom they select, and to worship or not worship as they believe.

A fifth need is *fun*. Glasser believes learning is often fun, which then is a great incentive to assimilate what we need to satisfy our needs. Classes without fun (those that are grim and boring) are major failings of our educational system. Laughing and humor help fulfill our needs for fun. Fun is such a vital part of living that most of us have trouble conceiving how life would be without it.

Glasser adds there may be other (yet unidentified) needs in addition to these basic five. He also notes that there are differences between individuals in the intensity of each of these needs. Few people, for example, have such an intense need for power as Adolph Hitler, who wanted to control the world.

Glasser asserts that any theory which contends our behavior is a response to outside stimuli or events is wrong. He rejects behaviorism's stimulus-response (S-R) system. He asserts people are in control of what they do. When a person is thirsty, and then seeks water (because a glass of water is a thirst-quenching picture in his or her head) then that person's behavior is that of a well-functioning control system. A S-R theory, in contrast, would suggest a person would keep drinking water (perhaps drinking himself to death) everytime he was handed a glass of water.

Neuro-Linguistic Programming

A variety of psychological frameworks and theories to explain the dynamics of human behavior have already been discussed in this chapter. One other recently developed model which helps in understanding human behavior is Neuro-Linguistic Programming.

Neuro-Linguistic Programming (NLP) was developed by John Grinder, Richard Bandler and others (Lankton, 1980). NLP is the study of the structure of subjective experience (Lankton, 1980, p. 13). It makes explicit patterns of behavior and change that have previously been only intuitively understandable. Although relatively recent in origin, it promises to have substantial applications in assessing human behavior, in developing rapport, in influencing others (in education, public speaking and sales) and in changing behavior (therapy).

The components of the term *neuro-linguistic programming* refer to the following:

neuro—nervous system through which experience is received and processed via the five senses.

linguistic—language and nonverbal communication systems through which neural representations are coded, ordered, and given meaning.

programming—ability to organize our communication and neurological systems to achieve specific desired outcomes.

This section will focus on summarizing concepts from NLP that are useful in assessing human behavior. For other uses of NLP, see Lankton (1980) and Laborde (1983).

Representational Systems

Before reading further, take a few minutes to identify what you remember most about the following:

The last grocery store you were in.
What you did on your last birthday.
Your most enjoyable sexual experience.

Everyone has, at most, five sensory systems through which they contact physical reality. These senses are the eyes (visual), ears (auditory), skin (kinesthetic), nose (smell), and tongue (taste). For each of these events, you probably responded with remembrances involving only one or two senses. Taking the grocery store question, you may have had an *image* of fresh fruits and vegetables; or *heard* the hustle and bustle of the activity; or remember *feeling* the Charmin bathroom tissue; or remember *smelling* the pleasant aromas of the fresh flowers; or remember *tasting* the free samples of freshly cooked pizza.

Anytime a person interacts with the external world, he does so through sensory representations. My sensory contact with a grocery store is apt to be quite different from yours. The same applies for everyone. Your most enjoyable sexual experience may be a visual one, while your partner's may be auditory or kinesthetic.

We operate out of our sensory representations of the world and not on reality itself. Our sensory representations provide us with a *map* of the territory. But it is important to note that the *map is not the territory*.

NLP asserts that in order to accurately assess another's actions, one needs to identify the sensory representational system being used by that person. If we are able to identify the other's representational system, and then join with that system in our interactions with that person, communication is apt to flow much more smoothly and rapport is enhanced. On the other hand, if two people are not able to join together with the same representational system, then communication is apt to be tangential, and rapport will be adversely affected. The importance of this point is immense. Successful sales persons, educators and therapists are those who are able to identify and join with the representational systems of the persons they are seeking to influence.

Representational System Predicates

The adverbs, adjectives, and verbs that people select while speaking reveal which sensory system they are most conscious of at that point in time. NLP calls these words predicates.

In our culture people primarily use the visual, auditory, and kinesthetic systems. (A few other cultures in other countries place greater emphasis on the senses of smell and taste.) Unless the listener is aware what sensory representational system the speaker is using, the listener may misinterpret what the speaker is intending. For example, when Mary says "I understand you," the intended message depends on the representational system she is in:

Visual—That looks real good to me

Auditory—I hear you clearly

Kinesthetic—What you are saying feels right to me

(See *Predicates to Identify Sensory Representational Systems* for further examples.)

The following case example may help to illustrate the importance of sensory representational systems.

A married couple sought counseling as they felt their sexual relationship was deteriorating rapidly. After rapport had been established, the counselor asked each, "What tends to turn you on sexually?" The husband mentioned it was hearing romantic things said to him, while the wife mentioned it was being softly touched in a variety of areas. Not too surprisingly, the husband

■ Predicates to Identify Sensory Representational Systems

Visual	*Auditory*	*Kinesthetic*
Appear	Audible	Back away
Blind to	Babble	Beside yourself
Clear	Boisterous	Break down
Cockeyed	Buzz	Bounce
Colors	Discord	Caress
Disappear	Dissonant	Catch
Enlighten	Double talk	Clutch
Farsighted	Drumming	Cold
Features	Earshot	Cut-up
Focus	Echo	Dig in
Foresee	Give a hoot	Feel
Glance	Grumble	Firm
Green with envy	Harmony	Get in touch
Hindsight	Hear	Grasp
Horizon	Hear from	Grope
Illusion	In tune with	Handle
Illustrate	Keep yours ears open	Hard
Image	Lend an ear	Have a feel for
In the clear	Listen	Hit me like a ton
In the dark	Loud	of bricks
Inspect	Muffled	Hold
Keen	Mumble	Hustle
Look	Murmuring	Impressed
Neat	Noisy	Iron out
Observe	Pronounced	Keep your shirt on
Overview	Prattle	Kiss
Perspective	Quiet	Lukewarm
Picture	Resound	Nudge
Point out	Ringing	Play
Red tape	Rings a bell	Poke
Resemble	Roar	Press
Scan	Rumbling	Rack your brains
Scope	Screech	Raising hell
See	Shriek	Ran up against
Seeing red	Silence	Rubs me the wrong
Show	Sound	way
Sketchy	Sound judgment	Run through
Tint	Sound off	Sensitive
Unsightly	Squawk	Sensuous
Vague	Squeal	Soft
Vision	Stammer	Stroke
Watch	Talk of the town	Stumble on
The whole picture	Thundering	Tender
	Unheard of	Tension
	Whispering	Tickle
		Toss around
		Touch
		Vibes

was trying to excite his wife by saying romantic things (without touching his wife much), while the wife was seeking to excite her husband by touching him while remaining silent. A simple description of the importance of joining with the other's representational system greatly enhanced their love life with the husband spending much more time in tenderly caressing his wife, and the wife romantically talking to her husband.

In the course of growing up, people learn to favor particular representational systems for particular events. People are not totally visual or auditory or kinesthetic. The sense in use depends on the situation or context. It appears, though, that people tend to have a primary mode, in that they have a tendency to use more of one mode than the others (Laborde, 1983, p. 57).

Mismatched predicates interfere with communication and rapport, as indicated by the following example:

Client: I *feel* so awful! The IRS has just audited me and I just can't *handle* it!

Counselor: I *hear* you. It *sounds* bad, *but tell* me what it is that's so bad.

Client: I just can't *lift* this *feeling*. It's so *heavy*!

Counselor: Yes, but I don't *hear* what the problem is. *Listen* to me and *tell* me what's so bad!

In this illustration, the client is apt to end up viewing the counselor as being insensitive. An example of matched predicates in this situation is:

Client: I *feel* so awful! The IRS has just audited me and I just can't *handle* it!

Counselor: You *feel* like you're *breaking down* because of the *heaviness* of the audit.

Client: That's exactly it. I'm *stumbling*, but yet *grasping to hold on*.

Counselor: What do you *feel* you need to *hold* on?

Client: *Support* and understanding from my wife, my tax accountant, and you.

In this example the counselor phrases his responses to be consistent with the client's representational system, which leads to better understanding, and increased trust and rapport.

Eye Accessing Cues

Listening to the predicates in another's speech is just one reliable way to determine which representational system is dominant at a given time. Eye accessing cues is another way (see Figure 9.2).

As always with rules there are exceptions; for example, some left handers' kinesthetic representational system is eyes down and to the left, with the eyes down and to the right being their auditory representational system. To test out this information, it is suggested that the reader ask friends or acquaintances questions such as "What do you remember most about your last vacation?" to watch how the eye accessing cues are apt to be consistent with responses that are either visual, kinesthetic or auditory.

The Four-Tuple

The four-tuple is a way of representing a person's sensory experience at a moment in time. Its general form is *V, K, A, O*. These capital letters are abbreviations for the major sensory channels: visual, kinesthetic, auditory, and olfactory/gustatory.

Distinguishing between experiences that are internally generated (remembering or imagining a visual image, feeling, sound, or smell), and experiences that are externally generated (sights, sensations, sounds, or smells that we receive from the external world) is useful. Therefore the superscript *e* is used to refer to external cues and to internal cues. The experience of someone whose senses are fully turned outward is: V^e, K^e, A^e, O^e. Someone attending fully to an internal event, oblivious of the immediate surroundings is: V^i, K^i, A^i, O^i.

Most of us at any point in time are generally in a mixed state in which some of our senses are outwardly attending and some of our experience is remembered or imagined. Many times one or more of the sensory systems will not be in use. The following example shows how this notational system can be used. Whenever Mrs. Worth *hears* about the Christmas season, she *visualizes* being at her husband's funeral several years ago. (He was killed in an automobile accident.) She remembers how depressed she *felt* afterwards. These cues in sequence are: A^e, V^i, K^i.

The usefulness of this concept can be readily demonstrated. Think about

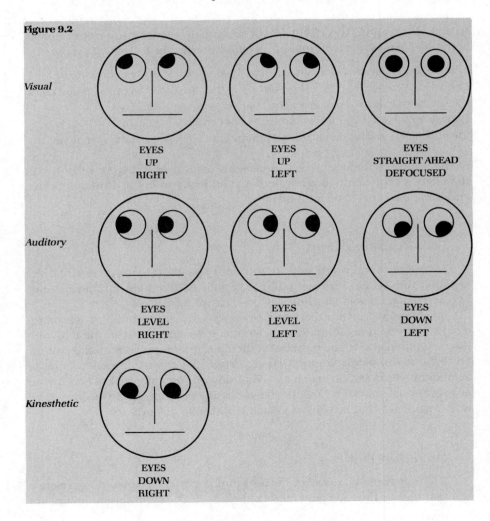

Figure 9.2

Visual

EYES
UP
RIGHT

EYES
UP
LEFT

EYES
STRAIGHT AHEAD
DEFOCUSED

Auditory

EYES
LEVEL
RIGHT

EYES
LEVEL
LEFT

EYES
DOWN
LEFT

Kinesthetic

EYES
DOWN
RIGHT

the last time you said something to someone and received an unusual response. Undoubtedly what happened was that your intended message led the listener to remember auditory, visual, kinesthetic, or olfactory events from the past, which then led the listener to respond primarily in terms of the internal cues. NLP makes an important point by asserting: *The meaning of a communication is the response it elicits, regardless of the intent.*

Summary

Erikson asserted that middle-aged adults face the developmental crisis of generativity versus stagnation. Peck theorized there are four psychological advances that are critical to successful adjustment in middle adulthood: (1) Emphasizing socializing rather than sexualizing in human relationships, (2) Valuing wisdom rather than physical powers, (3) Having cathetic flexibility rather than cathetic impoverishment, and (4) Having mental flexibility rather than mental rigidity.

This chapter also describes contemporary theories and models for assessing human behavior throughout the life span. Maslow's theory of hierarchy of needs has an ascending order of needs: physiological, safety, belongingness and love, self-esteem, and self-actualization. Analyzing human behavior in terms of games and life scripts provides another useful approach for understanding human behavior. In seeking to assess human behavior it is important to understand nonverbal communication.

William Glasser's control theory asserts that all human behavior is an attempt to reduce the differences between the pictures of what we want and the way we perceive situations in the world. Neuro-Linguistic Programming (NLP) is the study of the structure of subjective experience, and makes explicit patterns of behavior and change that have previously been only intuitively understandable.

Social Aspects of Middle Adulthood

George Andrus is spending 55 hours a week getting his insurance business going and uses his leisure time working around his house. Jenny Savano recently got a divorce, is trying to raise her three children on a meager monthly AFDC grant, and is attending a vocational school to receive training as a secretary. Tom and Eleanor Townsend have their careers well established, their two children have grown and left home, and they enjoy traveling to such exotic places as the Greek Isles. Joan Sarauer spends much of her day caring for her husband who is dying of emphysema. Dorothy and Michael Powers attend church every Sunday, and take leadership roles in church activities during the week.

■ A Perspective

There is obviously considerable variation in the major social interests of middle-aged adults. However, there are some fairly common themes:

> Settling in to a career
> Raising children and maintaining a household
> Participating in some hobbies
> Seeing the children leave home
> Becoming grandparents
> Adjusting to relationship changes with spouse
> and children after the children leave home
> Socializing with friends

This chapter will:

- Describe three major sociological theories about human behavior: functionalism, conflict theory, and interactionism. These theories are macro theories. (The differences between micro theories and macro theories will be described in the next section.)

- Discuss six social problems that middle-aged adults may encounter: poverty, worker alienation, unemployment, spouse abuse, empty shell marriages, and divorce. (As noted in Chapter 6, social problems can be viewed as a subcategory of life events in the Behavior Dynamics Assessment Model.)

Macro and Micro Theories

Social scientists over the years have developed a variety of theories to explain the nature of society and its problems. One way of categorizing these theories is by dividing them into macro theories and micro theories. *Macro theories* seek to make sense of the behavior of large groups of people and the workings of entire societies. This chapter will partly focus on describing the three most prominent macro theories in sociology: functionalism, conflict theory, and interactionism. (These theories are applicable to all age groups, including middle-aged adults.)

Micro theories, on the other hand, seek to make sense of the effects of group life on individuals. Prominent theories of this type include Erikson's theory which was summarized in Chapter 6 and learning theory which was summarized in Chapter 4.

Advocates of these various theories often disagree with one another. Each of these theories has certain merits and shortcomings. Some theories are more effective in analyzing a particular social problem, while other theories are more effective in analyzing other social problems. Therefore, it is helpful for assessors of human behavior to have a knowledge of all the contemporary theories in order to be able to select the theory or theories that are most effective in analyzing key dynamics of the social problem under study. Often, the greatest understanding of a social problem occurs when the insights gained from different theoretical perspectives are combined. The Behavior Dynamics Assessment Model encourages the use of both macro and micro theories in assessing human behavior.

The Functionalist Perspective

In recent years functionalism has been one of the most influential sociological theories. The theory was originally developed by Emile Durkheim, a French sociologist, and refined by Robert K. Merton, Talcott Parsons, and many others. The theory views society as a well-organized system in which most members agree on common values and norms. Institutions, groups, and roles fit together in a unified whole. Members of society do what is necessary to maintain a stable society because they accept its regulations and rules.

Society is viewed as a system composed of interdependent and interrelated parts. Each part makes a contribution to the operation of the system, thus enabling the entire system to function. The various parts are in delicate balance, with a change in one part affecting the other parts.

A simple way to picture this approach is to use the analogy of a human body. A well-functioning person has thousands of parts with each having a specific function. The heart pumps blood, the lungs draw oxygen into the body and expel carbon dioxide, the stomach digests food for energy, the muscles move bodily parts to perform a variety of functions, and the brain coordinates the activities of the various parts. Each of these parts is interrelated in complex ways to the others and is also dependent on them. Each performs a vital function, without which the entire system might collapse, as in the case of heart failure.

Functionalism asserts that the components of a society, similar to the parts of the human body, do not always work the way they are supposed to work. Things get out of whack. When a component of a society interferes with efforts to carry out essential social tasks, that part is said to be *dysfunctional*. Often, changes in society introduced to correct a particular imbalance may produce other imbalances, even when things are going well. For example, developing effective birth-control devices (such as the pill) and making these readily available is quite effective in preventing unwanted pregnancies. However, it may also be a factor leading to increased premarital and extramarital sexual relationships—which is viewed as a problem by some groups.

According to the functionalist perspective, all social systems have a tendency toward equilibrium—maintenance of a steady state, or particular balance, in which the parts of the system remain in the same relationship to one another. The approach asserts that systems have a tendency to resist social change, as change is seen as disruptive unless it occurs at a slow pace. Since society is composed of interdependent and interconnected parts, a change in one part of the system will lead to changes in at least some of the other parts. The introduction of the automobile, for example, into our society led to drastic changes: the decline of traveling by horses, people being able to commute large distances to work, vacation travel to distant parts of the country, the opening of many new businesses (service stations, car dealerships, etc.), and sharp increases in air pollution and traffic fatalities.

Some of the functions and dysfunctions of a social system are *manifest*, that is, obvious to everyone. For example, a manifest function of police departments is to keep crime rates low. Other functions and dysfunctions are *latent*—hidden and unintended. Sociologists have discovered that when police departments label people they arrest with such stigmatizing labels as "criminal," "outlaw," and "delinquent," a hidden consequence is that those so labeled may actually commit more crimes over the long run than they would if they had never been arrested in the first place. Thus, police departments (in trying to curb crime) may unintentionally, at times, contribute to its increase.

According to functionalists, social problems occur when society, or some part of it, becomes disorganized. *Social disorganization* occurs when a large organization or an entire society is imperfectly organized to achieve its goals and maintain its stability. When disorganization occurs, the organization loses control over its parts.

Functionalists see thousands of potential causes of social disorganization. However, underlying all these causes is rapid social change, which disrupts the balance of society, producing social disorganization. In recent years more technological advances (such as the development of telephones, television, robots, and heart transplants) have occurred in less time than at any other time in human history. These advances have led basic institutions (such as the family and the educational system) to undergo drastic changes. Technological advances have occurred at such a pace that other parts of the culture have failed to keep pace. This *cultural lag* between technological changes and our adaptation to them is viewed as one of the major sources of social disorganization.

Examples of such social disorganization abound. The development of nuclear weapons has the potential to destroy civilization. Advances in sanitation and medical technology have sharply lengthened life expectancy but have also contributed to a worldwide population explosion. Advances in artificial insemination have led to surrogate motherhood, and our society has not as yet decided whether to encourage or discourage this type of motherhood. The development of technological advances in performing abortions has led to the capacity to terminate pregnancies quite safely on request, but it has also led to a national controversy about the desirability of legalized abortions.

Critics of functionalism assert it is a politically conservative philosophy, as it takes for granted the idea that society as it is (the status quo) should be preserved. As a result, basic social injustices of society are ignored. Critics also argue that the approach is value laden, because one person's disorganization is another person's organization. For example, some people view divorce as being functional, as it is a legal way to terminate a relationship that is no longer working. Functionalism has also been criticized as being a philosophy that works for the benefit of the privileged social classes, while perpetuating the misery of the poor and those who are being victimized by discrimination.

The Conflict Perspective

Conflict theory views society as being a struggle for power among various social groups. Conflict is asserted to be inevitable and in many cases actually beneficial to society. For example, most Americans would view the struggle of the "freedom fighters" during the Revolutionary War as being highly beneficial to our society. (England saw them as ungrateful insurgents.)

The conflict perspective rests on an important assumption: there are certain things (such as power, wealth, and prestige) that members of society value highly, and most of these valued resources are in scarce supply. Because of their scarcity, conflict theory asserts that people—either individually or in groups—struggle with one another to attain them. Society is thus viewed as an arena for the struggle over scarce resources.

Struggle and conflict may take many forms: competition, disagreements, court battles, physical fights and violence, and war. If the struggles usually involved violence, then nearly everyone would be involved in violent activities, and society would be impossible. As a result, norms have emerged that determine what types of conflict are allowable for which groups. For example, participating in a labor strike or acquiring a higher education is an approved way of competing for the limited money available in our society, while robbery is not an acceptable way.

From the conflict perspective, social change mainly involves reordering the distribution of scarce goods among groups. Unlike the functionalism which views change as potentially destructive, the conflict approach views change as potentially beneficial. Conflict can lead to improvements, advancements, the reduction of discrimination against oppressed groups, and the emergence of new groups as dominant forces in society. Without conflict, society would become stagnant.

Functionalism and conflict theory differ in another way. Functionalists assert that most people obey the law because they believe the law is fair and just, while conflict theorists assert that social order is maintained by authority backed by the use of force. They assert that the privileged classes hold power legally and use the legal system to make others obey their will. They conclude that most people obey the law because they are afraid of being arrested, imprisoned, or even killed if they do not obey.

Functionalists assert that most people in society share the same set of values and norms. In contrast, conflict theorists assert that modern societies are composed of many different groups with divergent values, attitudes, and norms—and, therefore, conflicts are bound to occur. The abortion issue illustrates such a value conflict. Prolife groups and traditional Roman Catholics believe the human fetus at any stage after conception is a living human being and, therefore, aborting a pregnancy is a form of murder. In contrast prochoice advocates assert that an embryo for the first few months after conception is not yet a human being because it is unable to survive outside the womb. They also assert that if the state were to forbid a woman to obtain an operation that she desires, the state would be violating her right to control her life.

Not all conflicts stem from disagreements over values. Some conflicts arise in part *because* people share the same values. In our society, for example, wealth and power are highly valued. The wealthy spend considerable effort and resources to maintain their status quo position, while the poor and oppressed groups vehemently advocate for equal rights and a more equitable distribution of income and wealth. Labor unions and owners in many businesses are in a continual battle over wages and fringe benefits. Republicans and Democrats continually struggle with one another in the hopes of gaining increased political power.

In contrast to functionalism being criticized as being too conservative, conflict theory has been criticized for being too radical. Critics say that if there were as much conflict as these theorists claim, society would have disintegrated long ago. Conflict theory has also been criticized as encouraging oppressed groups to revolt against the existing power structure, rather than seeking to work within the existing system to address their concerns.

The Interactionist Perspective

The interactionist approach focuses on individuals and the processes of everyday social interaction between them, rather than on larger structures of society, such as the educational system, the economy, or religion. Interactionist theory views behavior as a product of each individual's social relationships. Dorwin Cartwright (1951, p. 383) has noted:

How aggressive or cooperative a person is, how much self-respect or self-confidence he has, how energetic and productive his work is, what he aspires to, what he believes to be true and good, whom he loves or hates, and what beliefs or prejudices he holds—all these characteristics are highly determined by the individual's group memberships. In a real sense, they are products of groups and of the relationships between people.

Interactionist theory asserts that human beings interpret or define each other's actions instead of merely reacting. This interpretation is mediated by the use of symbols (particularly the words and language that a person learns).

Interactionists study the socialization process in detail because it forms the foundation for human interaction. The approach asserts that people are the products of the culture and social relationships in which they participate. Coleman and Cressey (1984, p. 21) summarize this approach:

> People develop their outlook on life from participation in the symbolic universe that is their culture. They develop their conceptions of themselves, learn to talk, and even learn how to think as they interact early in life, with family and friends. But unlike the Freudians, interactionists believe that an individual's personality continues to change throughout life in response to changing social environments.

> The work of the American philosopher George Herbert Mead has been the driving force behind the interactionist theories of social psychology. Mead noted that the ability to communicate in symbols (principally words and combinations of words) is the key feature that distinguishes humans from other animals. Individuals develop the ability to think and to use symbols in the process of socialization. Young children blindly imitate the behavior of their parents, but eventually they learn to "take the role of the other," pretending to be "Mommy" or "Daddy." And from such role taking children learn to understand the interrelationships among different roles and to see themselves as they imagine others see them. Eventually, Mead said, children begin to take the role of a *generalized other*. In doing so, they adopt a system of values and standards that reflect the expectations of people in general, not just those in the immediate present. In this way *reference groups* as well as actual *membership groups* come to determine how the individual behaves.

Cooley (1902) observed that it is impossible to make objective measures of most aspects of our self-concept—such as how brave, likeable, generous, attractive and honest we are. Instead, in order to gauge the extent to which we have these qualities, we have to rely on the subjective judgments of the people we interact with. In essence, Cooley asserted, we develop our self-concept through "the looking-glass self process," which means we learn what kind of person we are by seeing and hearing how others react to us.

Another important concept is that social reality is what a particular group agrees it is. Social reality is not a purely objective phenomenon.

Interactionist theory views human behavior as resulting from the *interaction* of a person's unique, distinctive personality and the groups he or she participates in. Groups are a factor in shaping one's personality, but the personality is also shaped by the person's unique qualities.

The reality we construct is mediated through symbols. We respond to symbolic reality, not physical reality. Sullivan et al. (1980, p. 27) describes the importance of symbols in shaping our reality.

> Symbols are the principal vehicles through which expectations are conveyed from one person to another. A symbol is any object, word or event that stands

for, represents, or takes the place of something else. Symbols have certain characteristics. First, the meaning of symbols derives from social consensus— the group's agreement that one thing will represent something else. A flag represents love of country or patriotism; a green light means *go*, not *stop*; a frown stands for displeasure. Second, the relationship between the symbol and what it represents is arbitrary—there is no inherent connection. There is nothing about the color green that compels us to use that, rather than red, as a symbol for *go*; a flag is in reality a piece of cloth for which we could substitute anything, as long as we agreed that it stood for country. Finally, symbols need not be tied to physical reality. We can use symbols to represent things with no physical existence, such as justice, mercy, or God, or to stand for things that do not exist at all, such as unicorns.

A direct offshoot of the interactionist perspective is labeling theory. This theory holds that the labels assigned to a person have a major impact on that person's life. Labels often become self-fulfilling prophecies. If a child is continually called "stupid" by his or her parents, that child is apt to develop a low self-concept, anticipate failure in many areas (particularly academic), and thereby put forth little effort in school and in competitive interactions with others, and end up failing. If a teenage girl gets a reputation as being promiscuous, adults and peers may label her as such, with other girls then shunning her, and teenage boys ridiculing her, and perhaps some seeking to date her for a one-night stand. If a person is labeled an ex-con for spending time in prison, that person is likely to be viewed with suspicion, have trouble finding employment, and be stigmatized as being dangerous and untrustworthy, even though the person may be honest, conscientious, and hard working. Scheff (1966) has developed a labeling theory to explain why some people develop a career of being mentally ill. He asserts the act of labeling someone mentally ill is the major determinant for their acting as if they were mentally ill. Once labeled, others interact with them as if they were mentally ill, which leads them to view themselves as being mentally ill, and they then enact this role.

The most common criticism of interactionist theory is that the theory is so abstract and vaguely worded that it is nearly impossible either to prove or to disprove it (Coleman and Cressey, 1984, p. 22).

Poverty

The functionalist, conflict, and interactionist perspectives will be further illustrated by discussing how each of these theories explains poverty. Poverty is a problem that is faced by perhaps a majority of social welfare recipients.

The Rich and the Poor

Poverty and wealth are closely related. Throughout most countries in the world, wealth is concentrated in a small percentage of the population. Abundance for a few is often created by depriving others.

There are two ways of measuring the extent of economic inequality. *Income* refers to the amount of money a person makes in a given period. *Wealth* is a person's total assets—real estate holdings, cash, stocks, bonds, and so forth.

The distribution of wealth and income is highly unequal in our society.

Similar to most countries, the United States is characterized by *social stratification*—that is, it has social classes with the upper classes having by far the greatest access to the pleasures that money can buy.

Looking at wealth, the lowest fifth of American individuals owns only 0.2 percent of the wealth, while the richest fifth owns more than three-quarters of the wealth (Robertson, 1980, p. 177). This means 20 percent of the population has three times as much wealth as all of the rest of the people combined! There are over 200,000 millionaires in this country; there are over 150 families that are worth more than $100 million, and there are about 60 families that are worth more than $500 million (Robertson, 1980, pp. 175–79). The richest 2 percent of our population owns 62 percent of all privately held corporate stock (Julian and Kornblum, 1983, p. 238). It is estimated that approximately one fourth of the wealth in this country is controlled by the richest 1 percent of the population (Coleman and Cressey, 1980, p. 152). Almost 20 percent of all American families have a negative net worth, meaning they have more liabilities than assets. Paul Samuelson (1980, p. 34), an economist, provides a dramatic metaphor of the disparity that exists between the very rich and most people in the United States:

> If we made an income pyramid out of a child's blocks, with each layer portraying $1,000 of income, the peak would be far higher than the Eiffel Tower, but almost all of us would be within a yard of the ground.

■ The Ideology of Individualism

Wealth is generally inherited in this country. There are few individuals who actually move up the social status ladder. Having wealth opens up many doors (through education and contacts) for children of the wealthy to make large sums of money when they become adults. For children living in poverty, there is little chance to escape when they become older. Yet, there is the myth of individualism which is held by many. It states that the rich are personally responsible for their success, and that the poor are to blame for their failure. Joe Feagin (1975, pp. 91–92) has summarized the main points of this myth:

1. Each individual should work hard and strive to succeed in competition with others.

2. Those who work hard should be rewarded with success (seen as wealth, property, prestige, and power).

3. Because of widespread and equal opportunity, those who work hard will, in fact, be rewarded with success.

4. Economic failure is an individual's own fault and reveals lack of effort and other character defects.

The poor are blamed for their circumstances in our society. Blaming the poor has led to a stigma being attached to poverty, particularly to those who receive public assistance (welfare).

A few comments appear in order. Given the huge wealth of the richest fifth, it is clear that a simple redistribution of some of the wealth from the top fifth to the lowest fifth could easily wipe out poverty. Of course, that is not politically acceptable to members of the top fifth who have the greatest control of the government. Also many of these rich families are able to avoid paying income taxes by taking advantage of tax loopholes and tax shelters.

Similar disparities between the rich and the poor are found when looking at annual income instead of total wealth. The poorest fifth receives only 5 percent of the national income, while the richest fifth receives over 40 percent of the national income. This pattern has remained virtually unchanged since World War II (Coleman and Cressey, 1984, p. 159). In our society it is common for heads of major corporations to earn $250,000 or more per year. In 1983, 48 executives of corporations were each paid over $1 million (Alm and Morse, 1984). In addition, they enjoy many other tax-free benefits from their corporations: expense accounts, use of cars and private jets, paid memberships in health clubs, medical care, theater tickets, and vacations.

In contrast millions of Americans regularly do not get enough to eat because they are poor. A study in 1985 found that the number of people in our country who are hungry is higher than at any time since the 1930s (*Wisconsin State Journal*, February 27, 1985, p. 8). An estimated 20 million citizens are hungry at least some period of time each month. Some clinics in poor areas are seeing cases of kwashiorkor and marasmus, two third world diseases of advanced malnutrition in which the victims often die. The brain of an infant grows to 80 percent of its adult size within the first three years of life. If supplies of protein are inadequate during this period, the brain stops growing, the damage is irreversible, and the child will be permanently retarded (Robertson, 1980, p. 31).

Coleman and Cressey (1980, p. 152) describe the effects of having, and not having, wealth:

> The poor lack the freedom and autonomy so prized in our society. They are trapped by their surroundings, living in rundown, crime-ridden neighborhoods that they cannot afford to leave. They are constantly confronted with things they desire but have little chance to own. On the other hand, wealth provides power, freedom, and the ability to direct one's own fate. The wealthy live where they choose and do as they please, with few economic constraints. Because the poor lack education and money for travel, their horizons seldom extend beyond the confines of their neighborhood. In contrast, the world of the wealthy offers the best education, together with the opportunity to visit places that the poor haven't even heard of.
>
> The children of the wealthy receive the best that society has to offer, as well as the assurance that they are valuable and important individuals. Because the children of the poor lack so many of the things everyone is "supposed" to have, it is much harder for them to develop the cool confidence of the rich. In our materialistic society people are judged as much by what they have as by who they are. The poor cannot help but feel inferior and inadequate in such a context.

■ Wealth Perpetuates Wealth, and Poverty Perpetuates Poverty

C. Wright Mills (1956, pp. 69–70) describes one way that wealth educates wealthy children to be financially successful.

The exclusive schools and clubs and resorts of the upper social classes are not exclusive merely because their members are snobs. Such locales and associations have a real part in building the upper-class character, and more than that, the connections to which they naturally lead help to link one higher circle with another. So the distinguished law student, after prep school and Harvard, is "clerk" to a Supreme Court judge, then a corporation lawyer, then in the diplomatic service, then in the law firm again. In each of these spheres, he meets and knows men of his own kind, and, as a kind of continuum, there are the old family friends and the schoolboy chums, the dinners at the club, and each year of his life the summer resorts. In each of these circles in which he moves, he acquires and exercises a confidence in his own ability to judge, to decide, and in this confidence he is supported by his ready access to the experience and sensibility of those who are his social peers and who act with decision in each of the important institutions and areas of public life. One does not turn one's back on a man whose presence is accepted in such circles, even under most trying circumstances. All over the top of the nation, he is "in," his appearance, a certificate of social position; his voice and manner, a badge of proper training; his associates, proof at once of their acceptance and of his stereotyped discernment.

In contrast, Ben Bagdikian (1964, p. 75) describes how living in poverty leads to despair, hopelessness and failure.

It was midafternoon but the tenement was dark. Grey plastic sheeting was tacked to the insides of the living room windows. . . . Plaster was off an expanse of ceiling and walls. . . . In one corner of the kitchen was a small refrigerator, in another a table with three legs and one chair. There was a stained stove bearing a basin full of children's clothes soaked in cold soapy water. . . . Through one kitchen door was a bathroom dominated by a toilet covered by boards; it had frozen and burst during the winter. Through another door was "the kid's room." . . . In this room slept seven children, in two beds. Neither bed had a mattress. The children slept on the springs. . . .

Outside, Sister Mary William . . . said: "You figure out what's going to happen to Harry Martin when he finds out he's never going to be a lawyer. And his brother's never going to be a doctor. And his sister's never going to be a nurse. The worst most of us have to resign ourselves to is that there's no Santa Claus. Wait until this hits those kids."

The Problem

In 1984, 35 million Americans, 15 percent of our population, were living below the poverty line (*U.S. News & World Report*, March 26, 1984, p. 54). (The poverty line is the level of income that the federal government considers sufficient to meet basic requirements of food, shelter, and clothing.) One of the alarming elements about poverty is that the rate of poverty in recent years has been increasing. From 1978 to 1984 the rate went from 11 to 15 percent. The poverty rate in 1984 was as high as it was in 1966 (*Focus*, Winter, 1984, p. 1). In addition, there are many people who do not fall under the government's poverty line, but still have very limited income and a living standard that is similar to those below the poverty line.

Poverty does not simply mean that poor people in the United States are living less well than people of average income. It means eating diets largely of beans, macaroni and cheese, or, in severe cases, even dog and cat food. It may mean not having running water, living in substandard housing, and being exposed to rats, cockroaches, and other vermin. It means not having sufficient heat in the winter and being unable to sleep as the walls are too thin to deaden the sounds from the neighbors living next door. It means being embarrassed about the few ragged clothes that one has to wear. It means great susceptibility to emotional disturbances, alcoholism, and victimization by criminals, as well as having a shorter life expectancy. It means few opportunities to advance oneself socially, economically, or educationally. It often means slum housing, unstable marriages, and little opportunity to enjoy the finer things in life—traveling, dining out, movies, plays, concerts, sports events.

The infant mortality rate of the poor is almost double the rate of the affluent (Julian and Kornblum, 1983, p. 31). The poor have less access to medical services and receive lower quality care from health care professionals. The poor are exposed to higher levels of air pollution, water pollution, and unsanitary conditions. They have higher rates of malnutrition and disease. Schools in poor areas are of lower quality and have fewer resources. As a result the poor achieve less academically and are more apt to drop out of school. They are more apt to be arrested, indicted, imprisoned, and given longer sentences for the same offense. They are less likely to receive probation, parole, or suspended sentences (Julian and Kornblum, 1983, pp. 257–58).

■ The Poverty Trap

Louise Ferguson, age 33, has recently become a grandmother. Her oldest daughter, Teresa, is a 17-year-old unmarried mother. Today, July 27, is a significant day in their lives, as Louise and Teresa are applying at Milwaukee's Public Welfare Office to place baby Rufus' name on America's welfare rolls. He will represent the third successive generation in the Ferguson family to receive AFDC benefits.

Louise's parents migrated from Mississippi to Milwaukee in 1952, shortly after Louise's birth. Her father got a job as a janitor for the school system, and her mother has been a part-time nurse's aid at a hospital. Louise started high school and received above average grades. She had hopes of getting a student loan to go to college. She wanted to get out of the ghetto in which she was being raised.

However, at the age of 16, she became pregnant. Her parents talked her out of an abortion, and she gave birth to Teresa. Two months after the birth, she signed up for AFDC, at the urging of her parents and friends. It would only be temporary, she thought, until she could get a better handle on her life. She found going to school and caring for a baby to be too much work. So she dropped out of high school in her junior year. She no longer had the same interests as her former friends who did not have a baby to care for. At times Louise found it a joy to care for Teresa, and at other times the baby drove her up a wall. Louise went out as much as she could, when she had a little extra money and when she could find someone to babysit for her. Over the next 15 years, Louise had four other children. Only one of the five different fathers ever married her, and that marriage only lasted two and one-half years. He left home one day, complaining about children and responsibilities. He never returned, and Louise has never heard from him again.

Louise has tried a variety of jobs while on AFDC—nurse's aid, dishwasher, waitress, and service station attendant. She discovered that costs for transportation, clothes, and babysitting left her no better off financially than if she stayed home and received her monthly AFDC checks. Life has been hard for Louise. She feels like a second-class citizen and a charity case for being on welfare rolls. She has had to pinch pennies all her life to try to make ends meet. Countless days she has fed her children on beans and rice. She sharply regrets not being able to give her children the material things that many other children have. While some parents are buying computers for their children, she takes her children to Goodwill's clothing store to try to find bargains on second-hand sneakers, shirts, blue jeans, and jackets.

She is living in a ghetto area and is alarmed that her oldest son, Michael, is experimenting with heroin and other drugs. The school system is another concern—a high percentage of students drop out, the windows in the buildings are boarded up, vandalism is frequent, physical attacks on teachers sometimes occur, and the educational quality is known to be inferior.

When she discovered Teresa was sexually active at 15, she pleaded with her not to make the mistake she did. When she continued to be sexually active, she even took Teresa to Planned Parenthood to receive birth control pills. Louise's remaining dream is that her children will have a better life than hers. Tears often come to her eyes when she sees her children getting caught in the same poverty trap that she is in. Teresa took her pills for several months. When the supply ran out, she never got around to going back to Planned Parenthood to get her prescription refilled.

Yes, today is a significant day for Louise. Significant in the sense that it is sad, as the third generation in her family is now going on welfare. As Louise and Teresa are walking towards the welfare department, Louise is solemnly pondering why her life has turned out as it has and also wondering what it will take to give at least some of her children a chance for a better life.

Poverty also often leads to despair, low self-esteem, and stunting of one's physical, social, emotional, and intellectual growth. A second level of damage from poverty occurs from the *feeling* that lack of financial resources is preventing one from having equal opportunities and from the *feeling* then, that one is a second-class citizen. Poverty hurts most when it leads to viewing oneself as inferior or second class.

We like to think that America is a land of equal opportunity and that there is considerable upward class mobility for those who put forth effort. The reality is the opposite of the myth. Extensive research has shown that poverty is almost escape proof. Children raised in poor families are apt themselves to live in poverty in their adult years. Most people have much the same social status as their parents had. Movement to a higher social status is an unusual happening in practically all societies—including the United States (Julian and Kornblum, 1983, pp. 236–45).

In testimony before the Senate Select Committee on Nutrition and Human Needs, Robert Coles (1969), a physician, described the plight of those living in poverty:

> We had seen . . . not only extreme poverty, but gross, clinical evidence of chronic hunger and malnutrition—evidence that we as doctors found it hard to deal with ourselves, let alone talk about, because we had been unprepared by our own medical training for what we saw. Today's American physicians are simply not prepared by their education to find in this nation severe vitamin deficiency diseases, widespread parasitism, and among infants, a mortality rate that is comparable, say, to the underdeveloped nations of Asia or Africa. . . .
>
> I saw . . . malnourished children, children who are not getting the right amount and kinds of food, who suffer from several diseases and see no physician, who indeed were born in shacks without the help of a doctor and under conditions that are primitive, to say the least. . . . Why . . . must these children go hungry, still be sick? . . . Why do American children get born without the help of a doctor, and never, never see a doctor in their lives? It is awful, it is humiliating for all of us that these questions still have to be asked in a nation like this, the strongest and richest nation that ever was. . . .
>
> I do not understand why these things have to persist and why we have to talk about this again and again and again, and people like me have to come and repeat all these findings.

Who Are the Poor?

An encouraging trend is that the proportion of people below the poverty line has gradually been decreasing in the last 80 years. Prior to the 20th century a majority of the population lived in poverty. President Franklin D. Roosevelt (1937) stated, "I see one third of a nation ill-housed, ill-clad, ill-nourished." In 1962 the President's Council on Economic Advisors estimated one fifth of the population were in poverty (U.S. Bureau of the Census, 1982, p. 441). Now about 15 percent of the nation are estimated to be below the poverty line. An alarming concern is that since 1978 there has been an increase in the proportion of the population who are poor.

Michael Harrington (1962) points out that the poor are invisible in our society; that is, their clothes are not markedly different, our superhighways carry us quickly past dilapidated homes, and the poor are such a heterogeneous group that they are not politically organized to make their needs known.

Poverty is concentrated in certain population categories, including one-parent families, children, the elderly, large-size families, and minorities.

Educational level, unemployment, and place of residence are also factors related to poverty.

One-Parent Families. Most one-parent families are headed by a female. Thirty four percent of female-headed families are in poverty, compared to 7 percent for two-parent families (U.S. Bureau of the Census, 1982, p. 441). Single mothers who are members of a racial minority (e.g. black, Chicano, American Indian) are particularly vulnerable to poverty as they are subjected to double discrimination in the labor market due to both race and sex. Women who work full time are paid on the average only 60 percent of what men who work full time are paid (U.S. Bureau of the Census, 1982, p. 403). Many single mothers are unable to work due to lack of transportation, to the lack or high cost of daycare facilities, and to having received little training for available job openings. Unable to work, they have to rely on public assistance (benefits which are often below the poverty line) in the form of Aid to Families with Dependent Children (AFDC). Of the families living in poverty, half are headed by a single mother (U.S. Bureau of the Census, 1982, p. 441). The increase in one-parent families in the United States has led to an increase in the feminization of poverty. About one out of every five children in this country is now living apart from one parent, and because of increasing divorce rates, separations, and births outside of marriage, it is estimated that nearly one of two children born today will spend part of her or his first 18 years in a family headed by a single mother (Focus, 1984, p. 3).

Children. Approximately 35 percent of the poor are children under the age of 16. More than half of these children live in families where the father is absent. (*U.S. News & World Report*, March 26, 1984, p. 55). Many of these children rely on AFDC payments for meeting the basic necessities.

The Elderly. About 15 percent of the poor are people aged 65 and older (U.S. Bureau of the Census, 1982, p. 442). Many of the elderly depend on Social Security pensions or public assistance payments (in the form of Supplementary Security Income) to meet basic necessities. Over 43 percent of the elderly have pretransfer incomes below the poverty line (*Focus*, Winter 1984, p. 6). Significantly, almost one third of the elderly who live alone are poor, while less than one tenth of those who live in families are poor (Coleman and Cressey, 1984, p. 64).

Large-Size Families. Larger size families are more apt to be poor, partly because more income is needed as family size increases. It costs over $70,000 to raise a child from birth to age 18 (*U.S. News and World Report*, January 5, 1981, p. 77).

Minorities. Contrary to popular stereotypes, most poor people (over two thirds) are white (U.S. Bureau of the Census, 1982, p. 442). But members of most minority groups are disproportionately apt to be poor. Blacks, for example, compose about 12 percent of the total population, yet they constitute over one fourth of all the poor. One out of every three black persons is poor, compared to one out of ten white persons (U.S. Bureau of the Census, 1982, p. 442). Approximately one third of American Indian families live below the poverty line, and about 25 percent of Mexican Americans live in poverty—particularly migrant workers in agriculture (*Focus*, Winter 1984, p. 7). Racial discrimination is a major reason why most racial minorities are disproportionately poor.

Education. Achieving less than a ninth-grade education is a good predictor of being poor. Completing high school, however, is not a guarantee for earning adequate wages and for avoiding poverty, as many of the poor have graduated from high school. Obtaining a college degree is an excellent predictor of avoiding poverty as only a small proportion of those with a college degree are poor (Flynn, 1975, pp. 88–89).

Employment. Being unemployed is, of course, associated with poverty. However, being employed is not a guarantee of avoiding poverty, as over one million heads of families work full time, but earn less than the poverty level (U.S. Bureau of the Census, 1982, p. 445).

The general public (and many government officials) wrongly assume that obtaining jobs for unemployed adults is the key to ending poverty. However, jobs alone cannot end poverty.

Place of Residence. People who live in rural areas are more likely to be poor than people who live in urban areas. In rural areas wages are low, there is high unemployment, and work tends to be seasonal. The Ozarks, Appalachia, and the South have pockets of rural poverty with high rates of unemployment (Mann, 1982, pp. 31–36).

People who live in urban slums constitute the largest group in terms of numbers of people who are poor. The decaying cities of the Northeast and Midwest have particularly large urban slums. The urban poor are unable to take advantage of opportunities that are available to the affluent as they often lack job skills, transportation, a decent education, and they also may face racial or ethnic discrimination. Poverty is also extensive on Indian reservations and among seasonal migrant workers.

All these factors indicate some people are more vulnerable to poverty than others. Michael Harrington (1962, p. 21) notes that the poor made the simple mistake of:

> being born to the wrong parents, in the wrong section of the country, in the wrong industry, or in the wrong racial or ethnic group. Once that mistake has been made, they could have been paragons of will and morality, but most of them would never even have had a chance to get out of the other America.

What Causes Poverty?

There are a number of possible causes of poverty, including a high unemployment rate, poor physical health, emotional problems, drug addiction, low education level, racial and sexual discrimination, budgeting problems and mismanagement of resources, and mental retardation.

The above list is not exhaustive. However, it serves to show: (a) there are a large number of causes of poverty, (b) eliminating the causes of poverty would require a wide range of social programs, and (c) poverty interacts with almost all other social problems—such as emotional problems, alcoholism, unemployment, racial and sex discrimination, medical problems, crime, gambling, and mental retardation. The interaction between poverty and these other social problems is a contributing cause of poverty. Yet, for some social problems, poverty is also a contributing cause (such as emotional problems, alcoholism, and unemployment). And, being poor intensifies the effects (the hurt) of all social problems.

To some extent poverty is passed on from generation to generation. This cycle of poverty is diagrammed in Figure 10.1.

Figure 10.1   Cycle of Poverty

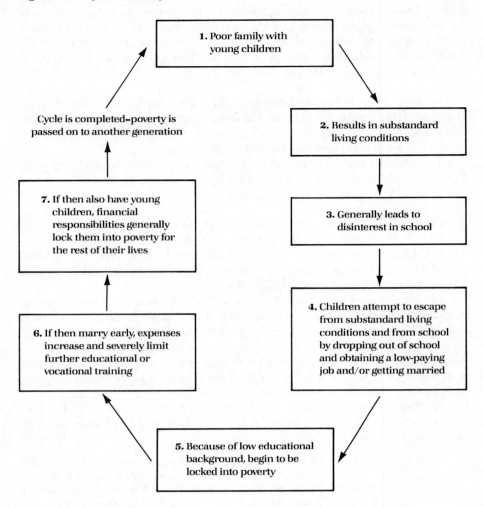

1. Poor family with young children

2. Results in substandard living conditions

Cycle is completed–poverty is passed on to another generation

3. Generally leads to disinterest in school

7. If then also have young children, financial responsibilities generally lock them into poverty for the rest of their lives

4. Children attempt to escape from substandard living conditions and from school by dropping out of school and obtaining a low-paying job and/or getting married

6. If then marry early, expenses increase and severely limit further educational or vocational training

5. Because of low educational background, begin to be locked into poverty

The Culture of Poverty

Why is poverty passed on from one generation to another? Some authorities argue that the explanation is due to a "culture of poverty." Oscar Lewis (1966), an anthropologist, is one of the chief proponents of the cultural explanation.

Lewis examined poor neighborhoods in various parts of the world, and concluded the poor are poor because they have a distinct culture or lifestyle. The key elements of Lewis' cultural explanation are as follows:

The culture of poverty arises after extended periods of economic deprivation in highly stratified capitalistic societies. Such economic deprivation is brought about by high rates of unemployment, underemployment for unskilled labor, and low wages for those who are employed. Such economic deprivation leads to the development of attitudes and values of despair and hopelessness. Lewis (1966, p. 23) describes these attitudes and values as follows:

The individual who grows up in this culture has a strong feeling of fatalism, helplessness, dependence and inferiority; a strong present-time orientation with relatively little disposition to defer gratification and plan for the future, and a high tolerance for psychological pathology of all kinds.

Once developed, this culture continues to exist, even though the economic factors that created it (for example, lack of employment opportunities) no longer exist. These attitudes, norms, and expectations of the poor serve to limit their opportunities and prevent their escape. A major reason they remain locked into their culture is that they are socially isolated. They have few contacts with groups outside their own culture and are hostile to the institutions (for example, social services and education) that might be able to help them escape poverty. They reject such institutions because they perceive them as belonging to the dominant class. Furthermore, since they view their financial circumstances as private matters and hopeless and they lack political and organizational skills, they do not take collective action to try to resolve their problems.

The culture of poverty theory has been controversial and widely criticized. Eleanor Leacock (1971) argues that the distinctive culture of the poor is not the cause, but the result of their continuing poverty. She agrees that the poor tend to emphasize instant gratification, which involves spending and enjoying one's money while it lasts. But she argues instant gratification is a result of being poor, rather than the cause, as it makes no sense to defer gratification when a person is pessimistic about the future. Deferred gratification is only a rational response when one is optimistic that postponing pleasures today by saving the money will reap greater benefits in the future. Interestingly, studies (Leacock, 1971) have found that when ghetto residents are able to obtain a stable, good-paying job, they then display the middle-class value of deferred gratification. Because of poverty, Leacock argues, the poor are forced to abandon middle-class attitudes and values, because such values are irrelevant to their circumstances. If they had stable, good paying jobs, they would likely take on the values of the middle class.

In an even stronger indictment, William Ryan (1976) criticizes the poverty culture theory as simply being a classic example of blaming the victim. Blaming the poor for their circumstances is a convenient excuse, according to Ryan, for avoiding developing the programs and policies thought necessary to eradicate poverty. The real culprit is the social system that allows poverty to exist. Ryan says bluntly that the poor are not poor because of their culture, but because they do not have enough money.

Pro and con arguments for the culture of poverty theory continue to persist. There are many reasons, both external and internal, as to why a person may be poor. External reasons include high rates of unemployment and underemployment, racial discrimination, automation which throws people out of work, lack of job training programs, sex discrimination, a shortage of programs to eradicate poverty, and inflation. Internal reasons include having a physical or mental impairment, being alcoholic, having obsolete job skills, becoming a parent at an early age, dropping out of school, and being uninterested in taking available jobs.

Poverty Is Functional

Obviously, poverty causes many dysfunctions, mainly to the poor themselves, but also to the affluent. However, realizing poverty has some functions helps us to understand why some decision makers are not actively seeking to eradicate poverty.

Eleven functions provided by the poor for affluent groups are summarized by Sullivan, et al. (1980, p. 390):

1. They are available to do the unpleasant jobs that no one else wants to do.
2. By their activities, they subsidize the more affluent (an example of such an activity is domestic service for low pay).
3. Jobs are established for those people, such as social workers, who provide services to the poor.
4. They purchase goods, such as those of poor quality, that otherwise could not be sold.
5. They serve as examples of deviance that are frowned on by the majority and that thereby support dominant norms.
6. They provide an opportunity for others to practice their "Christian duty" of helping the less fortunate.
7. They make mobility more likely for others because they are removed from the competition for a good education and good jobs.
8. They contribute to cultural activities by providing, for example, cheap labor for the construction of monuments and works of art.
9. They create cultural forms (for example, jazz and the blues) that are often adopted by the affluent.
10. They serve as symbolic opponents for some political groups and as constituents for others.
11. They often absorb the costs of change (for example by being the victims of high levels of unemployment that result from technological advances).

Also, denigrating the poor has the psychological function for some Americans of making them feel better about themselves.

Partly because poverty is functional, our society makes only a half-hearted effort to eradicate, or at least reduce, it. To eliminate it would mean a redistribution of income from the rich to the poor. Since the rich control the political power, they have generally been opposed to proposals that would eliminate poverty, such as guaranteed annual income programs. Gans (1968, pp. 133–35) emphasizes this point:

> Legislation in America tends to favor the interests of the businessman, not the consumers, even though the latter are a vast majority; of landlords, not tenants; of doctors, not patients. Only organized interest groups have the specific concerns and the time, staff, and money to bring their demands before government officials. . . . The poor are powerless because they are a minority of the population, are not organized politically, are often difficult to organize, and are not even a homogeneous group with similar interests that could be organized into a single pressure group. . . . Given the antagonism toward them on the part of many Americans, any programs that would provide them with significant gains are likely to be voted down by a majority. Legislative proposals for a massive anti-poverty effort . . . have always run into concerted and united opposition in Washington.

Our government has the resources to eliminate poverty—but not the will. It would cost less than one seventh of our annual expenditure on defense to raise the income of all Americans above the poverty line (U.S. Bureau of the Census, 1978, p. 8).

The Functionalist Perspective

Functionalists view poverty as being due to dysfunctions in the economy. A wide range of dysfunctions have been identified, some of which will be mentioned here. Rapid industrialization has caused disruptions in the economic system. For example, people who lack job skills are forced into menial work at low wages. Then when automation comes, they are discharged, without having work, money, or marketable job skills. Some products produced by industry also become outdated—such as steam engines, milk bottles, and horse carriages. When such products become obsolete, workers lose their jobs. In addition, work training centers and apprenticeship programs may continue to produce graduates whose skills are no longer in demand—for example, there no longer is a job market for people who are trained to repair adding machines and manual typewriters; and direct telephone dialing is sharply reducing the number of people needed as telephone operators.

Functionalists also note that the welfare system, which is intended to solve the problem of poverty, has a number of dysfunctions. Social welfare programs are sometimes established without sufficient funds to meet the needs of potential clients. Some bureaucrats are reluctant to bend the complex rules to help a deserving family who is technically ineligible for assistance. Social welfare programs at times have design dysfunctions in meeting the needs of recipients—for example, mothers of young children in some states are eligible for AFDC only when the husband is out of the home—with the result that some unemployed husbands are forced to desert their family in order for the family to be fed and sheltered. There are additional problems in the welfare system. Inadequate information systems fail to inform the poor about benefits to which they are entitled. Job training and educational programs sometimes train people for positions for which there are no employment openings.

According to functionalists, the best way to deal with poverty is to make adjustments to correct these dysfunctions. For example, the AFDC program should be amended (as many states have done) to allow AFDC payments in two-parent families when the combined income of husband and wife is below the eligibility guidelines.

Many functionalists view some economic inequality (that is, poverty) as being functional. Because the poor are at the bottom of the stratification system, they receive few of the material and social rewards in the society. Functionalists view the threat of being at the bottom of the heap as an important mechanism for motivating people to perform. According to functionalists, poverty becomes a social problem when it no longer performs the function of motivating people to make productive contributions to society. Poverty is also functional as the poor do the demeaning, difficult, and low-paying jobs that are essential but that no one else wants to do.

The Conflict Perspective

Conflict theorists assume that because there is such enormous wealth in modern societies, no one in such societies should go without their essential needs being met. These theorists assert poverty exists because the power structure wants it to exist. They assert that the working poor are being exploited, since they are paid poverty level wages so that their employers can reap higher profits.

The unemployed are also seen as being the victims of the power structure. Wealthy employers oppose programs to reduce unemployment (such as educational and job training programs) because they do not want to pay the taxes to support them.

Completing high school is no longer a guarantee of avoiding poverty. Even this college graduate's diploma does not ensure him against poverty. Yet he is unlikely to fall into the poverty trap since only a small portion of Americans with college degrees are poor. Contrary to popular belief, over two-thirds of America's poor are white. The fact that a disproportionate number of the poor belong to racial minority groups can be blamed, in part, on racial discrimination. (Gregg Theune)

This couple is seeking counseling to solve their marital problems. The marriage counselor, working with both spouses, helps them identify and resolve their problems. Marital problems are many and diverse, ranging from sexual and financial disagreements to conflicts on child rearing. To avoid marital problems, premarital counseling is becoming increasingly popular. The prospective mates learn to pinpoint, solve, and thereby bypass potentially troublesome spots in their prospective marriages. (Charles Zastrow)

This elderly bag lady is searching for food in a garbage bin across the street from the White House. Poverty is still a major national problem in America, striking about 15 percent of its senior citizens ages sixty-five and over. This needy group subsists on unbalanced, inadequate diets, lives in substandard housing, dresses in ragged clothing, and is prone to emotional disturbances. (Fran Buss)

Battered women who are abused by their husbands tend to be unemployed and financially insecure. They often feel trapped. The shelters for battered women that are springing up around the country offer these women a place to go when they flee their abusive homes. They often provide two additional services: employment counseling and legal help. The new hotlines that potential spouse abusers can call when they feel angry are another spouse-abuse deterrent. (Courtesy of United Way of America)

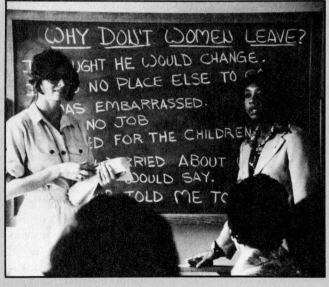

Wealthy people are apt to cling to the ideology of individualism, because they tend to view unemployment and poverty as stemming from a lack of effort rather than from social injustice or from other circumstances beyond the control of the individual. As a result, the wealthy ignore the economic and political foundations of poverty, and instead get involved in charitable efforts for the poor, which leaves them feeling they have done good deeds. Conflict theorists see charity and government welfare programs as a force in perpetuating poverty and economic inequality, as such programs quell political protests and social unrest that threaten the status quo. Conflict theorists also assert that many poor people eventually come to accept the judgments passed on them by the rest of society and adjust their aspirations and their self-esteem downward.

Conflict theorists do not see poverty as either essential or functional. They see poverty as arising because some groups benefit from seeing to it that the poor have less. From the conflict perspective, poverty becomes a social problem when some group feels the existing distribution of resources is unfair and unjust and that something can and should be done about it.

Conflict theorists believe poverty can best be dealt with by the poor becoming politically aware and active and organizing to reduce inequality through government action. These theorists view poor people's adjustments to poverty as being a set of chains that must be broken. Most conflict theorists believe poverty can only be significantly reduced through political action by poor people—action which receives at least some support from concerned members of the power structure.

The Interactionist Perspective

Interactionists emphasize the subjective nature of poverty. Poverty is viewed as being relative, since it depends on what it is compared to. Most poor people in the United States presently have a higher standard of living than middle class people did 200 years ago. Poor people in this country are also substantially better off than poor people in third world countries.

The main reference for poor people in this country is their poor neighbors. A successful person in some neighborhoods is someone who knows where the next meal is coming from, and a big success may be someone who gets a job on an assembly line. People with such attitudes become trapped in their own beliefs. Another value they acquire that traps them is instant gratification, in which they are not inclined to defer immediate rewards so that long-run goals, such as a college education, can be reached.

Interactionists also emphasize the psychological effects of being poor in a wealthy society. Through comparing themselves to people with wealth, many come to believe they are failures and attribute their failure to personal shortcomings rather than to social forces that are beyond their control. With such a failure identity, they may withdraw from society, develop emotional problems because of their perceptions of self, or turn to delinquency and crime to seek to obtain illegally material goods that they are unable to obtain legally.

Interactionists view poverty as a matter of shared expectations. The poor are negatively judged by influential groups. Those who are the objects of such labeling are stigmatized and may begin to behave in accordance with those expectations. Interactionists emphasize that poverty is not just a matter of economic deprivation, but involves the person's self-concept.

For example, a third generation welfare recipient is apt to view himself much more negatively than a person working his way through college, even though both may have the same income.

To resolve the poverty problem, interactionists urge that the stigma and negative definitions associated with poverty be eliminated. Positive changes in the poverty problem will not occur until the poor are convinced that they no longer are doomed to live in poverty. The poverty trap can be sprung with public assistance programs that bring the poor up to an adequate standard of living, *combined* with programs that open up opportunities to move up the socioeconomic ladder, and programs that encourage the poor to redefine their social environment.

Problems in the Work Setting

"What do you do for a living?" is a question that is commonly asked when two strangers meet. Work is a central focus of life, particularly for middle-aged adults who are generally at the peak of their work career in terms of earnings and prestige. Work not only enables a person to earn money to pay bills, it can also provide a sense of self-respect, provide a circle of colleagues and friends, and be a source of self-fulfillment. A challenging job can help a person to grow intellectually, psychologically, and socially. Work also largely determines a person's place in the social structure. (In the past, birth largely determined one's social position and vocational choices.) We have considerable choice in the vocations we select, and vocational choice largely determines our social status. We are largely defined by our work.

In our society we highly value the work ethic; that is, we consider work to be honorable, productive, and useful. Unemployed, able-bodied persons are often looked down on. The importance of work is shown in a study by Morse and Weiss (1955). They asked, "If by some chance you inherited enough money to live comfortably without working, do you think that you would work anyway, or not?" Eighty percent of the respondents stated they would prefer to keep on working.

Work has not always been so esteemed. The ancient Greeks, for example, viewed work as a curse imposed on humanity by the gods. Work was thought to be an unpleasant and burdensome activity that was incompatible with being a citizen. Citizens sought to have extensive leisure time so they could further develop their minds. The Greeks, therefore, used slaves, and justified slavery on the basis that it freed citizens to spend their time in philosophic contemplation and cultural enrichment. Aristotle remarked, "No man can practice virtue who is living the life of a mechanic or laborer." Most societies until the Protestant Reformation tended to disparage work, frequently viewing it as an undesirable but necessary burden to survive.

The Protestant Reformation which began in the 16th century brought about profound changes in social values concerning work. Work became for the first time highly valued. One of the Protestant reformers, Martin Luther, asserted that labor was a service to God. Since the time of Luther, work has continued to be viewed as being honorable and as having religious significance.

Another Protestant reformer, John Calvin, had even a more dramatic effect on changing the views toward work. Calvin preached that work is the will of God. Hard work, good deeds, and success at one's vocation were taken to be signs that one was destined for salvation. Calvin preached that

God's will was that people should live frugally (spending very little money) and should use profits from work to invest in new ventures, which, in turn, would bring more profits for additional investments, and so on. Hard work and frugality came to have great value. Idleness or laziness came to be viewed as sinful. One religious group that was most influenced by Calvin's teachings were the Puritans. The Puritans also developed a strong ascetic lifestyle; that is, the practice of denying worldly pleasures as a demonstration of religious discipline. Calvin's teachings were widely accepted and formed a new cultural value system which became known as the Protestant Ethic. This ethic had three core values: hard work, frugality, and asceticism.

■ Max Weber and the Protestant Ethic

In 1904 the German sociologist Max Weber (1958) published what has become one of the most provocative theories in sociology. In *The Protestant Ethic and the Spirit of Capitalism* Weber asserted that the Protestant Ethic encouraged, and made possible, the emergence of capitalism. Weber theorized that the ideas of puritanism (advocated by Martin Luther and John Calvin) provided the value system that led to the transformation from traditional society to the Industrial Revolution.

Weber noted that puritan Protestantism embraced the doctrine that people were divinely selected for either salvation or damnation. There was nothing people could do to alter their fate. No one knew for sure whether he or she was destined for eternal salvation or eternal damnation. However, people looked for signs from God to suggest their fate. Since they also believed that work was a form of service to God, they concluded that success at work (making profits) was a sign of God's favor. They, therefore, worked hard to accumulate as much wealth as possible.

Since the Protestant Ethic viewed luxury and self-gratification as sinful, the profits acquired were not spent on luxuries but were reinvested in new ventures to increase income.

Such new ventures included building factories and developing new machines. Thus, according to Weber, the Industrial Revolution began, and capitalism was born.

The values of hard work and saving that were advanced by the Protestant Ethic have continued throughout our history. For example, Benjamin Franklin (1980, p. 300) praised these values with:

"A penny saved is a penny earned"

"Time is money"

"After industry and frugality, nothing contributes more to the raising of a young man than punctuality"

"He who sits idle . . . throws away money"

"Waste neither time nor money; an hour lost is money lost."

Richard Nixon, while president, in a speech on welfare reform declared that labor has intrinsic value, has a strong American tradition, and is consistent with religious teachings. Nixon (1980) added, "Scrubbing floors and emptying bedpans have just as much dignity as there is in any work done in this country—including my own. . . . Most of us consider it immoral to be lazy or slothful."

Although we no longer value the frugal, ascetic lifestyle of Puritanism, we still believe strongly in the ethic of hard work. An able-bodied person, to gain approval from others, is expected to be employed (or at least to be receiving job training). People on welfare are often looked down on. There still remains a strong link between amount of income and personal worth. The more people are paid, the more highly they are regarded by others, and the more highly they regard themselves.

A government report, *Work in America* (1973) found that people in low-status jobs are generally unable to form a satisfying identity from their jobs. Having an assembly line job, for example, often leads workers to view themselves as being personally insignificant. They routinely perform the same task day in and day out—such as attaching nuts to bolts. Such jobs, *Work in America* (1973, p. 45) noted, lead to a worker having "an overwhelming sense of inferiority: he cannot talk proudly to his children of his job, and feels he must apologize for his status."

Since the status of our work has immense effects on our self-concept, having a degrading, boring, and dehumanizing job can have immense adverse effects on our psychological well-being. We judge ourselves not only by how much our job pays, but also on whether the job is challenging, satisfying and helps us grow and develop. Two of the most serious social problems in the work setting are worker alienation and unemployment.

Worker Alienation

Alienation has a specific sociological meaning. *It is the sense of meaninglessness and powerlessness that people experience when interacting with social institutions they consider oppressive and beyond their control.*

The term *worker alienation* was originally developed by Karl Marx. (Perhaps because Marx has been associated with communism, the subject of alienation has tended to be neglected in our country.) Marx suggested that worker alienation largely occurs because workers are separated from ownership of the means of production, and from any control over the final product of their labor. They feel powerless and view their work as meaningless. Marx (1964) described alienation as follows:

> In what does this alienation consist? First, that work is external to the worker, that it is not part of his nature, that consequently he does not fulfill himself in his work but denies himself, has a feeling of misery, not well-being, does not develop freely a physical and mental energy, but is physically exhausted and mentally debased. . . . His work is not voluntary but imposed, *forced* labor. . . . Finally, the alienated character of work for the worker appears in the fact that it is not his work but work for someone else, that in work he does not belong to himself but to another person.

Marx thought that specialization was a major cause of alienation. With specialization, workers are forced to repeatedly perform an unfulfilling task. People use only a fraction of their talents. Work becomes an enforced impersonalized activity, rather than a creative venture.

Specialization has been a continuing trend in our society. The producing of most products has now become fragmented into repetitive and monotonous tasks, with each worker contributing only a small portion of the final product. A worker on an assembly line commented (Wolfbein, 1971, p. 45):

> The assembly line is no place to work, I can tell you. There is nothing more discouraging than having a barrel beside you with 10,000 bolts in it and using

them all up. Then you get a barrel with another 10,000 bolts, and you know every one of those 10,000 bolts has to be picked up and put exactly in the same place as the last 10,000 bolts.

Specialization has contributed substantially to highly sophisticated products and services being developed and provided. But it has also created problems. Workers find it difficult to have much pride in their work when they realize they are merely a replaceable adjunct to a machine or a process, and when they contribute only a small part to the final product. Such specialization often results in job dissatisfaction. Those who are trained for a single, narrowly defined job which later becomes obsolete are often without marketable skills for other openings. Specialization has also created problems of worker cooperation and coordination that present difficult problems for managers of organizations. Finally our society has become highly interdependent due to specialization.

There are a number of other sources of alienation. Working for a large business or corporation and knowing you can readily be replaced leads to a sense of feeling powerless and having a meaningless job. Not being involved in the decision-making process, and being aware that supervisors do not want workers to make waves, also leads to a feeling of powerlessness and meaninglessness.

In some businesses, machines have been developed to do most of the work. This automation has led workers to feel they are insignificant cogs in the production process. Even the pace at which they work is controlled by the machinery. Having a job where one has little opportunity to be

■ Job Dissatisfaction

George Murdoch was born with a silver spoon in his mouth. His father was an accountant and his mother, a nurse. He was raised in an upper middle class suburb. The family had two late model automobiles, a sailboat, and an elegant home near a lake. The family took annual trips to such exotic places as the Greek Isles, Acapulco, France, and Hawaii.

George was an only child and in his younger years had a number of friends. George was primarily interested in sports and having a good time. He never applied himself in school. The main thing his parents nagged him about was his grades—he often received Cs and Ds and seldom studied. Why should he? He already had plenty of toys to play with. Even in high school, partying, skipping school, and being with his friends seemed like the thing to do, rather than studying.

After high school, his parents wanted George to go to college. Although George didn't want to go, they lured him into going by buying him a new Corvette. The offer was too good to refuse. He went and majored in partying. He was suspended because of low grades. His parents were furious with him but paid his way to go to another private college. The result was the same. His parents then sent him to a third college. After he flunked out from this college, his parents decided they had had enough. They informed George he was now on his own. Because he was drinking and partying heavily, they also told him he had to find his own place to live. They paid his rent for one month at a low budget apartment that George chose. His parents decided that the school of hard knocks might be the best teacher for George.

Over the next three years, George had a variety of low-skill, low-paying jobs: janitor, dishwasher, bartender, grocery store clerk, and service station attendant. He disliked each job, as it was monotonous and unchallenging. George also found that most of his former high school friends were now graduating from college and beginning their careers. He felt their interests had changed, that they were being snobby and he intensely disliked being asked what he was now doing.

While a bartender at a family restaurant, he met Kathy Reisner and they began dating. After six months of a courtship that was filled with a great deal of anger and hostility on both sides because both were dating others, Kathy became pregnant. George and Kathy married and several months later became the parents of a girl.

George now felt he had to provide for three people. His relationship with Kathy was filled with violent arguments. Because George had few other friends, he decided to try to preserve the marriage.

In order to increase the family income, he went to a diesel truck training school to learn to drive a semi. After this training, he got a job with Long Trucking Company. For the past four years he has been a truck driver. The pay is good, as he is now earning around $25,000 a year. But he dislikes the work. He describes it as follows:

How would you like to bounce around in a truck eight or nine hours a day? Sometimes I get so sleepy I'm afraid I'm going to dose off and hit a bridge abutment. If I'm a little late in delivering a load, I'm reamed out. If I'm early or on time, I almost never get any appreciation. I eat at greasy spoon truck stops, and when I'm on a long haul I usually sleep in the cab. In winter it's freezing cold, and in the summer it's blazing hot. There is also the danger that fog, icy roads, or even wet roads will cause this rig to jackknife.

I sure wish I could get another job. I need to be home more with my family. At times I think my wife is cheating on me when I'm away for 4 to 5 days at a time.

Some people think trucking is great because you get to see the country. That just isn't so. All I get to see are roads, bridges, truck stops, and warehouses. There has to be more to life than spending eight to nine hours a day bouncing around in a cab, knowing that if you fall asleep your life will be over. But I'm locked into this job for the next 20 to 30 years. I've got a family to support and no other job I can get will pay the bills.

creative, but does the same task over and over has also contributed to alienation—jobs such as typist, receptionist, janitorial work, garbage collector, assembly line work, and telephone operator.

Jobs that do not provide opportunities to learn, that do not provide a sense of accomplishment, that do not provide an opportunity to work with interesting or congenial people, also lead to alienation. Many authorities believe that alienation leads to acts of disruption in the production process—work of poor quality, high rates of absenteeism, and vandalism or theft of company property.

Job Satisfaction and Dissatisfaction

Dissatisfaction with one's job is a useful indicator of alienation at work. Studies on job satisfaction show wide differences, according to vocation, in worker satisfaction with their job.

Many people, if given a choice, would select a different career. Yet, it is noteworthy that when public opinion polls ask people if they are satisfied with their job, over 80 percent consistently answer "yes" (Robertson, 1980,

■ Percent of People in Occupational Groups Who Would Choose Similar Work Again

Professional and Lower White-Collar Occupations		Working-Class Occupations	
Urban university professors	93	Skilled printers	52
Mathematicians	91	Paper workers	42
Physicists	89	Skilled autoworkers	41
Biologists	89	Skilled steelworkers	41
Chemists	86	Textile workers	31
Firm lawyers	85	Blue-collar workers, cross section	24
Lawyers	83	Unskilled steelworkers	21
Journalists (Washington correspondents)	82	Unskilled autoworkers	16
Church university professors	77		
Solo lawyers	75		
White-collar workers, cross section	43		

SOURCE: *Work in America: Report of a Special Task Force to the Secretary of Health, Education, and Welfare* (Cambridge, Mass: The M.I.T. Press, 1973), p. 16.

p. 89). At the present time, it is unclear why some approaches to measuring job satisfaction show high levels of satisfaction, while other approaches suggest large numbers of workers are sufficiently dissatisfied that they would choose another occupation if given a choice.

Although the amount of pay received is an important factor in worker satisfaction, it appears it is not the most important factor. The *Work in America* (1973, p. 16) report asked workers to rank various aspects in order of importance. Respondents gave the following ranking:

1. Interesting work.
2. Enough help and equipment to get the job done.
3. Enough information to get the job done.
4. Enough authority to get the job done.
5. Good pay.
6. Opportunity to develop special abilities.
7. Job security.
8. Seeing the results of one's work.

Morton (1977, p. 64) reviewed a number of studies on job satisfaction and identified the following factors as the sources of job satisfaction:

- Psychological satisfaction. A satisfactory job provides a sense of accomplishment, provides an opportunity to learn, is closely matched to a worker's interests and abilities, and provides an opportunity to work with congenial or interesting people.
- Monetary compensation. Workers tend to be satisfied when they feel they are paid fairly.
- Physical factors. Job satisfaction is increased in a setting that is pleasant, is viewed as free from hazards, when commuting time to work is short, and when transportation to work is readily available.
- Control. Workers are more satisfied in jobs where they feel they have some decision-making responsibilities and have some control over their work schedules. Punching a time-clock is disliked, while flexitime is appealing. Flexitime seeks to

reduce alienation from work by making work schedules more flexible. The idea is to have most workers present during the busiest time of the day, but to then leave the remaining hours and days per week up to the discretion of the workers. Those who want to start earlier so they can leave earlier can do so. Those who want to start later and work later can do so. In some places it is possible with flexitime to work four days a week (10 hours per day) and thereby have an extra day off.

- Institutional aspects. Workers are more satisfied with jobs that have promotion-from-within policies, training programs, personnel policies that assure equal opportunity for advancement and education, and that have good physical facilities and conveniences—lounges, cafeterias, gyms, and the like.
- Economic, political, and social aspects. The national mood affects job satisfaction. In the late 1960s and 1970s there was severe discontent and controversy about the Vietnam War, which lowered job satisfaction. On the other hand, a feeling of national prosperity increases job satisfaction.

Unemployment

■ American Dream Becomes Economic Nightmare Through Unemployment

Lorraine and Jim Dedrick thought they had it made. They had a five-bedroom, stone-foundation home on a lake, a landscaped yard, two well-behaved children, a car, a van, a motor-powered boat, and a sailboat. The home, the vehicles, and the boats were bought on time payments. Since both were working, they were confident they could easily make the monthly payments. Mrs. Dedrick describes what happened.

My husband worked at Dana Corporation in Edgerton (Wisconsin). (Dana Corporation was a car and truck-axle manufacturing plant.) He was a crew supervisor and was making over $23,000 a year. I was, and still am, a legal secretary for a firm in Madison.

When the layoffs started in spring 1979, we didn't think it would touch Jim. He had six years of seniority. But by March of 1980, we knew a layoff was inevitable. Neither Dana, nor the whole American auto industry, were doing well. When the layoff came in June of 1980, we weren't surprised.

At first we weren't worried. Jim thought it would be nice to have a summer off and looked forward to doing some fishing and some fixing up around the house. Since he was 39 years old and had worked steady since he was 18, I also thought a few months break would do him good. He was, of course, able to draw unemployment benefits,

and with my salary I was certain we could get by. Surely the auto industry would recover, and he would be called back in fall.

In late summer, however, a rumor started and quickly spread throughout the plant that Dana was going to close its plant in Edgerton. In September they announced the plant was going to close.

Both of us immediately became alarmed. Jim started looking for other work in earnest. Unfortunately, there were no comparable jobs in the area—and for that matter the whole auto industry was suffering.

Jim applied at many different jobs but had no luck. I know of nothing worse than to see a once proud, secure person come home each evening with the look on his face that he had once again been rejected. Jim began developing stomach problems from the rejections, and I started having tension headaches. We used to go out a lot, laugh, and have a good time. Now, we not only cannot afford it, we no longer have an interest.

Jim grabbed at every straw. He even went to apply for jobs in Milwaukee and Chicago. In the last year he appears to have aged ten years.

In February of 1981, his unemployment benefits ended. Bill collectors began hounding us. We soon depleted all our savings. We got so many calls from bill collectors that we took out an unlisted telephone. Never before were we unable to pay our bills.

The months since February have been hell. Increasingly we have gotten into arguments. Whenever I bring my check home, Jim has a pained look on his face, as he feels he's not doing his share. I try to tell him that it's not his fault, but whenever we talk about it he gets hurt and angry.

At the end of February he began to advertise by word of mouth that he was an independent carpenter. He's good with his hands. Unfortunately, the few jobs he got have as yet not even paid for the extra tools he's had to buy. It has only gotten us deeper into debt.

When I drive to work, the tears often fall. It's my only time alone. Driving home I often cry as I think about our situation, and know I'll have to face Jim's sad look. We don't associate much with friends now. They either pity us or have that arrogant look that says "I told you so" in response to our optimism when Jim was first laid off.

It just doesn't look like Jim is going to be able to get a job in this area. Next week he's going to go to Houston—we've heard there are a lot of job openings there. (It was August 1981 when Mrs. Dedrick discussed her family's plight.)

Dennis, our 12 year old son, is alternately sad and angry about the possibility of leaving this area. He's got a lot of friends and loves to go boating, fishing, and sailing. Having to take your son away from something he really loves is one of the most difficult things I'll probably ever have to do.

Karen, our daughter who's 15, really had a bad year at school. Her grades fell, and when we asked why, she stated, "What's the use in studying—it won't help in getting a job." That remark hurt deeply, probably because it may have a ring of truth in it.

It looks like we're going to have to give up our dream house on this lake. (Tears came to Mrs. Dedrick as she spoke.) We've lived here for the past five years and really loved it. This is our first real home. We've added on a patio, a bedroom, and enlarged the living room. We also spent a lot of time in painting and fixing it up. It's really become a part of us. If Jim gets a job in Texas, we'll be forced to sell. We checked what market prices are, and there's no way we're going to get what we put into this house.

A few years ago we thought we were starting to live the American dream. This past year and a half has been hell. Here we are broke, unhappy, and about to lose our home. At our age starting over is almost more than we can take.

The Costs of Unemployment

Unemployment can have devastating effects (in inset). Most obvious, it reduces (sometimes to poverty levels) the amount of income that a family or single person receives. Short-term unemployment, especially when receiving unemployment compensation, may have only minor effects. But long-term unemployment may have numerous adverse effects.

Wilensky (1966, p. 129) found long-term unemployment often leads to extreme personal isolation. Work is a central part of many people's lives. When unemployment occurs, work ties are cut, and many of the unemployed see friends less, cut their participation in community life, and increasingly become isolated.

Braginsky and Braginsky (1975, p. 70) found long-term unemployment causes attitude changes which persist even after reemployment. Being laid off (or let go) is often interpreted by the unemployed as a sign of being incompetent and worthless. Self-esteem is lowered, they are apt to experience depression, and they feel alienated from society. Many suffer deep shame and avoid their friends. They feel dehumanized, insignificant, and that they are an easily replaced statistic. They also tend to lose faith in our political and economic system, with some blaming our political system for their problems. Even when they find new jobs, they do not fully recover their self-esteem.

Brenner (1973) found a strong association between unemployment and emotional problems. During an economic recession he found that mental hospital admissions increase. The suicide rate also increases, indicating an increase in depression. Also higher during times of high unemployment are the divorce rate, the incidence of child abuse, and the number of peptic ulcers (a stress-related disease).

In many cases the long-term unemployed are forced to exhaust their savings, sell their homes, and become public assistance recipients. A few turn to crime, particularly the young. The unemployed no longer enjoy the companionship of their fellow workers. They are apt to experience feelings of embarrassment, anger, despair, depression, anxiety, boredom, hopelessness, and apathy. Such feelings may lead to alcoholism, drug abuse, insomnia, psychosomatic illnesses, marital unhappiness, and even violence within the family. The work ethic is still prominent in our society—when people lose their job they devalue themselves and also miss the sense of self-worth that comes from doing a job well.

Widespread unemployment can have devastating effects on society. Those still working are apt to fear they may lose their jobs. Severe unemployment leads to disenchantment with (and sometimes even rebellion against) political and social institutions. Widespread unemployment also cuts sharply government tax revenues and government services. In the late 1970s and early 1980s the auto industry in Detroit and the state of Michigan had high rates of unemployment. Revenues for the city and state were sharply reduced, and Detroit and Michigan were forced to drastically cut services at a time when services were most needed. Such cuts further add to alienation and despair.

High unemployment also leads to high rates of underemployment. Underemployment is where people are working at jobs below their level of skill. A sizeable number of people who are unemployed during periods of high unemployment are forced to take whatever jobs are available. College graduates, for example, may be forced to take unskilled road construction work or become clerical workers.

Who Are the Unemployed?

In the past several years the unemployment rate nationally has ranged from 6 to 10 percent. Practically every worker risks being unemployed, and most are unemployed sometime during their working years. There is some variation from time to time in the groups that are subjected to unemployment. In the late 1970s and early 1980s unemployment was particularly high among steel workers and automobile workers. In the late 1970s school teachers had high unemployment rates. In the middle 1970s Ph.D.s in the liberal arts and social sciences had high unemployment rates. In the early 1980s the housing industry was in a slump, and there were high unemployment rates among carpenters and construction workers.

There are groups, however, that have chronically high rates. These groups include minorities, teenagers, women, older workers, the unskilled, and the semiskilled.

High unemployment among racial minorities is partly due to discrimination which makes it more difficult to obtain employment. Unfortunately there is truth in the cliche that minorities are "last to be hired, first to be fired." Another reason for high unemployment is due to their lower average level of educational achievement which leaves them unqualified for many of the available jobs. (Lower educational achievement levels and lack of marketable job skills are largely due to past discrimination.)

High unemployment among women is also partly due to discrimination. Many employers (most of them men) are still inclined to hire a man before a woman, and many jobs are still erroneously thought to be "a man's job." Women have also been socialized to seek lower paying jobs, to not be competitive with males, and to believe their place is in the home and not in the work force. (See Chapter 15 for a fuller discussion.)

There are many myths about older workers—age 40 and over—that make it more difficult to obtain a new job if they become unemployed. They are thought to be less productive, more difficult to get along with, more difficult to train, clumsier, more accident prone, less healthy, and more prone to absenteeism. Research has shown these beliefs to be erroneous. Older workers have lower turnover rates, produce at a steadier rate, make fewer mistakes, have lower absenteeism rates, have a more positive attitude toward their work, and exceed younger employees in health and low on-the-job injury rates (Butler, 1977). An additional problem for unemployed older workers is that younger workers are often available at salaries far below what the older applicants were paid at their last job.

Unemployment is high for teenagers and young people, partly because many have not received job skill training that would provide them with marketable skills.

Employers are willing to hire unskilled workers when they have simple, repetitive tasks to be performed. But unskilled workers are the first to be laid off when there is a business slump. Unskilled workers can readily be replaced if business picks up. Highly skilled workers are more difficult to replace, and employers often have much more invested in skilled workers as they have spent more time in training such workers.

Blue collar workers are more affected by economic slumps than white collar workers. Industries that employ large numbers of blue-collar workers—housing, road construction, manufacturing heavy equipment such as tractors, the auto industry—are the ones which are most quickly and deeply affected and are often forced to lay off workers. In addition, the number of blue collar jobs in the United States is decreasing, while white collar jobs are increasing. A major reason for this decline is automation. *Automation is the production technique where the system of production is increasingly controlled by means of self-operating machinery.* Examples of automation include the automobile assembly line and direct dialing of the telephone which displaced thousands of telephone operators. Robots are now starting to replace workers in many industries—particularly in doing the simple, repetitive tasks.

College graduates in recent years have become increasingly susceptible to underemployment. A distressing statistic is that only 20 percent of the jobs in this country require more than a high-school diploma, while approximately half of all high-school graduates go on to some form of higher education (Flint, 1978). This statistic strongly indicates that higher education is out of balance with the work needs of the labor force. It is, therefore, crucial that college students (if they want a job in their major field of study) select a major that helps prepare them for desired job opportunities. Admittedly this is difficult to do. One reason is that job prospects fluctuate. In 1980, for example, there were substantial openings in social service positions. However, after Ronald Reagan was elected president, and severe cuts were made in social service positions, the job market in social service positions in 1981 and 1982 was poor. Nursing used to be an area where jobs were plentiful. Then in 1984 and 1985 efforts by the federal government and health maintenance organizations (HMOs) to reduce the length of patient stay in hospitals has led to nurses being laid off and terminated at a number of hospitals. With such rapidly changing job prospects, it is difficult to predict what the job prospects will be like when graduation occurs in three or four years. This is one reason why a general or liberal arts education, though appearing less relevant to future employment in the short run, may be more useful in the long run. Students who have a solid general education adapt more readily to changing job conditions than students who have had a more narrow, technical education.

A major reason for the high unemployment rate in this country is that we have a structural unemployment problem, as large numbers of unemployed people are not trained for the positions that are open. In recent years a large number of blue collar jobs have closed (as in the steel industry), while at the same time a number of high skill jobs have opened in other areas (such as in the high technology field of computers). As people become trained for current positions, the employment needs of our economy will continue to shift so that there will continue to be disharmony between skills needed for vacant positions and skills held by unemployed people.

Factors That Reduce Unemployment

Many factors increase the number of jobs and thereby reduce the unemployment rate. Lower interest rates encourage consumers to purchase more items through loans and by credit. Consumers buying more stimulates companies to produce more to meet the demand and thereby to hire more people. Lower interest rates also have a direct effect on businesses. Businesses often borrow money to purchase capital items (e.g., additional machines to produce their goods, or buildings to expand the business) in order to increase the production. If interest rates are lower, businesses are more apt to borrow money to increase production—and when expansion in production occurs, additional jobs are usually created.

A war almost always reduces the unemployment rate. Some workers are drafted to fight as soldiers. Their former jobs are then available for those who are unemployed. In addition, many additional jobs are created to provide the military with the products needed to fight a war—bullets, bombs, tanks, fighter planes, food, medicine, and so on.

Businesses and governments in many other countries take a more humanistic approach to employees and to assuring there will be jobs available for those who are unemployed. In the United States when an economic slump occurs, businesses usually lay off workers. In Japan, in contrast, businesses are much less likely to lay off workers, and seek to have their employees spend their entire working lives with the same company. Governments in many other countries attempt to create jobs for those who are unemployed. West Germany, for example, pays the unemployed to receive work training. Russia and other countries in Eastern Europe have successfully controlled unemployment by creating government jobs—although some departments are at times considerably overstaffed.

The development of new products opens up many new jobs. The invention of the automobile, airplane, television set, hair dryer, and refrigerator have opened up many new jobs for not only factory workers, but also for managers, repair personnel, sales personnel, insurance personnel, and so on.

In the early 1960s the economy was in a slump, with the unemployment rate being fairly high. President Kennedy stimulated the economy through a tax cut to individuals and to businesses. With their additional money, individuals were able to buy more. Businesses had additional money to reinvest to increase production. Kennedy's plan worked—the economy was stimulated, production increased, more jobs were created, and the unemployment rate went down. In the early 1980s we were again in an economic slump—with both a high inflation and high unemployment rate. President Reagan's plan of tax cuts to individuals and to businesses was enacted in 1981 and was again successful in stimulating the economy; individuals were able to buy more, companies expanded production, more jobs were created, and the unemployment rate went down somewhat, although it is still at an unacceptably high level. Another problem has developed, however. By cutting taxes, the federal deficit has sharply increased. There is a danger that the huge federal deficit may heat up the rate of inflation and result in another recession. (Inflation is a general rise in prices.)

Economics is a complicated and complex area, with the leading economists often disagreeing on the approaches that should be taken to reduce both the unemployment rate and the inflation rate. Generally inflation and unemployment have an inverse relationship; an increase in one will usually lead to a decrease in the other. In times of high unemployment people have less money to spend. They purchase fewer goods and services, which reduces the demand for goods and services. When the demand goes down the price of the goods and services is not likely to rise and may even be depressed. Furthermore, when workers do not feel their jobs are secure due to high layoffs, they are unlikely to ask for large pay increases. When there is little pressure for price or wage increases, inflation is low.

On the other hand, when the unemployment rate is low, more people are working and are able to buy goods and services. This increased demand drives up prices. If the demand stays high, businesses produce more and make a higher profit. Labor unions want a share of this increased profit and so they ask for large wage and salary increases. The pay increases they receive are then passed on to consumers in the form of higher prices.

Spouse Abuse

Spouse abuse, particularly wife-beating, has only recently become an issue of national concern. Prior to this recognition, spouse abuse was unfortunately tolerated.

It is not just wives who are abused—husbands are slapped or shoved with about the same frequency as are wives (*U.S. News & World Report*, January 15, 1979, p. 62). The greatest physical damage, however, usually occurs to women. Studies show men cause more serious injuries, largely because they are physically stronger. Nearly 11 percent of all murder victims are killed by their spouses (*U.S. News & World Report*, January 15, 1979, p. 62). Women also tend to endure cruelty and abuse much longer, partly because they feel trapped because of unemployment and financial insecurity. Spouse abuse is sometimes victim precipitated—that is, the recipient of the abuse may be the first to use verbal or physical violence in the incident

(Gelles, 1974). However, the dominant theme in American spouse abuse is the systematic use of violence and the threat of violence by some men to "keep their wives in line." That is to say, some segments of our society believe that husbands have a right to control what their wives do and to force them to be submissive.

Incidents of physical abuse between spouses are not widely isolated, but tend to recur frequently in the marriage. Murray Straus et al. (1979) have noted spouse abuse occurs as often among the well educated as among those less educated. Murray Straus and his associates in 1979 conducted a survey for the National Commission on the Causes and Prevention of Violence. Interviews were held with over 2,000 couples who were a cross section of American families. The study concluded that each year 7.5 million couples in this country have a violent episode in which one spouse seeks to physically hurt the other. Wives use knives and other weapons more often than husbands do and are as likely to murder their spouses as husbands are. Disturbingly, the study found that one man in four, and one woman in six, approved of a husband slapping his wife under certain conditions. Most wives who are severely beaten by their husbands do not seek to end the marriage. Wives are more likely to remain in the home if (a) the violence is infrequent, (b) they were abused by their parents when they were children, or (c) they believe they are financially dependent on their husbands.

■ No Way Out for Maria Canseco

Maria Canseco finished her drink hastily at the Havana Club, a neighborhood bar in the Spanish-speaking section of Milwaukee. She had stopped for a drink with another beautician. She knew she had to be home before her common-law husband, Gregario Gomez, got home from work.

She made it home in time and started preparing dinner. Thirty-five minutes later Gregario came home, staggering. He too had stopped at a bar and had several drinks. Gregario asked where she had been after work. (A friend of his had told him she was at the Havana Club.) Maria, to avoid a fight, stated she came straight home. Gregario called her a liar and began accusing her of seeking to prostitute herself. As he had done often in the past, he grabbed her hair and started shaking her. He grabbed her throat, began choking her, and yelled obscenities at her. She feared he was going to kill her this time. She brought up her knee in a sharp, forceful kick into Gregario's groin. He screamed and let go of her. Maria tried to run around him to the door, but he grabbed her arm and began to beat her unmercifully with his fists. A neighbor heard the screaming and called the police. When the police arrived, Maria was unconscious. She was rushed to the hospital in an ambulance. She needed 42 stitches for her cuts and remained in the hospital for three days.

While at the hospital she decided not to see Gregario again. On her release she went to the police department and filed assault charges against Gregario. He was arrested and brought before a criminal court judge. The judge questioned Gregario, who stated he was very sorry for what he had done. The judge informed Gregario that Maria had signed an affidavit stating she no longer wants to live with him. The judge informed Gregario that if he agrees to no longer bother her, nor go near her, he would drop the charges against him. Gregario quietly stated he would never go near her again. Charges were dismissed.

Maria found a one-bedroom efficiency apartment. She hoped she would never see Gregario again, but Gregario found out where she had moved. Six days after she moved in, she heard a knock at her door. When she opened it, Gregario slammed the door open. He was again drunk. She tried to fight him off. He raped her, yelled obscenities at her, and then beat her severely. When Maria came to, Gregario had gone. She walked down to the same police station where she had filed charges the first time. The police placed her in a shelter for battered women and then arrested Gregario.

Gregario appeared before a different judge. The judge again lectured Gregario and extracted a promise from Gregario that if he would leave Maria alone, he would then be released. Gregario, of course, said he was very sorry and stated he never wanted to see Maria again as she had caused him too much trouble. He was released.

Maria spent a month at the shelter, and then moved to another neighborhood across town. The move was physically and emotionally hard for Maria. She was leaving the neighborhood where she was raised and now was moving to an all-white neighborhood that had a sharply different culture.

After several months, Maria felt she was finally getting her life going in the right direction. She began growing plants, got an older model car, and some new furniture for her apartment. Then one hot summer night when she had the patio door open, Gregario cut through the screen door. He was again drunk. Maria tried to call the police, but Gregario ripped the telephone cord from the wall. He grabbed her, and she tried to kick, bite, and scratch him with her fingernails. The more she fought, the more violent he became. He again raped her and knocked her unconscious. Before leaving, he smashed all her new furniture. With a leg of the table he hit her in the face and body. Neighbors who heard the screams called the police, and Maria was taken to the hospital in an ambulance.

This time Maria was unconscious for over 11 hours. Even worse, one of the blows from the splintered table leg severely damaged her right eye. Maria had 47 stitches in her face, and her right eye could not be saved. She was in the hospital for three weeks and was fitted with a glass eye. When the bandages were finally taken off, Maria looked in the mirror, and began to cry. Her face was badly scarred, and her eye was grotesque.

Maria again filed charges. She also hired an attorney to speak for her in court. The district attorney was sympathetic and presented in detail to the judge an account of the abuse that Maria had been subjected to in the past. The district attorney requested that Gregario be sentenced to prison for five years for assault and rape. The judge questioned Gregario at length. Gregario called him "sir" before answering each question and presented himself as being a hard working, remorseful person. The judge lectured Gregario and stated he would place him on probation for two years if he promised not to see Maria. With a slight smile on his face, Gregario promised and was released.

At this point Maria gave up hoping that she would ever escape from Gregario. He had brutally humiliated her in so many ways, and she now felt she was ugly. She went back to her apartment, knowing Gregario would return. She no longer put effort into her apartment and became listless and depressed. Two and one half months later Gregario again burst into her apartment and brutally abused her. She didn't fight this time. The neighbors heard little. When Maria regained consciousness, she went to the bathroom and took an overdose of sleeping pills.

In our society the courts severely punish someone for assaulting a stranger but usually look the other way if one repeatedly assaults one's spouse.

Many authorities believe spouse abuse is related to a norm of tolerating violence in American families. Straus (1977, p. 456) notes: "There seems to be an implicit, taken-for-granted cultural norm which makes it legitimate for family members to hit each other. In respect to husbands and wives, in effect, this means that the marriage license is also a hitting license."

Studies (Gelles, 1974) have found that a sizeable number of both men and women believe it is appropriate for a husband to physically hit his wife "every now and then." If a male child is a victim of physical abuse, that child is more likely as an adult to abuse his wife and children. Alcohol abuse is also often associated with wife beating.

A surprising number of battered women do not leave their husbands permanently. There appear to be a variety of reasons for this. Many are socialized to play a subordinate role to their husbands. Their husbands use violence and psychological abuse to make them feel too inadequate to live on their own. Some believe it is their moral duty to stick it out to the end—that marriage is forever, for better or for worse. Many hope (in spite of the continuing violence) that their husbands will change. A fair number do not view leaving as a viable alternative as they feel financially dependent on their husbands. Many have young children and do not believe they have the resources to raise children on their own. Some believe the occasional beatings are better than the loneliness and insecurity connected with leaving. Some dread the stigma associated with separation or divorce. These women are captives in their own homes.

Fortunately, new services in recent years have been developed for battered women. Shelter homes for battered women have been established in many communities. These shelters give abused women an opportunity to flee from the abusive situation. Such women also generally receive counseling, assistance in finding a job, and legal help. In some areas programs are also being established for the husbands, with efforts being made to provide marriage counseling to both spouses, and 24-hour hotlines being established that encourage potential spouse abusers to call when they are angry. Many communities also have public information programs (e.g., short television announcements) to inform battered women they have a legal right not to be abused and that there are resources (e.g. shelter homes and counseling services) to stop the abuse. As services for battered wives become more widely available, we may expect an increasing number of these women to flee from their homes and to refuse to return until they have some guarantee of their safety. (The topic of spouse abuse/battered women is discussed in greater detail in Chapter 15.)

Empty-Shell Marriages

In empty-shell marriages the spouses feel no strong attachments to each other. Outside pressures keep the marriage together. Such outside pressures include: business reasons (for example, an elected official wanting to convey a stable family image); investment reasons (for example, husband and wife may have a luxurious home and other property which they do not want to lose by parting) and outward appearances (for example, a couple living in a small community may remain together to avoid the reactions of relatives and friends to a divorce). In addition, a couple may believe that ending the marriage would harm the children or may believe that getting a divorce would be morally wrong.

John F. Cuber and Peggy B. Harroff (1971) have identified three types of empty-shell marriages. In a *devitalized relationship* husband and wife lack excitement or any real interest in their spouse or their marriage. Boredom and apathy characterize this marriage. Serious arguments are rare.

In a *conflict-habituated relationship* husband and wife frequently quarrel in private. They may also quarrel in public or put up a facade of being compatible. The relationship is characterized by considerable conflict, tension, and bitterness.

In a *passive-congenial relationship* both partners are not happy, but are content with their lives and generally feel adequate. The partners may have some interests in common, but these interests are generally insignificant. The spouses contribute little to each other's real satisfactions. This type of relationship generally has little overt conflict.

The number of empty-shell marriages is unknown—it may be as high as the number of happily married couples. The atmosphere in empty-shell marriages is without much fun or laughter. Members do not share and discuss their problems or experiences with each other. Communication is kept to a minimum. There is seldom any spontaneous expression of affection or sharing of a personal experience. Children in such families are usually starved for love and reluctant to have friends over as they are embarrassed about having their friends see their parents interacting.

The couples in these marriages engage in few activities together and display no pleasure in being in one another's company. Sexual relations between the partners, as might be expected, are rare and generally unsatisfying. Visitors will note that the partners (and often the children) appear insensitive, cold, and callous to each other. Yet, closer observation will reveal that the members are highly aware of each other's weaknesses and sensitive areas, as they manage to frequently mention these areas in order to hurt one another.

William J. Goode (1976, p. 543) compares empty-shell marriages to marriages that end in divorce:

> . . . most families that divorce pass through a state—sometimes *after* the divorce—in which husband and wife no longer feel bound to each other, cease to cooperate or share with each other, and look on one another as almost a stranger. The "empty-shell" family is in such a state. Its members no longer feel any strong commitment to many of the mutual role obligations, but for various reasons the husband and wife do not separate or divorce.

The number of empty-shell marriages ending in divorce is unknown. It is likely that a fair number eventually do. Both spouses have to put considerable effort into making a marriage work in order to prevent an empty-shell marriage from gradually developing.

Divorce

Our society places a higher value on romantic love than most other societies. In societies where marriages are arranged by parents, being in love generally has no role in mate selection. In our society, however, romantic love is a key factor in forming a marriage.

Children are socialized from an early age in this country to believe in the glories of romantic love. "Love conquers all," it is asserted. Magazines, films, TV programs, and books continually portray "happy ending" romantic adventures. All of these breathtaking romantic stories suggest that every normal person falls in love with that one special person, gets married, and lives happily ever after. This happily-ever-after ideal rarely happens.

Now, more than one out of three marriages ends in divorce (U.S. Bureau of the Census, 1984, p. 63). This high rate has gradually been increasing. Prior to World War I divorce was comparatively rare.

Divorce usually leads to a number of difficulties for those involved. First, those who are divorcing face emotional concerns, such as a feeling that they have failed, concern over whether they are able to give and receive love, a sense of loneliness, concern over the stigma attached to divorce, concern about the reactions of friends and relatives, concern over whether they are doing the right thing by parting, and concern over whether they will be able to make it on their own. Many people feel trapped as they believe they cannot live with their spouse and cannot live without them. Dividing up the personal property between the two is another area that frequently leads to bitter differences of opinions. If there are children, there are concerns about how the divorce will affect them.

Other issues also need to be decided. Who will get custody of the children? (Joint custody is now an alternative—with joint custody, each parent has the children for part of the time.) If one parent is awarded custody, controversies are apt to arise over visiting rights, and how much (if any) child support should be paid. Both spouses often face the difficulties of finding new places to live, making new friends, doing things alone in our couple-oriented society, financially trying to make it on one's own, and thinking about the hassles connected with dating.

Studies (Plateris, 1967) show that going through a divorce is very difficult. People are less likely to perform their jobs well and more likely to be fired during this period. Divorced people have a shorter life expectancy. Suicide rates are higher for divorced men.

Divorce per se is no longer automatically assumed to be a social problem. In some marriages where there is considerable tension, bitterness, and dissatisfaction, divorce is sometimes a solution. It may be a concrete step that some people take to end the unhappiness and to begin leading a more productive and gratifying life. It is also increasingly being recognized that a divorce may be better for the children, as they no longer may be subjected to the tension and unhappiness in a marriage that has gone sour.

Mary Jo Bane (1976, pp. 31–33) has noted that the rising divorce rate may not be as serious a threat to the institutions of marriage and family as some people believe:

> It is distressing in and of itself . . . only if staying together at all costs is considered an indicator of healthy marriages or healthy societies . . . Some things are fairly clear. The majority of marriages do not end in divorce. The vast majority of divorced people remarry. Only a tiny proportion of people marry more than twice. We are thus a long way from a society in which marriage is rejected or replaced by a series of short-term liaisons. . . . Society may be changing its attitudes toward the permanence of marriage and its notions of the roles of husbands and wives. It may simply be recognizing that there is no particular benefit to requiring permanence in unhappy marriages.

The rising rate of divorce does not necessarily mean that more marriages are failing. It may simply mean that in marriages which have gone sour, more people are dissolving the marriage than continuing to live unhappily.

Reasons for Marital Unhappiness

There are many sources of marital breakdown, including alcoholism, economic strife caused by unemployment or other financial problems, incompatibility of interests, infidelity, jealousy, verbal or physical abuse of spouse, and interference in the marriage by relatives and friends.

As noted earlier, many people marry because they believe they are romantically in love. If this romantic love does not grow into rational love (see Chapter 7 for a description of rational love), the marriage is apt to fail. Unfortunately, young people are socialized in our society to believe that marriage will bring them continual romance, resolve all their problems, be sexually exciting, thrilling, full of adventure and excitement, and will always be as wonderful as the courtship. (Most young people only need to look at their parents' marriage to realize such romantic ideals are seldom attained.)

Unfortunately, living with someone in a marriage involves carrying out the garbage, washing dishes and clothes, being weary from work, putting up with the partner's distasteful habits, changing diapers, dealing with conflicts over such things as how to spend a vacation, and differences in sexual interests. *To make a marriage work requires that each spouse puts considerable effort into making it successful.*

Another factor that is contributing to an increasing divorce rate is the unwillingness of some men to accept the changing status of women. Many men still prefer a traditional marriage where the husband is dominant, and the wife plays a supportive (subordinate role) as child-rearer, housekeeper, and emotional supporter to her husband. Many women no longer accept such a status and demand an equalitarian marriage in which making major decisions, doing the domestic tasks, raising the children, and bringing home paychecks are shared responsibilities.

About half of the adult women are now in the labor force (*U.S. News & World Report*, January 15, 1979, p. 64). This increase in the percent of working women means women are no longer as dependent financially on their husbands. Women who are financially able to support themselves are more likely to seek a divorce if their marriage goes sour.

Another factor contributing to the increasing divorce rate is the growth of individualism. Individualism involves the belief that people should seek to actualize themselves, to be happy, to develop their interests and capacities to the fullest, to seek to fulfill their own needs and desires. With individualism the interests of the individual take precedence over the interests of the family. People in our society have increasingly come to accept individualism as a way of life. In contrast, people in more traditional societies and in extended families are socialized to put the interests of the group first, with their own individual interests being viewed as less important. In extended families people view themselves as members of a group first and as individuals second. With America's growing belief in individualism, people who conclude they are unhappily married are much more apt to dissolve the marriage and seek a new life.

Another reason for the rise in the divorce rate is the growing acceptance of divorce in our society. With less of a stigma attached to a divorce, more people who are unhappily married are now ending the marriage.

An additional factor in the increasing divorce rate is that modern families no longer have as many functions as in traditional families. Education, food production, entertainment, and other functions once centered in the family are now largely provided by outside agencies. Kenneth Keniston (1977, p. 21) notes:

> In earlier times, the collapse of a marriage was far more likely to deprive both spouses of a great deal more than the pleasure of each other's company. Since family members performed so many functions for one another, divorce in the past meant a farmer without a wife to churn the cream into butter or care for him when he was sick, and a mother without a husband to plow the fields and bring her the food to feed their children. Today, when emotional satisfaction is the bond that holds marriages together, the waning of love or the emergence of real incompatibilities and conflicts between husband and wife leave fewer reasons for a marriage to continue. Schools and doctors and counselors and social workers provide their supports whether the family is intact or not. One loses less by divorce today than in earlier times, because marriage provides fewer kinds of sustenance and satisfaction.

■ Facts About Divorce

Age of spouses. Divorce is most likely to occur when the partners are in their twenties.

Length of engagement. Divorce rates are higher for those having a brief engagement.

Age at marriage. People who marry at a very young age (particularly teenagers) are more apt to divorce.

Length of marriage. Most divorces occur within two years after marriage. There is also an increase in divorce shortly after the children are grown—this may be partly because some couples wait until the children are ready to leave the nest before dissolving an unhappy marriage.

Social class. Divorce occurs more frequently at the lower socioeconomic levels.

Education. Divorce rates are higher for those with fewer years of schooling. Interestingly, divorce occurs more frequently when the wife's educational level is higher than the husband's.

Residence. Divorce rates are higher in urban areas than in rural areas.

Second marriages. The more often individuals have divorced, the more likely they are to divorce again.

Religion. The more religious individuals are, the less apt they are to become divorced. Divorce rates are higher for Protestants than for Catholics or Jews. Divorce rates are also higher for interfaith marriages than for single faith marriages.

SOURCE: William J. Goode, "Family Disorganization", in Robert K. Merton and Robert Nisbet, eds., *Contemporary Social Problems*, 4th ed. (New York: Harcourt Brace Jovanovich, 1976), pp. 511–56; Goode, *After Divorce* (New York: Free Press, 1956); Paul C. Glick, *American Families* (New York: John Wiley 1957); J. Richard Udry, *The Social Context of Marriage*, 2d ed. (Philadelphia: Lippincott, 1971); Joseph Julian and William Kornblum, *Social Problems*, 4th ed. (Englewood Cliffs, NJ: Prentice-Hall, 1983), pp. 413–14.

Children of Divorce

Kaluger and Kaluger (1984, p. 298) note that society places two conflicting demands on parents who are contemplating a divorce:

> One is that the couple's first concern should be with their parental roles and that they should try to put aside their marital problems, which imply that marriage roles are secondary to parental roles. Yet, in a society that places great emphasis on personal ego-need satisfaction in marriage, the placing of marriage in a secondary position may be difficult for the married person to accept.

A basic question parents contemplating divorce ask themselves is: Is it better for the children if we remain unhappily married or better if we end the marriage and thereby end the conflict and tension? A key to answering this question depends on what life will be like after the divorce.

■ The Effects of a Divorce on Children Depends on What Happens After the Divorce

The Haag Family

Mary Beth and Doug Haag obtained a divorce after nine years of marriage. They had two children, John (eight years old) and David (four years old). The divorce process was filled with a fair amount of emotional trauma, as both partners were uncertain whether to end the marriage. But both partners were honest in answering their children's questions about the divorce and made crystal clear to them that they were in no way at fault for the marriage ending. Mary Beth and Doug decided to each take custody of a child, partly because John wanted to live with Doug. Doug took custody of John, and Mary Beth took custody of David. The reasons for separating the children were carefully explained to them. The children frequently visited each other on weekends, holidays, and during the summer. Telephone calls between the children were frequent and encouraged.

Mary Beth and Doug respected each other after the divorce and no longer fought. Doug was an accountant, and Mary Beth, an elementary school teacher—both earned enough so that neither was in serious financial difficulty. Doug married a year and a half later to a woman who understood the harmonious relationship that had developed between Doug and Mary Beth after the divorce.

Mary Beth occasionally dates, but largely concentrates her free time on attending college to obtain her masters degree and on spending time with David. The home environment is now much better for all the Haags than it was in the final years of a marriage which was filled with bitterness and hostility.

The Denny Family

Robert and Corine Denny divorced after 13 years of marriage. Robert, a dentist, asked for the divorce because he was involved with one of his dental assistants. Corine was furious when she found out. Since she had stayed home to raise the children for the last 12 years, she got the larger part of the divorce settlement. She received the house, the year old Buick, custody of the three children, and $1,200 per month in child support. The reasons for the divorce were never fully explained to the children, because the parents wanted to hide the fact that Robert had been dating someone else for two years prior to the divorce. As a result, the children assumed they were responsible for causing the tension and arguments prior to the divorce and felt guilty because they thought they were responsible for their parents' separating.

Corine became depressed after the divorce and sought to drown her misery in vodka. She also began going out with a woman friend who was also divorced. Frequently she brought men home to stay overnight. Her standard of living dropped sharply. She refused to look for a job or seek job training and sought to live off of the child support payments. When the children visited their father (which was infrequent as Corine tended to sabotage such visits), Robert sought to dazzle his children with how well his life was now going. Both Robert and Corine sought to use the children as pawns to get back at each other. Corine viewed Robert as someone who had destroyed her comfortable life. Robert viewed Corine as a lush who was being irresponsible and who was spending his hard earned money on partying.

The children suffered greatly. Their grades dropped sharply in school. They were embarrassed to have friends over as their house was a mess, and they never knew when their mother would be intoxicated. The oldest daughter, Jill (12 years old) began skipping school and is now sexually active without using birth control. Bob, 10 years old, was recently caught for shoplifting and is on informal supervision at the juvenile probation department. Dennis, 8 years old, has withdrawn. He spends most of his free time watching rock videos on TV. In school he makes practically no effort, has few friends, and is receiving Ds and Fs in all his classes.

Within five years after a divorce, three quarters of all divorced people are remarried (Kaluger and Kaluger, 1984, p. 298). Therefore, most children of divorce eventually return to living in a family having an adult male and female.

In most cases the mother receives custody of the children, and most divorced women conquer the difficult process of taking over the role of the father. Kaluger and Kaluger (1984, p. 298) note:

Divorced mothers, as well as all other parents without partners, feel that not having to share daily parental decisions with a partner who might not agree with his/her strategy is an advantage. They feel that the parental partner can be a great asset if the two parents agree, but if this is not usually true, one parent can probably do a better job alone.

Papalia and Olds (1981, p. 326) summarize some of the problems children face in growing up in one-parent families:

Children growing up in one-parent homes undoubtedly have more problems and more adjustments to make than children growing up in homes where there are two adults to share the responsibilities for child rearing, to provide a higher income, to more closely approximate cultural expectations of the "ideal family," and to offer a counterpoint of sex-role models and an interplay of personalities. But the two-parent home is not always ideal, and the one parent home is not necessarily pathological.

Rutter (1979) found that children grow up better adjusted when raised in a single parent family in which they have a good relationship with that parent than when they are raised in a two-parent family which is filled with discontent and tension.

The breakup of a marriage is traumatic not only for the parents but also for the children. Children appear to react more severely to a divorce than they do to the death of a parent, as suggested by the fact that children of divorce are more likely to get into trouble with the law than those in which a parent has died (Rutter, 1979). This delinquent behavior appears to be more of a reaction to the discontent in the home that caused the divorce, rather than a reaction to the separation and divorce itself as children from intact homes where there is considerable conflict also are more likely to commit delinquent acts (Rutter, 1979).

When parents end a marriage, the children are apt to be fearful of the future, to feel guilty for their own (usually fantasized) role in causing the breakup, to be angry at both parents, and to feel rejected by the parent who moves out. They may become irritable, accident-prone, depressed, bitter, hostile, disruptive, and even suicidal. They may suffer from skin disorders, inability to concentrate, fatigue, loss of appetite, and insomnia. They may also show less interest in their school work and their social lives (Sugar, 1970; McDermott, 1970).

Hetherington, Cox, and Cox (1975) studied 48 divorced families for the first two years after the breakup to assess the effects of divorce on the children. They found that immediately after a breakup there is considerable disruption and disorganization in family life. The parents have a variety of stresses to deal with—including economic pressures (partly the result of now maintaining two households), restrictions on recreational and social activities (more so for the mother, especially if she is unemployed), and the needs for affectionate and intimate heterosexual relationships. A number of changes also occur in parent-child interactions. Divorced parents make fewer demands on the children, are less consistent in discipline, communicate less well with them, and have less control over them. These differences are greatest during the first year after the breakup. By the end of the second, a reequilibration appears to take place, particularly between mothers and children. In this study the mothers primarily received custody, and the fathers gradually became less available to their children. The study concluded that the first two years after a breakup are stressful for everyone in the family.

A child's reaction to a divorce is affected by a variety of factors, including the age and sex of the child, the length of time of severe discord in the marriage, and the length of time between the first separation and the formal divorce (Sugar, 1970). A key factor in how traumatic the divorce will be for the child is how well the parents deal with the child's concerns, fears, questions, and anxieties. It is much more traumatic when parents do not explain that is not the child's fault for the breakup and if the divorce and custody arrangements are hotly contested. Another factor that increases the trauma is when one or both of the parents seek to turn the child against the other parent. Transferring anger and bitterness about the breakup to the child also increases the child's trauma.

Papalia and Olds (1981, p. 328) summarize some things that parents can do to reduce the trauma:

> One of the most important tasks of parents facing divorce is the need to reassure their children that they are not responsible for the break. Parents also can help their children by reestablishing regular routines, by finding adults who can fill the gap left by the missing parent, and by not forcing the children to take sides. The emotional aspects of divorce, rather than the legal considerations, are hardest on children. . . . The initial break is always painful, but many children thrive in an atmosphere that brings hope for a better life after the end of a troubled marriage.

Marriage Counseling

The primary social service for people who are considering a divorce or who have an empty-shell marriage is marriage counseling. (Those who do obtain a divorce may also need counseling to work out adjustment problems—such as adjusting to single life. Generally such counseling is one-on-one, but at times may include the ex-spouse and the children, depending on the nature of the problem.)

Marriage counseling is provided by a variety of professionals, including: social workers, psychologists, guidance counselors, psychiatrists, and members of the clergy. Marriage counseling is provided (to a greater or lesser extent) by most direct social service agencies.

Marriage counselors generally use a problem-solving approach in which: (a) problems are first identified, (b) alternative solutions are generated, (c) the merits and shortcomings of the alternatives are examined, (d) the clients select one or more alternatives to implement, and (e) the extent to which the problems are being resolved by the alternatives are later assessed. Since the spouses own their problems, they are the primary problem solvers.

A wide range of problems may be encountered by married couples. A partial list of such problems include sexual problems, financial problems, communication problems, problems with relatives, interest conflicts, infidelity, conflicts on how to discipline and raise children, and drug abuse problems. Marriage counselors seek to have spouses precisely identify their problems and then use the problem-solving format to seek to resolve the issues. At times, some couples may rationally decide a divorce is in their best interests.

Marriage counselors try to see both spouses together during sessions. Practically all marital conflicts involve both partners and, therefore, are best resolved when both partners work together on resolving the conflicts. (If the spouses are seen separately, each spouse is apt to become suspicious of what the other is telling the counselor.) By seeing both together, the counselor can facilitate communication between the partners and have the partners work together on resolving their concerns. (When spouses are seen individually, they are also more apt to compose exaggerated stories of the extent to which their mate is contributing to the disharmony.) Seeing both partners together allows each partner the opportunity to refute what the other is saying. Only in rare cases is it desirable to hold an individual session with a spouse. For example, if one of the partners wants to work on unwanted emotions dealing with an incestual relationship in the past, meeting individually with that spouse might be desirable. (When an individual session is held, the other spouse should be informed of why the session is being held and of what will be discussed.)

If some of the areas of conflict involve other family members (such as the children), it may be desirable to include these other family members in some of the sessions. For example, if a father is irritated that his 14-year-old daughter is often disrespectful to him, the daughter may be invited to the next session to work on this subproblem.

Although marriage and divorce counseling are the primary social services that are available for resolving marital conflicts, there are a variety of other related services.

Premarital counseling services are designed for those considering getting married. Such services help such clients assess whether marriage is in their best interests, to prepare for the realities of marriage, deal with conflicts that people are having while dating, and explore birth control.

The self-help organization of Parents Without Partners serves divorced people, unwed mothers or fathers, and stepparents. It is partially a social organization, but also an organization to help members with adjustment problems of raising a family alone.

A recent development in social services is divorce mediation, which helps spouses who have decided to obtain a divorce to resolve such issues as dividing the personal property, resolving custody and child support issues, and working out possible alimony arrangements.

Some agencies are now offering relationship workshops and encounter couple groups which are designed to help those who are dating or who are married to improve their relationships through sharing concerns and improving communication patterns.

Summary

Three theories about human behavior are summarized—functionalism, conflict theory, and interactionism. Functionalism views society and other social systems as composed of interdependent and interrelated parts. In contrast to functionalism, conflict theory is more radical, and views society as being a struggle for scarce resources among individuals and social groups. Interactionist theory views human behavior as resulting from the interaction of a person's unique, distinctive personality and the groups she or he participates in.

Much of the chapter focuses on describing the following social problems that middle age adults (and other age groups) may encounter—poverty, worker alienation, unemployment, spouse abuse, empty-shell marriages, and divorce. Those most vulnerable to being poor include one-parent families, children, the elderly, large size families, minorities, those without a high school education, and those living in urban slums. Worker alienation and unemployment are two of the major problems in the work setting; both have devastating effects on those affected.

Spouse abuse appears to be related to a tradition of tolerating violence in American families. Three types of empty-shell marriages are: devitalized relationships, conflict-habituated relationships, and passive-congenial relationships. Although a divorce is traumatic for everyone in the family, it appears children grow up better adjusted when raised in a single parent family in which they have a good relationship with that parent, than when they are raised in a two-parent family which is filled with discontent and tension.

Later Adulthood

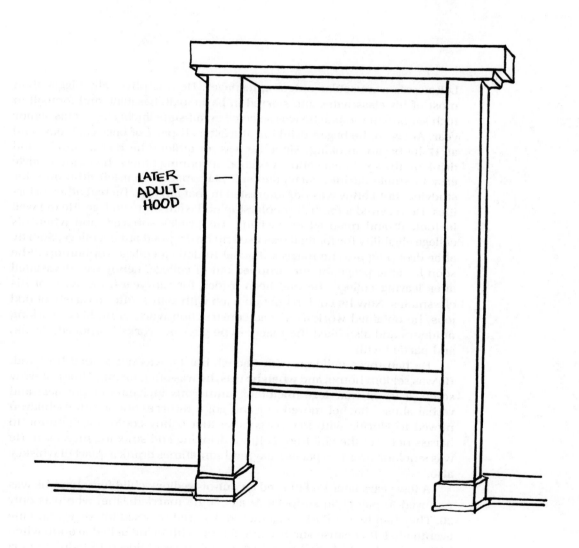

LATER
ADULT-
HOOD

Biological Aspects of
Later Adulthood

LeRoy was a muscular outgoing teenager. He was physically bigger than most of his classmates and starred in basketball, baseball, and football in high school. In football he was selected an all-state linebacker in his senior year. At age 16 he began drinking at least a six pack of beer each day, and at 17 he began smoking. Since he was an athlete, he had to smoke and drink on the sly. Since LeRoy was good at conning others, he found it fairly easy to smoke, drink, party, and still play sports. That left little time for studying, but LeRoy was not interested in that anyway. He had other priorities. He received a football scholarship and went on to college. He did well in football and majored in partying. His grades suffered, and when his college eligibility for football was used up he dropped out of college. Shortly after dropping out, he married Rachel Rudow, a college sophomore. She soon became pregnant and dropped out of college. LeRoy was devastated after leaving college. He had been a jock for ten years, the envy of his classmates. Now he couldn't obtain a job with status. After a variety of odd jobs, he obtained work as a road-construction worker. He liked working outdoors and also liked the macho-type guys he worked, smoked, drank, and partied with.

He had three children with Rachel, but he was not a good husband. He was seldom home, and when he was, he was often drunk. After a stormy seven years of marriage (including numerous incidents of physical and verbal abuse) Rachel moved out and got a divorce. She and the children moved to Florida with her parents so that LeRoy could not continue to harass her and the children. LeRoy's drinking and smoking increased. He was smoking over two packs a day, and sometimes drank a quart of whiskey also.

A few years later he fathered an out-of-wedlock child for whom he was required to pay child support. At age 39 he married Jane, who was only 20. They had two children together and stayed married for six years. Jane eventually left because she became fed up with being belted around when LeRoy was drunk. LeRoy now had a total of six children to help support and seldom saw any of them. LeRoy continued to drink and also ate to excess. His weight went up to 285 pounds, and by age 48 he was no longer able to keep up with the other road construction workers. He was discharged by the construction company.

The next several years saw LeRoy taking odd jobs as a carpenter. He

didn't earn much, and he spent most of what he earned on alcohol. He was periodically embarrassed by being hauled into court for failure to pay child support. He was also dismayed because he no longer had friends who wanted to get drunk with him. When he was 61, the doctor discovered he had cirrhosis of the liver and informed him he wouldn't live much longer if he continued to drink. Since LeRoy's whole life centered around drinking, he chose to continue to drink. LeRoy also noticed that he had less energy and frequently had trouble breathing. The doctor indicated that he probably had damaged his lungs by smoking and now had a form of emphysema. The doctor lectured LeRoy on the need to stop smoking, but LeRoy didn't heed that advice either. His health continued to deteriorate, and he lost 57 pounds. At age 64, while drunk, he fell over backwards and fractured his skull. He was hospitalized for three and one-half months. The injury permanently damaged his ability to walk and talk. He now is confined to a low-quality nursing home. He is no longer allowed to smoke or drink. He is frequently angry, impatient, and frustrated. He no longer has any friends. The staff detests working with him; his grooming habits are atrocious, and he frequently yells obscenities. LeRoy frequently expresses a wish to die to escape his misery.

ElRoy's early years were in sharp contrast to his brother LeRoy. ElRoy had a lean, almost puny muscular structure, and did not excel at sports. LeRoy was his parents' favorite and also dazzled the young females in school and in the neighborhood. ElRoy had practically no dates in high school and was viewed as a prude. He did well in math and the natural sciences. He spent much of his time studying and reading a variety of books and liked taking radios and electrical appliances apart. At first, he got into trouble because he was not skilled enough to put them back together but soon became known as someone who could fix radios.

He went on to college and studied electrical engineering. He had a zero social life, but graduated with good grades in his major. He went on to graduate school and obtained a masters degree in electrical engineering. On graduation he was hired as an engineer by Motorola in Chicago. He did well there, and in four years was named manager of a unit. Three years later he was lured to RCA with a handsome salary offer. The group of engineers he worked with at RCA made some significant advances in television technology.

At RCA ElRoy began dating a secretary, Elvira McCann, and they were married when he was 36. Life became much smoother for ElRoy after that. He was paid well and enjoyed annual vacations with Elvira to such places as Hawaii, Paris, and the Bahamas. ElRoy and Elvira wanted to have children, but could not. In ElRoy's early 40s, they adopted two children, both from Korea. They bought a house in the suburbs and also a sailboat. ElRoy and Elvira occasionally had some marital disagreements, but generally got along well. In their middle adult years, one of their adopted sons, Kim, was tragically killed by an intoxicated automobile driver. That death was a shock and very difficult for the whole family to come to terms with. But the intense grieving gradually lessened, and after a few years ElRoy and Elvira put their lives back together.

Now, at age 67, ElRoy is still working for RCA and loving it. In a few years he plans to retire and move to the Hawaiian island of Maui. ElRoy and Elvira have already purchased a condominium there. Their surviving son, Dae, has already graduated from college and is working for a life insurance company. ElRoy is looking forward to retiring so he can move to Maui, and get more involved in his hobbies of photography and making model railroad displays. His health is good, and he has a positive outlook on life. He occasionally thinks about his brother and sends him a card at Christmas and at his birthday. Since ElRoy never had much in common with LeRoy, he seldom visits him.

■ A Perspective

At age 73, Ronald Reagan won reelection as president of the United States. At 80, George Burns received his first academy award for his role in *The Sunshine Boys*. At 81, Benjamin Franklin mediated the compromise that led to the adoption of the U.S. Constitution. Konrad Adenauer was chancellor of Germany at age 88. At 89 Arthur Rubinstein gave a critically acclaimed recital in Carnegie Hall, and at the same age Albert Schweitzer was directing a hospital in Africa. Pablo Picasso, at 90, was producing engravings and drawings. At 94, Bertrand Russell headed international peace drives. Grandma Moses began painting at age 78 and was still painting at age 100. (*U.S. News & World Report,* Sept. 1, 1980, pp. 52–53). These internationally noted individuals document that age need not be a barrier to making major contributions in life. Unfortunately the discrimination against the elderly in our society prevents many of them from having a meaningful and productive life.

The Behavior Dynamics Assessment Model enables us to examine numerous biological aspects of later adulthood. This chapter will:

- Define old age.
- Describe the physiological and mental changes that occur in later adulthood.
- Present contemporary theories on the causes of the aging process.
- Describe common diseases and major causes of death among the elderly.
- Present material on stress management and on other ways to maintain good physical and mental health throughout life.

What Is Old Age?

Later adulthood is the last major segment of the life span. Sixty-five has usually been cited as the dividing line between middle age and old age (Hareven, 1976). There is nothing magical or particularly scientific about age 65. Wrinkles do not suddenly appear on the 65th birthday, nor does the hair suddenly turn gray or fall out. In 1883, the Germans set age 65 as the criterion of aging for the world's first modern social security system (Sullivan et al., 1980, pp. 335–70). When our Social Security Act was passed in 1935, the United States followed the German model by selecting 65 as the age of eligibility for retirement benefits.

The elderly are an extremely diverse group, spanning an age range of over 30 years. Biologically, psychologically, and sociologically there are a number of differences between Sylvia Swanson, age 65, and her mother Maureen Methuselah. Sylvia owns and operates a boutique, making frequent buying trips to Paris, Mexico City, and San Francisco, while Maureen has been a resident of a nursing home since the death of her husband 13 years ago.

Gerontologists have attempted to deal with these age-related differences among the elderly by dividing later adulthood into two groups: *young-old*, ages 65 to 74 years, and *old-old*, ages 75 years and above (Hall, 1980).

Our society tends to define old age mainly in terms of chronological age. In primitive societies, old age is generally determined by physical and mental conditions rather than by chronological age. Such a definition is more accurate than ours. Everyone is not in the same mental and physical condition at age 65. Aging is an individual process that occurs at different rates in different people, and sociopsychological factors may retard or accelerate the physiological changes.

Senescence

The process of aging is called *senescence*. Senescence is the normal process of bodily change that accompanies aging. Senescence affects different persons at different rates and in various parts of the body. Some parts of the body resist aging more than others. In this section we will look at how the aging process in later adulthood affects appearance, senses, teeth, voice, skin, psychomotor skills, intellectual functioning, skeleton and joints, homeostasis, muscular structure, nervous system, digestive system, respiration, heart, and sexuality.

Appearance. Changes in physical appearance include increased wrinkles, reduced agility and speed of motion, stooping shoulders, increased unsteadiness of the hands and legs, increased difficulty in moving, thinning of hair, and the appearance of varicose veins. The wrinkling of the skin is caused by the partial loss of elastic tissue and of the fatty layer of the skin (Rossman, 1977).

Senses. The acuity of the senses generally deteriorate in later years. The sense of touch declines with age because there is drying, wrinkling, and toughening of the skin. The skin also has increased sensitivity to changes in temperature. Since the automatic regulation of bodily functions have a slower rate of responding, elderly persons often "feel the cold more."

The sense of hearing gradually deteriorates. The ability to hear very high tones is generally affected first. As time goes on, the level of auditory acuity becomes progressively lower. Many of the elderly find it difficult to follow a conversation when there is a competing noise, as from a radio, television, or the buzz of other people talking (Kalish, 1975). Impairment in hearing is five times as common in persons aged 65 to 79 as it is in individuals between the ages of 45 and 64 years. Elderly men are more apt to experience hearing impairments than elderly women (Kaluger and Kaluger, 1984, p. 582).

The senses of taste and smell have reduced functional capability during advancing years. Much of this reduced sensitivity appears more related to illness and a poor health condition rather than to a deterioration of sense organs due to age (Rovee et al., 1975).

Vision also declines. Most people over age 60 need glasses or contact lenses to see well. The decline in vision is usually caused by deterioration of the lens, cornea, retina, iris and optic nerve (Botwinick, 1970). The power of the eye to adjust to different levels of light and darkness is reduced, and color perception is also reduced. The elderly are likely to have 20/70 vision or less, are not as able to perceive depth, and cannot see as well in the dark, a problem that keeps many of them from driving at night. (Corso, 1971). Half of the legally blind persons in the United States are over 65 (Papalia and Olds, 1981, p. 509).

In many of the elderly, the eyes eventually appear sunken due to a gradual loss of orbital fat. The blink reflex is slower, and the eyelids hang loosely because of reduced muscle tone. The old-old are much more apt to have a decline in vision than the young-old.

Cataracts are a common concern of the elderly. A cataract is a clouding of the lens of the eye or of its capsule which obstructs the passage of light. The consequences of a cataract for visual functioning depend on its location. The most common form of a cataract involves a hardening of cell tissues in the nucleus of the lens. In severe cases double vision may result. Cataracts can generally be surgically removed, with a substitute lens being implanted. After cataract surgery, the use of contact lenses is usually recommended. A Duke University study by Anderson and Palmore (1974) found that the incidence of cataracts in persons in their 60s, 70s and 80s was respectively 9, 18, and 36 percent. Fortunately, with the development of corrective lenses and of new surgical techniques for the removal of cataracts, many vision losses are at least partially correctible.

The vestibular senses whose function it is to maintain posture and balance also lose some of their efficiency. As a result, the elderly are more prone to fall than younger adults. The elderly are also more apt to suffer from dizziness, which increases the likelihood they will fall.

Teeth. As people grow older, the gums gradually recede, and the teeth increasingly take on a yellowish color. Periodontal disease becomes an increasing problem. More than half of the elderly eventually lose all their teeth, with the problem being more severe for people from low income levels (Papalia and Olds, 1981, p. 511). Having to have the teeth replaced with dentures takes several weeks to get adjusted to, and the person will not be able to eat or sleep as well during this adjustment period. Poorer teeth or the use of dentures may also be traumatic as it drives home the fact that the person is aging physically. A person's disposition can be ad-versely affected. On the other hand, dentures for some people improve their appearance and may lead to an improved self-concept. Many of the facial evidences of old age may be prevented by proper dental care throughout life or by using dentures. Dental health is due to a combination of innate tooth structure and lifelong eating and dental health habits.

Voice. Gradually the voice becomes higher pitched, and in advanced old age it may become less powerful and restricted in range. Public speaking and singing abilities generally deteriorate earlier than normal speaking skills. All of these changes are partly due to the hardening and decreasing elasticity of the laryngeal cartilages. Speech often becomes lower, and pauses become longer and more frequent. If there are pathological changes in the brain, slurring may occur.

Skin. The skin in many of the elderly becomes somewhat splotchy, paler in color, and loses some of its elasticity. Some of the subcutaneous muscle and fat disappear, resulting in the skin hanging in folds and wrinkles.

Psychomotor Skills. The elderly can do most of the same things that younger people can do, but they do them more slowly. Birren (1974) asserts that a key factor in the high accident rates of the elderly is a slowdown in the processing of information by the central nervous system. It takes the elderly longer to move in order to assess their environment, longer to make a decision after assessment, and then longer to implement the right action. This slowness in processing information shows up in many aspects of the elderly's lives. Their rate of learning new material is slowed, and the rate at which they retrieve information from memory is reduced.

Have you ever been irritated when an elderly person was driving a car slowly in front of you? Perhaps you even blasted your car horn to attempt to hurry him along. We need to remember the elderly are probably functioning at the fastest pace that is safe for them.

The slower processing times and reaction times have practical implications for drivers. The elderly have accident rates much higher than middle-age adults. Their rates are similar to those for teenagers (Zylman, 1972). However, the reasons for these relatively high accident rates differ (Kaluger and Kaluger, 1984). Teenagers frequently have accidents because they tend to be more reckless and often take risks. The elderly, on the other hand, tend to have accidents because of being slower in getting out of the way of potential problems and of difficulties in recovering balance. The elderly have as great a need to drive as others. Being able to drive often makes the difference between actively participating in society or facing a life of enforced isolation. Papalia and Olds (1981, p. 511) suggest what needs to be done:

> Instead of discouraging them from driving, we need to institute measures that will protect them and others and yet enable those who can continue to drive to do so. This would include regular retesting of older drivers' vision, coordination, and reaction time. It might also include staggering the work times of older workers so that they would not have to battle rush-hour traffic. And it might include a shorter work day, in recognition of the fact that many older drivers cannot see well enough in the dark to drive at night.

Physical exercise and mental activity appear to reduce losses in psychomotor skills, such as in the areas of speed, strength, and stamina. Regular exercise also helps to maintain the circulatory and respiratory systems and helps people be more resistant to physical ailments that might be fatal, such as heart attacks (Bromley, 1974).

Intellectual Functioning. The notion that there is a general intellectual decline in old age is largely a myth (Balter and Schaie, 1974, p. 35). Most intellectual abilities hold up well with age. The elderly do tend to achieve somewhat lower scores on IQ tests than younger people, and the scores of the elderly gradually decline as the years pass (Papalia and Olds, 1981, p. 518). In explaining such differences Papalia and Olds (pp. 518–20) note that a distinction needs to be made between *performance* and *competence.* It could well be that while the elderly show a decline in performance on IQ tests, their actual intellectual competence may not be declining. Their lower performance on IQ tests could be due to a variety of factors. With diminished capacities to see and hear they have more difficulty perceiving instructions and executing tasks. Due to reduced powers of coordination and agility, they may perform less well. They may be more fatigued when older, and fatigue has been found to suppress intellectual performance (Furry and Baltes, 1973). Speed is a component of many IQ tests, and the elderly have a decline in speed because it takes them longer to perceive, longer to assess, and longer to respond (Birren, 1974). In addition, when elderly people know they are being timed, their anxiety increases as they are aware that it takes them longer to do things than it used to; such increased anxiety may actually lower performance (Papalia and Olds, 1981, p. 521). IQ tests primarily have test items that are designed to test intelligence in younger people; as a result, some of the items may be less familiar to older people which lowers their scores. The elderly are consistently more cautious than the young, which may hinder their performance on IQ tests which generally emphasize risk taking and speed (Botwinick, 1966). The elderly are more apt to have self-defeating attitudes about their abilities to solve problems; such attitudes may become self-fulfilling prophecies on IQ tests as they are inhibited from doing as well as they could.

The reduced performance by the elderly on IQ tests may also be partly due to a lessening of continued intellectual activity in later adulthood. It appears that reduced use of one's intellectual capacities results in a reduction of intellectual ability. Such a proposition underscores the need for the elderly to remain intellectually active.

Riegel and Riegel (1972) have found that there is a *terminal drop* in intelligence; that is, there is a sudden drop in intellectual performance a few weeks or a few months before death. Terminal drop is not limited to the elderly, as it is also found in younger people who have a terminal illness.

It is at this time not possible to draw definitive conclusions as to whether intellectual functioning actually declines in later adulthood. IQ scores do go down, but that does not mean intellectual competence declines, for the reasons cited. Continued intellectual activity serves to maintain intellectual capacities.

Skeleton and Joints. The maximum height of a person is reached by the late teens or early twenties. In future years there is little or no change in the length of the individual bones. In elderly persons there may be a small reduction in overall height which is due to a progressive decline in

■ **The Myth of Senility**

Senility can be defined as an irreversible mental and physical deterioration associated with later adulthood. Many people erroneously believe that every elderly person will eventually become senile. That is simply not accurate. Although the physical condition of the elderly deteriorates somewhat, the elderly can be physically active until near death. Furthermore, the vast majority of the elderly show no signs of mental deterioration for as long as they live (Heinig, 1978).

Regarding the term *senility* Butler (1975, p. 232) notes: "[Senility] is not a medical diagnosis, but a wastebasket term for a range of symptoms that, minimally, includes some memory impairment or forgetfulness, difficulty in attention and concentration, decline in general intellectual grasp and ability, and reduction in emotional responsiveness to others."

Those elderly persons who do appear disoriented and confused are apt to be suffering from one or more of over 100 illnesses, many of which are treatable (Heinig, 1978). Infections, undiagnosed diabetes, strokes, cerebral arteriosclerosis (hardening of the blood vessels in the brain), Alzheimer's disease, anemia, brain tumors, and thyroid disorders are only a few of the medical conditions that can cause a person to have senilelike symptoms.

the discs between the spinal vertebrae (Garn, 1975). The bones of the body also become less dense and more brittle due to changes in chemical composition. Such changes increase the risk of breakage. Joint movements also become stiffer and more restricted, and the incidence of diseases (such as arthritis) affecting the joints increases with age. The elderly need to stay physically active to exercise their joints, as the joints will increase in stiffness if there is little activity.

Homeostasis. Frolkis (1977) has found that homeostasis becomes less efficient in later adulthood. The stabilizing mechanisms become sluggish, and the physiological adaptability of the person is reduced. The heart and breathing rates take longer to return to normal. Wounds take longer to heal. The thyroid gland shrinks, resulting in a lower rate of basal metabolism. The pancreas loses part of its capacity to produce the enzymes that are used in protein and sugar metabolism.

Muscular Structure. After around age 30 there is a gradual reduction in the power and speed of muscular contractions and the capacity for sustained muscular effort decreases. After the age of around 50 the number of active muscle fibers gradually decreases, resulting in the older person's muscles being reduced in size. The hand grip strength of a 75-year-old man is only about 55 percent of that of a 30-year-old man (Kaluger and Kaluger, 1984, p. 586). The ligaments tend to harden and contract, and sometimes result in a hunched-over body position. The reflexes respond more slowly, and incontinence (loss of bowel or bladder control) sometimes occurs. The involuntary smooth muscles that are part of the autonomic system show much less deterioration than the other muscle groups.

Nervous System. Although there is little functional change in the nerves with increasing age, some of the nerve tissue is gradually replaced by fibrous cells. Reflex and reaction times of an older person become slower. The total number of brain cells may decrease, but the brain continues to function normally unless its blood supply is blocked. The brain weight of an average 75-year-old man is only 56 percent of the brain weight of a 30-year-old man (Kaluger and Kaluger, 1984, p. 586). People with certain medical conditions (such as cerebral arteriosclerosis) will have progressive deterioration of brain tissue. If such deterioration takes place, the person is apt to have a loss of recent and/or past memories, to become apathetic, to be less coordinated in body movements, to give less attention to grooming habits, and may have some personality changes (such as being more irritable, confused, and frustrated). In many of the elderly the cortical area of the brain that is responsible for organizing the perceptual processes gradually shows degenerative changes.

Digestive System. With increased age there is a reduction in the amount of enzyme action, gastric juices, and saliva, which upsets the digestion process (Rockstein, 1975). Complaints about digestive disorders are among the most common complaints of the elderly. Since the digestive system is highly sensitive to stress, to emotional disturbances, and to anxieties that accompany old age, many of the digestive disorders may be due to these factors rather than to age per se. The regularity of bowel movements also is more of a problem in later adulthood, resulting in diarrhea or constipation.

Respiration. The lungs decrease in size, resulting in a decrease of oxygen utilization. Some air sac membranes are replaced by fibrous tissue, which obstructs the normal exchange of gases within the lungs. The maximum breathing capacity and maximum oxygen intake in a 75-year-old are about 40 percent of a 30-year-old (Kaluger and Kaluger, 1984, p. 586). Moderate exercise throughout life is important for keeping oxygen intake and blood flow at their highest levels, thereby slowing down the aging process.

Heart. The heart and the blood vessels are the bodily parts in which aging produces the most destructive changes. The heart and arteries are the weakest link in the chain of life, as most of the other organs would probably last for 150 years if they received an adequate blood supply (Harris, 1975). The heart is affected by aging in a variety of ways. The heart shrinks in size, and the percentage of fat in the heart increases. The heart muscles tend to become stringy and dried out. Deposits of a brown pigment in the cells of the heart partly restrict the passage of blood and interfere with the absorption of oxygen through the heart walls. The elasticity in the valves of the heart is reduced, and deposits of cholesterol and calcium in heart valves also decrease valve efficiency. The heart of an older person pumps only 70 percent as much blood as that of a younger person (Harris, 1975). The rhythm of the heart becomes slower and more irregular. Deposits of fat begin to accumulate around the heart and interfere with its functioning. Blood pressure also rises. These changes are not necessarily dangerous, provided the heart is properly treated. A nutritious diet, moderate exercise, adequate sleep, and a positive mental attitude will help keep the heart functioning properly.

In later life the coronary artery has a tendency to harden and become narrow, which may lead to a partial blockage. The coronary artery is the site of many heart attacks that are brought on by increased emotional stress or physical effort. Hardening of the coronary artery may also increase blood pressure and may reduce the flow of blood to many parts of the body. Poor circulation of blood may cause a variety of problems. For example, poor circulation to the brain may lead to brain deterioration and to personality changes. Poor circulation to the kidneys may result in kidney problems and even kidney failure.

Sexuality. There is a common misconception that older people lose their sexual drive. It is true that both sexual interest and sexual activity gradually decline among the elderly (Jacobson, 1974). Elderly men tend to be more sexually active than elderly women. This may be the result of factors other than differences in sex drive, such as a larger percentage of women living longer than their spouses and thereby finding themselves without a sexual partner (Aiken, 1978).

Newman and Nichols (1970) found that 54 percent of persons between the ages of 60 and 75 reported they were still sexually active. After the age of 75, only 27 percent reported they were sexually active.

The most noted studies of sexual behavior among the elderly were conducted by Kinsey et al. (1948, 1953), Masters and Johnson (1966, 1968, 1970), and Pfeiffer (1974). All found that the elderly who are in fairly good health are physiologically able to be sexually active well into their 70s and beyond. As far as sexuality is concerned in older years there is truth to the colloquial saying that "If you don't use it, you'll lose it". The studies found that those who were most active sexually during youth and middle age usually maintained their sexual vigor and interest longer into old age. The study by Pfeiffer (1974) was particularly interesting as 15 percent of the elderly reported a rising rate of sexual activity as they were growing older. (The nature of sexual activity in this study included both activity with a partner and self-stimulation.)

If sexual behavior does decline in later years, it probably is due more to social reasons than physical. Masters and Johnson (1966) found the most important deterrents to sexual activity when one is older are the lack of a partner; boredom with one's partner; overindulgence in drinking or eating; poor physical or mental health; fear of poor performance; negative attitudes toward menopause; and negative attitudes toward sex, such as the erroneous belief that sex is inappropriate for the elderly. Other factors deter sexual activity. One is the lack of privacy in many living arrangements, such as in nursing homes. Butler and Lewis (1977) note that the fear of death due to a stroke or heart attack deters some of the elderly from sexual activity. A variety of feelings—guilt, anxiety, depression, or hostility—also deter sexual activity. Because of some of these reasons there is usually more interest in sex than there is sexual activity. (This last statement is applicable, however, to practically all age groups.)

The attitudes of younger adults as to what is appropriate sexual behavior for the elderly commonly create problems. Many younger people express beliefs that it is inappropriate for an unmarried elderly person to become romantically involved with someone. A widower or widow at times faces strong opposition to remarrying from other family members. Negative views are often strongest when an elderly person becomes involved with someone younger who will become an heir if the older person dies.

Fortunately, the attitudes toward sexuality in old age are changing. Taber (1975, pp. 356–57) notes:

> With the changing attitudes of younger people to alternatives to the traditional family, some older people are finding informal arrangements for living together attractive. The couple who do not have a marriage ceremony can share all the companionship and sexual satisfactions without upsetting inheritance rights and retirement benefits. When they become aware of it, their children may accept such a pattern because they find it preferable to remarriage. We have no idea of the numbers that are involved, but the old as well as the young have new options as societal norms change. The popularity of living together without marriage will probably increase.

The elderly have a right to sexual expression, as long as they do not hurt anyone. Think how angry you feel if someone tries to control your sexual activity. Few efforts are made to control the sexual expressions of middle-age people. It seems absurd for society to put more restrictions on people as they move from middle adulthood to later adulthood. Being touched and receiving affection is something that everyone needs at all ages to promote self-worth and personal satisfaction.

Many of the current living arrangements for the elderly (group homes, nursing homes, and foster homes) have overlooked the need for privacy. Many nursing homes, for example, place two women or two men in a small room. Butler and Lewis (1976) suggest that future care facilities for the elderly be designed to provide privacy.

What Causes Aging?

Everyone who lives to later adulthood will experience some of the physiological changes that are described in the preceding material. But what causes these changes? No one knows all of the reasons. A number of theories have been developed which involve biological, sociological, environmental, and psychological factors. Most of the theories involve biological factors.

Genetic Theories. These theories hypothesize that aging occurs due to damage or change in the genetic information involved in the formation of cellular proteins. Such changes cause cells to die, which results in aging. The following theories have been classified as genetic theories.

Cellular genetic theory of DNA damage asserts that damages or changes to DNA molecules alter the genetic information and result in the cell being unable to manufacture essential enzymes. (DNA molecules in each cell contain the genetic information of each person. Amazingly, each cell of the body is literally a blueprint of the composition of a person.) Without essential enzymes, it is theorized that aging occurs as cells gradually die.

The running-out-of-program theory asserts there is a set amount of basic genetic material (DNA molecules) in each cell. As the cells age, the DNA is used up and the cells die. Hayflick's research (1974) supports this theory as his findings showed human cells will divide only a limited number of times, usually about 50.

The somatic mutation by radiation theory postulates that aging occurs due to abnormal chromosomes developing after exposure to radiation. Recent research suggests radiation is not the major factor causing the aging process (Shock, 1977).

The error theory of aging asserts that aging is due to an accumulation of errors involved in transmission of information from the DNA molecule to the final protein product. Such accumulation of errors results in "error catastrophe," which eventually leads to the death of cells.

Nongenetic Cellular Theories. This category of theories postulates that changes take place in the cellular proteins after they have been formed. Such changes cause some cells to die, which results in aging. The following theories have been classified as nongenetic cellular theories.

Deprivation theory assumes that aging is caused by vascular changes which deprive cells of essential nutrients and oxygen.

Accumulation theory asserts that aging results from the accumulation of harmful substances in the cells of an organism. When the accumulation builds up, the cells eventually begin to die. The specific substances involved have not as yet been identified.

Wear and tear theory asserts that cells begin to die after long use and exposure to stressful elements during the process of living.

Free radical theory hypothesizes there are chemicals, called free radicals, that contain oxygen in a highly activated state that react with other molecules in their vicinity. Such reactions are postulated to damage and kill some cells.

Cross-linkage theory asserts that cross-linkages or bonds develop between molecules or between components of the same molecules. These bonds supposedly change the chemical and physical properties, which cause some cells to function improperly and gradually die.

Physiological Theories. These theories explain aging as being due to either the breakdown of an organ system or to an impairment in physiological control mechanisms. The following theories have been classified as physiological theories.

Single organ system theory asserts that aging is due to an essential system breaking down. The precise system that is thought to control aging has not been identified, but various systems have been suggested. Those suggested include the thyroid gland, which is involved with metabolism, sex glands which regulate hormone secretions, the cardiovascular system which controls oxygen and blood flow, and the pituitary gland which regulates secretions from other glands.

Endocrine control system theory postulates that hormones control the aging process. There is evidence that hormones are involved in puberty and menopause. There is also evidence that the functions of the endocrine system decline with age.

Stress theory asserts aging is due to the accumulation of the effects of the stresses of living. Each stress encountered is thought to leave a small residual of accumulants and impairments, which results in bodily systems then aging. This theory is consistent with cliches about how stressful events will turn a person's hair gray or cause the hair to fall out.

Immunological theory assumes that individuals have an immune system which protects the body from invading bacteria, micro-organisms, and atypical mutant cells that may form. As a person grows older, it is hypothesized that fewer antibodies are produced, which decreases the protection ability of the immune system. Gradually, invading micro-organisms begin to engulf and digest body cells, which results in aging.

Because over three-quarters of the elderly have chronic medical conditions, regular check-ups are particularly essential. But many of the their medical ailments don't need medical treatment. Personal and social stress cause the illnesses that shorten their lives. The following are a few ways to slow down the aging process: maintain a healthy diet; learn how to relax and manage stress; remain physically and mentally active; learn to think positively. (Courtesy of United Way of America)

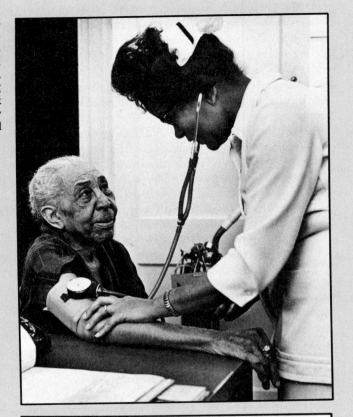

Do the elderly lose their sexual drive? A common misconception in our society is that sex over sixty cannot and should not continue. But modern studies show that healthy elderly people can be sexually active well into their seventies and beyond. And just as important as coitus itself is the showing of affection through touching that sexual activity provides. The elderly definitely need both the sexuality and intimacy that are part of a love relationship. (Courtesy of United Way of America)

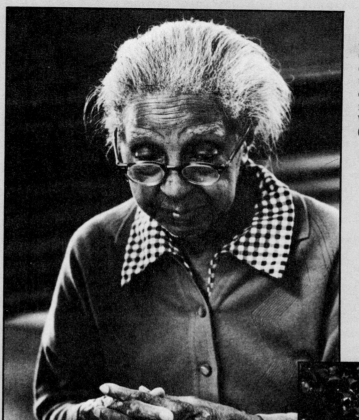

During senescence, physical changes such as increased wrinkles, unsteadiness of the hands and legs, and stooping shoulders develop. Vision declines, and many elderly people develop cataracts, or a clouding over the lense of the eye that obstructs the passage of light. But with the development of new surgical techniques and corrective lenses, vision can be partially restored. What auditory changes occur during senescence? (Courtesy of United Way of America)

What is this elderly woman gaining by working in her garden? Garden work is providing her with exercise that keeps her physically fit and enables her to better handle the stressful crises she encounters. She gets psychological gains from her gardening, too. When she is feeling tense, she concentrates on the physical work she is doing and switches her thoughts away from her daily concerns. Reaping the fruits of her labor reinforces her positive feelings about herself. (Fran Buss)

Control mechanisms theory of the central nervous system asserts that mechanisms in the central nervous system are responsible for aging. A variety of mechanisms may be involved. For example, the mechanisms that control the autonomic nervous system may function less effectively, which causes the autonomic nervous system to gradually degenerate. Or control mechanisms may cause the endocrine system to function less effectively, which results in a gradual reduction in the functions of practically every system in the body.

Everyone grows old, so the conclusion is obvious that nature has a built-in mechanism that promotes aging. We still do not know what this mechanism is. As yet, sufficient evidence has not been presented to prove which (if any) theory is valid.

Factors That Influence the Aging Process

Aging is a very complex process. There seem to be many variables that accelerate and decelerate the process. A person who has a serious, long-term illness, or a severe impairment, will often age much faster and earlier than someone who is healthy (Makinodan, 1974). The precise reasons why such conditions accelerate the aging process are not known. More rapid aging in such individuals may be due to decreased exercise, or to unknown biochemical changes, or to greater stress.

Bierman and Hazzard (1973) have found that a large number of "biological insults" hastens the aging process. Such insults include accidents, broken bones, severe burns, severe psychological stress, and severe alcohol or drug abuse. Poor eating habits also accelerate aging (Kent, 1980).

Environmental factors influence the aging process. Being physically and mentally active tends to slow down the aging process. Inactivity speeds it up. A positive outlook (positive thinking) tends to slow down the aging process. Insecurity, lack of someone to talk to, negative thinking, and being in a strange environment tend to accelerate the aging process (Rosenmayr, 1980). Prolonged excessive heat or cold will also speed up the aging process. (Shock, 1977).

Genetic inheritance also plays a role. People whose parents lived a long time have a longer life expectancy than people whose parents lived a shorter period of time (with the assumption that they died from natural causes). Our bodies apparently have a genetic time clock. Some individuals have a longer time than others. Within a family group, the rate of aging shows a high positive correlation for the different family members. It seems that some kind of a timing device causes tissues and organ systems to break down at specific times (Shock, 1977). This timing device can be accelerated or decelerated by a variety of factors.

Diseases and Causes of Death of the Elderly

Over three quarters of the elderly have a chronic medical condition, and almost half have two or more. Almost one in ten is bedridden (Flynn, 1980, p. 352). Four out of ten have physical impairments that interfere with performing major self-care tasks (Flynn, 1980, p. 352). Older persons see their doctor more frequently, spend a higher proportion of their income on prescribed drugs, and, once in the hospital, they stay longer. As might be expected, the health status of the old-old (75 and over) is worse than the young-old.

The medical expenses of an elderly person average six times more than those of a young adult (Robertson, 1980, p. 307). One of the reasons medical costs are high is because the elderly suffer much more from long-term illnesses—such as cancer, heart problems, diabetes, and glaucoma.

The physical process of aging is a factor in the elderly having a higher rate of health problems. However, research in recent years has demonstrated that personal and social stresses also play major roles in causing diseases. The elderly face a wide range of stressful situations: death of family members and friends, retirement, loneliness, changes in living arrangements, reduced income, loss of social status, and a decline in physical capacities and physical energy. Medical conditions also may result from inadequate exercise, substandard diets, cigarette smoking, and excessive drinking of alcoholic beverages.

A special problem for the elderly is that when they become ill, their new illness is often imposed on an assortment of preexisting chronic illnesses and on organ systems which no longer are functioning very well. The health of elderly patients is thus more fragile, and even a relatively minor illness such as a flu can lead to major consequences, and even death (Estes, 1969, p. 124).

The most common conditions that limit the activities of the elderly are high blood pressure, heart conditions, rheumatism, arthritis, orthopedic impairments, and emotional disorders. Many of these disorders begin to appear among people in their 30s, such as arthritis and heart conditions (Ledger, 1978). Other common chronic conditions among the elderly include cataracts, varicose veins, hemorrhoids, obesity, abdominal-cavity hernias, and prostate disorders.

The discussion of these health problems needs to be put in context. The elderly have higher rates of illnesses than younger people, but it needs to be emphasized that a majority of the elderly are reasonably healthy. People over 65 do have a health advantage over younger persons in a few areas as they have fewer flu infections, colds, and acute digestive problems. The reasons are unclear. They may be more immune to common germs, or they may go out less and, therefore, be less exposed to germs.

Life Expectancy

The average life expectancy in ancient Rome and during the Middle Ages was between 20 and 30 years. The life expectancy for Americans has gradually been increasing. At the middle of the 19th century Americans lived an average of 40 years. At the turn of the 20th century, the age was 49 years. The average life expectancy in 1982 was 75 years (United States Bureau of the Census, 1984). These gains have resulted from improvements in medical care, diets, and sanitation. Particularly significant in leading to these gains has been immunization against many diseases that used to kill (such as whooping cough, polio, and diphtheria) and the development of antibodies to reduce the severity of such illnesses as strep throat, bronchitis, and pneumonia.

Rowland (1977) sought to identify life events that predict death in the elderly. In a review of the literature, only two items were found to have predictive significance: death of a spouse and environmental relocation (primarily a move to nursing home). A partial explanation for both of these life events is that those who lose their spouse or are moved to a nursing home may no longer have a will to live, which then hastens their death. For those being moved to a nursing home, an additional partial explanation for a higher death rate is that such individuals may be in poorer health and, therefore, more apt to die.

■ **Leading Causes of Death among the Elderly in 1980**

Cause of Death	Of Those Who Died, Proportion Who Died of This Cause	Cause of Death	Of Those Who Died, Proportion Who Died of This Cause
1. Diseases of the heart	44.2	8. Diabetes	1.8
2. Malignant neoplasms (Cancer)	19.7	9. Nephritis, nephrotic syndrome, and nephrosis (diseases of kidney)	1.0
3. Cerebrovascular diseases	10.5	10. Chronic liver disease and cirrhosis	.7
4. Chronic obstructive pulmonary diseases (lung diseases)	3.5	11. Suicide	.4
5. Pneumonia and influenza	3.4	12. Homicide	.1
6. Atherosclerosis (hardening of the arteries)	2.0	13. Other	10.8
7. Accidents and adverse effects	1.9		100.0%

SOURCE: United States Bureau of the Census, *Statistical Abstract of the United States, 1984* (Washington, D.C.: U.S. Government Printing Office, 1984), p. 79.

How Long Will You Live?

This is a rough guide for calculating your personal longevity. The basic life expectancy for males is age 71 and for females it is age 78. Write down your basic life expectancy. If you are in your fifties or sixties, you should add 10 years to the basic figure because you have already proven yourself to be quite durable. If you are over age 60 and active, add another 2 years.

Basic Life Expectancy _____

Decide how each item below applies to you and add or subtract the appropriate number of years from your basic life expectancy.

1. Family history

   Add 5 years if two or more of your grandparents lived to 80 or beyond. _____

   Subtract 4 years if any parent, grandparent, sister, or brother died of heart attack or stroke before 50. Subtract 2 years if anyone died from these diseases before 60. _____

   Subtract 3 years for each case of diabetes, thyroid disorders, breast cancer, cancer of the digestive system, asthma, or chronic bronchitis among parents or grandparents. _____

2. Marital status

If you are married, add 4 years. _____

If you are over 25 and not married, subtract 1 year for every unwedded _____
decade.

3. Economic status

Subtract 2 years if your family income is over $40,000 per year. _____

Subtract 3 years if you have been poor for greater part of life. _____

4. Physique

Subtract 1 year for every 10 pounds you are overweight. _____

For each inch your girth measurement exceeds your chest measure- _____
ment deduct 2 years.

Add 3 years if you are over 40 and not overweight. _____

5. Exercise

Regular and moderate (jogging 3 times a week), add 3 years. _____

Regular and vigorous (long-distance running three times a week), add _____
5 years.

Subtract 3 years if your job is sedentary. _____

Add 3 years if it is active. _____

6. Alcohol

Add 2 years if you are a light drinker (1–3 drinks a day). _____

Subtract 5 to 10 years if you are a heavy drinker (more than 4 drinks _____
per day).

Subtract 1 year if you are a teetotaler. _____

7. Smoking

Two or more packs of cigarettes per day, subtract 8 years. _____

One to two packs per day, subtract 4 years. _____

Less than one pack, subtract 2 years. _____

Subtract 2 years if you regularly smoke a pipe or cigars. _____

8. Disposition

Add 2 years if you are a reasoned, practical person. _____

Subtract 2 years if you are aggressive, intense, and competitive. _____

Add 1–5 years if you are basically happy and content with life. _____

Subtract 1–5 years if you are often unhappy, worried, and often feel _____
guilty.

9. Education

Less than high school, subtract 2 years. _____

Four years of school beyond high school, add 1 year. _____

Five or more years beyond high school, add 3 years. _____

10. Environment

If you have lived most of your life in a rural environment, add 4 _____
years.

Subtract 2 years if you have lived most of your life in an urban _____
environment.

11. Sleep

   More than 9 hours a day, subtract 5 years. _____

12. Temperature

   Add 2 years if your home's thermostat is set at no more than 68°F. _____

13. Health care

   Regular medical checkups and regular dental care, add 3 years. _____
   Frequently ill, subtract 2 years. _____

SOURCE: From *The Psychology of Death, Dying and Bereavement*, by Richard Schultz, Table 5.1, Pages 97–98. Copyright © 1978 by Newbery Award Records, Inc. Reprinted by permission of Random House, Inc.

Significant sex differences are found in life expectancies. In 1982 females in the United States had a life expectancy at birth of 78 years while males had a life expectancy of only 71 years (United States Bureau of the Census, 1984, p. 73). For every 100 white women age 65 and over, there are only 69 white men. For those 75 years of age and older, there are only 58 white men to every 100 white women. Sex differences in life expectancy are less pronounced for blacks and Hispanics, although differences are still present (Papalia and Olds, 1981, p. 508).

In later life there appear to be both environmental and biological reasons for the higher mortality rates among men. Environmental factors are demonstrated by the fact that men are more likely to die from suicide, accidents, and homicide (U.S. Bureau of the Census, 1984, p. 79). Men are also more likely to die from lung cancer, heart disease, emphysema, and asthma, all of which have been linked to such environmental causes as smoking and alcohol abuse (U.S. Bureau of the Census, 1984, p. 79). A partial explanation for sex differences in mortality rates is that sex role stereotypes allow women to be much more expressive of their feelings than men. It may be that suppression of feelings leads to anger, frustration and other unwanted emotions being bottled up inside, which increases stress, results in higher stress-related disorders in men, and then shortens their life span.

Biological factors are probably also involved in leading to higher mortality rates among men. The higher mortality rate among males in the fetal stage and in infancy supports the notion of an inborn difference in resistance. Additional evidence was found in a study by Madigan and Vana (1957) which looked at life expectancy rates of men and women who had similar kinds of lifestyles in Roman Catholic teaching orders. The nuns were found to have a longer life expectancy than the brothers.

The fact that there are many more women over age 65 than men means that women are much more apt to be widows than men are apt to be widowers. Since there is a social custom in our society for males to marry someone younger, husbands are even more likely to die before their wives. Women are thus much more likely than men to spend their later years alone.

■ Alzheimer's Disease

Tony Wiggleworth is 68 years old. Two years ago his memory began to falter. As the months went by, he even forgot what his wedding day to Rose was like. His grandchildren's visits slipped from his memory in two or three days.

The most familiar surroundings have also become strange to him. Even his friends' homes seem like places he has never been before. When he walks down the streets in his neighborhood, he frequently becomes lost.

He is now quite confused. He has difficulty speaking and can no longer do such elementary tasks as balance his checkbook. At times, Rose, who is taking care of him, is uncertain whether he knows who she is. All of this is very baffling for Tony. Until he retired three years ago, he had been an accountant and excelled at remembering facts and details.

Tony has Alzheimer's disease, a form of senile dementia. The disease now affects more than 1 million Americans and kills about 100,000 Americans annually (Raeburn, 1984, p. 1). In its final stages, Alzheimer's leads to progressive paralysis and breathing difficulties. The breathing problems often result in pneumonia, the most frequent cause of death for Alzheimer's victims. Other symptoms of Alzheimer's include irritability, restlessness, agitation, and impairments of judgment.

An examination of the brains of victims has found a distinctive tangle of protein filaments in the cortex, the part of the brain responsible for intellectual functions. This research shows that there are biochemical causes for the disease and leads to the conclusion that aging does not automatically include senility. The exact causes of Alzheimer's are as yet unknown, but it is definitely a disease. During the early phases, the patient can usually be treated at home, but as it progresses a nursing home placement is usually necessary.

There is evidence of an inherited predisposition toward the illness, as it is clearly passed on from one generation to the next in about 15 percent of the cases (Raeburn, 1984). Scientists are now investigating a number of hypotheses as to what causes Alzheimer's. One intriguing finding is that victims of Down's syndrome (a severe form of mental retardation due to a chromosome defect) who survive into their 30s frequently develop symptoms indistinguishable from Alzheimer's. Such a similarity may provide a clue as to the causes of Alzheimer's. There is high hope that the causes of Alzheimer's can be found soon, and treatment developed.

Wellness

The preceding material echoes over and over a central theme. Elderly people are apt to experience little physical or mental deterioration (until near death) if they have a nutritious diet, are successful in managing stress, and stay mentally and physically active. A real key to good mental and physical health in later years is having a lifestyle throughout life that incorporates health maintenance principles. Health is one of our most important resources.

Traditionally, the health profession in this country has focused on treatment of diseases rather than on prevention. The Chinese approach to medicine has focused on helping patients maintain good health. The holistic concept of treating the whole person is gaining ground in America. There is now greater emphasis on prevention, wellness, and treating a patient psychologically and socially as well as physically (Rosen and Wiens, 1979).

■ **Health and Longevity**

In a study of 6,928 adults, Nedra Belloc and Lester Breslow found that the following seven health practices are positively related to good health and longevity:

Eating breakfast

Exercising regularly

Staying within 10 percent of your proper weight

Not smoking cigarettes

Not drinking to excess

Not eating between meals

Sleeping seven to eight hours a night

At age 45, a person who follows these practices has a life expectancy that is 11 years longer than a person who follows fewer than four. A 70-year-old who practices all seven is apt to be as healthy as a 40-year-old who follows only one or two.

SOURCE: A. F. Ehrbar, "A Radical Prescription for Medical Care," *Fortune*, February 1977, p. 169.

Physical Exercise

For people who have had poor health maintenance habits, it is nearly never too late to start. For example, Arehart-Triechel (1977) reported on a study in which a group of 70-year-old inactive men participated in a daily exercise program; at the end of a year they had regained the physical fitness levels normally associated with 40-year-olds. There is also evidence that continued exercise as people grow older reduces the degree of physical and mental slowness that occurs in many of the elderly. Before middle age and older adults embark on an exercise program (if they have been relatively inactive for a number of years), they should have a physical examination by their physician to identify heart conditions and other medical problems that may be unduly aggravated by exercise. DeVries (1975) suggests poorly conditioned elderly should begin an exercise program of such activities as brief walks, and perhaps later incorporate a jog-walk routine under proper medical supervision. Swimming in moderation is also suggested.

Mental Activity

Just as physical exercise maintains the level of physiological functioning, mental exercise maintains good cognitive functioning. Denny (1982) concludes there are some age-related declines in cognitive functioning, but if a person is mentally active the declines begin to appear at a later age and to be less severe. The specific declines in intellectual functioning have been described earlier.

Our society needs to put more emphasis on assuring that the elderly are exposed to intellectual stimulation. Some nursing homes and retirement communities now have daily programs that provide such stimulation; national issues or local issues are discussed and guest speakers on a variety of subjects are sometimes brought in.

One innovative program is Elderhostel which offers low-cost, summer college courses designed for the elderly. The elderly sign up for one-, two- or three-week sessions to study a variety of topics at a relaxed pace. Some public universities also have provisions for the elderly to attend regular classes with either reduced or no tuition. The elderly have generally responded well to adult educational courses. Some want to update earlier studies, and others want to pursue educational programs to enrich their lives. Some want to acquire basic learning skills, and some want to attain a high school or college diploma.

Traveling is yet another way for the elderly to stay mentally active. Some organizations, such as the American Association of Retired Persons (AARP), offer travel tours within the United States and to other parts of the world.

Most authorities on aging now believe that intellectual decline in old age is largely a myth. It thus appears that our society is largely wasting a precious resource—an elderly population with extensive experience, training, and intelligence. Our society needs to develop more educational programs to help the elderly maintain their intellectual functioning, and find additional ways to allow the elderly to be productive, contributing members to society.

Sleep Patterns

Many of the elderly have one or more sleep disturbances, such as insomnia, difficulty in falling asleep, restless sleep, falling asleep when company is present, frequent awakening during the night, and feeling exhausted or tired after having a restless night of sleeping.

What is a healthy sleep pattern for the elderly? The stereotype that the elderly need more sleep appears to be erroneous. It appears the elderly in fairly good health require no more sleep than those in middle adulthood (Kaluger and Kaluger, 1984, p. 591).

Sleep disturbances that the elderly experience tend to be a result of anxiety, depression, worry, or illness. Restless sleep is common for those who are inactive, those who catnap too much, and those who have physical discomforts (such as arthritic pains).

Some normal changes occur in sleep patterns for the elderly. Deep sleep (stage 4 of sleep) virtually disappears (Kales, 1975). The elderly generally take a longer time to fall asleep and have more frequent awakenings. More importantly, the elderly distribute their sleep somewhat differently. They generally have several catnaps of 15 to 60 minutes during the day. Pfeiffer (1974) indicates such catnaps are normal, and caution should be used in attempting to use sleep medication to keep an elderly person asleep for eight hours throughout the night as they need less sleep when they have catnaps. People develop their sleep patterns according to their physical needs and according to the responsibilities and activities they have.

Nutrition and Diet

Over 80 percent of deaths caused by malnutrition involve people over age 65 (Pepper, 1980). A majority of the elderly have inadequate diets (Kaluger and Kaluger, 1984, p. 590). Because of the relationship between diet and cardiac problems, physicians recommend that the elderly have low-fat, high-protein diets.

The elderly are the most undernourished group in our society (Ferguson, 1975, p. 238). A number of reasons can be given for chronic malnutrition of the elderly: lack of money, transportation problems, lack of incentives to prepare a nutritious meal when one is living alone, inadequate cooking and storage facilities, poor teeth and lack of good dentures, and lack of knowledge about proper nutrition.

Some of the elderly have a tendency to overeat. One way for people to occupy their free time is to eat, and most of the elderly have a lot of free time. The caloric requirements decrease somewhat in the later years, and the excess calories that are consumed turn into fat, which increases the risks of heart disease and other medical conditions.

To improve the nutritional needs of the elderly, some programs have been developed. Many communities, with the assistance of federal funds, now provide meals for the elderly at group eating sites. These meals are generally provided four or five times a week and usually are luncheon meals. These programs improve the nutrition of elderly persons and offer opportunities for socialization.

Meals on Wheels is a service which delivers hot and cold meals directly to house-bound recipients (many of whom are elderly) who are incapable of obtaining or preparing their own meals, but who can feed themselves.

Stress and Stress Management

Learning how to manage stress is important for the physical and emotional health of all age groups. Because of its importance, we will look at stress and at techniques to manage stress in considerable detail.

Importance of Managing Stress

Stress is a contributing factor in causing a wide variety of emotional and behavioral difficulties, including anxiety, child abuse, spouse abuse, temper tantrums, feelings of inadequacy, physical assaults, explosive expressions of anger, feelings of hostility, impatience, stuttering, suicide attempts, and depression (Greenberg, 1980, pp. 39–49).

Stress is a contributing factor in most physical illnesses. (Pelletier, 1977). These illnesses include hypertension, heart attacks, migraine headaches, tension headaches, colitis, ulcers, diarrhea, constipation, arrhythmia, angina, diabetes, hay fever, backaches, arthritis, cancer, colds, flus, insomnia, hyperthyroidism, dermatitis, emphysema, Raynaud's disease, alcoholism, bronchitis, infections, allergies, and enuresis. Stress-related disorders have not been recognized as being our number-one health problem (McQuade and Aikman, 1974).

Becoming skillful in learning how to relax is important in treating and facilitating the recovery from both emotional and physical disorders. The therapeutic value of learning how to manage stress has been dramatically demonstrated by Simonton and Simonton (1978) who have had considerable success in treating terminal cancer patients by instructing them on how to manage and reduce stress.

The increased recognition of stress management in treating physical and emotional disorders is gradually altering the traditional physician-patient relationship. Instead of being passive participants in the treatment process, patients are increasingly being taught (by social workers and other health professionals) how to prevent illness and how to speed up the recovery from illness by learning stress management strategies (Brown, 1977).

People who are successful in managing stress have a life expectancy which is several years longer than those who continually are at high stress levels. (Pelletier, 1977). Effective stress management is a major factor in enabling people to live fulfilling, healthy, satisfying and productive lives (Tubesing, 1981).

Conceptualizing Stress

Stress can be defined as the physiological and emotional reactions to stressors. A stressor is a demand, situation, or circumstance which disrupts a person's equilibrium (internal balance) and initiates the stress response. There are an infinite variety of possible stressors: loss of a job, loud noise, toxic substances, retirement, arguments, death of a spouse, moving to a nursing home, heat, cold, serious illness, lack of purpose in life, etc. Every second we are alive our bodies are responding to stressors that call for adaptation or adjustment. Our bodily reactions are continually striving for "homeostasis" or balance.

Selye (1956), one of the foremost authorities on stress, found the body reacts to stressors in the same way regardless of the source of stress. This means the body reacts to positive stressors (e.g., a romantic kiss) in the same way that it reacts to negative stressors (e.g., an electric shock). Selye found that the body has a three-stage reaction to stress: (a) the alarm phase, (b) the resistance phase, and (c) the exhaustion phase. Selye called this three-phase response the General Adaptation Syndrome (GAS).

In the alarm phase the body recognizes the stressor and responds by preparing for fight or flight. The body's reactions are numerous and complex and will only be briefly summarized here. The body sends messages from the hypothalamus (a section of the brain) to the pituitary gland to release its hormones. These hormones trigger the adrenal glands to release adrenaline. The release of adrenaline and other hormones results in the following:

- Increased breathing and heartbeat rates.
- A rise in blood pressure.
- Increased coagulation of blood, which minimizes potential loss of blood in case of physical injury.
- Diversion of blood from the skin to the brain, the heart, and contracting muscles.
- A rise in serum cholesterol and blood fat.
- Mobility of the gastrointestinal tract decreases or stops.
- Dilation of the pupils.

These changes result in a huge burst of energy, better vision and hearing, and increased muscular strength—all changes which increase our capacities to fight or to flee. (A major problem of the fight-or-flight reaction for us is that we often cannot deal with a threat by fighting or by fleeing. In our complex civilized society fighting or fleeing generally runs counter to sophisticated codes of acceptable behavior. The fight-or-flight response was once functional for primitive humans, but now seldom is.)

In the resistance phase (the second phase) bodily processes seek to return to homeostasis. The body seeks during this phase to repair any damage caused by the stressors and may adapt to such stressors as hard physical labor and intense heat. In handling most stressors the body generally only goes through the two phases of alarm and repair. During a lifetime a person goes through these two phases thousands of times.

The third phase of exhaustion only occurs when the body remains in a state of high stress for an extended period of time. If the body remains at a high level of stress, it is unable to repair damage that has occurred. If exhaustion continues, a person is apt to develop a stress-related illness.

There are two components of a stressor—experiences or events which are encountered and our thoughts and perceptions about these events (Tubesing, 1981). See *Conceptualizing Stressors, Stress, and Stress-Related Illnesses.*

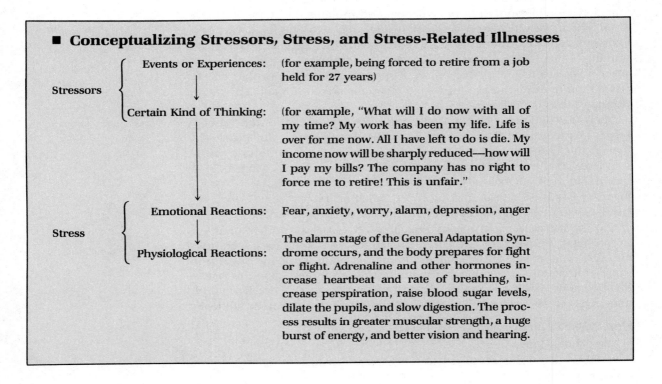

■ **Conceptualizing Stressors, Stress, and Stress-Related Illnesses**

Stressors

Events or Experiences: (for example, being forced to retire from a job held for 27 years)

Certain Kind of Thinking: (for example, "What will I do now with all of my time? My work has been my life. Life is over for me now. All I have left to do is die. My income now will be sharply reduced—how will I pay my bills? The company has no right to force me to retire! This is unfair."

Stress

Emotional Reactions: Fear, anxiety, worry, alarm, depression, anger

Physiological Reactions: The alarm stage of the General Adaptation Syndrome occurs, and the body prepares for fight or flight. Adrenaline and other hormones increase heartbeat and rate of breathing, increase perspiration, raise blood sugar levels, dilate the pupils, and slow digestion. The process results in greater muscular strength, a huge burst of energy, and better vision and hearing.

If the body remains at a high level of stress for a prolonged period, a stress-related disorder is apt to develop.

Stress is heavily dependent on what a person thinks about events. The following example shows how a person's thinking about a positive event can be a source of negative stress.

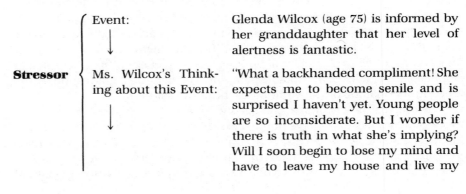

Stressor

Event: Glenda Wilcox (age 75) is informed by her granddaughter that her level of alertness is fantastic.

Ms. Wilcox's Thinking about this Event: "What a backhanded compliment! She expects me to become senile and is surprised I haven't yet. Young people are so inconsiderate. But I wonder if there is truth in what she's implying? Will I soon begin to lose my mind and have to leave my house and live my remaining years in confusion in a nursing home? It seems there are things I'm starting to forget more frequently than I did in the past."

Stress {

Emotion: → Anger, anxiety, worry, alarm

Physiological Reaction: The alarm stage of the GAS is occurring. If sustained and intensive, conditions exist for a stress-related illness to develop.

Certainly not all stress is bad. Life without stress would be boring. Selye (1972, p. 83) indicates stress is often "the spice of life," and that it is impossible to be alive without experiencing stress. Dreaming even produces some stress. Stress at times is often beneficial to us. It stimulates and prepares us to perform a wide variety of tasks. Students, for example, often find they need to feel a moderate level of stress before they can study for an exam—too little stress results in their being unable to concentrate and may even result in their falling asleep, while too high a level of stress results in too much anxiety and interferes with their concentration. High levels of the alarm phase of the GAS are very desirable during emergencies where physical strength is needed—such as in lifting a heavy object which has fallen on someone.

The kind of stress which is harmful has been called *distress* by Selye (1974). Long-term distress generally results in the formation of a stress-related physical illness. Distress occurs when the stressors are prolonged, and a person becomes exhausted.

■ Stress Signals

A number of signals can be used to measure whether we are at a good level of stress, or whether we are at too high a level of stress. You have to use your own judgment based on these signals to determine whether your stress level is too high.

Good Level	Too High
1. *Behaviors*	
Creative, make good decisions	High-pitched nervous laughter
Friendly	Lack of creativity
Generally successful	Poor work quality
Able to listen to others	Overdrink or overeat
Productive—get a lot done	Smoke to excess
Appreciate others, sensitive to others, and recognize contributions of others	Stutter
	Inability to concentrate
Smile, laugh, joke	
	Easily startled by small sounds
	Impatient
	Easily irritated

2. *Feelings*

Feeling of confidence

Calm, relaxed

Feelings of pleasure and enjoyment

Feelings of excitement and exhilaration

3. *Body Signals*

Restful

Absence of aches and pains

Coordinated body reactions

Unaware of body which is functioning smoothly

Good health, absence of stress
related illnesses

Unpleasant to be around

Put others down

Engage in wasted activity and motion

Resentful, bitter, dissatisfied, angry

Timid, tense, anxious, fearful

Paranoid

Weary, depressed, fed up

Feelings of inadequacy or failure

Confused, swamped, overwhelmed

Feelings of powerlessness or helplessness

Loss of appetite, diarrhea, or vomiting

Accident prone

Frequent need to urinate

Trembling, nervous tics

Feelings of dizziness or weakness

Frequent colds and flus

High blood pressure

Tight or tense muscles

Asthma or breathing irregularities

Skin irritations, itches and rashes

Sleep problems

Upset stomach or ulcers

Various aches and pains—muscle aches,
backaches, neck aches, and headaches

Approaches to Stress Management

There are five major categories of approaches to stress management, only three of which are constructive. The three constructive approaches are (1) changing the distressing event; (2) changing one's thinking about the distressing event; and (3) taking one's mind off the distressing event, usually by thinking about something else.

There are also two destructive ways that some people use to relieve stress. One way is by resorting to alcohol or drugs. Perhaps the major reason for abusing alcohol and other drugs is to seek relief from stress and unwanted emotions. Drugs will provide temporary relief, but the next day a person's problems still remain, and there is a serious danger that drug abuse may become a destructive habit. The other destructive way of escaping stress is by suicide, which, sadly, some people turn to. Most of our attention will focus on constructive ways of relieving stress.

Changing a Distressing Event. As indicated earlier, there are an infinite number of distressing events. When distressing events occur it is desirable to confront them directly to try to improve the situation. If someone is grieving from the death of someone close, discussing the grief with others and perhaps seeking professional counseling can be helpful. If an elderly person is concerned about what to do with his time after retiring, the person needs to work on finding meaningful and enjoyable activities to become involved in. If a person is concerned about a deterioration in health, it is desirable to see a physician and receive medical treatment. Many distressing events can be improved by confronting them head on, and taking constructive action to change them.

Changing One's Thinking About a Distressing Event. Some events cannot be changed. For example, Carlton Komarek does not want to retire from a meat packing plant when he reaches age 70 in May, but the company has a rigid rule not to make any exceptions. Since Carlton cannot change the situation, the only constructive remaining alternative is to accept it and find meaningful activities after he retires. It is counterproductive to nag, complain, or get upset about something that cannot be changed. Bullet-biting acceptance of the situation will also improve Carlton's disposition.

One of the structured techniques to change one's thinking about a distressing event is to challenge and change the negative and irrational thinking through doing a Rational Self-Analysis, as described in Chapter 7.

Positive Thinking. When anticipated and unanticipated events occur, we have a choice to either take a positive view or a negative view. If we take a negative view we are apt to experience more stress, and also apt to alienate friends and acquaintances. Here is a summary of some of W. Clement Stone's (1966, pp. 9–10) basic tenets of positive thinking:

> Give a smile to everyone you meet (smile with your eyes)—and you'll smile and receive smiles. . . .
>
> Give honor, credit and applause (the victor's wreath)—you will be honorable and receive credit and applause. . . .
>
> Give time for a worthy cause (with eagerness)—you will be worthy and richly rewarded. . . .
>
> Give hope (the magic ingredient for success)—you will have hope and be made hopeful. . . .
>
> Give cheer (the verbal sunshine)—you'll be cheerful and cheered. . . .
>
> Give good thoughts (nature's character builder)—you will be good and the world will have good thoughts for you. . . .

Some books on positive thinking have become best sellers (Schuller, 1973; Ringer, 1977).

Akin to positive thinking is having a philosophy of life which allows us to take crises in stride, to travel through life at a relaxed pace, to allow us to look at the scenery with enjoyment, to approach work in a relaxed fashion so as to permit greater creativity, to enjoy and use leisure time to develop more fully as a person, and to find enjoyment in each day.

Talking to Others. Every person needs someone to share good times with and to talk about personal difficulties. Sharing concerns with someone helps to vent emotions. Talking a concern through often helps in two ways to reduce stress. It may lead to a new perspective on how to resolve the distressing event, or it may help by changing one's thinking about the distressing event to a more positive and rational attitude. The listener may be a neighbor, friend, member of the clergy, professional counselor, etc.

Closely related to discussing the distressing event with someone is having a social support group. Support groups allow people to share their lives, to have fun with others, to let their hair down, and to be a resource for help when emergencies and crises arise. Possible support groups include friends in a retirement community, one's family, one's coworkers, a church group, a community group, and so on.

Taking One's Mind Off the Distressing Event, Usually by Thinking About Something Else. This category is the third and final constructive approach to reducing stress. There are a variety of ways to stop thinking about a distressing event.

Relaxation Approaches. Deep breathing relaxation, imagery relaxation, progressive muscle relaxation, meditation, and biofeedback are effective techniques in reducing stress and inducing the relaxation response (becoming relaxed). For each of these techniques the relaxation response is facilitated by sitting in a comfortable position, in a quiet place, with closed eyes (Zastrow, 1985).

Deep breathing relaxation helps you to stop thinking about day-to-day concerns and concentrate your thinking on your breathing processes. For 5 to 10 minutes, slowly and gradually inhale deeply and exhale, while telling yourself something like "I am relaxing, breathing smoother. This is soothing, and I'm feeling calmer, renewed and refreshed." Continued practice of this technique will enable a person to become more relaxed whenever in a tense situation—such as prior to giving a speech.

Imagery relaxation involves switching your thinking from your daily concerns to focusing your thinking (for 10 to 15 minutes) on your ideal relaxation place. It might be lying on a beach by a scenic lake in the warm sun. It might be relaxing in warm water while reading a magazine. Savor all the pleasantness, the peacefulness—focus on everything that you find calming, soothing, relaxing. Sense your whole body becoming refreshed, revived, and rejuvenated.

Progressive muscle relaxation is based on the principle that a person cannot be anxious if the muscles are relaxed (Jacobson, 1938). The approach is learned by having a person tighten and then relax a set of muscles. When relaxing the muscles, the person is advised to concentrate on the relaxed feeling while noting that the muscles are becoming less tense. The following excerpt from Watson and Tharp (1973, pp. 182–83) gives a brief description of the initial steps in this procedure:

> Make a fist with your dominant hand (usually right). Make a fist and tense the muscles of your (right) hand and forearm; tense it until it trembles. Feel the muscles pull across your fingers and the lower part of your forearm... Hold this position for 5 to 7 seconds, then ... relax... Just let your hand go. Pay attention to the muscles of your (right) hand and forearm as they relax. Note how those muscles feel as relaxation flows through (20 to 30 seconds).

The procedure of tensing and then relaxing is continued three or four times until the hand and forearm are relaxed. Next, other muscle groups are tensed and relaxed in the same manner, one group at a time. These groups might include: left hand and forearm, right biceps, left biceps, forehead muscles, upper lip and cheek muscles, jaw muscles, chin and throat muscles, chest muscles, abdominal muscles, back muscles between shoulder blades, right and left upper leg muscles, right and left calf muscles, and toes and arches of the feet. With practice, capacity to relax simply by visualizing the muscles is developed.

There are a variety of meditative approaches being used today. (Imagery relaxation is an example of a meditative approach.) Benson (1975) has identified four basic components common to meditative approaches which induce the relaxation response. These components are: (1) Being in a quiet environment free from external distractions, (2) Being in a comfortable position, (3) Having an object to dwell on, such as a word, sound, chant, phrase, imagery of a painting, etc. Since any neutral word or phrase will work, Benson suggests (1975) repeating silently to yourself the word *one*, and (4) Having a passive attitude in which you stop thinking about day-to-day concerns. This last component, Benson asserts, is the key element in inducing the relaxation response.

Biofeedback equipment provides mechanical feedback to a person about her or his level of stress. Such equipment is able to inform people about levels of stress which they are usually unaware of until a markedly high level is reached. For example, a person's hand temperature may vary 10 to 12 degrees in an hour's time, with an increase in temperature indicating an increase in becoming calm and relaxed. With biofeedback equipment, numerous physical functions can be measured and fed back, such as blood pressure, hand temperature, muscle tension, heart beat rate, and brain waves. With biofeedback training a person is first instructed in recognizing high levels of anxiety or tenseness. Then the person is instructed on how to reduce such high levels by either closing the eyes and adopting a passive letting-go attitude or by thinking about something pleasant or calming. Often, relaxation approaches are combined with biofeedback to elicit the relaxation response. Biofeedback equipment provides immediate feedback to a person about the kind of thinking that is effective in reducing stress (Brown, 1977).

Exercise. Stress prepares the body to move and to become involved in large muscle activity (including fight or flight). Since the body automatically prepares us for large muscle activity, it makes sense to exercise. Through exercising, we use up fuel in the blood, reduce blood pressure and heart rate, and reverse the other physiological changes set off during the alarm stage of the general adaptation syndrome. Exercising helps keep us physically fit so we have more physical strength to handle stressful crises. Exercising also reduces stress and relieves tension, partly by switching our thinking from our daily concerns to the exercise we are involved in. For these reasons one needs to have an exercise program. A key to making ourselves exercise daily is selecting a program we enjoy. A wide variety of exercises are available including walking, jogging, isometric exercises, jumping rope, swimming and so on.

Pleasurable Goodies. Pleasurable goodies relieve stress, change our pace, are enjoyable, make us feel good and are in reality personal therapies. What is a goody (pleasurable experience) to one person may not be to another. Common goodies are being hugged, listening to music, going shopping, taking a hot bath, going to a movie, having a glass of wine, taking part in family and religious get togethers, taking a vacation, singing, and so on. Such goodies remind us we have worth and add spice to life.

Personal pleasures can also be used as payoffs to ourselves for jobs well done. Most of us would not seek to short-change others for doing well; we ought not to short-change ourselves. Such rewards make us feel good and are a motivator to move on to new challenges.

Having enjoyable activities beyond work and family responsibilities also are pleasurable goodies which relieve stress. Research (Schafer, 1978) has found that stress reduces stress; that is, an appropriate level of stressful activities in one area helps reduce excessive stress in others. Getting involved in enjoyable outside activities switches our negative thinking from our daily concerns to positive thoughts about the enjoyable activities. Therefore, it is stress reducing to become involved in activities we enjoy. Such activities may include golf, tennis, swimming, scuba diving, taking flying lessons, traveling, and so on.

Summary

Later adulthood begins around age 65. The elderly are an extremely diverse group, spanning an age range of over 30 years. Later adulthood is an age of recompense as it is a time when people reap the consequences of the kind of life they have lived. The process of aging affects different persons at different rates. Nature appears to have a built-in mechanism that promotes aging, but it is not known what this mechanism is.

There are a variety of factors that accelerate the aging process: poor diet, overwork, alcohol or drug abuse, prolonged illnesses, severe disabilities, prolonged stresses, negative thinking, exposure to prolonged heat or cold, and serious emotional problems. Factors that slow down the aging process include a proper diet, skill in relaxing and managing stress, being physically and mentally active, a positive outlook on life, and learning how to control unwanted emotions.

The elderly are much more susceptible to physical illnesses than younger people; yet, a majority of the elderly are reasonably healthy. The two leading causes of death are diseases of the heart and cancer. The chapter ended with a discussion of the effects of stress, and a description of stress management techniques.

Psychological Aspects of Later Adulthood

Mrs. Sandra Lombardino is 69 years old. Except for being overweight and having arthritis, she is in fairly good health. She is personable, well-groomed, kind, and articulate. She retired two years ago as an elementary school teacher; she was well liked by students and fellow staff in her thirty-three years of teaching. She raised four children, all of whom have long since left home and started careers and families of their own.

Mrs. Lombardino would like to use her retirement years to travel and to do volunteer work. She has worked hard for many years and has looked forward to enjoying her retirement.

She is increasingly frustrated because her husband's demands and offensive behavior are destroying her retirement dreams. Her husband, Benedito, has a number of health care needs. Benedito used to be a carpenter, and at one time was a good athlete. But Benedito has been a heavy drinker for over 40 years. When drunk he has been physically and verbally abusive to his wife and to his children. His children left home to escape from him as soon as they were financially self-supporting. The children love their mother, but despise their father.

In many ways Sandra Lombardino has been a martyr. She took a marriage vow to live together for better or worse until death. She has fulfilled that vow, in spite of the urgings of her friends and relatives to seek a divorce. Several years ago Benedito was discovered to have cirrhosis of the liver and had to stop working. He now receives a monthly disability check. Despite his illness, Benedito has continued to drink heavily and has developed high blood pressure and diabetes. He is grossly overweight and is often incontinent. The drinking and illnesses have caused brain deterioration and he now has difficulty walking, talking, and grooming himself, and he frequently hallucinates. His offensive behavior has resulted in a loss of friends. Benedito has been pressured into attending a number of alcoholism treatment programs, including Alcoholics Anonymous, but he has always returned to drinking.

Sandra Lombardino is in a quandry about what she should do. She is angry that she now has to spend most of her waking hours caring for someone who is obnoxious and verbally abusive to her. She resents not being able to travel and do volunteer work. Sometimes she wishes her husband would die, so that she could get on with her life. At other times she feels guilty about wishing her husband would die.

She has contemplated getting a divorce, but such a process would mean

her husband would get half of the property that she has worked so many years to acquire. She also has considered placing Benedito in a nursing home, but she feels an obligation to care for him and realizes that the expenses of a nursing home would deplete her life savings. Mrs. Lombardino feels that the cruelest injustice would be for her to die before her husband, so that she would be robbed of her chances to achieve her retirement dreams.

■ A Perspective

As suggested by the Behavior Dynamics Assessment Model, there are a number of psychological adjustments that people need to make at all ages for their lives to be meaningful and fulfilling. Later adulthood is no exception. This chapter will:

- Describe developmental tasks of old age.
- Present theoretical concepts about developmental tasks in later adulthood.
- Summarize theories of successful aging.
- Discuss the impact of key life events on the elderly.
- Present guidelines for positive psychological preparation for later adulthood.
- Summarize material on grief management and death education.

Developmental Tasks of Old Age

Most of the developmental tasks that the elderly encounter are psychological in nature. We will look at a number of these tasks, using Douglas and Norma Polser as an example.

Retirement and Lower Income

In 1970 Douglas Polzer retired from being a road construction foreman in Dubuque, Iowa. Two years earlier his wife, Norma, had retired from the post office. Retirement brought a number of changes to their lives. For several months after retiring Douglas had difficulty in finding things to do with his time. His work had been the center of his life. He no longer saw much of his former co-workers, and he had practically no hobbies or interests. When he was working, he always had many stories to tell about unusual situations that happened. He no longer had much to talk about. Another problem for the Polzers was that they had a lower standard of living. Their main sources of income were social security benefits and Norma's federal pension.

Living With One's Spouse in Retirement

Prior to retiring Norma and Douglas did not see each other very much. Both worked during the week, and Norma worked on Saturday. Each tended to socialize with their co-workers. Norma and Douglas tended to get on each other's nerves if they were together a lot.

After Douglas retired, both were generally home. Since Norma had always done most of the domestic tasks, she kept busy. Finding things to do was not very difficult for her.

For the first few months after Douglas retired he followed Norma around the house telling her how she should do her work. That didn't go over very well. They got on each other's nerves and had a number of arguments. As time passed, Douglas became more interested in fishing, taking walks, and getting together with his retired friends. Gradually, with Douglas being gone more, the arguments faded.

Affiliating with Individuals of One's Own Age Group or with Associations for the Aged

The Polzers joined the Senior Citizens Leisure Club in Dubuque. Norma participated more frequently than Douglas. The club had a variety of activities: luncheons; speakers, bus tours, painting and craft sessions, bowling, and golf. The club also had a small library.

Maintaining Interest in Friends and Family Ties

Norma and Douglas formed a number of new friendships with members they met in the club. Through conversing with such friends, Norma and Douglas were able to gain new perspectives on the adjustments they had to make.

Most of the Polzers' friends prior to retiring were co-workers. After retirement, they gradually saw less and less of these friends, since their interests were growing in different directions. These former friends still talked a great deal about what was happening at work, and both Norma and Douglas now thought such conversations were boring.

The Polzers usually got together on Sunday with their son, Kirk, and his family who lived in Dubuque. Their daughter, Devi, had left home at age 17 to marry. After three children, she obtained a divorce and was on AFDC for four years until she remarried. She is now living in California and has had two more children. The Polzers seldom see her, but their relationship with her has improved since her adolescent years. Doug and Norma wish they could see Devi and her children more.

Continuing Social and Civic Responsibilities

Douglas has continued to be a volunteer night watchman for the county fair that is held for four days during the summer. Since they retired, Doug and Norma have been more active in attending their church and participating in church activities; Doug has become an elder for the church and Norma has become more active in the ladies aid society.

Coping with Illness and Loss of Spouse and/or Friends

After four years of retirement, life was going fairly smoothly for the Polzers. Then in 1974 Doug had a stroke which left him partly paralyzed. Doug and Norma's lives changed radically. Douglas almost never went outside the house. He became irritable, incontinent, and needed constant attention. Visiting nurse services provided some help, and so did the Polzer's son and daughter-in-law. But the major burden was Norma's. She was forced to drastically reduce her church and club activities. For the next two years she spent most of her time caring for Douglas. He never said "thank you," and he verbally abused her. At times Norma wished he would die. Then in 1976 he did.

Norma's world again changed. For the first time in many years, she was living alone. Douglas' death was very hard for her. She felt guilty since she had wished Douglas would die and believed that this may have magically contributed to his death. Initially, she was lonely. But, as the months began to pass, she gradually started putting her life back together. She became active again in the church and in the senior leisure club. Sharing her grief with other club members helped. As the years passed more of her friends died, and Norma found herself attending more funerals.

Finding Satisfactory Living Arrangements at the Different Stages of Old Age

After Douglas died, Norma was depressed and had less energy. Kirk helped, but he had his own family, career, and home to care for. Norma realized she was slowing down physically. After two years, Kirk began to encourage her to sell the house and move into an apartment complex that was especially built for the elderly. Norma resisted for over a year. Then, in 1979 Norma slipped on a stair and broke her leg. She had to crawl to the telephone. Kirk came and took her to the emergency room where her leg was put in a cast. When she got out of the hospital, Kirk took her to his home. Norma's house was put up for sale.

Having to leave her house was almost as great a loss as when Douglas died. She spent two months with Kirk's family, but she did not get along with Kirk's wife. Each had different ways of doing things and different ideas on how children should be raised. When relationships became severely strained, Norma moved to an apartment for the elderly. The move meant that many cherished possessions had to be discarded. Norma began to realize that if her mental or physical condition deteriorated further, her next move would be to a nursing home; at times she thought she would rather die than enter a nursing home. The move also meant Norma had to establish new relationships; that went smoother than even Norma hoped as she was warmly welcomed.

Adjusting to Changing Physical Strength and Health and Overcoming Bodily Preoccupation

For many years Norma had struggled to get used to gray hairs, wrinkles, and all the other physical changes of aging. Her arthritis often caused swelling and pain in her joints, and she no longer had as much energy and stamina as in the past.

Reappraising Personal Values, Self-Concept, and Personal Worth in Light of New Life Events.

A major adaptation task of the elderly, according to Butler and Lewis (1977), is to conduct an evaluative life review. During this review they reflect on their failures and accomplishments, their disappointments and satisfactions and hopefully come to a reasonably positive view of their life's worth. Failure to arrive at a positive view can result in overt psychopathology.

After Norma became settled in her apartment, she again had a lot of free time. She was now 76 years old, and her health was declining. She spent a lot of time thinking about the past. She had enjoyed the early years of retirement, but she acknowledged that the five years since Douglas' first stroke had been rocky.

Accepting the Prospect of Death

It is now 1985, and Norma has been living in her apartment for six years. Her arthritis is worse, and she has cataracts. But her last six years have been fairly uneventful. Kirk and his family visit almost every Sunday, and she has made a number of friends at her apartment complex. She has attended a number of funerals, and still occasionally mourns the death of Douglas, especially on holidays and on their wedding anniversary. Norma feels her life has been fairly full and meaningful. These assessments have also led her to think about her eventual death. She worries about the pain she may experience and is fearful about slowly deteriorating. To avoid being kept alive after her mental capacities have deteriorated, she has signed a "living will" which declares that if she becomes unconscious for a prolonged period of time she does not want heroic measures to be used to keep her alive. She is fully aware and accepting of the fact that she will die in the not-to-distant future. Since her life has been full and positive, she is prepared for death. Her religion asserts there is a life after death; she is uncertain whether an afterlife exists, but if it does she is hoping to be reunited with Douglas, and to see many of her friends who have died.

Theoretical Concepts About Developmental Tasks in Later Adulthood

In this section we will examine the following theoretical concepts: integrity versus despair, shifting from work-role preoccupation to self-differentiation, shifting from body preoccupation to body transcendence, shifting to self-transcendence, life review, self-esteem, and low status and ageism.

Integrity versus Despair

The final stage of life according to Erickson (1963) involves the psychological crisis of *integrity versus despair*. The attainment of integrity comes only after considerable reflection about the meaning of one's life. Integrity refers to an ability to accept the facts of one's life and to face death without great fear. The elderly who have achieved a sense of integrity view their past in an existential light. They have a feeling of having achieved a respected position during their lifetime and have an inner sense of completion. They accept all of the events that have happened to them, without trying to deny some unpleasant facts or to overemphasize others. Integrity is an integration of one's sense of past history with one's present circumstances, and a feeling of being content with the outcome. In order to experience integrity, the elderly must incorporate a lifelong sequence of failures, conflicts, and disappointments into their self-image. This process is made more difficult by the fact that the role of the elderly is devalued in our society. There are a lot of negative attitudes being expressed in our society which (often erroneously) suggest the elderly are incompetent, dependent, and old-fashioned. The death of close friends and relatives and the gradual deterioration of one's physical health makes it additionally difficult for the elderly to achieve integrity.

The opposite pole of integrity is despair. Despair is characterized by a feeling of regret about one's past and includes a continuous nagging desire to have done things differently. Despair makes an attitude of calm acceptance of death impossible, as those who despair view their life as being incomplete and unfulfilled. They either seek death as a way of ending a miserable existence, or they desperately fear death because it makes any hope of compensating for past failures impossible. Some of the elderly who despair commit suicide (see Figure 12.1).

Buhler conducted a study of the extent to which the elderly achieve integrity. The study found that integrity and despair were largely ideal concepts. Most of the people she studied showed neither of the extremes of integrity or despair. Instead, most of the elderly exhibited a combination of partial fulfillment of a life well lived and of goals met, tempered by many disappointments and culminating in a state of resignation. Buhler's study suggests that while Erickson's concepts of integrity versus despair may have conceptual value in describing the polar extremes of adjusting to later adulthood most of the elderly make an adjustment that falls somewhere between these polar extremes.

Three Key Psychological Adjustments

Peck (1968) suggests there are three primary psychological adjustments that must be made in order to make later adulthood meaningful and grat-

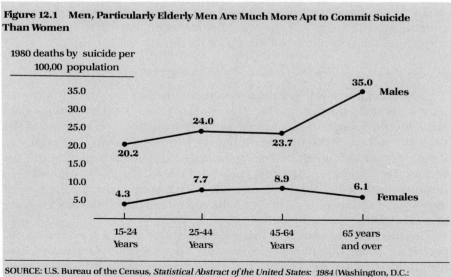

Figure 12.1   Men, Particularly Elderly Men Are Much More Apt to Commit Suicide Than Women

SOURCE: U.S. Bureau of the Census, *Statistical Abstract of the United States: 1984* (Washington, D.C.: U.S. government Printing Office) 1984.

ifying. The first adjustment is shifting from work-role preoccupation to self-differentiation. Since retirement is a crucial shift in one's life, a new role must be acquired. The elderly person has to adjust to the fact that she or he will no longer go to work and needs to find a new identity and new interests. People who are in the process of making this adjustment must spend time assessing their personal worth. (A woman whose major work has been being a wife and a mother faces this adjustment when her children leave home or her husband dies.) A crucial question to resolve at this point is: "Am I a worthwhile person only insofar as I can do a full-time job or can I be worthwhile in other different ways . . . (Peck, 1968, p. 90)?" In making this adjustment, people need to recognize that they are richer and more diverse than the sum of their tasks at work.

A second adjustment is shifting from body preoccupation to body transcendence. Health problems increase for the elderly and energy levels decrease. One's physical appearance also shows signs of aging such as graying and thinning of hair and increasing wrinkles. Many older people, as a result, become preoccupied with their state of health and their appearance. Others, however, transcend these concerns and are able to enjoy life in spite of declining health. Those who make this transcendence have generally learned to define comfort and happiness in terms of satisfying social relationships or creative mental activities.

The third adjustment is shifting to self-transcendence. The inevitability of death must be dealt with. Although death is a depressing prospect, Peck (1968) indicates a positive acceptance can be achieved by shifting one's concerns from "poor me" to "what can I do to make life more meaningful, secure, or happier for those who will survive me?"

Life Review

Most older persons conduct an evaluative life review in which they assess their past life and consider the future in terms of the inevitability of death. Frenkel-Brunswick (1970) refers to this life review as "drawing up the balance sheet of life." The two key elements in this review are concluding that the past was meaningful and learning to accept the inevitability of death. Those who psychologically achieve this are apt to be content and comfortable with their later years; those who conclude that life has been empty and who do not as yet accept death are apt to despair.

Self-Esteem

Self-esteem (the way people regard themselves) is a key factor in overall happiness and adjustment to life. According to Cooley's (1902) "looking glass self-concept," people develop their sense of who they are in terms of the ways that others relate to them. If elderly people are treated by others as if they are old-fashioned, senile, dependent, and incompetent, they are apt to view themselves in the same way. With losses of friends and relatives through death, with the loss of the work role, and with a decline in physical appearance and in physical abilities, the elderly are vulnerable to a lowering of self-esteem.

In order for the elderly to feel good about themselves, they need feedback from others that they are worthwhile, competent, and respected. Like people in all other age groups, the elderly thrive by demonstrating their competence. People tend to feel competent when they exert control over their own lives. The more options they have, the more in control they are, the higher their self-esteem will be. Schwartz (1975) has noted that privacy is a factor in furthering competence and self-esteem. People who have a private place to go can decide when they want to be with other people and when they want to be alone. In a nursing home those who have a private room can retreat to it whenever they find something distasteful, or too noisy, or whenever they want to rest. A private room gives them a way to control their environment.

Low Status and Ageism

The elderly suffer psychologically because our society has generally been unsuccessful in finding something important or satisfying for them to do. Roscow (cited in McTavish, 1971, p. 90) has noted: "It should be clear that the crucial people in the aging problem are not the old, but the younger age groups, for it is the rest of us who determine the status and position of the older person in the social order." The young and the middle aged not only determine the future for the elderly, they also determine their own future as they will someday be elderly.

In most primitive and earlier societies, the elderly were respected and viewed as useful to their people to a much greater degree than is the case in our society. Industrialization and the growth of modern society have robbed the old of their high status in our society. Prior to industrialization, older people were the primary owners of property. Land was the most important source of power; and therefore, the elderly controlled much of the economic and political power. Now, people primarily earn their living in the job market, and the vast majority of the aged own little land and are viewed as having no salable labor. In earlier societies the elderly were also valued because of the knowledge they possessed. Their experiences enabled them to supervise planting and harvesting and to pass on knowledge about hunting, housing, and crafts. The elderly also played key roles in preserving and transmitting the culture. But the rapid advances of science and technology have tended to limit the value of the technological knowledge of the elderly, and books and other memory-storing devices have made old people less valuable as storehouses of culture and records.

Papalia and Olds (1981, p. 536) summarize our society's treatment of the elderly:

> Our society does not allow many of our elderly to experience their last years positively. We don't respect old people for their wisdom and experience, but instead dismiss their ideas as outdated and irrelevant. We don't allow them to use their abilities productively, but force them into retirement when they are still eager and able to work. We don't sustain them financially, but allow them to waste away in a state of poverty that crushes the spirit.

The low status of the elderly is closely associated with ageism. The term *ageism* refers to having negative images of and attitudes toward people simply because they are old. Today, the reaction to the elderly by many people is a negative one. Ageism is similar to sexism or racism as it involves discrimination and prejudice against all members of a particular social category.

The negative stereotypes about the elderly appear to be ingrained in our society. Third graders have been found to have generally negative stereotypes of the elderly—as being very mean or very kind, and as being very lonely, bored and inactive (Hickey, Hickey and Kalish, 1968). Many children's books do not have elderly characters, and those that do usually portray the elderly unfavorably (Flaste, 1977).

The prejudice against the elderly is shown in everyday language by the use of such terms as "old biddy," and "old fogey."

Ageism is an additional burden that the elderly encounter. Some of the elderly, particularly among the young old, are able to refute ageism stereotypes by being productive and physically and mentally active. Unfortunately for others, ageism stereotypes become self-fulfilling prophecies. The elderly are treated as if they are incompetent, dependent, and senile; such treatment lowers their self-esteem, and some end up playing the roles suggested by the stereotypes. As suggested by the Behavior Dynamics Assessment Model, ageism adversely impacts on the elderly and restricts the roles and alternatives available to the elderly.

Theories of Successful Aging

The three theories of how to age successfully include activity theory, disengagement theory, and social reconstruction theory.

Activity Theory

This theory asserts that the more physically and mentally active the elderly are, the more successfully they will age. Components of this theory were discussed at length in Chapter 11. One component of the theory asserts that the sexual response can be maintained in later adulthood by being sexually active. There is considerable evidence that being physically and mentally active will help to maintain the physiological and psychological functions of the elderly.

Disengagement Theory

Cumming and Henry (1961) coined the term *disengagement* to refer to a process whereby people respond to aging by gradually withdrawing from the various roles and social relationships they occupied in middle age. Such disengagement is claimed to be functional for the elderly as they are thought to be gradually losing the energy and vitality to sustain all the roles and social relationships held in younger years.

Disengagement theory refers not only to the elderly withdrawing from society but also to society withdrawing from the elderly, or *societal disengagement* (Atchley, 1983, p. 97). It is claimed it is functional for our society (which values competition, efficiency, and individual achievement) to disengage from the elderly, who have the least physical stamina and the highest death rate. Societal disengagement occurs in a variety of ways: employers may seek to force the elderly to retire, the elderly may not be sought out for leadership positions in organizations, their children may involve them less in making family decisions, and the government may be less responsive in meeting their needs as compared to people who are younger. Societal disengagement is often unintended and unrecognized by employers, younger relatives, and other younger members of society. Disengagement theory also asserts that the elderly welcome this withdrawal and contribute to it.

Disengagement theory has generated much research over the years. There is controversy regarding whether disengagement is functional for the elderly and for our society. Research has found some people undeniably do voluntarily disengage as they grow older. However, critics assert that disengagement is related less to old age itself than to the factors associated with aging, such as retirement, poor health, death of spouse and of close friends, and impoverishment. For example, when people are forced to retire they tend to disengage from co-worker friendships, union activities, professional friendships, and reading in their field. Once retired, they also have less money to spend on entertainment, so disengagement from some activities is forced.

Disengagement is neither universal nor inevitable. Contrary to the theory's predictions, most older persons maintain extensive associations with friends, and active involvement in voluntary organizations (such as church groups and fraternal organizations). Also, some of the elderly, after retiring, develop new interests, expand their circle of friends, join clubs, and do volunteer work. Others rebel against society's stereotypes and refuse to be treated as if they had little to offer to society. Many of these people are marshaling political resources to force society to adapt to their needs and skills.

Disengagement theory at times advocates the exact opposite of activity theory. Activity theory asserts it is beneficial for the elderly to be physically and mentally active, while disengagement theory asserts it is beneficial to withdraw from a variety of activities (many of which provide physical and mental stimulation).

A severe criticism of disengagement theory is that the theory may be used to justify society's failure to help the elderly maintain meaningful roles. It may also be used to justify ageism. Disengagement theory may, at best, be merely a description of the age/youth relationships (and reactions to them) which we should combat as we try to combat ageism.

Social Reconstruction Syndrome Theory

This theory was developed from the *social breakdown syndrome* which was conceptualized by Zusman (1966). Zusman indicated social breakdown occurs for the elderly because of the effects of labeling. The process occurs as follows. Society has unrealistic standards or expectations that all adults should work and be productive; other people label the elderly as being incompetent or lacking in some ways; the elderly accept the label and view themselves in terms of the label; they then learn behavior consistent with the label and downplay their previous skills. As a result, they become more dependent, incompetent, and feel inadequate.

Kuypers and Bengston (1973) assert that this negative interaction between the elderly's environment and self-concept explains many of the problems of aging in our society. To break the vicious cycle of this labeling process, they recommend the *social reconstruction syndrome*, which has three major recommendations. First, our society should liberate the elderly from unrealistic standards and expectations. The belief that self-worth depends on a person's productivity has adverse consequences for the elderly who are retired. Kuypers and Bengston (1973) recommend that society be reeducated to change these unrealistic standards. Fischer (1977, p. 33) specifies the direction such reeducation should take:

> The values of our society rest upon a work ethic—an ethic of doing—that gives highest value to people in the prime of their productive years. We should encourage a plurality of ethics in its place—not merely an ethic of doing, but also an ethic of feeling, an ethic of sharing, an ethic of knowing, an ethic of enduring, and even an ethic of surviving.

The second recommendation of Kuypers and Bengston (1973) is to provide the elderly with the social services they need. Such services include transportation, medical care, housing, help with housekeeping, and programs that provide physical and mental activity.

The third recommendation is to find creative ways to give the elderly more control over their lives. Bengsten (1973, p. 49) for example, recommends that at nursing homes the decision-making bodies should be "exclusively comprised of the elderly themselves. While the nursing and social service staff, for example, might be younger people, they are servants of the elderly board of directors, the elderly committee structure and the elderly administrators."

■ Successful Aging

Leaf (1973) studied three societies where the elderly live much longer (some over 100 years) and remain more vigorous than in most other places around the world. These societies were located in Abkhazia in the southern part of the Soviet Union; the principality of Hunza in Pakistani-controlled Kashmir; and an Andean village in Ecuador.

Leaf (1973) studied the question of why the elderly in these three societies are vigorous, healthy, and live long lives. He found that several aspects of their lives, involving psychological and physical factors, were very different from the lifestyles in our society. The social status of the elderly in these societies is high. They live with members of their family who respect them and who appreciate the useful contributions they make to the family and to the community. In Hunza, 20 elderly men compose a council of elders who meet daily to resolve disputes among citizens.

There is no forced retirement, and the elderly work as long as they are able to. On a daily basis they perform such tasks as doing laundry, feeding poultry, planting and harvesting crops, tending animals, and caring for small children. They have a different outlook toward life and old age. They expect to be healthy and to live a long time and consider the normal life span to be about 100 rather than 70. They view people as being young

for a long time, and believe that youth extends to about 80 years of age.

In all three communities the people eat less than we do. The average American adult consumes about 3,300 calories a day, while people in these three societies consume a low-calorie diet throughout life, usually less than 2,000 calories a day. They eat very few fats of animal origin and few dairy products. Such dietary habits may delay the development of *atherosclerosis* (fatty deposits in the arteries). The elderly Abkhasians drink some vodka and some homemade wine regularly. Almost none of the people studied are obese.

People in all three societies have a high level of physical activity. They walk up and down mountainous terrain and are involved in such physical activities as hunting, farming, and sheep herding which maintains cardiovascular fitness and good muscle tone.

Genetic factors may also be involved in leading to their longevity. People in these societies (just as people who live a long time in our society) generally have parents who lived to advanced ages. It could well be that people who live to advanced ages do not have genes that carry predispositions to disabling or fatal diseases.

The elderly in these societies also have an active interest in the opposite sex. They continue to have sexual intercourse with their partners well into their advancing years.

It is impossible to tell with exactness which (if any) of the above factors are responsible for people in these societies being in good health and living to advanced ages. The study, however, does suggest a number of factors that *may* make old age a good age. Having a life of quality in old age, as these elderly appear to have, is much more important than living to an advanced age.

The Impact of Life Events on the Elderly

Consistent with the behavior dynamics assessment model described in Chapter 1, we will look at a number of life events that impact on life in later adulthood. The events we will examine are marriage, death of spouse, widowhood, never having been married, remarriage, family relationships, and grandparenthood. These events directly affect the behavior of the elderly and often limit the alternatives available to them.

Marriage

Because people are living longer, many marriages are lasting longer as well. Today, fiftieth wedding anniversaries are much more common than they were in the past. But divorces are more common too.

Couples who are still married in their later years are less likely than younger couples to see their marriages as full of problems (Papalia and Olds, 1981, p. 545). There could be a variety of reasons. They may well have worked out their major conflicts. Since divorce is now quite accessible, those marriages that survive many years may be the happier and more conflict-free ones. Or, the difference may be one of development; as people learn to cope with crises and conflicts.

The level of happiness and satisfaction in the marriages of elderly people appear to be higher than that of younger couples. Stennett, Carter and Montgomery (1972) studied 408 married elderly men and women. Nearly 95 percent rated their marriages as very happy or happy. More than half stated that the happiest time of married life was the present and that their marriages had become better over the years. The researchers also examined what makes a marriage happy. The respondents continued to be romantics as they stated being in love was a key factor in achieving a successful marriage. Also important were respect for each other and the sharing of common interests. The most rewarding aspects were companionship and being able to express their true feelings to each other. Most reported their marriages were now trouble free. Those who did have conflicts stated the sources were differences in interests, in values, and in philosophies of life.

Married elderly people are happier than the unmarried and particularly happier than the widowed and the divorced (Lee, 1978). Lee (1978) also found that the extent to which the elderly are satisfied with their marriage influences their overall sense of well-being, particularly women. Health and satisfaction with one's standard of living were also found to positively correlate with overall sense of well-being. Chronic illness has a negative effect on the morale of couples, even when only one is ill. The healthy partner may become depressed, angry, or frustrated with the responsibilities of taking care of the ill spouse and having to do most of the tasks to maintain the household. Ill health of one spouse may also reduce the opportunities for enjoyable activities together, may drain financial resources, and may reduce sexual involvement.

Clark and Anderson (1967) found that happily married elderly couples lived less by rigidly defined sex roles than unhappily married elderly couples. Happily married elderly couples were found to be more flexible about who does what in the marriage and tended to ignore sex-role expectations as far as carrying out household and domestic responsibilities.

Death of Spouse

The death of a spouse is traumatic at any age. It is more apt to occur in later adulthood as death rates are considerably higher in this age group. The surviving spouse in later adulthood faces a variety of emotional and practical problems. The survivor has lost a lover, a companion, a good friend, and a confidant. The more intertwined their life has become, the greater the loss is apt to be felt. In most marriages household maintenance responsibilities gradually become divided. The survivor now finds he or she has a lot more tasks to do, some of which were never learned.

One's social life changes also. At first relatives, friends, and neighbors will usually rally to give the survivor sympathy and emotional support. But, gradually they will return to their own lives, leaving the widower or widow to form a new life. Friends and relatives are apt to also grow tired of listening to the survivor talk about his or her loss and grief and withdraw emotional and practical help. The survivor may have to make such decisions as moving to a smaller place that is easier to maintain and facing the problem of going to social events alone. Some survivors withdraw because they feel like a "fifth wheel" especially with other couples.

Partly because of the greater number of elderly single women, widowers are more likely to form new relationships and to remarry. Widows are more likely to establish relationships with other widows, but have a harder time finding available men.

Widowhood

Less than half of all women over 65 have husbands, while 8 out of 10 elderly men are married (National Council on Aging, 1978). This difference is largely due to the tendency of men to marry younger women and to women having a greater life expectancy. The effects of widowhood are poignantly summarized by a 75-year-old widow, "As long as you have your husband, you're not old. But once you lose him, old age sets in fast." (Quoted in Papalia and Olds, 1981).

Lopata (1973) surveyed the experiences, attitudes, and lifestyles of 301 widows who were 50 years of age and over. The respondents stated that loneliness was the worst problem of widowhood. They missed their husband's companionship and love.

Widowhood affects different people in diverse ways. Interestingly, women who had serious marital conflicts had more trouble adjusting to the death of their husband. Perhaps they felt guilty for things they did or said, or felt guilty for things they failed to say or do.

The study also found that the more a woman has been dependent on her husband for her identity, the more deeply she feels his absence. This finding suggests that women should develop a strong sense of their own identity and assume a large role in family decision-making activities, including the financial areas in order to prepare themselves for the probability of eventual widowhood.

A majority of the respondents felt their life had changed significantly in one or more ways as a result of widowhood; most of these respondents stated the change was positive. Even many of the women who had been happily married came to consider themselves more competent and independent following the death of their spouse. Women who reported there were no significant changes after the death of their spouse tended to be more socially isolated and to have less education than women who reported changes.

Never Married

Gubrium (1975) surveyed 22 people who had never been married and who ranged in age between 60 and 94 years. They expressed fewer feelings of loneliness than those who had once been married. Perhaps they had made an adjustment to being single a long time ago (or even preferred to be single) and, therefore, were not as bothered by being alone as those who were once married. These single people also seemed to be more independent, had fewer social relationships, were generally satisfied with their lives, and seemed to be less concerned about their age than most elderly persons. Gubrium (1975) suggests they may have a unique social personality in which they generally prefer to be by themselves.

Remarriage

Our society has generally opposed the elderly dating and remarrying. We think nothing of younger people hugging and kissing each other, but such behavior by an elderly couple is met with stares and often crude remarks. Children of the elderly are sometimes opposed to their mother or father remarrying. (They may be concerned about inheritance, or they may believe starting a new relationship is being unfaithful to or dishonoring the parent who has died.) Yet, remarriage in later adulthood is becoming an increasing phenomenon (U.S. Census Bureau, 1984, p. 84). More than 35,000 couples are getting married annually in which at least one member is over age 65.

Vinick (1968) interviewed 24 elderly couples who had remarried after both partners were over 60 years of age. Most of the respondents had been widowed rather than divorced. Most had either known each other during their previous marriages or were introduced to each other by a friend or relative. The male usually took the initiative in beginning the relationship. More than half married within the year in which they began dating.

The couples remarried for companionship. The female respondents also tended to mention emotional feelings toward the man they married and noted certain positive personal qualities. Most of these couples were supported in their decision to marry by their adult children. Some reported receiving negative feedback from a few friends, partly because the friends felt either envious or abandoned.

Almost all these spouses reported being very happily married. A typical response was "We're like a couple of kids. We fool around—have fun. We go to dances and socialize a lot with our families. We enjoy life together. When you're with someone, you're happy." (Vinick, 1978, p. 362). These spouses tended to have a "live and let live" attitude toward each other and to have less conflict.

For a variety of reasons it appears our society should change its negative attitudes about remarriage in later adulthood. Married elderly are happier than those who are widowed or divorced. They have companionship, can share interests, provide emotional support, and can assist each other in household maintenance tasks. It is also cost effective for society to support the single elderly in remarrying as they are then less likely to need financial assistance and social services and are less likely to be placed in nursing homes (Papalia and Olds, 1981, p. 548).

In regards to love and remarriage in later adulthood, Henri Rousseau, age 65, noted:

> One can still be in love at any age without being ridiculous. It's not the same sort of love that young people go in for, but must one resign oneself to living alone just because one's old? It's dreadful going back to lonely lodgings. It's at my age that one most needs one's heart warmed up again.... It's not right to laugh at old people who get married again; you need the company of someone you love (Quoted in Papalia and Olds, 1981, p. 548).

Family Relationships

There is a popular belief that the elderly have disengaged somewhat from their adult children and their grandchildren. There is also apt to be a generation gap (conflict in values) between the elderly and their younger family members. These beliefs suggest the elderly may have strained and somewhat unfavorable family relationships.

A study by Seelbach and Hansen (1980), however, suggests the elderly person's family relationships are generally quite positive. These researchers asked 367 elderly people how satisfied they are with various aspects of family relations. (About 40 percent of the respondents were institutionalized, primarily in nursing homes.) Eighty-eight percent of the respondents stated they were perfectly satisfied with the treatment they received from their families. Those who were over age 80 were more satisfied than the "young-old" (age 65 to 80 in this study). Eighty-seven percent said they were now receiving as much love and affection from their families as they ever had. Fewer than one in three wished their families would pay more attention to them. Such positive replies were surprising; most of the institutionalized elderly did *not* appear estranged from their families, even though their families were involved in placing them in a nursing home. The results suggest family relationships with the elderly are substantially better than suggested by popular beliefs.

In most instances, the elderly and their adult children do not live together for a variety of reasons. Many people live in small quarters that makes it inconvenient to house another person. The elderly are reluctant to move in as they may fear they will have little privacy. They may fear there will be somebody else's rules to follow and it may limit who they have over to visit. They may resent having to account to their children for how they spend their time. They may fear their children may put pressure on them to make lifestyle changes, such as giving up smoking, changing their eating habits, and reducing the intake of alcoholic beverages. They may also fear inconveniencing or becoming a burden to their children's families. And, many simply do not want to leave their own home (castle) where they feel comfortable and have pleasant memories.

Although most of the elderly do not live with their children, they tend to live close to them and to see them frequently. A study reported by Rabushk and Jacobs (1980) found that 8 out of 10 elderly persons had seen at least one of their children during the past week.

Most of the elderly do not want to live with their children. Of the few who do, most are female and widowed (Papalia and Olds, 1981, p. 553). Lopata (1973) in a survey of widows who did not live with their children found that these respondents felt it would be difficult to live with their married children's families. They felt they would have trouble remaining silent about mistakes they saw their children making in such areas as handling finances, raising children, and getting along in their marriages. They felt the advice they would be compelled to give would be unwelcomed.

Our society has the exact opposite views about the contributions of the elderly as held by most primitive societies. In primitive societies the advice and knowledge of the elderly are actively sought, and the elderly usually live with their children and receive needed care. In our society the role of adult children in caring for their aged parents is confused. Middle age adults tend to feel their first priorities are to meet their needs and the needs of their children. The fact that many adults would rather see their parents cared for in a nursing home than living with them suggests adults do not feel as great an obligation to their parents as do members of primitive societies. The question of whether to place one's partly incapacitated elderly parent in a nursing home or to provide care in one's own home is a question that many middle age adults struggle with.

Most adult children help their parents in many ways. Hill (1965) found that grandparents receive substantial help from both their children and their adult grandchildren in such areas as household tasks, emotional support, and assistance during periods of illness. The grandparents in this study were more apt to receive help than to give it.

Help often goes in both directions. Grandparents may care for young grandchildren when both parents work or when the parents go out for an evening. Grandparents and parents may jointly work together helping each other around their homes. Grandparents may open their home to a son or daughter who is divorced or separated or who is temporarily unemployed.

Parent Abuse

An increasing number of incidents of elderly parents being abused by their children are being reported to adult protective service units in social service agencies. Although the public is virtually unaware of parent abuse, there is an estimated 1 million or more elderly people who are abused by their adult children (Koch and Koch, 1980, p. 14). One example follows:

In Chicago, a 19-year-old woman confessed to torturing her 81-year-old father and chaining him to a toilet for seven days. She also hit him with a hammer when he was asleep: "I worked him over real good with it. Then after I made him weak enough, I chained his legs together. After that, I left him and rested. I watched TV for a while" (Koch and Koch, 1980, p. 14).

Koch and Koch (1980, p. 14) report that the following four types of parent abuse are the most prevalent, as reported to adult protective services.

- Physical abuse (three-fourths of the cases) which included direct beating and the withholding of personal care, food, medicine, and necessary supervision.
- Psychological abuse (almost half of the cases) involving verbal assaults and threats provoking fear.
- Material abuse or theft of money or personal property.
- Violation of rights (nearly all of the cases) such as forcing a parent out of his or her own dwelling, usually into a nursing home.

Adult children may abuse their parents for a variety of reasons. They may be responding to the stress of their own personal problems or to the stress of time, energy and finances in caring for another person. They may be paying back their parent for having been abusive to them when they were younger. They may be upset with their elderly parent's emotional reactions, physical impairments, lifestyle, or personal habits such as excessive drinking. They may be intentionally abusing the parent to force him or her to move out of their home. When the elderly person is living with the abuser, finding alternative living arrangements is often necessary.

Grandparenthood

Neugarten and Weinstein (1964) identified five major styles of grandparenting in our society. The *fun seeker* is a playmate to the grandchildren in a mutual relationship that both enjoy. The *distant figure* has periodic contact with the grandchildren, generally on birthdays and holidays, but is quite uninvolved with their lives. The *surrogate parent* assumes considerable caretaking responsibilities, usually because the grandchildren's parents are working, or because the mother is single and working. The *formal figure* leaves all child-rearing responsibilities to the parents and limits his or her involvement with the grandchildren to providing special treats and occasional babysitting. The *reservoir of family wisdom* takes on an authoritarian role and dispenses special resources and skills.

In a study of 70 sets of grandparents Neugarten and Weinstein (1964) found that half the grandparents were either distant figures or fun seekers. Grandparents are not necessarily elderly adults; some are as young as 35–40 years. In Neugarten and Weinstein's (1964) study those grandparents over age 65 were more apt to be formal figures. Perhaps as people become older they may be less interested in playing with young children and also less interested in assuming parenting responsibilities.

Kahana and Kahana (1970) asked children who ranged in age from 4 to 12 a variety of questions about relationships with their grandparents. These children generally felt closest to the maternal grandparents, with the favorite grandparent usually being the mother's mother. The youngest children preferred the formal figures who gave them treats, food, love and presents. The 8- and 9-year-olds preferred the fun seekers, and the oldest children preferred the formal figures. Kahana and Kahana (1970, p. 99) conclude, "It is possible that different styles of grandparenthood fit in best with the child's needs at different stages in his development." Kahana and Coe (1969) found that grandparents feel increasingly distant from their grandchildren as the children become older.

Because the elderly are living longer, four and even five generational families are becoming more common. Future research will need to focus on the relationships that develop.

Guidelines for Positive Psychological Preparation for Later Adulthood

Growing old is a lifelong process. Becoming 65 does not destroy the continuities between what a person has been, presently is, and will be. Recognition of this fact should lessen the fear of growing old. For those who are financially sound, in good health, and who have prepared thoughtfully, later adulthood can be a period, if not of luxury, then at least of reasonable pleasure and comfort.

Some may be able to start small home businesses based on their hobbies or become involved in meaningful activities with churches and other organizations. Others may relax while fishing and/or slowly traveling around the country. Still others may continue such interests as woodworking, reading, needlework, painting, weaving, and photography.

Our lives largely depend on our goals and our efforts to achieve these goals. How we live prior to retiring will largely determine whether old age will be a nightmare or whether it will be gratifying and fulfilling. The importance of being physically and mentally active throughout life was discussed at length in Chapter 11.

Close Personal Relationships

Close relationships with others is important throughout life. The elderly who have close friends are more satisfied with life (Lemon, Bengston, and Peterson, 1972). Practically everyone needs a confidant, a person to confide one's private thoughts and feelings. The elderly who have a confidant are better able to handle the trials and tribulations of aging (Lowenthal and Haven, 1968). Through sharing their deepest concerns with a confidant, people are able to ventilate their feelings and also talk through their problems so that they are often better able to arrive at some strategies for handling such problems.

Lowenthal and Haven (1968) found in a study of the elderly that those who are married are more likely than the widowed to have confidants; the widowed were more likely to have confidants than single people. For those who are married, the spouse is apt to be the confidant, especially for the men. The wives sometimes had other confidants, such as a child, a relative, or a friend. Vinick (1978) also found that elderly women were more apt than elderly men to have close friendships with children, other relatives, and with other people.

Finances

In a study of elderly adults Markides and Martin (1979) found that health and income are the two factors most closely related to life satisfaction in later adulthood. When people feel good and have money, they can be more active. These researchers found those who are active—who go out to eat,

There are several different styles of grandparenting. This seventy-two-year-old grandfather is a surrogate parent. Because his granddaughter's parents both work, he fills in as her prime caretaker after school. Some grandparents are "fun seekers," and like to be their grandchildren's playmates. Others are "distant figures," quite uninvolved in their grandchildren's lives. Still others are either authoritarian or prefer to leave all child-rearing responsibilities to the children's parents. (Courtesy of United Way of America)

It is not easy for the elderly to maintain a high sense of self-esteem. This is the time when their close friends and relatives die, their work roles often end, and their physical appearance and abilities decline. Yet the happy, elderly women pictured take pride in themselves and their accomplishments. Like all elderly people, they react to the way they are treated by those around them. Regarded as vital, independent, and competent, that's exactly the way they act. (Courtesy of United Way of America)

This elderly couple, both recently retired, are enjoying sights seen from a tour bus. For financially secure adults in good health, entering late adulthood is a satisfying and often exciting experience. They are frequently on the go, eating out, visiting museums, attending meetings, or going to picnics and religious services. Their lives are much more satisfying than those of other elderly couples who must, or choose to, stay at home. (Courtesy of United Way of America)

According to the "activity theory" of aging, the more physically and mentally active the elderly remain, the more successfully they will age. The woman in this photograph seems to agree. The "disengagement theory" takes an opposite view, holding that the elderly will age better if they disengage themselves from former roles and activities, slow down, and adapt to more age-appropriate skills. What is the third theory on successful aging? (Karen Kirst-Ashman)

go to meetings or museums, go to church, go on picnics or travel—are happier than those who tend to stay at home.

Saving money for later years is important and so is learning to manage or budget money wisely. Two savings programs that are encouraged by the federal government are IRA (Individual Retirement Account) programs for wage and salary earners and Keogh plans for self-employed individuals.

Interests and Hobbies

Psychologically, people who are traumatized most by retirement are those whose self-image and life interests center around their work. People who have meaningful hobbies and interests look forward to retirement in order to have sufficient time for their hobbies and interests.

Self-Identity

People who are comfortable and realistic about who they are and what they want out of life are better prepared to deal with stresses and crises that arise.

Looking Toward the Future

A person who dwells in the past or rests on past achievements is apt to find the older years depressing. On the other hand, a person who looks to the future generally has interests that are alive and growing and is thereby able to find new challenges and new satisfactions in later years. Looking toward the future involves planning for retirement, including deciding where you would like to live, in what type of housing and community, and what you look forward to doing with your free time.

Coping With Crises

If a person learns to cope effectively with crises in younger years, these coping skills will remain when a person is older. Effective coping is learning to approach problems realistically and constructively.

Reactions to Death in Our Society

People in primitive societies handle death better than we do. They are more apt to view death as a natural occurrence, partly because they have a shorter life expectancy. They also frequently see friends and relatives die. Because they view death as a natural occurrence they are better prepared to handle the death of loved ones.

In our society we tend to shy away from thinking about death. The terminally ill generally die in institutions (hospitals and nursing homes) away from our homes. Therefore, we are seldom exposed to people dying. Many people in our society seek to avoid thinking about death. They avoid going to funerals and avoid conversations about death. Many people live as if they believe they will live indefinitely.

In a very real sense we are all terminal from birth. We need to become comfortable with our own eventual death. If we do that, we will be better prepared for the deaths of close friends and relatives. We will also then be better prepared to relate to the terminally ill and better able to help survivors who have experienced the death of a close friend or relative.

Funerals are needed for survivors. Funerals help initiate the grieving process so people can work through their grief. (If a close survivor delays in going through the grieving process, the eventual grief may be intensified.) Funerals also serve a function of demonstrating that the person is dead. If survivors do not see the dead body there is a very real danger that some survivors may mystically believe the person is still alive. For example, John F. Kennedy was assassinated in the early 1960s and had a closed casket funeral. Because the body was not shown, rumors abounded for many years that he was still alive.

Sudden deaths of young people are more difficult to cope with for three reasons. First, we do not have time to prepare for the death. Second, we feel the loss as being more severe because we feel the person is missing out on many of the good things in life. Third, we do not have the opportunity to obtain "closure" to the relationship; we may feel we did not have the opportunity to tell the person how we felt about him or her or we may feel we did not get the opportunity to resolve interpersonal conflicts. (Because the grieving process is intensified when closure does not occur, it is advisable to actively work towards closure in the relationships we have with others.)

Children should not be sheltered from death. Children should be taken to funerals of relatives and friends, and their questions answered honestly. It is a mistake to say, "Grandmother has gone on a trip and won't be back." The child will wonder if others who are close will also go on a trip and won't be back; or, the child may be confused about why grandmother won't return from the trip. It is much better to explain to children that death is a natural process of life. It is desirable to state that death is unlikely to occur until a person is elderly, but that there are exceptions—as from an automobile accident. Parents who take their children to funerals almost always find the children handle the funeral better than expected. Funerals help children learn that death is a natural process of life.

Grief counselors worry about survivors who seek to appear strong at funerals and who try to not appear emotionally upset by the death of a close friend or relative. Usually they are seeking to avoid dealing with their loss, and there is a danger when they start grieving they will experience intense grief—partly because they will feel guilty about denying they are hurting, and partly because they will feel guilty that they deemphasized the importance of the person who died.

Many health professionals find death difficult to handle. Health professionals are committed to recovery, to healing. When someone is found to have a terminal illness, health professionals are apt to experience a sense of failure. In some cases they experience guilt that they cannot do more, or that they might have made a mistake that contributed to a terminal illness. Therefore, do not be too surprised if you find that some health professionals do not know what to say or do when confronted by terminal illness.

The Grieving Process

Nearly all of us are currently grieving about some loss that we have had. It might be the end of a romantic relationship, or moving away from friends and parents, or the death of a pet, or failing to get a grade we wanted, or the death of someone.

It is a mistake to believe that grieving over a loss should end in a set amount of time. The normal grieving process is often the life span of the griever. When we first become aware of a loss of very high value, we are apt to grieve intensively—by crying or by being depressed. Gradually we will have hours, then days, then weeks, then months where we will not think about the loss and will not grieve. However, there will always be something that reminds us of the loss (such as anniversaries), and we will again grieve. The intense grieving periods will, however, gradually become shorter in duration, occur less frequently, and gradually decrease in intensity.

Two models of the grieving process will be presented: the Kübler-Ross (1969) model and the Westberg (1962) model.

Kübler-Ross Model

Stage one. Denial. During this stage we tell ourselves "No, this can't be." "There must be a mistake." "This just isn't happening." Denial is often functional as it helps cushion the impact of the loss.

Stage two. Rage and anger. During this stage we tell ourselves "Why me?" "This just isn't fair." For example, terminally ill patients resent the fact that they will soon die, while other people remain healthy and alive. During this stage God is sometimes a target of the anger. The terminally ill, for example, blame God as unfairly imposing a death sentence.

Stage three. Bargaining. During this stage people with a loss attempt to strike bargains to seek to regain all or part of the loss. For example, the terminally ill may seek to bargain with God for more time. They promise to do something worthwhile or to be good in exchange for another month or year of life. Doctor Kübler-Ross indicates even agnostics and atheists sometimes attempt to bargain with God during this stage.

Stage four. Depression. During this stage those having a loss tell themselves, "The loss is true, and it's really sad. This is awful."

Stage five. Acceptance. During this stage the person fully acknowledges the loss. The terminally ill tell themselves, "I will soon pass on, and it's all right." Those who are not terminally ill accept the loss, and begin working on alternatives to cope with the loss, and to minimize the loss.

The Westberg (1962) Model

Shock and Denial. Many people when informed of a tragic loss are so numb and in such a state of shock that they are practically devoid of feelings. It could well be that when emotional pain is unusually intense that the system temporarily "blows out" so that the person hardly feels anything, and the person then acts as if nothing has happened. Denial is a way of avoiding the impact of a tragic loss.

Emotions Erupt. As the realization of the loss becomes evident, the person expresses the pain by crying, screaming, or sighing.

Anger. At some point a person usually experiences anger. The anger may be directed at God for causing the loss. The anger may be partly due to the unfairness of the loss. If the loss involves the death of a loved one, there is often anger at the dead person for "desertion."

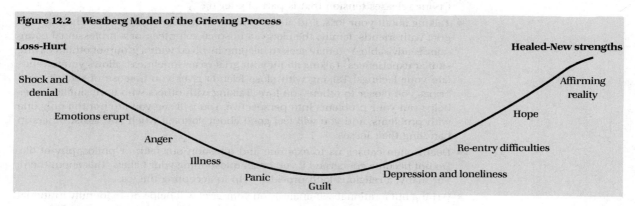

Figure 12.2   Westberg Model of the Grieving Process

Illness. Since grief is stress-producing, stress-related illnesses are apt to develop, such as colds, flus, an ulcer, tension headaches, diarrhea, rashes, insomnia, and so on.

Panic. Because the grieving person realizes he or she does not feel like the "old self," the person may panic and worry about going insane. Nightmares, unwanted emotions that appear uncontrollable, and physical reactions contribute to the panic.

Guilt. The grieving person may blame himself or herself for having done something that contributed to the loss or feel guilty for not doing something which might have prevented the loss.

Depression and Loneliness. At times the grieving person is apt to feel very sad about the loss and also has feelings of isolation and loneliness. The grieving person may withdraw from others who are viewed as not being supportive or understanding.

Reentry Difficulties. At this point the grieving person makes efforts to put his or her life back together. Reentry problems are apt to arise: the person may resist letting go of attachments to the past, and loyalties to memories may hamper pursuing new interests and activities.

Hope. Gradually hope of putting one's life back together returns and begins to grow.

Affirming Reality. The grieving person puts his or her life back together again, and the old feeling of having control of one's life returns. The reconstructed life is not the same as the old, and memories of the loss remain. However, the reconstructed life is satisfactory. The grieving person resolves that life will go on.

For both of these models Kübler-Ross and Westberg note the following. Some people remain grieving and never do reach the final stage (the acceptance stage in the Kübler-Ross model and the affirming reality stage in the Westberg model). Kübler-Ross and Westberg also caution it is a mistake to rigidly believe everyone will progress through these stages as diagrammed. There is often considerable movement back and forth in these stages. For example, in the Kübler-Ross model a person may go from denial to depression, to anger and rage, back to denial, then to bargaining, then to depression, back to anger and rage, and so on.

How to Cope with Grief. The following suggestions are given to help those who are grieving.

- Crying is an acceptable and valuable expression of grief. Cry as you feel the need. Crying releases tension that is part of grieving.

- Talking about your loss, and about your plans, is very constructive. Sharing your grief with friends, family, the clergy, a hospice volunteer, or a professional counselor is advisable. You may seek to become involved with a group of others having similar experiences. Talking about your grief eases loneliness, allows you to ventilate your feelings. Talking with close friends gives you a sense of security and brings you closer to others you love. Talking with others who have similar losses helps put your problems into perspective. You will see you are not the only one with problems, and you will feel good about yourself when you assist others in handling their losses.

- Death often causes us to examine and question our faith or philosophy of life. Do not become concerned if you begin questioning your beliefs. Talk about them. For many, a religious faith provides help in accepting the loss.

- Writing out a rational self-analysis on your grief will help you to identify irrational thinking that is contributing to your grief (see Chapter 7). Once your irrational thinking is identified, you can relieve much of your grief through rational challenges to your irrational thinking.

- Try not to dwell on how unhappy you feel. Become involved and active in life around you. Do not waste your time and energy on self-pity.

- Seek to accept the inevitability of death, yours and others'.

- If the loss is the death of a loved one, holidays and the anniversaries of your loved one's birth and death can be stressful. Seek to spend these days with family and friends who will give you support.

- You may feel that you have nothing to live for and may even think about suicide. Understand that many people who encounter severe losses feel this way. Seek to find assurance in the fact that a sense of purpose and meaning will return.

- Intense grief is very stressful. Stress is a factor that leads to a variety of illnesses, such as headaches, colitis, ulcers, colds, and flus. If you become ill, seek a physician's help, and tell the physician you believe your illness may be related to grief you are experiencing.

- Intense grief may also lead to sleeplessness, sexual difficulties, loss of appetite, or overeating. If a loved one has died, do not be surprised if you dream the person is still alive. You may find you have little energy and cannot concentrate. All of these reactions are "normal." Do not become worried that you are going crazy or losing your mind. Seek to take a positive view. Seek to eat a balanced diet, to get ample rest, and to exercise moderately. Every person's grief is individual—if you are experiencing unusual physical reactions (such as nightmares) try not to become overly alarmed.

- Medication should be taken sparingly and only under the supervision of a physician. Avoid trying to relieve your grief with alcohol or other drugs. Many drugs are addictive and may stop or delay the necessary grieving process.

- Recognize that guilt, real or imagined, is a normal part of grief. Survivors often feel guilty about things they said or did, or feel guilty about things they think they should have said or done. If you are experiencing intense guilt, it is helpful to share it with friends or with a professional counselor. It might also be helpful to write a rational self-analysis of the guilt. Learn to forgive yourself. All humans make mistakes. If you didn't make mistakes you wouldn't be human.

- You may find that friends and relatives appear to be shunning you. If this is happening they probably are uncomfortable around you as they do not know what to say or do. Take the initiative and talk with them about your loss. Inform them about ways in which you would like them to be supportive of you.

- If possible, put off making major decisions (changing jobs, moving, etc.) until you become more emotionally relaxed. When you're highly emotional, you're more apt to make undesirable decisions.

How to Relate to a Dying Person

First, you need to accept your own eventual death, and view death as a normal process of life. If you cannot accept your own death, you will probably be uptight about talking to someone who is terminally ill, and will not be able to discuss the concerns that the dying person has in an understanding and positive way.

Second, convey verbally and with body language that you are willing to talk about any concerns that the other person has. Touching or hugging the dying person is very helpful. (Remember the person has a right not to talk about concerns if he or she chooses). What you want to seek to convey is that you are emotionally ready and supportive, that you care, and that you are available.

Third, answer questions as honestly as you can. If you do not know an answer, seek out a physician who will accurately provide the requested information. Evasion or ambiguity in response to a dying person's questions only increases his or her concerns. If there is a chance for recovery, this should be mentioned. Even a small margin of hope can be a comfort. The chances for recovery, however, should not be exaggerated.

Fourth, a dying person should be allowed to accept the reality of the situation at his or her own pace. Relevant information should not be volunteered nor should it be withheld. People who have a terminal illness have a right to have access to all the relevant information.

Fifth, if people around the dying person are able to accept the death, it helps the dying person accept the death. Therefore, it is therapeutic to help close family and friends of the dying person accept the death. Remember, they may well have a number of concerns they want to share and may need help with.

Sixth, if you do have trouble in talking about certain subjects involving death, inform the dying person of your limitations. This takes the guesswork out of the relationship.

Seventh, the religious or philosophical viewpoint of the dying person should be respected. Your own personal views should not be pressed.

How to Relate to Survivors

These suggestions are similar to those given to relating to a dying person. It is very helpful to become accepting of your own death. If you are comfortable about your own death, you will be better able to calmly listen to the concerns being expressed by survivors.

It is helpful to initiate the first encounter with a survivor by saying something like "I'm sorry," and then touching or hugging the person. Then convey that if he or she wants to talk or needs help, you're available. Take your lead from what the survivor expresses. You should seek to convey that you care, that you share his or her loss and that you're available if he or she wants to talk.

It is helpful to use active listening with both survivors and persons who are terminally ill. In using active listening, the receiver of a message feeds back only what he or she feels the sender's message meant. In using this approach, the receiver does *not* send a message of his or her own—such as a question, giving advice, personal feelings, or an opinion (Gordon, 1970).

Continue to visit the survivors, if they show interest in such visits. It is also helpful to express your caring and support through a card, a little gift, or a covered dish. If a survivor is unable to resume the normal functions of living, or remains deeply depressed, it is advisable to suggest seeking professional help. Joining a survivor's self-help group is another possible suggestion.

The religious or philosophical viewpoint of survivors should be respected. You should not seek to press your views upon the survivors.

How to Become Comfortable with Your Own Eventual Death

Perhaps the main reason people are uncomfortable about death is that in our culture we are socialized to avoid seeing death as a natural process of life. We would be more comfortable with our own death if we would more openly talk about it and actively seek answers to questions and concerns that we have. Comfort with our own death helps us to relate to and understand those who are dying in a more supportive manner. If you are uncomfortable about death, including your own eventual death, there are a number of suggestions for things you can do to become more comfortable.

Identify what your concerns are and then seek answers to these concerns. A number of excellent books provide information on a wide range of subjects involving death and dying. Many colleges, universities, and organizations provide workshops and courses on death and dying. If you have intense fears related to death and dying, you may consider talking to authorities in the field, such as professional counselors or to clergy with experience and training in grief counseling.

Taboos against talking about death and dying need to be broken in our society. You may find that tactfully initiating discussions about death and dying with friends and relatives will be helpful to you, and to people close to you.

It is probably accurate that we will never become fully accepting of our own death, but we can learn a lot more about the subject and obtain answers to many of the questions and concerns we have. In talking about death it is advisable to avoid using euphemisms such as "passed on," "gone to heaven," and "taken by the Lord." It is much better to be accurate and say the person has died. Using euphemisms gives an unrealistic impression of death and is part of the avoidance approach to facing death. Fortunately, an open communications approach about death is emerging in our society.

There are a number of additional ways to become more informed about death and dying: attending funerals, watching quality films and TV programs that cover aspects of dying, providing support to friends or relatives who are terminally ill, being supportive to survivors, talking to people who do grief counseling to learn about their approach, keeping a journal of your thoughts and concerns related to death and dying, and planning the details of your funeral. The following questions will help to assess attitudes toward grief, death, and dying.

■ Questions About Grief, Death, and Dying

1. Which of the following describe your present conception of death:
   a. Cessation of all mental and physical activity
   b. Death as sleep
   c. Heaven-and-hell concept
   d. A pleasant after-life
   e. Death as being mysterious and unknown
   f. The end of all life for you
   g. A transition to a new beginning
   h. A joining of the spirit with an unknown cosmic force
   i. Termination of this physical life with survival of the spirit
   j. Something other than this list

2. Which of the following aspects of your own death do you find distasteful:
   a. What might happen to your body after death
   b. What might happen to you if there is a life after death
   c. Concerns about what might happen to your dependents
   d. The grief that it would cause to your friends and relatives
   e. The pain you may experience as you die
   f. The deterioration of your body before you die
   g. All your plans and projects coming to an end
   h. Something other than this list

3. If you could choose, what age would you like to be when you die?

4. When you think of your own eventual death, how do you feel?
   a. Depressed
   b. Fearful
   c. Discouraged
   d. Purposeless
   e. Angry
   f. Pleasure in being alive
   g. Resolved as you realize death is a natural process of living
   h. Other (specify)

5. For what or for whom would you be willing to sacrifice your life?
   a. An idea or moral principle
   b. A loved one
   c. In combat
   d. An emergency where another life could be saved
   e. Not for any reason

6. If you could choose, how would you prefer to die?
   a. A sudden violent death
   b. A sudden but nonviolent death
   c. A quiet and dignified death
   d. Death in the line of duty
   e. Suicide
   f. Homicide victim
   g. Death after you have achieved your life goals
   h. Other (specify)

7. If it were possible, would you want to know the exact date on which you would die?

8. Would you want to know if you had a terminal illness?

9. If you had six more months to live, how would you want to spend this time?
   a. By satisfying hedonistic desires such as sex
   b. By withdrawing
   c. By contemplating or praying
   d. By seeking to prepare loved ones for your death
   e. By completing projects and tying up loose ends
   f. By considering suicide
   g. Other (specify)

10. Have you seriously contemplated suicide? What are your moral views of suicide? Are there circumstances under which you would take your life?

11. If you had a serious illness, and the quality of your life had substantially deteriorated, what measures do you believe should be taken to keep you alive?
    a. All possible heroic medical efforts
    b. Medical efforts being discontinued when there is practically no hope of returning to a life with quality
    c. Other (specify)

12. If you are married, would you prefer to outlive your spouse? Why?

13. How important do you believe funerals and grief rituals are for survivors?

14. If it were up to you, how would you like to have your body disposed of after you die?
   a. Cremation
   b. Burial
   c. Donation of parts of your body for organ transplants
   d. Donation of your body to medical school or to science
   e. Other (specify)

15. What kind of funeral would you prefer:
   a. A church service
   b. As large as possible
   c. Small with only close friends and relatives present
   d. A lavish funeral
   e. A simple funeral
   f. Whatever your survivors want
   g. Other (specify)

16. Have you made a will? Why or why not?

17. Were you able to arrive at answers to most of these questions? Were you uncomfortable in answering these questions? If you were uncomfortable, what were you feeling, and what made you uncomfortable? For the questions you do not have answers to, how might you arrive at answers?

Mwalimu Imara (1975) views dying as having a potential for being the final stage of growth. Learning to accept death is similar to learning to accept other losses such as the breakup of a romantic relationship or leaving a job we cherished. If we learn to accept and grow from the losses we encounter, such experiences will help us in facing the deaths of loved ones and our own eventual death.

Having a well-developed sense of identity (that is who we are, and what we want out of life) is an important step in learning to become comfortable with our own eventual death. If we have a well-developed blueprint of what will give meaning and direction to our lives, we are emotionally better prepared to accept the fact that we will eventually die.

■ Life After Life

Raymond Moody (1975) interviewed a number of people who had near-death experiences. These people had been pronounced clinically dead, but then shortly afterwards were revived. Moody provides the following composite summary of typical experiences that are being reported. (It is important to bear in mind that the following narrative is not a representation of any one persons' experience, rather it is a composite of the common elements found in many accounts.)

A man is dying and, as he reaches the point of greatest physical distress, he hears himself pronounced dead by his doctor. He begins to hear an uncomfortable noise, a loud ringing or buzzing, and at the same time feels himself moving very rapidly through a long dark tunnel. After this, he suddenly finds himself outside of his own physical body, but still in the immediate physical environment, and he sees his own body from a distance, as though he is a spectator. He watches the resuscitation attempt from this unusual vantage point and is in a state of emotional upheaval.

After a while, he collects himself and becomes more accustomed to his odd condition. He notices that he still has a "body," but one of a very different nature and with very different powers from the physical body he has left behind. Soon other things begin to happen. Others come to meet and to help him. He glimpses the spirits of relatives and friends who have already died, and a loving, warm spirit of a kind he has never encountered before—being of light—appears before him. This being asks him a question, nonverbally, to make him evaluate his life and helps him along by showing him a panoramic, instantaneous playback of the major events of his life. At some point he finds himself approaching some sort of barrier or border, apparently representing the limit between earthly life and the next life. Yet, he finds that he must go back to the earth, that the time for his death has not yet come. At this point he resists, for by now he is taken up with his experiences in the afterlife and does not want to return. He is overwhelmed by intense feelings of joy, love, and peace. Despite his attitude, though, he somehow reunites with his physical body and lives.

Later he tries to tell others, but he has trouble doing so. In the first place, he can find no human words adequate to describe these unearthly episodes. He also finds that others scoff, so he stops telling other people. Still, the experience affects his life profoundly, especially his views about death and its relationship to life.*

No one is sure why such experiences are being reported. A variety of explanations have been suggested (Siegel, 1981). One is that it suggests there may be a pleasant after-life. This explanation gives comfort to those who dislike seeing death as an absolute end. Another explanation, however, is that these near-death experiences are nothing more than hallucinations triggered by chemicals released by the brain or induced by lack of oxygen to the brain. Scientists involved with near-death research acknowledge that so far there is no conclusive evidence that these near-death experiences prove there is life after death.

*Reprinted from Raymond A. Moody, Jr., *Life After Life*, New York: Bantam Books, 1975, pp. 21–23. Reprinted by permission of the copyright owner, Mockingbird Books, St. Simons Island, GA.

Summary

There are a number of psychological developmental adjustments that the elderly need to make, such as adjusting to retirement and lower income, and to changing physical strength and health. Theoretical concepts about developmental tasks in later adulthood include: integrity versus despair; shifting from work-role preoccupation to self-differentiation; shifting from body preoccupation to body transcendence; shifting from self-preoccupation to self-transcendence; conducting a life review; the importance of self-esteem; and the negative effects of low status and ageism.

Three theories of successful aging are the activity theory, disengagement theory, and social reconstruction syndrome theory. Suggestions for positive psychological preparation by younger adults for later adulthood include: forming close personal relationships, making financial preparation, having interests and hobbies, forming a positive self-identity, looking toward the future, learning to cope with crises, and learning to cope with death. The chapter ends with guidelines on coping with grief, relating to a dying person, relating to survivors, and becoming more comfortable with one's own eventual death.

Social Aspects of Later Adulthood

On July 14, 1981, David Pearsall had his seventieth birthday, and it was a day to remember. It was not only his birthday, but his last day of work, at the company he worked for, Quality Printers. That evening the owners of Quality Printers gave a retirement party for Dave. He received a gold watch, and the owners and many of his fellow printers gave brief testimonial speeches about how much Dave had contributed to the morale and productivity of the company. Dave was deeply honored, and tears occasionally came to his eyes.

Dave felt strange waking up the next morning. He was used to getting up early to go to work. Work had become the center of his life. He even socialized with his fellow printers. This morning he had nothing planned and nothing to do. He lay in bed thinking about what the future would hold for him. Dave had generally muddled through life. His father had helped him obtain a position as a printer, and Dave seldom gave much attention to planning for the future. For example, while he thought it would be nice to retire, he had given little consideration to it.

Dave got up, looked in a mirror, and noticed his thinning, gray hair, the wrinkles on his face and hands, and the tire around his waist. In concluding that the best part of his life had passed him by, he anxiously wondered what the future would hold for him, and he contemplated what he should do with all of his time—he had no idea.

For the next few weeks he followed his wife, Jeanette, around the house. David began giving Jeanette his suggestions on how he thought she could be more efficient and productive around the house. After a few weeks of such advice, Jeanette angrily told David to get off her back. He visited the print shop where he used to work but soon realized everyone was too busy to spend time talking with him. He also stopped socializing with these printers, since they tended to talk about work. He felt useless. As the months went by, he spent most of his time sitting at home and watching TV. Occasionally he went to a neighborhood bar, where he drank to excess.

David and his wife never gave much attention to long-range financial planning. They both had worked for many years and tended to spend their paychecks shortly after they received them. When they bought their house five years ago, they gave little thought to how they would make their mortgage payments after retiring. David had hoped the social security system would take care of his bills.

David and Jeanette were in for a shock when they retired. The monthly

social security checks were much less than what they had anticipated. They stopped going out to eat, to movies and to ballgames. A few months after David retired, they realized they no longer could make the mortgage payments. They put the house up for sale and sold it four and one-half months later, at a price much lower than what the house was worth. Both were very sad about leaving their home, but financially they had no other choice. They moved into a two bedroom apartment. Both became even more inactive, as they no longer had yard work and fewer home maintenance tasks. One neighbor played a stereo late into the night and the Pearsalls had trouble sleeping.

In February 1983, Jeanette had a major heart attack. She was in the hospital for nearly two weeks and was then placed in an intensive care nursing home. David became deeply depressed and missed the companionship of his wife. He wished she could come home, but her medical needs wouldn't allow that, so he visited her every day. Since David had never learned to cook much, and because he was depressed, his diet consisted mainly of cheese sandwiches and TV dinners. In November 1983, Jeanette died of another heart attack.

David became even more distressed and depressed. He no longer shaved or bathed. He no longer cleaned his apartment, and neighbors began to complain about the odors. David gave up the will to live. He seldom heard from his son, Donald, who was living in a distant city. David sought to drown his unhappiness in whiskey. One night in January 1985 he passed out in his apartment with a lighted cigarette in his hand, which set his couch on fire. David died of smoke inhalation.

David's later years raise some questions for our society. Have we abandoned the elderly to a meaningless, unfulfilling existence? Is it a mistake for the elderly to count on the social security system to meet their financial needs when they retire? How can our society provide a more meaningful role for the elderly?

■ A Perspective

This chapter will focus on the social problems encountered by the elderly. According to the Behavior Dynamics Assessment Model, social problems can be viewed as a subcategory of life events that influence an individual's

growth and development. The plight of the elderly has now become recognized as a major problem in the United States. The elderly face a number
of personal problems: high rates of physical illness and emotional difficulties, poverty, malnutrition, lack of access to transportation, low status,
lack of a meaningful role in our society, and inadequate housing. To a large
extent, the elderly are a recently discovered minority group. Similar to
other minority groups, the elderly are victims of job discrimination, are
excluded from the mainstream of American life on the basis of supposed
group characteristics, and are subjected to prejudice which is based on
erroneous stereotypes. This chapter will:

- Explain the specific problems faced by the elderly and the causes of these problems.
- Describe current services to meet these problems and identify gaps in these
  services.
- Discuss the emergence of the elderly as a significant political force in our society.
- Present a proposal to provide the elderly with a meaningful, productive, social
  role in our society.

A Recently Discovered Minority Group

Throughout time, some tribal societies have abandoned their enfeebled old.
The Crow, Creek, and Hopi tribes, for example, built special huts away from
the tribe where the old were left to die. The Eskimos left the incapacitated
elderly in snowbanks or had them paddle away in a kayak. The Siriono of
the Bolivian forest simply left them behind when they moved on in search
of food (Moss and Moss, 1975, p. 18). Even today, the Ik of Uganda leave the
elderly and disabled to starve to death (Turnbull, 1972). Generally, the primary reason such societies have been forced to abandon the elderly is scarce
resources.

Although we might consider such customs to be barbaric and shocking,
have we not also abandoned the old? We force them to retire when many
are still productive. All too often, when a person is forced to retire, his or
her status, power, and self-esteem are lost. Also, in a physical sense, we
seldom have a place for large numbers of older people. Community facilities—parks, subways, libraries—are oriented to serving children and young
people. Most housing is designed and priced for the young couple with
one or two children and an annual income of over $20,000. If the elderly
are not able to care for themselves (and if their families are unable or
unwilling to care for them), we store them away from society in nursing
homes. Our abandonment of the elderly is further indicated by our taking
little action to relieve the financial problems of the elderly—nearly a quarter
of the elderly have incomes close to or below the poverty line (U.S. Bureau
of the Census, 1984). (In one sense, our abandonment of the elderly is more
barbaric than that of tribal societies who are forced by survival pressures
to abandon the elderly.) Our treatment of the elderly has only recently come
to be viewed as a major social problem.

The aged are subjected to various forms of discrimination—for example,
job discrimination. Older workers are erroneously believed to be less productive. Unemployed workers in their 50s and 60s have greater difficulty

finding new jobs and remain unemployed much longer than younger unemployed workers. The elderly are given no meaningful role in our society. Our society is a youth-oriented society, which devalues growing old. Our society glorifies the body beautiful and physical attractiveness and, thereby, shortchanges the elderly. The elderly are viewed as out of touch with what's happening, and their knowledge is seldom valued or sought. Intellectual ability is sometimes thought to decline with age, even though research shows intellectual capacity, barring organic problems, remains essentially unchanged until very late in life. (Birren, 1968, p. 19).

The elderly are erroneously thought to be senile, resistant to change, inflexible, incompetent workers, and a burden on the young. Given opportunities, elderly individuals usually prove such prejudicial concepts to be wrong.

The aged generally react to prejudice against them in the same way that racial and ethnic minorities react—by displaying self-hatred and by being self-conscious, sensitive, and defensive about their social and cultural status (Barron, 1971). As we have mentioned previously, individuals who frequently receive negative responses from others eventually tend to come to view themselves negatively.

Problems Faced by the Elderly

The social problems of the elderly are considered to be problems for two reasons. Some of the problems are conditions that the elderly encounter, such as poverty, malnutrition, poor health, and lack of transportation. Other problems are difficulties incurred by society in caring for the elderly, such as increased taxes for medical care. A point to remember is that, unlike other minorities, the problems of the elderly are problems that we all encounter eventually assuming we do not die prematurely. By the time most of today's students reach middle age (presumably their peak earning years), a large proportion of the adult population may well be in retirement, depending mainly on social security, medicare, etc., for their daily and medical needs. If we do not face and solve the problems of the elderly now, we will be in dire straits in the future.

Emphasis on Youth

Our society fears aging more than do most other societies. Our emphasis on youth is illustrated by our dread of getting gray hair and wrinkles or becoming bald and by our being pleased when someone guesses our age to be younger than it actually is.

Our society places a high value on youthful energy and action. We like to think we are doers. But why is there such an emphasis on youth in our society? Industrialization has resulted in a demand for laborers who are energetic, agile, and strong. Rapid advances in technology and science have made obsolete past knowledge and certain specialized work skills. Pioneer living and the gradual expansion of our nation to the west required brute strength, energy, and stamina. Competition has always been emphasized and has been reinforced by Darwin's theory of evolution, which highlighted survival of the fittest. The cultural tradition of valuing youth in our society has resulted in a devaluation of the elderly.

An Increasing Aged Population

The aged are partially a problem for our society because there are now eight times as many people age 65 and older than there were at the turn of the century. The number and proportion of older people have steadily been increasing.

• Composition of U.S. Population Aged 65 and Over

Years	1900	1950	1970	1980
Number of Older Persons (in millions)	3	12	20	25
Percent of Total Population	4	8	9.5	11

SOURCE: Beth J. Soldo, *America's Elderly in the 1980s* (Washington, D.C.: Population Reference Bureau, 1980), p.7

Several reasons can be given for the phenomenal growth of the older population. The improved care of expectant mothers and newborn infants has reduced the infant mortality rate. New drugs, better sanitation, and other medical advances have increased the life expectancy of Americans from 49 years in 1900 to 75 years in 1984 (U.S. Bureau of Census, 1984).

Another reason for the increasing proportion of the aged is that the birthrate is declining—fewer babies are being born, while more adults are reaching old age. After World War II, there was a baby boom lasting roughly from 1947 to 1960. Children born during these years flooded our schools in the 1950s and 1960s. Today, they are crowding the labor market. At the turn of the century, this generation will reach retirement. After 1960, there was a baby bust, a sharp decline in birthrates. The average number of children per woman went down from a high of 3.8 in 1957 to a low of 1.8 in 1976 (U.S. Bureau of the Census, 1984).

The increased life expectancy, with the baby boom followed by the baby bust, will significantly increase the median age of Americans in future years. The median age is increasing dramatically. The long-term implications will be considerable, as the United States will probably undergo a number of cultural, social, and economic changes.

The Fastest Growing Age Group Is the Old-Old

As our society is having more success in treating and preventing heart disease, cancer, strokes and other killers, more and more elderly are living into their 80s and beyond. People age 85 and over constitute the fastest growing age group in the United States.

In 1940, only 365,000 Americans were 85 or over, a mere 0.3 percent of the total population. By 1982, the number had zoomed to 2.5 million, or 1.1 percent of the population. By the year 2000 the Census Bureau predicts this oldest old group will top 5.1 million, almost 2 percent of all Americans. By the year 2000, more than 100,000 Americans will be 100 or over, three times the present number (Otten, 1984).

We are witnessing "the graying of America." This population revolution is rather quietly occurring in our society.

Those who are age 85 and over will create a number of problems and difficult decisions for our society. Otten (1984, p. 1) notes:

> It is these "oldest old"—often mentally or physically impaired, alone, depressed—who pose the major problems for the coming decades. It is they who will strain their families with demands for personal care and financial support. It is they who will need more of such community help as Meals on Wheels, homemaker services, special housing. It is they who will require the extra hospital and nursing-home beds that will further burden federal and state budgets.
>
> And it is they whose mounting needs and numbers already spark talk of some sort of rationing of health care. "Can we afford the very old?" is becoming a favorite conference topic for doctors, bioethicists and other specialists.

Elaine Brody (quoted in Otten, 1984, p. 10) briefly summarizes the number of old-old who need extensive health care:

> From the population of very old people come most of the million and more who are so disabled that they require round-the-clock care in nursing homes, the two million who are equally disabled but who are not in institutions, and many of the six million more who require less intensive services.

Many of the old-old suffer from a multiplicity of chronic illnesses. Common medical problems of the old-old include arthritis, heart conditions, hypertension, osteoporosis (brittleness of the bones), Alzheimer's disease, incontinency, hearing and vision problems, and depression.

While only 6.4 percent of the 75- to 84-year-olds are in nursing homes, 21.6 percent of the 85-or-over are in nursing homes (Otten, 1984). The cost to society for such care is expensive, as it costs around $20,000 per year per person to provide nursing home care. Despite the widespread image of families dumping aged parents into nursing homes, most frail elderly are still outside institutional walls, being cared for by a spouse, a child, or a relative. Some middle-aged people are now simultaneously encountering demands to put children through college and to support an aging parent in a nursing home.

The number of years spent in retirement is considerable. To maintain the same standard of living after retiring requires immense assets.

Rising health care costs and superlongevity have ignited controversy over whether to ration health care to the very old. For example, should people over age 75 be prohibited from receiving liver transplants or kidney dialysis? Discussion of euthanasia (the practice of killing individuals who are hopelessly sick or injured) has also been increasing. In 1984 Governor Richard Lamm of Colorado created a controversy when he asserted the terminally ill have a duty to die. Dr. Eisdor Fer (quoted in Otten, 1984, p. 10) stated:

> The problem is age-old and across cultures. Whenever society has had marginal economic resources, the oldest went first, and the old people bought that approach. The old Eskimo wasn't put on the ice floe; he just left of his own accord and never came back.

Mandatory Retirement and Early Retirement

The maintenance of a high rate of employment in our society is a major goal. One instrument that our society used in the past to keep the workforce reduced to a level in line with demand was mandatory retirement at a certain age, such as 65 or 70. In 1986, Congress (recognizing that mandatory retirement was overtly discriminatory against the elderly) outlawed most mandatory retirement policies. In many occupations, the supply of labor is exceeding the demand. An often-used remedy for the oversupply of available employees is the encouragement of ever-earlier retirement. Forced retirements often create financial and psychological burdens that retirees usually face without much assistance or preparation.

Many workers who retire early supplement their pension by obtaining another job, usually of a lower status. Nearly 90 percent of Americans 65 years of age and older are retired, even though many are intellectually and physically capable of working (U.S. Bureau of Census, 1984).

Our massive social security program supports early retirement at the age of 62. Pension plans of some companies and craft unions make it financially attractive to retire as early as 55. Perhaps the extreme case is the armed forces, which permits retirement on full benefits after 20 years' service or as early as age 38.

While early retirement has some advantages to society, such as reducing the labor supply and allowing younger employees to advance faster, there are also some serious disadvantages. For society, the total bill for retirement pensions is already huge and still growing. For the retiree, it means facing a new life and status without much preparation or assistance. While our society has developed educational and other institutions to prepare the young for the work world, it has not developed comparable institutions to prepare the elderly for retirement.

In our society, we still view people's worth partly in terms of their work. People often develop their self-image in terms of their occupation. Because the later years generally provide no exciting new roles to replace the occupational roles lost on retirement, retirees cannot proudly say, "I am a . . . ." Instead, they must say, "I *was* a . . . ." The more a person's life revolves around work, the more difficult retirement is apt to be.

Retirement often removes people from the mainstream of life. It diminishes their social contacts and their status and places them in a *roleless role*. People who were once valued as salespeople, teachers, accountants, barbers, or secretaries are now considered noncontributors in a roleless role on the fringe of society.

There are several myths about the older worker that have been widely believed by employers and the general public. Older workers are thought to be less healthy, clumsier, more prone to absenteeism, more accident-prone, more forgetful, and slower in task performance (Butler and Lewis, 1977). Research has shown these beliefs to be erroneous. Older workers have lower turnover rates, produce at a steadier rate, make fewer mistakes, have lower absenteeism rates, have a more positive attitude toward their work, and exceed younger employees in health and low on-the-job injury rates (Butler and Lewis, 1977). However, when older workers do become ill, they usually take a somewhat longer time to recover (Butler and Lewis, 1977).

A key question regarding early retirement is the age at which people want to retire. Gerontologists have studied this question. Younger workers generally state they prefer to retire before age 65. Older workers indicate they desire to retire later than the conventional age of 65 (Ekerdt, Boss, and Mogey, 1980). The explanation for this difference appears to be partly economic. Since social security benefits and pension plans are usually insufficient to provide the same standard of living as when the elderly are working, the elderly see an economic need to continue working beyond age 65. An additional explanation is sociopsychological. With retirement often being a roleless role in our society, older workers may gradually identify more and more with their work and prefer it over retirement.

Adjustment to retirement varies for different people. One study found that at least one third of retired people have adjustment problems (Atchley, 1978). The two most common problems were adjusting to a reduced income and missing their former jobs. Those who had the most difficulty in adjusting either tended to be rigid or overly identified with their work by viewing their job as being their primary source of satisfaction and self-image. Those who were happiest were able to replace job prestige and financial status with values stressing self-development, personal relationships, and leisure activities.

The golden age of leisure following retirement appears to be largely a myth. Lawton (1978) found that life in retirement is apt to be sedentary, with TV-viewing and sleep outranking such traditional leisure time activities as gardening, sports, clubs and other pastimes. Julian and Kornblum (1983, pp. 384–85) attribute such leisure activities to the past experiences of today's elderly:

> This elderly age cohort was born in an era when the average work week was 50 hours long. Their own working lives began in the period of the 48-hour work week, when vacations were rare and holidays were few. Homemakers cared for larger houses and larger families, and they had few labor-saving devices or products. These people had little opportunity to develop an understanding or appreciation of leisure. Moreover, many elderly people are poorly educated— a factor that makes them less likely to enjoy reading or activities that focus on new knowledge or self-improvement. The gross reduction in income, fear of crime, lack of transportation, and reduced mobility also contribute to the sedentary life of the old.
>
> Future generations of retirees will probably be different. Those who have enjoyed affluence, travel and education are more likely to enjoy retirement. This trend is already surfacing in the form of retirement communities that offer golf, swimming, and recreational centers.

Financial Problems of the Elderly

Many of the elderly live in poverty. A fair number lack adequate food, essential clothes and drugs, and perhaps a telephone in the house to make emergency calls. Nearly one fourth of the elderly have incomes close to or below the poverty line; less than 1 percent have incomes of $25,000 or more, and only 10 percent have incomes of at least $10,000 (Julian and Kornblum, 1983, p. 354). Only a small minority of the elderly have substantial savings or investments.

Gordon and Waster Moss (1975, pp. 17–18) describe the plight of someone who is old and poor:

> An old woman turned quickly away from the dismal scene outside her Florida hotel room window. Listlessly, she mixed her own breakfast: a cup of Sanka and a small glass of Tang. After finishing her breakfast, she looked at her wardrobe. It contained a few unwanted dresses given to her by a relative and one she had bought herself seven years ago. After choosing one, she made her bed and dusted her dresser, two small tables, and their lamps. She then turned on a small fan in anticipation of a hot, muggy day, wound her clock, straightened her small pile of old books, blew dust from the artificial flowers in a cheap vase,

This elderly woman works part time, spending a few hours a day making and selling quilts. Her work gives her positive feelings about herself, and also brings her pocket money. The elderly, who are still functioning well and want to work, should be encouraged to do so. Part-time work is often a perfect solution for them, allowing them to feel vital, but not overtaxing their strength. (Courtesy of United Way of America)

Nursing homes were created as an alternative to other costly medical care facilities for the elderly. Unfortunately, some of these homes are run poorly and negligently. But all nursing homes are not grim. Many, like the one where these elderly live, are quite pleasant. The administration provides healthy care and enjoyable, stimulating activities for its residents. (Courtesy of United Way of America)

Besides her plants, this impoverished, elderly woman has little to occupy her time. Mandatory retirement has removed her from the mainstream of life, diminished her social contacts, and taken away her previous work status. As is the case with many other retirees, her social security benefits and pension plan are inadequate and don't provide her with the standard of living she enjoyed while employed. She feels "roleless" and no longer valued in society. (Fran Buss)

This woman, who has lived through the painful loss of friends and relatives, is thinking about her own end. Hoping to keep her mental facilities intact, she dreads the disability, pain, and possible suffering she may have to endure before death. She wants a dignified death, in her own home, with friends and family nearby. But her resources are low and she's afraid that she won't even have a dignified funeral. (Fran Buss) and sat down in her only chair to watch television. Finally, it was noon, time for her to go down to the church for a hot lunch. In the afternoon, she would watch television soap operas or perhaps spend an hour or two visiting with the many other widows in the hotel.

All the while, uncertainty gnawed at her. Already, she was paying over half of her small retirement and welfare income for rent; and if the rent went up anymore, she would be unable to stay. The hot lunch, sponsored by the federal government, cost her only 50 cents and helped a little. Nevertheless, due especially to medical bills, she frequently ran out of money before the end of the month.

Her ulcer was her biggest worry. A few weeks earlier, it had started to bleed, and she had passed out. She had lain helpless for some time before finally managing to crawl to the phone. The desk clerk and some friends had then helped her get to the hospital. She had been more fortunate than some others in the hotel. Their lives had ended in their rooms, because they had been too weak from malnutrition to crawl for help.

The financial problems of the elderly are compounded by additional factors. One factor is the high cost of health care as previously discussed. A second factor is inflation. Inflation is especially devastating to those on fixed incomes. Most private pension benefits do not increase in size after a worker retires. For example, if living costs rise annually at 7 percent (which is the approximate rate of increase in the past decade) a person on a fixed pension would in 20 years be able to buy only one fourth as many goods and services as he or she could at retirement (*U.S. News & World Report*, Feb. 26, 1979, p. 57). Fortunately, in 1974, Congress enacted an automatic escalator clause in social security benefits, providing a 3 percent increase in payments when the Consumer Price Index increased a like amount. However, social security benefits were never intended to make a person financially independent—it is nearly impossible to live comfortably on monthly social security checks.

The most important source of income for the elderly is social security benefits, primarily: the Old-Age, Survivors, Disability, and Health Insurance Program and the Supplemental Security Income Program. These programs are described later in this chapter.

The importance of financial security for the elderly is emphasized by Sullivan et al. (1980, pp. 357–58) as follows:

> Financial security affects one's entire lifestyle. It determines one's diet, ability to seek good health care, to visit relatives and friends, to maintain a suitable wardrobe, and to find or maintain adequate housing. One's financial resources, or lack of them, play a great part in finding recreation (going to movies, plays, playing bridge or bingo, etc.) and maintaining morale, feelings of independence, and a sense of self-esteem. In other words, if an older person has the financial resources to remain socially independent (having her own household and access to transportation and medical services), to continue contact with friends and relatives, and to maintain her preferred forms of recreation, she is going to feel a great deal better about herself and others than if she is deprived of her former style of life.

The Social Security System

The social security system was never designed to be the main source of income for the elderly. It was originally intended as a form of insurance that would *supplement* other assets when retirement, disability, or death

Year	Maximum Tax Rate	Maximum Taxable Earnings	Tax
1971	5.2%	$7,800	$405.60
1972	5.2%	$9,000	$468.00
1973	5.85%	$10,800	$631.80
1974	5.85%	$13,200	$772.20
1975	5.85%	$14,100	$824.85
1976	5.85%	$15,300	$895.05
1977	5.85%	$16,500	$965.25
1978	6.05%	$17,700	$1070.85
1979	6.13%	$22,900	$1403.77
1980	6.13%	$25,900	$1587.67
1981	6.65%	$29,700	$1975.05
1982	6.7%	$32,700	$2190.90
1985	7.05%	$43,500	$3066.75
1986	7.15%	$47,700	$3410.55
1990	7.65%	$66,900	$5117.85

SOURCE: Social Security Administration, Department of Health and Human Services, *Income and Resources of the Aged* (Washington, D.C.: U.S. Government Printing Office, 1980.

of a wage-earning spouse occurred. Yet, many of the elderly do not have investments, pensions, or savings to support them in retirement, and, therefore, social security has become the major source of income for the elderly.

The social security system was developed in the United States in 1935. Financially, the system has been fairly solvent until recently. For the first few decades after the social security system was enacted in 1935 more money was paid into the system from social security taxes on employers and employees than was paid out. This was largely due to the fact that life expectancy was only somewhat over 60 years of age. Life expectancy, however, has gradually increased to 75 in 1984 (U.S. Bureau of the Census, 1984). The system is now paying out more than it is taking in. Social security taxes have been sharply increased in recent years, but with the old-old being the fastest growing age group in our society and with the proportion of the elderly increasing in our society, the system is going bankrupt.

The *dependency ratio* is the ratio between the number of working people and the number of nonworking people in the population. As the proportion of elderly people increases, the nonworkers will represent a greater and greater burden on the workers. Authorities predict that by the year 2020 the dependency ratio will decline from the 1983 level of 3.3 workers for every nonworking person to a ratio of about 2 to 1 (Julian and Kornblum, 1983, p. 388).

Some serious problems now exist with the system. First, the benefits are too small to provide the major source of income for the elderly. Even with payments from social security included, an estimated 80 percent of retirees are now living on less than half of their preretirement annual income. And the monthly payments from social security are generally below the poverty line (Koeppel, 1975). Second, it is unlikely that the monthly benefits will be raised much, as the system is already losing money. Our society faces some hard choices about keeping the social security system solvent in future years. Benefits might be lowered, but this would even further impoverish the recipients. Social security taxes might be raised, but there is little public support for this. Social security taxes are already increasing dramatically. The maximum tax that is paid will increase from $405.60 in 1971 to $5,117.85 in 1990.

The future of the social security system is unclear. The system is likely to continue to exist, but reduced benefits are a distinct possibility. Young people are well-advised to plan for retirement through savings, investment, and pension plans that are independent of the social security system.

Death

Preoccupation with dying, particularly with the circumstances surrounding it, is an ongoing concern of the elderly. For one reason, they see their friends and relatives dying. For another, they realize they've lived many more years already than they have left.

The elderly's concern about dying is most often focused on dreading the disability, the pain, and long periods of suffering that may precede death (Moss and Moss, 1975, p. 72). They generally would like a death with dignity, where they could die in their own homes, with little suffering, with mental faculties intact, and with families and friends nearby. Old people are also concerned about the costs of their final illness, the difficulties they may cause others by the manner of their death, and whether their resources will permit a dignified funeral.

In modern America, more than two thirds of all deaths occur in nursing homes or hospitals surrounded by medical staff (Kübler-Ross, 1969). Such deaths often occur without dignity.

Fortunately, the hospice movement has been developing in recent years to attempt to counter death without dignity. A hospice is a program which is designed to allow the terminally ill to die with dignity—to live their final weeks in the way they want to. Hospices have their origin among European religious groups in the Middle Ages who welcomed travelers who were sick, tired, or hungry (Sullivan et al., 1980, p. 363).

Hospices serve patients in a variety of settings—in hospitals, in nursing homes, and in the dying person's home. Medical services and social services are provided in hospices, and extensive efforts are made to allow the terminally ill to spend their remaining days as they choose. Hospices sometimes have educational and entertainment programs, and visitors are common. Pain relievers are extensively used, so that the patient is able to live out the final days in relative comfort.

Hospices view the *disease*, not the patient, as terminal. Their emphasis is on helping patients to use the time that is left, rather than trying to keep people alive as long as possible. Many hospice programs are set up to assist patients to live their remaining days at home. In addition to medical and visiting nurse services, hospices have volunteers to help the patient and family members with such services as counseling, transportation, filling out insurance forms and other paperwork, and respite care (that is, staying with the patient to provide temporary relief for family members).

Emotional Problems

The older person is often a lonely person. Most people 70 years of age or older are widowed, divorced or single. When someone has been married for many years and the spouse dies, a deep sense of loneliness usually occurs which seems unbearable. The years ahead often seem full of nothing but emptiness. It is not surprising, then, that depression is the most common emotional problem of the elderly. Symptoms of depression include feelings of uselessness, of being a burden, of being unneeded, of loneliness, of hopelessness. Somatic symptoms of depression include loss of weight and appetite, fatigue, insomnia, and constipation. (It is often difficult to determine whether such somatic symptoms are due to depression or to an organic disorder.)

Depression can alter the personality of an elderly person. Depressed people may become apathetic, withdrawn, and show a slowdown in behavioral actions. Levy et al. (1980) have found that an elderly person's reluctance to respond to questions is apt to be due to depression rather than to the contrariness of old age.

Those who have unresolved emotional problems in earlier life will, of course, continue to have them when older. Often, these problems will be intensified by the added stresses of aging.

There appears to be two major barriers to good mental health in the later years: failure to bounce back from psychosocial losses (such as the death of a loved one) and failure to have meaningful life goals (Skidmore and Thackeray, 1976, p. 226). Old age is a time when there are drastic changes thrust on the elderly that may create emotional problems: loss of a spouse, loss of friends and relatives through death or moving, poorer health, loss of accustomed income, and changing relationships with one's children and grandchildren.

Unfortunately, there is an erroneous assumption that *senility* and *mental illness* are inevitable and untreatable. On the contrary, Robert Butler (1970) has found that old people respond well to both individual and group counseling. In addition, even many 90-year-olds show no sign of senility. Senility is by no means an inevitable part of growing old.

Where the Elderly Live

We have heard so much about nursing homes in recent years that few people realize that 95 percent of the elderly do not live in nursing homes or any other kind of institution (Moss and Moss, 1975, p. 47). About 70 percent of all elderly males are married and live with their wives (Flynn, 1980, p. 352). Because females tend to outlive their spouses, nearly two thirds of women over age 65 live alone (Flynn, 1980). Nearly 80 percent of older married couples maintain their own households—in apartments, mobile homes, condominiums, or their own houses (Moss and Moss, 1975, pp. 49–56). In addition, nearly half of the single elderly (widows, widowers, divorced, never married) live in their own homes (Moss and Moss, 1975). When the aged do not maintain their own households, they most often live in the homes of relatives, primarily one of their children.

Old people who live in rural areas generally have a higher status than those living in urban areas. People living on farms can retire gradually.

People whose income is in land, rather than a job, can retain importance and esteem to an advanced age.

However, almost three fourths of our population live in urban areas, and the elderly often live in poor-quality housing. At least 30 percent of the elderly live in substandard, deteriorating, or dilapidated housing (Soldo, 1980, p. 24). Many of the elderly in urban areas are trapped in decaying, low-value houses needing considerable maintenance and often surrounded by racial and ethnic groups different from their own. Many of the urban elderly live in the urban inner cities in hotels or apartments with inadequate living conditions. Their neighborhoods may be decaying and crime-ridden, where the elderly are easy prey for thieves and muggers.

Fortunately, many mobile home parks, retirement villages, and apartment complexes geared to the needs of the elderly are being built throughout the country. Many such communities for the elderly provide a social center, security protection, sometimes a daily hot meal, and perhaps help with maintenance.

Transportation

Owning, maintaining, and driving a car is a luxury only the more affluent and physically vigorous elderly can afford. The lack of convenient, inexpensive transportation is a problem faced by most elderly.

Crime Victimization

Having reduced energy, strength, and agility, the elderly are easily victimized by crime, particularly robbery, aggravated assault, burglary, larceny, vandalism, and fraud. Many of the elderly live in constant fear of being victimized, although actual victimization rates for the elderly are lower than rates for younger people.[1] Some are extremely hesitant to leave their homes for fear they will be mugged or from fear their homes will be burglarized while they are away. A Louis Harris poll among the elderly showed fear of becoming a victim of crime was their major concern—it was ranked higher than poverty, isolation, sickness, loneliness, and other problems associated with old age (described in Schack and Frank, 1978, p. 83). When the elderly are victims of crimes of physical assault, they are more likely than younger people to sustain serious injury and to recover more slowly.

Malnutrition

The elderly are the most uniformly undernourished segment of our population (Ferguson, 1975, p. 238). Chronic malnutrition of the elderly exists because of transportation difficulties in getting to grocery stores; lack of knowledge about proper nutrition; lack of money to purchase a well-balanced diet; poor teeth and lack of good dentures, which greatly limits the diet; lack of incentives to prepare an appetizing meal when one is living alone; and inadequate cooking and storage facilities.

---

[1]The actual victimization rates for the elderly may be considerably higher than official crime statistics indicate, because many of the elderly feel uneasy about becoming involved with the legal and criminal justice systems. Therefore, they may not report some crimes which they are victims of. Some of the elderly are afraid of retaliation from the offenders if they report the crimes, and some of the elderly dislike the legal processes they will have to go through if they press charges.

As described in Chapter 11, the elderly are more apt to have chronic illnesses, and their average health care costs are six times higher than for younger people. The old-old, those over age 75, are particularly apt to have long-term illnesses.

Current Services

Present services and programs for the elderly are primarily maintenance in nature, as they are mainly designed to meet basic physical needs. Nonetheless, there are a number of programs, often federally funded, to provide services needed by the elderly. Before we briefly review many of these programs, we will look at the Older Americans Act of 1965, which has set objectives for programs that serve the elderly.

Older Americans Act of 1965

The Older Americans Act of 1965 created an operating agency (Administration on Aging) within the Department of Health, Education, and Welfare (as of 1980, the Department of Health and Human Services). This law and its amendments are the basis for financial aid by the federal government to assist states and local communities to meet the needs of the elderly. The objectives of the act are to secure for the elderly:

- An adequate income.
- Best possible physical and mental health.
- Suitable housing.
- Restorative services for those who require institutional care.
- Opportunity for employment.
- Retirement in health, honor, and dignity.
- Pursuit of meaningful activity.
- Efficient community services.
- Immediate benefit from research knowledge to sustain and improve health and happiness.
- Freedom, independence, and the free exercise of individual initiative in planning and managing their own lives (U.S. Department of Health, Education, and Welfare, 1970).

Although these objectives are commendable, in reality these goals have not been realized for many of the elderly.

■ Gerontology and Geriatrics Are Not the Same

Gerontology is the scientific study of the aging process from a physiological, pathological, psychological, sociological, and economic point of view (Kaluger and Kaluger, 1984, p. 570).

Geriatrics is a branch of medicine that deals with the diseases and problems of later adulthood and the elderly.

White House Conferences on Aging

The problems of the elderly have now been focused on by the public spotlight and have become a popular cause. There have been three White House Conferences on Aging—in 1961, 1971, and 1981. Many states have state offices on aging, and some municipalities and counties have established community councils on aging. A number of universities have established centers for the study of gerontology and nursing, medicine, sociology, social work, architecture. Government research grants are being given to encourage the study of the elderly and their problems. Publishers are now producing books and pamphlets to inform the public about the elderly, and a few high schools are beginning to offer courses to help teenagers understand the elderly and their circumstances.

A number of programs, often federally funded and administered at state or local levels, provide funds and services needed by the elderly. A number of these programs are briefly described in the following material.

Old Age, Survivors, Disability, and Health Insurance (OASDHI)

The OASDHI social insurance program[2] was created by the 1935 Social Security Act. OASDHI is usually referred to as social security by the general public. It is an income insurance program designed to partially replace income lost when a worker retires or becomes disabled. Cash benefits are also paid to survivors of insured workers.

Payments to beneficiaries are based on previous earnings. Rich as well as poor are eligible if insured. Benefits are provided to fully insured workers at age 65 or older (age 62 if somewhat smaller benefits are taken). Dependent husbands and wives over 62 and dependent children under 18 (no age limit on disabled children who become disabled before 18) are also covered under the retirement benefits.

Participation in this insurance program is compulsory for most employees, including the self-employed. The program is generally financed by a payroll tax (FICA—Federal Insurance Contributions Act) assessed equally to employer and employee. The rate has gone up gradually. Eligibility for benefits is based on the number of years in which social security taxes have been paid and the amount earned while working.

Supplemental Security Income (SSI)

Under the SSI program, the federal government makes monthly payments to people in financial need who are 65 years of age or older or who are blind or disabled at any age. In order to qualify for payments, applicants must have no (or very little) regular cash income, own little property, and have little cash or few assets that could be turned into cash (such as jewelry, stocks, bonds, and other valuables).

The SSI program became effective January 1, 1974. The word supple-

---

[2]Social insurance programs are financed by a tax on employees, or on employers, or on both. In contrast, public assistance benefits are paid from general government revenues (such as revenues through income taxes). In our society receiving social insurance benefits is generally considered a right, while receiving public assistance is usually considered charity and is stigmatized.

mental in the term *supplemental security income* is used because, in most cases, payments *supplement* whatever income may be available to the claimant. Since OASDHI monthly payments are often low, SSI sometimes supplements even that income source.

SSI provides a guaranteed minimum income (an income floor) for the aged, the legally blind, and the disabled. Administration of SSI has been assigned to the Social Security Administration. Financing of the program is through federal tax dollars, primarily income taxes.

Medicare

In 1965, Congress enacted the medicare program (Title XVIII of the Social Security Act). Medicare helps the elderly pay the high cost of health care. It has two parts: hospital insurance (Part A) and supplementary medical insurance (Part B). Everyone 65 or older who is entitled to monthly benefits under the Old Age, Survivors, and Disability Insurance program gets Part A automatically, without paying a monthly premium. Practically everyone in the United States 65 or older is eligible for Part B; Part B is voluntary, and beneficiaries are charged a monthly premium. Disabled people under age 65 who have been getting social security benefits for 24 consecutive months or more are also eligible for both Part A and Part B, effective on the twenty-fifth month of disability.

Part A. Hospital insurance helps pay for time-limited care in hospitals and skilled nursing facilities and for home health visits (such as visiting nurses). Coverage is limited to 90 days in a hospital and to 100 days in a nursing facility. If patients are able to be out of a hospital or nursing facility for 60 consecutive days following confinement, they are again eligible for coverage. Covered services in a hospital or skilled nursing facility include the cost of room and meals in a semiprivate room, regular nursing services, and cost of drugs, supplies, and appliances.

Part B. Supplementary medical insurance helps pay for physicians' services, outpatient hospital services in an emergency room, outpatient physical and speech therapy, and a number of other medical and health services prescribed by a doctor, such as diagnostic services, X-ray or other radiation treatments, and some ambulance services.

Medicaid

This program was established in 1965 by Title XIX of the Social Security Act. Medicaid primarily provides medical care for recipients of public assistance. It enables states to pay hospitals, nursing homes, medical societies, and insurance agencies for services provided to recipients of public assistance. Many of these recipients are indigent elderly, some of whom are in nursing homes. The federal government shares the expenses with the states on a 55–45 basis to recipients of public assistance, primarily those covered by Supplemental Security Income. Medical expenses that are covered under medicaid include diagnosis and therapy performed by surgeons, physicians, and dentists; nursing services in the home or elsewhere; and medical supplies, drugs, and laboratory fees.

Under the medicaid program benefits vary from state to state. The original legislation encouraged states to include coverage of all self-supporting persons whose marginal income made them unable to pay for medical care.

However, this inclusion is not mandatory, and the definition of medical indigence has generally been defined by states to provide insurance coverage primarily to recipients of public assistance.

Food Stamps

The food stamp program is designed to combat hunger. Food stamps are available to public assistance recipients and to other low-income families. These stamps are then traded in for groceries.

Adult Protective Services

One of the services that is offered in practically all communities, usually by public welfare departments, is adult protective services. Although offered widely, the public is largely unaware of it. One in every 20 elderly people probably needs some form of protective services, and this proportion is expected to increase as the proportion of people over age 75 increases (Atchley, 1977, p. 267). Protective services are for adults who are being neglected or abused or for adults whose physical or mental capacities have substantially deteriorated. The aim of protective services is to help the elderly meet their needs in their own home if possible. Alternative placements include foster care, group home care, and elderly housing units (such as apartments for the elderly). Services provided include homemaker services, counseling, rehabilitation, medical services, visiting nurse services, counseling, rehabilitation, medical services, visiting nurse services, Meals on Wheels, and transportation.

■ Adult Protective Services

Dodge County Public Welfare Department received a complaint from a neighbor of Jack and Rosella McArron that the McArrons were living in health-threatening conditions and that Mr. McArron was frequently abusing his wife.

Vincent Rudd, adult protective service worker, investigated the complaint. When he arrived at the door, Jack McArron appeared in shabby, filthy clothes with a can of beer in his hand and refused entry to Mr. Rudd. Mr. Rudd heard someone moaning in the background, so he went to the nearest service station where he called the police department. Together, Mr. Rudd and a police officer returned to the McArrons. The officer informed Mr. McArron that a protective service complaint had been made, and that an investigation must be made. Mr. McArron grudgingly let the officer and Mr. Rudd in.

The inside of the house had the appearance of having been hit by a cyclone. Newspapers and dirty clothes were heaped together in piles on the floor. The dining room table was covered by several inches of dust, cigarette butts, beer cans, whiskey bottles, and dirty dishes. The plumbing was not working. Cockroaches were seen. The house had a woodstove that was covered with dirt and a burnt crust. At the very least the place appeared to be a fire trap. There was a stench that appeared largely due to urine.

Mr. McArron appeared to be intoxicated. Mrs. McArron was found moaning, in the bedroom. Mr. McArron stated she had arthritis and had slipped on the stairway. He further stated her demands and her behavior were driving him to drink. Her hair was greasy and appeared not to have been washed for months. She was wearing a torn nightgown which smelled of urine. She was very thin, wrinkled, and had a variety of cuts and bruises. Her mutterings were difficult to understand, but she appeared to be stating her husband had been battering her for months.

She was taken to a hospital where she spent two and one-half weeks. (She was found to be 66 years old, and her husband, 69.) At first she wouldn't eat, so she was fed intravenously. After several days she became more alert. Daily baths improved her appearance. It became clear that she had frequently been abused by her husband for more than a decade. She was also found to have severe arthritis and diabetes. In the hospital she stated she did not want to return to live with her husband because of the beatings. She, therefore, was placed in a foster home.

The neighbors of the McArrons were interviewed; it was found that Jack McArron had had a drinking problem for years and that the neighbors seldom saw him sober. The neighbors were afraid of what he might do when intoxicated. He frequently beat his wife, was loud and obnoxious, and the neighbors were fearful he might kill someone while driving under the influence. Mr. McArron was taken to a 30-day drug treatment center. Records showed he had been admitted to this center on seven previous occasions. This time a physician found evidence that Mr. McArron was suffering fairly serious brain deterioration due to chronic alcoholism. He appeared paranoid as he talked about his neighbors being gangsters. He stated they were stealing his possessions. As the days went by, he started blaming the police and protective services for kidnapping his wife and talked about getting her back. He stated "I'm goin' lookin' for her with my shotgun, and I'll blast anyone who gets in my way." With his increasing paranoid statements, the staff was reluctant to let Mr. McArron return to his home as it was felt that if he became intoxicated he could potentially be dangerous. His mental capacities were deteriorating, and he was found to have a severe case of cirrhosis of the liver. As a result, procedures were followed to have a court declare him incompetent, to appoint a younger cousin as guardian, and to then place Mr. McArron in a nursing home.

After Mrs. McArron was placed in a foster home for several weeks, she said that she wanted to return to live with her husband. She was informed that her husband was in a nursing home. She visited him on several occasions and became increasingly depressed about his deteriorating condition. She began talking about wanting to die. About a year and a half later she did die of a massive heart attack. Her husband's condition in the nursing home has continued to deteriorate.

Vincent Rudd often reflected about this case. It seemed that the intervention which resulted in Jack and Rosella being separated from each other was in some way a factor in facilitating both their mental and emotional deterioration. Breaking a husband-wife bond has unexpected adverse consequences. But what were the alternatives? They seemed to be killing each other by living together. Mr. Rudd realized intervention in social work is a matter of judgment, and all anyone can do is give it their best shot.

Additional Programs

Additional programs for the elderly include the following:

- Meals on Wheels provide hot and cold meals to house-bound recipients who are incapable of obtaining or preparing their own meals, but who can feed themselves.
- Senior-citizen centers, golden age clubs, and similar groups provide leisure time and recreational activities for the elderly.
- Special bus rates reduce bus transportation costs for the elderly.
- Property tax relief is available to the elderly in many states.
- Housing projects for the elderly are built by local sponsors with financing assistance by the Department of Housing and Urban Development.
- Reduced rates at movie theaters and other places of entertainment are often offered voluntarily by individual owners.
- Home health services provide visiting nurse services, physical therapy, drugs, laboratory services, and sickroom equipment.
- Nutrition programs provide meals for the elderly at group eating sites. (These meals are generally provided four or five times a week and usually are luncheon meals.)
- Homemaker services provide household tasks that the elderly are no longer able to do for themselves.

- Day care centers for the elderly provide activities that are determined by the needs of the group.
- Telephone reassurance is provided by volunteers, often older persons, who telephone elderly people who live alone. (Such calls are a meaningful form of social contact for both parties and also ascertain whether any accidents or other serious problems have arisen which require emergency attention.)
- Nursing homes provide residential care and skilled nursing care when independence is no longer practical for the elderly who cannot take care of themselves or for the elderly whose families can no longer take care of them.
- Nursing Home Ombudsman Program investigates and acts on concerns expressed by residents in nursing homes.

Nursing Homes

Nursing homes were created as an alternative to expensive hospital care and are substantially supported by the federal government through medicaid and medicare. Over 1 million older people now live in extended-care facilities, making nursing homes a billion-dollar industry. There are more patient beds in nursing homes than in hospitals (U.S. Bureau of the Census, 1984, p. 112). Over 40 cents of each Medicaid dollar goes to nursing homes. (Trafford, 1978, p. 56).

Nursing homes are classified according to the kind of care they provide. At one end of the scale, there are residential homes that provide primarily room and board, with some nonmedical care (such as help in dressing). At the other end of the scale are nursing-care centers that provide skilled nursing and medical attention 24 hours a day. The more skilled and extensive the medical care given, the more expensive the home. The costs vary from a few hundred dollars to more than $2,000 per month. Although only about 5 percent of the elderly live permanently in homes, many spend some time convalescing in them. Most of the elderly eventually die in a nursing home, so the odds are that most of the elderly will live for awhile in a nursing home.

Several years ago, Ralph Nader released a report highly critical of nursing home care. The report cited instances of patients heavily tranquilized so that they were easier to manage, use of patients as guinea pigs in drug experiments, abysmal neglect and dehumanization, and kickbacks to nursing home administrators from druggists (Townsend, 1971).

One scandal after another characterizes care in nursing homes. A few years ago in Houston, an elderly woman was so neglected in a nursing home that her death was not discovered until rigor mortis had set in. Another woman in the same home was hospitalized from rat bites (Trafford, 1978). It has been charged that some doctors are giving needless repeated injections to nursing home patients in order to make high profits (Butler, 1975). In 1980, a nursing home in Madison, Wisconsin, strapped a 37-year-old stroke patient into her wheelchair for over 40 minutes at a time when the patient had no bladder or bowel control. She was not assisted to the toilet despite her repeated cries to help (Paley, 1980).

Robert Butler (1975) visited a number of nursing homes and found patients lying in their own feces or urine. He also found that the food was so unappetizing that residents at times refused to eat it, that many homes had serious safety hazards, and that boredom and apathy were common among staff as well as residents.

In spite of the criticisms, nursing homes are needed. If nursing homes were abolished, other institutions, such as hospitals, would have to serve the elderly. Life in nursing homes need not be bad. Where homes are properly administered, residents can expand, rather than restrict, their life experiences.

At the present time, people of all ages tend to be prejudiced against nursing homes, even those that are well run. Frank Moss (1977, p. 9) describes the elderly person's view of nursing homes: "The average senior citizen looks at a nursing home as a human junkyard, as a prison—a kind of purgatory, halfway between society and the cemetery—or as the first step of an inevitable slide into oblivion." There is some truth to the notion that most nursing homes are places where the elderly wait to die.

Not all of the residents in nursing homes need to be there. One estimate is that fewer than half of the current residents would need nursing home care if occasional medical and personal assistance were provided (Moss and Moss, 1975, p. 61). According to this course, about 30 percent of nursing homes are really undesirable places to live, 30 percent are reasonably adequate, and 40 percent are good.

■ Community Options Program

Community Options Program (COP) is an innovative program in Wisconsin to provide alternatives to nursing homes. COP is funded by the state and by the federal government and is administered by county social services departments.

To qualify for the program a person must have a long-term or irreversible illness or disability and be a potential or current resident of a nursing home or of a facility for the developmentally disabled. The person must also have income and assets that are below the poverty line. If these eligibility guidelines are met, a social worker and a nurse assess the applicant for social and physical abilities and disabilities to determine the types of services needed.

If an alternative to nursing home placement is available, is financially feasible, and, most importantly, is preferred by the applicant, a plan for services is drawn up, and a start date for in-home or in-community services is determined.

A wide variety of services may be provided which are designed to be alternatives to placement in nursing homes. Typical services include homemaker services, visiting nurse services, home delivered meals, adult foster care, group home care, and case management. COP is a coordinated program which makes use of a number of resources from a variety of agencies. Wisconsin is finding that the program is not only cost effective in comparison to nursing home care, but is also preferred over nursing home care by service recipients.

The most common complaint against nursing homes is the lack of well-trained professional staff trained in the special needs of the aged (Moss and Moss, 1975, p. 61). Nursing home administrators in some states need only be 18 years old and have taken a six-month training course in nursing home administration. Few homes have social workers, occupational therapists or physical therapists.

The cost of care for impoverished nursing home residents is largely paid by the medicaid program. Since the federal government has set limits on what will be reimbursed under medicaid, other problems may arise. There may be an effort to keep salaries and staff to a minimum. A home may postpone repairs and improvements on the facilities. Food is apt to be inexpensive—such as macaroni, which is high in fats and carbohydrates.

Congress has mandated that every nursing home patient on medicaid is entitled to a monthly personal spending allowance. The homes have control over these funds, and some homes keep this money (Moss, 1977, p. 9).

Gordon Moss and Walter Moss (1975, p. 65) present additional complaints:

> The quality of care from both particular staff members and from the institution as a whole is another major source of problems and complaints. There may be much delay or no response to calls for help. Patients may be left sitting for a long time on bedpans. The staff may harass patients they dislike or consider to be insufficiently docile by doing these things or by withholding services, isolating them in separate rooms in little-used parts of the building, or forcing them to remain bedridden.

Complaints about the physical facilities of nursing homes include not enough floor space or too many people in a room. The call light by the bed may be difficult to reach, or the toilets and showers may not be conveniently located. The building may be decaying.

It has been charged that as high as 40 to 50 percent of drugs prescribed to residents of nursing homes may be administered in error, resulting in adverse reactions and occasional death (Moss and Moss, 1977, p. 9). A Senate Committee on Aging reported in 1977 after eight years of investigation that "the evidence is overwhelming that many pharmacists are required to pay kickbacks to nursing home operators as a precondition of obtaining a nursing home's business" (*Wisconsin State Journal*, July 17, 1977, p. 11).

Frank Moss (1977, p. 9), along with a number of other authorities, is critical of our society's response to the problems of the elderly:

> The phenomenon of large numbers of ill elderly is a comparatively recent problem in the United States, as is our "solution"—nursing homes. The solution reflects today's society: the sick and the aged are an embarrassment; they remind us of our own mortality and therefore should be removed from view.

The Elderly Are Emerging as a Powerful Political Force

In spite of all the maintenance programs that are now available for the elderly, the key problems of the elderly remain to be solved. A high proportion of the elderly do not have meaningful lives, respected status, adequate income, transportation, living arrangements, diet, or health care.

We are beginning to hear about a new kind of discrimination: ageism: prejudice against the elderly. How can we defend urging people to retire when they are still productive? How can we defend the living conditions within some of our nursing homes? How can we defend our restrictive attitudes toward sexuality among the elderly? How can we defend providing services to the elderly that are limited to maintenance and subsistence? Gordon and Walter Moss (1977, p. 79) comment, "Just as we are learning that black can be beautiful, so we must learn that gray can be beautiful, too. In so learning, we may brighten the prospects of our old age."

In the past, prejudice has been most effectively combated when those being discriminated against join together for political action. It, therefore, seems apparent that if major changes in the elderly's role in our society are to take place it will have to be done through political action.

Older people are, in fact, becoming increasingly involved in political activism and, in some cases, even radical militancy. Two prominent organizations are the American Association of Retired Persons and its affiliated group, the National Retired Teachers Association. These groups are lobbying for the interests of the elderly at local, state, and federal levels of government.

An action-oriented group that has caught the public's attention is the Gray Panthers. This organization argues that a fundamental flaw in our society is the emphasis on materialism and on the consumption of goods and services, rather than on improving the quality of life for all citizens (including the elderly). The Gray Panthers seek to end ageism and to advance the goals of human freedom, human dignity, and self-development. This organization uses social action techniques, including getting the elderly to vote as a bloc for their concerns. The founder of the group, Maggie Kuhn (quoted in Butler, 1975, p. 341), states, "We are not mellow, sweet old people. We have got to effect change, and we have nothing to lose."

There are clear indications that the politics of age have arrived. The elderly are rapidly becoming one of the most politically organized and influential groups in America.

The last 20 years have seen some significant steps toward securing a better life for the elderly: increased social security payments, enactment of the medicare and medicaid programs, the emergence of hospices, and the expansion of a variety of other programs for the elderly. With the elderly becoming a powerful political bloc, we are apt to see a number of changes in future years to improve the status of the elderly in our society.

Finding a Social Role for the Elderly

At the present time the early retirement policies of many employers and the stereotypic expectations of the elderly often result in the elderly being unproductive, inactive, dependent, and unfulfilled. To develop a productive and meaningful role for the elderly in our society, the stereotypic expectations of the elderly need to be changed. Consistent with the Behavior Dynamics Assessment Model described in Chapter 1, providing the elderly with more social options allows them more alternatives.

The elderly who want to work and are still able should be permitted to continue working well past age 65 or 70. Also, it is suggested here that if an elderly person wants to work half time or part time, this should be encouraged. For example, two elderly persons working half time could fill a full-time position. Consultant roles might also be created for the elderly after they retire in the areas where they possess special knowledge and expertise. For those who do retire, there should be educational and training programs to help them develop their interests and hobbies (such as photography) into new sources of income.

Having the elderly working longer in our society would have a number of payoffs for the elderly and for society. The elderly would continue to be productive, contributing citizens. They would have a meaningful role. They would continue to be physically and mentally active. They would have higher self-esteem. They would begin to break down the stereotypes of the elderly being unproductive and a financial burden on society. They would be paying into the social security system rather than drawing from it.

What is being proposed here is a system for the elderly to have a productive role, either as paid workers or as volunteers. The authors contend that in our materialistic society the only way for the elderly to have a meaningful role is to be productive. The elderly face the choice (as do younger people) between having adequate financial resources through productive work or inadequate financial resources by not working.

Objections to such a system may be raised by those who maintain that some of the elderly are no longer productive. This may be true, but some younger people are also unproductive. What is needed to make the proposed system work is jobs having realistic, objective, and behaviorally measurable levels of performance. Those at any age who do not meet the performance levels would first of all be informed about the deficiencies, would be given training to meet the deficiencies. If the performance levels were still not met, discharge processes would be used as a last resort. (For example, if a tenured faculty member was deficient in levels of performance—as measured by student-course evaluations, peer faculty evaluations of teaching, record of public service, record of service to the department and to the campus, and record of publications—that faculty member would first of all be informed of the deficiencies. Training and other resources to meet the deficiencies would be offered. If the performance does not improve to acceptable standards, then dismissal proceedings would be initiated. Some colleges and universities are now moving in this direction.)

In the productivity system that is being suggested, the elderly would have an important part to play. They would be expected to continue to be productive within their capacities. By being productive, they would serve as examples to counter the current negative stereotypes of the elderly.

Another objection these authors have heard to this new system is that the elderly have worked most of their lives, and, therefore, deserve to retire and live in leisure with a high standard of living. It would be nice if the elderly really had this option. However, that is not realistic. Most of the elderly do not have the financial resources after retiring to maintain a high standard of living. When most of the elderly retire, their income and their standard of living are sharply reduced. The choice in our society is really between working and thereby maintaining a high standard of living or retiring and having a lower standard of living.

We are already seeing a number of the elderly heading in a more productive direction. A number of organizations have been formed to promote the productivity of the elderly. Three examples of these organizations are Retired Senior Volunteer Program, Service Corps of Retired Executives, and Foster Grandparent Program.

The *Retired Senior Volunteer Program (RSVP)* offers people over age 60 the opportunity of doing volunteer service to meet community needs. RSVP agencies place volunteers in hospitals, schools, libraries, day care centers, courts, nursing homes, and a variety of other organizations.

The *Service Corps of Retired Executives* (SCORE) offers retired businessmen and businesswomen an opportunity to help owners of small businesses and managers of community organizations who are having management problems. Volunteers receive no pay but are reimbursed for out-of-pocket expenses.

The *Foster Grandparent Program* employs low-income older people to provide personal care to children who live in institutions. These children include the mentally retarded, developmentally disabled, and the emotionally disturbed. Foster grandparents are given special assignments in child care, speech therapy, physical therapy, or as teacher's aides. This program has been shown to be of considerable benefit to both the children and to the foster grandparents (Atchley, 1977, p. 267). The children served become more outgoing and have improved relationships with peers and staff. They have increased self-confidence, improved language skills, and decreased fear and insecurity. The foster grandparents have an additional (although small) source of income, increased feelings of vigor and youthfulness, an increased sense of personal worth, a feeling of being productive, and a renewed sense of personal growth and development. For society, foster grandparents provide a vast pool of relatively inexpensive labor that can be used to do needed work in the community.

The success of these programs illustrates that the elderly can be productive in both paid and volunteer positions. Atchley (1977, p. 269) makes the following recommendations for using elderly volunteers:

> First, agencies must be flexible in matching the volunteer's background to assigned tasks. If the agency takes a broad perspective, useful work can be found for almost anyone. Second, *volunteers must be trained.* All too often agency personnel place unprepared volunteers in an unfamiliar setting. Then the volunteer's difficulty confirms the myth that you cannot expect good work from volunteers. Third, a variety of placement options should be offered to the volunteer. Some volunteers prefer to do familiar things; others want to do *anything but* familiar things. Fourth, training of volunteers should not make them feel that they are being tested. This point is particularly sensitive among working-class volunteers. Fifth, volunteers should get personal attention from the placement agency. There should be people (perhaps volunteers) who follow up on absences and who are willing to listen to the compliments, complaints, or experiences of the volunteers. Public recognition from the community is an important reward for voluntary service. Finally, transportation to and from the placement should be provided.

Summary

People 65 and older now comprise over one tenth of our population. The old-old are now the fastest growing age group in our society. The elderly tend to encounter a number of problems in our society: low status, lack of a meaningful role, the emphasis on youth in our society, health problems, inadequate income, inadequate housing, transportation problems, malnutrition, crime victimization, emotional problems (particularly depression), and concern with circumstances surrounding dying. A majority of the elderly depend on the social security system as their major source of income. Yet, monthly payments are inadequate and the system may be going bankrupt.

In many ways, the elderly are victims of ageism. Increasingly, the elderly are becoming politically active and organized to work toward improving their status.

In order to provide the elderly with a productive, meaningful role in our society it is proposed here that the elderly should be encouraged to work (either in paid work or as volunteers) as long as they are productive and have an interest in working to maintain their standard of living. Helping the elderly to stay productive in their lives is predicted to have a number of personal payoffs for them, and to be highly beneficial to society.

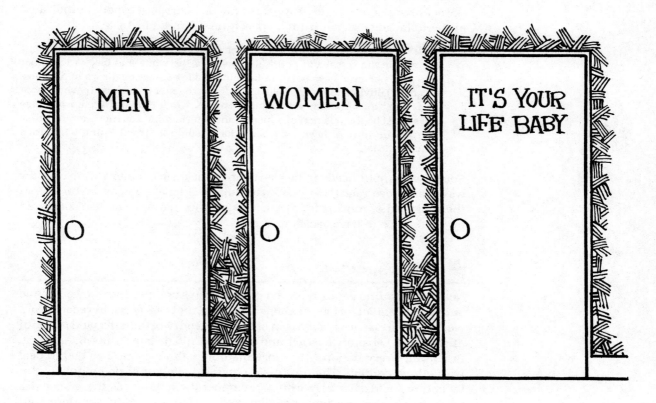

Ethnocentrism and Racism

Abraham Lincoln has the reputation of being the key person in ending slavery in our country. Yet, it appears Lincoln held racist beliefs, as indicated in the following excerpt from a speech he delivered in 1858:

> I will say, then, that I am not, nor ever have been in favor of bringing about in any way the social and political equality of the white and black races; that I am not, nor ever have been, in favor of making voters or jurors of Negroes, nor of qualifying them to hold office, nor to inter-marry with white people . . . and inasmuch as they cannot so live, while they do remain together there must be the position of superior and inferior, and I as much as any other man am in favor of having the superior position assigned to the white race (Lincoln, 1858).

Such a statement needs to be viewed in its historical context. Our country was even more racist 130 years ago than it is today. Lincoln, who was in the vanguard of moving for greater equality for blacks, was also socialized by his culture to have racist attitudes.

■ A Perspective

Nearly every time we turn on the evening news on television we see ethnic and racial conflict—riots, beatings, murders, and civil wars. In recent years we have seen clashes resulting in bloodshed from Northern Ireland to South Africa, from Lebanon to Israel, and from the United States to South America. Practically every nation with more than one ethnic group has had to deal with ethnic conflict. The oppression and exploitation of one ethnic group by another is particularly ironic in democratic nations, as these societies claim to cherish freedom, equality, and justice. In reality, the dominant group in all societies that controls the political and economic institutions rarely agrees to share (equally) its power and wealth with other ethnic groups. According to the Behavior Dynamics Assessment Model, ethnocentrism and racism are factors that can adversely affect the growth and development of minority group members.

This chapter will:

- Define and describe ethnic groups, ethnocentrism, racial groups, racism, prejudice, discrimination, and institutional discrimination.

Chapter

14

- Outline the sources of prejudice and discrimination.
- Summarize the effects and costs of discrimination, and describe effects of discrimination upon human growth and development.
- Suggest strategies to combat discrimination.
- Outline some guidelines for social work practice with racial and ethnic groups.
- Forecast the pattern of race and ethnic relations in the United States in the future.

Ethnic Groups and Ethnocentrism

An ethnic group has a sense of togetherness, a conviction that its members form a special group, and a sense of common identity or peoplehood. Milton M. Gordon (1964, pp. 27–28) defines an ethnic group as

> . . . any group which is defined or set off by race, religion, or national origin, or some combination of these categories [which] have a common social-psychological referent, in that all of them serve to create, through historical circumstances, a sense of peoplehood.

Practically every ethnic group has a strong feeling of *ethnocentrism*. Ethnocentrism is "the tendency to view the norms and values of one's own culture as absolute and to use them as a standard against which to judge and measure all other cultures" (*Encyclopedia of Sociology*, 1974, p. 101). Ethnocentrism leads members of ethnic groups to view their culture as the best, as being superior, as being the one that other cultures should adopt. Ethnocentrism also leads to prejudice against foreigners, who may be viewed as barbarians, heathens, uncultured people, or savages.

Feelings of ethnic superiority within a nation are usually accompanied by the belief that political and economic domination by one's own group is natural, is morally right, is in the best interest of the nation, and perhaps also is God's will. Ethnocentrism has been a factor in leading to some of the worst atrocities in history—Adolf Hitler's mass executions of an estimated 6 million European Jews and Gypsies, and the colonists' nearly successful attempt to exterminate the native population of America.

■ Violence against Minorities in the United States

Minorities have been subjected to extensive violence by whites in our society. (It has been a two-way street as a number of whites have been subjected to violence by non whites.)

During the second half of the nineteenth century frequent massacres of Chinese mining and railroad workers occurred in the West. During one railroad strike in 1885, white workers stormed a Chinese community in Rock Springs, Wyoming, murdered 16 persons, and burned all the homes to the ground. No one was arrested. In 1871 a white mob raided the Chinese community in Los Angeles, killing 19 persons and hanging 15 to serve as a warning to survivors (Pinkney, 1972, p. 73).

Pinkney (1972, p. 73) comments on the treatment of black slaves by their white owners.

> Few adult slaves escaped some form of sadism at the hands of slaveholders. A female slaveholder was widely known to punish her slaves by beating them on the face. Another burned her slave girl on the neck with hot tongs. A drunken slaveholder dismembered his slave and threw him piece by piece into a fire. Another planter dragged his slave from bed and inflicted a thousand lashes on him.
>
> Slaveowners often used a whip, made of cowskin or rawhide, to control their slaves. An elaborate punishment system was developed, linking the number of lashes to the seriousness of the offenses with which slaves were charged.

Shortly before the Civil War, roving bands of whites commonly descended on black communities and terrorized and beat the inhabitants. Slaves sometimes struck back and killed their slaveowners or other whites. During Reconstruction, it has been estimated over 5,000 blacks were killed in the South by white vigilante groups (Pinkney, 1972, p. 79).

Following the Civil War lynching of blacks increased and continued into the 1950s. Blacks were lynched for such minor offenses as peeping into a window, attempting to vote, using offensive remarks, seeking employment in a restaurant, getting into a dispute with a white person, and expressing sympathy for another black who had already been lynched. Arrests for lynching black people have been rare. Lynch mobs not only included men, but sometimes also women and children. Some lynchings were publicly announced and the public invited to participate. The public often appeared to enjoy the activities and urged the active lynchers on to greater brutality.

Race riots between whites and blacks have also been common since the Civil War. During the summer of 1919, for example, 26 major race riots occurred, the most serious of which was in Chicago. In this riot, which lasted from July 27 to August 2, 38 persons were killed, 537 were injured, and over 1,000 were left homeless (Waskow, 1967).

Native Americans have been subjected to kidnapping, massacre, conquest and forced assimilation, and murder. Some tribes have been completely exterminated. The treatment of Native Americans by whites in North America stands as one of the most revolting series of acts of violence in history.

The extermination of Native Americans began with the early Christian Pilgrims. They were the first to establish a policy to massacre and exterminate Native Americans in this country. In 1636 the Massachusetts Bay Puritans sent a force to massacre the Pequot, a division of the Mohegan tribe. The dwellings were burned, and 600 inhabitants were slaughtered (Pinkey, 1972, p. 96).

In 1642 the governor of New Netherlands began offering bounties for Native American scalps. A year later this same governor ordered the massacre of the Wappinger tribe. Pinkney (1972, p. 96) describes the massacre:

> During the massacre infants were taken from their mother's breast, cut in pieces and thrown into a fire or into the river. Some children who were still alive were also thrown into the river, and when their parents attempted to save them they drowned along with their children. When the massacre was over, the members of the murder party were congratulated by the grateful governor.

A major motive for this violence was that the European settlers were land hungry. The deliberate massacre and extermination of Native Americans continued from the 1600s throughout most of the 1800s. The whites frequently made and broke treaties with Native Americans during these years—and ended up taking most of their land and sharply reducing their population. For example, in a forced march on foot covering several states, an estimated 4,000 Cherokees died from cold and exhaustion in 1838 (Pinkney, 1972, p.

107). During these years Native Americans were considered savage beasts. Whites felt, "The only good Indian is a dead one," and they exterminated Native Americans because it was felt they impeded economic progress.

Today, racial clashes between minority group members still occur on a smaller scale on the street and in some of our schools. Recent years have seen a resurgence of the Ku Klux Klan, the American Nazi Party, and other white power groups in many areas of the country. Demonstrations by these organizations have led to several bloody clashes. The worst in recent years was a shoot-out in Greensboro, North Carolina, in 1979 in which five anti-Klan protestors were killed.

In interactions between nations, ethnocentric beliefs sometimes lead to wars and serve as justifications for foreign conquests. At practically any point in the last several centuries at least a few wars have occurred between nations in which one society has been seeking to force its culture on another. In the past few decades, the United States and Russia have been engaged in a struggle to extend their influence on other cultures. We hold a number of negative stereotypes about the Russian culture, and their citizens have a number of negative stereotypes about our culture. Other countries have also been involved in bitter struggles, for example Israel and other Arab countries in the Middle East.

Race and Racism

Although a racial group is often also an ethnic group, the two groups are not necessarily the same. A *race* is believed to have a common set of physical characteristics. But the members of a racial group may or may not share the sense of togetherness or identity that holds an ethnic group together. A group that is both a racial group and an ethnic group is Japanese-Americans, as they are thought to have some common physical characteristics and also have a sense of peoplehood. (Coleman & Cressey, 1984, pp. 188–190). On the other hand, white Americans and white Russians are of the same race, but they hardly have a sense of togetherness. In addition, there are ethnic groups that are composed of a variety of races. For example, a religious group (such as Roman Catholic) is sometimes considered an ethnic group and is composed of members from diverse racial groups.

In contrast to ethnocentrism, racism is more likely to be based on physical differences than on cultural differences. Racism is "...a belief in racial superiority that leads to discrimination and prejudice toward those races considered inferior" (*Encyclopedia of Sociology*, 1974, p. 236). However, similar to ethnocentric ideologies, most racist ideologies assert that members of other racial groups are inferior. Some white Americans in this country have gone to extreme and morally reprehensible limits to seek to attain greater control and power over other racial groups.

Prejudice and Discrimination

Prejudice, in regard to race and ethnic relations, is making negative prejudgments. Gordon Allport (1954, p. 7) defines *prejudice* as thinking negatively of others without sufficient justification. His definition has two elements: an unfounded judgment and a feeling of scorn, dislike, fear, and aversion. Prejudiced people apply racial stereotypes to all or nearly all members of a group according to preconceived notions of what they believe the group to be like and how they think the group will behave. Racial prejudice results from the belief that people who have different skin color and other physical characteristics also have innate differences in behaviors, values, intellectual functioning, and attitudes.

The term *discriminate* has two very different meanings. It may have the positive meaning to be discerning and perceptive. However, in minority group relations, it involves making categoric differentiations based on a social group ranked as inferior, rather than judging an individual on his or her own merits. Racial or ethnic discrimination involves denying to members of minority groups equal access to opportunities, residential housing areas, membership in religious and social organizations, involvement in political activities, access to community services, and so on.

Prejudice is a combination of stereotyped beliefs and negative attitudes, so that prejudiced individuals *think about people* in a predetermined, usually negative, categorical way. *Discrimination* involves physical actions, unequal *treatment of people* because they belong to a category. Discriminatory behavior often derives from prejudiced attitudes. Robert Merton (1949), however, notes prejudice and discrimination can occur independently of each other. Merton (1949, p. 47) describes four different types of people:

1. *The unprejudiced nondiscriminator*, in both belief and practice, upholds American ideals of freedom and equality. This person is not prejudiced against other groups and, on principle, will not discriminate against them.

2. *The unprejudiced discriminator* is not personally prejudiced but may sometimes, reluctantly, discriminate against other groups because it seems socially or financially convenient to do so.

3. *The prejudiced nondiscriminator* feels hostile to other groups but recognizes that law and social pressures are opposed to overt discrimination. Reluctantly, this person does not translate prejudice into action.

4. *The prejudiced discriminator* does not believe in the values of freedom and equality and consistently discriminates against other groups in both word and deed.

An example of an unprejudiced discriminator is the unprejudiced owner of a condominium complex in an all-white middle-class suburb who refuses to sell a condominium to a black family because of fear (founded or unfounded) that the sale would reduce the sale value of the remaining units. An example of a prejudiced nondiscriminator is a personnel director of a fire department who believes Mexican-Americans are unreliable and poor fire fighters but yet complies with affirmative action efforts to hire and train Mexican-American fire fighters.

It is very difficult to keep personal prejudices from eventually leading to some form of discrimination. Strong laws and firm informal social norms are necessary to break the relationship between prejudice and discrimination.

Discrimination is of two types. *De jure discrimination* is legal discrimination. The so-called Jim Crow laws in the South gave force of law to many discriminatory practices against blacks, including denial of the right to trial, prohibition against voting, and prohibition against interracial marriage. Today, in the United States, there is no de jure racial discrimination, as such laws have been declared unconstitutional.

De facto discrimination refers to discrimination that actually exists, whether legal or not. Most acts of de facto discrimination abide by powerful informal norms that are discriminatory. Marlene Cummings (1977, p. 200) gives an example of this type of discrimination and urges victims to confront assertively such discrimination:

> Scene: department store. Incident: Several people are waiting their turn at a counter. The person next to be served is a black woman; however, the clerk waits on several white customers who arrived later. The black woman finally demands service, after several polite gestures to call the clerk's attention to her. The clerk proceeds to wait on her after stating, "I did not see you." The clerk is very discourteous to the black customer; and the lack of courtesy is apparent, because the black customer had the opportunity to observe treatment of the other customers. De facto discrimination is most frustrating . . .; the customer was served. Most people would rather just forget the whole incident, but it is important to challenge the practice even though it will possibly put you through more agony. One of the best ways to deal with this type of discrimination is to report it to the manager of the business. If it is at all possible, it is important to involve the clerk in the discussion.

Racial and Ethnic Stereotypes

Racial and ethnic stereotypes involve attributing a fixed and usually inaccurate or unfavorable conception to a racial or ethnic group. Stereotypes are closely related to the way we think—as we seek to perceive and understand things in categories. We need categories to group things that are similar in order to study them and to communicate about them. We have stereotypes about many categories, including mothers, fathers, teenagers, communists, Republicans, school teachers, farmers, construction workers, miners, politicians, Mormons, and Italians. These stereotypes may contain some useful and accurate information about a member in any category. Yet, each member of any category will have many characteristics that are not suggested by the stereotypes and may even have some characteristics that run counter to some of the stereotypes.

Racial stereotypes involve differentiating people in terms of color or other physical characteristics. For example, as we have previously mentioned, history has seen the erroneous stereotype that Native Americans become easily intoxicated and irrational when using alcohol. This belief was then translated into laws that prohibited Native Americans from buying and consuming alcohol. A more recent stereotype is that blacks have a natural ability to play basketball and certain other sports. While at first glance, such a stereotype appears complimentary to blacks, it has broader, negative implications. The danger is that, if people believe the stereotype, they may also feel that other abilities and capacities (such as intelligence, morals, and work productivity) are also determined by race. In other words, believing this positive stereotype increases the probability that people will also believe negative stereotypes.

Racial and Ethnic Discrimination Is the Problem of Whites

Gunnar Myrdal (1944) points out that minority problems are actually majority problems. The white majority determines the place of nonwhites and other ethnic groups in our society. The status of different minority groups varies in our society because whites apply different stereotypes to various groups; for example, blacks are viewed and treated differently from Japanese. Elmer Johnson (1973, p. 344) notes, "Minority relationships become recognized by the majority as a social problem when the members of the majority disagree as to whether the subjugation of the minority is socially desirable or in the ultimate interest of the majority." Concern about discrimination and segregation has also received increasing national attention because of a rising level of aspiration among minority groups who demand (sometimes militantly) equal opportunities and equal rights.

Our country was supposedly founded on the principle of human equality. The Declaration of Independence and the Constitution assert equality, justice, and liberty for all. Yet, in practice, our society has always discriminated against minorities.

From its earliest days, our society has singled out certain minorities to treat unequally. A *minority* can be defined as a group which has a subordinate status and is being subjected to discrimination.

The categories of people who have been singled out for unequal treatment in our society have changed somewhat over the years. In the late 1800s and early 1900s, people of Irish, Italian, and Polish descent were discriminated against, but that discrimination has been substantially reduced. In the nineteenth century, Americans of Chinese and Japanese descent were severely discriminated against. However, this has also been declining for many decades.

Race Is a Social Concept

Ashley Montague (1964) considers the concept of race to be one of the most dangerous and tragic myths in our society. Race is erroneously believed by many to be a biological classification of people. Yet, there are no clearly delineating characteristics of any race. Throughout history, the genes of different societies and racial groups have occasionally been intermingled. No racial group has any unique or distinctive genes. In addition, biological differentiations of racial groups have gradually been diluted through various sociocultural factors. These factors include changes in preferences of desirable characteristics in mates, effects of different diets on those who reproduce, and such variables as wars and diseases in selecting those who will live and reproduce (Johnson, 1973, p. 350).

In spite of definitional problems, it is necessary to use racial categories in the social sciences. Race has important (though not necessarily consistent) social meanings for people. In order to have a basis for racial classifications, a number of social scientists have used a social, rather than a biological, definition. A social definition is based on the way in which members of a society classify each other by physical characteristics. For example, a frequently used social definition of a black person in America is anyone who either displays overt black physical characteristics or is known to have a black ancestor (Rose, 1964). The sociological classification of races is indicated by different definitions of a race among various societies; for example, in the United States, anyone who is known to have a black ancestor is considered to be black; while in Brazil, anyone known to have a white ancestor is considered to be white (Ehrlich and Holm, 1964).

Race, according to Montague (1964), becomes a very dangerous myth when it is assumed that physical traits are linked with mental traits and cultural achievements. Every few years, it seems, some noted scientist stirs the country by making this erroneous assumption. For example, Arthur Jensen (1969) asserted that whites, on the average, are more intelligent, as IQ tests show whites average scores of 10 to 15 points higher than blacks. Jensen's findings have been sharply criticized by other authorities as falsely assuming that IQ is largely genetically determined (Montague, 1975). These authorities contend that IQ is substantially influenced by environmental factors, and it is likely that the average achievement of blacks, if given similar opportunities to realize their potentialities, would be about the same as whites. Also, it has been charged that IQ tests are racially slanted. The tests ask the kinds of questions which whites are more familiar with and thereby more apt to answer correctly.

Elmer Johnson (1973, p. 50) summarizes the need for an impartial, objective view of the capacity of different racial groups to achieve:

> Race bigots contend that, the cultural achievements of different races being so obviously unlike, it follows that their genetic capacities for achievement must be just as different. Nobody can discover the cultural capacities of any population or race...until there is equality of opportunities to demonstrate the capacities.

Most scientists, both physical and social, now believe that, in biological inheritance, all races are alike in everything that really makes any difference (such as problem-solving capacities, altruistic tendencies, and communication capacities). With the exception of several very small, inbred, isolated, primitive tribes, all racial groups appear to show a wide distribution of every kind of ability. All important race differences that have been noted in personality, behavior, and achievement (e.g., a higher percentage of white students graduate from high school as compared to black students) appear to be due to environmental factors.

Institutional Discrimination

While personal discrimination does occur, the results of *institutional discrimination* affect more people and are generally more serious. Institutional discrimination is discrimination against minority groups that is built into economic, educational, and political institutions. A subcategory of institutional discrimination is *institutional racism*, which refers to discriminatory acts and policies against a racial group that pervade the major institutions of society, such as the legal system, politics, the economy, and education. Some of these discriminatory acts and policies are illegal, while others are not.

Carmichael and Hamilton (1969, p. 4) make the following distinction between individual racism and institutional racism:

> When white terrorists bomb a black church and kill five black children, that is an act of individual racism, widely deplored by most segments of society. But when in the same city...five hundred black babies die each year because of the lack of proper food, shelter, and medical facilities, and thousands more are destroyed and maimed physically, emotionally, and intellectually because of conditions of poverty and discrimination in the black community, that is a function of institutional racism.

Discrimination is built, often unwittingly, into the very structure and form of our society. The following examples reflect institutional discrimination. A family counseling agency with branch offices assigns less-skilled counselors and provides lower-quality services in an office located in a minority neighborhood. A public welfare department encourages white applicants to request funds for special needs (e.g., clothing) or to use certain services (e.g., day care and homemaker services with the costs charged to the agency), while nonwhite clients are not informed or are less enthusiastically informed of such services. A public welfare department takes longer to process the requests of members of minority groups for funds and services. A police department discriminates against nonwhite staff in work assignments, hiring practices, promotion practices, and pay increases. A probation and parole agency tends to ignore minor violations of the rules for parole of white clients but seeks to return to prison nonwhite parolees having minor violations of parole rules. A mental health agency tends to assign psychotic labels to nonwhite clients, while assigning labels indicating a less serious disorder to white clients. White staff at a family counseling center are encouraged to provide intensive services to clients with whom they have a good relationship (often white clients). On the other hand, they are told to give less attention to those clients "they aren't hitting it off well with" (these clients may be disproportionately nonwhite).

■ Institutional Discrimination in Mexican-American Barrios

Joan Moore (1976, p. 64) provides the following description of institutional discrimination in Mexican-American barrios. The description applies to many other ethnic slums as well.

The Mexican-American *barrios* are often of a quality that reflects . . . the peculiar lack of institutional response to their problems. Thus when a visitor enters Mexican-American *bar-*rios in many urban areas, ordinary urban facilities tend to disappear. Streets are unpaved; curbs and sidewalks and street lights disappear, traffic hazards go unremedied, and the general air of decay and neglect is unmistakable. Abandoned automobiles, uncollected refuse, and the hulks of burned-out buildings are monuments to the inadequacy of public services in such areas.

Globe Magazine (1971, p. 6) carried a news story of a case example of institutional discrimination that ended in tragedy. During the evening of April 27, 1971, the mother of Claris Blake (a 12-year-old black girl) called police requesting help in searching for her daughter who failed to return after going to a corner grocery store. The police never made a search, and the FBI refused to enter the case. On May 7, Claris called her mother and asked if her mother loved her—the phone then clicked. On May 15, Claris' body was found; she had been shot to death. Explained one official, "Look, let's face it; the wheel turned damned slowly in this case. It's not just the police. It's the double standard of our whole society. If a 12-year-old girl disappears on her way to the store and she's *white,* the assumption is she's met foul play. If a little girl disappears on her way to the store and she's *black,* everyone assumes she's just run away."

The unemployment rate for nonwhites has consistently been over twice that for whites. The infant mortality rate for nonwhites is nearly twice as high as for whites. The life expectancy age for nonwhites is several years less than for whites. The average number of years of educational achievement for nonwhites is considerably less than for whites (Julian, 1980, pp. 290–93).

Many examples of institutional racism are found in the school system. Schools in white suburbs generally have better facilities and more highly trained teachers than in minority neighborhoods. Minority families are, on the average, less able to provide the hidden costs of free education (higher property taxes, transportation, class trips, clothing, and supplies), and, therefore, their children become less involved in the educational process. Textbooks generally glorify the white race and give scant attention to minorities. Jeannette Henry (1967, p. 22) writes about the effects of history textbooks on Native American children:

> What is the effect upon the student, when he learns from his textbooks that one race, and one alone, is the most, the best, the greatest; when he learns that Indians[1] were mere parts of the landscape and wilderness which had to be cleared out, to make way for the great "movement" of white population across the land; and when he learns that Indians were killed and forcibly removed from their ancient homelands to make way for adventurers (usually called "pioneering goldminers"), for land grabbers (usually called "settlers"), and for illegal squatters on Indian-owned land (usually called "frontiersmen")? What is the effect upon the young Indian child himself, who is also a student in the school system, when he is told that Columbus discovered America, that Coronado "brought civilization" to the Indian people, and that the Spanish missionaries provided havens of refuge for the Indians? Is it reasonable to assume that the student, of whatever race, will not discover at some time in his life that Indians discovered America thousands of years before Columbus set out upon his voyage; that Coronado brought death and destruction to the native peoples; and that the Spanish missionaries, in all too many cases, forcibly dragged Indians to the missions?

Our criminal justice system also has elements of institutional racism. Our justice system is supposed to be fair and nondiscriminatory. The very name of the system, *justice,* implies fairness and equality. Yet, in practice, racism is evident. Although blacks compose only about 12 percent of the population, they make up 41 percent of the jail population. (There is considerable debate as to what extent this is due to racism as opposed to differential crime rates by race.) The average prison sentence for murder and kidnapping is longer for blacks than for whites. Fully half of those sentenced to death are black (Julian and Kornblum, 1983, pp. 298–99). Police departments and district attorney's offices are more likely to enforce vigorously the kinds of laws broken by lower-income groups and minority groups than by middle- and upper-class white groups. Poor people are substantially less likely to be able to post bail. As a result, they are forced to remain in jail until their trial, which often takes months or sometimes more than a year—until their case comes up. Unable to post bail, they are

[1]The term *Indian* was originally used by early European settlers to describe the native populations of North America. Because of its nonnative derivation and the context of cultural domination surrounding its use, many people, particularly Native Americans, object to the use of the word. The term *Native American* is now generally preferred.

more likely to be found guilty, as Paul Wice (1973, p. 23) notes:

> Numerous studies clearly show that detained defendants are far more likely to be found guilty and receive more severe sentences than those released prior to trial. Limited visiting hours, locations remote from the counsel's office, inadequate conference facilities, and censored mail all serve to impede an effective lawyer-client relationship.

The Sources of Prejudice and Discrimination

No single theory provides a complete picture of why racial and ethnic discrimination occurs. By being exposed to a variety of theories, the reader should at least be better sensitized to the nature and sources of discrimination. The sources of discrimination come from inside and outside a person.

Projection. Projection is a psychological defense mechanism in which one attributes to others characteristics that one is unwilling to recognize in oneself. Many people have personal traits they dislike in themselves. They have an understandable desire to get rid of such traits, but this is not always possible. Such people may project some of these traits onto others (often to some other group in society), thus displacing the negative feelings they would otherwise direct at themselves. In the process, they then reflect and condemn those onto whom they have projected the traits.

For example, a minority group may serve as a projection of a prejudiced person's fears and lusts. People who view blacks as lazy and preoccupied with sex may be projecting their own internal concerns about their industriousness and their sexual fantasies onto another group. While some whites view blacks as being promiscuous, historically, it has generally been white men who pressured black women (particularly slaves) into sexual encounters. It appears many white males felt guilty about these sexual desires and adventures and dealt with their guilt by projecting their own lusts and sexual conduct onto black males.

Frustration-aggression. Another psychic need satisfied by discrimination is the release of tension and frustration. All of us at times become frustrated when we are unable to achieve or obtain something we desire. Sometimes we strike back at the source of frustration, but many times direct retaliation is not possible—for example, we are reluctant to tell our employers what we think of them when we feel we are being treated unfairly, as we fear repercussions.

Some frustrated people displace their anger and aggression onto a *scapegoat*. The scapegoat may not be a particular person but may be a group of people. Similar to people who take out their job frustrations at home on their spouses or family pets, some prejudiced people vent their frustrations on minority groups. (The term scapegoat derives from an ancient Hebrew ritual, in which the goat was symbolically laden with the sins of the entire community and then chased into the wilderness. It escaped, hence the term scapegoat. The term was gradually broadened to apply to anyone who bears the blame for others.)

Countering Insecurity and Inferiority. Still another psychic need that may be satisfied through discrimination is the desire to counter feelings of insecurity or inferiority. Some insecure people seek to feel better about themselves by putting down another group, as they then can tell themselves that they are better than these people.

Authoritarianism. One of the classic works on the causes of prejudice is *The Authoritarian Personality* (Adorno, Frenkel-Brunswik, Devinson, and Sandord, 1950). Shortly after World War II, these researchers studied the psychological causes of the development of European fascism and concluded there was a distinct type of personality associated with prejudice and intolerance. The *authoritarian personality* is inflexible and rigid and has a low tolerance for uncertainty. This type of personality has a great respect for authority figures and quickly submits to their will. Such a person highly values conventional behavior and feels threatened by unconventional behavior of others. In order to reduce this threat, such a personality labels unconventional people as being immature, inferior, or degenerate and thereby avoids any need to question his or her own beliefs and values. The authoritarian personality views members of minority groups as being unconventional, degrades them, and tends to express authoritarianism through prejudice and discrimination.

History. Historical explanations can also be given for prejudice. Marden and Meyer (1962) note that the groups now viewed by white prejudiced persons as being second class are groups that have been either conquered, enslaved, or admitted into our society on a subordinate basis. For example, blacks were imported as slaves during our colonial period and stripped of human dignity. The Native Americans were conquered, and their culture was viewed as inferior. Mexican-Americans were allowed to enter this country primarily to do seasonal, low-paid farm work.

Competition and Exploitation. Our society is highly competitive and materialistic. Individuals and groups are competing daily with one another to acquire more of the available goods. These attempts to secure economic goods usually result in a struggle for power. In our society, whites have historically sought to exploit nonwhites. As previously mentioned, they have either conquered, enslaved, or admitted nonwhites into our society on a subordinate basis. Once the white group achieved dominance, it then used (and still is using) its power to exploit nonwhites through cheap labor—for example, as sweatshop factory laborers, migrant farm hands, maids, janitors, and bellhops.

Members of the dominant group know they are treating the subordinate group as inferior and unequal. To justify such discrimination, they develop an ideology (set of beliefs) that their group is superior—and that it is right and proper that they have more rights, goods, etc. Often, they assert God divinely selected their group to be dominant. Furthermore, they assign inferior traits to the subordinate group (lazy, heathen, immoral, dirty, stupid) and conclude that the minority needs and deserves less, as it is biologically inferior. Throughout history in most societies, the dominant group (which has greater power and wealth) has sought to maintain the status quo by keeping those who have the least in an inferior position.

Socialization Patterns. Prejudice is also a learned phenomenon and is transmitted from generation to generation through socialization processes. Our culture has stereotypes of what different minority group members "ought to be" and the ways minority group members "ought to behave" in relationships with members of the majority group. These stereotypes provide norms against which a child learns to judge persons, things, and ideas. Prejudice, to some extent, is developed through the same processes by which we learn to be religious and patriotic or to appreciate and to enjoy art or to develop our value system. Prejudice, at least in certain segments in our society, is thus a facet of the normative system of our culture.

In the Eye of the Beholder. No one theory explains all causes of prejudices, as prejudices have many origins. Taken together, however, they identify a number of causative factors. All theories assert that the causative factors of prejudice are in the personality and experiences of the person holding the prejudice and not in the character of the group against whom the prejudice is directed.

A novel experiment documenting that prejudice does not stem from contact with the people toward whom prejudice is directed was conducted by Eugene Hartley (1946). Hartley gave his subjects a list of prejudiced responses to Jews and blacks and to three groups that did not even exist: Wallonians, Pireneans, and Danireans. Prejudiced responses included such statements as all Wallonians living here should be expelled. The respondents were asked to state their agreement or disagreement with these prejudiced statements. The experiment showed that most of those who were prejudiced against Jews and blacks were also prejudiced against people whom they had never met or heard anything about.

The Effects and Costs of Discrimination

Grace Halsell is a white woman who, through chemical treatments, changed the color of her skin to look like a black person for a brief period of time in order to determine what it means to live black in a white world. Halsell (1969, pp. 156–57) reports on her experiences in working one day as a maid for a white woman in the South:

> Long before I have one job completed, there are new orders: "Now sweep off the front porch, the side porch, the back porch, and mop the back porch." The tone is unmistakably that of the mistress-slave relationship—
>
> I feel sorry for her. We are two women in a house all day long, and I sense that she desperately wants to talk to me, but I can never be as an equal. She looks on me as less than a wholly dignified and developed person . . .
>
> My eight hours are up. She asks if I know where to catch the bus. No, I say, should I turn left or right "when I go out the front door?" The *front* door comes out inadvertently, because I am only trying to get an idea of directions. She hands me five dollars and ushers me to the back door, quite pointedly.
>
> Two bus transfers and an hour later, I am back in "nigger-town." Near the Summers Hotel, young bright-eyed Negro[2] children I've come to know wave, smile, and say "hi!"

---

[2]When this was written in 1969, the term *Negro* was still used widely; but, in the 1970s, the preferred term changed to *black*, and the term *Negro* now is sometimes used to suggest a black person who interacts submissively with whites.

I want to tell each one of them because I feel so degraded, so morally and spiritually depressed, "Don't do what I did! Don't ever sell yourself that cheap! Don't let it happen to you."

And I want to add, "...whatever you do, don't do what I did." The assault upon an individual's dignity and self-respect has intolerable limits, and I believe at this moment my limits have been reached.

Racial discrimination is an extra handicap. Everyone in our competitive society seeks to obtain the necessary resources to lead a contented and comfortable life. Being a victim of discrimination is another obstacle which has to be overcome. Being discriminated against due to race makes it more difficult to obtain adequate housing, financial resources, a quality education, employment, adequate health care and other services, equal justice in civil and criminal cases, and so on.

Discrimination also has heavy psychological costs. All of us have to develop a sense of identity—who we are and how we fit into a complex, swiftly changing world. Ideally, it is important that we form a positive self-concept and strive to obtain worthy goals. Yet, as we have noted before, according to Cooley's (1902) "Looking Glass Self," our idea of who we are and what we are is largely determined by the way others relate to us. When members of a minority group are treated by the majority group as if they are inferior, second-class citizens, it is substantially more difficult for such members to develop a positive identity. Thus, people who are the objects of discrimination encounter barriers to developing their full potentials as human beings.

In 1965, prior to most "black pride" movements, Kenneth Clark (1965) described the devastating effects of discrimination on blacks:

> Human beings who are forced to live under ghetto conditions and whose daily experience tells them that almost nowhere in society are they respected and granted the ordinary dignity and courtesy accorded to others will, as a matter of course, begin to doubt their own worth. Since every human being depends upon his cumulative experiences with others for clues as to how he should view and value himself, children who are consistently rejected understandably begin to question and doubt whether they, their family, and their group really deserve no more respect from the larger society than they receive. These doubts become the seeds of pernicious self- and group-hatred, the Negro's complex and debilitating prejudice against himself.... Negroes have come to believe in their own inferiority.

Young children of groups who are the victims of discrimination are likely to develop low self-esteem at an early age. Porter (1971) has found black children who have been subjected to discrimination have a preference for white dolls and white playmates over black.

Discrimination also has high costs for the majority group. It impairs intergroup cooperation and communication. Discrimination also is a factor in contributing to social problems among minorities—for example, high crime rates, emotional problems, alcoholism, drug abuse—all of which have cost billions of dollars in social programs. Albert Szymanski (1976) argues that discrimination is a barrier to collective action (e.g., unionization) among whites and nonwhites (particularly people in the lower-income classes) and, therefore, is a factor in perpetuating low-paying jobs and poverty. Less affluent whites who could benefit from collective action are hurt.

The effects of discrimination are even reflected in life expectancy. The life expectancy of minority members is substantially lower than whites of European ancestry in our country. For example, blacks and Mexican-Americans live, on the average, six years less than the average white, and the life expectancy of Native Americans is 28 years less than that of whites (Coleman and Cressey, 1984, pp. 206–7). Coleman and Cressey (1984, p. 207) note, "The plain fact is that these people die earlier than others because they receive inferior food, shelter, and health care."

Finally, discrimination in the United States undermines some of our nation's political goals. Many other nations view us as hypocritical when we advocate human rights and equality. In order to make an effective argument for human rights on a worldwide scale, we must first put our own house in order by eliminating racial and ethnic discrimination. Few Americans realize the extent to which racial discrimination damages our international reputation. Nonwhite foreign diplomats to America often complain about being victims of discrimination, as they are mistaken for being members of American minority groups. With most of the nations of the world being nonwhite, our racist practices severely damage our influence and prestige.

The Effects of Discrimination on Human Growth and Development

The effects of discrimination will be illustrated by examining the research conducted on blacks, the largest racial minority group, composing about 12 percent of the population. We shall begin by examining some background material on the history and culture of blacks in our society.

History and Culture of Blacks

The United States has always been a racist country. Although our forefathers talked about freedom, dignity, equality, and human rights, our economy prior to the Civil War depended heavily on slavery.

Many slaves came from cultures that had well-developed art forms, political systems, family patterns, religious beliefs, and economic systems. However, their home culture was not European, and, therefore, slave owners viewed it as being of no consequence and prohibited slaves from practicing and developing their art, their language, their religion, and their family life. For want of practice, their former culture soon died in America.

The life of a slave was harsh. Slaves were not viewed as human beings, but as chattel to be bought and sold. Long, hard days were spent working in the field, with the profits of their labor going to their white owners. Whippings, mutilations, and hangings were commonly accepted white control practices. The impetus to enslave blacks was not simply racism, as many whites believed that it was to their economic advantage to have a cheap supply of labor. Cotton growing, in particular, was thought to require a large labor force that was also cheap and docile. Marriages among slaves were not recognized by the law, and slaves were often sold with little regard to effects on marital and family ties. Throughout the slavery period and even after it, blacks were discouraged from demonstrating intelligence, initiative, or ambition. For a period of time, it was even illegal to teach blacks to read or write.

Some authorities (Henderson and Kim, 1975, p. 180) have noted the opposition to the spread of slavery preceding the Civil War was primarily due to the Northern fears of competition from slave labor and the rapidly increasing migration of blacks to the North and West rather than to moral concern for human rights and equality. Few whites at that time understood or believed in the principle of racial equality—not even Abraham Lincoln, who believed blacks were inferior to whites.

Following the Civil War, the federal government failed to develop a comprehensive program of economic and educational aid to blacks. As a result, most blacks returned to being economically dependent on the same planters in the South who had held them in bondage. Within a few years, laws were passed in the Southern states prohibiting interracial marriages and requiring racial segregation in schools and public places.

A rigid caste system in the South hardened into a system of oppression known as Jim Crow laws. The system prescribed how blacks were supposed to act in the presence of whites, asserted white supremacy, embraced racial segregation, and denied political and legal rights to blacks. Blacks who opposed Jim Crow laws were subjected to burnings, beatings, and lynchings. Jim Crow laws were used to teach blacks to view themselves as inferior and to be servile and passive in interactions with whites.

World War II opened up new employment opportunities for blacks. A large migration of blacks from the South began. Greater mobility afforded by wartime conditions led to upheavals in the traditional caste system. Many blacks served in the armed forces during this war, fought and died for their country, and yet their country maintained segregated facilities. Awareness of disparity between the ideal and reality led many people to try to improve race relations, not only for domestic peace and justice, but to answer criticism from abroad. With each gain in race relations, more blacks were encouraged to press for their rights.

A major turning point in black history was the U.S. Supreme Court decision in *Brown* v. *Board of Education* in 1954, which ruled that racial segregation in public schools was unconstitutional. Since 1954, there have been a number of organized efforts by both blacks and certain segments of the white population to secure equal rights and opportunities for blacks. Attempts to change deeply entrenched racist attitudes and practices have produced much turmoil: the burning of our inner cities in the late 1960s, the assassination of Martin Luther King, Jr., and clashes between black militant groups and the police. There have also been significant advances. Wide-ranging civil rights legislation, protecting rights in areas such as housing, voting, employment, and use of public transportation and facilities, has been passed. Charles Henderson and Bok-Lim Kim (1975, p. 180) summarize the current situation:

> Blacks are on the move physically, economically, and socially. In the 1960s and early 1970s, blacks migrated from the rural South into the cities of the nation's North and West. There, with greater choices, many have been progressing from unskilled, low-paid jobs into white-collar and skilled occupations. In search of better housing and better jobs, many have been moving from the city to the surrounding suburbs. A migrant population has been giving way to settled, urban dwellers, as increasing numbers are moving economically and socially from extreme poverty into middle-class status.
>
> Many blacks, however, are left behind both in the rural backwaters of the South and in urban ghettos. In many instances, white progress has been so much greater that it overshadows black gains.

The children in this picture, who are racially different, attend a racially integrated school. They each have physical characteristics unique to their own racial groups. Unlike a racial group, an ethnic group comprises people with a sense of common identity. But a racial group can also be an ethnic group. One example are the Japanese-Americans. They have both a sense of "peoplehood" and physical characteristics in common. (Courtesy of United Way of America)

Social workers should be keenly aware of the many effective ways of promoting racial integration. Encouraging children to join interracial groups fosters integration. The social worker should learn about the culture of the group or groups that he or she is leading. But since social workers, too, are raised in a society where racial and ethnic prejudices exist, they must first examine and rid themselves of their own racial prejudices. (Courtesy of United Way of America)

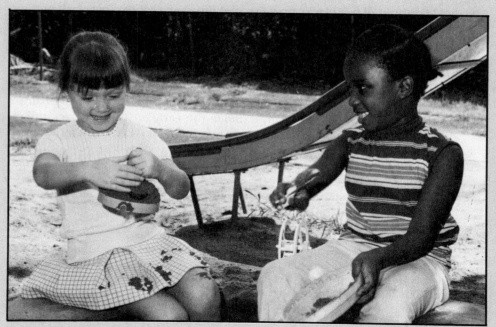

Increased contact between minority groups and majority groups doesn't always alleviate prejudice. In fact, in some cases, such contact heightens prejudice. A good way to put an end to prejudice is to put people in an "equal status" situation. These two children are at play in an equal status situation. They have overcome prejudice and are sharing two things that have nothing to do with racial or ethnic matters: toys and play time. (Courtesy of United Way of America)

How effectively is prejudice obliterated in equal rights situations? As these children at play demonstrate, equal rights can be extremely effective in bringing about interracial harmony. Over three decades ago, equal rights laws were put in effect in the areas of housing, voting, public accommodation, and education. Unfortunately, some officials still find ways of circumventing these laws. But the laws are an important first step in banishing prejudiced attitudes and practices. (Courtesy of United Way of America)

Four out of five blacks now live in metropolitan areas, over half of them in our central cities (*Statistical Abstract of the United States, 1984*). American cities are still largely segregated, with blacks primarily living in black neighborhoods. In recent years, the main thrust of the civil rights movement among blacks has been economic equality. The economic gap between blacks and whites continues to be immense. Black families are three times as likely as white families to fall below the poverty line (*Statistical Abstract of the United States, 1984*, p. 471). Since the early 1950s, the black unemployment rate has been approximately twice that for whites. Unemployment is an especially severe problem for black teenagers, whose rate of unemployment is substantially higher than for white youth and has run as high as 50 percent (Robertson, 1980, p. 216).

Occupational status in our society is crucially related to self-esteem and lifestyle, as demonstrated in the following statement by a 39-year-old black male:

> How can you have any pride? I'm a part-time worker—a part-time husband. I guess I'm really a part-time man. I can't find enough to do to keep food on the table. Guess some people would think that I'm the sorriest man that ever wore out shoe leather. It ain't that I don't have no get-up, it's just that I can't find nothing to do. I had to leave home so the children could eat. While I'm sitting here with you, they're out looking for me. That ain't so bad—what really hurts is that my wife is going to tell them people down at the welfare that some other man is the baby's daddy, or else she thinks she can't get no aid. If they take her off welfare, she'll starve. So every time she has another baby, she gives a different guy's name—excuse me for bawling, man, I just can't help it—but it sure ain't no justice when a man's got to make his own children bastards in order to feed them (Moore, 1969, p. 71).

We, as a nation, have come a long way since the U.S. Supreme Court's decision in 1954. But we still have a long way to go before we eliminate black poverty and respond to the deep frustrations of blacks in our ghettos. Living conditions in black ghettos remain as bleak as they were when our inner cities erupted in the late 1960s.

Most blacks live in census tracts that are 50 percent or more black (Cottingham, 1975). This means that despite the racial diversity of American society, a majority of black children are raised in black neighborhoods, with limited exposure to the dominant white society.

Most black children live in homes where the median income is lower than that in the homes of most white children. In recent decades there has been a significant growth of the black middle class, which has been partly due to increased college education among blacks and to affirmative action programs. Anderson and Dumpson (1978) have noted that middle-class blacks are as segregated from low-income blacks as rich whites are from poor whites. Although there is a growing black middle class, there continues to be a large lower socioeconomic black underclass. Many members of this underclass are jobless and live in inner cities. In many jobless low-income black families, the children lack resources to develop to their maximum potential.

■ Anacostia—A Black Neighborhood Near the White House

People in Anacostia can stand on their porches and see one of the grandest views in America—the dome of the nation's capitol, the top of the Washington Monument, and the spires of the National Cathedral.

In many ways Anacostia is a microcosm of urban, black America. The view in Anacostia includes boarded-up windows, trash, potholes, broken-down autos, and decaying buildings. The glitter of the nation's capitol, only a few miles away, does not reach Anacostia. There are no fancy restaurants or shopping malls. Street corners are often the sites of drug deals. Anacostia is a mostly poor, mostly black neighborhood in southeast Washington, D.C.

Much of the federal aid that Anacostia once had was lost to Reagan administration budget cuts. Anacostians believe that Washington's predominantly black-run city government has neglected them (*U.S. News and World Report*, Dec. 10, 1984, p. 74). Some sections have no streetlights. Buses are overcrowded, even at midday. Most cabs, even with black drivers, refuse to go to Anacostia. Crime rates are high—including high rates of burglary, robbery, larceny, rape, aggravated assault, arson, and homicide.

Most of the housing is low income, much of it old and in need of repair. Many houses are owned by absentee landlords and have been subdivided into three or more units. Many small merchants in the area conduct business behind bulletproof glass.

What is the remedy for combating urban blight in our society? Many programs have been tried. The Model Cities Program grew out of the War on Poverty and the 1964 Equal Opportunity Act. Urban blight areas in several cities were targeted for massive federal intervention aimed at improving housing, employment, health care, educational opportunities, and reducing poverty. The results have not been very successful. Our inner cities are in as bad a state of urban decay as they were two or three decades ago (Hull, 1984, pp. 435–36). Anacostia is just one of the numerous inner city blight areas where a feasible intervention approach has not as yet been identified.

Nearly half of all black children are being raised in single-parent families. Morton (1983) notes, however, that many black children living in single-parent families are living in family structures composed of some variation of the extended family. Many single-parent families move in with relatives during adversity, including economic adversity. In addition, black families of all levels rely on relatives to care for their children while they work. Notes Norton (1983, p. 183):

> Many middle-class families pay an aunt or cousin or mother to come into their homes and babysit, with formal salary arrangements. Having reached financial stability themselves, they not only share that stability by providing economic opportunity for other family members but also assure that their children will receive responsible, loving and interested family-oriented child-care. Other, less well off families drop their children at the home of relatives, making financial arrangements that are probably lower in cost. For others, there are no financial arrangements, but reciprocity is given in returned child-care, sharing of food, clothing or shelter.

Solomon (1983, p. 420) has noted " . . . black culture contains elements of 'mainstream' white culture, elements from traditional African culture, and elements from slavery, reconstruction and subsequent exposure to racism and discrimination."

Subcultures of blacks have vocabularies and communication styles that differ from the dominant white culture. Young children raised in these subcultures often have difficulty understanding the English language spoken in schools. Black American dialects appear to be the result of a creolized form of English that was at one time spoken on Southern plantations by black slaves (Dillard, 1972). (*Creolize* refers to a language based on two or more languages that serves as the native language of its speaker.) It has been estimated that approximately 80 percent of blacks speak a "radically nonstandard" English (Wilson, 1978). Present-day black English is a combination of the linguistic remnants of its Southern plantation past and a reflection of the current black sociocultural situation. As such, it is important to recognize it as a dialect in its own right and not perceive it as just a distortion of standard English. Most adult blacks are at least bicultural, being fluent in a black American dialect and in standard English.

Religious organizations that are predominantly black have tended to have not only a spiritual mission, but also have been highly active in social action efforts to combat racial discrimination against blacks. Many prominent black leaders, such as Martin Luther King, Jr., and Jesse Jackson, have been members of the clergy. Black churches have served to develop leadership skills. They have served as social welfare organizations to meet basic needs, such as clothing, food, shelter. Black churches are natural support systems for troubled black individuals and families.

Many blacks have had the historical experience of being subjected to negative evaluations by school systems, social welfare agencies, health care institutions, and the justice system. Because of their past experiences, blacks are likely to view such institutions with apprehension. Schools, for example, have erroneously perceived blacks as being less capable of developing cognitive skills. Such perceptions about school failure are often a self-fulfilling prophecy. If black children are expected to fail in school systems, teachers are likely to put forth less effort in challenging them to learn, and black children may then put forth less effort to learn, resulting in a lower level of achievement.

Black response to discrimination may be expressed in a variety of ways: anger, hostility, passiveness, dependency, distrust, frustration, and feelings of powerlessness.

Black Reactions to Discrimination

William Grier and Price Cobb (1968, p. 204) have identified three possible defensive postures taken by blacks in their interactions with whites:

1. Cultural paranoia that assumes that anyone white or any social institution dominated by whites will potentially act against a black's best interests.
2. Cultural depression that is a consequence of life experiences and serves to define a black as less capable, less worthy than whites.
3. Cultural antisocialism that develops from a black's experience with laws, policies, and institutional procedures, which have no respect for him or her as an individual or blacks as a group; the black, in turn, has no respect for, or obligation to conform to, these laws, policies, or procedures.

In developing their personalities, blacks have the task of achieving a balanced response to the experience of racism and discrimination. Chestang (1972) contends that blacks have dual personality components. One is a depreciated element that recognizes the low status that society ascribes to them and responds with feelings of hopelessness and worthlessness. The other is a transcendent element that seeks to overcome this low status and to actualize the potential for successful psychosocial functioning. If either of these two elements becomes too dominant, problems are likely to arise. For example, the overly depreciated personality conveys an image of a deserving victim, while the overly transcendent personality conveys a self-centered, conceited image.

Some of the attitudes and behaviors exhibited by blacks who seek services from white social agencies are often labeled resistance. However, the attitudes and behaviors can better be viewed as attempts at coping with powerlessness and racism. For example, if there are delays in provision of services, blacks may convey apathy or disparage the agency as they interpret the delay as being due to racism and then respond in ways they have learned in the past to handle discrimination.

Effects of Discrimination on Development of Self-Concept

The term *self-concept* refers to the positive and negative thoughts and feelings that one has towards one's self. It is often used interchangeably with such terms as self-image, sense of self, self-esteem, and identity. A positive self-concept is a key element in school achievement, in positive social interactions with others, and in emotional, social, and intellectual growth (Moss and Kagan, 1958).

Barnes (1972) reviewed the theoretical perspectives on self-concept. He notes that black families have been socialized to believe they are substandard human beings and that black children learn that their black skin color and hair texture is culturally viewed as being undesirable. He concludes such discrimination is apt to lead to the following in a black child: "incomplete self-image; negative self-image and preference for white; and rejection of and expressed hostility toward his own group" (p. 168). Barnes (1972, p. 169) also concludes the black child's cognitive status, emotional well-being, and achievement orientation are apt to be adversely affected by discrimination in the following ways:

- High anxiety level.
- High level of maladjustment.
- Neuroticism and rejection of other Afro-Americans.
- Inability to delay gratification.
- Low-level orientation toward achievement.
- Proneness toward delinquency.
- Confusion of sexual identity or sex role adoption.
- Sense of little personal control over the environment.
- Low achievement motivation.
- Unrealistically high aspirations.

Barnes' major conclusion is that the possibilities of a black child developing a positive self-concept in this society are nil. Most authorities are not as pessimistic as Barnes.

Solomon (1983) notes that if black adults accept society's label of inferiority, they are likely to convey such thoughts and feelings to their children. Such children are not only likely to develop a negative self-concept, but then are also likely to put less effort into developing cognitive skills, and less effort into achieving in school. Because of low self-esteem and under-developed cognitive skills they are less likely to develop interpersonal or technical skills, which then results in having difficulties in social interactions and to being restricted in adulthood to low-paying, low-skill jobs. The vicious circle is then completed when such difficulties confirm and reinforce feelings of inferiority and of negative value, which are then begun to be passed on to their children.

A number of studies have in recent years been conducted on the extent to which discrimination adversely affects self-concept development in black children. Very significantly, these studies indicate that the black child's conceptualization of self does not necessarily have to be impaired by racism. Concludes Powell (1983, p. 73):

> Afro-Americans have survived a harsh system of slavery, repression, and racism. Although there have been casualties, there have been many more survivors, achievers, and victors. The cultural heritage of coping with adversity and overcoming has been passed on from generation to generation, laced with stories of those with remarkable courage and fortitude.

Given the pervasiveness of racism and discrimination in our society, why is it that many black children overcome this obstacle in self-concept development, and develop a fairly positive sense of self-esteem? The reason appears to involve the fact that every person is embedded simultaneously in at least two systems: one is the larger society and the other is one's immediate social and physical environment. The latter environment includes family members, other relatives, peers, friends, and neighbors. One's immediate environment appears to be the predominant system in shaping one's self-concept. It appears that the child who is loved, accepted and supported in his immediate environment comes to love and respect himself as someone worthy of love.

Black children, as they grow older, learn of the larger society's devaluation. Practically all black children are aware by age seven or eight of the social devaluation placed on their racial group (Baumrind, 1972). The awareness of this devaluation does not necessarily extend to the black child's evaluation of himself as an individual. The sense of self developed in the immediate environment acts as a buffer against the potential devaluation by the larger society.

Certainly racism has the potential for adverse effects on the self-esteem development for black children. In spite of racism in our economic, political, and social structures, black families have not only survived but have interacted with their children in ways that foster the development of a positive identity.

Strategies to Combat Discrimination

A wide range of strategies have been developed to reduce racial and ethnic discrimination. These strategies include the following: mass media appeals, strategies to increase interaction among racial and ethnic groups, civil rights laws, activism, school busing, affirmative action programs, human relations programs, and confrontation of racist and ethnic remarks and actions. Since racism is a more serious problem in our society than ethnocentrism, most of the strategies against discrimination primarily focus on curtailing racial discrimination.

Mass Media Appeals

Newspapers, radio, and television present programs that are designed to explain the nature and harmful effects of prejudice and promote the harmony of humanity. Mass media are able to reach large numbers of people simultaneously. By expanding public awareness of the existence of discrimination and its consequences, the media may strengthen control over racial and ethnic extremists. But mass media have limitations in changing prejudiced attitudes and behaviors; they are primarily a provider of information and seldom have a lasting effect in changing deep-seated prejudices through propaganda. Broadcasting such platitudes as "all people are brothers and sisters" and "prejudice is un-American" is not very effective. Highly prejudiced persons are often unaware of their own prejudices. Even if they are aware of their prejudices, they generally ignore mass media appeals as irrelevant to them or dismiss the appeals as propaganda. However, the media probably have had a significant impact in reducing discrimination through showing nonwhites and whites harmoniously working in commercials, on news teams, and on TV shows.

Greater Interaction between Minority Groups and the Majority Group

Increased contact between minority groups and the majority group is not in itself sufficient to alleviate prejudice. In fact, increased contact may, in some instances, highlight the differences between groups and increase suspicions and fear. Simpson and Yinger (1965, p. 510) reviewed a number of studies and concluded that prejudice is likely to be increased when contacts are tension laden or involuntary. Prejudice is likely to subside when individuals are placed in situations where they share characteristics in nonracial and nonethnic matters; for example, as coworkers, fellow soldiers, or classmates. Equal status contacts, rather than inferior-superior status contact, are also more apt to reduce prejudices (Sullivan, 1980, p. 437).

Civil Rights Laws

In the past 30 years, equal rights have been legislated in areas of employment, voting, housing, public accommodation, and education. A key question is "How effective are laws in changing prejudice?"

Proponents of civil rights legislation make certain assumptions. The first is that new laws will reduce discriminatory behavioral patterns. The laws define what was once normal behavior (discrimination) as now being deviant behavior. Through time, it is expected that attitudes will change and become more consistent with the forced nondiscriminatory behavior patterns.

A second assumption is that the laws will be used. Civil rights laws were enacted after the Civil War but were seldom enforced and gradually were eroded. It is also unfortunately true that some officials will find ways of evading the intent of the law by eliminating only the extreme, overt symbols of discrimination, without changing other practices. Thus, the enactment of a law is only the first step in the process of changing prejudiced attitudes and practices. However, as Martin Luther King, Jr., noted, "The law may not make a man love me, but it can restrain him from lynching me, and I think that's pretty important."

Activism

The strategy of activism attempts to change the structure of race relations through direct confrontations of discrimination and segregation policies. Activism has three types of politics: the politics of creative disorder, the politics of disorder, and the politics of escape (Johnson, 1973, pp. 374–79).

The *politics of creative disorder* operates on the edge of the dominant social system and includes school boycotts, rent strikes, job blockades, sit-ins, public marches, and product boycotts. This type of activism is based on the concept of nonviolent resistance. A dramatic illustration of nonviolent resistance began on December 1, 1955 in Montgomery, Alabama, when Rosa Parks refused to give up her seat on a bus to a white person. Alabama and many other Southern states at that time had Jim Crow laws which were designed to enforce segregation. One such law required blacks to sit in the back seats of buses. Mrs. Parks refused to get up and move to the back. She was arrested, and the famous Montgomery Bus Boycott ensued. The boycott lasted for a year and resulted in a U.S. Supreme Court ruling that declared ordinances which required segregated seating on public conveyances to be unconstitutional. The boycott had an even more important psychological impact, as it suggested that minority citizens had rights equal to those of whites and that united nonviolent resistance could overturn discriminatory laws (Cummings, 1977, pp. 197–206).

The *politics of disorder* reflects alienation from the dominant culture and disillusionment with the political system. Those being discriminated against resort to mob uprisings, riots, and other forms of violence.

In 1969, the National Commission on Causes and Prevention of Violence reported that 200 riots had occurred in the previous five years, when our inner cities erupted (Sullivan et al., 1980, p. 438). In the early 1980s, we have again seen some riots in Miami and in some of our other inner cities. The focus of most of these riots has been minority group aggression against white-owned property.

The *politics of escape* engages in rhetoric about how minorities are being victimized. But, since the focus is not on arriving at solutions, the rhetoric is not productive, except perhaps for providing an emotional release.

The principal value of social protest seems to be the stimulation of public awareness of certain problems. The civil rights protests in the 1960s made practically all Americans aware of the discrimination to which nonwhite groups were being subjected. With this awareness, at least some of the discrimination has ceased, and race relations have improved. Continued protest beyond a certain (although indeterminate) point, however, appears to have little additional value (Sullivan et al., 1980, p. 376).

School Busing

Housing patterns in many large metropolitan centers have led to de facto segregation; that is, blacks and certain other nonwhite groups live in one area, while whites live in another. This segregation has affected educational opportunities for nonwhites. Nonwhite areas have fewer financial resources, and, as a result, the educational quality is often substantially lower than in white areas. In recent years, courts in a number of metropolitan areas have ordered that a certain proportion of nonwhites must be bused to schools in white areas, and that a certain proportion of whites must be bused to schools in nonwhite areas. The objectives are twofold: to provide equal educational opportunities and to reduce racial prejudice through interaction.

In some areas, school busing has become accepted and appears to be meeting the stated objectives. In other areas, however, the approach is highly controversial and has exacerbated racial tensions. Busing in these areas is claimed to be highly expensive; to be destructive of the neighborhood school in which the facility serves as a recreational, social, and educational center of the community; and to result in lower-quality education. A number of parents in these areas feel so strongly about busing that they are sending their children to private schools. In addition, some have argued that busing increases white flight from neighborhoods where busing has been ordered (Sullivan et al., 1980, p. 439). In 1970, William Raspberry, a columnist for the *Washington Post*, commented about the effects of busing in Washington, D.C.: "We find ourselves busing children from all-black neighborhoods all the way across town to schools that are rapidly becoming all-black" (*Washington Post*, 1970).

Additional concerns have been expressed about busing. Busing children a long distance is very costly and uses funds that could otherwise be used to improve the quality of education. Busing lessens local control and interest in schools, and it makes it less practical for parents to become involved in school affairs, as the school is less accessible.

Busing may also intensify racial tensions. For example, in Boston in 1975, a federal judge ordered school busing in order to counter housing segregation patterns. The Irish and Polish descendants of South Boston (who saw themselves as oppressed ethnic minorities) violently opposed the busing, and racial tensions intensified for several years. Sociologists also voice concern that school busing in an atmosphere of hostility may reduce the quality of education and increase racial prejudices and tensions.

School busing to achieve integration was vigorously pursued by the court system and the federal Justice Department in the 1970s. In 1981, the Reagan administration stated it would be much less active in advocating that busing be used as a vehicle to achieve integration. Both the Reagan administration and the Justice Department have been slow to press for busing to achieve integration in the 1980s.

Affirmative Action

Affirmative action programs require that employers demonstrate they are actively employing minority applicants. Employers can no longer defend themselves by claiming that a decision not to hire a minority group member was based on some criterion other than ethnic group membership. If the percentage of minority group members in their employ is significantly lower than the percentage in the workforce, employers must accept a goal for minority employment and set up timetables stating when these goals are likely to be met.

Affirmative action programs provide for preferential hiring and admission requirements (e.g., admission to medical schools) for minority applicants. Affirmative action programs cover all minority groups including women. These programs also require that employers make active efforts to locate and recruit qualified minority applicants and in certain circumstances, have hard quotas under which specific numbers of minority members, regardless of their qualifications, must be accepted to fill vacant positions (e.g., a university with a high proportion of white, male faculty may be required to fill half of its faculty vacancies with women and other minority groups). Affirmative action programs require that employers must demonstrate according to a checklist of positive measures that they are not guilty of discrimination.

A major dilemma with affirmative action programs is that preferential hiring and quota programs involve reverse discrimination, where qualified majority-group members are sometimes arbitrarily excluded. Several successful lawsuits have claimed reverse discrimination. The best-known case to date has been that of Alan Bakke, who was initially denied admission to the medical school at the University of California at Davis in 1973. He alleged reverse discrimination, as he had higher grades and higher scores on the Medical College Admissions Test than several minority applicants who were admitted under the university's minorities quota policy. In 1978, his claim was upheld by the U.S. Supreme Court in a precedent-setting decision (Sindler, 1978). The court ruled that strict racial quotas were unconstitutional, but the court did not rule out that race might be used as one among many criteria in making admissions decisions. Undoubtedly more court cases will be decided before a coherent policy emerges in this area.

Charles Henderson et al. (1980, p. 403) summarize some of the views of whites and minority groups about affirmative action:

> The minority worker in white agencies often asks himself: "Why have I been hired?" . . . . The worker may meet resistance from white colleagues if he or she is a product of "affirmative action," seen by some white people as simply "reverse discrimination." Whites may be quick to say that competence is what counts. Blacks perceive this as saying that they are not competent. Considering the many ways in which whites have acquired jobs, blacks wonder why competence is now suggested as the only criterion for employment. For every white professional who may dislike affirmative action to compensate for past exclusions and injustices, there is a black professional who feels that it is tragic that organizations have had to be forced to hire minorities.

Supporters of affirmative action programs also note that the majority group expressed little concern about discrimination when its members were the beneficiaries instead of the victims of discrimination. They also assert there is no other way to make up rapidly for past discrimination against minorities—many of whom may presently score slightly lower on qualification tests simply because they did not have the opportunities and the quality of training that the majority group members have had.

With affirmative action programs, some minority group members are given preferential treatment, which results in some whites being discriminated against. But minority group members still face more employment discrimination than whites do.

Affirmative action programs raise delicate and complex questions about achieving equality through giving preferences in hiring and admissions to minorities. Yet, no other means has been found to end subtle discrimination in hiring and admissions.

Admission to educational programs and securing well-paying jobs are crucial elements in working toward integration. The history of immigrant groups who have made it (such as the Irish, Japanese, and Italians) suggests equality will only be achieved when minority group members gain middle- and upper-class status. Once such status is achieved, the minority group members become an economic and political force with which to be reckoned. The dominant groups then are pressured into modifying their norms, values, and stereotypes. For this reason, a number of authorities have noted that the elimination of economic discrimination is a prerequisite for achieving equality and harmonious race relations (Featherman and Hauser, 1976, pp. 621–51). Achieving educational equality between races is also crucial, as lower educational attainments lead to poorer jobs, lower incomes, lower-living standards, and the perpetuation of racial inequalities from one generation to the next.

Human Relations Programs

Some school systems have human relations programs, which are designed to alleviate prejudice and discrimination. One program has been developed by the public school system in Madison, Wisconsin (Buchanan and Cummings, 1975). The goal is to help children gain a better awareness of themselves as individuals and a better understanding of, and respect for, individual differences in others.

The program has several steps, along with some suggested activities, books, and other helpful hints for parents and teachers to use with their children. Some of the key concepts are the following:

- Each person is unique, with all people having common needs.
- Each person can do some things better than other things. It is a serious mistake to use yourself as a yardstick to measure others' abilities or to use others as a yardstick to measure yours. Words such as "stupid" or "dumb" hurt deeply, especially when one is doing one's best.
- Each person has different attitudes, ideas, beliefs, and values. Although the beliefs of others may differ from one's own, they are no less important.
- Prejudice differs from a dislike. Prejudice is defined broadly as "when you are against someone you do not know because of some/one of their differences" (Buchanan and Cummings, 1975, p. 13).

The program assists children in learning personal differences and how a lack of understanding about these differences can be related to prejudice. The program explains that melanin is the pigment responsible for light and dark skin color differences. The more melanin you have, the darker you are; but melanin, of course, in no way governs the personality or behavior of a person. Tanning occurs because the skin produces more melanin to protect it from the hot sun; yet tanning does not change the inner self, only the outside wrapping. Students are given an understanding of other individual differences such as retardation, religious differences, epilepsy, and hearing impairments so that they can be more respectful of such differences. The program also assists students in learning about and appreciating cultural and ethnic differences.

Such programs offer considerable promise of being a highly effective strategy in alleviating discrimination in the following areas: race, sex, ethnic or cultural differences, religious or political differences, and physical or mental handicaps.

Racist jokes and sarcastic remarks help shape and perpetuate stereotypes and prejudices. It is important that both whites and nonwhites tactfully but assertively indicate they do not view such remarks as being humorous or appropriate. It is also important that people tactfully and assertively point out the inappropriateness of racist actions by others. Such confrontations make explicit that subtle racist remarks and actions are discriminatory and harmful, which has a consciousness raising effect. Gradually, it is expected that such confrontations will reduce racial prejudices and actions.

Noted author, lecturer, and abolitionist Frederick Douglass (1977, p. 201) stated:

> Power concedes nothing without a demand—it never did, and it never will. Find out just what people will submit to, and you've found out the exact amount of injustice and wrong which will be imposed upon them. This will continue until they resist, either with words, blows, or both. The limits of tyrants are prescribed by the endurance of those whom they oppress.

Social Work Practice with Racial and Ethnic Groups

Social workers and other helping persons have many of the prejudices, stereotypes, and misperceptions of the general society. There is a danger that a social worker will use his own cultural, social, or economic values in assessing and providing services to clients.

The problematic nature of cross-cultural social work does not, however, preclude its effectiveness. While many white practitioners can establish productive working relationships with minority clients, others cannot. In other instances, minority practitioners are sometimes effective and sometimes not with others of the same race or ethnic group (Mizio, 1972). This concept is illustrated by the following statement by a client who is black and Catholic:

> In answering the question of whether a white middle-class psychiatrist can treat a black family, I cannot help but think back over my own experiences. When I first came to New York and decided to go into psychotherapy I had two main thoughts: (1) that my problems were culturally determined and (2) that they were related to my Catholic upbringing. I had grown up in an environment in which the Catholic Church had tremendous influence. With these factors in mind, I began to think in terms of the kind of therapist I could best relate to. In addition to being warm and sensitive, he had to be black and Catholic. Needless to say, that was like looking for a needle in a haystack. But after inquiring around, I was finally referred to a black Catholic psychiatrist.
>
> Without going into too much detail, let me say that he turned out to be not so sensitive and not so warm. I terminated my treatment with him and began to see another therapist who was warm, friendly, sensitive, understanding and very much involved with me. Interestingly enough, he was neither black nor Catholic. As a result of that personal experience, I have come to believe that it is not so much a question of whether the therapist is black or white but whether he is competent, warm and understanding. Feelings, after all, are neither black nor white (Sager, Brayboy, and Waxenberg, 1970, pp. 210-11).

In order for a worker to be effective in working with diverse racial and ethnic groups, the worker needs to learn the culture of the group or groups he is working with; be aware of his own values, prejudices, and stereotypes; and learn which intervention approaches are apt to be effective, and which are apt to be ineffective, with the group or groups he is working with.

Learning the Culture of the Group

In working with a diverse culture the following questions are crucial: How are the members likely to view someone from a different culture? What kinds of communications and actions are likely to lead to the development of a relationship? How do members view asking for help from a social agency? If the agency is viewed as being part of the dominant white society which has devalued this group in the past, how are the members likely to view the social agency? What are the values of the group? When the members of this group need help, who are they most likely to turn to—relatives, friends, neighbors, church, social agencies, school system, or local government? What are culturally acceptable ways of providing help to people in need?

If a white worker is serving low-income, inner-city, black clients, Barbara Draper (1979, p. 279) briefly describes in the following excerpt some of the ways to learn about the culture:

> The white worker must try to enter the life space of the black client. He/she must listen to the expression of black language, its sounds and meaning. Read black literature and newspapers. Listen to black radio stations to get with the tempo and temper of blacks' feelings. Leave the office and walk around in black neighborhoods—look at the parts that are slums, but also acknowledge the blocks that are kept with pride . . . . Look at the addict and the pimp but also see those who carry themselves with dignity. Look at the hustler but also see the shopkeeper, the dentist, the doctor. Go with the black client to the hospital and the social service agency. Notice the very real differences in the way services are often given to black and white clients . . . . There is infinite variety among blacks whether in the metropolis or the small town.

As a corollary of becoming accepted by clients of diverse racial or ethnic groups, the worker must live his or her personal life in a manner that will not offend important values and mores of these groups.

Self-Awareness of Values, Prejudices, and Stereotypes

Since workers are raised in a society where racial and ethnic prejudices abound, workers also have prejudices and stereotypes.

Let us directly ask the reader a few questions at this point. In the past year have you listened to some racial or ethnic jokes? Did you laugh? If you did laugh, do you think your laughter, in a minute way, was perpetuating some of the racial or ethnic stereotypes that exist? Have you told in the past year some racial or ethnic jokes? If yes, was the content derogatory? By telling such jokes, are you demonstrating some of your prejudices and stereotypes? By telling such jokes, are you not, in a small way, reinforcing some of the harmful stereotypes and prejudices that exist in our society?

Racial and ethnic prejudices can be demonstrated by the following exercise: "Assume you are single; place a checkmark by the following ethnic and racial groups that you would be hesitant or reluctant to marry a member of."

___ Iranian	___ American Native	___ Puerto Rican
___ Chinese	___ Italian	___ German
___ Japanese	___ Mexican	___ Vietnamese
___ Samoan	___ Egyptian	___ French
___ Filipino	___ Irish	___ Russian
___ Black	___ Cuban	

If you have checked some of these (and most people check several), analyze your thoughts as to why you would be hesitant to marry those you have checked. There is a fair chance that such an analysis will help you identify some of your prejudices.

Since practically everyone has racial and ethnic stereotypes and prejudices, one needs to be aware of them in order to remain objective in working with clients. When a helping professional is working with a client of a racial or ethnic group that he or she has negative perceptions about, the helping professional should continually be asking the following questions: Am I individualizing this person as a unique person with worth, or am I making the mistake of viewing this person in terms of my prejudices and stereotypes? Am I working up to my full capacities with this individual, or am I seeking to cut corners by probing less deeply, by not fully informing this person of the services he or she is eligible for, by wanting to end the interview before fully exploring all the client's problems or fully exploring all possible alternatives?

Techniques of Intervention

The third area is for the worker to learn which intervention approaches are likely to be effective, and which are likely to be ineffective with the ethnic or racial group he or she is working with. Several guidelines will be presented for illustrative purposes.

Workers should seek to use their own patterns of communication and avoid the temptation to adopt the client's accent, vocabulary or speech (Hull, 1985, p. 254). The worker who seeks to do the latter is apt to make mistakes in enunciations, and thereby come across as a phony, or may offend the client if the client interprets the worker's communication to be mimicry.

A worker with an urban background who has a job in a small rural community needs to live his personal life in a way that is consistent with community values and standards. A worker who gains a reputation as being a violator of community norms will not be effective in a small community. Neither the power structure nor a majority of clients are likely to give such a worker credibility. A worker in a small community needs to identify community values in areas such as the following: religious beliefs and patterns of expression, dating and marriage patterns, values towards domestic and wild animals (for example, opposing deer hunting in many communities may run counter to strong local values), drug usage, political beliefs and values, and sexual mores. Once such values are identified, the worker needs to seek to achieve a balance between the kind of lifestyle he wants and the kind of lifestyle the community expects he will live.

Kadushin (1972) recommends using all of the formalities in initial meetings with adult clients of diverse racial and ethnic groups. Such usage should include the formal title (Mr., Miss, Mrs., Ms.), the client's proper full name, greeting with a handshake, and the other courtesies usually extended. In initial contacts workers should also usually show their agency identification and state the reasons for the meeting.

Agencies and workers should establish working hours that coincide with the needs of the groups being served. Doing so may mean having evening and weekend hours to avoid forcing clients, already with financial difficulties, to lose time from their job.

In the area of group services to racially diverse clients, Davis (1979) recommends that membership be selected in such a manner that no one race vastly outnumbers the others. Sometimes it is necessary to educate clients about the processes of individual or group counseling. Using words common to general conversation is much better than using technical and sophisticated jargon that clients are not likely to comprehend.

In working with adult clients who are not fluent in the English language, it is generally a mistake to use bilingual children of the clients as interpreters (Norton, 1978, p. 22). Having children as interpreters is embarrassing to the parents as it places them in a position of being partially dependent on their children and erroneously suggests the parents are deficient in learning essential communication mechanisms. In addition, children often lack an adult's knowledge, which reduces their values as interpreters. Also, in using interpreters the worker should direct his conversation to the client and not to the interpreter. To talk to the translator diverts attention from the client and places the client in the position of bystander, rather than central figure in the relationship.

Native Americans place a high value on the principle of self-determination (*Good Tracks*, 1973, p. 30). This sometimes provides a perplexing dilemma for a worker who wonders "How can I help if I can't intervene?" Native Americans will request intervention only infrequently, and the white worker needs to have patience and wait for the request. How long this will take varies. During the waiting period the non-Native American worker should be available and may offer assistance as long as there is no hint of coercion. Once help is accepted, the worker will be tested. If the client believes the worker has been helpful, the word will spread and the worker is likely to have more requests for help. If the client concludes the worker is lacking in helpful capacities, this assessment will also spread, and the worker will have an even more difficult task in being sought out by potential clients.

In establishing rapport with black, Hispanic, Native American, or clients of other groups who have suffered from racial oppression, a peer relationship should be sought in which there is mutual respect and mutual sharing of information. A white superiority type of relationship should be rejected totally, as it is likely to be interpreted by racially diverse clients as being offensive—which in fact it is.

The Future of American Race and Ethnic Relations

Minorities will assertively and sometimes aggressively pursue a variety of strategies to change racist and ethnocentric prejudices and actions. Counteractions by certain segments of the white dominant group are also likely to occur. (Even in the social sciences, every action elicits a reaction.) For example, in recent years, there have been increased memberships in organizations such as the Ku Klux Klan and the John Birch Society that advocate white supremacy. To a lesser extent, the Reagan administration appears more interested in furthering the interests of middle- and upper-class Americans, which might have a negative effect on the poor, who consist to a large extent of minorities.

Minorities have been given hope of achieving equality of opportunity and justice. Their hope has been kindled, and they will no longer submit to a subordinate status. Struggles to achieve racial equality will continue.

What will be the pattern of race relations in the future? Milton Gordon (1961, pp. 363–65) outlined three possible patterns of intergroup relations: Anglo-conformity, melting pot and cultural pluralism:

> *Anglo-conformity* assumes the desirability of maintaining modified English institutions, language, and culture as the dominant standard in American life. In practice, "assimilation" in America has always meant Anglo-conformity, and the groups that have been most readily assimilated have been those that are ethnically and culturally most similar to the Anglo-Saxon group.
>
> The *melting pot* is, strictly speaking, a rather different concept, which views the future American society not as a modified England but rather as a totally new blend, both culturally and biologically, of all the various groups that inhabit the United States. In practice, the melting pot has been of only limited significance in the American experience.
>
> *Cultural pluralism* implies a series of coexisting groups, each preserving its own tradition and culture but each loyal to an overarching American nation. Although the cultural enclaves of some immigrant groups, such as the Germans, have declined in importance in the past, many other groups, such as the Italians, have retained a strong sense of ethnic identity and have resisted both Anglo-conformity and inclusion in the melting pot.

Members of some European ethnic groups such as the British, French, and Germans have assimilated the dominant culture of the United States and are now integrated. Other European ethnic groups such as the Irish, Italian, Polish, and Hungarians are now nearly fully assimilated and integrated.

Cultural pluralism, however, appears to be the form that race and ethnic relations are presently taking. Renewed interest on the part of a number of ethnic European Americans in expressing their pride in their own customs, religions and linguistic and cultural traditions is evident. Slogans on buttons and signs say "Kiss me I'm Italian," "Irish Power," and "Polish and Proud." Blacks, Native Americans, Hispanics and Asian Americans are demanding entry into mainstream America but are not demanding assimilation. They are demanding coexistence in a plural society, while seeking to preserve their own traditions and cultures. They are finding a source of identity and pride in their own cultural backgrounds and histories.

Some progress has been made toward ending discrimination since the *Brown* v. *Board of Education* decision in 1954. Yet equal opportunity for all people in America is still only a dream (see inset).

■ A Dream of the End of Racism

In 1963 Martin Luther King, Jr., delivered a speech in which he stated a hope and a goal that racism will one day be ended. An excerpt from that speech follows:

> I say to you today, my friends, though, even though we face the difficulties of today and tomorrow, I still have a dream. It is a dream deeply rooted in the American dream. I have a dream that one day this nation will rise up, live out the true meaning of its creed: "We hold these truths to be self-evident, that all men are created equal."
>
> I have a dream that one day on the red hills of Georgia sons of former slaves and the sons of former slave-owners will be able to sit down together at the table of brotherhood. I have a dream that one day even the state of Mississippi, a state sweltering with the heat of injustice, sweltering with the heat of oppression, will be transformed into an oasis of freedom and justice.
>
> I have a dream that my four little children will one day live in a nation where they will not be judged by the color of their skin, but by the content of their character.
>
> When we allow freedom to ring—when we let it ring from every city and every hamlet, from every state and every city, we will be able to speed up that day when all of God's children, black men and white men, Jews and Gentiles, Protestants and Catholics, will be able to join hands and sing in the words of the old Negro spiritual, "Free at last, Free at last, Great God Almighty. We are free at last." (Bishop, 1971, pp. 327–28).

For most nonwhite Americans this dream is still far from being a reality.

Summary

Our country has always been racist and ethnocentric. Discrimination continues to have tragic consequences for those who are victims. In our country's history, racial discrimination has had violent and tragic consequences for many nonwhite groups. Individuals who are targets of ethnic or racial discrimination are excluded from: certain types of employment, educational and recreational opportunities, certain residential housing areas, membership in certain social and religious organizations, certain political activities, access to some community services, and so on. Discrimination is also a serious obstacle to developing a positive self-concept, and has heavy psychological and financial costs. Internationally, racism and ethnocentrism severely damage our credibility in promoting human rights.

Theories of the sources of discrimination include: projection, frustration-aggression, countering insecurity and inferiority, the authoritarian personality, historical explanations, competition and exploitation, and socialization processes. There are numerous racial and ethnic groups in our society. These groups each have a unique culture, language, history, and special needs. This uniqueness needs to be understood and appreciated if we are to achieve progress towards ethnic and racial equality.

Strategies against discrimination include mass media appeals, increased interaction between minority groups and the majority group, civil rights legislation, protests and activism, affirmative action, school busing, human relations programs in school systems, and confronting racist and ethnic remarks and actions. Three possible patterns of intergroup ethnic and race relations in the future are Anglo-conformity, melting pot, and cultural pluralism. Cultural pluralism is the form that race and ethnic relations are presently taking, and may well take in the future.

Gender Roles and Sexism

Girls are pretty. Boys are strong.

Girls are emotional. Boys are brave.

Girls are soft. Boys are tough.

Girls are submissive. Boys are dominant.

Girls are promiscuous. Boys are sexually active.

These ideas refer to some of the traditional stereotypes about how men and women should be. A *stereotype* is "a fixed mental image of a group that is applied to all its members" (Zastrow, 1984, p. 545). The problem with such fixed images is that they allow no room for individual differences within the group. One of the major values adhered to in social work is that each individual has the right to self-determination. Clinging to stereotypes violates this basic value.

Stereotypes about men and women are especially dangerous because they affect each and every one of us. To expect all men to be successful, strong, athletic, brave leaders places an impractical burden on them. To expect all women to be sweet, submissive, pretty, and born with a natural love of scrubbing kitchen floors places tremendous pressure on them to conform.

■ A Perspective

Sexism may be defined as "prejudice, discrimination, and stereotyping based on gender" (Zastrow, 1984, p. 544). Prejudice involves negative attitudes and prejudgments about a group. Discrimination involves the actual treatment of that group's members in a negative or unfair manner. As the Behavior Dynamics Assessment Model predicts, aspects of human diversity affect people's behavior and their transactions with the impinging environment. The aspect of diversity addressed here is gender. Since men in our society have traditionally held the vast majority of positions of power, this chapter will focus on the state and status of women as victims of sexism.

This chapter will

• Identify and discuss traditional gender role expectations and stereotypes as they affect people over the life span.

516

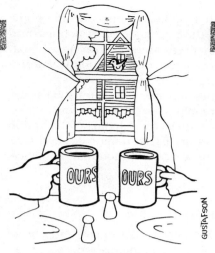

- Assess the impacts of sexism on both men and women.
- Examine some of the differences between men and women including personality, abilities, and communication styles.
- Recognize and emphasize the basic similarities between men and women.
- Discuss and examine the issues of comparable worth, sexual harassment, sexist language, rape and sexual assault, and battered women.
- Present strategies for combating sexism and achieving sexual equality.

Gender Role Stereotypes

From the moment they're born, boys and girls are treated very differently. Girls are wrapped in pink blankets and parents are told that they now have "a beautiful little girl." Boys, on the other hand, are wrapped in blue blankets and parents are told that they now are the proud parents of "a bouncing baby boy." The process of gender stereotyping continues through childhood, adolescence, and adulthood. Gender stereotyping involves expectations about how people should behave based upon their gender. Female stereotypes include being "passive, unaggressive, not intellectually inclined, emotional, nurturant, and irresponsible with money" (Hyde, 1982, p. 323). Male stereotypes include being "aggressive, athletic, successful, unemotional, brave, and instantly aroused by attractive women" (Hyde, 1982, p. 326). These stereotypes have nothing to do with an individual's personality, his or her own personal strengths and weaknesses, or likes and dislikes.

A major problem with gender-based stereotypes is that they often limit people's alternatives. Pressure is exerted from many sources on people to conform to gender-based expectations. In accordance with the Behavior Dynamics Assessment Model, this pressure affects the individual and affects the alternatives available to him or her.

For example, until 1920, when women finally were allowed to vote, concrete political input was simply not available to them. Prior to that time, the political macrosystem (the United States government) dictated that women could not vote. Gender-based stereotypes about women which helped maintain that stance may have included the ideas that women were not bright enough to partake in decision making; that women belonged in the home caring for husband and children, not in the hectic world of politics; and that women were destined to be the virtuous upholders of purity and human dignity (Rottman, 1978), qualities not to be muddied in the political arena. For whatever reasons, women were simply not allowed to vote.

In order to understand and assess human behavior, one must be aware of the pressures that gender-based stereotypes bring to bear on people. Social workers need to understand how human diversity affects behavior. Gender is one critical type of diversity. Gender-based differences and stereotypes will be examined within the contexts of childhood, adolescence, young adulthood, and later adulthood.

Childhood and Gender Stereotypes

Although there appear to be few differences in the innate behavior of boys and girls at birth (Hyde and Rosenberg, 1980), infants are treated differently by virtue of their gender from the moment they are born. Parents are more likely to treat boys more actively and roughly than girls (Maccoby and Jacklin, 1974) who are more likely to be talked to and looked at (Lewis, 1972). Perhaps this differential treatment reinforces aggressive behavior in boys and verbal behavior in girls. In one interesting study, young mothers were divided into two groups and given the same six-month-old infant to handle and play with (Walum, 1977). For one group the infant was dressed in a ruffled pink dress and called Beth. For the other group the same infant was called Adam and dressed in blue overalls. In their interactions with "Beth" mothers were much more likely to smile at the infant, give her a doll to play with, and perceive the infant as being sweet than when the same baby was "Adam." Such differences in treatment tend to become greater and more encompassing as children grow older (Block, 1976). Even parents who state that they consciously try to avoid imposing gender stereotypes on their children still treat boys and girls differently (Scanzoni and Fox, 1980).

It is appropriate and relevant to mention here the age-old nature-nurture argument regarding why people become the people they do. Supporters of the nature idea argue that people are innately programmed with inborn, genetic, or natural predispositions. But according to the nurture perspective, people are the product of their environment. That is, people are affected by what happens to them from the day they're born. They learn from their environment and are shaped by it. Both sides of the debate have evidence and research to support their perspective. The real answer is not clear. Probably the answer lies somewhere in the middle. People are probably born with certain potentials and predispositions which are then shaped, strengthened, or suppressed by their environments.

Two differences in behavior appear early in life (Hyde, 1982, pp. 323–24). One is a difference in aggressive behavior. As soon as children are old enough to maneuver by themselves, boys behave more aggressively than girls. Perhaps the fact that boys are treated more aggressively from birth has something to do with this. The other early behavioral difference is in toy preference. By age three or four girls begin choosing to play with dolls and participate in sewing and housekeeping play. Boys, on the other hand, are oriented toward more masculine toys such as trucks and guns. The reasons for these differences are not clear. Perhaps children play with the toys they are given and encouraged to play with. One study did indeed find that boys and girls tended to have different types of toys (Rheingold and Cook, 1975). Girls' rooms are filled with dolls and items devised for playing house. Boys' rooms, on the other hand, display various action-oriented toys such as cars, trucks, guns, and sports equipment. Another reason for the differences in toy preference may be that children, who become conscious of gender by age two and one half or three (Masters and Johnson, 1985, p. 272), learn early on how they should be playing. They watch television and observe Mommy and Daddy; they learn that girls and boys should like to do different things.

Differences continue to be apparent as children reach school age. Girls tend to do better academically in school than do boys (Hyde, 1982, p. 324). Several possible reasons can be given for this. First, 90 percent of grade school teachers are women (Guttentag and Bray, 1977). Perhaps it is easier to be taught from a same-gender role model with which one can identify more easily. Second, boys are generally rougher and more action oriented than girls. Logically this may result in more behavior management problems which might affect their schoolwork. Third, boys lag behind girls in their physiological development. It may be more difficult for them to master academic material at the same level than girls.

One interesting aspect about childhood is that girls are allowed more freedom in their gender-stereotyped behavior than are boys (Hartley, 1959). Girls who are tomboys are tolerated and even considered normal (Green, 1974). When boys, however, manifest so-called feminine behavior such as playing with dolls, such behavior is frequently thought to be seriously abnormal, related to homosexuality, and something to be corrected (Lebovitz, 1972; Green, 1974; Newman, 1976).

Boys are discouraged from crying. If six-year-old Susie falls, skins her knee, and comes into the house crying, her mother might respond, "You poor thing. Did you hurt yourself? It's okay now. Let me kiss it and make it better." However, if six-year-old Bill falls, skins his knee, and runs into the house, he might get a somewhat different reception. His mother might respond, "Now, now, Billy, big boys don't cry. It'll be okay. Let me put a Band-aid on it." Even very little boys are often encouraged to be strong, brave, and bereft of outward emotion. A tragic result of this is that as adults, males often maintain this facade. This sometimes creates problems in adult love and sexual relationships where men are expected to express their feelings and communicate openly (Gross, 1978).

Adolescence and Gender Stereotypes

Because it is a time of change, adolescence can be difficult. Bodies change drastically, sexual desires emerge, peers exert tremendous pressure to conform, personal identities are struggling to surface, and conflicts with parents are rampant. In addition to these other issues, adolescents must deal with powerful pressures to conform to gender stereotypes.

Masters and Johnson (1985, p. 276) indicate that there are three basic rules by which male adolescents are expected to abide. First, they must achieve success at athletics. Second, they have to become enthralled with girls and sex. Third, they don't dare show any interest in feminine things or manifest any feminine behavior. Young men who violate these rules are subject to social ostracism and ridicule. Masters and Johnson continue that the reasons for these pressures to conform are probably twofold. The first reason is that masculinity and femininity are often seen as two opposite extremes. If a male shows any signs of leaning toward feminine behavior, he may be shifted into the feminine category. The second reason is to avoid any suspicion that he may be homosexual (See Chapter 16).

Adolescent girls, on the other hand, have problems of their own. Until adolescence, girls have tended to excel over boys in their levels of academic achievement. However, as they approach adulthood, the concept of achievement conflicts with other gender role stereotypes such as dependence, submissiveness, and nurturance. It's difficult for women to achieve at higher levels than men and still be passive, dependent, and submissive at the same time. This problem is termed *femininity-achievement incompatibility* (Horner, 1972; Hyde and Rosenberg, 1980). For arbitrary reasons femininity and achievement traditionally have not been considered compatible in our society. A female adolescent gets messages from many sources that achieving academically will detract from her femininity (Weitzman, 1975; Frieze et al., 1978). Parents, teachers, and school guidance counselors may encourage young women to learn domestic or secretarial skills instead of working toward a profession.

For example, one 17-year-old female high school senior happened to be tall, beautiful, and poised. She was also ranked sixth academically in a class of 467 students at a prestigious suburban high school. Her high school guidance counselor emphatically urged her to think about selling fashion clothing for some large department store. No mention was made of becoming an astrophysicist, a corporation attorney, or a brain surgeon. Those, of course, were so-called masculine professions. But the fact is that femininity and achievement are two unrelated concepts. One has nothing to do with the other.

There might be change for the better. Now women are entering the workforce to a much greater extent and assuming positions of power and influence. If more alternative options are available to women in the future, women will have greater freedom to choose what they would like to do with their lives.

Abolition of stereotypes would give men more options. It would give them more freedom to express feelings. The pressure for them to succeed and lead all the time would be lessened. It would also give them greater opportunities to participate in domestic and childrearing tasks. Many men miss many of the joys of watching their children grow up simply by not being around them very much.

Young Adulthood and Gender Stereotypes

Women are taught that they can be fulfilled by becoming wives and mothers (Hyde, 1982, p. 325). Men, on the other hand, are taught that their main source of self-satisfaction should come from their jobs (Hyde, 1982, p. 328). The pressures and expectations resulting from both of these stereotypes often create serious problems for the gender involved.

A woman who devotes herself entirely to being a wife and homemaker makes herself entirely and helplessly dependent on her husband. If her husband dies, becomes ill, or leaves her, such a woman has left herself in a very vulnerable position. As of 1979, one out of three marriages ended in divorce (U.S. Bureau of the Census, 1980). This striking rate has gradually been increasing. Divorce was a rare occurrence prior to World War I.

Gove (1979, pp. 39–40) identifies various other problems with which women in traditionally stereotyped roles are confronted. First, by putting all of their eggs in one basket, or directing all of their energy toward one goal, women limit their sources of gratification. Men, on the other hand, have both their work lives and their home lives from which they can derive pleasure. Second, many women find the tasks involved in childrearing and housework to be unrewarding and are disenchanted with the low status typically attributed to this work. Others find the unstructured and repetitive tasks of homemaking to be boring. Third, even when married women work outside of the home, they are still expected to do most of the domestic tasks.

Men don't have the best situation in the world either. Not only is a man expected to hold a steady job outside of the home, but he's also expected to be successful at it (Tavris, 1977). The man of the house is expected to be a strong leader all of the time. Not everyone is, can be, or even wants to be a leader. Such gender expectations place great burdens on men who are naturally passive, easygoing, or nonassertive. Whereas women are expected to lean all of the time, men are expected to bolster and support all of the time.

Later Adulthood and Gender Stereotypes

As they reach middle age some women suffer from what has been called the *empty-nest syndrome* (Bart, 1971). This involves the sense of depression and loss that can occur when children grow up and leave home. It is logical that a woman who has focused all of her efforts on her family needs to reevaluate her position when her major function, namely that of being a mother, almost disappears. Some recent research conflicts with the idea that middle-aged mothers have to suffer the empty-nest syndrome (Rubin, 1979). Interviews with women during this period revealed that they were not so much depressed as they were relieved. They indicated that for the first time in a long time, they felt free. The implication is that women at this point need to take control and pursue other interests rather than wallow in their loss. Perhaps women who have diversified their interests and talents prior to this time in their lives have an easier time with such transitions.

Another problem that plagues women as they get older is losing their physical beauty and attractiveness. Our society places a lot of emphasis on beauty. All one needs to do is watch a television commercial depicting a woman having a bad date because she didn't use the right kind of lipstick. Look at all the advertisements in the media for wrinkle removers, exercise programs, and hair tints. As women age, it becomes much more difficult to maintain a beautiful appearance. Unless women put beauty in perspective as being only one minor aspect affecting the quality of life, they have a greater potential for suffering serious problems with both adjusting to the aging process and maintaining self-esteem.

Men in middle age are affected by different gender stereotypes. Whereas a great deal of a woman's worth is traditionally based on her beauty, much of a man's worth is traditionally based on his ability to succeed (Hyde, 1982, p. 313). For example, rich, successful men are frequently associated with gorgeous women. Physically attractive women do tend to marry men of higher social and economic status (Elder, 1969).

But not all men are or can be successful. Even men who are moderately successful tend to enter a midlife crisis (Kaluger and Kaluger, 1984, pp. 538–39). This is a time when men, who were supposed to be successful in their careers, reevaluate their accomplishments and their expectations. At least half of a man's life is probably over by this time. It is a time for facing the fact that if he hasn't become president of the United States or even of the company by now, there is a good chance that he never will. At age 20 many more career options look (and indeed probably are) possible than at age 50. By middle age, men who had worked very hard at their jobs and careers and who had espoused traditional values tend to raise serious questions about what all that hard work and commitment to values really means (Levinson, 1977). Some of the crises and difficulties middle aged men experience include addressing the emergence of some of the more feminine portions of their identities and choosing what aspects of their lives need to be changed and adjusted (Levinson et al., 1978). (For a fuller discussion of midlife crisis, see Chapter 12).

Gender stereotypes pressure people to conform. Perhaps a more effective way of dealing with midlife crises for men is to be more flexible throughout life. If gender stereotypes begin to dissolve, maybe people will become more objective in assessing themselves from youth on. Then they may not feel pressured to be something they're not. Abolishing gender stereotypes may give people the freedom to develop more realistic expectations and to live the way they choose.

Male/Female Differences

Some differences do emerge between males and females. To what extent they are due to biological predisposition or to environmental effects is unknown. These differences are evident in personality, in abilities, and in communication styles.

Personality Differences

Males do tend to be physically and verbally more aggressive than females (Maccoby and Jacklin, 1974). This difference begins to emerge at age two and continues throughout life. As with other traits, it's very difficult to determine to what extent this is an innate difference and to what extent it is learned.

Some evidence shows that females tend to have less self-esteem than males (Block, 1976). This has several negative implications for females. People who are less aggressive may also be less assertive in climbing a career ladder. People who have lower self-esteem may not have the confidence it takes even to attempt to achieve and climb that ladder.

Ability Level of Males and Females

Although there are no differences between males and females in terms of intellectual ability or IQ, differences are found in some abilities to perform academic tasks (Maccoby and Jacklin, 1974). Females tend to be superior to males on most tests of verbal ability. Males, on the other hand, tend to do better than females on tests which emphasize mathematical and spatial ability. This tendency might be due to the experiences provided each gender. From birth females are talked to more frequently and are encouraged to express their feelings. Males, on the other hand, are encouraged to develop interests and skills in mechanical and technical areas. Activities in these areas help to develop skills in spatial perception and manipulation (Weitzman, 1979, p. 43).

Communication Styles of Males and Females

One other area where differences between males and females are evident is in verbal and nonverbal communication style (Deaux, 1976, Key, 1975). Contrary to popular belief, men spend more time talking than do women (Henley and Freeman, 1984, p. 472). Again contrary to popular belief, men also interrupt conversations more than women do (Deaux, 1976). If people are interrupted while speaking, they tend to submit to others whom they feel are superior (Eakin and Eakin, 1976). The implication is that in conversational contexts, women frequently place themselves and/or are placed in inferior positions.

Women are also more likely to give information or make self-disclosures than men are (Cozby, 1973). Self-disclosure can place a person in a vulnerable or inferior position. It involves increasing the other person's power (Henley and Freeman, 1984, p. 469). The person who receives the information can choose to criticize the discloser or give the information to other people. Research has indicated that people working in business organizations are more likely to disclose themselves to their supervisors than to those they supervise (Slobin et al., 1968).

Nonverbal behavior also differs between men and women. Men more frequently touch other people, while women are most likely to be the ones who are touched (Henley, 1973a). Touching has also been found to be associated with status (Henley, 1973b). Persons of higher status are much more likely to touch persons of lower status than vice versa. The fact that women are more likely to be touched implies that somehow they are perceived to have a lower status.

Another difference in communication styles is that women often tend to be coy in their behavior. Henley and Freeman (1984, pp. 472–473) define being coy as involving gestures of submission including lowering the eyes from another's gaze, falling silent (or not beginning to speak at all) when interrupted or pointed at, and cuddling to the touch. These may be considered by some to be typically "feminine" behaviors. Picture the stereotypical nineteenth-century southern belle fluttering at every eligible man around. Being coy, along with its sexual connotations, conveys deference, dependence, and a sense of needing leadership and protection.

Although many of these differences in communication styles are subtle and minor, in combination they mean a lot. Many of women's most salient issues involve unfairness and victimization due to sexism. To begin to examine the issues and to initiate change, some of the foundations of sexism need to be understood. Changes in these behaviors, when they're all considered together, may bring about significant change.

People

People are people; men and women are more similar than dissimilar. The differences we're referring to are differences in treatment and differences in what people have learned. Sexism needs to be addressed because it's unfair. It causes people to be treated differently because of their gender when there are no objective reasons for differential treatment.

Each individual, whether male or female, has the right to make choices. Cutting through and obliterating gender stereotypes and sexism will give people as individuals more freedom. Each individual will then have a better chance of being the way he or she naturally is comfortable being. The idea is to confront the hidden rules which pressure people to conform on the basis of gender. Women can then be assertive without being pushy. Men won't have to be strong all of the time and will be freer to express their feelings. Tasks and the burdens of leadership can then be shared or divided on the basis of mutual decision making. The best of each individual's personality traits can then blossom and be nurtured.

Significant Issues and Events in the Lives of Women

Women have been the victims of sexism in many striking and concrete ways. They historically have had fewer rights and are financially less well off to a significant degree. They are victims of life events (e.g. rape and domestic violence) which don't generally touch the lives of men.

The issues addressed here were selected on the basis of prevalence, severity, and current relevance. The issues include comparable worth, sexual harassment, sexist language, sexual assault, and battered women.

Comparable Worth

The principle of comparable worth may be defined as "calling for equal pay for males and females doing work requiring comparable skill, effort, and responsibility under similar working conditions" (Bellak, 1984, p. 75). That is, questions are being raised regarding the fact that men make substantially more money doing work requiring similar levels of preparation and skill than women do. Comparable worth does not refer to jobs which are identical, but rather which are similar. For example, a male janitor might receive a substantially higher salary than a female secretary, even though both jobs might require similar levels, not types, of training and experience.

It is a concept that needs to be introduced within the context of women's earning power, employment picture, and political status within this society.

The majority of American women work outside of the home (Fox and Hesse-Biber, 1984, p. 1). Their work is critical to their livelihood and, in many cases, to their self-concept. However, women tend to be clustered in occupations which historically are relatively low paying.

■ Employment Positions Held by Women

Position	Percentage held by women	Position	Percentage held by women
Secretaries	98.3	Child-care workers	97.4
Dental assistants	98.2	Receptionists	96.9

Position	Percentage held by women	Position	Percentage held by women
Registered nurses	96.0	Writers, artists, entertainers	42.5
Typists	95.7	Accountants	40.9
Telephone operators	92.8	Cleaning-service workers	39.0
Bank tellers	91.4	Financial managers	36.8
Bookkeepers	91.2	College teachers	36.6
Health service workers	90.3	Sales managers	29.7
Hairdressers, cosmetologists	89.8	Lawyers and judges	16.2
Librarians	85.9	Physicians	16.0
General office clerks	85.1	Police officers	10.8
Elementary school teachers	84.6	Psychologists	9.4
Cashiers	83.8	Dentists	6.2
File clerks	82.6	Engineers	6.2
Office-machine operators	69.8	Architects	2.4
Social workers	64.1	Fire fighters	.7
Food-service workers	64.0		
Real estate agents	48.2		

U.S. Bureau of the Census, *Statistical Abstract of the United States, 1986* (Washington, D.C.: U.S. Government Printing Office, 1986), pp. 402–403.

These occupations include secretaries, child-care workers, receptionists, typists, nurses, hairdressers, and cashiers (U.S. Bureau of the Census, 1981). Men, on the other hand, tend to work in better-paying occupations, as physicians, lawyers, managers, engineers, and construction workers. Perhaps an even more striking finding is that for most of these job categories (including those which are viewed as being feminine and those viewed as being masculine) women will earn less than men in the same job category (U.S. Bureau of the Census, 1978). Additionally, very few women hold top management jobs in this country. Women hold less than 1 percent of all the top-level corporation management positions, less than 2 percent of top corporation directorships, and only 5 or 6 percent of all the middle-management positions in this country (New York Times, 1977). On the average, women who work full time earn about 59 percent of what men working full time earn; this has dropped from 64 percent in 1955 (U.S. Department of Commerce, 1982; U.S. Department of Labor, 1977). Some of the reasons proposed to explain these differences will be discussed later on in the chapter.

Women also have less direct political power in terms of the actual number of political offices they hold. In 1980, women held fewer than 10 percent of all the elected offices in the country. Only 2 of the 100 U.S. Senators and 18 of the U.S. Representatives were women. Of all 50 state governors, only 1 was a woman (Congressional Directory, 1981, pp. 208–26, 388). Despite the fact that women make up over half of the nation's voters, they hold only 5 percent of all the available elected offices (Stockard and Johnson, pp. 22–24). In view of these statistics, one must appreciate what an awesome hurdle it must have been for Geraldine Ferraro to be nominated for vice president by one of the nations' two major political parties.

In view of women's status and of their disadvantaged situation, comparable work has risen to become one of most poignant issues for women.

Comparable Worth and the Law

Bellak (1984) describes the comparable worth situation to date. Although many state laws refer to the concept of comparable worth either directly or indirectly, they tend not to be very specific about what should be done, if anything, to remedy problematic situations. Currently, only the state governments, not private businesses and corporations, have even attempted to address the issue. Comparable worth is being used as a basis for an increasing number of pay discrimination suits. It appears that comparable worth is not clearly law at this time; it probably won't be until either Congress passes more specific laws or the courts make clear determinations about what must be done. However, six states currently have laws concerning comparable worth which are directed only at themselves as employers. Thirteen states have laws that apply not only to themselves, but to all employers. Additionally, ten more states are entertaining legislation on comparable worth, as is Congress concerning its own federal employees.

Comparable worth is anything but a simple concept. Those on both sides of the issue have developed rationales for their perspectives. Since money lies at the base of the issue, the answer cannot be easy. To better grasp the essence of the debate, some of the arguments for and against comparable worth will be discussed below.

For Comparable Worth

The core of the argument for comparable worth concerns fairness and values (Schwab, 1984, p. 90). That is, it is simply not fair that women, for whatever reasons, earn less than men for similar efforts. The Equal Pay Act passed in 1963 dictates that both men and women should be paid equally for equal work (Grune, 1984, p. 166). Comparable worth takes this basic right one step further. Women have the right to receive equal pay or to have pay equity for doing work comparable to that which men traditionally do. The intent of comparable worth is to overcome any effects of discrimination which have built up and multiplied over time.

Against Comparable Worth

Perhaps the nucleus of the argument against comparable worth concerns both the cost it would involve (Newman and Owens, 1984, p. 146) and the infringement on the freedom of organizations and businesses to hire at the rate established by market value. Salaries of workers, primarily female, in those jobs determined as being unfairly paid would have to be raised because it probably would not be feasible to cut salaries in the "masculine" professions in order to spread the money out more evenly. Therefore, more money would have to be found or raised or taxed to increase the salaries of those in the "feminine" professions.

Opponents also charge that comparable worth threatens the freedom of organizations and businesses. The market value of workers and jobs is related to supply and demand. When there is a large supply of workers and few jobs, workers will probably be willing to accept relatively low pay levels.

In other words, the demand for workers is low although the supply of workers is high. Opponents of comparable worth worry that implementing comparable worth will curb the freedom and competitiveness now available in the job market. Employers might no longer be able to adjust the salaries that they offer according to supply and demand principles. Organizations might have to offer a controlled set of salary levels based on the principles of comparable worth and not on how much an individual's job performance would be worth on the open market.

There have also been criticisms concerning the establishment and implementation of job evaluation systems. Job evaluation is not a new concept. (Schwab, 1984, p. 86).

Implementing Comparable Worth

Questions have been raised regarding how comparable worth would actually work, (Remick 1984). First, what factors would be chosen as the basis for job comparison? For example, what factors could be used in comparing driving a cement truck and pouring cement, with handing out paychecks at a cashier's window? Second, how would these factors be rated? How would the amount of strength needed and physical fatigue involved in working a drill press be weighed against the amount of skill necessary to type 80 words per minute? Third, how would the evaluation system be applied? Who would make decisions about how the categories were determined? Would everyone in an organization be involved including the top executives, or would just certain levels of employees be included? Fourth, how would salaries for each job classification be determined? How much salary would people in each job classification get?

First, a system of job evaluation would have to be developed. Job evaluation would involve evaluating each job in an organization on the basis of "skill requirements, effort, responsibility, and working conditions" (Schwab, 1984, p. 86). A system would have to be worked out whereby these job aspects could be analyzed, compared, and rated on a scale. The end result would be comparable job classifications with comparable salaries.

The second recommendation for implementing the doctrine of comparable worth would be to establish legislation to mandate compliance. That is, laws would have to be created to require both governmental and private business organizations to abide by comparable worth. This would require the development of job evaluation systems. It would also necessitate careful monitoring of organizations to make certain that they comply with or obey the rules.

The Future of Comparable Worth

We have just touched on a few of the basic issues involved in the comparable worth debate. Only the future can tell to what extent the doctrine will be implemented and how effective it will be. However, a few recent developments merit attention.

What has been referred to as the Tanner decision in *AFSCME* v. *the State of Washington* (Bellak, 1984, pp. 75–76) seems to have raised some eyebrows. Although the decision was later overturned by a higher court, U.S. District Court Judge Jack E. Tanner initially ruled that the state of Washington knowingly had failed to pay people in female-dominated jobs as much as people in male-dominated jobs after it had initiated, on its own accord, a job evaluation study. In other words, Washington failed to compensate people even after it knew that inequities existed. This was really a "failure to pay" suit rather than strictly a comparable worth suit. However, it still suggests the possibility that people can file suits concerning issues which involve comparable worth. The fact that the initial win was later overturned complicates the matter.

Minnesota, on the other hand, presents an example of a state which has moved actively and quickly to establish comparable worth salary adjustments (Steinberg, 1984, p. 114). A bill was passed in March 1982, which provided a gradual phasing in of equity salary adjustments. The cost was relatively minimal, adding up to 4 percent of the state of Minnesota's total payroll (Rothchild, 1984, p. 125).

Sexual Harassment

Sexual harassment is a serious form of sex discrimination which recently has gained public attention. It affects business, industrial, academic, and public work environments.

Sexual harassment is illegal. Title VII of the Civil Rights Act of 1964 outlaws discrimination on the basis of sex along with discrimination on the basis of race. Legal precedents have been established which include sexual harassment as a form of sex discrimination (Maypole and Skaine, 1983). Additionally, individual state laws can prohibit sexual harassment and provide legal recourse to victims.[1] Title IX of the Higher Educational Amendments of 1972 prohibit sex discrimination from taking place specifically on university campuses. Finally, individual agencies, organizations, or universities may have established policies prohibiting sexual harassment.[2]

The following section will define sexual harassment. Research concerning how frequently it occurs will be presented. Effects on victims will be addressed. Finally, some strategies for confronting sexual harassment will be proposed.

■ Vignettes of Sexual Harassment

Ann's boss states that if she doesn't go to bed with him, she won't make it through her six-month probationary period. She really needs the job. She doesn't know what to do.

Barbara's male supervisor likes to sneak up behind her and surprise her by putting his arms around her. This makes her feel very uncomfortable. However, he's responsible for scheduling her hours, evaluating her, and giving her raises. She is terrified of confronting him.

Harry really needs to get a good grade in his course with a female professor, Dr. Getsom, in order to keep his scholarship and stay in school. So far he has a "D+" in the course. When he goes to see Dr. Getsom, she likes to touch him a lot and acts very friendly. Last Thursday she said she would "see what could be done about helping him with his grade" if they'd start dating. He feels trapped. He doesn't know what to do.

One of the other financial assistance workers in the county social services department really annoys Buella. The man is constantly telling dirty jokes about women. Additionally, he likes to whistle at any woman under 25 who passes his desk.

---

[1]For example, the state of Wisconsin's Fair Employment Act as amended in 1978 prohibits sexual harassment.

[2]For example, the University of Wisconsin System Board of Regents have stated in their Resolution #2384 of May 8, 1981, that sexual harassment "is unacceptable and impermissible conduct which will not be tolerated."

The Definition of Sexual Harassment

Sexual harassment involves unwelcome sexual advances, requests for sexual favors, and other verbal or physical conduct of a sexual nature under the following conditions: First, submission to such conduct is required as a condition of employment or education. Second, submission to such conduct is used as a basis for decisions which affect an individual's employment or academic achievement. Such conduct results in a hostile, intimidating, or anxiety-producing work or educational environment.[3]

Sexual harassment occurs when a female employee is made to tolerate the regular touching of her arms, waist, neck, and buttocks by her male supervisor in order to ensure that she gets good supervisory reviews. Sexual harassment exists when a female administrative assistant is pressured to become sexually involved with the vice president she works for if she wants to keep her job. Sexual harassment also is evident when a male college professor likes to touch young male students in suggestive ways and refers to them as "pretty boys."

Sexual harassment almost always involves elements of unequal power and coercion. Sometimes it involves promising a victim a reward or threatening a punishment on the basis of the victim's sexual cooperation. Other times it involves becoming overly and inappropriately personal with a victim, either by sharing intimacies or prying into the victim's personal life.

Although most victims are women, sexual harassment can be directed at either males or females. In this respect it can be considered a human rights issue. A member of either gender may be the victim of harassing, offensive behavior of a sexual nature. Homosexual people are also victims. They can be targets of inappropriate sexual advances, threats, and promises when such overtures involve someone of their same gender.

Sexual harassment can also take place when verbal remarks make the work or academic atmosphere offensive or stifling. Sexual remarks which are not related to the work at hand can interfere with productivity and performance. For example, female students might be forced to endure condescending, derogatory remarks of a male instructor which focus on women's anatomy and on their inferior ability. Or female employees might force themselves to tolerate their supervisor's annoying behaviors. These might include a male's constant reference to women as "girls," his comments that "it must be that time of month" whenever a woman is moody, his remarks about how he likes "his girls" to wear short skirts, and his placing of pictures of naked women on the office bulletin board. Any of these behaviors act to disrupt a positive, productive working environment.

The Extent of Sexual Harassment

An accurate, specific profile of when, where, how, and to whom sexual harassment occurs does not exist. However, some recent surveys suggest that it is quite prevalent in a variety of settings. Almost 90 percent of women who voluntarily responded to the *Redbook* survey (Safran, 1976) indicated that they had been victims of sexual harassment at some time during their

---

[3]The definition of sexual harassment is taken from Resolution #2384 of the Board of Regents of the University of Wisconsin System dated May 8, 1981. The Equal Employment Opportunity Commission has published a similar definition of sexual harassment in "Guidelines on Discrimination because of Sex, Title VII, Sec. 703," *Federal Register*, 45, (April 11, 1980).

working careers. This survey also found that typical victims were married women in their 20s and 30s.

Universities also provide settings for sexual harassment. Approximately 20 percent of 300 female graduate students surveyed at the University of California at Berkeley indicated that they had felt harassed by male faculty (1977). A study of Cornell University students found that over 90 percent of the women who responded felt that sexual harassment was a serious problem. Of these, 70 percent stated that they had experienced it themselves.

Perhaps the most massive study to date was undertaken by the U.S. Merit Systems Protection Board (MSPB 1981). A stratified random sampling procedure was used to involve over 23,000 federal employees. Of the female employees surveyed, 42 percent stated that they are victims of sexual harassment of some kind during the two-year period prior to the survey. Only 1 percent reported being victims of actual sexual assault. However, 29 percent indicated that "severe sexual harassment" had occurred to them. This included harassing telephone calls, unsolicited touching and embracing, and unwanted pressure to participate in sexual activities. An additional 12 percent experienced "less severe harassment." This included inappropriate sexual jokes and comments, leering looks, and excessive pressure to date the harasser.

Interestingly enough, women were not the only ones to consider themselves victims of sexual harassment. Fifteen percent of the men in the MSPB study felt that they also had been harassed.

Several variables made victimization more likely according to the MSPB research. Youth was one variable. A woman under age 20 was twice as likely to be sexually harassed as one between age 20 and 40. A second variable was marital status. Unlike findings in the *Redbook* survey, divorced and single women were more likely to be harassed than women who were married or widowed. Finally, education appeared to be a variable related to sexual harassment. Unlike what might be expected, sexual harassment was more likely to occur to women with higher levels of education. Perhaps this latter finding was due to the fact that more highly educated women were more aware of sexual harassment issues and also to the fact that more highly educated women assumed job positions traditionally not held by women.

Sexual harassment appears to be a serious problem. Despite the lack of a definitive profile of its occurrence, sexual harassment occurs frequently in a variety of employment and educational settings.

Effects of Sexual Harassment

Negative psychological effects of sexual harassment include humiliation and anger. One study which examined the various emotional reactions to sexual harassment indicated that over three quarters of the victims felt angry (Silverman, 1976–77). Additionally, almost half felt upset, almost one fourth felt afraid, and more than one fourth felt other negative emotions such as feelings of isolation, desertion, loneliness and guilt.

Despite such negative consequences, many women feel it is hopeless to complain about sexual harassment. Only one fourth of the women in the *Redbook* (1976) survey felt that it would do any good to complain. Most women preferred to cope by assuming an air of cold indifference or by wearing extremely unrevealing, sexually conservative clothing.

The MSPB (1981) survey revealed that only 2 percent of the women who were victimized by sexual harassment actually filed a formal complaint. Of those who did, half felt their complaints were unsuccessful.

Sexual harassment incurs financial costs as well. The MSPB study estimated that sexual harassment costs the federal government about $50 million annually. Contributing to this figure were job turnover costs such as hiring and training new employees, costs due to absenteeism and increased health problems, and reduced worker productivity due to emotional stress. The personal and emotional costs placed on the victims themselves cannot even be measured.

■ Confronting Sexual Harassment

Victims of sexual harassment have several alternative routes available to them. Each has its own potential positive and negative consequences. Alternatives include ignoring the harassing behavior, avoiding the harasser, or asking the harasser to stop (Martin, 1984). The MSPB (1981) study found that ignoring the behavior had virtually no effect. Asking the harasser to stop, however, effectively stopped the harassment in half of the cases.

Avoiding the harasser is another option. A severe shortcoming of this approach is that the victim is the one who must expend the effort. The ultimate avoidance measure is actually quitting the job or dropping the class in order to avoid contact with a sexual harasser. This is the least fair (and potentially most damaging) alternative to the victim.

There are, however, several other suggestions to help victims confront sexual harassment. In many cases using these strategies will stop harassment. First, a victim needs to know his or her rights. A call to the Equal Employment Opportunity Commission (EEOC), the federal agency designated to address the issue of sexual harassment, is helpful. Many women can obtain necessary information about their rights and the appropriate procedures to follow for filing a formal complaint.

Many states also have state laws which make sexual harassment illegal. Such states often have agencies or offices that victims may call for help and information. For example, the state of Wisconsin has the Wisconsin Equal Rights Division to address such issues. Additionally, organizations and agencies also have specific policies against sexual harassment. Filing a formal complaint through established procedures is often an option.

Most victims, however, choose not to pursue the formal complaint route (Martin, 1984; MSPB, 1981). Some victims fear reprisal or retaliation; others don't want to be labeled troublemakers. Still others don't choose to expend the time and effort necessary in carrying out a formal process. Most victims simply want the harassment to end so that they can do their work peacefully and productively.

In addition to knowing your rights, the following suggestions can be applied to most situations where sexual harassment is occurring:

1. Confront your harasser. Tell the harasser which specific behaviors are unwanted and unacceptable. If you feel you cannot handle a direct confrontation, write the harasser a letter. It is helpful to criticize the harasser's behavior rather than the harasser as a person. The intent is to stop the harassment and maintain a pleasant, productive work environment. There is also the chance that the harasser was not aware that his or her behavior was offensive. In this case, giving specific feedback is frequently effective.

2. Be assertive. When giving the harasser feedback, look him or her directly in the eye. Look like you mean what you're saying. Don't smile or giggle even though you're uncomfortable. Rather, look the harasser directly in the eye, stand up straight, adopt a serious expression, and calmly state, "Please stop touching me by putting your arms around me and rubbing my neck. I don't like it." This is a serious matter. You need to get a serious point across.

3. Document your situation (Farley, 1978). Record every incident that occurs. Note when, where, who, and what was said or done, what you were wearing, and any available witnesses. Be as accurate as possible. Documentation does not have to be elaborate or fancy. Simple handwritten notes including the facts will suffice. It is also a good idea to keep copies of your notes in another location.

4. Talk to other people about the problem. Get support from friends and colleagues. Sexual harassment often erodes self-confidence. Victims do not feel they are in control of the situation. Emotional support from others can bolster self-confidence and give victims the strength needed to confront sexual harassment. Frequently sharing these problems with others will also allow victims to discover they're not alone. Corroboration with other victims will not only provide emotional support, but it will also strengthen a formal complaint if that option needs to be taken sometime in the future.

5. Get witnesses. Look around when the sexual harassment is occurring and note who can observe it. Talk to these people and solicit their support. Try to make arrangements for others to be around you when you anticipate that sexual harassment is likely to occur.

Sexist Language

One form of sexual harassment involves making verbal remarks that establish an offensive or stifling work or educational environment. Such language can include jokes with inappropriate sexual connotations. It can also include derogatory comments about ability based on gender. For example, a male professor might say to his students, "Girls don't usually do very well in this major. They're usually not as bright as men. They just run off and get married anyway." Such a comment is discriminatory. The professor is making an unfounded, unfair prediction. He is not attending to each student's ability to perform on an individual basis.

Many times English words themselves reflect an aura of sexism and unfairness. For instance, the word *man* seems to occur everywhere. Consider such words and phrases as *mankind, chairman, salesman, congressman,* and *the best man for the job.* Such terms often imply that women are included, but in a subsidiary way.

Another example of how sexism has infiltrated the English language is in the proper titles for men and women. On reaching adulthood, a man becomes a "Mr." for the remainder of his life. This is a polite term which makes no reference to the status of a man's personal life. A woman, however, starts as a "Miss." She becomes a "Mrs." on marriage, which clearly establishes her marital status. At least it establishes the fact that at one time or another she has been married.

■ Suggestions for Using Nonsexist Language

There are ways to minimize the use of sexist language. Frequently, all it takes is becoming accustomed to a different way of phrasing words and sentences. The following are some suggestions aimed at maximizing fairness and objectivity through language:

1. Replace the term *man* with other more inclusive terms such as *human* or *person.* For example, *mankind* can become *humankind, chairman* can become *chairperson* or *chair,* and the nature of *man* can become the nature of *humankind.*

2. Use the term *Ms* instead of *Miss* and *Mrs.* *Ms* and *Mr.* are equivalent terms. Such usage will seem natural once people become accustomed to using the new term.

3. Try to phrase sentences so that the masculine pronouns *he, him,* and *his* can be avoided.

This can be done in several ways (McGraw-Hill, 1974). First, pronouns can be eliminated altogether. For example,

"The average American likes to drink his coffee black."
can be changed to:
"The average American likes black coffee."

Second, phrases can frequently be rephrased into the plural:
"Average Americans like their coffee black."

Third, masculine pronouns can be substituted with one, you, or his or her. For example, a statement could be phrased in the following manner:

"The average American likes to have his or her coffee black."

4. Avoid using patronizing and derogatory stereotypes (McGraw-Hill, 1974). These include phrases such as *sweet young thing, the little lady, bubble-brained blonde, hen-pecked husband, frustrated spinster, nagging mother-in-law, dirty old man,* and *dumb jock.*

Many good suggestions can be found for using nonsexist language. However, the main idea is for a person to be sensitive to what he or she is saying. Subtle implications need to be examined in order to communicate accurately and objectively. This is especially true for social workers, and is pertinent to what they say and write.

Rape and Sexual Assault

The most intimate violation of a person's privacy and dignity is sexual assault. Sexual assaults involve any unwanted sexual contact where verbal or physical force is used. A commonly used legal definition of rape involves a sexual assault where penile penetration of the vagina occurs without mutual consent (Masters and Johnson, 1985, p. 464).

Throughout their lives the fear of assault and rape lingers in the minds of women. It is an act of violence over which they have neither control nor protection. Several aspects of sexual assault and rape will be addressed here to give an understanding of the effects on women and how women might best cope with the fact that rape exists. They include the frequency with which rapes occur, some theoretical perspectives on why rape exists in our culture, some common myths about rape, typical victim reactions to rape, and some suggestions for counseling rape victims.

Incidence of Rape

The FBI indicates that over 87,000 rapes were reported in the United States during 1985 (FBI Uniform Crime Reports, 1986). Most experts agree that the vast majority of rapes, perhaps four out of five, are never reported (Amir, 1971; FBI, 1973; Hyde, 1982; Masters and Johnson, 1985). Nevertheless, one recent source indicates that as many as one of every six women will be the victim of an attempted assault at some time during her life; 1 in 24 women will be raped (Nelson, 1980).

Women fail to report being raped for many reasons. Victims whose bodies have been brutally violated often desperately want to forget that the horror ever happened. To report it means dwelling on the details and going over the event again and again in their minds. Other victims fear retribution from the rapist. If they call public attention to him, he might do it again to punish them. No police officer will be available all of the time for protection. Other victims feel that people around them will think less of them because they've been raped. It's almost as if a part of them has been spoiled, a part which they would prefer to hide from other people. Rape is an ugly crisis which takes a great amount of courage to face.

Theoretical View of Rape

Albin (1977) summarizes three theoretical perspectives on why rape occurs. These include theories on victim precipitation of rape, the psychopathology of rapists, and the feminist perspective. The intent is not to state which one is the best theory, but to present three different ways of conceptualizing or thinking about rape.

Victim-Precipitated Rape

This perspective assumes that the victim is actually to blame for the rape. The idea is that the woman "asked for it." Perhaps she was wearing provocative clothing. A common belief is that women subconsciously desire to be raped (Strong and Reynolds, 1982, p. 507). This view focuses on how women really want to be overpowered and taken by force.

An unfortunate example of how destructive this perspective can be is provided by a young female student who came to her instructor seeking help for her friend. Her friend, age 18, had attended a local festival during the prior summer. The woman somehow got separated from her friends and found herself talking and flirting with two men about age 20. As it had been a hot July day, the woman was wearing a halter top and jeans. Suddenly, before she realized what had happened, the men shoved her into the car and swept her away to some city apartment. There they raped her throughout the night.

The next morning the men put her into the car and dropped her off back at the festival entrance. In terror and tears, she called her father and, sobbing, explained to him what had happened. His response to her was, "I told you not to ask for it. Why do you have to dress like that?" The woman was crushed.

This father had adopted the victim-precipitated view of rape. He immediately assumed it was his daughter's fault. Unfortunately, the young woman did not recover very well. What she had really needed from her father was support and help. What she had gotten was blame. Six months later the young woman found herself terrified of men. Her reaction was so extreme that on New Year's Eve at midnight, she could not bear to watch people give each other New Year's kisses. She rushed from the room crying.

The instructor listening to the story strongly suggested that the young rape victim get counseling help. She needed to work through her feelings and put the blame where it belonged, namely, on her attackers.

Many male students have also found the victim-precipitated view rather offensive. The implication is that men are rather animalistic and cannot control their own impulses. Various men have indicated that they find this you-know-how-men-are point of view as degrading as women might find the you-know-how-women-are perspective. Neither perspective takes into account individual differences or personal morals and values.

Rapist Psychopathology

A second theoretical perspective concerns rapist psychopathology. This view proposes that the rapist is emotionally disturbed or mentally unbalanced. He rapes because he is sick. This view places virtually none of the blame on society or on social attitudes.

The Feminist Perspective on Rape

The feminist perspective emphasizes that rape is the logical reaction of men who are socialized to dominate women. Rape is seen as a manifestation of men's need to aggressively maintain power over women. It has little to do with sexuality. Sexuality only provides a clearcut means for exercising power. Rape is seen as a consequence of attitudes toward women that are intimately intertwined throughout the culture. The feminist perspective sees rape as a societal problem, rather than only an individual one.

Herman (1984) elaborates on this view. She points out that both aggressors and victims are brought up to believe that sexual aggression is natural. As a result, victims often blame themselves for the assault. The rationale is that they should have expected to be raped. They should have been prepared or have done something to prevent it.

An analogous situation concerning self-blame is the example of a woman who has her purse snatched while shopping on a Saturday afternoon. If the self-blame concept were applied, it would follow that the woman would blame herself for the incident. She would chastise herself by saying it was her fault. She never should have taken her purse with her to shop in the first place. Maybe she should only do shopping by catalog from now on. Of course, taking that course of action would be absurd. It was not the woman's fault. It was the purse snatcher who broke the law. He is the one who should be held responsible.

Blaming oneself for being raped is inappropriate. The feminist view holds that society is wrong for socializing people to assume that male sexual aggression is natural. Socializing women to consider themselves weak and nurturant also contributes to the problem. It helps to develop a victim mentality, that is, an expectation that it's natural for women to be victims. The feminist perspective emphasizes that these attitudes need to be changed. Only then can rape as a social problem disappear.

Common Myths about Rape

Various myths about rape need to be examined and corrected. Women need accurate information in order to make responsible decisions. They need to learn what types of conditions and circumstances prompt rape so that they may be avoided.

Spontaneous Rape

Most rapes are thought to occur with spontaneous bursts of aggression and/or sexual desire. To the contrary, most rapes are planned in advance. Some research discloses that in 71 percent of all reported rapes, the rapists made arrangements in advance and in an additional 11 percent, at least some planning was involved (Amir, 1967). In planning, they usually try to maximize their victim's vulnerability.

The Dark Alley Rape

Another myth is that rapes tend to occur in dark alleys. Although some circumstances such as hitchhiking or walking home alone in the dark tend to increase the chances of being raped, there is some indication that half

This formerly battered wife succeeded in leaving her abusive husband and is building a new life for herself. But many battered wives cannot extract themselves from their turbulent homes. They may be economically dependent on their husbands, not have the necessary qualifications to obtain jobs, or have no one to care for their children even if they do find employment. Sadly, even abused wives who are financially independent often don't feel capable of leaving their abusive husbands. (Fran Buss)

This man's work conforms to the stereotypical male profession. Like most men, he was encouraged to develop his spatial perception and manipulation skills from an early age. Traditionally, girls have been discouraged from learning these skills. They are trained to be homebodies, as well as passive and submissive "little ladies" who play with dolls and wear frilly dresses. As society places less emphasis on gender-based stereotypes, the more self-satisfied men and women will become. (Karen Kirst-Ashman)

This mother is already teaching her son to be a "little man," an aggressive person who doesn't cry, even when he feels sad or is in pain. She has neither learned nor accepted the concept of "adrogyny." Adrogynous children have the capacity to take on some traditionally "masculine" characteristics and qualities and some traditionally "feminine" ones. Androgynous men express emotional feelings and androgynous women feel freer to be assertive, and have a greater share in leading and decision making. (Charles Zastrow)

One way the social worker can help combat sexism in the home is by encouraging couples to divide up both household tasks and responsibility for earning the family's income. The couple may receive a lot of outside pressure and criticism from family and friends who are not used to traditional role reversal. But with the social worker's counseling, they can learn to ignore it. (Karen Kirst-Ashman) of all rapes occur in the victim's own home (Medea and Thompson, 1974) (McIntyre, 1980). In these cases the victim is very likely to know the rapist. This presents a problem as people tend to feel safe when they're in their own homes with a person they know (Schneider et al., 1981). However, knowledge of this fact is important if it helps people be more cautious.

One incident emphasizes the importance of caution. A 20-year-old female student sheepishly approached her instructor and finally blurted out that she had been raped at a party the past Saturday night. Although it was not in her own home, it was in the home of a good friend of hers. Apparently, people attending the party were drinking and not concerning themselves with the noise level. The student found herself talking with a young male lawyer while sitting on the bed in one of the bedrooms. Suddenly, the lawyer closed and locked the door. He pinned her to the bed and began to rape her. She was awestruck that this could be happening. Although he was not a good friend, he was an acquaintance of hers. They shared several mutual friends. After all, he was even a lawyer. She resisted to the best of her ability. She was too ashamed to scream.

As she was talking about the incident several days later, her main concern was what her friends would think about her if they ever found out. Although she dreamed about getting revenge, she didn't want to jeopardize her reputation. As she continued to relate her story, her instructor discussed her feelings, the potential physical ramifications, and potential legal alternatives. Her instructor also helped the student gain a more objective perception of the incident. It was especially important for this victim to place the blame where it belonged, namely on the rapist. Finally, her instructor referred her to counseling to give her a chance to work out and deal with the feelings she had about having such a horrible experience.

Stranger Rape

Another myth is that only strangers are potential rapists. At least half of all reported rapes are inflicted by someone the victim knows (Strong and Reynolds, 1982, p. 512). Of approximately 106,000 women responding to a 1980 Cosmopolitan poll, 24 percent stated they had been rape victims. Of those who had been raped, 51 percent stated that the rapist was a friend. Thirty-seven percent were victimized by a stranger, 18 percent by a relative, and 3 percent by their own husbands.

It appears that rape by someone known to the victim causes the most severe psychological trauma (Bart, 1975). Perhaps the trauma has to do with the violation of trust. If a woman is not safe with a person she knows and trusts, who might she be safe with? This thought is frightening.

Interracial Rape

Most rapes are committed by a member of the same race as the victim (Herman, 1984, p. 27). The traditional, prejudicial perspectives that black men rape white women and white men rape black women are not true. The vast majority of rapes are intraracial, not interracial. The unfortunate myth of black/white rape may be perpetuated by the inordinate amount of media attention given these incidents when they do occur (Comment, 1968, p. 318).

Victim Age

Women have been raped at ages as young as six months and as old as 93 years (Herman, 1984, p. 28). Most rapes occur to younger woman. One study found that 20 percent of rape victims were between ages 10 and 14, with an additional 25 percent ranging in age from 15 to 19 (Amir, 1971). Another study found that 41 percent of rape victims seen in a Philadelphia hospital emergency room were age 16 or younger, with most being between ages 13 and 16 (Women Organized Against Rape, 1975). Another source indicates that the majority of rapes happen to women aged 16 to 25 (Meeks and Heit, 1982, p. 447). It appears that young women in their teens and early 20s are at the greatest risk of rape, although rape may occur at virtually any age.

Profile of a Rapist

Most rapists are young. Over half of all rapists are under age 25 (Federal Bureau of Investigation, 1981), and three fourths are under age 30 (Masters and Johnson, 1985, p. 476). Many tend to repeat their crime (Cohen et al., 1971). Most have a prior criminal record and about half were drinking heavily when they committed rape (Masters and Johnson, 1985, p. 476).

A problem with looking at a profile of convicted rapists is that the profile only reflects those who have been brought to court and found guilty. Only a fraction of rapes are reported in the first place. Consequently, not all alleged rapists are convicted. Many cases are unfounded, that is, police decide not to recommend that the case be prosecuted (Herman, 1984, p. 28). Several reasons for unfounding are given. First, sometimes a moral evaluation of the victim is made, for example that the victim had been drinking (Comment, 1968, p. 318) or there were allegations of prior sexual activity such as prostitution (Wood, 1973). Second, police may discover that the victim and the attacker had had a prior relationship (Comment, 1968, p. 304). In these cases there was a tendency to blame the victim for taking a risk with someone she knew. Third, there is a tendency for unfounding cases when a lack of force is used (Chappell, 1981, p. 180). An accurate profile of all the people who commit rape might be very different than the picture of only those who are convicted for the crime.

It is also important to understand that most rapists are not murderers (Selkin, 1975). Many attackers may threaten victims with violence or even murder. Knowing that most rapists are not murderers, women may respond more assertively. Instead of submitting out of fear, a woman may be more likely to resist forcefully and thereby prevent the rape.

Gang Rape

One study found that 43 percent of rapes are gang rapes (performed by two or more persons) (Amir, 1971). Herman (1984, p. 25) proposes that a man participating in this behavior "is not only expressing his hostility toward women and asserting his masculinity to himself but also proving his manhood to others." These rapes tend to be characterized by violence (Medea and Thompson, 1974, p. 34) and often involve sexual humiliation

(Brownmiller, 1975, p. 196). It appears that rape in these cases provides a means for these men to exercise dominance over women in a way that gains recognition and attention from others.

Victim Reactions to Rape

Burgess and Holmstrom (1974(a); 1974(b)), studying the reactions of 92 rape victims, found that women can experience serious psychological effects that can persist for a half year or more following a rape. They call these emotional changes the *rape trauma syndrome*. The syndrome has two basic phases. The first is the acute phase, which involves the woman's emotional reactions immediately following the rape and up to several weeks thereafter. The victim reacts in one of two ways. She may show her emotions by crying, expressing anger, or showing fear. On the other hand, she may try to control these intense emotions and keep them from view. Emotions experienced during the acute phase range from humiliation and guilt to shock to anger and desire for revenge.

Additionally, during this phase women will often experience physical problems including difficulties related directly to the rape, such as irritation of the genitals or rectal bleeding from an anal rape. Physical problems also include stress-related discomforts such as headaches, stomach difficulties, or inability to sleep.

The two primary emotions experienced during the acute phase are fear and self-blame. Fear results from the violence of the experience. Many rape victims report that during the attack they felt their life had come to an end. They had no control over what the attacker would do to them and were terrified. Such fear can linger. Oftentimes victims fear that rape can easily happen again. The second emotion, self-blame, results from society's tendency of blaming the victim as discussed in the theory of victim-precipitated rape and the feminist perspective on rape.

The second stage of the rape trauma syndrome is the long-term reorganization and recovery phase. The emotional changes and reactions of this phase may linger on for years. Nadelson et al. (1982) found that three fourths of rape victims felt that the rape had changed their lives in one way or another. Reported reactions included fear of being alone, depression, sleeplessness, and, most frequently, an attitude of suspicion toward other people. Other long-term changes that sometimes occur include avoiding involvement with men (Masters and Johnson, 1985, p. 474) and suffering various sexual dysfunctions such as lack of sexual desire, aversion to sexual contact, or difficulties in having orgasms (Kolodny et al., 1979).

It is very important for victims of rape to deal with even the most negative feelings and get on with their lives. In some ways rape might be compared to accepting the death of a loved one. The fact that either has occurred cannot be changed, despite the fact that each is very painful. However, it is crucial for survivors and victims to cope. Life continues.

■ One Rape Victim's Story

The following is an account shared by a social work student who is the mother of three teenage children. She wrote it in reaction to a class presentation on rape and rape counseling. A film was shown which portrayed the story of the rape of a young female hitchhiker. After the film, comments were made in class about what the young woman could have or should have done to prevent the rape. Some of the discussion focused on how women sometimes ask for it by the way they dress provocatively or by the way they act. This narrative is included here because nothing can portray the mighty impact of rape more than such a personal account. Here is her story.

The act of rape is only the beginning of a traumatic experience for which the victim has no end.

It's been 12 years now for me, but my first thought when I heard that the film in class was going to be about rape was to get out of the room. Once the film started, it was too late. The panic and fear hit, and I couldn't move. My palms were sweating and I wanted to throw up.

I have two reasons for sharing this. One is to help people understand and the second is to get my own perspective back.

I certainly do not mean to put anyone down for their comments about what the girl in the film could have or should have done. As I said I only want to help people understand. I knew my assailant for two years and my first reaction was shock and disbelief and certainly the first reaction of a woman attacked by a stranger would be the same. Once you realize what's really happening and if you have a moment of rational thought before the fear and panic hit, you may have lost any edge, if there was one. By the time I realized what was really happening to me, my hands were tied behind my back and my mouth was gagged. I fought as much as I could with my legs, but the more I fought the more violent he became so I stopped. At this point all I wanted to do was to stay alive.

Rape is a violation of the entire being. Physically, you may heal with no signs of your attack. Emotionally you will never completely heal.

In order for a rape victim to again function as a whole and healthy person, they must learn to love and respect themselves again, to be able to trust again, and very importantly learn how to deal with the fear and panic which will reoccur.

I've spent a lot of time trying to understand the causes of rape and other acts of violence towards women such as wife abuse. Many times we refer to these men as sick, but I believe they are just carrying out their attitudes toward women. These attitudes come from our oldest written laws including the Bible. Throughout these old laws women are referred to by terms such as "inferior," "lustful," and "deceitful," just to name a few. It is also stressed that men must control women. Women have been oppressed, suppressed, tortured, and murdered in the name of law and religion from the beginning. For example, the witch hunts where thousands of women were tortured and murdered were sanctioned by law and the church. The witch hunts began in 1486 and continued with great force for over 100 years in Europe. In one village in Germany 368 women were hanged or burned in the name of religion. Many of these women's only sin was that they dared to be different or assert their independence.

Certainly we've come a long way since the witch hunts, or have we really? Only recently have abused women found any protection and their situations been treated in a serious manner. Likewise in the cases of husbands raping their wives.

What's the answer? Certainly we must work hard for legislation to protect and designate women's rights, but attitudes cannot be legislated. Each of us must look deeply and honestly at our own attitudes and at how we interact with other people. Parents must look at the attitudes they are passing on to their children.

Awareness is the key. No attitude can be changed unless we're aware that it exists.

Finally, I am a woman and proud to be so, and I will not dress in an unattractive manner.

Suggestions for Counseling Rape Victims

Three basic issues are involved in working with a victim of rape. First, she is most likely in a state of emotional upheaval. Her self-concept is probably seriously shaken. Various suggestions for helping a rape victim in such a traumatic emotional state will be provided. Second, the rape victim must decide whether to call the police and press charges. Third, the rape victim must assess her medical status following the rape, for example, injuries or potential pregnancy.

Emotional Issues

Collier (1982) suggests that counseling victims of rape involves three major stages. First, the counselor or social worker needs to provide the victim with immediate warmth and support. The victim needs to feel safe; she needs to feel free to talk. She needs to ventilate and acknowledge her feelings before she can begin to deal with them. To the extent possible, the victim should be made to feel she is now in control of her situation. She should not be pressured to talk, but rather encouraged to share her feelings.

Although it is important for the victim to talk freely, it is also important that she not be grilled with intimate, detailed questions. She will have to deal with those enough if she reports the incident to the police.

Frequently, the victim will dwell on what she could have or should have done. It is helpful to emphasize what she did right. After all, she is alive, safe, and physically not severely harmed. She managed to survive a terrifying and dangerous experience. It is also helpful to talk about how she reacted normally, as anyone else in her situation would most probably have reacted. This does not mean minimizing the incident. It does mean objectively talking about how traumatizing and potentially dangerous the incident was. One other helpful suggestion for dealing with a rape victim is to help her place the blame where it belongs, namely on the rapist. He chose to rape her. It was not her doing. Research bears out the fact that the majority of rapes have absolutely nothing to do with the behavior of the victim (Amir, 1971).

The second stage of counseling, according to Collier (1982), involves creating support from others. This support may include that of professional resources such as local rape crisis centers as well as support from people who are emotionally close to the victim. Sometimes those close to the victim need to be educated. They need to find out that what the victim needs is warmth and support, and to feel loved. Questions which emphasize her feelings of self-blame such as why she didn't fight back or why she was wearing a low-cut blouse should be completely avoided.

Collier's (1982) third stage of counseling involves rebuilding the victim's trust in herself, in the environment around her, and in her other personal relationships. Rape weakens a woman. It destroys her trust in herself and in others. This stage of counseling needs to focus on the victim's objective evaluation of herself and her situation. Her strong points need to be clarified and emphasized so that she may gain confidence in herself.

The victim also needs to look objectively at her surrounding environment. She cannot remain cooped up in her apartment for the rest of her life. It is impractical and unfair. She can take precautions against being raped, but needs to continue living a normal life.

Finally, the victim needs to assess her other personal relationships objectively. Just because she was intimately violated by one aggressor, this has nothing to do with the other people in her life. She needs to concentrate on the positive aspects of her other relationships. She must not allow the fear and terror she experienced during that one unfortunate incident to color and taint other relationships. She must clearly distinguish the rape from her other relationships in her mind.

A raped woman may initially want to talk with another woman. However, it might also be important to talk to men, including those close to her. It is important for the victim to realize that not all men are rapists. Sometimes there is a male partner. His willingness to let the victim express her feelings, and in return offer support and empathy, is probably the most beneficial thing that can be done for the victim (Masters and Johnson, 1985, pp. 474–75).

Reporting to the Police

The initial reaction to being raped might be to call the police and relate the incident. However, many victims choose not to do this. Masters and Johnson (1985, p. 470) list numerous reasons why this is so. Included are fear that the rapist will try to get revenge, fear of public embarrassment and derogation, an attitude that it won't matter anyway because most rapists get off free, and fear of the legal process and questioning. It's financially expensive and emotionally draining to take a rape case to court (Herman, 1984, p. 30). In reality, even when they are persistent, women have found it difficult to have rapists prosecuted. In many cases, as we've already discussed, police determine that the case is unfounded. In cases where police do believe that a rape occurred, only half of the alleged rapists are apprehended and arrested (Herman, 1984, p. 32). Even fewer of these are actually convicted.

Some positive changes are occurring in police investigation of rape cases (Moody and Hayes, 1980) and in legal handling (Lasater, 1980). Many police departments are trying to deal with rape victims more sensitively. Some departments in larger cities have special teams trained specifically for dealing with rape victims. In many states information about the victim's past sexual history is no longer permissable for use in court. When such information is introduced, it can serve to humiliate and discredit the victim. Some states have more progressive laws. Wisconsin,[4] for example, has established four degrees of sexual assault in addition to forbidding the use of the victim's past sexual conduct in court. According to Wisconsin law the severity of the crime and the corresponding severity of punishment is based on the amount of force used by the rapist and on the amount of harm done to the victim. A wife is also able to prosecute her husband for sexual assault when sexual relations are forced on her.

Despite the potential difficulties in reporting a rape, the fact remains that if the victim does not report it, the rapist will not be held responsible for his actions. A rape victim needs to think through the various alternatives that are open to her and weigh their respective positive and negative consequences in order to come to this often difficult decision.

In the event that a victim decides to report, she should not take a shower. Washing will remove vital evidence. However, victims often feel defiled and dirty, and it is a logical initial reaction for them to want to cleanse themselves

---

[4]See Wisconsin State Statue 940.225.

and try to forget that the incident ever occurred. In counseling situations, it's important to emphasize the reason for not washing immediately.

Reporting a rape should be done within 48 hours at the absolute longest. The sooner the rape is reported and the evidence gathered, the better the chance of being able to get a conviction.

Medical Status of the Victim

A third major issue that rape victims need to address is their medical status following the assault. At some point the victim needs to attend to the possibility of pregnancy. She should be asked about this issue at an appropriate time and in a gentle manner. She should be encouraged to seek medical help both for this possibility and for screening sexually transmitted diseases. The negative possibilities should not be emphasized. However, the victim needs to attend to these issues at some point. And the victim should, of course, be urged to seek immediate medical care for any physical injury.

■ Suggestions for Rape Prevention

Rape is not the victim's fault. Women do not have control over being attacked. However, there are some measures that women can take to minimize their chances of being assaulted. Most of these suggestions are simply matters of common sense. It is unfortunate that women must be extra cautious, must plan ahead, and sometimes must change patterns of behavior in minor ways. However, it is necessary.

The following suggestions are included among those made by Women Organized Against Rape (WOAR)* in order to avoid being raped.

The first suggestion is to be aware of the things around you. Notice the people and cars in your immediate surroundings. Think ahead about what areas might be especially dangerous in your usual walking routes. If you have to travel through such areas, think ahead about what you would do if you were attacked. Try to stay in well-lighted areas and walk in the middle of the sidewalk. Walking in the middle of the street when there is little traffic is also a possibility. If you can, use different routes to get where you are going, especially at night. Avoid establishing a predictable pattern for a potential assailant.

Also try to be aware of your own behavior. Notice how you're standing or walking, and how you might appear to other people. Always walk with an air of confidence and strength. Try not to appear confused, vulnerable, or preoccupied, as attackers often look for such people. Walking with others or taking public transportation are other good options.

If you think someone is following you, don't be afraid to look behind you. You might want to cross the street or travel in another direction. If you continue to have the feeling that someone is following you, it's best to go to the nearest lighted store or house and call a friend or the police for help. Don't hesitate to scream for help if you feel you are in danger. Screaming such words as "fire" or "police" is usually better than screaming the words "help" or "rape."

Some specific suggestions can also be followed for avoiding sexual assault when you are in situations involving driving your car. First of all, try to park in well-lighted areas and have your car keys ready to use. Check the back seat before getting in. While driving, keep your car doors locked and your windows partly rolled up. If approached by someone while at a stoplight, put your hand on your horn and be ready to blow it. It's also a good idea to keep at least a quarter tank of gas in the car whenever you drive to avoid running out of gas in potentially dangerous situations.

If you should have car trouble, pull over to the side of the road and stay in the car with doors locked and windows raised. When no one is around, get out and raise the car's hood to alert others to your distress. It's best to wait until police come to assist you. In the event that a man should stop and volunteer help, roll your window down only slightly and ask that he call for police help. Although such persons offering assistance may have only the best intentions, there is no way to know for sure.

Hitch-hiking is very dangerous and should be

avoided. The best way to prevent sexual assault when hitch-hiking is simply not to hitch-hike at all.

There are also ways to maintain your safety at home. Outside entrances and hallways should all be well lighted. Doors should have good dead-bolt locks instead of simple key locks which offer virtually no protection. Windows should also have locks so that potential assailants cannot enter in that manner. Women who live by themselves or with other women should use only their first initials on mailboxes, which helps prevent potential assailants from targeting women. It's also very helpful to know your neighbors even if you live in a large, relatively impersonal apartment complex. You should know where you can go for help when you need it. Don't allow strangers in your home. If a man knocks on your door and says he's a serviceman, ask for identification and have him slide it under the door, or call his company for identification.

In the event of an attack, there are some guidlines which may help to lessen the probability of being raped (Sexual Assault Treatment Center, 1979). The first suggestion is simply to run. It's more advantageous to get angry instead of scared and to react immediately. Screaming loudly is also suggested.

Traditional weapons such as guns or knives usually do not provide an effective defense. It's too easy for the attacker to take them away and use them on the victim. Rather, carrying ordinary objects such as whistles, keys, rings, umbrellas, or hatpins is helpful. To fight back, aim for the face, including eyes, ears, nose, and mouth, which are more sensitive to pain. Pulling hair is another option and loud screams in the attacker's ear will stun him. Biting or kicking sometimes is effective. A kick aimed at his knees may be more effective in order to knock an attacker off balance, as he will be most likely to protect his genitals first.

*WOAR is located at 1220 Sansom Street, Philadelphia, PA 19107, telephone (215) 922-7400.

Battered Women

Terms associated with wife beating include domestic violence, family violence, spouse abuse, and battered women. Strong et al. (1983, p. 403) describe battering as a catch-all term that includes, but is not limited to, the practices of slapping, punching, knocking down, choking, kicking, hitting with objects, threatening with weapons, stabbing, and shooting. The *battered woman syndrome* implies the systematic and repeated use of one or more of the above against a woman by her husband or lover.

Some of the myths about battered women include the following (Cultural Information Service, 1984):

- Battered women aren't really hurt that badly.
- Beatings and other abuses just happen; they aren't a regular occurrence.
- Women who stay in such homes must really enjoy the beatings they get.
- Wife-battering only occurs in lower-class families.

It is estimated that 1.8 million women in America will suffer severe beatings in their own homes each year (Straus et al., 1981). Every 30 seconds a woman is beaten somewhere in this country (McGrath, 1980). One estimate indicates that wives will be the victim of violence in two thirds of all American marriages (Roy, 1982). Ninety-five percent of all spouse abuse is committed by men on their wives (Cultural Information Service, 1984). One third of all murdered women are killed by their husbands or lovers (McGrath, 1980). Although there has been some mention in the media of battered husbands, the overwhelming majority of domestic violence victims are women (Gelles, 1979).

Battery victims don't like to be beaten. Women go to domestic violence programs for help in stopping the beatings and yet maintaining their marriages (Norman and Mancuso, 1980, p. 115). They don't enjoy the pain and suffering. For reasons which will be discussed later, they tolerate it.

Wife battering is not limited to poor families, minorities, people in blue-collar occupations, or families of lower socioeconomic status (Gelles, 1974). Battered wives come from virtually every socioeconomic level. It's more likely for wife battering to be reported to police, public agencies, and hospitals when it happens in lower-case families (Stark and McEvoy, 1970). Middle- and upper-class families have more resources available to them either to deal with battering in other ways or to keep it hidden from public scrutiny.

A Profile of the Victim

Walker (1979) describes the battered woman as tending to have certain characteristics. First, she has very low self-esteem. Social workers who counsel battered women indicate that psychological abuse is frequently also involved. The battering husbands tend to criticize their wives and make derogatory remarks. They also tend to emphasize how their wives couldn't possibly survive without them. Over an extended period of time, their wives start to believe them.

A second characteristic of battered women is their tendency to believe in the common myths about battering. These women are especially likely to believe that the battering is somehow their own fault. The typical battered woman believes that it is her responsibility to nurture and maintain the marriage and will often blame herself completely for a bad one (Martin, 1976, p. 81).

A third characteristic is the battered women's traditional beliefs concerning gender roles. They tend to believe in men being the dominant decision-makers and leaders of the family, and they feel women should be submissive and obedient. Perhaps they feel they deserve to be beaten for not adequately obeying their husbands and doing what they are told. Walker (1979, p. 51) refers to a sense of learned helplessness which may develop. She states, "Women are systematically taught that their personal worth, survival and autonomy do not depend on effective and creative responses to life situations, but rather on their physical beauty and an appeal to men. They learn that they have no control over the circumstances of their lives." The more they are battered, the more helpless they feel and the less they are able to see their way out of their plight.

The Abusive Husband

Strong et al. (1983, pp. 405–6) propose a series of traits that tend to characterize men who batter their wives. Many of the attitudes and beliefs resemble those of their wives. For instance, they tend to have low self-esteem, to believe in the common myths about battering, and to firmly maintain traditional gender-role stereotypes. Additionally, men who batter are frequently emotionally immature and tend to use wife beating as a means of alleviating stress. Abusive men, in their personal insecurity, frequently become very jealous and possessive of their wives. Much of the research about the battered woman syndrome suggests that alcohol is frequently involved (Norman and Mancuso, 1980, p. 117).

Some evidence is found that men who batter have learned from their own parents to use aggressive behavior as a coping mechanism (Gelles, 1976; Marsden and Owens, 1975; Straus, 1974). This coincides with some of the ideas in learning theory. First, the male child can learn abusive behavior by observing the behavior modeled by his parents. For the male adult, the battering itself becomes reinforcing. It can be negatively reinforced when the wife is made to stop doing whatever it is she's not supposed to be doing. The battering can be a positive reinforcer when it provides the satisfaction of being able to exert control at least over something in life.

The fact that battering is rarely punished might also encourage it. As McGrath (1980) states, wife battering incidents "have had a police priority somewhere just above that of cats stuck in trees." Perhaps this indifference has to do with the assumption that domestic matters are no one's business but the marital partners involved. It may also stem from the traditional idea that women are something to be owned like property (Norman and Mancuso, 1980, p. 119). Therefore, the husband has the right to keep control. Also, battered women have been known to actually protect and defend their battering spouse when police enter a home and try to intervene in a violent argument. Finally, intervening is downright dangerous for the officers. Twenty-two percent of all police deaths and 40 percent of all injuries happen while they're trying to intervene in domestic violence disputes (McGrath, 1980).

The Battering Cycle

Walker (1979) found that wife abuse tends to occur in three basic phases. The first phase involves building up stress and tension. The wife tries to make things okay and avoid confrontations. There may be a few minor abusive incidents. However, this phase is primarily characterized by the build-up of excessive tension.

The second phase in the battering cycle is the explosion. This is when the tension breaks, the batterer loses control, and the battering occurs. This is generally the shortest of the three phases, but it may last for up to several days.

The third phase involves making up. Since his tension has been released, the batterer now adamantly states that he is truly sorry for what he has done. He swears he will never do it again. The battered woman relents and believes him. He is forgiven and all seems well, that is, until the cycle of violence begins again.

Why Does She Stay?

One of the most frequently asked questions about domestic violence is why the battered woman remains in the home and in the relationship. Approximately 60 to 70 percent of women who seek help from shelters and even those who initiate separation through the courts eventually return to their abusive home situations (Normal and Mancuso, 1980, p. 120). There are many reasons why these women return. Reasons include lack of self-confidence, traditional beliefs, guilt, economic dependence, fear of the abuser, fear of isolation, fear for her children, and love.

Lack of Self-Confidence. Because battered women frequently have low levels of self-esteem, it takes great initiative and courage to leave even a painful situation and strike out for the unknown. The unknown is frightening. At least if the battered woman stays in the home, she knows she has a place to stay.

Adherence to Traditional Beliefs. Because battered women tend to believe in traditional gender-role stereotypes, they believe in their husbands as caretakers and providers. They dislike the alternatives of being separated or divorced. It's often difficult for them to comprehend what they would do on their own.

Guilt. As discussed, many feel that it is their own fault that they are abused. To some extent this guilt may be due to their husbands telling them that they're to blame for causing trouble. Perhaps because of their low levels of self-esteem, it's easy for them to be critical of themselves. Their beliefs in traditional gender-role stereotypes may cause them to wonder how they have failed in their submissive, nurturant role of wife.

Economic Dependence. Many battered women are not financially secure in their own right. Many do not have the skills and training necessary to obtain jobs where they could maintain their current standard of living.

Fear of the Abuser. It is logical for a battered woman to fear brutal retaliation by her husband if she leaves him. A person who has dealt with stress by physical brutality before might do so again when it is initiated by the stress of his wife leaving him. The battered woman might even fear being murdered by an abandoned husband.

Fear of Isolation. Battered women often try to keep the facts of their battery a secret. They may feel isolated from friends and family. They may indeed actually be isolated by the time their battery reaches such crisis proportions. Many times "familial ties have been strained over the years, and closeness is lacking" (Norman and Mancuso, 1980, p. 120).

Fear for Her Children. The battered woman might also fear for the safety of her children. First, she might be worried about her ability to support them financially without her husband. Second, she may firmly believe the traditional belief that children need a father. She may believe that a father who abuses his wife is better than no father at all. Third, she may even fear that she may lose the custody of her children. Her husband may threaten to take them. She may have little knowledge of the complicated legal system and may believe that he can and will do it.

Love. Battered women still love their abusive husbands. Most abused women who seek help still would prefer to remain in their marriages if the battering could be stopped (Geller, 1978). Walker (1979) cites one elderly woman's reactions to the death of her husband, who had battered her throughout their 53-year marriage. The woman stated, "We did everything together. . . . I loved him; you know, even when he was brutal and mean. . . . I'm sorry he's dead, although there were days when I wished he would die. . . He was my best friend. . . . He beat me right up to the end. . . . It was a good life and I really do miss him."

■ The Burning Bed*

March 9, 1977. Francine Hughes has been arrested for setting fire to her house while her ex-husband, Mickey, was sleeping. He died in the blaze. She is charged with premeditated murder. In the county jail, Fran recounts her story to Ayron Greydanus, a court-appointed attorney.

The trouble begins soon after their 1964 marriage. Out of work, living with his parents, Mickey becomes intensely possessive of Fran and jealous of her interests. One day he slaps her for "sassing him" in front of his friends. It is only the first of many incidents. The violence escalates to regular beatings in which Fran is often literally knocked across the room. The battering continues after the births of their three children.

In 1971, Fran decides she must do something about her situation. Informed by the welfare office that she will have to divorce her husband in order to qualify for financial aid, Fran leaves Mickey and moves into an apartment. However, that same year, he is seriously injured in an automobile accident. She gives in to pressure from his family to visit him in the hospital. Later, she takes a place near his mother's house, intending to stay only until he recuperates.

Although they are divorced, Mickey begins to pay regular visits to her house. When she rejects his advances, he beats her in front of the children. Terrified, Fran hides in a closet. She appeals to his parents and the police for help, but nothing changes. Mickey threatens that if she leaves him, "those kids aren't going to have a mother."

After one brutal battering, Fran runs away with the children to her mother's house. Mickey appears at the door demanding the children, and to appease him, Fran's mother sends them out to him. Convinced that he will kill her, Fran again goes to the authorities, but she cannot even get the children back. Meanwhile, Mickey tries to persuade her that he has changed. He has quit drinking and promises he will not hurt her again.

In the courtroom, the trial of Francine Hughes is in progress. Mickey's mother testifies, and Christy Hughes, Fran's oldest daughter, describes her father's violence and threats. Then Fran is called to the stand to tell her side of the story.

Fran had been reunited with her children and had enrolled at a local community college. On the evening of March 9, she returned home late to find Mickey drunk and angry. Insisting that she quit school, he ripped up her notebooks and ordered her to burn them. After beating her nearly senseless, he demanded that they have sex.

Fran waited until he had fallen asleep. She told the children to get in the car. She poured gasoline around his bed and started the fire. As the house burst into flames, Fran and the children drove away.

In the courtroom, Fran explains her feelings that night: "I thought about all the things that had happened to me; how much he had hurt me my whole life." The jury returns the verdict for the murder charge: not guilty by reason of temporary insanity.

*This information is reprinted with permission from a "Viewer's Guide" prepared by Cultural Information Service (CISems, Inc.) in consultation with The National Coalition Against Domestic Violence. "The Burning Bed" was a two-hour made-for-television movie presented by the NBC Television Network in October, 1984. The story is a true narration of the life of Francine Hughes, a Michigan woman who took the law into her own hands after enduring 12 years of domestic abuse. The story is based on the 1980 book *The Burning Bed* by Faith McNulty.

Counseling Battered Women: Their Alternatives

Despite the difficulties in dealing with domestic violence, there are definite intervention strategies that can be undertaken. They involve police departments, shelters, and specific counseling approaches (Hutchins and Baxter, 1980).

The Police and Battered Women

It is likely that police officers will be the first outside means of intervention involved in episodes of domestic abuse (Hutchins and Baxter, 1980, p. 201). Many police departments, despite their previously mentioned reluctance, are taking an increasingly active interest in addressing family violence (Hutchins and Baxter, 1980, p. 203). Because of the seriousness of the issue and the high potential for fatality and injury, they are acknowledging that something must be done. For example, training programs targeting domestic violence are being developed for police personnel (Bard and Zacker, 1971). One thrust of such programs is the development of specialized interpersonal skills for dealing with such situations. There is also a growing awareness that female officers may play a special beneficial role in the intervention process (Hutchins and Baxter, 1980, p. 203).

Shelters for Battered Women

The most immediate need of a battered woman who seeks to flee the situation is a place to go. For this purpose, shelters have been developed around the country. Late 1973 marked the opening of the first American shelter for battered women, Rainbow Retreat, in Phoenix, Arizona (Hutchins and Baxter, 1980, p. 206).

All such programs provide a safe place where battered women can go to obtain temporary shelter. Hutchins and Baxter (1980) conceptualize the range in philosophies adopted by such shelters. At one end of the continuum are the more traditionally oriented agencies. These emphasize the traditional values of keeping the family together. They orient themselves toward helping women resolve their problems with their mates, stopping the battering, and enabling these women to safely return home.

At the other end of the continuum are those shelters adopting a purely feminist perspective. For these, "wife abuse is seen as a social problem, rooted in sexism and manifested in the suffering of countless individual women. The women are regarded as victims in need of immediate protection and long-term life change. Some of the refuges with this philosophy actively encourage permanent separation of the couple" (Hutchins and Baxter, 1980, p. 207). Here the idea is that women need not be dependent on men, especially those who have been cruelly abusive to them. Rather, such abused women need to nurture confidence in themselves and to develop their own alternatives.

Many shelters, however, adopt philosophies somewhere in between the purely traditional and the purely feminist. These shelters encourage women to think through their own individual situations, evaluate their own alternatives, and make their own decisions concerning what they feel is best for them.

Counseling Strategies

The following are some basic suggestions gathered from a range of sources regarding how social workers and counselors can help battered women:

Offer Support. A battered woman has probably been weakened both physically and emotionally. She needs someone to empathize with her and express genuine concern. She needs some time to sit back, experience some relief, and think.

Review Alternatives. A battered woman may feel trapped. She may be so overwhelmed that alternatives other than surviving in her abusive situation may not even have occurred to her. Her alternatives may include returning to the marriage, getting counseling help for both herself and her husband, temporarily separating from her husband, establishing other means of financial support and independent living conditions for herself, or filing for divorce.

Furnish Information. Most victims probably don't have much information about how they can be helped. Information about available legal, medical, and social services may open up alternatives to them to better enable them to help themselves (Resnick, 1976).

Advocate. An advocate can seek out information for a victim and provide the victim with encouragement (Resnick, 1976). An advocate can also help the victim get in touch with legal, medical, and social service resources and help the victim find her way through bureaucratic processes.

Counselor Training

Resnick (1976) has developed a training manual for counselors of battered women. She makes some excellent and specific suggestions regarding the initial interview, the range of the victim's emotional reactions, and specific counseling techniques.

The Initial Interview. A battered woman is probably very anxious during her initial meeting with a social worker or counselor. She may be worried about what to say to the counselor. The counselor should try to make the victim as comfortable as possible and emphasize that she doesn't have to talk about anything she doesn't want to.

The victim may also feel that the counselor will be judgmental and critical. Resnick emphasizes that it is important that the counselor put personal feelings aside and not pressure the battered woman into any particular course of action. This may be especially difficult when the counselor has some strong personal feelings that the victim should leave the abusive situation. A basic principle is that it is the victim's decision regarding what she will choose to do. In those cases where the victim chooses to return home, it may be useful for the counselor to help her clarify the reasons behind this decision.

Confidentiality may also be an issue for the battered woman. She may be fearful of the abuser finding out that she is seeking help and of his possible retaliation. The counselor needs to assure her that no information will be given to anyone without her consent. In the event that the victim does need a place to go, it should be made clear to her that the shelter is available.

The victim may show some embarrassment at being "a battered woman." The label may make her feel uncomfortable. The counselor should make an effort to downplay any embarrassment by emphasizing that she is a victim and that her situation has nothing to do with her character or with her intrinsic human value.

Emotional Reactions. Many battered women will display a range of emotional reactions including helplessness, fear, anger, guilt, embarrassment, and even doubts about her sanity. The counselor needs to encourage the victim to get all of these emotions out in the open. Only then will she be able to deal with them. The counselor can then help the victim to look objectively at various aspects of her situation and help get control of her own life.

Specific Counseling Techniques. Resnick emphasizes that the foundation of good counseling is good listening ability. The victim needs to know that she can talk freely to the counselor.

A battered woman is often overwhelmed and confused. One of the most helpful things a counselor can do is to help her sort through her various problems. A victim cannot do everything at once. However, she can begin getting control of her life by addressing one issue at a time and making decisions step by step.

One aspect of counseling which is very easy to forget is focusing on the victim's strengths. A battered woman will probably be suffering from low self-esteem. She probably needs help in identifying her positive characteristics.

One other important counseling technique is helping the victim establish a plan of action. She needs to clearly understand and define what she chooses to do. This choice may include formulating major goals such as divorcing her husband. It may involve setting smaller subgoals such as developing a list of existing daycare centers she can call to find out available child care options.

■ Strategies for Combating Sexism and Achieving Sexual Equality

In many ways problems discussed in this chapter are simply manifestations of the core problem of sexism. Sexism refers to prejudice, discrimination, and stereotyping based on gender. Sexism, therefore, involves misinformation and attitudes that result in behavior which discriminates against women. Some basic suggestions for combating sexism involve supplying accurate information, revising attitudes, and changing behavior:

Become conscious of the gender-role stereotypes affecting people from birth on. Don't force boys to be little men who must be actively aggressive and never dare cry when they're sad or hurting. Likewise, don't force girls to be little ladies who must wear frilly pink dresses, play with dolls, and be appropriately passive and submissive. The concept of *androgyny* may be helpful here. Androgyny refers to the capacity to have both traditionally feminine and masculine characteristics and qualities at the same time. It does not mean that men should be like women, or that women should be like men. Instead, androgyny implies that each individual, regardless of gender, be allowed to develop positive personal qualities. It means that males could be freer to express their

emotional feelings and develop their communication skills. It also means that women could be freer to be assertive and have a greater share in leadership and decision making.

Throughout life place less emphasis on the need to conform with gender-based stereotypes. If less pressure was placed on men to be dominant, successful leaders, perhaps the midlife crisis would no longer exist for most men. Likewise, if less emphasis was placed on women to be beautiful, docile homemakers, perhaps they would be happier, more self-satisfied, and more comfortable in their relationships with men.

To combat the discriminatory effects of sexism on women, encourage women to develop their assertiveness skills, enhance their self-confidence, and learn to develop and appreciate analytical and spatial manipulation skills, the lack of which seems to be barring them from many of the more profitable career alternatives. Encourage both males and females to pursue whatever interests they have from early on. Females should be encouraged to develop their mathematical ability. Males should be equally encouraged to develop their domestic skills.

Encourage more freedom in adult domestic relationships. Allow individual couples to negotiate both household tasks and outside work career goals without external pressure and criticism. Encourage men and women to share in child-caring tasks. Doing so would not only allow children to know their fathers better, but also fathers to know their children. Don't criticize men who opt to stay home and manage the house and women who choose to work outside the home.

Allow people the freedom to live their lives the way they want.

Confront laws and regulations that are discriminatory and restrictive on the basis of gender. Raise questions about them if you feel they're unfair. Vote for legislators and support administrators who adopt nonsexist stances. If necessary, fight for your own rights and advocate for the rights of your clients.

Summary

Traditional sex-role stereotypes pressure males to be strong, dominant, successful, and career-oriented; and females to be nurturant, passive, and beautiful homebodies. The socialization process and sex-role stereotyping have led to a number of problems. There is sex discrimination in employment, with men who work full time being paid nearly twice as much as women who work full time. There are double standards of conduct for males and females. There are power struggles between males and females because men are socialized to be dominant in interactions with women, while women increasingly seek equalitarian relationships. Sex-role stereotyping is pervasive in our society and can be found in child-rearing practices, the educational system, our language, the mass media, the business world, and marriage and family patterns.

Several significant issues and life events related to sexism are examined in this chapter, including: the concept of comparable worth, sexual harassment, the use of sexist language, rape and sexual assault, and battered women. Finally, general strategies for combating sexism are proposed. These strategies involve supplying accurate information, revising attitudes, and changing behavior.

Sexual Preference

John had been attending the state university for over a year now. He didn't have a chance to visit his parents in their small midwest town very often. When he did get home, his visits were usually limited to holidays. Thanksgiving of his sophomore year had finally rolled around, and he found himself hopping on the Greyhound bus headed for home.

This trip home was a problem for him. No matter how often or how deeply he mulled it over in his mind, he couldn't find an answer. He had something to tell his parents that he didn't think they would like very much. Over the past year John had come to realize something about himself. He had come out; he was gay.

As he watched the countryside roll by from his bus seat he thought. He thought about his childhood, about his high school friends, and even about the girl he had gone steady with for two and one-half years during high school. What would they think if they found out?

He had never really been interested in girls. Sure, he pretended to be. Once a guy got labeled a "fag," he might as well run off to a monastery. He had always been pretty bright. He had learned really fast how men were supposed to act. As all-conference fullback on the high school football team, he became quite adept at telling the appropriate locker room dirty jokes and at exaggerating the last weekend's conquests with women. He often wondered why he had to pretend so hard. The others seemed to really get into it. They seemed genuinely enthralled with the ideas of big breasted women and sex. He never dared mention the fact that he'd rather spend time with Dan or Chuck. He certainly never came close to mentioning any of his secret fantasies.

He even asked Millie to go steady with him. She was a nice girl, in addition to being cute and extremely popular. With her he didn't feel the pressure of constantly having to push for sex. Typically, every Saturday night, they'd go to a movie or basketball game or something like that. Then afterwards they'd "neck" in the driveway for just a bit. That couldn't last too long anyway because Millie's parents were pretty strict and imposed a midnight curfew. She was in by midnight or else. He always had to put a little bit of a move on her and try to get to second base. At that point she always stopped him, told him she loved him, and firmly stated she was waiting for marriage. What a relief.

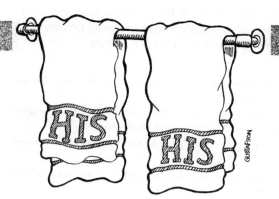

At college things were different. He had chosen the state university for a variety of reasons. He found that a person could do a lot of hiding among 40,000 other students. He also found that there were other men who felt just like he did. There was an exceptionally active gay rights group that sponsored a spectrum of social and recreational activities for gay men. Through one of these activities, he had met Hank. Lately they had been spending a lot of time together. He had never felt so comfortable in a relationship before. He found he could talk to Hank about his most intimate thoughts. He also discovered how much he enjoyed expressing his affection for Hank both verbally and physically.

John was jolted from his reverie as the bus pulled up to Drollinger's Drugstore, the local bus stop. He could see his parents waiting to pick him up. There was his father with a big smile on his face, waving at the son he was so proud of. John smiled, waved back, and thought, "Oh, boy. Well, here goes." He stepped off the bus.

Homosexuality is the focus of this chapter. Although most of us probably have a sexual preference for (or sexual orientation toward) the opposite gender, many of us do not. Many of us prefer and are attracted to members of the same gender and some to both genders.

For whatever reasons, the idea of homosexuality, which involves having a sexual preference for members of the same gender, frequently elicits a strong negative emotional response. As future professional social workers, you need to identify and address this negative response. The National Association of Social Workers' (NASW) Code of Ethics specifies that "the social worker should make every effort to foster maximum self-determination on the part of clients" (NASW, 1979). The right to determine one's own sexual preference clearly falls within the realm of self-determination.

■ A Perspective

This chapter will provide information about various aspects of homosexuality. The intent is to encourage readers to examine their own feelings and reactions. Understanding the effects of diverse sexual preferences upon human behavior is necessary for objective, professional social work practice. Assessing one's own values towards people's diverse sexual preferences is a major step in developing professional social work values.

This chapter will:

- Define and explain the meanings of homosexuality and bisexuality and discuss the terms used to refer to gay people.
- Report estimates of how many people are gay and discuss some of the theories attempting to explain why people have diverse sexual preferences.
- Address the issue of discrimination against gay people and discuss the concept of homophobia.
- Examine the psychological adjustment of gay people and review some of the myths and stereotypes about them.
- Describe the gay lifestyle including such aspects as gay relationships, sexual interaction, and typical meeting places.
- Identify some of the life situations and crises affecting gay people such as gay people and the law, coming out, gay people as parents, and gay people with AIDS.

Homosexuality and Bisexuality

A man is committed to prison and has sexual relations with other men. Is he a homosexual? A very shy, lonely woman who has never dated any men is approached by a lesbian friend. The lonely woman decides to have an affair with her friend. Is she a homosexual? Two 14-year-old male adolescents experiment with each other by hand-stimulating each other to orgasm. Are they homosexuals? While having sexual intercourse with his wife, a man frequently fantasizes about having sexual relations with other men. He has never had any actual sexual contact with a man in his adult life. Is he a homosexual?

The answers to these questions are not so easy. Placing people in definite, distinct categories is difficult. It is not always easy to draw a clear distinction between a heterosexual and a homosexual person. It may make us feel more secure and in control to cordon off the world into neat and predictable little boxes of black or white. However, in reality the world is an endless series of shades of gray. In other words, people frequently like to polarize others as being either heterosexual or homosexual. Perhaps such labeling makes situations appear to be more predictable. If a person is labeled a heterosexual, then many may assume that they know a lot of things about that person. For example, if a person is labeled a heterosexual female, then she will date males, is likely to marry, and is likely to become a mother and homemaker. Likewise, if a person is a homosexual male, then he will probably have his hair permed, wear hot pink sweaters, frequently flick his wrists, and inevitably become a hairdresser. In reality things are not so predictable and clear.

The problem with these neat little categories is that they foster stereotypes. A stereotype is a fixed mental image of a group that is frequently applied to all its members. Often the characteristics involved in the mental picture are unflattering. Stereotypes refuse to take into account individual differences. They negate the value and integrity of the individual.

What Does Being a Homosexual Mean?

For the purposes of this chapter, the terms *homosexual* or *gay* will be defined in the following arbitrary manner: A homosexual or gay person is a person who prefers sexual relations with persons of the same gender.

There are two aspects of this definition that merit attention. First of all, above anything else, a homosexual is a person. In the eyes of some heterosexuals the sexuality of a gay person often takes precedence over all other aspects of his or her personality. The person becomes lost or invisible. Figure 16.1 depicts this relationship. Most people have homophobia, which involves a fear of gay people. This fear of gay people warps their perception of homosexuals. The homosexuality becomes prominent at the expense of all other aspects of the gay person's personality. A more realistic view is one in which the viewer perceives homosexuality in context. The fact that a person is gay is only one slice in a person's personality pie. A realistic

Figure 16.1   The Personality Pie

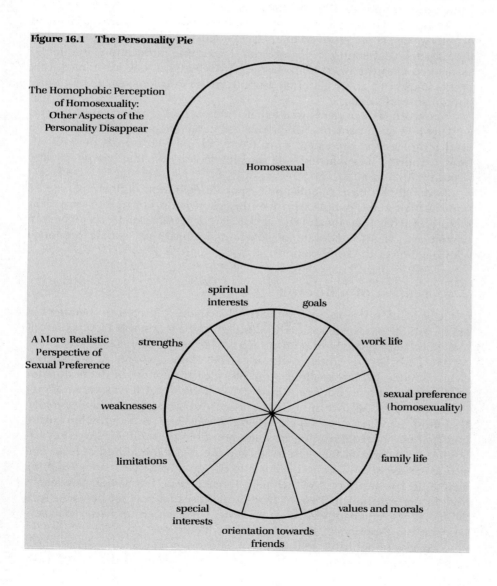

The Homophobic Perception of Homosexuality: Other Aspects of the Personality Disappear

Homosexual

A More Realistic Perspective of Sexual Preference

spiritual interests
goals
strengths
work life
weaknesses
sexual preference (homosexuality)
limitations
family life
special interests
values and morals
orientation towards friends

perspective allows the many various aspects of the personality to be acknowledged and appreciated.

The second part of the definition states that a homosexual is someone who prefers having sexual relations with people of his or her same gender. In other words, a male homosexual would choose to have sexual relations with another male over having them with a female. Likewise, a lesbian or female homosexual would opt to have sexual relations with another female instead of with a male. This part of the definition excludes people who under certain circumstances engage in homosexual activities. For instance, prisoners and other institutionalized persons might establish homosexual relationships with others simply because persons of the opposite gender are unavailable. These people will typically return to heterosexuality when the opportunity arises.

Historically, the word *homosexual* is derived from the Greek root "homo," meaning "same." The word *homosexual* itself, however, was not coined as a term until the late 1800's (Karlen, 1971).

Terms used to refer to gay people can be confusing. The term *gay* instead of *homosexual* is preferred by many gay people today because it has neither the direct sexual connotations nor the demeaning implications frequently associated with the word homosexual. Today either the word homosexual or gay is used to apply generally to both males and females, or in a more limited sense to males.

The word *lesbian* refers to a female homosexual. The word *lesbian* can actually be traced back to a Greek poetess named Sappho (c. 600 B.C.) who lived on the island of Lesbos, from which the term *lesbian* is derived. Although Sappho was married, she remains famous for the love poetry she wrote to other women.

Although we have established a specific definition of a gay person or homosexual, many people who use these terms do not have a very clear picture of what they mean. The words gay or homosexual may refer to a person with slight, moderate, or substantial interest or sexual experience with persons of the same gender.

Definition of a Bisexual

A bisexual refers to a person who is sexually attracted to members of either gender. A bisexual usually, although not always, has had sexual interactions with persons of both genders (Masters et al., 1982, p. 316).

We have already initiated the idea that homosexuality is not such a clear-cut concept. Bisexuality is even less clearly defined. In the first major study of sexuality in our era, Kinsey (1948) found that it was very difficult to categorize people in terms of being homosexual, bisexual, or heterosexual. He found many people who considered themselves as being heterosexual had had homosexual experiences at some time during their lives. For example, 37 percent of the men in his sample of 5,300 had had at least one sexual experience with another male to the point of orgasm after reaching age 16. In his study of 5,940 women, Kinsey (1953) found that between 8 and 20 percent had had some type of homosexual contact between ages 20 and 35. A significantly smaller percentage of each group had exclusively homosexual experiences throughout their lifetimes.

Because he found it so difficult to categorize people into distinct categories, namely those of homosexual and heterosexual, he developed a six-point scale which placed people on a continuum concerning their sexual experiences (see Figure 16.2). A rating of "0" on the scale meant that the individual was exclusively heterosexual: the person had never had any type of homosexual experience. On the other hand, a score of "6" on the scale indicated exclusive homosexuality: this individual had never experienced any form of heterosexual behavior. Those persons scoring "3" would have equal homosexual and heterosexual interest and experience.

More recent researchers have discovered similar difficulties in clearly categorizing people in terms of their sexual preference. Storms (1980) suggests that the Kinsey scale still failed to provide an accurate description. He developed a two-dimensional scheme to reflect sexual preference (see Figure 16.2). The two dimensions involved reflect homoeroticism (sexual interest in/experience with those of the same gender) and heteroeroticism (sexual interest in/experience with those of the opposite gender).

Additionally, sexual interest in general is portrayed. Those individuals who express high interest in both sexes are placed in the upper right-hand corner. They are considered bisexuals. Those persons who have a very low sexual interest in either gender are placed in the lower left-hand corner. They are considered asexuals. Persons with primary sexual interest in the

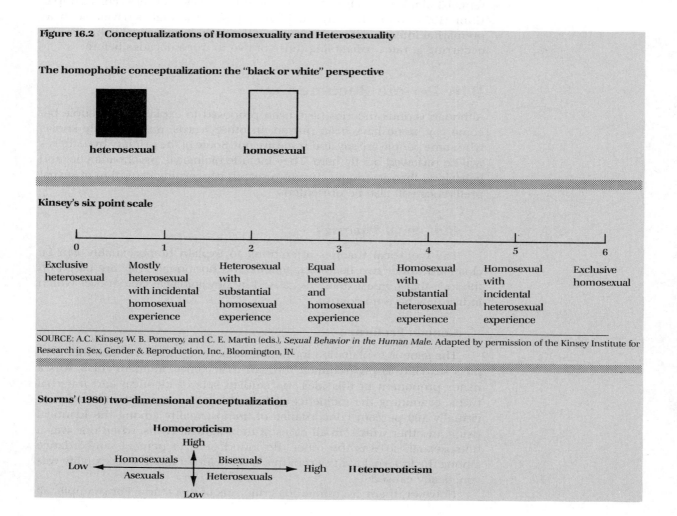

Figure 16.2   Conceptualizations of Homosexuality and Heterosexuality

The homophobic conceptualization: the "black or white" perspective

heterosexual   homosexual

Kinsey's six point scale

0	1	2	3	4	5	6
Exclusive heterosexual	Mostly heterosexual with incidental homosexual experience	Heterosexual with substantial homosexual experience	Equal heterosexual and homosexual experience	Homosexual with substantial heterosexual experience	Homosexual with incidental heterosexual experience	Exclusive homosexual

SOURCE: A.C. Kinsey, W. B. Pomeroy, and C. E. Martin (eds.), *Sexual Behavior in the Human Male.* Adapted by permission of the Kinsey Institute for Research in Sex, Gender & Reproduction, Inc., Bloomington, IN.

Storms' (1980) two-dimensional conceptualization

Homoeroticism

High

Low ← Homosexuals | Bisexuals → High   Heteroeroticism

Asexuals | Heterosexuals

Low

same gender, the homosexuals, are placed in the upper left-hand corner. Similarly, people with primary sexual interest in the opposite gender, the heterosexuals, are placed in the lower right-hand corner.

Numbers of Gay People

It is very difficult if not impossible to state exactly how many people are gay. However, it may be useful to consider the numbers of people who have adopted a primarily gay orientation over an extended period of time.

Kinsey found that, although over one-third of American men had homosexual experiences leading to orgasm during their adolescent or adult lives, only 10 percent of men were exclusively homosexual for a three-year period between ages 16 and 55. Only about 4 percent were gay throughout their lives.

Two to three times as many men as women are gay. Although Kinsey found that 19 percent of American women had homosexual experiences by the age of 40, only 2 to 3 percent of them remained gay throughout their lives.

More recent data has indicated that the incidence of homosexuality remains similar to that during the time of Kinsey's studies. For example, Hunt (1974) found that the incidence of some sexual behavior such as premarital intercourse was increasing. However, homosexual behavior was occurring at rates resembling those of two to three decades before.

Why People Become Gay

Although various theories have been proposed to explain why people become gay, none have been proven. In other words, no one really knows why some people are gay and some are not. Some of the primary hypotheses will be reviewed briefly here. They include biological, psychoanalytic, and behavioral theories. Some current research concerning causation of sexual preference will also be presented.

Biological Theories

The biological theories attempting to explain homosexuality can be clustered under two headings, genetic and hormonal. They are based on the idea that homosexuality is caused by physiological factors over which individuals have no control.

Genetic Factors

The genetic explanation for homosexuality supports the idea that people's sexuality is programmed through their genes. Kallman (1952) was a major proponent of this idea. He studied sets of identical and fraternal twins, examining the incidence of homosexuality among them. He found virtually 100 percent concordance of homosexuality among the identical twins. In other words, in all cases of the identical twins, when one was a homosexual, so was the other. He found only 14 percent concordance among the fraternal twins. From this he concluded that homosexuality was genetically caused.

However, there are numerous criticisms of this study. For example, all sets of twins were raised in the same home environment. Thus, environmental factors may have been responsibile to an undeterminable extent. Another question concerned the fact that the scientific method virtually never reveals perfect, 100 percent results. This fact alone raises serious concerns about the study. Finally, subsequent research has failed to corroborate the findings (Heston and Shields, 1968; Zuger, 1976). In summary, genetic explanations for homosexuality are generally disregarded today.

Hormonal Theories

Hormonal theories of homosexuality suggest that hormonal type and level cause homosexuality. One subset of these theories indicates that abnormal hormonal levels during the prenatal period may result in homosexuality (Dorner, 1976). However, no evidence exists to prove this. It might be logical to deduce from this theory that varying prenatal hormonal levels would also result in anatomical differences. However, research indicates that there are no anatomical differences between heterosexuals and homosexuals (Perloff, 1965; Wolff, 1971).

Another major subset of hormonal theories concerns differences in hormonal levels during adulthood. Tourney (1980) examined studies completed since 1969 which were oriented toward this issue. Earlier studies were not included because of their methodological problems. He found that results were extremely contradictory. Some studies indicate that homosexual men had lower levels of testosterone than heterosexual men (Loraine et al., 1970; Starka et al., 1975). Other studies found just the opposite, namely that testosterone levels were higher in homosexual men (Doerr et al., 1973). Yet other studies found no differences at all.

Some of the conflicting data may be due to methodological complications in the research. For example, one study done by Kolodny et al. (1971) found testosterone levels to be lower in homosexual men than in heterosexual men. However, on closer scrutiny it was found that some of the subjects in the study had also been smoking marijuana. Marijuana has been suspected of affecting testosterone levels. Therefore, it may have been the marijuana which caused lower testosterone levels, not the lower testosterone levels which caused homosexuality.

In view of the skepticism and conflicting evidence none of the hormonal theories are given much credence today. It is very doubtful that such a simple cause-effect relationship exists. Much more substantial, clear-cut research would be needed to verify hormonal theories.

Psychoanalytic Theories

Psychoanalytic theories postulate that homosexuality is caused by pathological family relationships occurring during childhood. Freud felt that at birth infants are essentially bisexuals. Through their family relationships they then become either normally heterosexual or abnormally homosexual. Homosexuality results from fixation at an earlier, more immature level of development.

Freud wrote relatively little concerning homosexuality. Available writings are rather vague. When he did comment, he seemed to assume a fairly neutral view of it (Masters and Johnson, 1982). However, later psychoanalytic theorists assumed more definite stances concerning the causes of homosexuality. Commonly cited among these theorists are Irving Bieber and Charlotte Wolff.

Bieber's Approach

Bieber (1962) studied 106 homosexual men and compared them to 100 heterosexual men. He found that homosexual men tend to have dominant mothers and passive, withdrawn fathers. He concluded that homosexuality results from fears of heterosexual interaction caused by these problems in early family relationships.

One of the problems with his study is that all of the subjects were in psychoanalysis at the time. The question might be raised whether the homosexual men were seeking therapy for reasons related to early family traumas which had nothing to do with their sexuality as such. Another problem with the research is that it relied on retrospective memories of childhood. Such accounts might be subject to forgetfulness or distortion. One even more disturbing criticism of the study concerned data collection. The information had not been gathered directly from subjects. Rather, questionnaires were forwarded to analysts who were providing therapy to the subjects. This provides a second possibility for distortion. Research using a more normal population and more valid methods might derive more believable results.

Wolff's Research

Wolff (1971) studied 100 lesbians who were not in therapy. She compared them with a control group of heterosexual women who were similar in terms of socioeconomic class and family background. She found that the lesbians were more likely to have rejecting or indifferent mothers and distant or absent fathers.

Wolff hypothesized that such family conditions tended to result in lesbianism. She suggested that when girls from such families grew up, they continued to seek love from women. They were in search of the love they never received from their own mothers. The other contributing factor was that such women never learned how to relate properly to men. Their fathers had not interacted with them enough to teach them.

Other research, however, indicates that many homosexuals grow up in normal, well-adjusted families (Tripp, 1975; Gagnon, 1977; Masters and Johnson, 1979). If family maladjustment were the only verified cause of homosexuality, then it follows that all gay people come from such backgrounds. Thus, as with the biological theories, many questions must be raised concerning the psychoanalytic theories of homosexuality.

Behavioral Theories

Behavioral theories emphasize that homosexual behavior is learned just as any other type of behavior is learned. Early in life homosexual behavior might be positively reinforced by pleasurable experiences and thereby strengthened. Likewise, such behavior may be punished by negative, punitive experiences and, as a result, be weakened.

For instance, a child who has several positive sexual contacts with members of the same gender might be positively reinforced or encouraged to seek out more such contacts. In a similar manner, a child who has a negative experience with a member of the same gender might be discouraged from having any more such encounters.

Feldman and McCulloch (1971) take this idea a step further. They suggest that an adult may change his or her sexual preference later in life through a series of such positive and negative experiences. In other words, even adults can learn to become gay according to behavioral theory. The fact that some female victims of sexual assault become lesbians after the very negative experience of being raped lends some support to this idea (Grundlach, 1977).

Two major shortcomings can be cited with respect to behavioral theories of homosexuality, however. First, there is a tremendous amount of negative feedback about homosexuality. Children learn early on that being called a "fag" is not a compliment. The question might be raised regarding how homosexual behavior would be reinforced and increase in frequency in view of such punitive circumstances.

Second, learning theory would imply that a person would first have a homosexual experience. Then, if the experience was positively reinforcing or personally rewarding, the person would seek out more such experiences. However, might it not be the case that individuals who have homosexual desires seek out sexual experiences with the same gender in the first place? In other words, might not the desire for sexual contact with the same gender be there even before any actions ever occur?

Recent Research on the Origins of Homosexuality

Bell, Weinberg, and Hammersmith (1981) undertook a massive investigation through the Alfred C. Kinsey Institute for Sex Research concerning the causes of homosexuality. They studied 979 gay men and women and compared them to 477 heterosexual men and women. Study participants were asked extensive questions about many aspects of their lives. A statistical method, *path analysis*, allowed the researchers to explore causal relationships between variables, such as parental characteristics and family relationships, and the development of sexual preference.

Three major findings surfaced from the research. First, sexual preference appears to emerge by the time both males and females reach adolescence. This is the case even when people have little or no sexual experience. Second, gay people have a similar amount of heterosexual experience during childhood and adolescence when compared to heterosexual people. There was one basic difference, however. Despite the fact that gay people participate in heterosexual activity, they do not enjoy it very much.

The study's third major finding involves the concept of gender nonconformity during childhood and the development of homosexuality. Gender nonconformity refers to a child's preference for play and activities which our society generally assumes appropriate for children of the opposite gender. For example, little girls usually choose to play with Barbie dolls and play dishes, while little boys generally prefer "GI Joe's" and toy bulldozers. A little girl who only plays with tanks and footballs or a little boy who only plays with Barbie dolls would provide examples of gender nonconformity. Gender nonconformity was a much stronger causal factor for gay men than for lesbians. Other factors such as family relationships have a stronger causal relationship with lesbianism.

This research indicates that sexual preference develops very early in life. It also suggests that whether a person is gay or heterosexual is not a matter of choice. Just as a heterosexual person might be sexually attracted to another heterosexual person, so is a gay person sexually attracted to another of the same gender. It appears that it would be just as impossible for a gay person to turn heterosexual as it would be for a heterosexual person to begin choosing sexual partners of the same gender.

The fact that many gay people externally assume heterosexual roles for appearance's sake is also logical. Numerous homophobic stigmas are placed on gay people. These people are often subjected to serious discrimination. People can choose to behave in a certain way. However, people cannot choose whom they will be sexually attracted to. In evaluating the consequences of the various alternatives open to them, some gay people may decide that it is too difficult to survive openly as a gay person (e.g., hold a job, relate to family members, participate in community activities). A gay person with a heterosexual facade is burdened with pretending to be someone he or she is not. Such pretense can violate individual dignity and freedom.

Discrimination: The Impacts of Homophobia

"Did you hear the one about the dyke who . . ."

"Harry sure has a 'swishy' way about him. You'd never catch me in the locker room alone with that guy."

"They're nothing but a bunch of lousy, Communist faggots."

Our common language is filled with derogatory terms referring to gay people. Just as other diverse groups are subject to arbitrary stereotypes and to discrimination, so are gay people. Because of negative attitudes and the resulting discriminatory behavior, alternatives for gay people are often different and limited. There are often other negative consequences. Other nonsexually related aspects of gay people's lives are affected because of their sexual preference.

For example, a male third grade teacher may live in deathly fear that the parents of his students will discover he's living with another man. He loves his job which he's had for nine years. If parents put pressure on the school administration about his homosexuality, he may get fired. He may never get another teaching job again.

Another example is provided by a female college student who expends massive amounts of energy to disguise the fact that she's a lesbian. She attends a state university in a small, midwest, rural town. She is terribly lonely. She keeps hoping that that special someone will walk into her life. However, she doesn't dare let her friends know she's gay or she really will be isolated. There wouldn't be anyone to talk to or to go to have dinner with. They would just never understand. People have committed suicide for less.

Gay people are frequently the victims of homophobia. Homophobia is the irrational hostility and fear that many people have towards homosexuality (Masters and Johnson, 1982, p. 323). It is not clear how homophobia originated. Maier (1984, p. 371) postulates that it may be people's attempts to deny homosexual feelings in themselves. Perhaps the more strongly homophobic people are, the more they are working to deny such feelings in themselves. Regardless of the cause, the manifestations and symptoms of homophobia are all around us.

Until very recently homosexuality was considered an illness. Not until 1974 did the American Psychiatric Association remove it from the list of mental illnesses.

Although there has been much psychological research on homosexuality, one survey of the research published between 1967 and 1974 found most of the studies sought to identify negative aspects of homosexuality (Morin, 1977). For example, over half of the publications addressed the causes of homosexuality and psychological adjustment of gay people. The implication is that the condition is something to be cured. Virtually none of the research addressed positive aspects of gay life such as establishing relationships and development of a positive self-concept.

The general public, as well as the professional literature, shows symptoms of homophobia. One national survey found almost three-quarters of its respondents view homosexuality as being "always wrong" (Nyberg and Alston, 1976). Such negative attitudes are likely to have some impact on gay people.

A potentially serious negative effect would be to internalize such negative attitudes. In other words, a gay person might think, "If being gay is bad, and I am gay, then that means that I am bad, too." Weinberg and Williams (1974) have found that only slightly more than one-tenth of all gay people feel that homosexuality is an illness. However, 80 percent of lesbians and 77 percent of gay men expressed having fears of others finding out about their sexual preference (Jay and Young, 1979). The implication is that they fear negative consequences such as job loss, exclusion from various opportunities, and social isolation might occur.

Psychological Adjustment of Gay People

Despite all of these difficulties, gay people have generally been able to maintain good psychological health. Hooker (1957) studied a group of 30 gay people. She compared them with a group of 30 heterosexuals matched for age, educational level, and intellectual capability. All of the subjects were administered a battery of personality tests. Professional clinicians were then asked to examine the tests. The clinicians were unable to discriminate between gay and heterosexual people on the basis of psychological adjustment. The implication is that gay people were neither more nor less psychologically disturbed than heterosexuals. Other research supports this (Evans, 1970; Green, 1972; Saghir and Robins, 1973).

■ Stereotypes about Gays

Not only are gay people the victims of homophobia, but they are also the target of derogatory, inaccurate stereotypes. Some of the more common ones include the ideas that gay people look "swishy" or "butchy," that they like to assume either a male or female role, and that they are potential child molesters (Hyde, 1982). All of these stereotypes are false.

The Queen and the Butch

A prevalent stereotype about gay people is that gay men typically look extremely feminine and that lesbians, on the other hand, appear very masculine. Terms used to refer to effeminate gay males include *swish, nellie,* and *queen.* Terms used to refer to masculine-looking lesbians include *dyke* and *butch* (Sagarin, 1970). In truth these stereotypes are not very accurate.

For example, male university athletes might be considered the epitome of masculinity in terms of traditional masculine stereotypes. Garner and Smith (1977) found that approximately 40 percent of such male athletes had participated in sexual relations to orgasm with another man in the two years preceding the study.

Only about 15 percent of gay men could readily be identified as gay by how they looked, acted, and dressed, according to Kinsey. More recently Voeller (1980) corroborated this statistic concerning male homosexuals. With the breakdown of some of the traditional gender roles, identifying homosexuals by appearance may be even less possible. Women normally wear slacks. Men normally can wear makeup and jewelry. They can even have their hair permed.

Much of the stereotypes about how gay people look is the result of confusion between two central concepts. These concepts are gender identity and choice of sexual partner (Hyde, 1982, p. 363). Gender identity refers to a "person's private, internal sense of maleness or femaleness—which is expressed in personality and behavior—and the integration of this sense with the rest of the personality and with the gender roles prescribed by society" (p. 62). In other words, gender identity refers to a person's self-concept of being either a male or a female. Choice of sexual partner, on the other hand, refers to "sexual attraction to members of the same gender, members of the other gender, or both" (p. 62). Here the emphasis is placed on sexual attraction.

These concepts should not be confused. For example, whether a man prefers to have sexual relations with another man has nothing to do with his own feeling that he is also a man. Most gay men think of themselves as being men (Storms, 1980). They neither think of themselves as being women, nor do they want to become women. Therefore, a gay man can logically look and act like any other man, yet still be attracted to men.

Likewise, gender identity and sexual preference should not be confused with respect to women. A woman may feel like a woman and think of herself as a woman, yet still also be attracted to women (Wolff, 1971). The two concepts are separate and distinct.

Playing Male and Female Roles

Another common stereotype about gay people is that in any particular pair, one will choose a "masculine" dominant role and the other a "feminine" submissive role. As with any heterosexual couple, this is rarely the case. Any individual, either homosexual or heterosexual, may play a more dominant or more submissive role depending on the particular mood, activity, or interaction involved. People are rarely totally submissive or totally dominant.

Gay people do not assume "male" and "female" roles on a regular basis (Peplau, 1981; Jay and Young, 1979). Even while engaged in sexual activity, few gay people limit themselves to only one role (Hooker, 1965). Most gay people practice a variety of sexual activities and exchange roles.

The Myth of Child-Molesting

One other derogatory stereotype targeting gay people is that they are inclined to molest children. This stereotype is especially deleterious for homosexual teachers in that it can cause them to lose their jobs.

In reality, 80 percent of all child molesting is performed by heterosexual men whose victims are young girls. Heterosexual teachers are proportionately more likely to molest children than are homosexual teachers (Newton, 1978).

The Gay Lifestyle

What is it like to be gay? How would life be different or similar if you awoke tomorrow morning and discovered that you were gay? What would happen to your relationships with family, friends, and colleagues?

No one typical type of lifestyle is practiced by all gay people. Gays have lives which are just as varied as those of heterosexuals. Being a gay man in Oconomowoc, Wisconsin, is different from being a gay man in a San Francisco suburb. Being a white lesbian mother on welfare in Utah is different from being a black upper class lesbian mother in New York City. However, some common patterns emerge in the lives of gay people. Several issues reflected by these patterns are addressed here. They include gay relationships, sexual interaction, and meeting places.

Gay Relationships

Individual relationships vary among gay people just as they do among heterosexuals. However, there is evidence that gay men have a greater number of partners than heterosexual men (Weinberg and Williams, 1974). The social and legal obstacles for gay people to establish long-term relationships may be one of the reasons for this. For example, opportunities for marriage aren't available to gay people. Gay marriages are illegal in every state (Peters, 1982, p. 24). Even if they are very much in love with each other and want to spend their lives together, social obstacles might exist such as pressure from family and heterosexual friends to form heterosexual relationships, marry, and have children.

Lesbians, on the other hand, tend to have substantially fewer partners than do gay men (Schafer, 1977). Likewise, a much higher proportion are involved in monogamous relationships (Rosen, 1974). Perhaps this is related to the fact that women in general traditionally have had fewer partners and less sexual experience than men.

Bell and Weinberg (1978) conducted a massive survey of gay people in the San Francisco area. They recruited 4,639 volunteer respondents through various means including notices in local newspapers, personal contacts, and notices at organizations and establishments oriented toward gay people. Respondents were given lengthy interviews concerning aspects of gay life. Additionally, the researchers made direct observations of gay behavior in various settings where gay people congregated.

A major criticism of the study is in its sampling methodology. First, all respondents were volunteers. The lack of a random sample representing the entire gay population raises questions whether findings can be applied to all gay people. Second, all respondents came from one limited geographical area. This raises doubts whether results accurately reflect the behavior and attitudes of gay people who live elsewhere. Nonetheless, there were many interesting findings including some concerning gay relationships.

Bell and Weinberg found that relationships between gay people tend to fall within five major categories. These include close-coupled, open-coupled, functionals, dysfunctionals, and asexuals.

Close-Coupled Relationships. Bell and Weinberg resisted the temptation of labeling gay people in close-coupled relationships as being happily married. However, these relationships most closely resembled marriage in terms of closeness. Ten percent of the males and 28 percent of the females lived in such relationships. These relationships were characterized by monogamy, closeness, and much mutual time spent together. These couples appeared to be happy and very satisfied with this lifestyle. An interviewer

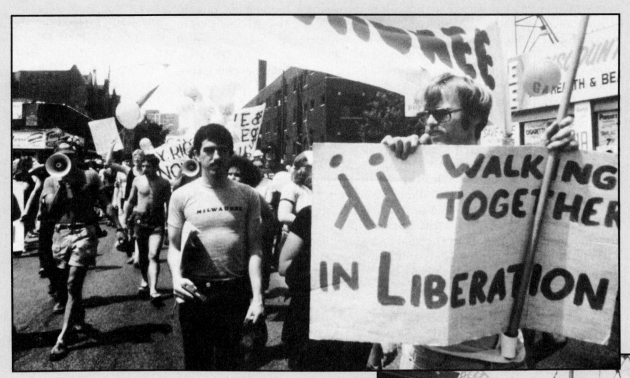

The gays demonstrating in this parade show a good deal of courage. "Coming out of the closet," or acknowledging homosexuality, can be a long and difficult process because of the homophobia and stereotypical feelings gays face. In order to help their clients, social workers must first examine their own attitudes toward homosexuality. They should then become familiar with the gay lifestyle and community. Then they will be better able to help their clients identify and evaluate alternative life choices.
(David Runyon)

Annual Gay Pride parades have provided gays with both a sense of community and an opportunity to confront homophobic people's restrictive values by expressing their gayness publicly.
(David Runyon)

There is nothing new about homosexuality. But just mention the word and there's frequently a strong negative response. The sign in the picture names prominent people in history whom the sign bearers believe to have been gay. The term *homosexual* comes from the Greek root, *homo* meaning *same*. The word itself was not coined until the late 1800s. Today the term *gay* is preferred by many homosexual people. The terms apply to both males and females. (David Runyon)

Gay people are often subject to discrimination. They are also frequent victims of homophobia, an irrational fear many people have toward homosexuality. Some believe that homophobia stems from people's attempts to deny their own homosexual feelings. The more strongly homophobic an individual is, the more he or she may be working to deny these feelings. Since there is already discrimination in our society against blacks, the gay, black men holding this sign are subject to double discrimination. (David Runyon)

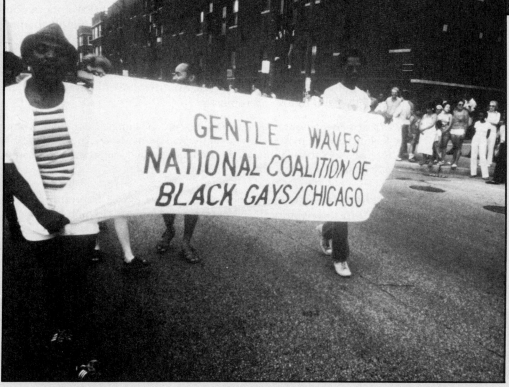

described one of the closed-couples in the following manner:

> She and her roommate were obviously very much in love. Like most people who have a good, stable, five-year relationship, they seemed comfortable together, sort of part of one another, able to joke, obviously fulfilled in their relationship. They work together, have the same times off from work, do most of their leisure activities together. She is helping her roommate to learn to paint, while her roommate is teaching her about photography. They sent me home with a plateful of cookies, a good symbolic gesture of the kind of welcome and warmth I felt in their home (p. 220).

Open-Coupled Relationships. As with closed-coupled relationships, people falling in this category lived with one special partner. However, the relationship was sexually open in that each partner could also seek out other sexual partners. Eighteen percent of the gay males and 17 percent of the females had this type of relationship.

These relationships tended not to be as happy as the closed-coupled ones. Partners tended to look for satisfaction outside of the relationship. More difficulties concerning sexual activity, communication, and jealousy were apparent than in closed-coupled relationships. The following are comments an interviewer used to describe a person involved in an open-coupled relationship:

> He tries to give the appearance of happiness with his roommate but cruises continually, feels grave guilt about this, and says that it contributes to his domestic travail. He stopped me from introducing myself to his roommate, as if I were a pickup he wanted to keep secret (p. 222).

Functionals. People falling in the functional category tended to orient the rest of their lives around their sexual interests. Bell and Weinberg compared them to heterosexual swinging singles. They participated in more sexual activity with a greater number of partners than did people in any of the other categories. Fifteen percent of the males and 10 percent of the females were included here. They seemed to be energetic, involved people who were generally happy with their lives. An interviewer characterizes one respondent using the following remarks:

> He was a very energetic and open kid, looking much younger than 27. He seemed to be feeling very happy, likes his job in the Merchant Marine, and enjoys being back for just short stays. Although this militates against long-term relationships, he really enjoys his feelings of independence (p. 224).

Dysfunctionals. Twelve percent of the males and 5 percent of the females fell within the dysfunctional category. Although sexually active, this group was characterized by relatively unhappy, troubled people. They tended to complain about sexual difficulties and suffer psychological problems. There was also a tendency to regret the fact that they were gay. One interviewer described a dysfunctional male as follows:

> He lives in an ugly, bleak two-bedroom apartment, where he seems to devote most of his time to watching TV. He has no close friends, and those he has he seldom sees. All relationships seem casual and unimportant to him (p. 226).

Asexuals. People in the asexual category tended to be little interested in sex, have few sexual experiences and generally spend their time alone.

They also tended to report having sexual problems. Sixteen percent of the males and 15 percent of the females were classified as asexuals. Bell and Weinberg attributed their solitary apathy more to psychological problems unrelated to sexuality than to the fact that they were gay. An interviewer described a lesbian asexual in the following account:

> She was a bit cool and businesslike. Her difficulties with interpersonal relations were hinted at when she said she tends to be suspicious of people who are "too nice." When the interview was over she was pleasant, but it felt superficial (p. 227).

Sexual Interaction

Many people find it hard to imagine what gay people do sexually. After all, they don't have the "necessary" ingredients of both penis and vagina. The fact is that gay people engage in the same types of activities that heterosexuals also enjoy. These include hugging, kissing, touching, fondling of the genitals, and oral sex.

The physiological responses of gay people are exactly the same as those of heterosexuals (Masters and Johnson, 1979). They become aroused or excited, enter a plateau stage of high arousal, have an orgasm, and go through a period of resolution during which the body returns to its normal, unaroused state. The process is the same for all people, male or female, gay or heterosexual.

One difference between gay and straight people is that gay people tend to be more open to new techniques, take more time, and pay more attention to the ways in which they interact sexually (Masters and Johnson, 1982, pp. 325–27). This may be partially due to the fact that there are fewer conventions or traditional rules about how sexual relations should be accomplished. For example, for heterosexual couples the missionary position, where the man lies on top of the woman and inserts his penis into her vagina, is the most frequently used position in the United States (Hyde, 1982, p. 204). There are no such historically established positions for gay people.

It's interesting that a major thrust of much sex therapy for heterosexual couples is to slow down, enjoy the many various aspects of sexual interaction, and avoid being so goal-oriented (Annon, 1976). Perhaps many heterosexual couples could learn a thing or two from many gay couples.

The frequency of homosexual activity (Bell and Weinberg, 1978) appears to resemble the frequency of heterosexual activity. American couples in their 20s tend to have sexual intercourse about two to three times per week. This figure tends to drop to approximately once a week after people reach age 45 (Hyde, 1982, p. 280). Frequency of sexual contact among gay people is broken down in Table 16.1.

Gay people participate in many of the same sexual activities as heterosexuals. As with heterosexuals, sexual preferences and techniques vary from individual to individual. However, some practices are more frequently used than others. The most common technique used by lesbians is manual stimulation of the genitals (Saghir and Robins, 1973; Bell and Weinberg, 1978). In order to reach orgasm, lesbians tend to prefer *cunnilingus*, a term for oral stimulation of the female genitals (Bell and Weinberg, 1978; Califia, 1979).

Fellatio, which refers to mouth stimulation of the male genitals, seems to be the most common sexual technique used by gay males (Saghir and

Table 16.1   Frequency of Homosexual Activity in Past Year

	Homosexual Males		Homosexual Females	
	White (N=574)	*Black* (N=111)	*White* (N=228)	*Black* (N=64)
Not at all	3%	0%	8%	3%
Once or a few times	3	1	6	9
Every other month	3	1	5	0
Once a month	7	3	10	8
2 to 3 times a month	17	13	20	14
Once a week	22	17	20	9
2 to 3 times a week	30	42	19	39
4 to 6 times a week	13	16	9	11
7 times a week or more	4	7	4	6

SOURCE: Adapted from Alan P. Bell and Martin S. Weinberg, *Homosexualities*, Copyright© 1978 by Alan P. Bell and Martin S. Weinberg. Reprinted by permission of Simon & Schuster, Inc.

Robins, 1973; Bell and Weinberg, 1978). *Anal intercourse*, which involves insertion of the penis into the rectum, also seems to be frequently used by many gay men (Saghir and Robins, 1973). However, this practice is not universal. Twenty-two percent of the white gay males in Bell and Weinberg's study (1978) had not participated in anal intercourse within the past year.

Meeting Places

Homosexuality cuts across virtually all socioeconomic levels and backgrounds. Therefore, it must be remembered that, like heterosexuals, gay people have vast individual differences concerning how they spend their time. However, there are a few common types of meeting places which provide opportunities to meet other gay people. Such places include gay bars and gay baths.

Gay Bars

Gay bars have been described as a sanctuary from the rest of the heterosexual world (Cory and LeRoy, 1963), a hub of communications for finding out about what's happening in the gay community (Hooker, 1967), and the major place for gay people to meet friends (Cory, 1951). Gay bars play an important place in gay life. They provide a place for gay people to socialize, relax, and dance without stigma. Bell and Weinberg (1978) found that almost half of the white gay males and almost two-thirds of the black gay males had patronized the bars at least once a week for the past year. For some people, the gay bar is the center of their social life (Warren, 1974).

Most gay bars orient themselves either to men or women (Rosen, 1974), although there are exceptions. Gay men tend to go to the bars in order to meet new sexual partners; lesbians, on the other hand, are more likely to go simply as a place to socialize with people they know (Maier, 1984, p. 364).

Gay Baths

Gay baths are gay men's health clubs, usually having a swimming pool or whirlpool. Additionally, they usually have a series of small rooms with beds in them where people can socialize and engage in sexual relations. Sexual activity is usually very impersonal (Bell and Weinberg, 1974). The baths, however, are not frequented nearly as often as the gay bars (Bell and Weinberg, 1978).

Significant Issues and Life Events

Diversity has serious impacts on gay people. They are the victims of stereotypes and homophobia. Discrimination may frequently limit the alternatives available to them. Social workers and other human service professionals need to be aware of the special issues and life events confronting gay people. In order to help clients define and evaluate the alternatives available to them, social workers must understand the effects of certain life events. Significant issues and life events examined here include gay people and the law, coming out, gay parents, and gay people with AIDS. Additionally, social work with gay people is addressed.

Gay People and the Law

For hundreds of years laws have been passed intended to suppress homosexuality. Although some progress has apparently been made by and on behalf of gay people in the last decade (Slovenko, 1980), homosexual acts are still illegal in many states (Maier, 1984, p. 376). Part of the reason for such antihomosexual bias lies in the homophobic fear that homosexuality will spread and prosper if legalized. Some people have expressed the fear that flagrant homosexuality would subvert the morality of society.

The Great Britain Committee on Homosexual Offenses and Prostitution (1963) came up with some findings quite to the contrary. To begin with, the committee concluded that outlawing homosexuality had no effect on the incidence of homosexual behavior. Additionally, they stated that it was beyond the realm of the law to regulate private morality. They recommended that adults be allowed to participate privately in homosexual behavior if they chose to do so. As an aside, the United States seems to have more laws on the subject of sexuality in general than all of the European countries put together (Slovenko, 1965, p. 9).

Gay people are prohibited from joining the CIA, the FBI, or even the armed forces (McCrary and Gutierrez, 1979/80). Leonard Matlovich perhaps provides the best and most publicized example of discrimination against gay people by the military. As the son of an Air Force sergeant, Matlovich was raised on air force bases. On high school graduation, he immediately joined the Air Force. He received numerous decorations for his service which included fighting in Vietnam. He was also labeled superior in his evaluations.

Years later, at age 30 Matlovich acknowledged that he was gay and became involved in gay activities. When he related this to his superiors, he was discharged with a general discharge, a type of discharge considered less than honorable. He eventually took his case to court. Although much attention was brought to the issue by this case, the fact still remains that no progress was made for other gay people interested in being members of armed forces.

Despite many backward laws, gay people have recently made some legal progress. Most federal agencies now prohibit discriminating against gay people in their own employment policies (Hedgpeth, 1979/80; Slovenko, 1980). Gay parents have begun to win child custody battles in courts (Green, 1978; Hitchens, 1979/80). Some states, counties, and cities no longer allow landlords to discriminate against gay people as tenants (Peters, 1982, p. 23).

People involved in gay liberation and gay rights organizations have provided much impetus to progress made in gay legal rights. Such groups exist in many communities, especially in urban settings. Group meetings often provide opportunities to discuss issues, plan political interventions, and get help and support concerning personal difficulties such as employment discrimination. Additionally, they provide a means of becoming acquainted with other gay people and with the gay community in general.[1]

Social workers need to attend to gay rights issues. Not only is an objective, open-minded attitude and belief in individual self-determination necessary, but an advocacy stance is also critical. Unfair, discriminatory rules in public and private agencies can be confronted. Attention can be called to any discrimination which does occur. Political candidates who encourage gay rights can be supported. Finally, others including friends, family, and professional colleagues can be educated about gay rights and encouraged to support them.

Coming Out

Coming out of the closet or coming out refers to the process of acknowledging oneself publicly as being gay. It is frequently a long and difficult process in view of the homophobia and stereotypes enveloping us.

Gay people usually become aware of the fact that they are different from most others in terms of sexual preference before the age of twenty (Moses and Hawkins, 1982). The process of coming out itself frequently takes one to two years (Jay and Young, 1979). Especially for adolescents who do not have much independence and who are subject to severe peer pressure, this period may be very difficult.

Moses and Hawkins (1982) describe the coming out process and elaborate on its implications. They explain that the first stage of coming out is coming out to oneself. It involves thinking about oneself as a person who is gay instead of as one who is heterosexual. The term used for this is *signification*. They suggest that there is often a period of identity shifting, during which individuals experiment with the label. They may begin conceptualizing themselves as gay and begin thinking about what such a label will mean concerning their own lifestyle.

Part of the signification process involves accepting a label about which society has had so many negative things to say. Some people feel much better about themselves after applying a label of being gay. It seems such a label helps in the process of establishing a self-identity. It also seems to give people permission to think and feel honestly about themselves. They then feel they can pursue new thoughts and experiences they feared and avoided before.

Moses and Hawkins (1982) suggest some excellent intervention strate-

---

[1]A National Gay Task Force, 80 Fifth Ave., New York, NY 10011 (212/741-1010) can provide further information about local groups.

gies for human service professionals when helping gay clients during their coming out period. To begin with, it is important to provide the client with information about what being gay is really like. Chances are that the client thinks in terms of some of the same stereotypes and has some of the same homophobic responses that many others in society do. A gay man who is coming out may need to be educated concerning the difference between gender identity and choice of sexual partner. He would also need to understand that he was not suffering from an illness.

The issue of self-concept may need to be addressed in counseling. Many times it is initially difficult for gay people to distinguish between society's somewhat negative view of homosexuals and their own views of themselves. They need to understand that they will not suddenly become different people with odd habits. Rather, they can be made to see that there are different options available to them which may provide them with greater freedom to be themselves.

Another suggestion is the realistic identification and evaluation of the alternatives open to a gay person. Signification may have advantages and disadvantages. Advantages might include the decreased fear and anxiety which result from pretending to be someone you're not. Another advantage might be the blossoming of new possibilities for social activities and support systems with other gay people. Referrals to local organizations would be helpful here.

Disadvantages also need to be confronted and evaluated. These might include the discrimination in employment and social settings sometimes suffered by gay people. Another disadvantage might be the potential loss of some friends and family members. Any anxiety about potential risks in telling people needs to be explored.

Moses and Hawkins (1982) make some specific suggestions for coming out to friends and family. First, the potential consequences need to be realistically examined. They emphasize that it may not be necessary to tell all close friends, relatives, and colleagues when the consequences for the gay person are likely to be negative.

For example, take a young man, a junior in college, who has recently come out. His relationship with his father has always been marginal in that they have never communicated well and do not feel very close to each other. However, they do attend family functions together and participate in the family system with other family members. The father has often made derogatory statements about gay people for as long as the son can remember. In this case, it may serve no purpose to come out to the father, since the relationship will probably not be improved. On the other hand, coming out may cause the son much painful criticism and potential ostracism from the family unit.

Moses and Hawkins (1982) reflect that many might consider it a conservative approach for a gay person to withhold the fact that he or she is gay. Others might think that this approach is not an honest one. (However, it is important for a gay person to evaluate the consequences of coming out versus not coming out.) A reality-oriented approach involves looking at all available alternatives. The positive and negative consequences for each alternative must be evaluated. The idea is to assist clients in making decisions which are in their best interests. Evaluating the consequences of various alternatives fits well into the Behavior Dynamics Assessment Model.

■ Cheryl's Exploration of Her Self-Identity and Sexual Preference

Cheryl, age 19, worked as a sales clerk at Shopko, the local discount store. Although she still lived with her parents primarily for financial reasons, she was starting to make her own decisions. She debated moving into an apartment with several female friends, and whether she should attend the local technical school or college part-time. These were not the issues she addressed, however, as she came in for counseling.

Cheryl hesitantly explained that she was very anxious about the sexual feelings she was having lately. Although she was steadily dating her high school sweetheart, he did not interest her sexually. She was thinking more and more about her sexual attraction toward other women. She had had these feelings for as long as she could remember. Lately she was becoming obsessed about them. She was very worried that she might be a lesbian.

On further discussion, she expressed fears about what being a lesbian would be like. She was concerned about starting to look too masculine and about becoming sex-starved for other women. Cheryl's counselor provided some information about what being gay is really like. They discussed and discarded some of Cheryl's negative stereotypes. The counselor referred Cheryl to some written material on lesbianism and to some local gay organizations so Cheryl could get more information.

As counseling progressed, Cheryl began to nurture her weakened self-image. Her years of anxiety and her efforts to hide her feelings had taken an emotional toll. Her counselor helped her to work through her confusion about all the negative things she'd heard about gays and her perception of herself. Cheryl began to look at herself more realistically. She began to focus on her personal strengths. These included her good sense of humor, her pleasant disposition, and her desire to become more independent and establish a career for herself. She found that these attributes and her personal identity had nothing to do with the negative stereotypes she had previously heard about homosexuality.

Finally, her counselor helped her to define and evaluate the various alternatives open to her. For the first time, she explored the possibility of breaking up with her stable, although somewhat boring, boyfriend. She considered the possibility of pursuing a sexual relationship with one of the women she had recently met at a gay rights organization meeting. She was already beginning to develop friendships with other women she'd met in a lesbian support group.

After several months of counseling, Cheryl had made several decisions. She had gone through the signification process. She had moved out of her parents' home and into an apartment with several of her female friends, none of whom were lesbians. After much fear and trepidation, she had come out to them. To her relief, they indicated that although they were surprised, it made no difference concerning their friendship. She had broken off with her boyfriend and had started a sexual relationship with another woman. Not only did she have no regrets about her new romantic situation, but she felt extreme relief, satisfaction, and a new sense of freedom.

Cheryl still had not decided whether to come out to her parents. She was still working on that. Nor had she yet decided what career route would be best for her. However, her new sense of self-identity provided her with new confidence and strength. The future looked hopeful and exciting instead of dull and restrictive.

Gay Parents

Many gay people have children. Bell and Weinberg (1978) found that about one-fourth of all their respondents had been married at one time. Of these, over a third of the lesbians had been married compared to less than a fifth of gay men. More than half of all the gay people who had been married also had children. Additionally, many gay people who never marry are also likely to have children.

Seeking Child Custody

One source reports that gay parents have only half as good a chance as heterosexual parents in winning a court battle for custody of their children (Moses and Hawkins, 1982, p. 202). Lesbian mothers are much more likely to be involved in decisions concerning custody than are gay fathers, who must even fight for the right to see their children (Hitchens, 1979/80). These are not very good odds, especially for lesbian mothers.

Cases have been cited where even when a lesbian mother receives custody of her child, she must abide by personal restrictions imposed by the courts. One good example is provided by a San Francisco mother who was awarded custody of her three children (Lewis, 1980). The court mandated that as a condition for custody the mother see her female lover only at specified times. These times included when her children were at school or when they visited their father. The question must be raised whether such conditions would have been imposed had her lover been a male.

Judges presiding over custody disputes can make arbitrary judgments concerning what is in the child's best interests (Moses and Hawkins, 1980, pp, 201–2). Some judges may have homophobic ideas. Such ideas have the potential of influencing their decisions.

Moses and Hawkins (1982, pp. 199–201) cite several myths about gay parenthood which might influence people against gay parents. First, there is the misconception that gay parents will influence their children to become gay. Second, there is the idea that children will be damaged by growing up in gay homes. Third, some people may mistakenly believe that gay people's parenting skills are inadequate. Finally, there is the myth that gay people are child molesters. Moses and Hawkins conclude that no evidence exists in support of any of these claims. If anything, there is supportive evidence that gay people are as good as heterosexuals as parents.

Gay people are slowly making progress in attaining more positive custody decisions (Green, 1978; Hitchens, 1979/80). Several suggestions can be made to human service professionals to help gay people fight and win these battles (Moses and Hawkins, 1982, pp. 204–5). First of all, the parent must realize that although progress has been made, the odds for gaining custody are still not very good. The parent needs to realize that such cases usually take considerable time and energy. Court cases also frequently cause burdensome stress for both parent and children, and are expensive. Teaching the client such skills as assertiveness, stress management, and problem-solving are frequently useful. Another suggestion is to make certain to get a highly competent attorney. Referring the gay parent to support groups is also helpful. Finally, educating the gay parent by providing reading material is often beneficial.

Coping with Children

Even when a gay parent gains custody of a child, there still may be some problems to overcome. For instance, lesbians with children place great importance on passing as heterosexuals (Pagelow, 1980, pp. 200–3). Losing a job or an apartment might have much greater impact on lesbians with children than lesbians who aren't parents. Much more may be at stake when the welfare, support, and living conditions of children must also be taken into consideration. Another typical worry of gay parents is that their children's friends might discover that they are gay (Lewis, 1979, pp. 121–23).

Several suggestions can be made to social workers and other human service professionals in their efforts to help gay people cope with parenthood (Moses and Hawkins, 1982, pp. 205–9). First, social workers can help the gay parent identify and emphasize the joys of parenthood. It might be all too easy to get lost in the additional problems of being gay and miss all of the normal pleasures of raising children.

Second, social workers can help gay parents address the issue of coming out to children. Berzon (1978) recommends that gay parents do this as soon as possible. This might avoid family stresses and problems in communication which could result from hiding such an important aspect about the parent. It might make daily living much more comfortable when the gay parent can openly interact with and express affection toward a partner, without excluding the children. Finally, sharing the truth with children might prevent them from finding out about it from someone else which, in turn, might cause them surprise and shock. Children might logically wonder why their parent hadn't told them. This secrecy might convey a very negative perspective about being gay.

Third, sometimes a gay parent will find a partner and decide to live with him or her. Social workers can help a gay parent address many of the same issues that need to be dealt with when a new heterosexual partner joins a household. Issues about child management need to be discussed. Expectations regarding how money will be shared or spent, how daily routines will be organized, and how the adults will act in front of the children need to be clarified openly.

Fourth, these parents may worry about the prejudice and discrimination their children might experience because of their parent's sexual preference. Wolf (1979) suggests teaching children situational ethics. The idea here is for gay parents to be open about their sexual preference. Children then can learn about being gay in a positive sense. However, at the same time, a gay parent can teach a child that it is more appropriate to refer to and talk about sexual preferences under some conditions than under others. For example, it is perfectly appropriate to be open about mother's female lover at home with the family. However, more discretion might have to be used when the child is giving a report before her class at school.

That children learn when certain behavior is appropriate or inappropriate is a normal part of growing up. One means of teaching the concept of appropriateness is to teach about individual differences (Moses and Hawkins, 1982, p. 209). Children understand that each person is different. Every individual has his or her own ideas and beliefs. Everyone lives life a bit differently. Differences in sexual preference are simply another type of human difference. As some people might have different ideas about sexual preference, they might be prejudiced about it. Therefore, it is not always wise to raise the issue.

Aids

Acquired Immune Deficiency Syndrome (AIDS) is a devastating disease which proportionately is much more likely to victimize gay men than most other groups in the population. Almost three-fourths of the people identified as having AIDS are sexually active gay and bisexual men. Other populations that have a higher risk of contracting AIDS include intravenous drug users (17 percent of all identified AIDS cases), persons (such as hemophiliacs) who have received blood transfusions contaminated with the AIDS virus (3 percent), and people having heterosexual relations with a person who has

From 1980 to 1985 the number of identified cases approximately doubled each year (*The Wall Street Journal*, August 5, 1985). Thus far, about half of all the people identified as having AIDS have died. Because of the life-threatening dangers of AIDS, gays have become more cautious in their sexual activities, and as a result the rate of identified AIDS cases is no longer projected to double each year ("AIDS Update," 1986).

What Causes AIDS?

AIDS is caused by a type of virus, a retrovirus, named HTLV-III/LAV. This retrovirus invades normal cells involved in the body's normal process of protecting itself from disease and causes these cells to produce more of the virus. Apparently HTLV-III/LAV then destroys normal white blood cells which are supposed to fight off diseases invading the body. As a result, the body is left defenseless and can fall easy prey to other infections. In other words, the virus destroys the body's immune or defense system so that other diseases invade and eventually cause death.

How Is AIDS Contracted?

The only documented ways in which AIDS can spread is by sexual intercourse, by using hypodermic needles which were also used by AIDS victims, and by receiving contaminated blood transfusions or other products derived from contaminated blood. Babies may also contract AIDS before or at birth from their infected mothers.

The virus has been found in both the blood and the sexual secretions of persons who have AIDS. Very small amounts of the virus have also been found in tears and saliva. However, many experts doubt whether there is enough of the virus to be transmitted in these fluids. They rule out casual kissing or swimming in pools as a means of contracting AIDS. Sneezing, coughing, crying, or handshakes also have not proven to be dangerous. Only the exchange of fluids through anal, oral, or genital intercourse permits infection ("AIDS Update," 1986). The virus is very fragile and cannot survive long without a suitable environment, nor is it able to penetrate the skin. In summary, evidence has not been found to show that AIDS can be spread through any type of casual contact.

Effects of AIDS

Initial effects of AIDS include persistent fever, fatigue, weight and appetite loss, diarrhea, and swollen glands. Persistent symptoms are those which last at least three months. The large majority (90 to 95 percent) of people who become infected with the HTLV-III/LAV virus do not go on to develop the life-threatening condition of AIDS with its deadly symptoms (*U.S. News & World Report*, September 30, 1985; pp. 48–49). For those who do develop AIDS, one common symptom is a sore on the tongue called a hairy leukoplakia. The more serious symptoms tend to develop six months to five years after initially being exposed to the disease. The average time before symptoms develop is two years. Two specific rare conditions tend to characterize 85 percent of AIDS victims. These include a type of pneumonia and a variety of skin cancer called Kaposi's sarcoma.

Another major health problem involves the majority of people who have been exposed to the virus who do not develop AIDS. These people can infect others, although they experience no life-threatening symptoms themselves.

Origin of AIDS

Two very different theories have been proposed to explain the development of AIDS (*The Milwaukee Journal*, Aug. 18, 1985, p. 7). One theory postulates that the virus first developed in Africa more than a decade ago. Samples of blood taken from Ugandan children in 1973 appeared to contain antibodies for the AIDS virus or a virus very similar to it. The presence of antibodies imply that these children had been exposed to the virus. Furthermore, the sudden appearance of AIDS may have resulted from the fast-paced urbanization of portions of Africa. Previously isolated enclaves harboring the disease might suddenly have been exposed to the outside world.

The second major theory explaining the origin of AIDS suggests that an older, less harmful version of the virus suddenly mutated into its current lethal form.

Treatment of AIDS

There is no cure for AIDS. The HTLV-III/LAV virus has been isolated and the process by which it attacks healthy, normal cells examined. However, a cure looks as if it may be years away. There are several reasons for this (*The Milwaukee Journal*, August 21, 1985, p. 8). First, many of the drugs being tested also have serious negative side effects including liver damage, fever, kidney problems, and destruction of cells necessary for blood clotting. Second, it is not yet possible to determine which of the many persons exposed to the HTLV-III/LAV virus will actually develop AIDS. Because the progression of the disease is little understood, it is very difficult to determine when and how experimental drugs should be administered. Third, little experimentation on people in general has been done. This is partially due to cost. A clinical trial on one human subject costs between $2,000 and $3,000 (*The Wall Street Journal*, August 5, 1985, p. 1).

Blood and AIDS

Many people were shocked by the discovery that people who were neither gay nor drug-abusive had contracted AIDS by receiving contaminated blood. The possibility that sperm banks and organ banks could also be contaminated exacerbated people's fears. Since July 31, 1985, screening tests have been used to distinguish contaminated from uncontaminated blood. Although not perfect, these tests should greatly curtail the risks of contracting AIDS from donated blood or procedures involving blood. It should be noted that there is no risk of contracting AIDS by being a blood donor.

■ Rock Hudson, an AIDS Victim, Dies at Age 59

Rock Hudson, the robustly handsome star of 62 movies and numerous television shows, died on October 2, 1985, at the age of 59. He was a victim of AIDS.

Hudson discovered that he was a victim of the disease in mid-1984. Although he attempted to participate in an experimental therapy program in Paris, his exceedingly poor health prohibited him from proceeding.

The 6'4" virile, attractive male actor had been admired by multitudes of women throughout his acting career. He starred in dozens of leading box office attractions throughout the 50s and 60s. These ranged from frivolous romantic comedies such as *Pillow Talk* and *Send Me No Flowers* co-starring actress Doris Day, to serious dramatic roles in *A Farewell to Arms* and *The Last Sunset*. His acting career culminated in 1956 when he earned an Oscar nomination for his performance with Elizabeth Taylor in the film *Giant*. More recently he starred in the television series "McMillan and Wife." Some of his final appearances occurred on the popular evening soap opera "Dynasty."

His early personal history was not always as exciting as his colorful acting career might imply. On November 17, 1925, Hudson was born Roy Scherer, Jr., in Winnetka, Illinois. He later became Roy Fitzgerald after assuming his stepfather's last name.

Even during his star-studded years, Hudson reportedly was a reserved individual. He appeared to lack the brash confidence which might be expected of such a famous star. He was often noted to be quite critical of himself.

In the past, rumors had circulated regarding Hudson's alleged homosexuality, despite his reputation as an idol of female fans. Even his acquired surname, "Rock," reflected a very macho image. In 1955 he married his agent's secretary, Phyllis Gates. One national magazine suggested that the marriage was arranged by his movie studio purely to quell any rumors that he was gay. The much publicized marriage ended shortly thereafter. The pair separated in 1956 and were divorced by 1958.

One source reports that Hudson's own publicist would give no confirmation regarding Hudson's sexual preference. The publicist allegedly remarked that even Hudson had never made a definite statement about this issue.

A positive aspect about this sad death was the publicity which it gave to AIDS. Many of Hudson's fellow performers, including Elizabeth Taylor, raised $1 million for AIDS research in a Hollywood benefit performance. The fact that such a famous and well-respected man could be victimized by AIDS perhaps contributed to public empathy regarding the condition and public financial support to help remedy it.

Perhaps Hudson stated this idea most articulately when he said, "I am not happy that I am sick. I am not happy that I have AIDS, but if that is helping others, I can, at least, know that my own misfortune has had some positive worth."

SOURCE: Most of the facts presented here were gathered from a newspaper article published in *The Racine (Wis.) Journal Times,* headlined "Rock Hudson Dies," and printed on October 2, 1985.

Ethical Issues Surrounding AIDS

Fear of AIDS and the unknown factors about how it is contracted has initiated and spotlighted several ethical issues. Various people including children, heterosexual partners of AIDS victims, and gays have been affected by these fears. In many cases, the result has been social isolation. About 6 percent have contracted AIDS without falling into one of the previously mentioned high-risk categories (*U.S. News & World Report,* September 30, 1985, p. 49). For many of these people, not enough personal information had been gathered to establish the source of infection.

About *150* of these victims were children under age 13 (*U.S. News & World Report,* September 30, 1985, p. 49). Many had been born to infected mothers; others had received contaminated blood. In a very few cases, no specific infectious source can be pinpointed.

Fear of the unknown has resulted in affected children being denied access to schools and affected adults being fired from their jobs. The state of Colorado became the first in the nation to mandate that anyone having a positive blood test indicating AIDS infection be reported to the state health department. Some insurance companies are considering barring AIDS victims from benefits. The core of the issue involves the right of the individual to continue to live as normal a life as possible, versus the right of the general public to protect itself from deadly health hazards.

Despite the fact that there appears to be no danger through everyday contact, gay people have been fired from their jobs, evicted from their apartments, and refused service from health care personnel. Some funeral directors have even refused to treat and embalm the dead who had been victims of AIDS. Federal guidelines urge individual evaluation of children who have AIDS to determine whether or not they will be admitted to schools (*U.S. News & World Report*, September 30, 1985, p. 49). Furthermore, these guidelines suggest that children who cannot control their body functions or who have behavioral problems involving biting their classmates automatically be excluded.

These matters merit serious consideration. A picture of Japanese-American citizens forced into concentration camps during World War II might flash before one's eyes. In those days irrational fear resulted in acts of discrimination against American citizens. Basic individual rights were seriously violated. The human dignity of those people who are unfortunate enough to contract this deadly disease deserves some attention. These people need compassion.

Impact of AIDS on Gay People and the Social Worker's Role

A major issue for many gay people has been the fact that relatively little funding was initially designated by government agencies for research on AIDS. Many gays felt this reflected discrimination and prejudice against their sexual preference. The first case of AIDS was reported and publicized in June 1981. However, relatively little public funding was made available for AIDS research until recently. Increased funding appeared to correspond with the public's awareness that AIDS was not limited to gay men, drug abusers, and foreigners, but that others could be infected.

Homophobic responses by heterosexual people and the idea that AIDS is a punishment for bad behavior may have been contributing factors to the relative inaction on the part of the public. Meanwhile, many gay men along with their friends, families, and lovers, were suffering desperately from the disease.

Caputo (1985) suggests that the social work roles of educator, advocate, mediator, social broker, and enabler can all be applied to working with AIDS victims. As an educator, the social worker can supply the victims and those close to them with information about the disease so that they are better prepared to cope with their situations. The advocate role allows the social worker to speak out on behalf of clients. A social worker can help clients to fight for their rights, especially in those cases where discrimination is occurring. As a mediator, the social worker may become a go-between between the AIDS victim/client and others with whom he's in conflict. For example, the client may have been shunned by his family or fired from his job. A social worker might help both sides better understand the concerns of the other and come to some mutually agreeable plan. The social worker as social broker can help the AIDS victim come into contact with needed health, financial, and social support sources. Finally, as enabler, the social worker may help the client cope with his situation. A social worker can help the client to express his feelings, look closely at his relationships, and make plans to do the best he can with each day of his life.

The *NASW Practice Digest* (Spring, 1984) addresses the issue of helping gay people with AIDS and discusses the Gay Men's Health Crisis program in New York City, which was developed for this purpose. It is an example of how AIDS victims and those close to them can be helped. A wide variety of services are provided, many by social workers. After an extensive assessment interview, victims are referred to the appropriate services. These may include legal assistance, financial aid, support groups, and recreational programming. Almost all AIDS victims receive crisis counseling. Victims suffer not only from the fact that they have contracted a deadly disease, but also as a result of attitudes of others who shun them, fire them, and evict them from apartments.

Luis Palacios is a social worker who runs crisis groups for the program. He describes the group process as taking members "from diagnosis to death" (*NASW Practice Digest*, 1984, p. 24). He believes that it is not only important for victims to deal with death but also with life. He emphasizes a "positive, life-affirming attitude." This helps people focus on the quality of life while they have it, instead of on the quantity. The idea is for AIDS victims to live life one day at a time and make each day as positive and happy as possible.

Social Work with Gay People

Social work has at least two important thrusts concerning working with gay people. One involves the individual practitioner's attitudes and skills. The other concerns agencies' provision of services to gay people.

Counseling Gay People

Josephine Stewart, who chairs the NASW National Committee on Lesbian and Gay Issues has made several suggestions for social work practitioners working with gay clients (*NASW Practice Digest*, 1984, pp. 28–30). For one thing, it is very important to confront one's own homophobia and become comfortable with one's own feelings. One of the worse things a practitioner can do is negatively label a gay client and criticize that client for his or her sexual preference. This contradicts the basic social work value of the client's right to self-determination. A negatively biased practitioner can work against a client's development and maintenance of a positive self-image. Alternatives involving a gay lifestyle and resources available in the gay community might be ignored or even rejected.

Another suggestion for working with gay people is to become familiar both with the gay lifestyle and with the gay community (Moses and Hawkins, 1982, p. 77; *NASW Practice Digest*, p. 30). This knowledge is necessary in order to help clients identify and evaluate the various alternatives available to them. It's also helpful to know people within the gay community who can update a practitioner on new events and resources.

Agency Provision of Services

The other issue concerning social work with gay people involves agencies' provision of services. Many services are needed by gay people which address specific aspects of gay life. These might include lesbian support groups, groups for gay men who are in the process of coming out, legal advice for gay parents seeking child custody, or couple counseling for gay partners. On the one hand, such services can be provided by agencies focusing on and serving only gay people. On the other hand, such services can be mainstreamed into traditional agencies.

There are several advantages of mainstreaming services into already existing social service agencies (*NASW Practice Digest*, 1984, pp. 5–7). First, a large traditional agency can provide a wider variety of services and serve more specific individual needs. For example, a lesbian mother might have access to agency-provided parent effectiveness training. She might have easy access to this service, even though it has nothing to do with her sexual preference.

Second, gay people do not have to be segregated from the rest of society. Gay people can go to a social service agency just as heterosexual people can. No stigma need be involved.

Third, mainstreaming provides the opportunity for heterosexual practitioners to interact with other practitioners who are familiar with the issues of gay life and serve a gay clientele. This provides an excellent opportunity for practitioners to learn from each other. Stereotypes can be addressed and homophobic responses confronted.

Regardless of where services are provided for gay people, the fact is that they are needed. Social workers need to learn about gay life. They need to confront their own feelings and apply social work values to gay clients. They need to learn about resources available for gay people and make appropriate referrals. They also need to educate others about the special issues confronting gay people in order to fight homophobia. Finally, many times social workers need to act as advocates for the rights of gay people. Sexual preference needs to be addressed as simply another aspect of human diversity. Sexual preference should be respected instead of denied. Political candidates in favor of gay rights need to be supported. Agencies which discriminate against gay people need to be confronted, educated, and pressured to provide needed services in a fair and unbiased manner.

Summary

A homosexual or gay person is someone who prefers sexual relations with persons of the same gender. A bisexual is a person who is sexually attracted to members of either gender. Because of the large numbers of people who have homosexual experiences at some time during their lives, most people do not fall within the distinct categories of gay or heterosexual. Although various theories attempt to explain why people become gay, no definite causes have been established. Recent research has found that most gay people establish their sexual preference by adolescence. A strong implication of the research is that people cannot choose whether to be gay or heterosexual.

Gay people are frequently the victims of homophobia, the irrational hostility and fear that many people have towards homosexuality. There are a number of inaccurate stereotypes that exist in our culture, such as the false notion that gay people are apt to molest children—the truth is that most child molesting is done by heterosexuals. There is no one type of lifestyle adopted by all gay people, just as there is no single lifestyle for all heterosexuals.

Several significant issues and life events tend to characterize the lives of gay people. Some laws permit discrimination against gay people. Coming out or acknowledging that one is gay sometimes is difficult in view of the homophobic fears and negative stereotypes about homosexuality. Many gay people, particularly lesbians, have children; and seeking custody of a child when the partner is heterosexual is often a difficult process. Acquired Immune Deficiency Syndrome (AIDS) victimizes gay men to a significantly higher degree than other groups in this country. Gay liberation and gay rights groups have made some progress in reducing the discrimination that gays are often subjected to.

BIBLIOGRAPHY

Abel, Ernest L. "Fetal Alcohol Syndrome." *Psychological Bulletin* 87 (1980):29–50.

Adams, M. "The Single Woman in Today's Society: A Reappraisal." *American Journal of Orthopsychiatry* 41, No. 5 (1971):776–86.

Adams, M. R. and G. Popelka. "The Influence of Time-Out on Stutterers and their Dysfluency." *Behavior Therapy* 2 (1971):334–39.

Adler, Ronald B. and Neil Towne. *Looking Out/Looking In.* 3d ed. (New York: Holt, Rinehart & Winston, 1981).

Adorno, T. W., E. Frenkel-Brunswik, D. J. Devinson, and R. N. Sandord. *The Authoritarian Personality* (New York: Harper & Row, 1950).

"AIDS Update: Myths and Realities" *Playboy Magazine,* June 1986, pp. 52–53 and 179.

Aiken, L. R. *The Psychology of Later Life* (Philadelphia: W. B. Saunders Co., 1978).

Albin, Rochelle S. "Psychological Studies of Rape." *Signs* 3 (1977):423–35.

Algozzine, R. "What Teachers Perceive—Children Receive" *Communication Quarterly* 24 (1976):41–47.

Allport, G. W. *Personality* (New York: Holt, 1937).

———. *The Nature of Prejudice* (Reading, Mass: Addison-Wesley, 1954).

———. *Pattern and Growth in Personality* (New York: Holt, Rinehart & Winston, 1961).

Alm, Richard and Robert J. Morse, "Growing Furor Over Pay of Top Executives." *U.S. News & World Report,* May 21, 1984, pp. 79–81.

Als, H., E. Tronick, B. M. Lester, and T. B. Brazelton, "Specific Neonatal Measures: The Brazelton Neonate Behavioral Assessment Scale." In J. D. Osofsky (Ed.), *Handbook of Infant Development* (New York: John Wiley & Sons, 1979).

Altus, W. D. "Birth Order Intelligence and Adjustment." *Psychological Reports* 5 (1959):502.

Amelar, R. D. *Infertility in Men* (Philadelphia: Davis, 1966).

American Academy of Pediatrics, Committee on Adolescence. "Pregnancy and Abortion Counseling." *Pediatrics* 63, No. 6 (1979):920–21.

American Cancer Society, *1976 Cancer Facts & Figures.* New York, 1975.

Ames, L. B. and J. Learned "Imaginary Companions and Related Phenomena." *Journal of Genetic Psychology* 69 (1946):147–67.

Amir, M. "Forcible Rape." *Federal Probation* 31, No. 1 (1967):51.

Anderson, B. and E. Palmore, "Longitudinal Evaluation of Ocular Function." In E. Palmore (Ed.), *Normal Aging* (Durham, N. C.: Duke University, 1974, pp. 24–32.

Anderson, B. E. and J. R. Dumpson, (Eds.) *The State of Black America* (New York: National Urban League, 1978).

Andrews, G., and Solomon, D., eds. *The Coca Leaf and Cocaine Papers* (New York: Harcourt Brace Jovanovich, 1975).

Annon, J. S. *The Behavioral Treatment of Sexual Problems: Brief Therapy* (New York: Harper & Row, 1976).

Apgar, V. "The Apgar Scoring Chart." *Journal of the American Medical Association* (1958):168.

———. "Perinatal Problems and the Central Nervous System." In U.S. Department of HEW, *The Child with Central Nervous System Deficit* (Washington, D.C.: U.S. Government Printing Office, 1967), pp. 75–76.

Arehart-Triechel, Joan. "It's Never Too Late to Start Living Longer." *New York Magazine,* April 11, 1977, p. 38.

Aristotle, *Politics,* Book 3, Section V (Jowlett translation).

Atchley, Robert C. *The Social Forces in Later Life: An Introduction to Social Gerontology.* 2d ed. (Belmont, CA: Wadsworth, 1977).

———. "Aging as a Social Problem: An Overview." In M. M. Seltzer, S. L. Corbett, and R. C. Atchley (Eds.), *Social Problems of the Aging* (Belmont, CA: Wadsworth, 1978).

———. *Aging: Continuity and Change* (Belmont, CA: Wadsworth, 1983).

Austin, V., D. Rulle, and T. Trabasso, "Recall and Order Effects as Factors in Children's Moral Judgments." *Child Development* 48 (1977):470–74.

Ayres, A. J. *Sensory Integration and the Child* (Los Angeles: Western Psychological Services, 1983).

Azrin, N. H. and W. C. Holz, "Punishment." In W. K. Honig (Ed.), *Operant Behavior: Areas of Research and Application* (New York: Appleton-Century-Crofts, 1966), pp. 380–447.

Babson, S. G., M. L. Pernoll, G. I. Brenda, and K. Simpson. *Diagnosis and Management of the Fetus and Neonate at Risk: A Guide for Team Care*, 4th ed. (St. Louis: C. V. Mosby, 1980).

Bachman, J. G. *Youth in Transition*. Vol. 2, *The Impact of Family Background and Intelligence on Tenth-Grade Boys* (Ann Arbor, MI: Institute for Social Research, University of Michigan, 1970).

Baer, Betty L. "Developing a New Curriculum for Social Work Education." In F. Clark and M. Arkava (Eds.), *The Pursuit of Competence in Social Work* (San Francisco: Jossey-Bass, 1979), pp. 96–109.

Baer, Betty L. and Federico, Ronald C. *Educating the Baccalaureate Social Worker* (Cambridge, Mass: Ballinger, 1978).

Bagdikian, Ben H. *In the Midst of Plenty: The Poor in America* (Boston: Beacon Press, 1964).

Baldwin, A. *Theories of Child Development* (New York: Wiley, 1968).

Baltes, P. and K. Schaie. "Aging and IQ: The Myth of the Twilight Years." *Psychology Today* 7, No. 10 (1974):35–38.

Bandura, A. *Principles of Behavior Modification* (New York: Holt, 1969).

Bane, M. J. "Marital Disruption and the Lives of Children." *Journal of Social Issues* 32 (1976):103–17.

———. *Here to Stay: American Families in the Twentieth Century* (New York: Basic Books, 1976).

Barbach, L. G. *Women Discover Orgasm* (New York: Free Press, 1980).

Bard, M., and J. Zacker. "The Prevention of Family Violence: Dilemmas in Community Intervention." *Journal of Marriage and the Family* 33 (1971):677–82.

Barnes, E. J. "The Black Community as the Science of Positive Self-Concept for Black Children: A Theoretical Perspective." In R. Jones (Ed.), *Black Psychology* (New York: Harper & Row, 1972).

Barron, Milton, L. "The Aged as a Quasi-Minority Group." In Edward Sagarin (Ed.), *The Other Minorities* (Lexington, Mass: Ginn, 1971).

Barry, John R. and C. Ray Wingrove, eds. *Let's Learn About Aging* (New York: John Wiley, 1977).

Barry, W. A. "Marriage Research and Conflict: An Integrative Review." *Psychological Bulletin* 73 (1970):41–45.

Bart, P. "Rape Doesn't End with a Kiss." *Viva* 11, No. 9 (June 1975):39–41, 100–101.

Bart, P. B. "Depression in Middle-Aged Women." In V. G. Gornick and B. K. Moran (Eds.), *Women in a Sexist Society* (New York: Basic Books, 1971).

Bar-Tal, D. and L. Saxe. "Perceptions of Similarity and Dissimilarity of Physically Attractive Couples and Individuals." *Journal of Personality and Social Psychology* 33 (1976):772–81.

Bartlett, Harriett, M. *The Common Base of Social Work Practice* (New York: National Association of Social Workers, 1970).

Baughman, E. E. *Black Americans: A Psychological Analysis* (New York: Academic Press, 1971).

Baumrind, D. "An Exploratory Study of Socialization Effects on Black Children: Some Black-White Comparisons." *Child Development* 43 (1972):261–67.

———. "A Dialectical Materialist's Perspective on Knowing Social Reality." *New Directions for Child Development.* 2 (1978).

Becher, E. M. "Marijuana: The Health Questions," *Consumer Reports*, March 1975, pp. 143–49.

Beck, A. T. *Depression* (New York: Harper & Row, 1967).

Belbin, R. M. "Middle Age: What Happens to Ability?" In R. Owen (Ed.), *Middle Age* (London: BBC, 1967).

Bell, A. P., and M. S. Weinberg, *Homosexualities: A Study of Diversity Among Men and Women* (New York: Simon & Schuster, 1978).

Bell, A. P., M. S. Weinberg, S. Martin, and S. K. Hammersmith, *Sexual Preference* (Bloomington, Indiana: Indiana University Press, 1981).

Bellak, A. O. "Comparable Worth: A Practitioner's View." In *Comparable Worth: Issue for the 80's, A Consultation for the U.S. Commission on Civil Rights* (June 6–7 1984):75–82.

Belloc, N. B. and L. Breslow. "Relationship of Physical Health Status and Health Practices." *Preventive Medicine* 1, No. 3 (1972):409–21.

Belmont, L. and A. F. Marolla. "Birth Order, Family Size, and Intelligence." *Science* 182 (1973):1096–1101.

Bengston, V. *The Social Psychology of Aging* (Indianapolis: Bobbs-Merrill, 1973).

Benson, Herbert. *The Relaxation Response* (New York: Avon Books, 1975).

Bermant, G., and J. M. Davidson. *Biological Bases of Sexual Behavior* (New York: Harper & Row, 1974).

Berne, Eric. *Games People Play* (New York: Grove Press, 1964).

———. *Principles of Group Treatment* (New York: Oxford University Press, 1966).

Berscheid, E., E. H. Walster, and G. Bohrnstedt. "The Happy American Body: A Survey Report." *Psychology Today* 7, No. 6 (1973):119–31.

Berscheid, E. and E. H. Walster, "Physical Attractiveness." In L. Berkowitz, (Ed.), *Advances in Experimental Social Psychology*. vol. 7 (New York: Academic Press, 1974), pp. 158–215.

Berzon, B. "Sharing Your Lesbian Identity with Your Children," in G. Vida (Ed.). *Our Right to Love: A Lesbian Resource Book* (Englewood Cliffs, NJ: Prentice-Hall, 1978).

Bieber, I. et al. *Homosexuality: A Psychoanalytic Study of Male Homosexuals* (New York: Basic Books, 1962).

Bierman, E., and W. Hazzard. "Biology of Aging." In D. Smith and E. Bierman (Eds.), *The Biologic Ages of Man* (Philadelphia: W. B. Saunders, 1973).

Biller, H. B. "Father Absence and the Personality Development of the Male Child," *Developmental Psychology* 2 (1970):181–201.

———. "Fatherhood: Implications for Child and Adult Development." In *Handbook of Developmental Psychology* (Englewood Cliffs, NJ: Prentice-Hall, 1982).

Birren, J. E., "Psychological Aspects of Aging and Intellectual Functioning." *The Gerontologist* 8, No. 1, part 2 (1968).

———. "Translations in Gerontology—from Lab to Life: Psychophysiology and Speed of Response." *American Psychologist*, 29, No. 11 (1974):808–15.

Birren, J. E., A. M. Woods, and M. V. Williams. "Behavioral Slowing with Age: Causes, Organization, and Consequences." In L. W. Poon (Ed.), *Aging in the 1980s* (Washington, D.C.: American Psychological Association, 1980).

Bishop, Jim. *The Days of Martin Luther King, Jr.* (New York: G. P. Putnam, 1971), pp. 327–28.

Black, J. K. "Are Young Children Really Egocentric?" *Young Children* 36 (1981):51–55.

Bliss, Tim. "Drugs—Use, Abuse and Treatment." In *Introduction to Social Welfare Institutions* (Homewood, IL: Dorsey Press, 1978).

Block, J. H. "Issues, Problems, and Pitfalls in Assessing Sex Differences." *Merrill-Palmer Quarterly* 22 (1976):283–308.

Blum, Richard H. et al. *Society and Drugs: Social and Cultural Observations* (San Francisco: Jossey-Bass, 1969).

Blum, S. "The Children Who Starve Themselves." *The New York Times Magazine*, November 10, 1974, pp. 63ff.

Boehm, D. "The Cervical Cap: Effectiveness as a Contraceptive." *Journal of Nurse-Midwifery* 28, No. 1 (1983):3–6.

Borke, H. "Piaget's Mountains Revisited: Changes in the Egocentric Landscape." *Developmental Psychology* 11 (1975):240–43.

Borskind-White, Marlene, and William C. White. *Bulimarexia* (New York: W. W. Norton, 1983).

Bostow, D. E. and J. B. Bailey. "Modification of Severe Disruptive and Aggressive Behavior Using Brief Time-Out and Reinforcement Procedures." *Journal of Applied Behavior Analysis* 2 (1969):31–37.

Botwinick, J. "Cautiousness in Advanced Age." *Journal of Gerontology* 21 (1966):347–353.

———. "Geropsychology." *Annual Review of Psychology*. 21 (1970):239–272.

———. "Intellectual Abilities." In J. E. Birren and K. W. Schaie (Eds.), *Handbook of the Psychology of Aging* (New York: Van Nostrand Reinhold, 1977).

Bouchard, T. J., Jr. "Current Conceptions of Intelligence and Their Implications for Assessment." P. McReynolds (Ed), *Advances in Psychological Assessment*, Vol. 1. (Palo Alto, CA: Science and Behavior Books, 1968).

Bowerman, D. E., and D. P. Irish. "Some Relationships of Stepchildren to Their Parents," *Marriage and Family Living* 24 (1962):113–21.

Bowman, H. A., *Marriage for Moderns*, 6th ed. (New York: McGraw-Hill, 1970).

Braginsky, D. D. and B. M. Braginsky. "Surplus People: Their Lost Faith in Self and System." *Psychology Today*, August 1975, p. 70.

Brazelton, H. M. "Neonatal Behavioral Assessment Scale." *Clinics in Developmental Medicine*, No. 50. (Philadelphia: J. B. Lippincott, 1973).

Brecher, E. M. et al. *Licit and Illicit Drugs: The Consumers Union Report on Narcotics, Stimulants, Depressants, Inhalants, Hallucinogens and Marijuana—Including Coffee, Nicotine, and Alcohol* (Boston: Little Brown, 1972).

Breland, H. "Birth Order, Family Configuration and Verbal Achievement." *Child Development* 45 (1974):1011–19.

Brenner, Harvey. *Mental Illness and the Economy* (Cambridge, MA: Harvard University Press, 1973).

Breuer, Joseph, and Sigmund Freud. *Studies in Hysteria* (London: Hogarth Press, 1895).

Brittain, C. "Adolescent Choices and Parent-Peer Cross-Pressures." *American Sociological Review* 28 (1963):385–91.

Bromley, D. B. *The Psychology of Human Aging*, 2d ed., (Middlesex, England, Penguin, 1974).

Bronfenbrenner, U. "The Changing American Family." In E. M. Hetherington and R. D. Parke (Eds.), *Contemporary Readings in Child Psychology* (New York: McGraw-Hill, 1977), pp. 315–30.

Brown, Barbara. *Stress and the Art of Biofeedback* (New York: Harper & Row, 1977).

Brown, Bertram S. "The Decriminalization of Marijuana." In *Hearings of the House Select Committee on Narcotic Abuse* (March 14, 1977), First session, 95th Congress.

Brownmiller, Susan. *Against Our Will: Men, Women and Rape* (New York: Bantam Books, 1975).

Bruck, H. *The Golden Cage: The Enigma of Anorexia Nervosa* (Cambridge: Harvard, 1978).

Bruner, J. S. "Nature and Uses of Immaturity." *American Psychologist* 27 (1972):687–708.

Bruner, J. S., R. R. Oliver, and P. M. Greenfield, *Studies in Cognitive Growth* (NY: John Wiley & Sons, 1966).

Buchanan, Roland L., and Marlene A. Cummings. *Individual Differences: An Experience in Human Relations for Children* (Madison, WI: Madison Public Schools, 1975).

Buhler, C. *Der Menschliche, Lebenslauf al Pschologishes Problem.* (Leipzig: Verlag von S. Herzel, 1933).

Buhler, C. "The Course of Human Life as a Psychological Problem" *Human Development* 11 (1968):184–200.

Burchard, J. D., and V. O. Tyler. "The Modification of Delinquent Behavior Through Operant Conditioning." *Behaviour Research and Therapy* 2 (1965):245–50.

Burgess, A. W. and L. L. Holmstrom. "Rape Trauma Syndrome." *American Journal of Psychiatry* 131 (1974):981–86 (a).

————. *Rape: Victims of Crisis* (Bowie, MD: Robert J. Brady, 1974). (b).

Bush, S. "Beauty Makes the Beast Look Better" *Psychology Today,* 10 (1976):15–16.

Butler, Robert N. "Myths and Realities of Aging." Address presented at the Governor's Conference on Aging, Columbia, MD, May 28, 1970.

Butler, Robert N. *Why Survive? Being Old in America* (New York: Harper & Row, 1975).

Butler, Robert N., and Myrna Lewis. *Sex After Sixty: A Guide for Men and Women for Their Later Years* (New York: Harper & Row, 1976).

————. *Aging and Mental Health: Positive Psychosocial Approaches.* 2d ed. (St. Louis: Mosby, 1977).

Bylinski, G. "What Science Can Do About Hereditary Disease." *Fortune,* September 1974, pp. 148–60.

Califia, P. "Lesbian Sexuality." *Journal of Homosexuality,* 4, No. 3 (1979):255–66.

Campbell, A. "The American Way of Mating: Marriage Si; Children Only Maybe" *Psychology Today,* 1975, 8, pp. 37–43.

Campbell, A. P. E. Converse, and W. L. Rodgers, *The Quality of American Life: Perceptions, Evaluations, and Satisfactions* (New York: Russell-Sage, 1976).

Caputo, Larry. "Dual Diagnosis: AIDS and Addiction," *Social Work,* 1985, 30(4), pp. 361–364.

Card, J. J. and L. L. Wise, "Teenage Mothers and Teenage Fathers: The Impact of Early Childbearing on the Parents' Personal and Professional Lives," *Family Planning Perspectives,* 1978, 10, pp. 199–205.

Carmichael, Stokely, and Charles V. Hamilton. *Black Power: The Politics of Liberation in America* (New York: Vintage Books, 1967).

Carroll, J. L., and J. R. Rest. "Moral Development" in B. B. Wolman (Ed.), *Handbook of Developmental Psychology* (Englewood Cliffs, NJ: Prentice-Hall, 1982).

Carter, E. A. and M. McGoldrick. *The Family Life Cycle: A Framework for Family Therapy* (New York: Gardner Press, 1980).

Cartwright, Dorwin. "Achieving Change in People: Some Applications of Group Dynamics Theory." *Human Relations* 4 (1951):381–92.

CBS Reports. "The Baby Makers." (Television program, October 1979).

Chappell, D. et al. "Forcible Rape: A Comparative Study of Offenses Known to the Police in Boston and Los Angeles." In J. M. Henslin (Ed.). *Studies in the Sociology of Sex* (New York: Appleton-Century-Crofts, 1971).

Chestang, Leon. "Character Development in a Hostile Environment." Occasional Paper No. 3 (Chicago: School of Social Science Administration, University of Chicago, 1972), pp. 7–8.

Child Welfare League of America. *Standards for Foster Family Care* (New York: 1959).

Christopher, Rita. "Mother's Little Helper." *Maclean's Magazine,* March 10, 1980, p. 10.

Clark, K. B. and M. P. Clark. "Racial Identification and Preferences in Negro Children." In G. E. Swanson, T. M. Newcomb, and E. L. Hartley (Eds.). *Readings in Social Psychology,* Rev. Ed. (New York: Holt, Rinehart & Winston, 1952).

Clark, M. and B. Anderson, *Culture and Aging* (Springfield, IL: Charles C Thomas, 1967).

Clarren, K. S., and D. W. Smith. "The Fetal Alcohol Syndrome," *New England Journal of Medicine* 298 (1978):1063–67.

Clayton, R. R. *The Family, Marriage and Social Change* (Lexington, Mass.: D. C. Heath & Co., 1975).

Clifford, E. "Body Satisfaction in Adolescents," *Perceptual and Motor Skills* 33 (1971):119–25.

Clifford, R. E. "Subjective Sexual Experience in College Women." *Archives of Sexual Behavior* 7 (1978):183–197.

Cohen, F. "Psychological Characteristics of the Second Child as Compared with the First," *Indian Journal of Psychology* 26 (1951):79–84.

Cohen, M. L., R. Garofalo, R. Boucher, and T. Seghorn. "The Psychology of Rapists." *Seminars in Psychiatry* 3 (1971):307–27.

Cole, M., J. Gay, J. Glick, D. Sharp. *The Cultural Context of Learning and Thinking* (New York: Basic Books, 1971).

Coleman, James W., and Donald R. Cressey, *Social Problems* (New York: Harper & Row, 1980).

Coleman, James W., and Donald R. Cressey. *Social Problems*. 2d ed. (New York: Harper & Row, 1984).

Coles, Robert. *Children of Crisis* (Boston: Atlantic Little Brown, 1967).

————. Testimony Before the Select Committee on Nutrition and Human Needs of the United States Senate, February 1969.

Collier, Helen V. *Counseling Women* (New York: Free Press, 1982).

Comment. "Police Discretion and the Judgment that a Crime has Been Committed—Rape in Philadelphia." *University of Pennsylvania Law Review* 117 (1968):2.

Conger, J. J. "Adolescence, A Time for Becoming." In M. E. Lamb (Ed.) *Social and Personality Development* (New York: Holt, 1978), pp. 131–54.

Consumers Union. *Licit and Illicit Drugs*, E. M. Brecher (Ed.) (Boston: Little, Brown, 1972).

Cooley, Charles H. *Human Nature and the Social Order* (New York: Scribner, 1902).

Coopersmith, S. *The Antecedents of Self-Esteem* (San Francisco: Freeman, 1967).

Coopersmith, S. "Studies in Self-Esteem." *Scientific American*, 218, No. 2 (1968):96–106.

Corso, J. F. "Sensory Processes and Age Effects in Normal Adults." *Journal of Gerontology* 26, No. 1 (1971):90–105.

Cory, D. W. *The Homosexual in America: A Subjective Approach* (New York: Greenberg, 1951).

Cory, D. W., and J. P. LeRoy, "Homosexual Marriage." *Sexology*, 29, No. 10 (1963):660–62.

Costa, P. T., Jr., and R. R. McCrae, "Still Stable After all These Years: Personality as a Key to Some Issues in Aging." In P. B. Baltes and O. G. Grin, Jr. (Eds.), *Life-Span Development and Behavior*, Vol. 3 (New York: Academic Press, 1980).

Costin, L. B. *Child Welfare: Policies and Practice* (New York: McGraw-Hill, 1979).

Cottingham, P. "Black Income and Metropolitan Residential Dispersion." *Urban Affairs Quarterly* 10 (March 1975):273–96.

Council on Social Work Education. *Curriculum Policy for the Masters Degree and Baccalaureate Degree Programs in Social Work Education* (New York, 1983).

Council on Social Work Education. *Handbook of Accreditation Standards and Procedures*. Rev. ed. (New York, July 1984).

Coyner, S. "Women's Liberation and Sexual Liberation." In S. Gordon, and R. W. Libby (Eds.), *Sexuality Today and Tomorrow* (North Scituat, MA: Duxbury Press, 1976).

Cozby, P. C. "Self-Disclosure: A Literature Review." *Psychological Bulletin* 79 (1973):73–91.

Craib, Ralph. "Sex and Women at UC [University of California] Berkeley—Two Surveys," *San Francisco Chronicle*, July 22, 1977.

Craig, G. J., and R. Specht. *Human Development*. 3d ed. (Englewood Cliffs, NJ: Prentice-Hall, 1983).

Craighead, W. E., M. L. Mahoney, and A. R. Kazdin. *Behavior Modification: Principles, Issues, and Applications* (Boston: Houghton-Mifflin, 1976).

Cuber, John F., and Peggy B. Harroff, "Five Types of Marriage." In Arlene S. Skolnick and Jerome H. Skolnick (Eds.), *Family in Transition* (Boston: Little, Brown, 1971), pp. 287–99.

Cultural Information Service "The Burning Bed: Viewer's Guide" (New York: CIStems, Inc., 1984).

Cumming, Elaine and W. E. Henry, *Growing Old: The Process of Disengagement* (New York: Basic Books, 1961).

Cummings, Marlene, "How to Handle Incidents of Racial Discrimination." In Charles Zastrow and Dae H. Chang, (Eds.), *The Personal Problem Solver* (Englewood Cliffs, NJ: Prentice-Hall, 1977), pp. 197–206.

Daley, M., and M. Wilson. *Sex, Evolution, and Behavior*. 2d ed. (Boston: Willard Grant, 1983).

Davis, Larry E. "Racial Composition of Groups." *Social Work*, 24 (May 1979):208–13.

Deaux, Kay. *The Behavior of Women and Men* (Belmont, CA: Brooks/Cole, 1976).

DeLury, G. E. *World Almanac* (Garden City, NY: Doubleday, 1974).

Denfield, D., and M. Gordon "The Sociology of Mate Swapping: Or the Family that Swings Together Clings Together." *Journal of Sex Research* 6 (1970):85–100.

Denney, N. W. "Aging and Cognitive Changes." In B. B. Wolman (Ed.), *Handbook of Developmental Psychology* (Englewood Cliffs, NJ: Prentice-Hall, 1982).

Dennis, W. "Creative Production Between the Ages of 20 and 80" *Journal of Gerontology* 21 (1966):8.

Deutsch, M. "Minority Group and Class Status as Related to Social and Personality Factors in Scholastic Achievement." *Monographs of the Society for Applied Anthropology* 2 (1960).

Devore, W., and E. G. Schlesinger. *Ethnic-Sensitive Social Work Practice* (St. Louis: C. V. Mosby, 1981).

DeVries, H. A. "Physiology of Exercise and Aging." In D. S. Woodruff and J. E. Birren (Eds.), *Aging: Scientific Perspectives and Social Issues* (New York: D. Van Nostrand, 1975).

Dewsburg, D. "Effects of Novelty on Copulatory Behavior: The Coolidge Effect and Related Phenomena" *Psychological Bulletin* 89 (1981):464–82.

Dickman, Irving R. *Winning the Battle for Sex Education* (New York: SIECUS, 1982).

Dillard, J. L. *Black English: Its History and Usage in the U.S.* (New York: Random House, 1972).

Division of Health Examination Statistics, National Center for Health Statistics: Data from the Health and Nutrition Examination Survey, 1971–1974.

Doerr, P. et al. "Plasma Testosterone, Estradiol, and Semen Analysis in Male Homosexuals," *Archives of General Psychiatry* 29 (1973):829–33.

Donaldson, M. "The Mismatch Between School and Children's Minds." *Human Nature* 2 (1979):158–62.

Dorner, G. *Hormones and Brain Differentiation* (Amsterdam: Elsevier, 1976).

Douglass, Frederick. Quoted in Charles Zastrow and Dae H. Chang (Eds.), *The Personal Problem Solver* (Englewood Cliffs, NJ: Prentice-Hall, 1977), p. 201.

Doyle, Sir Arthur Conan. "A Scandal in Bohemia." In *The Adventures of Sherlock Holmes* (London: John Murray, 1974).

Draper, Barbara Jones. "Black Language as an Adaptive Response to a Hostile Environment." In Carel B. Germain (Ed.), *Social Work Practices: People and Environments* (New York: Columbia University Press, 1979), pp. 274–283.

Dreher, K. F. and J. G. Fraser. "Smoking Habits of Alcoholic Outpatients." *International Journal of Addictions* 3 (1968):65–80.

Drill, V. A. "Oral Contraceptives: Relation to Mammary Cancer, Benign Breast, Lesions and Cervical Cancer." *Annual Review of Pharmocology*, 1975, 15, pp. 367–385.

Duberman, L. *The Reconstituted Family: A Study of Remarried Couples and Their Children* (Chicago: Nelson-Hall, 1975).

Duffy, M. "Calling the Doctor: Women Complain About Illness More Often than Men," *New York Daily News*, February 8, 1979.

Dunning, W. W. and D. H. Chang, "Drug Facts and Effects." In Charles Zastrow and Dae H. Chang, (Eds.) *The Personal Problem Solver* (Englewood Cliffs, NJ: Spectrum, 1977).

Duren, Ryne. Presentation on drug abuse at University of Wisconsin-Whitewater, October 18, 1985.

Dusay, John M., and Katherine M. Dusay. "Transactional Analysis." In Raymond J. Corsini (Ed.), *Current Psychotherapies*. 3d. ed., (Itasca, IL: F. E. Peacock, 1984), pp. 392–446.

Dytrych, Z., Z. Matejcek, V. Schuller, H. P. David, and H. L. Friedman. "Children Born to Women Denied Abortion." *Family Planning Perspectives* 7 (1975):165–171.

Eakins, B., and G. Eakins. "Verbal Turn-Taking and Exchanges in Faculty Dialogue." In B. L. Dubois and I. Crouch (Eds.), *Papers in Southwest English IV: Proceedings in the Conference on the Sociology of the Languages of American Women* (San Antonio, TX: Trinity University Press, 1976).

Earls, F., and B. Siegel, "Precocious Fathers." *American Journal of Orthopsychiatry* 50 (1980):469–80.

Eaton, J. T., D. B. Lippmann, and D. P. Riley. *Growing With Your Learning-Disabled Child* (Boston: Resource Communications, 1980).

Edwards, C. P. "The Comparative Study of the Development of Moral Judgment and Reasoning." In R. L. Monroe and B. B. Whiting (Eds.), *Handbook of Cross-Cultural Human Development* (New York: Garland Publishing, 1977).

Ehrbar, A. F. "A Radical Prescription for Medical Care" *Fortune*, February 1977, p. 169.

Ehrlich, Paul, and Richard Holm, "A Biological View of Race." In Ashley Montague (Ed.), *The Concept of Race* (New York: Free Press, 1964).

Einstein, E. "Stepfamily Lives." *Human Behavior*, April 1979, pp. 63–68.

Ekerdt, D. J., R. Bosse, and J. M. Mogey. "Concurrent Change in Planned and Preferred Age for Retirement" *Journal of Gerontology* 35 (1980):232–40.

Ekman, Paul, and Wallace V. Friesen. *Unmasking the Face* (Englewood Cliffs, NJ: Prentice-Hall, 1975).

Elder, Glen. "Appearance and Education in Marriage Mobility." *American Sociological Review* 34 (1969):519–33.

Elias, James and Paul Gebhard, "Sexuality and Sexual Learning in Childhood." *Phi Delta Kappan* 50 (1969):401–5.

Elkins, D. "Some Factors Related to the Choice Status of Ninety Eighth Grade Children in a School Society." *Genetic Psychology Monographs* 58 (1958):207–72.

Ellis, Albert. *Reason and Emotion in Psychotherapy* (New York: Lyle Stuart, 1962).

———. "Rational-Emotive Therapy." In Raymond Corsini (Ed.), *Current Psychotherapies* (Itasca, IL: F. E. Peacock Publishers, 1975), pp. 167–206.

————. "Rational-Emotive Therapy." In Raymond Corsini (Ed.), *Current Psychotherapies*, 2d ed. (Itasca, IL: F. E. Peacock Publishers, 1979), pp. 185–229.

Emlen, A. C. "Slogans, Slots, and Slander: The Myth of Day Care Need." *American Journal of Orthopsychiatry* 43, No. 1 (January 1973):23–36.

Encyclopedia of Sociology (Guilford, CN: Duskin Publishing Group, 1974).

Engen, T. "Taste and Smell" In J. E. Berrin and K. W. Schale (Ed.), *Handbook of the Psychology of Aging* (New York: Van Nostrand Reinhold, 1977).

England, P. "Explanations of Job Segregation and the Sex Gap in Pay." In *Comparable Worth: Issue for the 80's, A Consultation for the U.S. Commission on Civil Rights*, Vol. 1, June 6–7, 1984, pp. 54–64.

Erikson, E. H. *Childhood and Society* (New York: Norton, 1950).

————. "The Problem of Ego Identity." *Psychological Issues* 1 (1959):101–64.

————. *Childhood and Society*. 2d ed. (New York: W. W. Norton, 1963).

Espenshade, T. J. "The Economic Consequences of Divorce," *Journal of Marriage and the Family* 41 (1979):615–25.

Estes, E. H. "Health Experience in the Elderly." In E. Busse and E. Pfeiffer (Eds.), *Behavior and Adaptation in Late Life* (Boston: Little, Brown, 1969).

Evans, R. B. "Sixteen Personality Factor Questionnaire Scores of Homosexual Men." *Journal of Consulting and Clinical Psychology* 34 (1970):212–15.

Farberow, N. L. and R. E. Litman, "Suicide Prevention." In H. L. P. Resnick and H. L. Ruben (Eds.), *Emergency Psychiatric Care* (Bowie, MD: Charles Press, 1975), pp. 103–88.

Farley, Lin. *Sexual Shakedown: The Sexual Harassment of Women on the Job* (New York: Warner Books, 1978).

Faust, M. S. "Developmental Maturity as a Determinant in Prestige of Adolescent Girls." *Child Development* 31 (1960):173–84.

Feagin, Joe R. *Subordinating the Poor: Welfare and American Beliefs* (Englewood Cliffs, NJ: Prentice-Hall, 1975).

Featherman, David L., and Robert M. Hauser, "Changes in the Socioeconomic Stratification of the Races, 1962–73." *American Journal of Sociology*, November 1976, pp. 621–51.

Featherstone, J. "Open Schools—the British and U.S." *The New Republic*, September 11, 1971, pp. 20–25.

Federal Bureau of Investigation. *Uniform Crime Reports for the United States: 1985* (Washington, D.C.: U.S. Government Printing Office, 1986).

————. *Uniform Crime Reports for the United States* (Washington, D.C.: U.S. Government Printing Office, 1982).

Federico, R. *The Social Welfare Institution* (Lexington, MA: D. C. Heath, 1973), pp. 146–47.

Feldman, H. "The Effects of Children on the Family." In A. Michel (Ed.), *Family Issues of Employed Women in Europe and America* (Leiden, The Netherlands: E. F. Brill, 1971).

Feldman, H., and M. Feldman. "Effect of Parenthood at Three Points in Marriage." Unpublished manuscript, 1976–77.

Feldman, M. P., and M. J. MacCulloch. *Homosexual Behavior: Therapy and Assessment* (Oxford: Pergamon Press, 1971).

Ferguson, Elizabeth. *Social Work: An Introduction*. 3d ed. (Philadelphia: J. B. Lippincott, 1975).

Finn, Peter, and P. A. O'Gorman. *Teaching About Alcohol* (Boston: Allyn & Bacon, 1981).

Fischer, D. H. "Putting our Heads to the 'Problem' of Old Age." *The New York Times*, May 10, 1977, p. 33.

Fischer, J. *Effective Casework Practice: An Eclectic Approach* (New York: McGraw-Hill, 1978).

Fischer, J., and Gochros, H. L. *Planned Behavior Change: Behavior Modification in Social Work* (New York: Free Press, 1975).

Fish, J. E. and C. J. Larr, "A Decade of Change in Drawings by Black Children." *American Journal of Psychiatry* 129 (1972):421–26.

Flaste, R. "In Youngsters' Books, The Stereotype of Old Age" *The New York Times*, January 7, 1977, p. A12.

Flint, Jerry. "Oversupply of Young Workers Expected to Tighten Jobs Race." *New York Times*, June 25, 1978, pp. 1 and 34.

Flint, M. "Cross-Cultural Factors That Affect Age of Menopause." In P. A. Van Keep, R. B. Greenblatt, and M. Albeaux-Fernet (Eds.), *Consensus on Menopause* (Baltimore: University Park Press, 1976).

Flynn, Marilyn. "Poverty and Income Security." In Donald Brieland et al. (Eds.), *Contemporary Social Work* (New York: McGraw-Hill, 1975), pp. 87–108.

————. "Aging." In Donald Brieland, Lela Costin, and Charles Atherton (Eds.), *Contemporary Social Work*, 2d ed. (New York: McGraw-Hill, 1980), pp. 344–72.

Focus. "Poverty in the United States: Where Do We Stand Now?" 7 (Winter 1984):1.

Forssman, H., and I. Thuwe. "One Hundred and Twenty Children Born After Application for Therapeutic Abortion Refused." *Acta psychiatrica Scandinavica* 42 (1966):71–85.

Fort, J., and C. T. Cory. *American Drug Store* (Boston: Little, Brown, 1975).

Fosburgh, Lacey. "The Make-Believe World of Teenage Maternity." *New York Times Magazine,* August 7, 1977, p. 7.

Fox, M. F., and S. Hesse-Biber. *Women at Work (Palo Alto, CA: Mayfield, 1984).*

Franklin, Benjamin. Quoted in Thomas Sullivan et al. *Social Problems* (New York: John Wiley & Sons, 1980), p. 300.

Franklin, E. W. and A. M. Zeiderman. "Tubal Ectopic Pregnancy Etiology and Obstetric and Gynaecologic Sequelae." *American Journal of Obstetrics and Gynecology* 117 (1973):220–25.

Frazier, A., and L. K. Lisonbee, "Adolescent Concerns with Physique." *School Review* 58 (1950):397–405.

Freese, Arthur S. "Adolescent Suicide: Mental health Challenge." (New York: Public Affairs Pamphlets, 1979).

Frenkel-Brunswick, E. "Adjustments and Reorientation in the Course of the Life-Span." In R. G. Kuhlen and G. G. Thomson (Eds.), *Psychological Studies of Human Development.* 3d ed. (New York: Appleton-Century-Crofts, 1970).

Freud, Sigmund. Quoted in Ronald B. Adler and Neil Towne, *Looking Out, Looking In.* 3d ed. (New York: Holt, Rinehart & Winston, 1981), p. 253.

Friedlander, W. A., and Apte, R. Z. *Introduction to Social Welfare* (Englewood Cliffs, NJ: Prentice-Hall, 1980).

Friedlander, Walter A. *Introduction to Social Welfare* (Englewood Cliffs, NJ: Prentice-Hall, 1968).

Frieze, I. H. et al. *Women and Sex Roles: A Social Psychological Perspective* (New York: Norton, 1978).

Frolkis, V. V. "Aging of the Autonomic Nervous System" in J. E. Birren and K. W. Schaie (Eds.), *Handbook of the Psychology of Aging* (New York: Van Nostrand Reinhold Co., 1977).

Fuchs, V. R. *Who Shall Live? Health, Economics and Social Choice* (New York: Basic Books, 1974).

Furry, C. A. and P. B. Baltes. "The Effect of Age Differences on the Assessment of Intelligence in Children, Adults, and the Elderly" *Journal of Gerontology* 28, No. 1 (1973):73–80.

Furstenberg, F. F., Jr. "The Social Consequences of Teenage Parenthood," *Family Planning Perspectives* 8, No. 4 (July–August 1976):148–64.

Gallagher, J. M. "Cognitive Development and Learning in the Adolescent." In J. F. Adams (Ed.), *Understanding Adolescence.* 2d ed. (Boston: Allyn & Bacon, 1973).

Gans, Herbert J. *More Equality* (New York: Pantheon, 1968).

Garn, S. M. "Bone Loss and Aging." In R. Goldman and M. Rockstein (Eds.), *The Physiology and Pathology of Human Aging* (New York: Academic Press, 1975).

Garner, B., and R. W. Smith. "Are there Really Any Gay Male Athletes? An Empirical Survey." *Journal of Sex Research* 13 (1977):22–34.

Garrison, K. C. "Physiological Changes in Adolescence." In J. F. Adams (Ed.), *Understanding Adolescence: Current Developments in Adolescent Psychology* (Boston: Allyn & Bacon, 1968).

———. "Psychological Development." In J. F. Adams (Ed.), *Understanding Adolescence.* 2d ed. (Boston: Allyn & Bacon, 1973).

Garvey, C. *Play* (Cambridge, Mass: Harvard University Press, 1977).

Gebhard, P. H. "Postmarital Coitus Among Widows and Divorcees." In P. Bohannan (Ed.), *Divorce and After* (Garden City, NY: Doubleday, 1968).

Gelfand, D. M. "The Influence of Self-Esteem on Rate of Verbal Conditioning and Social Matching Behavior." *Journal of Abnormal and Social Psychology* 65 (1962):259–65.

Geller, H. and G. Steele, *Probability Tables of Deaths in the Next Ten Years from Specific Causes* (Indianapolis, IN: Department of Prospective Medicine, Methodist Hospital of Indiana, 1977).

Geller, J. "Reaching the Battered Husband," *Social Work with Groups* 1 (1978):27–37.

Gelles, R. J. *The Violent Home: The Study of Physical Aggression Between Husbands and Wives* (Beverly Hills, CA: Sage Publications, 1974).

———. "Abused Wives: Why Do They Stay?" *Journal of Marriage and the Family* 38 (1976):659–68.

———. "The Myth of Battered Husbands." *Ms.,* October 1979.

Germain, Carel B. "An Ecological Perspective in Casework Practice." *Social Casework* 54 (June 1973):323–30.

———. *Social Work Practice: People and Environments* (New York: Columbia University Press, 1979).

Germain, Carel B., and Gitterman, Alex. *The Life Model of Social Work Practice* (New York: Columbia University Press, 1980).

Gessell, A. *The First Five Years of Life: The Preschool Years* (New York: Harper & Row, 1940).

Gessell, A., and F. L. Ilg, *The Child from Five to Ten* (New York: Harper & Row, 1946).

Gessell, A., F. L. Ilg, and L. B. Ames. *Youth: The Years from Ten to Sixteen* (New York: Harper & Row, 1956).

Gil, D. G. *Violence Against Children* (Cambridge, Mass: Harvard University Press, 1973).

Gilligan, C. "In a Different Voice: Women's Conceptions of Self and of Morality." *Harvard Educational Review* 47, No. 4 (1977):481–517.

Girdano, D. A., and D. Dusek. *Drug Education: Content and Methods* (Philippines: Addison-Welsey Company, 1980).

Glass, D., J. Neulinger, and O. Brim. "Birth Order, Verbal Intelligence and Educational Aspirations." *Child Development* 45, No. 3 (1974):807–11.

Glasser, William. *Schools Without Failure* (New York: Harper & Row, 1969).

———. *The Identity Society* (New York: Harper & Row, 1972).

———. *Control Theory* (New York: Harper & Row, 1984).

Glick, P. C. "The Future of the American Family" *Current Population Reports*, Special Studies Series P-23, No. 78. Washington, D.C.: U.S. Government Printing Office, 1979.

Globe Magazine. In *The Boston Globe*, July 11, 1971.

Goldin, R. *Therapy as Education*. Unpublished dissertation, Boston University, 1977.

Goldmeier, J. "From Divorce to Family Reconstitution: A Clinical View." In C. Janzen and O. Harris (Eds.), *Family Treatment in Social Work Practice* (Itasca, IL: F. E. Peacock, 1980), pp. 259–83.

Goldstein, J., A. Freud, and A. J. Solnit, *Beyond the Best Interests of the Child* (New York: Free Press, 1973).

Good Tracks, Jimm G. "Native American Noninterference." *Social Work* 18 (November 1973): 30–34.

Goode, William J. "Family Disorganization." In Robert K. Merton and Robert Nisbet (Eds.), *Contemporary Social Problems*, 4th ed. (New York: Harcourt, Brace, Jovanovich, 1976), pp. 511–55.

Goodman, M. J., J. S. Grove, and F. Gilbert, Jr. "Age at Menopause in Relation to Reproductive History in Japanese, Caucasian, Chinese and Hawaiian Women Living in Hawaii." *Journal of Gerontology* 33 (1978):688–94.

Goodrich, W., R. G. Ryder and H. L. Rausch, "Patterns of Newlyweds." In M. E. Losswell and T. E. Losswell (Eds.), *Love, Marriage and Family: A Developmental Approach*, (Glenview, IL: Scott, Foresman, 1973).

Gordon, Milton. "Assimilation in America: Theory and Reality." *Daedalus* 90 (Spring 1961):363–65.

———. *Assimilation in American Life: The Role of Race, Religion, and National Origins* (New York: Oxford University Press, 1964).

Gordon, S. *The Sexual Adolescent* (North Scituate, MA: Duxbury Press, 1973).

Gordon, T. *Parent Effectiveness Training* (New York: Peter H. Wyden, 1970).

———. *Parent Effectiveness Training* (New York: New American Library, 1975).

Gottlieb, D. "Teaching and Students: The Views of Negro and White Teachers." *Sociology of Education* 37 (1966):345–53.

Gove, W. R. "Sex Differences in the Epidemiology of Mental Disorder: Evidence and Explanations." In E. S. Gomberg, and V. Franks (Eds.), *Gender and Disordered Behavior* (New York: Brunner-Mazel, 1979), pp. 23–68.

Grady, W. P. "Remarriages of Women 15–44 Years of Age Whose First Marriages Ended in Divorce: United States 1976." *Advancedata* 58 (1980):1–12.

Great Britain Committee on Homosexual Offenses and Prostitution. *The Wolfenden Report* (New York: Stein & Day, 1963).

Green, R. "Homosexuality as a Mental Illness." *International Journal of Psychiatry*, Vol 10, 1972, pp. 77–98.

———. *Sexual Identity Conflict in Children and Adults* (New York: Basic Books, 1974).

———. "Should Homosexuals Adopt Children?" In J. P. Brady, and H. K. Brodie (Eds.), *Controversy in Psychiatry* (Philadelphia: Saunders, 1978), pp. 813–28.

Greenberg, Herbert M. *Coping with Job Stress* (Englewood Cliffs, NJ: Prentice-Hall, 1980).

Greene, B. "Speck Admits Killing of 7 of 8 Chicago Nurses." *Wisconsin State Journal*, March 8, 1978, pp. 1–2.

Greene, B. L., R. R. Lee, and N. Lustig. "Conscious and Unconscious Factors in Marital Infidelity." *Medical Aspects of Human Sexuality*, 8 (1974):87–105.

Grier, William H., and Price M. Cobb, *Black Rage* (New York: Basic Books, 1968), pp. 200–213.

Gross, A. E. "The Male Role and Heterosexual Behavior." *Journal of Social Issues* 34, No. 1 (1978):87–107.

Grossman, H. J. (Ed.). *Manual on Terminology and Classification in Mental Retardation*. Rev. ed. (Washington, D.C.: AAMD, 1975).

Group for the Advancement of Psychiatry. *The Joys and Sorrows of Parenthood* (New York: Scribner's 1973).

Grundlach, R. "Sexual Molestation and Rape Reported by Homosexual and Heterosexual Women." *Journal of Homosexuality* 2 (1977):367–84.

Grune, J. A. "Pay Equity Is a Necessary Remedy for Wage Discrimination." In *Comparable Worth: Issue for the 80's, A Consultation for the U.S. Commission on Civil Rights*. 1 (June 6–7, 1984):165–76.

Grush, J. E., and J. G. Yehl. "Marital Roles, Sex Differences and Interpersonal Attraction." *Journal of Personality and Social Psychology* 37 (1979):116–23.

Gubrium, F. F. "Being Single in Old Age." *International Journal of Aging and Human Development* 6, No. 1 (1975):29–41.

Guilford, J. P. "Factorial Angles to Psychology." *Psychological Review* 68 (1961):1–20.

Guttentag, M., and H. Bray. "Teachers as Mediators of Sex Role Standards." In Alice Sargend (Ed.), *Beyond Sex Roles* (St. Paul: West, 1977), pp. 395–411.

Guyton, A. C. *Textbook of Medical Physiology*, 6th ed. (Philadelphia: Saunders, 1981).

Haith, M. M., and J. J. Campos, "Human Infancy" *Annual Review of Psychology* 28 (1977):251–293.

Hall, Edward T., *The Hidden Dimension* (Garden City, NY: Doubleday, 1969).

Hall, E. "Acting One's Age: New Rules for Old." *Psychology Today*, 1980, 13 (11), pp. 66–80.

Hall, R. V., S. Axelrod, M. Foundopoulos, J. Shellman, R. A. Campbell, and S. S. Cranston. "The Effective Use of Punishment to Modify Behavior in the Classroom." *Educational Technology* 11 (1971):24–26.

Hallberg, Edmund C. *The Gray Itch: The Male Menopause Syndrome*, (New York: Stein and Day, 1978).

"Hallucinogens and Narcotics Alarm Public." *Chemistry and Engineering News.* 48, 1976, pp. 44–45.

Halsell, Grace. *Soul Sister* (New York: Fawcett Crest, 1969).

Hareven, T. K. "The Last Stage: Historical Adulthood and Old Age." *Daedalus* 105, No. 4 (1976):13–27.

Harrington, Michael. *The Other America* (New York: Macmillan, 1962).

Harris, R. "Cardiac Changes with Age." In R. Goldman and M. Rockstein (Eds.), *The Physiology and Pathology of Human Aging* (New York: Academic Press, 1975).

Harris, Thomas. *I'm OK—You're OK* (New York: Harper & Row Publishers, Inc., 1969).

Hartley, Eugene. *Problems in Prejudice* (New York: King's Crown Press, 1946).

Hartley, R. E. "Sex-Role Pressures in the Socialization of the Male Child. *Psychological Reports* 5 (1959):457–68.

Harvey, O. J., M. Prather, B. J. White, and J. K. Hoffmeister. "Teacher's Beliefs, Classroom Atmosphere, and Student Behavior." *American Educational Research Journal* 5 (1968):151–66.

Hass, A. *Teenage Sexuality* (New York: Macmillan, 1979).

Hatcher, Robert A. et al. *Contraceptive Technology, 1976–1977.* 8th ed. (New York: Irvington, 1976).

———. *Contraceptive Technology, 1980–1981.* 10th ed. (New York: Irvington, 1980).

Hayflick, L. "The Strategy of Senescence." *The Gerontologist*, 14, No. 1 (1974):37–45.

Hearn, Gordon. *The General Systems Approach: Contributions Toward an holistic Conception of Social Work* (New York: Council on Social Work Education, 1969).

Hedgpeth, J. M. "Employment Discrimination Law and the Rights of Gay Persons." *Journal of Homosexuality* 5, Nos. 1, 2 (1978/80):67–78.

Hellman, L. M. and J. A. Pritchard. *Williams Obstetrics*. 14th ed. (New York: Appleton-Century-Crofts, 1971).

Henderson, Charles H., and Bok-Lim Kim. "Racism." In Donald Brieland, Lela Costin, and Charles Atherton (Eds.), *Contemporary Social Work* (New York: McGraw-Hill, 1975).

Henderson, Charles H., Bok-Lim Kim, and Ione D. Vargus. "Racism." In Donald Brieland, Lela Costin and Charles Atherton (Eds.), *Contemporty Social Work*. 2d ed. (New York: McGraw-Hill, 1980), p. 403.

Hendry, L., and P. Gillies. "Body Type, Body Esteem, School and Leisure: A Study of Overweight, Average, and Underweight Adolescents." *Journal of Youth and Adolescence* 7, No. 2 (1978):181–96.

Henig, R. M. "Exposing the Myth of Senility." *The New York Times Magazine.* December 3, 1978, p. 158.

Henley, N. M. "The Politics of Touch." In P. Brown (Ed.), *Radical Psychology* (New York: Harper & Row, 1973).

———. "Status and Sex: Some Touching Observations." *Bulletin of the Psychonomic Society* 2 (1973):91–93.

Henley, N. M., and J. Freeman. "The Sexual Politics of Interpersonal Behavior." In J. Freeman (Ed.), *Women: A Feminist Perspective* (Palo Alto, CA: Mayfield, 1984), pp. 465–77.

Henry, Jeannette. *The Indian Historian* 1 (December 1967).

Herman, Dianne. "The Rape Culture." In Jo Freeman (Ed.), *Women: A Feminist Perspective* (Palo Alto, CA: Mayfield, 1984), pp. 20–38.

Hess, E. H. "Imprinting." *Science* 130 (1959):133–41.

Hess, E. H., and J. M. Polt. "Pupil Size as Related to Interest Value of Visual Stimuli." *Science* 132 (1960):349–50.

Heston, L., and J. Shields. "Homosexuality in Twins." *Archives of General Psychiatry* 18 (1968):149–60.

Hetherington, E. M., M. Cox, and R. Cox. "Beyond Father Absence! Conceptualization of Effects of Divorce." Paper presented at the annual meeting of the Society for Research in Child Development, Denver, 1975.

————. "Beyond Father Absence: Conceptualization of Effects of Divorce." In E. M. Hetherington and R. D. Parke (Eds.), *Contemporary Readings in Child Psychology* (New York: McGraw-Hill, 1977), pp. 308–15.

Hetherington, E. M. and Parke, R. *Child Psychology: A Contemporary Viewpoint* (New York: McGraw-Hill, 1979).

Hickey, T., L. Hickey, and R. Kalish. "Children's Perceptions of the Elderly." *Journal of Genetic Psychology* 112 (1968):227–35.

Hilgard, E. R., and R. C. Atkinson. *Introduction to Psychology*. 4th ed. (New York: Harcourt Brace & World, 1967).

Hill, R. "Decision Making and the Family Life Cycle." In E. Shanas and G. Streib (Eds.), *Social Structure and the Family: Generational Relations* (Englewood Cliffs, NJ: Prentice-Hall, 1965).

Hitchens, D. "Social Attitudes, Legal Standards and Personal Trauma in Child Custody Cases." *Journal of Homosexuality* 5, No. 1–2 (1979/80):89–96.

Hobbs, D., and S. Cole. "Transition to Parenthood: A Decade Replication." *Journal of Marriage and the Family* 38 (1976):723–31.

Hobson, R. P. "The Question of Egocentrism: The Young Child's Competence in the Coordination of Perspectives." *Journal of Child Psychology and Psychiatry* 21 (1980):325–31.

Hodges, A., and B. Balow. "Learning Disability in Relation to Family Constellation." *Journal of Educational Research* 55 (1961):4–42.

Hoffman, L. W. and J. Manis "The Value of Children in the United States: A New Approach to the Study of Fertility." *Journal of Marriage and the Family* 41 (1979):583–96.

Holmes, D. L. and F. J. Morrison, *The Child: An Introduction to Developmental Psychology* (Monterey, CA: Brooks/Cole, 1979).

Holmes, T. H. and M. Masuda. "Psychosomatic Syndrome." *Psychology Today* 106 (1972):71–72.

Holmes, T. H., and R. H. Rahe. "The Social Readjustment Rating Scale." *Journal of Psychosomatic Research* 11 (1976):213.

Hooker, E. "The Adjustment of the Male Overt Homosexual," *Journal of Projective Techniques* 21 (1957):18–31.

————. "An Empirical Study of Some Relations Between Sexual Patterns and Gender Identity in Male Homosexuals." In J. Money (Ed.), *Sex Research: New Developments* (New York: Holt, 1965).

————. "The Homosexual Community." In J. H. Gagnon and W. Simon (Eds.), *Sexual Deviance* (New York: Harper & Row, 1967), pp. 167–84.

Hormer, M. S. "Toward an Understanding of Achievement—Related Conflicts in Women." *Journal of Social Issues* 28, No. 2 (1972):157–75.

Hosford, R. E., and Louis de Visser *Behavioral Approaches to Counseling: An Introduction* (Falls Church, VA: APGA Press, 1974).

Hoult, R. "Experimental Measurement of Clothing as a Factor in Some Social Ratings of Selected American Men." *American Sociological Review* 19 (1954):324–28.

Houseknecht, S. K. "Childlessness and Marital Adjustment," *Journal of Marriage and the Family* 41 (1979):259–66.

Howell, M. C. "Effects of Maternal Employment on the Child." *Pediatrics* 52(3) (1973):327–43.

Howie, L. H. and T. F. Drury. "Vital and Health Statistics, series 10, no. 126," National Center for Health Statistics, no. (PHS) 78-1554 (Washington, D.C.: U.S. Government Printing Office, September 1978).

Hsu, L., A. Crisp, and B. Harding. "Outcome of Anorexia Nervosa." *Lancet,* January 13, 1976, pp. 61–65.

Hull, Grafton H., Jr. "Urban Problems." In Charles Zastrow and Lee Bowker (Ed.), *Social Problems* (Chicago: Nelson-Hall, 1984), pp. 416–37.

————. "Social Work Practice with Diverse Groups." In Charles Zastrow (Ed.), *The Practice of Social Work.* 2d ed. (Homewood, IL: The Dorsey Press, 1985), pp. 244–271.

Hultsch, D. F., and F. Deutsch. *Adult Development and Aging: A Life Span Perspective* (New York: McGraw-Hill Book Co., 1981).

Hunt, B., and M. Hunt. *Prime Time* (New York: Stein and Day, 1974).

Hunt, L. G., and N. E. Zinberg. *Heroin Use: A New Look* (Washington, D.C.: Drug Abuse Council, 1976).

Hunt, M. *Sexual Behavior in the 1970s* (Chicago: Playboy Press, 1974).

Hunt, M., and B. Hunt. *The Divorce Experience* (New York: Signet, 1977).

Hunt, W. A., and J. D. Matarazzo. "Habit Mechanisms in Smoking." In W. A. Hunt (Ed.), *Learning Mechanisms of Smoking* (Chicago: Aldine, 1970).

Hutchins, T., and V. Baxter, "Battered Women." In N. Gottlieb, (Ed.), *Alternative Social Services for Women* (New York: Columbia University Press, 1980), pp. 179–234.

Hutt, P. J. "Rate of Bar Pressing as a Function of Quality and Quantity of Food Reward." *Journal of Comparative and Physiological Psychology* 47 (1954):235–39.

Hyde, J. S. *Understanding Human Sexuality* (New York: McGraw-Hill, Inc., 1982).

Hyde, J. S. and B. G. Rosenberg, *Half the Human Experience: The Psychology of Women.* 2d ed. (Lexington, Mass: Heath, 1980).

Imara, Mwalimu. "Dying as the Last Stage of Growth." In Elizabeth Kübler-Ross. *Death: The Final Stage of Growth* (Englewood Cliffs, NJ: Prentice-Hall, Inc., 1975); pp. 147–63.

Jacobs, H. C. "National Caucus on the Black Aged: A Progress Report." *Aging and Human Development* 3 (1971):226–31.

Jacobs, J., and J. Teicher. "Broken Homes and Social Isolation in Attempted Suicide of Adolescents." *International Journal of Social Psychology* 13 (1967):139–49.

Jacobson, Edmund. *Progressive Relaxation*. 2d ed. (Chicago: University of Chicago Press, 1938).

Jacobson, S. B. "The Challenge of Aging for Marriage Partners." In W. C. Bier (Ed.), *Aging: Its Challenge to the Individual and to Society* (New York: Fordham University Press, 1974).

Jacoby, Oswald. *Oswald Jacoby on Poker* (New York: Doubleday, 1974).

Jacques, J. M., and K. J. Chason. "Cohabitation: Its Impact on Marital Success." *The Family Coordinator* 28 (1979):35–39.

James, Muriel, and Dorothy Jongeward. *Born to Win: Transactional Analysis with Gestalt Experiments* (Reading, Mass: Addison-Wesley, 1971), p. 35.

James, W. H. "Marital Coital Rates, Spouses' Ages, Family Size and Social Class." *Journal of Sex Research* 10 (1974):205–18.

Jay, K., and A. Young. *The Gay Report* (New York: Summit Books, 1979).

Jenkins, A. H. *The Psychology of the Afro-American: A Humanistic Approach* (New York: Pergamon Press, 1982).

Jenkins, J. L., M. K. Salus, and G. L. Schultze, *Child Protective Services: A Guide for Workers* (Washington, D.C.: U.S. Department of Health, Education and Welfare, Publication No. (OHDS) 79-30203, 1979).

Jensen, Arthur. "How Much Can We Boost I.Q. and Scholastic Achievement?" *Harvard Educational Review* 39 (1969): pp. 1–123.

Jensen, Michael L. "Adolescent Suicide: A Tragedy of Our Times." *FLEducator*, Summer 1984, pp. 12–16.

Jersild, A. T. *The Psychology of Adolescence*, 2d ed. (New York: Macmillan, 1965).

Johnson, Elmer H. *Social Problems of Urban Man* (Homewood, IL: Dorsey Press, 1973).

Johnson, Louise C. *Social Work Practice: A Generalist Approach* (Boston: Allyn and Bacon, 1983).

Johnston, L. D., J. G. Bachman, and P. M. O'Malley, *1979 Highlights: Drugs and the Nation's High School Students: Five Year National Trends* (Rockville, MD: National Institute on Drug Abuse, 1979).

Jones, M. C. "The Later Careers of Boys Who Were Early or Late Maturing." *Child Development* 28 (1957):113–28.

———. "Psychological Correlates of Somatic Development," *Child Development*, 1965, 36, pp. 899–911.

———. "A Study of Socialization Patterns at the High School Level." *Journal of Genetic Psychology* 92 (1958):87–111.

Jones, M. C., and N. Bayley. "Physical Maturing Among Boys as Related to Behavior." *Journal of Educational Psychology* 41 (1950):129–48.

Jones, M. C., and P. H. Mussen. "Self Conceptions, Motivations, and Interpersonal Attitudes of Early and Late Maturing Girls." *Child Development* 29 (1958):491–501.

Julian, Joseph, and Kornblum, W. *Social Problems*. 3d ed. (Englewood Cliffs, NJ: Prentice-Hall, 1980).

Kadushin, A. *The Social Work Interview* (New York: Columbia University Press, 1972).

———. *Child Welfare Services* (New York: Macmillan, 1980).

Kahana, B., and E. Kahana. "Grandparents from the Perspective of the Developing Grandchild." *Developmental Psychology* 3, No. 1 (1970):98–105.

Kahana, E., and R. M. Coe "Perceptions of Grandparenthood by Community and Institutional Aged" *Proceedings of the Seventy-Seventh Annual Convention of the American Psychological Association* 4 (1969):735–36.

Kakvan, M., and S. D. Greenberg. "Cigarette Smoking and Cancer of the Lung: A Review." *Rhode Island Medical Journal* 60, No. 12 (1977):588–91, 606.

Kales, J. D. "Aging and Sleep." In R. Goldman and M. Rockstein (Eds.), *The Psychology and Pathology of Human Aging* (New York: Academic Press, 1975).

Kalish, R. A. *Late Adulthood: Perspectives on Human Development* (Monterey, CA: Brooks/Cole, 1975).

Kallman, F. J. "Comparative Twin Study on the Genetic Aspects of Male Homosexuality." *Journal of Nervous and Mental Disease*, 1952, 115, pp. 283–298.

Kaluger, G., and M. F. Kaluger. *Human Development: The Span of Life* (St. Louis: C. V. Mosby, 1979).

———. *Human Development: The Span of Life*. 3d ed. (St. Louis: Times Mirror/Mosby, 1984).

Kaluger, G., and C. J. Kolson. *Reading and Learning Disabilities* 2d ed. (Columbus, Ohio: Charles E. Merrill, 1978).

Kangas, J., and K. Bradway. "Intelligence at Middle Age: A Thirty-Eight-Year Follow-Up." *Developmental Psychology* 5 (1971):333–37.

Kaplan, H. S. *The New Sex Therapy* (New York: Brunner/Mazel, 1981).

Karlen, A. *Sexuality and Homosexuality: A New View* (New York: Norton, 1971).

Katz, P., and S. Zalk. "Modification of Children's Racial Attitudes." *Developmental Psychology* 14, No. 5, (1978):447–61.

Keating, N. C., and L. V. Clark. "Development of Physical and Social Reasoning in Adolescents." *Developmental Psychology* 16 (1980):23–30.

Keller, Mark, and C. Gurioli. *Statistics on Consumption of Alcohol and on Alcohol* (New Brunswick, NJ: Rutgers Center of Alcohol Studies, 1976).

Keniston, Kenneth. *All Our Children: The American Family Under Pressure* (New York: Harcourt Brace Jovanovich, 1977).

Kent, S. *The Life-Extension Revolution* (New York: William Morrow & Co., 1980).

Key, M. R. *Male/Female Language* (Metuchen, NJ: Scarecrow Press, 1975).

Kiev, Ari. "The Courage to Live." *Cosmopolitan,* September 1980, pp. 301–8.

Kimmel, D. C. *Adulthood and Aging* (New York: Wiley, 1974).

Kinsey, A. C., W. B. Pomeroy, and C. R. Martin. *Sexual Behavior in the Human Male* (Philadelphia: W. B. Saunders, 1948).

Kinsey, A. C., W. B. Pomeroy, C. E. Martin and P. H. Gebhard. *Sexual Behavior in the Human Female* (Philadelphia: W. B. Saunders Co., 1953).

Kirby, I. J. "Hormone Replacement Therapy for Postmenopausal Symptoms." *Lancet* 2 (1973):103.

Kircher, A. S., J. J. Pear, and G. L. Martin. "Shock as Punishment in a Picture-Naming Task with Retarded Children." *Journal of Applied Behavior Analysis* 4 (1971):227–33.

Kirkpatrick, C. *The Family as Process and Institution* (New York: Ronald Press, 1975).

Kirst-Ashman, Karen K. "Exploration of the Family Environment and Problems of Uncontrollable Adolescents." Doctoral Dissertation, University of Illinois at Urbana-Champaign, 1983.

Knapp, Mark L. *Nonverbal Communication in Human Interaction.* 2d ed. (New York: Holt, Rinehart and Winston, 1978).

Koch, H. L. "Sibling Influence on Children's Speech." *Journal of Speech Disabilities* 21 (1956):322–28.

———. "The Relation of Certain Formal Attributes of Siblings to Attitudes Held Toward Each Other and Toward Their Parents." *Monographs of the Society for Research in Child Development* 25 (1960):1–134.

Koch, J. P. "The Prentif Contraceptive Cervical Cap: A Contemporary Study of Its Safety and Effectiveness." *Contraception* 25 (1982):135.

Koch, Lewis and Joanne Koch. "Parent Abuse—A New Plague." *Parade Magazine,* January 27, 1980, p. 14.

Koeppel, B. "The Big Social Security Ripoff." *Progressive* 39, No. 7 (1975):13–18.

Kohlberg, Lawrence. "The Development of Children's Orientations Toward a Moral Order. I: Sequence in the Development of Moral Thought." *Vita Humana* 6 (1963):11–35.

———. "The Child as a Moral Philosopher." *Psychology Today* 2, No. 4 (1968):25–30.

———. *Stages in the Development of Moral Thought and Action* (New York: Holt, Rinehart & Winston, 1969).

———. "The Child as Moral Philosopher." In P. Cramer (Ed.), *Readings in Developmental Psychology Today* (Del Mar, Calif.: CRM, 1970).

———. "Revisions in the Theory and Practice of Moral Development." *New Directions for Child Development* 2, 1978.

———. *The Philosophy of Moral Development* (New York: Harper & Row, 1981).

Kohlberg, Lawrence, and C. Gilligan. "The Adolescent as a Philosopher: The Discovery of the Self in a Postconventional World." *Daedalus,* Fall 1971, pp. 1051–86.

Koll, Lawrence C., Viola Bernard, and Bruce P. Dohrenwend. "The Problem of Validity in Field Studies of Psychological Disorder." In Bruce P. Dohrenwend and Barbara Snell Dohrenwend (Eds.), *Urban Challenges to Psychiatry* (New York: John Wiley, 1969), pp. 429–60.

Kolodny, R. C., W. H. Masters, J. Hendryx, and G. Toro. "Plasma Testosterone and Semen Analysis in Male Homosexuals." *New England Journal of Medicine* 285 (1971):1170–74.

Kolodny, R. C., W. H. Masters, and V. E. Johnson. *Textbook of Sexual Medicine* (Boston: Little, Brown, 1979).

Kompara, D. "Difficulties in the Socialization on Process of Step Parenting." *Family Relations* 29 (1980):69–73.

Konig, K. *Brothers and Sisters: A Study in Child Psychology,* (New York: St. George Books, 1963).

Krasner, L. "Behavior Therapy." *Annual Review of Psychology* 22 (1971):483–532.

Krumboltz, J. D., and H. B. Krumboltz. *Changing Children's Behavior* (Englewood Cliffs, NJ: Prentice-Hall, 1972).

Kübler-Ross, E. *On Death and Dying* (New York: Macmillan, 1969).

Kushner, M. "Faradic Aversive Controls in Clinical Practice." In C. Neuringer and J. L. Michael (Eds.), *Behavior Modification in Clinical Psychology* (New York: Appleton-Century-Crofts, 1970), pp. 26–51.

Kuypers, J., and V. Benston. "Competence and Social Breakdown: A Social-Psychological View of Aging" *Human Development* 16, No. 2 (1973):37–49.

Laborde, Genie Z. *Influencing with Integrity* (Palo Alto, CA: Syntony Publishing, 1983).

Lankton, Steve. *Practical Magic: A Translation of Basic Neuro-Linguistic Programming into Clinical Psychotherapy* (Cupertino, CA: 1980).

Lasater, M. "Sexual Assault: The Legal Framework." In C. Warner (Ed.), *Rape and Sexual Assault* (Germantown, MD: Aspen Systems Corp., 1980), pp. 231–64.

Lasser Tax Institute, *J. K. Lasser's Your Income Tax: 1984* (New York: Simon and Schuster, 1984).

Lawton, M. P. "Leisure Activities for the Aged." *Annals of the American Academy of Political and Social Science* 438 (1978):71–79.

Leacock, Eleanor. *The Culture of Poverty: A Critique* (New York: Simon & Schuster, 1971).

Lebovitz, P. S. "Feminine Behavior in Boys: Aspects of Its Outcome." *American Journal of Psychiatry* 128 (1972):1283–89.

Ledger, M. "Aging." *Pennsylvania Gazette*, June 1978, pp. 18–23.

Lee, G. "Marriage and Morale in Later Life." *Journal of Marriage and the Family* 40 No. 1 (1978):131–39.

Lee, John. "Homosexuality: Tolerance vs. Approval." *Time Magazine*, 173, No. 2, (January 8, 1979):48–51.

Lehman, H. C. "The Most Creative Years of Engineers and Other Technologists." *Journal of Genetic Psychology* 108 (1966):263–77.

Leiber, C. S. "Alcoholic Fatty Liver: its Pathogenesis and Precursor Role for Hepatitis and Cirrhosis." *Panminerva Medica*, 18, No. 9–10 (1976):346–58.

Leifer, Myra. *Psychological Effects of Motherhood: A Study of First Pregnancy* (New York: Praeger 1980).

Lembo, John. *Help Yourself* (Niles, IL: Argus Communications, 1974).

Lemert, Edwin M. *Social Pathology* (New York: McGraw-Hill, 1951).

Lemon, B., V. Bengston, and J. Peterson, "An Exploration of the Activity Theory of Aging: Activity Types and Life Satisfaction Among In-movers to a Retirement Community." *Journal of Gerontology* 24, No. 4 (1972):511–23.

Lennard, H. L., and Associates. *Mystification and Drug Misuse* (San Francisco: Jossey-Bass, 1971).

Levinson, D. J. "The Midlife Transition: A Period in Adult Psychosocial Transition" *Psychiatry* 40 (1977):99–112.

Levinson, D. J., C. N. Darrow, E. B. Klein, M. H. Levinson, and B. McKee. "The Psychosocial Development of Men in Early Adulthood and the Mid-Life Tradition." In D. F. Ricks, A. Thomas, and M. Roff (Eds.), *Life History Research in Psychopathology* (Minneapolis: University of Minn. Press, 1974).

———. *The Seasons of a Man's Life* (New York: Alfred A. Knopf, 1978).

Levitt, E. E., and A. D. Klassen, Jr. *Public Attitudes Toward Sexual Behaviors: The Latest Investigation of the Institute for Sex Research* (Bloomington: Indiana University Press, 1973).

Levy, S. M., L. R. Derogatis, D. Gallagher, and M. Gatz, "Intervention with Older Adults and the Evaluation of Outcome." In L. W. Poon (Ed.), *Aging in the 1980s* (Washington, D.C.: American Psychological Association, 1980).

Lewin, K., R. Lippett, and R. K. White, "Patterns of Aggressive Behavior in Experimentally Created 'Social Climates,'" *Journal of Social Psychology*, 1939, 10, pp. 271–299.

Lewinsohn, Peter M., Ricardo F. Munoz, M. A. Youngren, and M. Z. Antonette, *Control Your Depression* (Englewood Cliffs, NJ: Prentice-Hall, 1978).

Lewis, K. "Children of Lesbians: Their Point of View." *Social Work* 25, No. 3 (1980):203.

Lewis, M. "State as an Infant—Interaction: An Analysis of Mother-Infant Interaction as a Function of Sex." *Merrill-Palmer Quarterly* 18 (1972):95–121.

Lewis, Oscar. "The Culture of Poverty." *Scientific American* 215 (October 1966):19–25.

Lewis, S. *Sunday's Women: a Report of Lesbian Life Today* (Boston: Beacon Press, 1979).

Libby, R. W. and G. D. Nass. "Parental Views on Teenage Sexual Behavior." *Journal of Sex Research* 7 (1971):226–36.

Lichtenwalner, J. S. and J. W. Maxwell. "The Relationship of Birth Order and Socioeconomic Status to the Creativity of Preschool Children." *Child Development* 40 (1969):1241–1246.

Liebow, Elliot. *Tally's Corner: A Study of Negro Street-Corner Men* (Boston: Little, Brown, 1967).

Lincoln, Abraham. Speech made in Charleston, Illinois, in 1858. As reported in Richard Hofstader, *The American Political Tradition* (New York: Alfred A. Knopf, 1948), p. 116.

Lindeman, R. D. "Changes in Penal Function." In R. Goldman and M. Rockstein (Eds.), *The Physiology and Pathology of Human Aging* (New York: Academic Press, 1975).

Livson, N., and H. Peskin. "Perspectives on Adolescence from Longitudinal Research." In A. J. Adelsen (Ed.), *Handbook of Adolescent Psychology* (New York: Wiley, 1980).

Loewenberg, F. M. *Fundamentals of Social Intervention* (New York: Columbia Press, 1977).

Lopata, H. "Living Through Widowhood." *Psychology Today* 7 No. 2 (1973):87–98.

Loraine, J. A. et al. "Endocrine Function in Male and Female Homosexuals," *British Medical Journal* 4 (1970):406–8.

Lovaas, O. I. and J. Q. Simmons. "Manipulation of Self-Destruction in Three Retarded Children." *Journal of Applied Behavior Analysis*, 2 (1969):143–57.

Lowenthal, M. F., and C. Haven, "Interaction and Adaptation: Intimacy as a Critical Variable." In B. Neugarten (Ed.), *Middle Age and Aging* (Chicago: University of Chicago Press, 1968).

Lowenthal, M. F. and D. Chiriboga. "Transition to the Empty Nest: Crisis, Change, or Relief?" *Archives of General Psychiatry* 26 (1972):8–14.

Lueck, M., A. Orr, and M. O'Connell. "Trends in Childcare Arrangements of Working Mothers." *Current Population Reports* Series P-23, No. 117 (1982):14.

Maas, H. S. *Five Fields of Social Work Practice* (New York: National Association of Social Workers, 1966).

Maccoby, E. E., and C. N. Jacklin, *The Psychology of Sex Differences* (Stanford, CA: Stanford University Press, 1974).

MacKinnon, Catherine A. *Sexual Harassment of Working Women: A Case of Sex Discrimination* (New Haven, CN: Yale University Press, 1979), p. xii.

Macmillan, D. L. *Behavior Modification and Education* (New York: Macmillan, 1973).

Madigan, F. C. and R. B. Vance. "Differential sex mortality: A research design." *Social Forces* 35 (1957):193–99.

Maier, R. A. *Human Sexuality in Perspective* (Chicago: Nelson-Hall, 1984).

Maier, R. A., and B. M. Maier. *Comparative Animal Behavior* (Belmont, CA: Brooks/Cole, 1970).

Makinodan, T. "Cellular basis of immunosenescence." In *Molecular and Cellular Mechanisms of Aging* Vol. 27 (Paris: INSERM, Coll. Inst. Nat. Sante Rec. Med., 1974), pp. 153–66.

Manley, Merlin. "How to Cope With a Sense of Failure." In Charles Zastrow and Dae Chang (Eds.), *The Personal Problem Solver* (Englewood Cliffs, NJ: Prentice-Hall, 1977), pp. 35–45.

Mann, James. "Poverty Trap: No Way Out?" *U.S. News & World Report*, August 16, 1982, pp. 31–36.

Mann, J. I., and W. H. Inman. "Oral Contraceptives and Death from Myocardial Infarction." *British Medical Journal* 2 (1975):245–48.

Manosevitz, M., N. M. Prentice, and F. Wilson. "Individual and Family Correlates of Imaginary Companions in Preschool Children." *Developmental Psychology* 8, No. 1 (1973):72–79.

Marcia, J. "Identity in Adolescence." In J. Adelson (Ed.), *Handbook of Adolescent Psychology* (New York: Wiley, 1980).

Marden, Charles F., and Gladys Meyer. *Minorities in American Society* (New York: American Book, 1962).

Marieskind, Helen I. *Women in the Health System* (St. Louis: C. V. Mosby, 1980).

Markides, K., and H. Martin. "A Causal Model of Life Satisfaction among the Elderly." *Journal of Gerontology* 34, No. 1 (1979):86–93.

Markman, H. J. "Prediction of Marital Distress: A 5-Year Follow-Up." *Journal of Consulting and Clinical Psychology* 49 (1981):760–62.

Marsden, D., and D. Owens. "The Jekyll and Hyde Marriage." *New Society* 32 (1975):334.

Marshall, Donald S. "Too Much in Mangaia." In Chad Gordon and Gayle Johnson (Eds.), *Readings in Human Sexuality: Contemporary Perspectives*. 2d ed. (New York: Harper & Row, 1980).

Martin, D. *Battered Wives* (San Francisco: Glide Publications, 1976).

Martin, S. E. "Sexual Harassment: The Link Between Gender Stratification, Sexuality, and Women's Economic Status." In Jo Freeman (Ed.), *Women: A Feminist Perspective* (Palo Alto, CA: Mayfield Publishing, 1984), pp. 54–69.

Marx, Karl. *Selected Writings in Sociology and Social Philosophy*, T. B. Bottomore, trans. (New York: McGraw-Hill, 1964).

Mashek, John W. "Massive Shift to Right: Story of '80 Elections." *U.S. News & World Report*, November 17, 1980, p. 29.

Maslow, A. H. *Motivation and Personality* (New York: Harper and Row, 1954).

––––––. *Toward a Psychology of Being*. 2d ed. (Princeton, N.J.: Van Nostrand, 1968).

––––––. *The Farther Reaches of Human Nature* (New York: Viking, 1971).

Maslow, A. H., and N. L. Mintz. "Effects of Esthetic Surroundings." *Journal of Psychology* 41 (1956):247–54.

Masters, W. H., and V. E. Johnson. *Human Sexual Response* (Boston: Little, Brown, 1966).

––––––. "Human Sexual Response: The Aging Female and the Aging Male." In B. L. Neugarten (Ed.), *Middle Age and Aging: A Reader in Social Psychology* (Chicago: The University of Chicago Press, 1968), pp. 269–79.

––––––. *Human Sexual Inadequacy* (Boston: Little, Brown, 1970).

Masters, W. H., V. E. Johnson, and R. C. Kolodny. *Human Sexuality*. (Boston: Little, Brown, 1979).

––––––. *Human Sexuality*. 2d ed. (Boston: Little, Brown, 1982).

––––––. *Human Sexuality*. 3d ed. (Boston: Little, Brown, 1985).

Maultsby, Maxie C., Jr. *Help Yourself to Happiness* (Boston, MA: Herman Publishing, 1975).

Maypole, D. E., and R. Skaine. "Sexual Harassment in the Workplace." *Social Work* 28, No. 5 (Sept./Oct., 1983): 385–90.

McAdoo, H. P. "The Development of Self-Concept and Race Attitudes in Black Children: A Longitudinal Study." In W. E. Cross, Jr. (Ed.), *Proceedings: The Third Annual Conference on Empirical Research in Black Psychology* (Washington, D.C.: U.S. Department of Health, Education, and Welfare, National Institute of Education, 1977).

McArthur, C. "Personalities of First and Second Children." *Psychiatry* 19 (1956):47–54.

McCary, James L. *Human Sexuality* (Princeton, NJ: Van Nostrand, 1973).

McCrary, J., and L. Gutierrez, "The Homosexual Person in the Military and in National Security Employment." *Journal of Homosexuality* 5, Nos. 1, 2 (1979/80):115–46.

McDermott, J. F. "Divorce and its Psychiatric Sequelae in Children." *Archives of General Psychiatry* 23, No. 5 (1970):421–27.

McDonald, Kim. "Rapid-Growth Genes Could Yield 'Super Livestock.'" *Chronicle of Higher Education*, February 8, 1984.

McGrath, C. "The Crisis of Domestic Order." *Socialist Review*, January/February 1980, pp. 11–30.

McGraw-Hill Book Co. "Guidelines for Equal Treatment of the Sexes" as reported in an article entitled, "Man!" *New York Times Magazine*, October 20, 1974.

McIntyre, J. "Victim Response to Rape: Alternative Outcomes." Final Report to the National Institute of Mental Health, ROIMH 29043, Rockville, MD, 1980.

McKay, J., L. Sinisterra, A. McKay, H. Gomez, and P. Lloreda, "Improving Cognitive Ability in Chronically Deprived Children." *Science* 200 (1978):270–78.

McKenry, P. C., L. H. Walters, and C. Johnson. "Adolescent Pregnancy: A Review of the Literature." *The Family Coordinator*, 23, No. 1 (1979):17–28.

McQuade, Walter, and Ann Aikman, *Stress* (New York: Bantam Books, 1974).

McTavish, D. G. "Perceptions of Old People: A Review of Research Methodologies and Findings." *The Gerontologist* 11 (1971):90–101.

McWhirter, J. J. *The Learning Disabled Child: A School and Family Concern* (Champaign, IL: Research Press, 1977).

Medea, A., and K. Thompson. *Against Rape* (New York: Farrar, Strauss and Giroux, 1974), pp. 4–5.

Meeks, L. B., and P. Heit. *Human Sexuality: Making Responsible Decisions* (Chicago: Saunders College Publishing, 1982).

Mehrabian, Albert. *Public Places and Private Spaces* (New York: Basic Books, 1976).

———— *Silent Messages.* 2d ed. (Belmont, CA: Wadsworth, 1981).

Meisels, A., R. Begin, and V. Schneider. "Dysplasias of Uterine Cervix. Epidemiological Aspects: Role of Age at First Coitus and Use of Oral Contraceptives." *Cancer* 40, No. 6 (1977):3076–81.

Mercer, J. R. "A Policy Statement: On Assessment Procedures and the Rights of Children." *Harvard Educational Review* 44 (February 1974): pp. 17–34.

Merton, Robert. "Discrimination and the American Creed." In Robert M. MacIver (Ed.), *Discrimination and National Welfare* (New York: Harper, 1949).

Metropolitan Life Insurance Company. "Recent Trends in Mortality from Cirrhosis of the Liver." (New York: 1977).

Middlebrook, P. N. *Social Psychology and Modern Life* (New York: Alfred A. Knopf, 1974).

Miles, C. P. "Conditions Predisposing to Suicide: A Review," *Journal of Nervous and Mental Disease* 164 (1977):231–46.

Mills, C. Wright. *The Power Elite* (New York: Oxford University Press, 1956).

Mills, J., and E. Aronson. "Opinion Change as a Function of the Communicator's Attractiveness and Desire to Influence." *Journal of Personality and Social Psychology* 1 (1965):73–77.

Milton, G. A. *Five Studies of the Relation Between Sex Role Identification and Achievement in Problem Solving.* Technical Report No. 3, Dept. of Industrial Administration, Department of Psychology, Yale University, December 1958.

The Milwaukee Journal. "Like Much About AIDS, Origin Is Uncertain." August 18, 1985, p. 7.

————. "Researcher Far from AIDS Care," August 21, 1985, p. 8.

Minahan, N. "Relationships Among Self-Perceived Physical Attractiveness, Body Shape, and Personality of Teen-Age Girls," *Dissertation Abstracts International* 32 (1971):1249–50.

Minuchin, S. *Families and Family Therapy* (Cambridge, MA: Harvard University Press, 1974).

Mischel, W. *Introduction to Personality.* 2d ed. (New York: Holt, Rinehart, & Winston, 1976).

Mizio, Emelicia. "White Worker-Minority Client." *Social Work*, 17 (May 1972):82–86.

Montagu, Ashley. *Man's Most Dangerous Myth: The Fallacy of Race.* 4th ed. (Cleveland, World, 1964).

————. *Touching: The Human Significance of the Skin* (New York: Harper & Row, 1971).

————, Ed. *Race & I.Q.* (London: Oxford University Press, 1975).

Moody, J., and V. Hayes. "Responsible Reporting: The Initial Step." In Warner, C. (Ed.), *Rape and Sexual Assault* (Germantown, MD: Aspen Systems, 1980).

Moore, C. "Cigarette Smoking and Cancer of the Mouth, Pharynx, and Larynx." *Journal of the American Medical Association* 218 (1971):553–58.

————. "Cigarette Smoking and Cancer of the Mouth, Pharynx, and Larynx." *Journal of the American Medical Association* 191 (1965):104–10.

Moore, William, Jr. *The Vertical Ghetto* (New York: Random House, 1969), p. 71.

Moos, R. H. and B. Humphrey. *Family, Work, and Group Environment Scales Manual* (Palo Alto, CA: Consulting Psychologists Press, 1974).

Morin, S. F. "Heterosexual Bias in Psychological Research on Lesbianism and Male Homosexuality." *American Psychologist* 32 (1977):629–37.

Morland, J. "A Comparison of Race Awareness in Northern and Southern Children." *American Journal of Orthopsychiatry* 36 (1966):22–31.

Moore, Joan W. *Mexican Americans.* 2d ed. (Englewood Cliffs, NJ: Prentice-Hall, 1976).

Morris, C. G. *Psychology: An Introduction* (Englewood Cliffs, NJ: Prentice-Hall, 1979).

Morse, Nancy C., and Robert S. Weiss. "The Function and Meaning of Work." *American Sociological Review,* April 1955, pp. 191–98.

Morton, Herbert C. "A Look at Factors Affecting the Quality of Working Life." *Monthly Labor Review,* October 1977, p. 64.

Moses, A. E., and R. O. Hawkins. *Counseling Lesbian Women and Gay Men: A Life-Issues Approach* (St. Louis: C. V. Mosby, 1982).

Moss, Frank. "It's Hell to be Old in the U.S.A." *Parade Magazine* (New York: Parade Publications), July 17, 1977, p. 9.

Moss, Gordon, and Walter Moss, *Growing Old* (New York: Pocket Books, 1975).

Moss, H. A., and Kagan J. "Maternal Influences and Early IQ Scores" *Psychological Reports* 4 (1958):655–61.

Motherner, I. "Teenage Mothers USA." *RF Illustrated,* Rockefeller Foundation 3, No. 3 (May 1977): unpaged.

Muson, H. "Moral Thinking: Can It Be Taught?" *Psychology Today* 12, No. 9 (1979):48–58, 67–68, 92.

Mussen, P. H., and M. C. Jones. "Self Conceptions, Motivations, and Interpersonal Attitudes of Late and Early Maturing Boys." *Child Development* 28 (1957):243–56.

Muuss, R. E. "Adolescent Development and the Secular Trend." *Adolescent* 5 (1970):267–84.

————. "Puberty Rites in Primitive and Modern Societies" *Adolescence.* 5 (1970):109–28.

Myers, Ursula S. "Illegitimacy and Services to Single Parents." In Charles Zastrow (Ed.), *Introduction to Social Welfare Institutions,* 2d ed. (Homewood, Il: 1982), pp. 164–97.

Myrdal, Gunnar. *An American Dilemma* (New York: Harper, 1944).

Nadelson, C. C. et al. "A Follow-Up Study of Rape Victims." *American Journal of Psychiatry* 39 (1982):1266–70.

National Academy of Sciences, *Marijuana and Health* (Washington, D.C.: U.S. Government Printing Office, 1982).

National Association of Social Workers. "Social Casework and Social Group Work: The Behavioral Approach." In *The Encyclopedia of Social Work* 2 (1977):1309–21.

————. "NASW Code of Ethics," as revised by the 1979 Delegate Assembly, National Association of Social Workers, Inc., Washington, D.C.

National Association of Social Work, *Practice Digest,* Spring, 1984.

National Center for Health Statistics: Final Mortality Statistics, 1977." Monthly Vital Statistics Report 27 (Supp.) February 5, 1979, pp. 1–27.

National Center for Social Statistics. *Children Served by Public Welfare Agencies and Voluntary Child Welfare Agencies and Institutions, March 1972* (Washington, D.C.: U.S. Government Printing Office, January 1974).

National Clearinghouse for Drug Abuse Information. *Amphetamine* (Rockville, MD: Alcohol, Drug Abuse, and Mental Health Administration, Report Series 28, No. 1, February 1974).

National Committee for the Day Care of Children, Inc. *Newsletter* 4, No. 5 (Spring 1965).

National Council on Aging, *Fact Book on Aging: a Profile of America's Older Population* (Washington, D.C.: NCOA, 1978).

National Institute on Drug Abuse. *Sedative-Hypnotic Drugs: Risks and Benefits* (Washington, D.C.: U.S. Government Printing Office, 1977).

National Institute on Drug Abuse. *Student Drug Use in America: 1975–1981* (Washington, D.C.: U.S. Government Printing Office, 1982).

Neiding, P. H., and D. H. Friedman. *Spouse Abuse: A Treatment Program for Couples* (Champaign, IL: Research Press, 1984).

Nelson, C. "Victims of Rape: Who Are They?" In Warner, C. (Ed.), *Rape and Sexual Assault* (Germantown, MD: Aspen Systems, 1980), pp. 9–26.

Neugarten, B. *Middle Age and Aging* (Chicago: University of Chicago, 1968).

Neugarten, B., and K. Weinstein. "The Changing American Grandparent." *Journal of Marriage and the Family* 26 (1964): 199–205.

Neugarten, B., V. Wood, R. Kraines, and B. Lommis. "Women's Attitudes Toward the Menopause." *Vita Humana* 6 (1963):140–51.

New York Times. "Women and Power—a Status Report." May 1, 1977, sec. 3, pp. 1, 4.

Newhouse, M. L. et al. "A Case Control Study of Carcinoma of the Ovary," *British Journal of Preventive and Social Medicine* 31, No. 3 September (1979):148–53.

Newman, Barbara M., and Philip R. Newman. *Development Through Life: A Psychosocial Approach* (Homewood, IL: Dorsey Press, 1984).

Newman, G., and C. R. Nichols. "Sexual Activities and Attitudes in Older Persons." In E. B. Palmore (Ed.), *Normal Aging* (Durham, NC.: Duke University Press, 1970).

Newman, L. E. "Treatment for the Parents of Feminine Boys." *American Journal of Psychiatry* 133 (1976):683–87.

Newman, W., and C. Owens. "Race-and Sex-Based Wage Discrimination Is Illegal." In *Comparable Worth: Issue for the 80's*, A Consultation for the U.S. Commission on Civil Rights. (June 6–7, 1984):131–47.

Newton, D. E. "Homosexual Behavior and Child Molestation: A Review of the Evidence." *Adolescence* 13 (1978):29–43.

Newton, Esther. *Mothercamp: Female Impersonators in America* (New Jersey: Prentice-Hall, 1972).

Nixon, Richard. Quoted in Ian Robertson. *Social Problems*. 2d ed. (New York: Random House, 1980), p. 87.

Noble, Ernest P. *Alcohol and Health: Third Special Report to the United States Congress* (Rockville, MD: U.S. Public Health Service, June 1978).

Norman, E., and A. Mancuso. *Women's Issues and Social Work Practice* (Itasca, Il: F. E. Peacock, 1980).

Norton, Dolores G. "Environment and Cognitive Development: A Comparative Study of Socioeconomic Status and Race." Bryn Mawr: Doctoral Dissertation: Graduate School of Social Work and Social Research, Bryn Mawr College, 1969.

———. "Incorporating Content on Minority Groups into Social Work Practice Courses." In *The Dual Perspective* (New York: Council on Social Work Education, 1978).

———. "Black Family Life Patterns, the Development of Self and Cognitive Development of Black Children." In Gloria J. Powell (Ed.), *The Psychosocial Development of Minority Group Children* (New York: Brunner/Mazel, 1983) pp. 181–93.

Novak, E. R., G. S. Jones, and H. W. Jones. *Novak's Textbook of Gynecology*, 9th ed. (Baltimore: Williams & Wilkins, 1975).

Nyberg, K. L., and J. S. Alston. "Analysis of Public Attitudes Toward Homosexual Behavior." *Journal of Homosexuality* 2 (1976/77):99–107.

Nye, F. I. "Child Adjustment in Broken and Unhappy Unbroken Homes." *Marriage and Family Living* 19 (1957):356–61.

O'Brien, F., N. H. Azrin, and C. Bugle. "Training Profoundly Retarded Children to Stop Crawling." *Journal of Applied Behavior Analysis* 5 (1974):131–37.

Offer, Daniel, and Melvin Sabshin. *Normality: Theoretical and Clinical Concepts in Mental Health* (New York: Basic Books, 1966).

Offir, C. W. *Human Sexuality* (New York: Harcourt Brace Jovanovich, 1982).

Ogburn, W. F., and M. F. Nimkoff. *Technology and the Changing Family* (New York: Houghton Mifflin, 1955).

Olds, S. W. "Menopause: Something To Look Forward To?" *Today's Health*, May 1970, p. 48.

O'Leary, K. D., and G. T. Wilson. *Behavior Therapy: Application and Outcome* (Englewood Cliffs, NJ: Prentice-Hall, 1975).

O'Neill, George, and Nena O'Neill. *Open Marriage* (New York: M. Evans, 1971).

Orbach, Susie. *Fat Is a Feminist Issue* (New York: Paddington Press, 1978).

Orlofsky, J., J. Marcia, and I. Lesser. "Ego Identity Status and the Intimacy Versus Isolation Crisis of Young Adulthood." *Journal of Personality and Social Psychology* 27, No. 2 (1973):211–19.

Osofsky, J. D. et al. "Psychologic Effects of Legal Abortion," *Clinical Obstetrics and Gynecology* 14, No. 1 (1971):215–34.

Osofsky, J. D., and H. J. Osofsky. "The Psychological Reactions of Patients to Legalized Abortions." *American Journal of Orthopsychiatry* 42 (1972):48–60.

Otten, Alan S. "Ever More Americans Live Into 80s and 90s, Causing Big Problems." *The Wall Street Journal*, July 30, 1984, pp. 1, 10.

Otto, W. "Family Position and Success in Reading." *Reading Teacher*, November 1965.

Ouellette, E. et al. "Adverse Effects on Offspring of Maternal Alcohol Abuse During Pregnancy." *New England Journal of Medicine* 297 (1977):528–30.

Padilla, E. R., and G. E. Wyatt. "The Effects of Intelligence and Achievement Testing on Minority Group Children." In G. J. Powell (Ed.), *The Psychosocial Development of Minority Group Children* (New York: Brunner/Mazel, 1983), pp. 417–37.

Pagelow, M. "Heterosexual and Lesbian Single Mothers: A Comparison of Problems, Coping, and Solutions." *Journal of Homosexuality* 5, No. 3, (1980):189–204.

Palen, J. John *Social Problems* (New York: McGraw-Hill, 1979), p. 544.

Paley, D. "Nursing Home Is Cited Again." *Wisconsin State Journal*, May 23, 1980, Section 4, p. 1.

———. "Cocaine Becoming 'Acceptable.' " *Wisconsin State Journal*, December 13, 1982, Section 1, p. 1.

Papalia, Diane E., and Sally Wendkos Olds, *Human Development*. 2d ed. (New York: McGraw-Hill, 1981).

Parke, R. S. "Some Effects of Punishment on Children's Behavior-Revisited." In E. M. Hetherington and R. D. Parke (Eds.), *Child Psychology: A Contemporary Viewpoint* (New York: McGraw-Hill, 1977), pp. 208–20.

Parnell, R. W. *Behavior and Physique: An Introduction to Practical and Applied Somatometry* (London: Edward Arnold, 1958).

Parten, M. "Social Play Among Preschool Children." *Journal of Abnormal and Social Psychology* 27, (1932):243–69.

Patel, N. S. "Attempted and Completed Suicide." *Medical Science Law* 14, (1974):273–79.

Patterson, G. R. *Families: Applications of Social Learning to Family Life* (Champaign, IL: Research Press, 1975).

Patterson, G. R., and J. B. Reid. "Reciprocity and Coercion: Two Facets of Social Systems." In C. Neuringer and J. L. Michael (Eds.) *Behavior Modification in Clinical Psychology* (New York: Appleton-Century-Crofts, 1970), pp. 133–77.

Patterson, William M. et al. "Evaluation of Suicidal Patients, The Sad Persons Scale." *Psychosomatics* 24, No. 4, (April 1983):343–49.

Pauker, J. D. "Fathers of Children Conceived Out of Wedlock: Prepregnancy, High School, Psychological Test Results." *Developmental Psychology* 4, No. 2, (1971):215–18.

Peck, R. C. "Psychological Development in the Second Half of Life." In B. L. Neugarten (Ed.), *Middle Age and Aging* (Chicago: University of Chicago Press, 1968).

Pelletier, Kenneth R. *Mind as Healer, Mind as Slayer* (New York: Dell Publishing, 1977).

Pendergrass, V. E. "Timeout from Positive Reinforcement Following Persistent High-Rate Behavior in Retardates." *Journal of Applied Behavior Analysis* 5, (1972):85–91.

Peplau, L. A. "What Homosexuals Want in Relationships." *Psychology Today* 15, No. 3, (March, 1981):28–38.

Pepper, C. "Will There Be a Brighter Tomorrow for the Nation's Elderly?" *USA Today* 108, No. 2420, (1980):14–16.

Perez, J. F. *Family Counseling: Theory and Practice* (New York: D. Van Nostrand Co. 1979).

Perloff, W. H. "Hormones and Homosexuality." In J. Marmor (Ed.), *Sexual Inversion: The Multiple Roots of Homosexuality* (New York: Basic Books, 1965).

Peters, H. "The Legal Rights of Gays." In A. E. Moses and R. O. Hawkins (Eds.), *Counseling Lesbian Women and Gay Men: A Life Issues Approach* (St. Louis: C. V. Mosby, 1982), pp. 21–26.

Peters, R. *Mammalian Communicaton: A Behavioral Analysis of Meaning* (Monterey, CA: Brooks/Cole, 1980).

Pfeiffer, E. *Successful Aging* (Durham, N. C.: Duke University Center for the Study of Aging and Human Development, 1974).

Phillips, D. L. "Rejection: A Possible Consequence of Seeking Help for Mental Disorder." *American Sociological Review*, 1963, 28, pp, 963–73.

Piaget, J. *The Origins of Intelligence in Children* (New York: International Universities Press, 1952).

Piaget, J. "Intellectual Development from Adolescence to Adulthood." *Human Development* 15, (1972):1–12.

Pierce, Ponchitta. "Male Change of Life." *Ebony* 30, (1976):122–28.

Pincus, A., and A. Minahan. *Social Work Practice: Model and Method* (Itasca, IL: F. E. Peacock, 1973).

Pines, A., and E. Aronson. *Burnout: From Tedium to Personal Growth* (New York: Free Press, 1981).

Pinkney, Alphonso. *The American Way of Violence* (New York: Random House, 1972).

Planned Parenthood Association of Wisconsin, Inc. "Facts About Oral Contraception," undated handout.

Plateris, Alexander A. *Increases in Divorces: United States—1967* (Washington, D.C.: U.S. Government Printing Office, 1967).

Porter, Judith. *Black Child, White Child: The Development of Racial Attitudes* (Cambridge, MA: Harvard University Press, 1971).

Powerdermaker, Hortense. *Life in Lesu* (New York: Norton, 1933), pp. 276–77.

Powell, Gloria J. "Coping With Adversity: The Psychosocial Development of Afro-American Children." In Gloria J. Powell (Ed.), *The Psychosocial Development of Minority Group Children* (New York: Brunner/Mazel, 1983).

Power, C., and J. Reimer. "Moral Atmosphere: An Educational Bridge Between Moral Judgment and Action." *New Directions in Child Development* 2, (1978).

Prather, H. *Notes to Myself* (Moab, Utah: Real People Press, 1970).

Price-Bonham, S., and P. Skeen. "A Comparison of Black and White Fathers With Implications for Parent Education." *The Family Coordinator* 28, (1979):53–59.

Prochaska, James O. *Systems of Psychotherapy* (Homewood, IL: Dorsey Press, 1979).

Rabushk, A., and B. Jacobs. "Are Old Folks Really Poor? Herewith a Look at Some Common Views." *The New York Times*, February 15, 1980, p. A29.

Rachal, J. V. et al. *A National Study of Adolescent Drinking Behavior, Attitudes, and Correlates* (Research Triangle Park, NC: Research Triangle Institute Project No. 23U–891, 1975).

Raeburn, Paul. "Alzheimer's: Disease of the Aged." *Wisconsin State Journal*, March 5, 1984, Section 2, p. 1.

Ramsay, O. A., and E. H. Hess. "A Laboratory Approach to the Study of Imprinting." *Wilson Bulletin* 66, (1954):196–206.

Reevy, William R. "Child Sexuality." In A. Ellis and A. Abarbanel (Eds.), *The Encyclopedia of Sexual Behavior* (New York: Hawthorn, 1967).

Reilly, Philip. *Genetics, Law and Social Policy* (Cambridge, MA: Harvard University Press, 1977).

Reitz, Rosetta. *Menopause: A Positive Approach* (Radnor, PA: Chitton Book Company, 1977).

Remick, Helen. "Dilemmas of Implementation: The Case of Nursing." In Helen Remick (Ed.), *Comparable Worth and Wage Discrimination* (Philadelphia: Temple University Press, 1984).

Resnick, H. L. P. "Suicide." In H. I. Kaplan, A. M. Freedman, and B. J. Sadock (Eds.), *Comprehensive Textbook of Psychiatry*. 3d ed. (Baltimore: Williams & Wilkins, 1980), pp. 2085–98.

Resnick, M. *Wife Beating Counselor Training Manual No. 1* (Ann Arbor, MI: 1977 AA NOW/WIFE Assault, 1976).

Rest, J. R. "The Hierarchical Nature of Moral Judgment: The Study of Patterns of Comprehension and Preference with Moral Stages" *Journal of Personality* 41, No. 1, (1974):92–93.

Rheingold, H. L., and K. V. Cook. "The Contents of Boys' and Girls' Rooms as an Index of Parents' Behavior." *Child Development* 46, (1975):459–63.

Rice, F. P. *The Adol.: Development Relationships and Culture*, 2d ed. (Boston: Allyn & Bacon, 1978).

Richmond, Mary. *Social Diagnosis* (New York: Free Press, 1917).

Riegel, K. F., and R. M. Riegel. "Development, Drop, and Death." *Developmental Psychology* 6, No. 2, (1972):306–19.

Rifken, L. "Who Should Play God?" (New York: Dell Publishing, 1977).

Rinehart, W., and Piotrow, P. T. "OCs: Update on Usage, Safety, and Side Effects." *Population Reports*, Series A (5), January 1979.

Ringer, Robert. *Looking Out for #1* (New York: Fawcett Crest, 1977).

Rioux, J. W. "The Disadvantaged Child in School." In J. Helmuth (Ed.), *The Disadvantaged Child* (New York, Brunner/Mazel, 1968).

Risley, T. R. "The Effects and Side Effects of Punishing the Autistic Behavior of a Deviant Child." *Journal of Applied Behavior Analysis* 1, (1968):21–34.

Road Traffic Board of South Australia. *The Points Demerit Scheme as an Indication of Declining Skill with Age*, 1972.

Roberts, Elizabeth J., and Steven A. Holt. "Parent-Child Communication About Sexuality." SIE-CUS Report 8, No. 4 (March 1980):1–2, 10.

Robertson, Ian. *Social Problems*. 2d ed. (New York: Random House, 1980).

Robinson, D. "Our Surprising Moral Unwed Fathers." *Ladies Home Journal*, August 1969, pp. 49–50.

Roche, A. F., and G. H. Davila. "Late Adolescent Growth in Stature." *Pediatrics* 50, No. 6, (1972):874–80.

Rockstein, M. "The Biology of Aging in Humans: An Overview." In R. Goldman and M. Rockstein (Eds.), *The Physiology and Pathology of Human Aging* (New York: Academic Press, 1975).

Rogers, C. R. "A Theory of Therapy, Personality and Interpersonal Relationships, as Developed in the Client-Centered Framework." In S. Koch (Ed.), *Psychology: A Study of a Science*. Vol. 3 (New York: McGraw-Hill, 1959), pp. 184–256.

Rohn, R., R. Sarles, T. Kenny, B. Reymonds, and F. Heald. "Adolescents Who Attempt Suicide." *Journal of Pediatrics* 90, No. 4, (1977):636–38.

Rollin, B. "Motherhood: Who Needs It?" *Look*, September 22, 1970, pp. 15–17.

Rollins, B., and R. Galligan. "The Developing Child and Marital Satisfaction of Parents." In R. Lerner and G. Spanier (Eds.), *Child Influences on Marital and Family Interaction: A Life-Span Perspective* (New York: Academic Press, 1978), pp. 71–105.

Romero, E. R., and V. Bernal del Rio. "Mental Health Needs and Puerto Rican Children." In G. J. Powell (Ed.), *The Psychosocial Development of Minority Group Children* (New York: Brunner/Mazel, 1983), pp. 330–43.

Roosevelt, Franklin D. Second inaugural address, January 20, 1937.

Rorvik, David M. "Making Men and Women Without Men and Women." *Esquire Magazine*, April 1969, pp. 110–15.

Rose, Arnold. *The Negro in America* (New York: Harper & Row, 1964).

Rose, S. R. *Treating Children in Groups* (San Francisco: Jossey-Bass, 1973).

Rosen, D. H. *Lesbianism: A Study of Female Homosexuality* (Springfield, IL: Charles C Thomas, 1974).

Rosen, J., and A. Wiens. "Changes in Medical Problems and Use of Medical Services Following Psychological Intervention." *American Psychologist* 34, (1979):420–31.

Rosenberg, L. et al. "Oral Contraceptive Use in Relation to Nonfatal Myocardial Infarction." *American Journal of Epidemiology* 111, (1980):59–66.

Rosenberg, S. D., and M. P. Farrell. "Identity and Crisis in Middle-Aged Men." *International Journal of Aging and Human Development* 7, (1976):153–70.

Rosenhan, D. L. "On Being Sane in Insane Places." *Science* 179, (1973):250–57.

Rosenmayr, L. "Achievements, Doubts and Prospects of the Sociology of Aging." *Human Development* 23, (1980):46–62.

Rosenthal, Robert, and Lenore Jacobson. *Pygmalion in the Classroom* (New York: Holt, Rinehart & Winston, 1968).

Rossman, J. "Anatomic and Body Composition Changes with Aging." In C. E. Finch and L. Hayflicks (Eds.), *Handbook of the Biology of Aging* (New York: Van Nostrand Reinhold, 1977).

Rothman, Sheila M. *Woman's Proper Place* (New York: Basic Books, 1978).

Rovee, C. K., R. Y. Cohen, and W. Shlapack. "Life Span Stability in Olfactory Sensitivity." *Developmental Psychology* 11, (1975):311–18.

Rowland, K. "Environmental Events Predicting Death for the Elderly." *Psychological Bulletin* 84, (1977):349–72.

Roy, Maria (Ed.). *The Abusive Partner: An Analysis of Domestic Battering* (New York: Van Nostrand Reinhold, 1982).

Rubin, G. L. "Ectopic Pregnancy in the United States: 1970 Through 1978." *Journal of the American Medical Association* 249, (1983):1725–29.

Rubin, K., T. Maioni, and M. Hornung. "Free Play Behaviors in Middle-Class and Lower-Class Preschoolers: Parten and Piaget Revisited." *Child Development* 47, (1976):414–19.

Rubin, K., and K. Trotten. "Kohlberg's Moral Judgment Scale: Some Methodological Considerations." *Developmental Psychology* 13, No. 5, (1977):535–36.

Rubin, L. B. *Women of a Certain Age: The Midlife Search for Self* (New York: Harper & Row, 1979).

Rubin, Z. *Liking and Loving* (New York: Holt, Rinehart & Winston, 1973).

Russell, C. "Transition to Parenthood: Problems and Gratifications." *Journal of Marriage and the Family* 36, (1974):294–302.

Russell, M. A. H. "Cigarette Smoking: Natural History of a Dependence Disorder." *British Journal of Medical Psychology* 44 (March 1971).

Rutter, M. "Separation Experiences: A New Look at an Old Topic." *Pediatrics* 95, No. 1, (1979):147–54.

Ryan, William. *Blaming the Victim* Rev. Ed. (New York: Vintage, 1976).

Safran, Claire. "What Men Do to Women on the Job: A Shocking Look at Sexual Harassment." *Redbook,* (November 1976).

Sagarin, E. "Language of the Homosexual Subculture." *Medical Aspects of Human Sexuality* 4 (1970).

Sager, Clifford J., Thomas L. Brayboy, and Barbara R. Waxenberg. *Black Ghetto Family in Therapy: A Laboratory Experience* (New York: Grove Press, 1970).

Saghir, M. T., and E. Robins. *Male and Female Homosexuality* (Baltimore: Williams & Wilkins, 1973).

Saltz, E., D. Dixon, and J. Johnson. "Training Disadvantaged Preschoolers on Various Fantasy Activities: Effects on Cognitive Functioning and Impulse Control." *Child Development* 48, (1977):367–80.

Samuelson, Paul. Quoted in P. Blumberg. *Inequality in an Age of Decline* (New York: Oxford University Press, 1980).

Sarri, Rosemary C. "Adolescent Status Offenders—A National Problem." In Alfred Kadushin (Ed.), *Child Welfare Strategy in the Coming Years* (U.S. Department of Health, Education and Welfare, Publication No. (OHDS) 78-30158, 1978).

Sawin, D. B., and R. D. Parke. "Adolescent Fathers: Some Implications from Recent Research on Parental Roles." *Educational Horizons* 55, (1976):38–43.

Scales, P. "Males and Morals: Teenage Contraceptive Behavior Amid the Double Standard." *The Family Coordinator* 26, (1977):211–22.

Scanlon, J. *Young Adulthood* (New York: Academy for Educational Development, 1979).

Scanzoni, J., and G. L. Fox, "Sex Roles, Family and Society: The Seventies and Beyond." *Journal of Marriage and the Family* 42, (1980):743–58.

Schachter, S. "Birth Order, Eminence and Higher Education." *American Sociological Review* 28, (1963):764–67.

Schack, Steven, and Robert S. Frank. "Police Service Delivery to the Elderly." *The Annals of the American Academy of Political and Social Science* 438, (July 1978):83.

Schaefer, C. E. "Imaginary Companions and Creative Adolescents." *Developmental Psychology* 1, (1969):747–49.

Schafer, S. "Sociosexual Behavior in Male and Female Homosexuals: A Study in Sex Differences." *Archives of Sexual Behavior* 6, (1977):355–64.

Schafer, Walt, *Stress, Distress and Growth* (David, CA: International Dialogue Press, 1978).

Schanche, D. "What Really Happens Emotionally and Physically When a Man Reaches 40?" *Today's Health,* March 1973, pp. 40–43, 60.

Schatten, G., and H. Schatten. "The Energetic Egg." *The Sciences* 23, No. 5, (1983):28–34.

Scheck, D. C., R. Emerick, and M. M. El-Assal. "Adolescents' Perceptions of Parent-Child Relations and the Development of Internal-External Control Operation." *Journal of Marriage and the Family* 35, (1973):643–54.

Scheff, Thomas. *Being Mentally Ill* (Hawthorne, NY: Aldine Publishing, 1966).

Scheflen, Albert. *How Behavior Means* (Garden City, NY: Anchor Books, 1974).

Scherz, F. H. "Theory and Practice of Family Therapy." In R. W. Roberts and R. H. Nee (Eds.), *Theories of Social Casework* (Chicago: University of Chicago Press, 1970), pp. 219–64.

Schlesinger, B. "One-Parent Families in Great Britain." *Family Coordinator* 26, (1977):139–41.

Schmidt, G. W., and R. Ulrich. "Effects of Group Contingent Events Upon Classroom Noise." *Journal of Applied Behavior Analysis* 2, (1969):171–79.

Schneck, H. M., Jr. "Trend in Growth of Children and Lags." *The New York Times*, June 10, 1976, p. 13.

Schneider, Jean et al. "Some Factors for Analysis in Sexual Assault." *Social Science and Medicine* 15A, No. 1, (January 1981):55–61.

Schuller, Robert. *Move Ahead with Possibility Thinking* (Moonachie, NJ: Pyramid Publications, 1973).

Schultz, T. "Does Marriage Give Today's Women What They Want?" *Ladies Home Journal*, June 1980, pp. 89–91, 146–155.

Schutte, R. C., and B. L. Hopkins. "The Effects of Teacher Attention on Following Instructions in a Kindergarten Class." *Journal of Applied Behavior Analysis* 3, (1970):117–22.

Schwab, D. P. "Using Job Evaluation to Obtain Pay Equity." In *Comparable Worth: Issue for the 80's, A Consultation for the U.S. Commission on Civil Rights.* Vol. 1, June 6–7, 1984, pp. 83–92.

Schwartz, A., and I. Goldiamond. *Social Casework: A Behavioral Approach* (New York: Columbia University Press, 1975).

Schwartz, G. E. "Biofeedback, Self Regulation, and the Patterning of Physiological Processes." *American Scientist* 63, (1975):314–24.

Sears, R. R. "Ordinal Position in the Family as a Psychological Variable." *American Sociological Review* 15, (1950):397–401.

————. "Sources of Life Satisfaction of the Terman Gifted Men." *American Psychologist* 32, (1977):119–28.

Seelbach, W. C., and C. J.Hansen. "Satisfaction with Family Relationships Among the Elderly." *Family Relations* 29, No. 1, (1980):91–96.

Selkin, J. "Rape." *Psychology Today* 8, No. 8, (1975), p. 70.

Selye, Hans. *The Stress of Life* (New York: McGraw-Hill, 1956).

————. *Stress Without Distress* (New York: Signet, 1974).

Settlage, D. S. F., et al. "Sexual Experience of Younger Teenage Girls Seeking Contraceptive Assistance for the First Time." *Family Planning Perspectives* 5, (July/Aug., 1973):223–26.

Sexual Assault Treatment Center of Greater Milwaukee. "If You Are Attacked." (Milwaukee, WI: handout, 1979).

Shah, F., M. Zelnik, and J. Kantner, "Unprotected Intercourse Among Unwed Teenagers." *Family Planning Perspectives* 7, No. 1, (1975):39–44.

Shane, J. M., I. Schiff, and E. A. Wilson. "The Infertile Couple: Evaluation and Treatment." *Clinical Symposia* 28, No. 5, (1976).

Sheldon, W. H. (with the collaboration of S. S. Stevens). *The Varieties of Temperament: A Psychology of Constitutional Differences* (New York: Harper & Row, 1942).

Sherman, J. A. *On the Psychology of Women: A Survey of Empirical Studies* (Springfield, IL: Charles C Thomas, 1971).

Shock, N. W. "Biological Theories of Aging." In J. E. Birren and K. W. Schaie (Eds.) *Handbook of the Psychology of Aging* (New York: Van Nostrand Reinhold Co., 1977), pp. 103–12.

Shostak, A., G. McLouth, and L. Seng, *Men and Abortions: Lessons, Losses, and Love* (New York: Praeger, 1984).

Shulman, L. *Identifying, Measuring, and Teaching Helping Skills* (New York: Council on Social Work Education, 1981).

Siegel, Ronald K. "Accounting for 'Afterlife' Experiences." *Psychology Today*, January 1981:66–69.

Silverman, Dierdre. "Sexual Harassment: Working Women's Dilemma." *Quest: A Feminist Quarterly* Winter 1976-77, p. 3.

Simonton, O. Carl, and Stephanie Matthews-Simonton, *Getting Well Again* (Los Angeles: J. P. Tarcher, 1978).

Simpson, George E., and J. Milton Yinger. *Racial and Cultural Minorities.* 3d ed. (New York: Harper & Row, 1965).

Sinclair, Esther. "Important Issues in the Language Development of the Black Child." In G. J. Powell (Ed.), *The Psychosocial Development of Minority Group Children* (New York: Brunner/Mazel, 1983), pp. 490–98.

Sindler, Allan P. *Bakke, DeFunis and Minority Admissions: The Quest for Equal Opportunity* (New York: Longmans, Green, 1978).

Singer, J. E. "The Use of Manipulative Strategies: Machiavellianism and Attractiveness." *Sociometry* 27, (1964):128–51.

Siporin, Max. *Introduction to Social Work Practice* (New York: Macmillan, 1975).

Skidmore, Rex A., and Milton Thackeray, *Introduction to Social Work*. 2d ed. (Englewood Cliffs, NJ: Prentice-Hall, 1976).

Skinner, B. F. *Science and Human Behavior* (New York: Free Press, 1953).

Slobin, D. I., S. H. Miller, and L. W. Porter. "Forms of Address and Social Relations in a Business Organization." *Journal of Personality and Social Psychology* 8, (1968):289–93.

Slovenko, R. *Sexual Behavior and the Law* (Springfield, IL: Charles C Thomas, 1965).

Slovenko, R. "Homosexuality and the Law: From Condemnation to Celebration." In Marmor, J. (Ed.), *Homosexual Behavior* (New York: Basic Books, 1980), pp. 194–218.

Smart, R. G., and Blair, N. L. "Drug Use and Drug Problems Among Teenagers in a Household Sample." *Drug and Alcohol Dependence* 5, (1980):171–79.

Snyder, D. "Multidimensional Assessment of Marital Satisfaction." *Journal of Marriage and the Family* 41, (1979):813–23.

Soldo, Beth J. *America's Elderly in the 1980s* (Washington, D.C.: Population Reference Bureau, 1980).

Solender, E. K., and E. Solender. "Minimizing the Effect of the Unattractive Client on the Jury: A Study of the Interaction of Physical Appearance with Assertions and Self-Experience References." *Human Rights* 5, 1976, pp. 201–14.

Solomon, Barbara Bryant. "Social Work with Afro-Americans." In Armando Morales and Bradford W. Sheafor (Eds.), *Social Work: A Profession of Many Faces*. 3d ed. (Boston: Allyn Bacon, 1983), pp. 414–36.

Sommer, Robert. *Personal Space: The Behavioral Basis of Design* (Englewood Cliffs, NJ: Prentice-Hall, 1969).

Sorensen, R. C. *Adolescent Sexuality in Contemporary America* (New York: World, 1973).

Speroff, L., R. H. Glass, and N. G. Kase, *Clinical Gynecologic Endocrinology and Infertility* (Baltimore: Williams & Wilkins, 1973).

Spitz, Rene. "Hospitalization: Genesis of Psychiatric Conditions in Early Childhood." *Psychoanalytic Study of the Child*, 1945, p. 53.

Sprey, J. "Extramarital Relationships," *Sexual Behavior* 2, (1972):34–40.

Stack, C. *All Our Kin: Strategies for Survival in a Black Community* (New York: Harper & Row, 1974).

Stark, R., and J. McEvoy. "Middle Class Violence." *Psychology Today* 4, (1970):54–56, 110–112.

Starka, L. et al. "Plasma Testosterone in Male Transsexuals and Homosexuals." *Journal of Sex Research* 11, (1975):134–38.

Stein, P. J. "Being Single: Bucking the Cultural Imperative." Paper presented at the 71st annual meeting of the American Sociological Association, September 3, 1976.

Steinberg, R. J. "Identifying Wage Discrimination and Implementing Pay Equity Adjustments." In *Comparable Worth: Issue for the 80's, A Consultation for the U.S. Commission on Civil Rights*, Vol. 1, June 6–7, 1984, pp. 99–116.

Stennett, N., L. Carter and J. Montgomery. "Older Persons' Perceptions of Their Marriages." *Journal of Marriage and the Family* 34, (1972):665–70.

Stinnet, N., and J. Walters. *Relationships in Marriage and Family* (New York: Macmillan, 1977).

Stockard, J., and M. M. Johnson. *Sex Roles* (Englewood Cliffs, NJ: Prentice-Hall, 1980).

Stoltz, H. R., and L. M. Stoltz. "Adolescent Problems Related to Somatic Variation." In N. B. Henry (Ed.), *Adolescence: 43rd Yearbook of the National Committee for the Study of Education* (Chicago: Department of Education, University of Chicago, 1944).

Stone, W. Clement. "Be Generous." In Og Mandino (Ed.), *A Treasury of Success Unlimited* (New York: Hawthorn Books, 1966).

Storms, M. D. "Theories of Sexual Orientation," *Journal of Personality and Social Psychology* 38, (1980):783–92.

Stout, H. R. *Our Family Physician* (Peoria: Henderson and Smith, 1885):333–34.

Straus, M. A. *Behind Closed Doors: Violence in the American Family* (New York: Doubleday, 1980).

Straus, Murray. "Leveling, Civility and Violence in the Family." *Journal of Marriage and the Family* 36, (1974):13–29.

————. "Wife Beating! How Common and Why?" *Victimology* 2, No. 3–4, (Fall-Winter 1977):443–58.

Straus, Murray, Richard Gelles, and Suzanne Steinmetz. *Behind Closed Doors: A Survey of Family Violence in America* (Garden City: Doubleday, 1977).

Strong, B. et al. *The Marriage and Family Experience* (New York: West, 1983).

Strong, Bryan, and Rebecca Reynolds. *Understanding Our Sexuality* (New York: West Publishing, 1982).

Stuart, Richard B. *Trick or Treatment* (Champaign, IL: Research Press, 1970).

Stubblefield, H. "Contributions of Continuing Education." *Vocational Guidance Quarterly* 25, (1977):351–55.

Sugar, M. "Children of Divorce." *Pediatrics* 46, No. 4, (1970):588–95.

Sullivan, Thomas J. et al. *Social Problems* (New York: John Wiley, 1980).

Super, C. M. "Cognitive Development: Looking Across at Growing Up." In C. M. Super and S. Harkness (Eds.), *New Directions for Child Development*, No. 8: Anthropological Perspectives on Child Development (San Francisco: Jossey-Bass, 1980).

Sutton-Smith, B., and B. G. Rosenberg. *The Sibling* (New York: Holt, Rinehart & Winston, 1970).

Szasz, Thomas S. *The Myth of Mental Illness* (New York: Hoeber-Harper, 1961).

_____. "The Myth of Mental Illness." In *Clinical Psychology in Transition,* compiled by John R. Braun (Cleveland: Howard Allen, 1961).

_____. *Law, Liberty and Psychiatry* (New York: Macmillan, 1963).

Szymanski, Albert. "Racial Discrimination and White Gain." *American Sociological Review* 41, (June 1976):403–14.

Taber, Merlin. "The Aged." In Donald Brieland et al. *Contemporary Social Work* (New York: McGraw-Hill, 1975).

Tanner, J. M. "The Adolescent Growth-Spurt & Developmental Age." In G. A. Harrison, J. S. Werner, J. M. Tannert, and N. A. Barnicot (Eds.), *Human Balance: An Introduction to Human Evolution, Variation, and Growth* (Oxford: Clarendon Press, 1964), pp. 321–39.

_____. "Puberty." In A. McLaren (Ed.), *Advances in Reproductive Physiology,* Vol. 11 (New York: Academic Press, 1967).

_____. "Earlier Maturation in Man." *Scientific American,* 218, (1968):21–27.

_____. "Physical Growth." In P. H. Mussen (Ed.), *Carmichael's Manual of Child Psychology,* Vol. 1, (3rd. ed.), (New York: Wiley, 1970).

_____. "Sequence, Tempo, and Individual Variation in the Growth & Development of Boys & Girls Aged Twelve to Sixteen," *Daedelus,* 100, (1971):907–30.

_____. *Fetus into Man: Physical Growth from Conception to Maturity* (Cambridge, MA: Harvard, 1978).

Tate, B. G., and G. S. Baroff. "Adversive Control of Self Injurious Behavior in a Psychotic Boy." *Behavior Research and Therapy* 4, (1966):281–87.

Tavris, C. "Masculinity." *Psychology Today* 10, No. 8, (1977):34.

Tavris, C., and S. Sadd. *The Redbook Report on Female Sexuality* (New York: Delacorte Press, 1977).

Taylor, R. L. "Psychosocial Development Among Black Children and Youth: A Reexamination." *American Journal of Orthopsychiatry* 46, (1976):4–19.

Terman, Lewis Madison. *Stanford–Binet Intelligence Scale.* Manual for the third revision form L-M by L. M. Terman and M. A. Merrill (Boston: Houghton Mifflin, 1960).

Thomas, E. J. "Behavioral Modification and Casework." In R. W. Roberts, and R. H. Nee (Eds.) *Theories of Social Casework* (Chicago: University of Chicago Press, 1970).

Thorndike, E. L. *The Fundamentals of Learning* (New York: Teachers College, 1932).

Thurstone, L. L. "Primary Mental Abilities" *Psychometric Monographs* 1, 1938.

Timiras, P. S. *Developmental Physiology and Aging* (New York: Macmillan, 1972).

Timiras, P. S., and A. Vernadakis. "Structural, Biochemical, and Functional Aging of the Nervous System." In P. S. Timiras (Ed.), *Developmental Physiology and Aging* (New York: Macmillan, 1972).

Tobias, S. Chapter 3, "Mathematics and Sex." In *Overcoming Math Anxiety* (New York: W. W. Norton, 1978).

Toffler, Alvin. *Future Shock* (New York: Bantam Books, 1970).

Tomeh, A. K. "Birth Order and Friendship Associations." *Journal of Marriage and the Family* 32, (1970):361–62.

Tourney, G. "Hormones and Homosexuality." In J. Marmor (Ed.), *Homosexual Behavior* (New York: Basic Books, 1980), pp. 41–58.

Townsend, Claire. *Old Age: The Last Segregation* (New York: Grossman, 1971).

Trafford, Abigail. "The Tragedy of Care for America's Elderly." *U.S. News & World Report,* April 24, 1978, p. 56.

Trager, G. L. "Paralanguage: A First Approximation." *Studies in Linguistics* 13, (1958):1–12.

Troll, L. *Early and Middle Adulthood* (Belmont, CA: Wadsworth, 1975).

Trussell, James, and Charles F. Westoff. "Contraceptive Practice and Trends in Coital Frequency." *Family Planning Perspectives* 12, No. 5, (1980):246–49.

Tubesing, Donald A. *Kicking Your Stress Habits* (Duluth, MN: Whole Person Associates, 1981).

Turnbull, Colin M. *The Mountain People* (New York: Simon & Schuster, 1972).

Tyler, V. O., and G. D. Brown. "The Use of Swift, Brief Isolation as a Group Control Device for Institutionalized Delinquents." *Behavior Research and Therapy* 5, (1967):1–9.

U.S. Bureau of the Census. "Money Income in 1976 of Families and Persons in the United States." *Current Population Reports,* Series P-60, No. 114 (Washington, D.C.: U.S. Government Printing Office, 1978).

_____. "Money Income and Poverty Status of Families and Persons in the United States: 1977." *Current Population Reports* Advanced Report, Series P-60, No. 16 (Washington, D.C.: U.S. Government Printing Office, 1978).

_____. *Current Population Reports, Series P-20, No. 349, December 1980.*

————. *Statistical Abstract of the United States, 1979* (Washington, D.C.: U.S. Government Printing Office, 1980).

————. *Statistical Abstract of the United States, 1980* (Washington, D.C.: U.S. Government Printing Office, 1981), pp. 418–20.

————. *Money Income and Poverty Status of Families and Persons in the United States:* 1981 Advance Report Current Population Report Series, P-60, No. 134 (Washington, D.C.: U.S. Government Printing Office, July 1982), pp. 13–14.

————. *Statistical Abstract of the United States: 1982–83* (Washington, D.C.: U.S. Government Printing Office, 1982).

————. *Statistical Abstract of the United States, 1984* (Washington, D.C.: U.S. Government Printing Office, 1984), p. 465.

————. *Statistical Abstract of the United States, 1986* (Washington, D.C.: U.S. Government Printing Office, 1986).

U.S. Bureau of Labor Statistics. "Labor Force Statistics Derived from the Current Population Survey: A Databook" Vol. 1 (Washington, D.C.: U.S. Government Printing Office, 1982).

U.S. Department of Health, Education and Welfare. *Older Americans Act of 1965, as Amended, Text and History* (Washington, D.C.: U.S. Government Printing Office, 1970).

————. *Health, United States, 1975* DHEW Publication No. (HRA) 76–1232. Rockville, MD: National Center for Health Statistics, 1976.

————. Office of the Assistant Secretary for Planning and Evaluation, *The Appropriateness of the Federal Interagency Day Care Requirements (FIDCR), Vol. 1: An Overview of the Study and Findings*, discussion draft, Feb. 17, 1978, P II-7.

————. *Resource Materials: A Curriculum on CAN* DHEW Public. No. (OHDS) 79–30221 September, 1979.

————. *Smoking and Health* (Washington, D.C.: U.S. Government Printing Office, 1979).

————. *Surgeon-General's Report on Smoking and Health* (Washington, D.C.: U.S. Government Printing Office, 1979).

U.S. Department of Labor, Bureau of Labor, Bureau of Labor Statistics. *U.S. Working Women: A Databook.* Bulletin No. 1977 (Washington, D.C.: U.S. Government Printing Office, 1977), p. 35.

U.S. Department of Labor, Employment Standards Administration, Women's Bureau. *20 Facts on Women Workers* (Washington, D.C., 1975).

U.S. Government Printing Office. *Marihuana: A Signal of Misunderstanding, First Report of the Commission on Marihuana and Drug Abuse* (Washington, D.C., 1972).

U.S. Merit Systems Protection Board (MSPB). *Sexual Harassment in the Federal Workplace: Is It a Problem?* (Washington, D.C.: U.S. Government Printing Office, 1981).

U.S. News & World Report. "A Rush of Test-Tube Babies." August 7, 1978, p. 22).

————. "Battered Families: A Growing Nightmare." January 15, 1979, pp. 60–62.

————. "Working Women." January 15, 1979, p. 64.

————. "Will Inflation Tarnish Your Golden Years?" February 26, 1979, p. 57.

————. "Where Jobs Will Be in the 1980s." October 15, 1979, p. 76.

————. "Age Need Not Be a Barrier to Making Major Contributions," September 1, 1980, pp. 52–53.

————. "To Raise a Child Today." January 5, 1981, p. 77.

————. "The Desperate World of America's Underclass." March 26, 1984, p. 54–56.

————. "Anacostia, an Orphan at Steps of Nation's Capital." December 10, 1984, pp. 74–75.

————. "Rx for AIDS: A Grim Race Against the Clock." Sept. 30, 1985, pp. 48–49.

————. "Threat of AIDS Widening to the General Public." Sept. 30, 1985, p. 49.

U.S. Printing Office. *1981 Congressional Directory* 97th Congress (Washington, D.C.: 1981).

Ubell, Earl. "A World Without Disease." *Parade Magazine*, January 27, 1985, pp. 11–13.

Vener, A. M., and C. S. Stewart. "Adolescent Sexual Behavior in Middle America Revisited: 1970–1973." *Journal of Marriage and the Family* 36, (November 1974):728–34.

Verbrugge, L. M. "Marital Status and Health." *Journal of Marriage and the Family* 41, No. 2. (1979):267–85.

Vinick, B. "Remarriage in Old Age." *The Family Coordinator* 27, No. 4, (1978):359–63.

Voeller, B. "Society and the Gay Movement." In J. Marmor (Ed.), *Homosexual Behavior* (New York: Basic Books, 1980), pp. 232–54.

Wagonseller, B. R., M. Burnette, B. Salzberg, and J. Burnett, *Behavior Management Techniques: Discipline* (Champaign, IL: Research Press, 1977).

Walberg, H. J., and S. P. Rasher. "The Ways Schooling Makes a Difference." *Phi Delta Kappa* 58, (1977):703–7.

Walker, L. E. *The Battered Woman* (New York: Harper & Row, 1979).

Walker, W. J. "Changing United States Life-Style and Declining Vascular Mortality: Cause or Coincidence?" *New England Journal of Medicine* 297, No. 3, (1977):163–65.

The Wall Street Journal. "Gains Against AIDS Have Come Rapidly But a Cure is Distant." August 5, 1985, pp. 1, 12.

Walum, L. R. *The Dynamics of Sex and Gender: A Sociological Perspective* (Chicago: Rand McNally College Publishing Co., 1977).

Warren, C. A. B. *Identity and Community in the Gay World* (New York: Wiley, 1974).

Warren, C. L., and R. St. Pierre. "Sources and Accuracy of College Students' Sex Knowledge." *Journal of School Health* 43, (1973):588–90.

Washington Post, February 20, 1970.

Waskow, Arthur I. *From Race Riot to Sit-In* (Garden City, NY: Doubleday, 1967).

Watson, D. L., and R. G. Tharp, *Self-Directed Behavior* (Monterey, CA: Brooks/Cole, 1973).

Weatherly, D. "Self-Perceived Rate of Physical Maturation and Personality in Late Adolescence." *Child Development* 35, (1964):1197–1210.

Weber, Max. *The Protestant Ethic and the Spirit of Capitalism*, re-released (New York: Charles Scribner's Sons, 1958).

Webster's New Collegiate Dictionary (Springfield, MA: G. & C. Merriam Company, 1977).

Wegscheider, Sharon. *Another Chance: Hope and Health for the Alcoholic Family.* (Palo Alto, CA: Science and Behavior Books, 1981).

Weinberg, S., and C. Williams. *Male Homosexuals: Their Problems and Adaptations* (New York: Oxford University Press, 1974).

Weiss, L. and M. Lowenthal. "Life-Course Perspectives on Friendship." In M. Lowenthal, M. Thurner and D. Chiriboga (Eds.), *Four Stages of Life* (San Francisco: Jossey-Bass, 1975).

Weitzman, L. J. "Sex-Role Socialization." In J. Freeman (Ed.), *Women: A Feminist Perspective* (Palo Alto, CA: Mayfield, 1975).

———. *Sex Role Socialization* (Palo Alto, CA: Mayfield, 1979).

Welford, A. T. "Motor Performance." In J. E. Birren and K. W. Schaie (Eds.), *Handbook of the Psychology of Aging* (New York: Van Nostrand Reinhold, 1977).

Westberg, Granger. *Good Grief* (Philadelphia: Fortress Press, 1962).

Westoff, C. F. "Coital Frequency and Contraception." *Family Planning Perspectives* (1974):136–41.

White, G. D., G. Nielsen, and S. M. Johnson. "Timeout Duration and the Suppression of Deviant Behavior in Children." *Journal of Applied Behavior Analysis* 5, (1972):111–20.

Wice, Paul Bernard. *Bail and Its Reform: A National Survey* (Washington, D.C.: U.S. Government Printing Office, 1973).

Widgery, R. N., and B. Webster. "The Effects of Physical Attractiveness Upon Perceived Initial Credibility." *Michigan Speech Journal* 4, (1969):9–15.

Wilensky, Harold L. "Work as a Social Problem." In Howard Becker (Ed.), *Social Problems* (New York: John Wiley, 1966).

Williams, C. D. "The Elimination of Tantrum Behavior by Extinction Procedures." *Journal of Abnormal and Social Psychology* 59, (1959):269.

Williams, R. L., and L. W. Rivers. "The Use of Standard and Non-Standard English in Testing Black Children." A paper presented at the Annual Meeting of the American Psychological Association, Honolulu, Hawaii, September 1972.

Williamson, N. "Boys or Girls? Parents' Preferences and Sex Control." *Population Bulletin* (Washington, D.C.: Population Reference Bureau, 1978).

Wilson, A. N. *The Developmental Psychology of the Black Child* (New York: African Research Publication, 1978).

Wilson, J. G. "Embryotoxicity of Drugs in Man." In Wilson, J. G., and Fraser, F. C. (Eds.), *General Principles and Etiology Handbook Teratology.* Vol. 1. (New York: Plenum Press, 1977), pp. 309–55.

Winick, M. *Malnutrition and Brain Development* (New York: Oxford University Press, 1976).

Wisconsin State Journal. "Medicaid Kickbacks Called 'Way of Life.'" July 17, 1977, Section 1, p. 11.

———. "Exclusive Sperm Bank Rekindles Controversy." March 1, 1980, Section 1.

———. "Abortion Foes Gain Victory." July 1, 1980, Section 1, p. 1.

———. "Healthy Baby is Born from Donated Embryo." February 4, 1984, Section 1, p. 2.

———. "Embryo Case Opens New Debate." June 19, 1984, pp. 1–2.

———. "Study Cites Hunger in U.S." February 27, 1985, Section 1, p. 8.

Wise, F., and N. B. Miller. "The Mental Health of the American Indian Child." In G. S. Powell (Ed.), *The Psychosocial Development of Minority Group Children* (New York: Brunner/Mazel, 1983), pp. 344–61.

Wolf, D. *The Lesbian Community.* (Berkeley: University of California Press, 1979).

Wolf, M. M., T. Risley, J. Johnston, F. Harris, and E. Allen. "Application of Operant Conditioning Procedures to the Behavior Problems of an Autistic Child: Follow-Up and Extension." *Behaviour Research and Therapy* 5, (1967):103–11.

Wolff, C. *Love Between Women* (New York: Harper & Row, 1971).

Wolfbein, Seymour. *Work in American Society* (Glenview, IL: Scott, Foresman, 1971).

Wolpe, J. *The Practice of Behavior Therapy* (Elmsford, NY: Pergamon Press, 1974).

Women Organized Against Rape, W.O.A.R. *Data* (Philadelphia: mimeo, 1975), p. 1.

Wood, P. L. "The Victim in a Forcible Rape Case: A Feminist View." *American Criminal Law Review* 7, No. 2, (1973):348.

Wooden, K. *Weeping in the Playtime of Others* (New York: McGraw-Hill, 1976).

Woodworth, R., and H. Schlosberg. *Experimental Psychology* (New York: Holt, 1954).

Work in America: Report of a Special Task Force to the Secretary of Health, Education, and Welfare (Cambridge, MA: M.I.T. Press, 1973), p. 45.

Wynder, E. L., L. S. Covey, K. Mabuchi, and D. Mushinski. "Environmental Factors in Cancer of the Larynx: A Second Look." *Cancer* 35, (1976):1591–1601.

Yancy, W. S., P. R. Nader, and K. Burnham. "Drug Use and Attitudes of High School Students." *Pediatrics* 50, No. 5, (1972):739–45.

Yussen, S. "Characteristics of Moral Dilemmas Written by Adolescents." *Developmental Psychology* 13, No. 2, (1977):162–63.

Zabin, L. S., J. F. Kantner, and M. Zelnik. "The Risk of Adolescent Pregnancy in the First Months of Intercourse." *Family Planning Perspectives* 11, No. 4, (1979):215–22.

Zaludek, Gloria M. "How to Cope with Male Menopause." *Science Digest*, 1976, pp. 74–79.

Zastrow, Charles. *Talk to Yourself: Using the Power of Self-Talk* (Englewood Cliffs, NJ: Prentice-Hall, 1979).

———. *The Practice of Social Work* (Homewood, IL: Dorsey Press, 1981).

———. *Introduction to Social Welfare Institutions: Social Problems, Services, and Current Issues* (Homewood, IL: Dorsey Press, 1982).

———. *The Practice of Social Work*. 2d ed. (Homewood, IL: Dorsey Press, 1985).

Zastrow, Charles, and Lee Bowker, *Social Problems* (Chicago: Nelson-Hall, 1984).

Zastrow, Charles, and Ralph Navarre, "Self-Talk: A New Criminological Theory." *International Journal of Comparative and Applied Criminal Justice*, Fall 1979, pp. 167–76.

Zelnick, M., and J. F. Kantner, "The Resolution of Teenage First Pregnancies." *Family Planning Perspectives* 6, (Spring 1974):74–80.

Zelnick, M., Y. J. Kim, and J. F. Kantner. "Probabilities of Intercourse and Conception Among U.S. Teenage Women, 1971 and 1976." *Family Planning Perspectives* 11, No. 3, (1979):177–83.

Zodhiates, K., Feinbloom, R., and Sagov, S. "Contraceptive Use of Cervical Caps." (letter) *New England Journal of Medicine*, 304, No. 15, (1981):915.

Zuger, B. "Monozygotic Twins Discordant for Homosexuality: A Report of a Pair and Significance of the Phenomenon." *Comprehensive Psychiatry* 17, (1976):661–69.

Zusman, J. "Some Explanations of the Changing Appearance of Psychotic Patients: Antecedents of the Social Breakdown Syndrome Concept." *The Millbank Memorial Fund Quarterly* 64, No. 1, (1966):20.

Zylman, R. "Age Is More Important Than Alcohol in the Collision Involvement of Young and Old Drivers." *Journal of Traffic Safety Education* 20, No. 1, (1972):7–8, 34.

Name Index

616

Subject Index

Hyde amendment, 57
Hyperactivity, 101
  use of amphetamines in treating, 227
Hypochrondria, 264
Hypothalamus, 167
Hypothetical-deductive reasoning, 88
Hysterotomy, 59

I

Id, 73
Ideal mate theory, of mate choice, 251
Identification, 75
Identity, versus role confusion, 199
Identity achievement, 204
Identity confusion, 200
Identity crisis, in middle adulthood,
      287–88
Identity diffusion, 204–5
Identity formation, 197
  foreclosure, 204
  identity achievement, 201–2, 204
  identity diffusion, 204–5
  implications of, in adolescence,
      200–5
  moratorium, 205
  psychosocial theory, 197, 198
    stages of human development,
      198–200
Illegitimate births, problem of, 276–78
Imagery relaxation, and stress
      management, 420
Imaginary friends, 153
I-messages, 244
Immunological theory of aging, 403
Imprinting, 40
Impulsivity, and suicide, 214
Income, definition of, 352
Independence, achievement of, in
      adolescence, 242–43, 246–49
Individualism
  effect of, on divorce rate, 384
  and human development, 39
  ideology of, and wealth, 353
Induced labor, 59
Industry, versus inferiority, 199
Infancy and childhood
  biological aspects of, 24–69
  psychological aspects of, 70–73
  social aspects of, 106–61
Infant mortality, and poverty, 355–56
Infant stimulation programs, 48
Inferiority
  countering feelings of, 493
  versus industry, 199
Infertility, 26, 62–63, 262
  alternatives available for dealing with,
      64–68
  causes of, 63–64
  definition of, 63
  psychological reactions to, 64
  treatment of, 64
Initiative, versus guilt, 198–99
Input, 8, 112–13
Institutional discrimination, 489–92
Integrity, versus despair, 200, 428–29
Intellectual functioning
  in the elderly, 398, 412–13
  in middle age, 288–90

Intelligence, definition of, 95
Intelligence testing, 95
  cultural biases and, 98–99
  mental retardation, 96–98
  potential problems with scores, 98
  Stanford-Binet IQ test, 95–96
Interactionist perspective, 350–52
  criticisms of, 352
  on drug use, 234
  of poverty, 366–67
Interaction play levels
  associative play, 152
  cooperative play, 152
  onlooker play, 151
  parallel play, 151
  solitary play, 151
  unoccupied behavior, 151
Interdependence, 9–10
Interface, 9
Intermittent reinforcement, 133–34
Interracial rape, 538
Intervention, techniques of, 512–13
Intimacy, versus isolation, 199
In vitro fertilization, 67–68
In vivo desensitization, 120
Irreversibility, 83
Isolation, versus intimacy, 199
IUD (intrauterine device), 191–92

J

Jim Crow laws, 486, 497
Job Corps, 10
Job dissatisfaction, 370–71
Job satisfaction, 371–73
John Birch Society, 514
Joints, changes in, and aging, 399
Juvenile delinquency, 274–76

K

Kaposi's sarcoma, 580
Kissing, as form on nonverbal
      communication, 326
Knowledge, relationship between
      assessment and, 238–39
Ku Klux Klan, 514

L

Labeling theory, as offshoot of
      interactionist theory, 352
Labels, impact of, on identity
      formation, 202
Laissez-faire leadership, 153–54
Lamaze Method, 35
Language disorders, 100–1
Later adulthood. See Aging;
      Elderly
Leadership style, in the classroom,
      153–54
Learning disabilities, 100
  definition of, 100
  dyslexia, 101
  effects of, 99, 102
  hyperactivity, 101
  language disorders, 100–1
  motor disabilities, 101
  and sensory integration, 54

treatment for, 102–3
  visual perceptual disorders, 101
Learning theory, 117–18
  and the A.B.C.'s of behavior, 122
  applications of, to parenting, 128–38
  extinction, 127
  and homosexuality, 563
  measuring improvement in behavior,
      140–42
  modeling, 120–21
  operant conditioning, 121
  punishment, 126, 127
  reinforcement, 122–23, 126, 127
  respondent conditioning, 119–20
Lesbian, 558. See also Homosexuality
Librium, 225
Life events
  as aspect of behavioral dynamic
      assessment, 13–14
  impact of, on adolescence and young
      adulthood, 180–90, 212–38
  impact of, on the elderly, 435–41
Life expectancy, 407–10
  and the elderly, 458
  and health, 412
Life review, conducting of, by older
      persons, 430
Life script analysis, 318–22
Lifestyle
  of the elderly, 467–69
  and homosexuality, 566–67, 570–73
  in young adulthood, 178–80
Locker room, 228
Logical thinking, barriers to
      development of, 82–83
Loneliness, and suicide, 213
Looking glass concept, 202, 266, 351,
      430, 495
Love, romantic versus rational, 249–50,
      383
LSD (D-lysergic acid diethylamide), 230
Lung cancer, 179

M

Macro-events, 14
Macro theory, 347
Male/female differences, 522
  ability levels, 522–23
  communication styles, 523
  personality differences, 522
Malnutrition, and the elderly, 468–69
Manic-depression, 264
Marijuana, 222, 231–32
Marriage, 250–51
  adjusting to death of spouse, 436
  benefits of, 253–54
  and cohabitation, 254–55
  and divorce, 382–88
  and the elderly, 435–38
  empty-shell, 381–82
  guidelines for successful, 253
  open versus closed, 254
  predictors of success, 251–52
  reasons for unhappiness in, 383–
      84
  and remarriage, 437–38
  sex in middle age, 298–300